Building English Skills Green Level

Contents of the Teacher's Edition

Components of the *Building English Skills Series . . .*

	Pink Level Grade 1	**Plum Level** Grade 2	**Brown Level** Grade 3	**Aqua Level** Grade 4
Student Text		 Available in hard- and softcover.		
Teacher's Edition				
Skills Practice Books	Reinforcement worksheets are provided in the Teacher's Edition of the *Pink Level.*	Reinforcement worksheets are provided in the Teacher's Edition of the *Plum Level.*	Skills Practice Book	Skills Practice Book
Diagnostic and Mastery Tests	Tests are provided in the Teacher's Edition of the *Pink Level.*	Tests are provided in the Teacher's Edition of the *Plum Level.*	Diagnostic and Mastery Tests	Diagnostic and Mastery Tests
Duplicating Masters ■ Skills Practice ■ Diagnostic and Mastery Tests	Duplicating Masters	Duplicating Masters	Duplicating Masters	Duplicating Masters
Teacher's Resource Kit				
	Building English Skills 1 Teacher's Resource Kit	Building English Skills 2 Teacher's Resource Kit	Building English Skills 3 Teacher's Resource Kit	Building English Skills 4 Teacher's Resource Kit

a Complete English Program for Grades K-12

(See page T-4 for Kindergarten and Grades 9–12.)

Silver Level Grade 5   **Gold Level** Grade 6   **Red Level** Grade 7   **Green Level** Grade 8

Additional Levels of the *Building English Skills* Series

Grades 9-12

Building English Skills, 9 to 12, continues the *BES* teaching approach, providing for a smooth transition and consistency from the elementary grades through high school.

Orange Level
Grade 9

Blue Level
Grade 10

Yellow Level
Grade 11

Purple Level
Grade 12

Program Components

Student Text (hardcover)

Teacher's Manual

Skills Practice Book

Duplicating Masters

Diagnostic and Mastery Tests

Kindergarten

Building Learning Skills, a comprehensive kindergarten program with a strong language arts development strand, is coordinated with *Building English Skills*.

Building Learning Skills
Kindergarten

Program Components

Student Text (softcover)

Teacher's Edition
(spiral-bound softcover)

Duplicating Masters

Single Image Cards

Significant Features of the *Building English Skills* Series

Building English Skills is a complete, developmental English program for grades K-12. Based on the suggestions of practicing classroom teachers, the series is designed to lead students toward mastery of essential writing and related language skills. Learner-verified and classroom-tested, *Building English Skills* offers these significant features:

Sound Organization

A consistent, developmental approach...within each grade, and from one grade to the next ... ensures transference of learning (see page T6).

Thorough Instruction

Step-by-step instruction ... with explanations, examples, and exercises ... provides for steady development in the use of language (see page T8).

In-depth Development of the Process of Writing

Building English Skills presents writing as a continuous process of thinking and rethinking, writing and revising (see page T10).

Clear Presentation of Grammar

In *Building English Skills*, grammar becomes an effective communication tool that students can use in their writing (see page T16).

Balanced Study of Language Arts

Building English Skills offers a complete, balanced presentation of all seven strands of language arts study: composition; grammar and usage; speaking and listening; vocabulary development; appreciation of literature; study and research skills; and the mechanics of writing (see page T18).

Sound Organization

A consistent, developmental approach ... within each grade, and from one grade to the next ... ensures transference of learning.

Building English Skills presents a complete, consistent series for teaching basic English skills in grades K-12. The philosophy, terminology, teaching approach, and topical emphasis are consistent from grade to grade. Skills are developed sequentially from one grade to the next, with each grade reinforcing and extending the skills introduced earlier.

In order to achieve a logical, developmental presentation of skills, this book divides concepts into two main sections. The first half of the text concerns composition and related skills such as vocabulary development, study and research skills, and library skills. The second half of the book deals with grammar, usage, and mechanics. It is meant to be used throughout the school year as a means of further improving student writing.

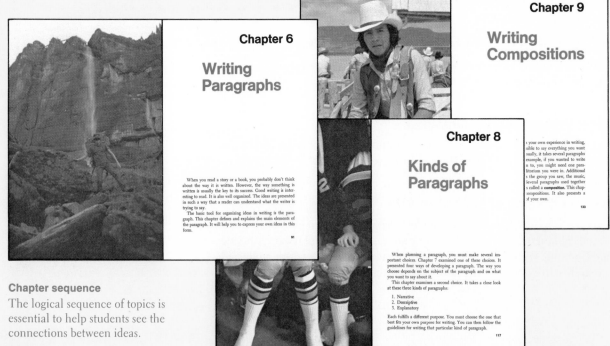

Chapter 6

Writing Paragraphs

When you read a story or a book, you probably don't think about the way it is written. However, the way something is written is usually the key to its success. Good writing is interesting to read. It is also well organized. The ideas are presented in such a way that a reader can understand what the writer is trying to say.

The basic tool for organizing ideas in writing is the paragraph. This chapter defines and explains the main elements of the paragraph. It will help you to express your own ideas in this form.

91

Chapter 9

Writing Compositions

...your own experience in writing, ...sible to say everything you want ...ually, it takes several paragraphs ...example, if you wanted to write ...n to, you might need one para-...litorium you were in. Additional ...s the group you saw, the music, ...several paragraphs used together ...s called a **composition**. This chap-...ompositions. It also presents a ...of your own.

133

Chapter 8

Kinds of Paragraphs

When planning a paragraph, you must make several important choices. Chapter 7 examined one of these choices. It presented four ways of developing a paragraph. The way you choose depends on the subject of the paragraph and on what you want to say about it.

This chapter examines a second choice. It takes a close look at these three kinds of paragraphs:

1. Narrative
2. Descriptive
3. Explanatory

Each fulfills a different purpose. You must choose the one that best fits your own purpose for writing. You can then follow the guidelines for writing that particular kind of paragraph.

117

Chapter sequence

The logical sequence of topics is essential to help students see the connections between ideas.

Chapter 8

Kinds of Paragraphs

When planning a paragraph, you must make several important choices. Chapter 7 examined one of these choices. It presented four ways of developing a paragraph. The way you choose depends on the subject of the paragraph and on what you want to say about it.

This chapter examines a second choice. It takes a close look at these three kinds of paragraphs:

1. Narrative
2. Descriptive
3. Explanatory

Each fulfills a different purpose. You must choose the one that best fits your own purpose for writing. You can then follow the guidelines for writing that particular kind of paragraph.

117

Single-concept chapters

Each chapter focuses on a single concept and develops it completely before moving on to another. Later lessons review and build on the concept so that students retain what they've learned. With this approach, students gain a sense of the relative importance of ideas because they are presented logically.

Introduction

Chapter introductions tell students what they are about to learn. This new learning is related to previous chapters, always building on what students already know.

Visual organization

Artwork and color are used as organizational devices. Photos, for example, signal the beginning of new chapters.

Skill-building

Lessons are often introduced with a reference to previous learning.

Using Details

Vivid details are important in a narrative paragraph because they help the reader to share the writer's experience. Notice the many details in the following paragraph.

I was the last contestant in the bubble gum contest at school, and I was determined to win. Constant practice had limbered my jaw and improved my technique. I chewed the sugary wad of gum confidently until it arrived at the properly smooth texture. I inhaled deeply; then I blew. The bubble was the size of a marble—the size of an egg—the size of a baseball. When it finally burst, like a rubbery pink balloon, the class cheered. I was clearly the new bubble gum champ of York Junior High.

The details in this paragraph help you to imagine the taste and texture of the gum, the increasing size of the bubble, and the bursting "rubbery pink balloon." These details allow you to share the action with the contestant.

Exercise Writing First-Person Narrative Paragraphs

Choose two of the following topic sentences (reword them if you wish) or make up sentences of your own. Then, using your imagination or personal experience, develop each sentence into a first-person narrative paragraph. Include specific details that will help to make the experience come alive for the reader.

Do not forget the three main steps in the Process of Writing: Pre-Writing, Writing the First Draft, and Revising. Use the Guidelines for the Process of Writing on page 89.

1. After I left school yesterday afternoon, things really began to go wrong.
2. It was our family's first visit to a big city.
3. I finally decided to have my hair cut.
4. At last I found a path through the woods.
5. It was the hardest job I ever had to do.
6. I had a good excuse for being late.

120

7. I was alone in the dark old house.
8. It was my first try at skiing, and I was scared.
9. One event taught me never to fight again.
10. Yesterday I learned that Pete is a coward.

Part 2 The Descriptive Paragraph

A narrative paragraph tells "what happened." A descriptive paragraph, on the other hand, has little or no action. Its purpose is to paint a picture with words.

A descriptive paragraph appeals to one or more of the five senses. In Chapter 4, you sharpened your awareness of the senses and practiced using words with sensory appeal. In Chapter 7, Part 1, you learned to develop a paragraph by using sensory details. Now, you will concentrate on paragraphs that appeal to the senses of sight and hearing. These are highly developed senses and are the basis for most descriptive paragraphs.

Using Specific Details

Imagine that you are describing a man walking down the street. Simply to write, "The man walked down the street," does not paint much of a picture. A reader might ask, Is he a young man? a middle-aged man? an old man? How is he walking? slowly? briskly? Is it a quiet neighborhood street or a busy downtown street?

To make your word-picture more exact, you might change the verb *walked* to a more specific verb such as *sauntered*. Next, you might add an adverb such as *happily* to tell the reader a little more about the way the man was walking. As a last step, you might add adjectives such as *young* to describe *man* and *busy* to describe *street*. A paragraph, developed from this revised sentence, might resemble the following:

The young man sauntered happily down the busy street. His head was high, his chin was up, and his long arms swung in

121

Thorough Instruction

Step-by-step instruction ... with explanations, examples, and exercises ... provides for steady development in the use of language.

Building English Skills develops each topic or skill completely, one step at a time, in one unit or chapter. Research by Jerome Bruner and others has shown that any topic can be taught successfully if it is presented in a logical, step-by-step, success-directed way — with illustrations, models, and exercises that are directly related to the student's needs and experiences.

Explanations
The one-step-at-a-time approach offers clear, to-the-point explanations.

Points of emphasis
For further reinforcement and reference, important definitions, rules, and generalizations are highlighted.

Part 1 The Parts of a Sentence

A sentence expresses a complete thought; that is, it makes a complete statement, asks a question, tells someone to do something, or expresses strong feeling. It always has two grammatical parts. One part tells whom or what the sentence is about. This is the **subject**. The second part tells something about the subject. This is the **predicate**.

| Subject | Predicate |
(Who or what)	*(What is said about the subject)*
Beth	smiled.
The boys	had gone.
The two cars	nearly collided.
Each participant	received a certificate.

An easy way to understand the parts of a sentence is to think of the sentences as telling who did something or what happened. The subject tells *who* or *what*. The predicate tells *did* or *happened*. You can divide sentences, then, in this way:

Who or What	Did or Happened
Juanita	arrived.
The ice	melted.
The subway	was crowded with people.
A roar of anger	rose from the crowd.
The runner in the red shirt	won the race.

320

The subject of the sentence names someone or something about which a statement is to be made.

The predicate of the sentence tells what is done or what happens.

Exercises Find the subjects and predicates.

A. Copy these sentences. Draw a vertical line between the subject and the predicate.

EXAMPLE: The whole crowd | cheered.

1. Karen wrote the weekly sports news.
2. Both dogs circled the water hole.
3. Thunder rumbled in the distance.
4. The boy across the street raises rabbits.
5. Terry saw the skydiving show on Channel 4.
6. A large crowd watched the basketball game.
7. My brother went home after the game.
8. Nancy collects foreign postage stamps.
9. Joe's Labrador retriever jumped the fence.
10. The yardstick snapped in two.

B. Copy these sentences. Draw a vertical line between the subject and the predicate.

1. An alligator slid into the water.
2. Elaine collects antique dolls.
3. The sand dunes baked in the sun.
4. Both of my sisters have graduated from high school.
5. Several students at Central School drew the posters.
6. My little sister knows the rules for the game.
7. Greg's brother builds historical model boats.
8. The girl in the yellow slicker missed the bus.
9. The man snored like a distant vacuum cleaner.
10. Two boys from our neighborhood went on a canoe trip.

321

Exercises
Short, structured oral and/or written exercises give students the reinforcement they need.

Examples
Examples are careful demonstrations of the skill or topic to be learned.

Explanations

The explanations are clear, complete, and follow a logical expansion of ideas.

Examples

Numerous examples or models clarify each explanation or definition.

Analysis

An explanation of the examples helps students analyze and identify the elements involved.

Points of emphasis

For further reinforcement and reference, important definitions, rules, and generalizations are highlighted.

Exercises

Short, structured oral or written exercises allow students to apply the new skill immediately.

Both preparation and presentation are basic to speaking in front of people. *The way you present your information and yourself affects the interest of your audience and determines the success of your talk.*

Part 2 Types of Informal Speaking

Making Announcements

In school you hear announcements several times a day. Some of them you remember, but others never seem to catch your attention. Announcements are short and simple, but the information should be clear and include the following details:

> **Information for Announcements**
>
> **Who** is involved or sponsoring the event?
> **What** is happening?
> **Where** is it taking place?
> **When** is it happening (time)?
> **Why** should the listener be interested?

Many people don't listen until they hear something in particular that interests them. That's why it is important to get their attention first. Always repeat the most important facts, especially the *where* and *when*.

Announcements fall into two basic categories: those about future events and those about events that have already taken place. When reporting events that have already happened, you can add many more details. Look at the following examples.

Announcement of a Future Event

Have you ever seen your name in print? Do you know who made basketball and cheerleading tryouts? Are you up-to-date on the latest gossip? Now you have a chance to find the answers

266

---

to these questions and many more. Tomorrow, Wednesday, October 15, the first issue of the school paper, *The Eagle's Eye*, will be sold in the school cafeteria during all lunch periods. The cost is only 10¢. Don't forget—tomorrow, Wednesday, the school paper will be sold in the cafeteria. There's something in it for everyone, so don't forget your dime.

Announcement of a Past Event

Last Saturday, April 12, at Heritage Park, our baseball team won its first victory by slaughtering the Holmes Lions, 12 to 5. Bob Jansen struck out ten batters while infielders Campbell, Juarez, and Lee pulled off six double plays. The team really worked together for this great victory. Everyone come to the next game and support our team. Be there on Saturday, April 19, at 7 P.M. at Heritage Park and watch our Eagles stampede those McArthur Mustangs. That's Saturday, April 19, at 7 P.M. at Heritage Park. See you there.

Announcements can be fun. Be sure to include all of the necessary details and review the information on preparation and presentation.

Exercises Making Announcements

A. Make an announcement to the class. Use two of the following events or two events that are going to take place in your school. If you wish, make up events, but be sure to include the specific information that is required.

a student council event	tryouts for a play
a club meeting	an assembly
a bake sale	talent show competition
an athletic event	a field trip

B. With a small group of three or four other people, plan a short newscast using announcements of future events and past events. You can center your newscast on one subject area, such as sports or politics, or you can present a typical newscast with several subject areas.

267

Giving Directions

Remember your first day in school, when you seemed totally lost? You probably received directions like these:

> Oh, the music room. Just go down the hall, through the double doors, and it's on your right.

You followed the directions and ended up at a janitor's closet, not a very good start for your first day. With this kind of experience, you can see the importance of using complete and accurate details. Look at the difference details can make:

> To get to the music room, continue going down this hall. As soon as you pass the entrance to the gym, you will see a hall on your left. Go down that hall and through the double doors. The music room door is the first on your right, across from the water fountain.

With these details you have a much better chance of finding your way.

When you give directions, remember that you know where the location is but that the other person does not. Do not take any clue for granted. Use accurate details and be as clear as possible. To be sure that you have given good directions, either repeat the directions or have the person repeat them to you.

Exercises Giving Directions

A. Give directions on how to get from the school to your house. Assume that the person who needs the directions does not know your town. Calculate your distances carefully and point out landmarks that might be helpful.

B. Each member of the class is to write out directions for another class member to follow. Try to make the directions as exact as possible. Your directions should be limited to activities inside the classroom. Do not try to trick anyone. Just give accurate directions about what to do. Try to include several different tasks, such as

268

---

selecting books, sharpening pencils, or opening windows. Don't leave out important details, such as opening a closet door. When it's your turn, follow only the directions on the paper—not what you guess the person meant.

Giving a Demonstration Talk

> How do you ride a bike?
> Just hold on to the handlebars, push the pedals with your feet, and go.

It sounds easy enough, but if you explain it that way to a child who has never done it, he or she will fall right over.

When you demonstrate how to do something, you have to be as exact as when you are giving directions. The following steps will help you to give an informative demonstration.

> **Steps for a Demonstration Talk**
>
> 1. **Know your subject.** The best demonstration will be about something you know how to do well. Also, choose a subject that you know will interest your audience.
>
> 2. **Organize your material.** Your audience will understand your demonstration best if the information is presented in the proper order. If you present each step in the order it occurs, your demonstration will make sense.
>
> 3. **Check your equipment.** Most demonstrations involve some form of equipment. Some require many utensils or tools. To keep yourself organized, make a list of the equipment you will need for each step. However, try to choose a subject that is not too complicated.
>
> 4. **Be interesting.** Start with a positive statement that gets your audience immediately involved. The people in your audience need to know why they should be interested in your subject.

269

T9

In-depth Development of the Process of Writing

Building English Skills presents writing as a continuous process of thinking and rethinking, writing and revising.

In *Building English Skills*, the process of writing is presented with consistency and in depth. Writing is approached as an ongoing process—of thinking as well as writing—so that students' analytical skills, as well as their creative skills, are fully developed.

The Philosophy

All teachers are aware of the difficulties some students have when asked to compose a paragraph or composition. The products of such assignments often seem to indicate that the writers have little ability to express thoughts clearly, develop content adequately, or organize ideas into a logical presentation. In reality, the problem is often not one of ability, but of technique. The students may simply never have been taught what writing really is, or the best way to approach it.

One of the biggest handicaps in writing is the tendency to view it in terms of a final product rather than as an ongoing process. In other words, many students are, in effect, beginning the writing process at the end. Having adopted the belief that writing is the ability to produce well-developed, well-organized ideas as soon as one sets pen to paper, these students attempt to produce a final product on the first attempt. There is little or no planning of ideas, and only a superficial revision of content. Such an approach invariably results in a poor piece of writing, as well as a frustrated writer.

It is important to make students recognize that few people know exactly what they want to say when they begin a piece of writing. In fact, it is usually the act of writing itself that enables us to discover exactly what it is we are thinking or feeling. As ideas are written down, worked, and reworked, they crystallize in our own mind. Only then are we able to begin developing and organizing them with any confidence.

Since this is the case, writing must be viewed as a thinking process, a means of first finding out what we want to say, and then deciding on the best way to present it. This belief is the cornerstone of the entire writing philosophy of *Building English Skills*. The text teaches students to approach writing with the understanding that writing is a *process* of thinking and rethinking, writing and revising. This process is essential to any good writing, and should be reinforced in all subject areas. A summary of the process is provided below.

The Process

1. Pre-Writing. The pre-writing stage can also be called the planning stage. It is one of the most basic and essential parts of the writing process. The purposes of the pre-writing stage are to explore possibilities for topics and presentation, and to begin gathering and organizing the details that will be used to develop the main idea. To help students accomplish these goals, the teacher should encourage them to complete the following pre-writing steps every time they write:

1. Choose and narrow a topic.
2. Decide on the purpose of writing.
3. Identify the audience who will read the final version.
4. Gather details that develop the topic and suit the purpose and audience.
5. Put the ideas into a logical order.

The teacher should also remind students that pre-writing is only a way to begin sorting through ideas, and that the notes made at this stage of the process may be modified, changed, or deleted altogether.

2. Writing the First Draft. The purpose of a first draft is basically to get some ideas down on paper. Even as they write this draft, students will find that they are discovering new ideas and refining others. This will lead to a need to reevaluate other aspects of the writing, such as organization and the choice of supporting details. A first draft, therefore, is simply that—the first attempt by the writer to find out what he or she wants to say. A student should be prepared to work through several versions of any piece of writing before reaching a final product.

It is important that students learn not to break the flow of ideas at this point to worry about grammar, usage, and mechanics. There will be time to concentrate on these later, during the revision process.

3. Rewriting, or Revising. Some writers make the mistake of equating revision with proofreading. Although checking for errors in grammar, usage, and mechanics is important, the greatest part of revising time should actually be spent on content. As previously noted, the first draft is primarily a way of discovering the ideas that are to be used. The most crucial part of writing occurs on successive drafts, during the revision process. When revising, a student should do the following:

1. Check to see that all ideas and details are related to the topic and purpose.
2. Refine good ideas, and add any new ones that could improve the writing.
3. Make certain that the purpose of the paper is clear, and that the content of the writing suits that purpose.
4. Refine the organization of the ideas.
5. Check to see that each sentence flows smoothly to the next.
6. Make sure that the language and content are suitable for the audience.
7. Substitute vivid words for vague language.
8. Proofread for errors in grammar, usage, and mechanics.

Students should be made to see that revising a piece of writing is like working with a clay statue—the material is constantly reshaped until the desired result is achieved. See the composition chapters for examples of how the revision process is treated in this text. See also the teaching suggestions in this Teacher's Edition for suggested revising techniques.

4. Preparing the Final Copy. Only after the first three steps are completed should a student consider making the final copy. This version incorporates all of the thoughts and improvements of the rest of the process.

One important point needs to be made about the process of writing as taught in this book. To aid student understanding, the process is often presented in a step-by-step manner. However, the teacher should make certain that the students always treat writing as more of a circular process. In other words, a writer should have every element of the process in mind at all times. Organization, for example, could be reworked any time, not just during the pre-writing stage. Details may constantly be added and deleted. The process of writing is primarily a process of continual revision.

The Follow-Through

Throughout the student texts, students are called upon to apply the process of writing to all of their writing tasks. Such consistent follow-through is imperative if students are to improve their writing habits. See pages T12–T15 of this Teacher's Edition for examples from the student texts.

Another important aspect of follow-through must be the area of evaluation. Evaluation of student writing is a crucial part of the teaching of writing. See pages T28–T30 for a thorough presentation of **Guidelines for Evaluating Composition**.

For a further, detailed discussion of the teaching of writing, refer to the separate booklet **Teaching and Evaluating Student Writing**.

Throughout the composition chapters, students learn and practice the pre-writing, writing, and revising skills that can be applied to any writing task. In addition, they learn different types of organization and development to suit various writing purposes.

Pre-Writing

Building English Skills guides the student through the preparations for writing.

Choosing and narrowing the topic

The text asks thought-provoking questions to help students think for themselves.

Special feature of the Teacher's Edition

For each writing lesson, the Teacher's Edition suggests a wealth of ideas for pre-writing activities: brainstorming, journal-writing, idea-sharing, and discussions. These provide a springboard for writing topics.

Determining purpose

Each chapter on writing—paragraphs, stories, descriptions, compositions, reports, or other forms—contains models that show what that particular kind of writing can do.

Determining audience

The series stresses awareness of audience as an important pre-writing consideration.

Part 1

Objectives

1. To understand how to choose and limit a topic
2. To understand how to make pre-writing notes
3. To learn to identify audience and purpose

Presenting the Lesson

1. Read and discuss the explanation of the five pre-writing steps on pages 82-83. As you cover these steps, assure students that each step is explained further in subsequent chapters. Stress that the purpose of the planning or pre-writing stage is to give the writer a focus for the writing and an opportunity to organize ideas.

2. You may want to introduce students to the following pre-writing techniques that can help them find ideas for their writing:

Brainstorming — talking freely as a class or in a small group. The group may simply discuss topics in general, or share ideas for solving a specific problem.

Journal-writing — diary-like jottings of interesting experiences or thoughts, striking observations, or unusual descriptions.

Idea starters — exposure to new situations or new ways of looking at ordinary situations that can provide material for writing. These include trips, film, art, poetry, photography, and speakers.

Discussion — talking about an assignment or debating ideas to clarify attitudes and opinions.

82

Part 1 Pre-Writing: Choosing and Limiting a Subject

You may be assigned reports in any of your subjects—science, English, social studies, math, art, or music. It is important that you know how to prepare these reports on your own. As with any composition, your first step is to choose and limit a subject. Begin by making a list of subjects that interest you and that you feel would be of interest to your readers. Next, make certain that these subjects do not involve you personally and can be developed from outside s___ such as Navajo sand painting, ___ meet these requirements. If yo___ made an inappropriate choice.

Once you have found a gen___ row to it to an idea that can be ___ length of the report. Which ___ would make a good five-paragr___

1. The geography of Latin ___
2. The Viking spacecraft's ___

The second topic, of course ___ cerns one particular space fli___ to be explained in a short, info___ however, needs to be narrow___

In order to limit a subject, ___ is available on it and how lon___ ing. Narrow the subject acco___ Try looking at a general ency___ an idea of just how large your ___ possibilities for limiting it.

154

Exercise Choosing and Narrowing Your Subject

From the list of subjects you made in the preceding exercise, choose the one subject you would like to write about. Study it carefully. Decide if it is narrow enough to be covered in five paragraphs. If it is too general, narrow it so that it is a workable topic. You may wish to check your final topic with your teacher.

Putting Down Ideas

You have decided on a general subject, then narrowed it to the point where it can be easily covered in a few paragraphs. If you have chosen your subject well, ideas will start to jump around in your mind. The next step is to get all of these ideas out of your head and down on paper. Do not worry about order or format at this point. Just write.

As you record your ideas, you may find that you have more thoughts than you can handle. To help you make some preliminary decisions as to which ideas will be useful and which will not, take a moment to think about these two things:

Purpose. What are you trying to accomplish with your composition? If you are telling a story, use only the ideas that will help further the action. If you are describing a person or place, stick to the details that will help your reader paint a mental picture of your subject. If you are explaining an idea or process, include only the information that will help your reader understand.

Audience. Who will read your composition? How much do your readers know about your subject? If they are familiar with your topic, leave out the more elementary ideas. If the subject is new to them, include all the background they will need to understand it completely.

The writer who chose the topic "Summer Jobs for Young People" decided that she wanted to write an informative composition directed at others of her own age group. Here is her

115

Part

O___
plac___
pre-___
writ___

It is ___
pre-___
plan___

1. C___
  In___
  W___
subj___
to s___
pen___
out ___

  *H___
will ___
may ___
idea ___
if yo___
you ___
had ___
you

2. ___

Once you have selected a topic, you must ___ what you intend to do with it. These qu___ ones to answer each time you write.

  What do I want to say about my topic? ___ scribe it, criticize it, or explain it? Do you

82

---

write down as many ideas and details as you can. If you are presenting opinions or observations, think through your subject thoroughly. Write down all the important points you want to make.

The writer who wanted to tell about his sister wrote down these notes. He may add or delete ideas later, but these notes give him a starting point for his writing.

Stacy saw runners in Olympics
Decided to become a runner
Stacy didn't look like a runner
Practiced every day
Read books on running, watched televised races
Family not sure she had a chance
Stacy joined the school track team
She got sick, injured herself
The day of the race
The lesson we learned from her

Exercise Writing Down Details

Think about the subject you have chosen for your composition. Write down all the details you can about your subject. Save this list. Add to it at any time.

Part 4 Pre-Writing: Organizing the Composition

Once you have made notes on your ideas, you are ready to plan the body of your composition. This involves three steps:

1. Identifying your main ideas
2. Organizing your ideas into logical order
3. Adding details to your list

The more time and attention you give to these steps, the easier the actual writing of the composition will be.

140

Listing Main Ideas

Begin the planning process by rereading your notes. You will find that most of the details you listed fit under a few key ideas. Identify these key ideas and list them, as in the following example:

Stacy's desire to be a runner
The first race
Her preparation for the team
Stacy's experiences on the team

After you have listed your main ideas, you may be able to decide on a title for your composition. The writer of this story decided on "A Lesson from My Sister."

Arranging Ideas in Logical Order

You now have a list of main ideas. The next step is to organize your main ideas so that the body of the composition will be easy to write and to read.

The order you choose for your composition will depend on your subject and the type of composition you are writing. Narrative compositions are often best ordered in time sequence. Spatial order works well for most descriptive compositions. The details in an explanatory composition could be arranged in time sequence, or from least important to most important.

The ideas for "A Lesson from My Sister" were reorganized into a time sequence, the order in which things happened. At this point, the writer also decided to use the first idea as an introduction to the composition.

A LESSON FROM MY SISTER

Introduction: Stacy's desire to be a runner
First Main Idea: Her preparation for the team
Second Main Idea: Stacy's experiences on the team
Third Main Idea: The first race

141

Gathering information
Students are given suggestions for gathering information.

Organizing information
Students learn to organize information in a way that is appropriate to the type of writing they are doing.

Writing the First Draft

Students are shown how putting ideas down on paper lets the writer discover what he or she wants to say.

Using pre-writing notes
Students refer to their pre-writing notes as they begin to get their ideas down on paper.

Concentrating on meaning
The emphasis in this stage is on meaning rather than form. Students are not concerned with grammar, usage, and mechanics.

Developing the topic
Students expand their ideas and develop the topic.

Part 5 Writing the First Draft

Once you have collected and organized your ideas, you are ready to begin a rough draft of your composition. Remember that at this stage in the writing process, you should be concerned only with getting your ideas down on paper and making them flow smoothly. You will have the opportunity to fine-tune your writing later, in the revision process.

Writing the Introduction

You want to give your reader a clear idea of what your composition is about. You also want that person to read the entire composition. It is important, therefore, to write an introductory paragraph that both informs the reader and catches his or her interest. Read this introductory paragraph:

My sister Stacy is a wonderful person. Once she did something that surprised the entire family. It had to do with running.

This paragraph gives the reader an idea as to what the composition is going to be about. However, it is not interesting enough to make the reader want to go any further. Now read this paragraph, which the writer arrived at after several revisions:

From the day she first saw the Olympic games on TV, my sister Stacy had wanted to be a runner. The rest of the family would look at her stocky body and short legs, and smile. Stacy was wonderful, and she might be any one of several things some day, but we knew she would never be a runner.

The writer of the above paragraph has fulfilled the two purposes of an introduction. He has given the reader an idea of what the composition is going to be about. He has also tempted the reader to go beyond the opening paragraph.

143

Revising

In revising, students first look at meaning. Students are guided by a checklist of questions on content to make sure the writing says what they want it to say.

Revising for content
Students check content for unity, coherence, organization, and choice of language.

Marking content changes
The revised copy shows the rethinking, replacing, and reorganizing that is a part of revising.

Using proofreading symbols
Students are introduced to and encouraged to use basic proofreading symbols.

Analysis of revised copy
Students analyze the thinking process that goes into any good revision.

Following guidelines for revising
A checklist guides students in checking for interest, clarity, organization, and sense.

Special feature of the Teacher's Edition
Lesson suggestions advise you of numerous group and teacher-directed techniques to be used in revising.

Part 6 Revising Your Composition

A piece of writing is never perfect after the [first draft. It] needs to be reworked—polished into a good final [copy.]

Read through your composition. Check to s[ee that your] ideas flow well. Reorganize them if you have t[o. Cut out un]necessary information and add needed details. [Replace dull] words and phrases with lively, colorful ones. Ch[eck your work] in grammar, capitalization, punctuation, and sp[elling. Use the] Guidelines on pages 59 and 131 for more help wi[th revising.]

The writer of "Summer Jobs in Your Neighbo[rhood" decided] that her composition could be improved. Look a[t the revision] of her rough draft. It shows some of the chan[ges she made] during the revision process.

SUMMER JOBS IN YOUR NEIGHBOR[HOOD]

relax and have fun
Summer is a good time to ~~goof off~~. But twelve [weeks with]out school or homework leaves a lot of free time. M[uch to your] surprise, you may find your self getting bored. One [way to turn] those long lazy hours ~~into a neat profit~~ is with a s[ummer] job. With a little creative thinking, you can find [a job that] *increase* will help to make your summer super—and may[be even]
account
~~piggybank~~ at the same tim[e.]

The first jobs that come [to mind]
such as
~~bys~~ like babysitting and [mowing lawns.]
~~time~~, teenagers have been [babysitting]
~~and mowing lawns~~. These [jobs]
ordina
because they are so ~~comm~~[on]
that so many people need [them done.]

126

Analyzing the Revision

Now examine the revised draft again. Look for the following changes, which the writer felt would improve her composition:

1. Vague language was replaced by precise words and phrases. For example, the word "prune" was substituted for the word "cut," and "ordinary" replaced "common." In addition, words and phrases were added to clarify or modify other words.
2. Formal language was substituted for informal language. Phrases such as "goof off" and "old standbys" were replaced.
3. Ideas were rearranged. The writer decided that the idea of day camps in paragraph two worked better in paragraph three, so she moved it. She also moved another sentence in that paragraph. These changes made the paragraph flow more smoothly.
4. Errors in grammar and mechanics were spotted and corrected. An error in subject-verb agreement was corrected in paragraph two, as was a run-on sentence. Mistakes in grammar, capitalization, punctuation, and spelling were corrected throughout the composition.

[...] were made [...] readers. In [...] he writer de[...] too young for [...] adult phrase. [...] refully. The [...] a great deal.

[...] changes you [...] er's marks to

Guidelines for Writing and Revising Compositions

As you write a composition, follow the steps in the Guidelines for the Process of Writing on page 59. Use these additional Guidelines as you revise your first draft.

1. Has the subject been narrowed to a single topic or idea that can be covered in a few paragraphs?

2. Does the composition have an introduction, a body, and a conclusion?

3. Does the **introduction** present the main idea? Does it catch the reader's interest?

4. Does each **body** paragraph explain or support the main idea? Do the paragraphs work together to develop that idea?

5. Does each paragraph begin with a clear and interesting topic sentence? Are there sufficient details to develop each topic sentence?

6. Does the **conclusion** summarize the information or comment on it?

7. Is the composition appropriate for the audience for which it is i[...]

Proofreading is presented as a necessary step following revising for content. Checklists help students make sure that the writing will be clear to its audience.

Making a Final Copy

When you are satisfied with your story, make a final, neat copy. Use whatever heading your teacher directs. Make sure you leave sufficient margins at the top, bottom, and sides of your paper.

When you have completed your final copy, proofread it one more time. Check for errors in grammar, capitalization, punctuation, and spelling.

Read through the corrected copy of "Summer Jobs in Your Neighborhood." Notice how all the changes from the rough draft have been used in the final paper.

SUMMER JOBS IN YOUR NEIGHBORHOOD

Summer is a good time to relax and have fun. But twelve weeks without school or homework leaves a lot of free time. Much to your surprise, you may find yourself getting bored. One way to fill those long, lazy hours is with a neighborhood job. With a little creative thinking, you can find a job that will help to make your summer super—and maybe increase your bank account at the same time.

The first summer jobs that come to mind are usually the familiar ones, such as babysitting, mowing lawns, and other odd jobs. These jobs should not be overlooked just because they are so ordinary. The reason they are plentiful is that so many people need these services. No matter how many of your friends are doing these chores, dozens of your neighbors will still be eager to hire someone to wash windows, prune plants, or paint porches. Just knock on a few doors and you'll soon have several customers.

If you want to do something a little different, try starting a business of your own. Many teenagers have been quite successful with this approach. Consider your skills and interests and try to make them profitable. For example, two twelve-year-olds I know do bike repairs. Another girl does magic shows at children's parties. Three eighth-graders raise and sell plants.

129

Proofreading

In composition chapters, students are referred to the proofreading checklist, which provides a handy summary of proofreading steps.

Making a clean copy

Students make a clean copy, incorporating all changes and corrections.

Making a final check

Students check their work one more time to make sure that all changes have been made.

Guidelines for the process of writing

This chart is a handy reference tool for students to use in all their writing.

Special feature of the Teacher's Edition

A discussion of two types of evaluation (holistic and analytic) and guidelines for holistic evaluation are provided in this Teacher's Edition. Three kinds of evaluators (self-, peer, and teacher) are also discussed. (See pages T28-T31 on Evaluating Composition.)

Guidelines for the Process of Writing

Pre-Writing
1. Select a topic and narrow it.
2. Decide on your purpose and audience.
3. Gather details to help you develop your topic.
4. Organize and strengthen your list of details.

Writing the First Draft
1. With your purpose and audience in mind, begin to write.
2. Do not be concerned with grammar or mechanics at this stage.

Rewriting, or Revising
1. Did you stick to your topic? Does your writing have unity?
2. Have all important details been included?
3. Are the topic sentences strong and interesting?
4. Do the ideas flow smoothly? Are ideas in a logical order?
5. Is the language vivid and precise?
6. Have you accomplished your purpose?

Proofreading Additional instruction on these concepts may be found in the indicated sections.

Grammar and Usage
Are there any sentence fragments or run-ons? (Sect. 1)
Do all verbs agree with their subjects? (Sect. 9)
Have you used the correct form of each pronoun? (Sect. 3)
Have you used adjectives and adverbs correctly? (Sect. 5)

Punctuation
Does each sentence have the proper end mark? (Sect. 12)
Are marks such as colons, semicolons, apostrophes, hyphens, and quotation marks used correctly? (Sect. 12)

Capitalization
Did you capitalize first words and all proper nouns and adjectives? (Sect. 11)

Spelling
Did you check all unfamiliar words in the dictionary? (Sect. 13)
Are plurals and possessive forms spelled correctly? (Sect. 2, 3)

Form
In your final copy, is the writing legible?
Have you used the proper heading and margins?

59

Clear Presentation of Grammar

In *Building English Skills,* grammar becomes an effective communication tool that students can use in their writing.

Grammar and usage skills are given thorough coverage in *Building English Skills.* The sentence, parts of speech, and usage rules are explained in clear, understandable language. Presentation is straightforward; drill is abundant; and application is explicit and useful.

Rules and generalizations
Important points are summarized and set off in color or boldface type.

Definitions
Definitions are exceptionally clear so that all students can understand them.

Terms
Important terms are highlighted in boldface type.

Explanations
Explanations explore the concepts in greater depth.

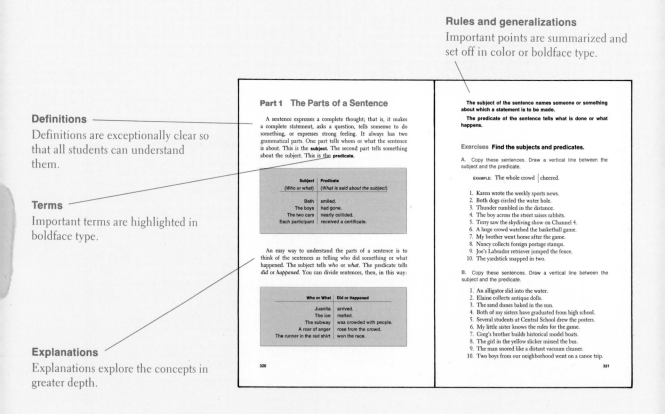

Part 1   The Parts of a Sentence

A sentence expresses a complete thought; that is, it makes a complete statement, asks a question, tells someone to do something, or expresses strong feeling. It always has two grammatical parts. One part tells whom or what the sentence is about. This is the **subject**. The second part tells something about the subject. This is the **predicate**.

Subject (Who or what)	Predicate (What is said about the subject)
Beth	smiled.
The boys	had gone.
The two cars	nearly collided.
Each participant	received a certificate.

An easy way to understand the parts of a sentence is to think of the sentences as telling who did something or what happened. The subject tells *who* or *what.* The predicate tells *did* or *happened.* You can divide sentences, then, in this way:

Who or What	Did or Happened
Juanita	arrived.
The ice	melted.
The subway	was crowded with people.
A roar of anger	rose from the crowd.
The runner in the red shirt	won the race.

320

The subject of the sentence names someone or something about which a statement is to be made.

The predicate of the sentence tells what is done or what happens.

Exercises Find the subjects and predicates.

A. Copy these sentences. Draw a vertical line between the subject and the predicate.

EXAMPLE: The whole crowd │ cheered.

1. Karen wrote the weekly sports news.
2. Both dogs circled the water hole.
3. Thunder rumbled in the distance.
4. The boy across the street raises rabbits.
5. Terry saw the skydiving show on Channel 4.
6. A large crowd watched the basketball game.
7. My brother went home after the game.
8. Nancy collects foreign postage stamps.
9. Joe's Labrador retriever jumped the fence.
10. The yardstick snapped in two.

B. Copy these sentences. Draw a vertical line between the subject and the predicate.

1. An alligator slid into the water.
2. Elaine collects antique dolls.
3. The sand dunes baked in the sun.
4. Both of my sisters have graduated from high school.
5. Several students at Central School drew the posters.
6. My little sister knows the rules for the game.
7. Greg's brother builds historical model boats.
8. The girl in the yellow slicker missed the bus.
9. The man snored like a distant vacuum cleaner.
10. Two boys from our neighborhood went on a canoe trip.

321

Skill-building

Lessons are often introduced with a reference to previous learning.

Practical techniques

The text suggests techniques to aid students in using the skill or concept on their own.

Success-directed practice

Exercises are structured to give students confidence and practice in applying the skill.

Part 2 Verbs and Direct Objects

In many sentences the thought is complete when there are just a verb and its subject.

Subject	Verb
Snow	fell.
Everyone	laughed.
John	stared.

In other sentences the thought is not completed until other words are added.

Roger cut _____   Linda closed _____

You wonder *what* Roger cut and *what* Linda closed. Suppose we completed the sentences as follows:

Roger cut the *rope*.   Linda closed the *door*.

In the first sentence, the word *rope* receives the action of the verb *cut*. It is the **direct object** of the verb.

In the second sentence, *door* receives the action of *closed*. It is the **direct object** of the verb.

The direct object tells what receives the action.

Recognizing Direct Objects

To find the direct object in a sentence, first find the verb. Then ask *what?* or *whom?* after the verb.

The mayor introduced his assistant.
Nancy finished the assignment.

VERB	WHAT OR WHOM (DIRECT OBJECT)
introduced	assistant
finished	assignment

356

Note: Direct objects answer only *what?* or *whom?* after the verb. They do not tell *when* or *where* or *how*. Notice that there are no direct objects in the following sentences:

Lena spoke softly.   A bear lives in that cave.

Exercises Find the direct objects.

A. Copy the following sentences. Underline the verb twice and draw a circle around the direct object.

EXAMPLE: The veterinarian scratched her head.

1. Mud splattered the windshield.
2. The players rushed the goalie.
3. Suddenly a breeze puffed the sail.
4. The jug contains pure water.
5. Dandelions covered the lawn.
6. He always starches his collars.
7. Allison designed the covers.
8. Pete mopped the floor.
9. Mrs. Marshall lost her watch.
10. Judge Harvey drives a Cutlass.

B. Find and write the direct objects in these sentences.

1. Together Pat and Sandra painted the wall.
2. Protect the wildlife.
3. Why did Tina crumple all that newspaper?
4. The store pipes music into every department.
5. Please cut the pie now.
6. Bob raised his eyebrows.
7. Give an example.
8. Have you finished your project yet?
9. Mr. White was constantly wiping his brow.
10. Did you finish your report?

357

Abundant exercises

Chapter parts include at least two sets of exercises that concentrate exclusively on the skill taught in that part.

Reinforcement exercises/Review

Additional reinforcement exercises appearing at the end of each chapter can be used for more practice on a specific topic, or as a chapter review.

Using grammar in writing

Writing activities apply the skill or concepts of grammar taught in the lesson. In addition, the Teacher's Edition provides numerous exercises for the application of grammar in writing (see page T24).

Reinforcement Exercises — Review

The Sentence and Its Parts

A. Find the subjects and predicates.

Copy these sentences. Draw a vertical line between the subject and the predicate.

1. All the water leaked out.
2. Chris wound the thread around the bobbin.
3. His tool box belongs in the shed.
4. The pies smell delicious.
5. Meredith followed the parade over the bridge.
6. The large brown dog breathed down my neck.
7. The gardener grafted the new branch onto an old tree.
8. Peter eased his bicycle over the ditch.
9. The sleet was falling at a 40° angle.
10. Our entire school attended the play-off.

B. Find the verbs and their simple subjects.

Number your paper 1–10. For each sentence write the verb and then its subject.

1. The door swung soundlessly on its hinges.
2. Ann's older sister babysat for the neighbors.
3. The bluejays zigzagged past the clothesline.
4. That little blue Volkswagen squeezed into our parking place.
5. An undercoating protects an automobile from salt corrosion.
6. The measurements of the room surprised my mother.

346

7. In April, the edges of the swamp reverberated with peeper frogs.
8. The computer revealed the mistake.
9. Warm weather makes me happy.
10. In the square, beautiful gardens surrounded the fountain.

C. Find the verbs.

The verb may express an action you cannot see or a state of being. Write only one word for the verb.

1. The Campbells had guests for Thanksgiving.
2. The sky appeared calm.
3. The porch steps are dangerous.
4. Terry had a hard time.
5. Their suspicion is mutual.
6. Fran had a job at the pool for two years.
7. Mrs. Watson feels much better.
8. The farmers hoped for rain.
9. I am from Missouri.
10. The issues in the debate became interesting.

D. Find the main verbs and helping verbs.

Write down the helping verb and main verb for each sentence. Label them HV (helping verb) and MV (main verb).

1. The hikers have looked everywhere for the rope.
2. The actors in the school play were practicing in a Spanish accent.
3. Laura had done all the work before breakfast.
4. The pair had played badminton in the tournament.
5. Roberto did believe the story.
6. The typist had done everything by three o'clock.
7. Karen has had enough sleep.

347

T17

Balanced Study of Language Arts

***Building English Skills* offers a complete, balanced presentation of all language arts skills.**

Part 3 Speaking Formally

When you are asked to speak about a specific topic, to a specific group, for a specific purpose, you will be presenting a ... A formal talk is longer and requires more prepara-... m informal talk. You might think that speaking ... harder and more complicated than speaking in-... t if you follow the step-by-step procedures in this ... will soon learn the routine.

Steps for Preparing a Formal Talk

Know your audience.

Select a topic.

Define your purpose.

Select a theme.

Gather your material.

Organize your material.

Practice your presentation.

Part 2 Poetry

A SONG OF GREATNESS

When I hear the old men
Telling of heroes,
Telling of great deeds
Of ancient days,

When I hear that telling
Then I think within me
I too am one of these.

When I hear the people
Praising great ones,
Then I know that I too
Shall be esteemed,
I too when my time comes
Shall do mightily.

—MARY AUSTIN

Poetry is one of the oldest forms ...
as people were "telling of great de...
posing songs and verse. A **poem** is a...
an emotion, giving an opinion, or te...
to have its own language—one of s...
these elements makes a special co...

The Sound of Poetry

Poetry is most enjoyable when it...
cause one of its most noticeable...
pattern of sound in a poem can h...
produce a musical effect. A poet...
variety of literary devices to create...

Alliteration. One device often u...
Alliteration is the repetition of the...

294

Part 1 Root Words

In Chapter 1, you saw that words or parts of words can some-times be put together to make new words. The words *hangup* and *smog* were made this way.

Another way to make a new word is to add a beginning or an ending to a word. What word was used to make the words in the following list?

> breaker
> breakable
> unbreakable

The word, of course, is *break*. The endings *-er* and *-able* were added to it. The beginning *un-* was also added.

In *breaker*, *breakable*, and *unbreakable*, the **root word** is *break*. You can think of the other words as "growing from" the root word *break*. In each of the other words *break* has had a beginning or ending added to it.

Exercise Root Words

Copy each of the following words on a sheet of paper. Find the root word in each. Write the root word after each word.

illegal	preheat
unable	player
instantly	infection
horizontal	miscalculate
prankster	helpful
patriotism	helpless
indigestion	unbeatable
misfire	dangerous
nonfattening	superpower
useful	poisonous

22

Speaking and listening

Oral language skills are developed through a steadily increasing range of creative and functional language experiences. Students learn to present, evaluate, and appreciate both formal and informal oral presentations. They are also taught the specialized speaking and listening skills needed for group discussion.

Appreciation of literature

The literary appreciation strand gives students a background for understanding and appreciating what they read. Students are gradually introduced to the five main classifications of literature: oral literature, poetry, drama, prose fiction, and prose nonfiction. The texts also provide opportunities for students to write in those forms.

Vocabulary development

Vocabulary development chapters provide transferable skills—a basis for understanding and using new words. Students learn the ways in which new words are formed, how to find the meaning of an unfamiliar word in the dictionary, and how to find the meaning in context.

Study and research skills

Study and research skills include finding word meanings from context, using the dictionary, thinking clearly, using critical thinking, avoiding generalizations, and distinguishing between fact and opinion. The text also includes an introduction to the SQ3R method of study, as well as suggestions for test-taking.

SQ3R

Survey Look over the material to get a general idea of what it is about. Read the titles and subtitles; notice the illustrations; read the introduction and summary.

Question Find out what ⌐
able to answer
Preview any stu⌐
at the end of th⌐
your teacher. Y⌐
own questions ⌐
headings into q⌐
maps, tables, o⌐
as the basis for⌐

Read Read the select⌐
the questions. I⌐
thoughts in eac⌐

Recite After reading, r⌐
your answers t⌐
brief notes to h⌐
answers, as wel⌐
points from the⌐

Review Try to answer e⌐
questions witho⌐
If you can't, rev⌐
the answer. The⌐
impress the mat⌐
you will be able⌐

Exercise Using SQ3R

Use the SQ3R method to stud⌐
bered questions will help you.

224

---

4. **Subject:** an evaluation of rock music of the 1980's
   Source: an interview with a classical pianist

5. **Subject:** the effect of TV on recent political elections
   Source: a study of the TV debates by presidential candidates published in 1966

Part 7   Taking Tests

The word "test" sometimes makes people nervous. Test-taking need not be any more threatening than any other part of your schoolwork, however. It is simply another skill, and like any skill it can be improved once you understand what is involved.

Understanding Test Questions

You already know the kinds of questions that appear on tests. They fall into five main categories. Study these categories, as well as the suggestions for dealing with them.

1. **True-False.** You are given several statements, and are asked to decide whether each one is true or false. Read such questions carefully. Words like "always," "never," "all," or "none" often make a statement false.

   ___F___ The first colonists landed at Plymouth Rock.

2. **Multiple Choice.** Here, you are provided with several possible answers for one question. Read all the choices carefully and select the *best* answer.

   An unproved theory is called a/an
   a) equation
   b) rule
   c) hypothesis
   d) none of the above

232

Use a period after each number or letter that shows a division of an outline or that precedes an item in a list.

AN OUTLINE	A LIST
I. Trees	1. meat
A. Shade trees	2. potatoes
1. Elms	3. ice cream

The Question Mark

Use a question mark at the end of an interrogative sentence.

An **interrogative sentence** is a sentence that asks a question.

Has anyone seen my dog?

The above sentence gives the exact words of the person who asked the question. It is called a *direct question*. A question mark is used only with a direct question.

Do not use a question mark with an indirect question. Instead, use a period.

An *indirect question* is the part of a statement that tells what someone asked, without giving the exact words.

Kelly asked *whether anyone had seen her dog.*

The Exclamation Point

Use an exclamation point at the end of an exclamatory sentence.

An **exclamatory sentence** is a sentence that expresses strong feeling.

What a terrific game that was!

An exclamation point is also used at the end of an imperative sentence that expresses excitement or emotion.

Hurry up!

544

The mechanics of writing

The chapters on mechanics of writing, such as capitalization, punctuation, and outlining, present rules in an orderly, easy-to-consult form. Because each rule is presented developmentally, with explanations, examples, and exercises, these chapters can be used three ways: for independent student work, for teacher-directed lessons, or as a reference source for students.

Components of This Level

Student Text
See pages T6-T19 for significant features of the Student Text.

Teacher's Edition
See pages T22-T31 for significant features of the Teacher's Edition.

Skills Practice Book
Thousands of additional skill-building exercises in composition, vocabulary, grammar, usage and mechanics are included in this workbook. Each page is a self-contained unit offering explanations, examples, and exercises. Additional pages are provided for mixed practice, cumulative review, and using grammar in writing.

Diagnostic and Mastery Tests
Consumable test booklets offer easy-to-use tests: diagnostic tests to help determine the direction of your teaching; and mastery tests to help you check progress throughout the year. The test booklets are available separately or in a Test Package, which contains 25 test booklets, an answer key, a class record, and an individual student's record.

Duplicating Masters

The Skills Practice Book exercises and the Diagnostic and Mastery Tests are also available in duplicating master form.

Teacher's Resource Kit

The Teacher's Resource Kit offers time-saving instructional aids for reinforcement, evaluation, and record-keeping. Each kit contains:

- Teacher's Edition
- ***Practice and Extension Exercises*** Book of Copy Masters
  Composition
  Vocabulary
  Grammar
  Usage and Mechanics
  Mixed Practice
  Cumulative Review
  Using Grammar in Writing

- ***Management, Testing, and Evaluation*** Book of Copy Masters
  Diagnostic Tests
  Mastery Tests
  Alternate set of Mastery Tests
  Individual Student's Record
  Class Record Sheet
  Composition Evaluation Form
  Letters to Parents

- ***Teaching and Evaluating Student Writing*** Booklet
- ***Ideas for Creative Teaching*** Booklet
- Overhead Transparencies for teaching the Process of Writing
- Classroom Posters
- Cumulative Record Folder

Software

Microcomputer software programs to accompany *Building English Skills* are in preparation. Please write for details.

How To Use the Teacher's Edition

Teaching Suggestions

The Teacher's Edition provides clear, well-paced teaching aids for introducing each chapter, for individualizing each lesson, and for reviewing, extending, and maintaining skills.

In addition to the regular chapter features, special features throughout the Teacher's Edition offer suggestions for

- **Optional activities** to reinforce a variety of language skills
- **Individualizing the lesson,** for less-advanced and advanced students
- **Pre-writing activities** to promote creativity
- **Using grammar in writing** assignments

Introducing the Chapter

Full-size student pages
For ease in reading, the entire student text is reproduced full size.

On-page teaching suggestions
All teaching suggestions are printed in the margins beside the student text.

Chapter 1

The Story of Our Language

There are more than half a million words in the English language. Where did they all come from? We could give a quick answer to that question by saying that most of the words in English were "borrowed" from other languages. There is more to the story than that, however. To tell the whole story we have to begin in prehistoric times.

In this chapter you will learn how words started and how different languages began. You will learn how the English language developed and how it is continuing to grow.

1

Chapter Objectives

1. To trace the history and ancestry of the English language from prehistoric times to the present
2. To recognize six ways that new words are added to our language: by borrowing, by compounding and blending older words, by clipping, by using acronyms, by using the names of people or places, and by imitating sounds.

Preparing the Students

Write these Old English lines on the board. Tell the students that this form of English is over a thousand years old.

Faeder ure
Thu the eart on heofonum
Si þin nama gehalagod.

See if the class can interpret the passage. Then tell the students that it is the first line of the "Lord's Prayer." Explain that language is in a sense a living thing because it is always growing and changing. This chapter will explain how it has changed in the past and show how and why it continues to change.

Additional Resources

Mastery Test—See pages 9–10 in the test booklet. Recommended for use after teaching the chapter.
Skills Practice Book—pages 1–5.
Duplicating Masters—pages 1–5.

Chapter objectives
Each chapter opener lists the skills to be mastered in the chapter.

Preparing the students
Suggested lessons or activities introduce students to the subject of the chapter.

Additional resources
A detailed list, with page references, directs you to extra practice, review, and testing resources.

Individualizing the Lesson

Lesson objectives
Clear objectives are stated in terms of learner outcomes.

Presenting the lesson
Step-by-step teaching suggestions for presenting each part in the chapter stress points of emphasis and suggest ways to use the exercises most effectively.

Individualizing
Specific teaching approaches are suggested for adjusting the basic lesson to different levels of ability or skill development.

Less-advanced Students
Advanced Students

Optional practice
Additional teaching ideas are provided for drill, review, or reinforcement.

Extending the lesson
The text suggests an enrichment lesson or exercise that approaches the material in a different way.

Answers
For easy reference, answers to the exercises are overprinted in blue.

Part 2

Objective

To use pronouns correctly as subjects and predicate pronouns .

Presenting the Lesson

1. Read and discuss pages 412 and 413. Refer to the subject forms on the chart on page 410, and stress that only these forms may be used for subjects and predicate pronouns. Since predicate pronouns in the nominative case may sound unusual to some students, read aloud many sentences using predicate pronouns correctly. Note that these pronouns come after linking verbs and are linked to the subject.
2. Do Exercise A on page 413 orally.

Individualizing the Lesson

Less-Advanced Students

Let the students work in pairs to complete Exercise B. Remind them that linking verbs used with predicate pronouns act as equal signs. Have them check their answers by switching predicate pronouns to the subject position. Sentences should still sound correct.

Advanced Students

Have the students diagram sentences with predicate pronouns, as described on page 399.

Part 2 The Subject Form of Pronouns

The subject forms of pronouns are used as subjects. They are also used as predicate pronouns. A **predicate pronoun** is a pronoun that follows a linking verb and is linked by the verb to the subject.

Study these examples:

SUBJECT		PREDICATE PRONOUN	
She and *I*	went.	The students were	*she* and *I*.
You and *he*	came.	The visitors were	*you* and *he*.

The correct use of predicate pronouns is not difficult. But you must be sure that you understand what these pronouns are and how they are used. Otherwise you may become confused.

If you have trouble recognizing predicate pronouns, remember these points:

1. Predicate pronouns follow linking verbs such as *is*, *was*, *were*, and *will be*.

2. The predicate pronoun usually means the same thing as the subject.

3. A sentence with a predicate pronoun will usually make sense if the subject and the predicate pronoun are reversed.

Study the following example.

SUBJECT	VERB	
The visitor	was	he.
He	was	the visitor.
The captains	were	Rita and I.
Rita and I	were	the captains.

Always use the subject form of a pronoun for subjects and predicate pronouns.

Exercises Choose the right pronoun.

A. Number your paper 1–10. Choose the right pronoun in each of the following sentences.

1. Kathy and (me, I) work together.
2. Chrisy and (her, she) are coming.
3. The base runners were Mark and (I, me).
4. The boys are Al's brothers. Al and (them, they) live next door.
5. (We, Us) and the Bradleys play touch football.
6. It was Todd and (me, I) to the rescue.
7. It is (she, her).
8. There are Ginny and (I, me) on TV!
9. (Us, We) and about half the class were tennis players.
10. The baseball experts are (they, them) and their brothers.

B. Number your paper 1–10. Choose the right pronoun in each of the following sentences.

1. (Him, He) is the boy at the door.
2. The Big Hawk Pack and (us, we) became friends at camp.
3. The winners are Trudy and (I, me).
4. Scott and (her, she) are cousins.
5. Robin and (her, she) both roasted marshmallows.
6. (He, Him) and Michael are always together.
7. (Her, She) and (me, I) will see you tonight.
8. The boy on the right is (he, him).
9. Michele and (they, them) kept movie scrapbooks.
10. Peter and (we, us) were almost late to homeroom.

413

Reinforcement Exercise

Assign and discuss Exercise B on page 423.

Optional Practice

Write the following sentences on the chalkboard:

I was the first person in line.
She was the best player.
He was the winner.
We were the youngest ones.
They are the tallest ones.

Have the students reverse these sentences, making the subjects into predicate pronouns. Read aloud the correct answers.

Extending the Lesson

Have each of the students circle all pronouns used as subjects or predicate pronouns in a magazine article. Have them check to see if these are all subject forms. Ask students to read aloud the sentences using predicate pronouns.

Reviewing, Extending, and Maintaining Skills

More exercises/Reinforcement exercises

Alternate uses of the review pages are suggested.

Mixed review exercises

For independent work or as a test of the chapter content, these exercises provide a cumulative review.

Reinforcement Exercises

These Reinforcement Exercises may be used for additional practice as needed. Each Exercise should be used after the text page indicated in parentheses.

Review

If you have not assigned these Exercises before this time, you can use them as an excellent Section Review.

Mixed Review

The following exercises provide review of the concepts and skills presented in this chapter.

A. Find the verbs and their subjects. Write the complete verb and its subject from each sentence. The parts may be compound. Underline subjects once and verbs twice.

1. Two reporters and a photographer covered that story.
2. Sandy selected and planted all of those flowers.
3. The leopards in that cage look sleek and strong.
4. The planes have already landed and are now moving toward the terminals.
5. The heavy snow and strong winds have made travel dangerous.
6. Julie and Steve did not finish their story.
7. Have all the guests arrived?
8. The coach and the referee disagreed about the penalty.
9. The runner had started toward second base but was seen by the

---

Reinforcement Exercises — Review

The Sentence and Its Parts

A. Find the subjects and predicates. (Use after page 321.)

Copy these sentences. Draw a vertical line between the subject and the predicate.

1. All the water leaked out.
2. Chris wound the thread around the bobbin.
3. His tool box belongs in the shed.
4. The pies smell delicious.
5. Meredith followed the parade over the bridge.
6. The large brown dog breathed down my neck.
7. The gardener grafted the new branch onto an old tree.
8. Peter eased his bicycle over the ditch.
9. The sleet was falling at a 40° angle.
10. Our entire school attended the play-off.

B. Find the verbs and their simple subjects.

Number your paper 1–10. For each sentence write the verb and then its subject. (Use after page 326.)

1. The door swung soundlessly on its hinges.
2. Ann's older sister babysat for the neighbors.
3. The bluejays zigzagged past the clothesline.
4. That little blue Volkswagen squeezed into our parking place.
5. An undercoating protects an automobile from salt corrosion.
6. The measurements of the room surprised my mother.

---

6. (Who, Whom) is your doctor?
7. (Who, Whom) did you invite?
8. (Who, Whom) will the judges choose?
9. (Who, Whom) won the 1983 World Series?
10. (Who, Whom) is that man in the gray suit?

F. Find the antecedents. (Use after page 420.)

Make two columns on your paper. Place the pronouns in one column and their antecedents in the other.

1. The chair has lost three of its rungs. *its chair*
2. The girls have a new game. They played it last night. *They girls   it game*
3. Mother called Pete. She asked him to help. *She Mother   him Pete*
4. The hikers were studying their maps. *their hikers*
5. That book has its cover on upside down. *its book*
6. Ms. Evans bought a car. It cost $5,500. *It car*
7. Grandfather is a welder. He wears goggles at work. *He grandfather*
8. Donna sent Kent a card. She mailed it on Friday. *She Donna   it card*
9. Glen inspected the mills. He saw everything in them. *He Glen   them mills*
10. Rosita rearranged the rec room. It looked great. *It room*

G. Use the correct possessive pronouns with indefinite pronouns. (Use after page 420.)

Number your paper 1–10. Choose the correct possessive pronoun from those in parentheses.

1. Nobody hits (his, their) stride in the first mile.
2. Somebody has (their, her) eyes shut.
3. Has anybody got (her, their) tools handy?
4. Both accepted (his, their) awards personally.
5. No one has bought (his, their) ticket yet.
6. Has everybody made (their, his) bed?
7. Many of the students typed (his or her, their) papers.
8. Each of the girls was in (her, their) place.
9. Several forgot (his, their) lines.
10. Everybody has (her, their) ups and downs.

425

Using Grammar in Writing

1. Show your students a picture of a group of people doing something, and ask the students to write an imaginary narrative based on the picture. Have the students circle all personal pronouns and decide what noun each stands for.

2. Have the students write three headlines for advertisements for a new brand of toothpaste. Tell the students that each headline must use a possessive pronoun.

3. Have the students combine the following sentence pairs, using a pronoun as an object:

Tina called Maggie. Tina apologized to Maggie.

The dog likes Kevin. It follows Kevin everywhere.

The coach talked to the pitchers. He gave the pitchers a new strategy.

4. Tell the students to imagine that the school is forming a new all-girls or all-boys service club. Have students write statements of goals for the club concerning what the club might do to improve the school. All sentences should use we or us girls or we or us boys.

5. Have each student write paragraphs describing each member of his or her family. Then have the students underline all pronouns and draw arrows to their antecedents. Finally, have the students exchange papers to check for pronoun-antecedent agreement.

6. Show the students pictures of groups of people engaged in an activity together. Have the students write sentences describing what everyone in the picture has in common. Tell them to begin each sentence with an indefinite pronoun, such as everybody or all, and to use another pronoun with it correctly.

Using grammar in writing

The text suggests a variety of creative writing activities designed to help students apply the concepts of grammar or mechanics in their writing.

Management Aids

In addition to the items provided in the Teacher's Resource Kit, these convenient evaluation forms can be used throughout the year for evaluation and record keeping (see page T1 for exact page references).

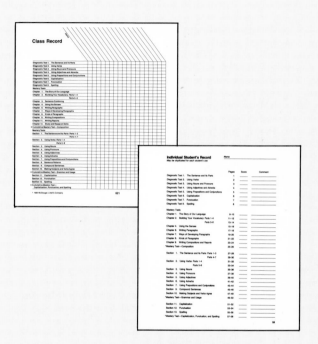

Class Record Sheet

For your convenience, a reproducible class record lists all the diagnostic and mastery tests and provides a chart on which to record student scores.

Individual Student's Record

To help you keep a concise record of each student's work, an individual record sheet is provided. This chart may also be duplicated and given to the students so that they may keep track of their own progress.

Composition Evaluation Form

Based on the Process of Writing as developed in the text, this form may be used during self-, peer, and teacher evaluation. The form also serves as a useful record of the student's development in writing (see page T31).

Cumulative Record Folder

In addition to the materials in the Teacher's Edition, cumulative record folders are available to provide a record of each student's performance from grade 1 through grade 8 of the program.

Management Guidelines

The following guidelines are designed to help a teacher adapt the materials in *Building English Skills* to suit his or her particular needs and schedule.

Determining the Topics To Be Covered

Before initiating the *Building English Skills* program, teachers should review the topics to be covered in light of these questions:

1. What are the curriculum requirements of the district?
2. How much time is available for the teaching of English?
3. What topics, if any, are taught elsewhere or as a separate course (for instance, library skills or spelling)?

These questions should help the teacher narrow down the topics to be covered in the time allotted.

Diagnosing Student Strengths

Next, teachers should administer the Diagnostic Tests to students to gain insight into the strengths and weaknesses of the class as a whole and of individual students. The results of these tests, combined with samples of student writing, will help determine which areas will require the most time and emphasis.

A Typical Schedule of Instruction

Here is a typical schedule of instruction:

	Suggested Number of Weeks	
Skills Taught	Grade 7	8
Composition	16	15
Grammar	14	14
Related Language Art Skills	6	7

Most teachers will spend approximately one week on each chapter. However, some chapters will require more time for in-depth coverage.

A Unique Service for Teachers:
Custom Designed Management Plan

For school districts adopting *Building English Skills*, McDougal, Littell & Company will, upon request, provide a customized time management plan geared to the curriculum requirements and time allotments in your district. Please write for details.

Individualizing

Initially, each chapter should be taught to the class as a whole. It may then be necessary for the teacher to provide additional help for some students while continuing to challenge the others. Suggestions for such individualization are provided in the teaching suggestions under these headings:

Less-advanced Students	Reinforcement Exercises
Advanced Students	Mixed Review
Optional Practice	Using Grammar in Writing
Extending the Lesson	

Teachers should become familiar with the suggestions before beginning to teach the lesson, and plan sufficient time to incorporate them as necessary. (See pages T23 and T24).

Combining Grammar and Composition

This text is divided into two parts: the first concerns composition and related skills, and the second concentrates on grammar, usage, and mechanics. Since the emphasis of the series is on composition, it is recommended that these chapters form the main framework of the course. Sections dealing with grammar, usage, and mechanics should be incorporated on a regular basis—with the frequency of presentation and the emphasis to be determined by the students' needs.

Managing Program Resources

In the *Building English Skills* series, all materials essential to the student for achieving the stated objectives are provided in the student text. All the materials essential to the teacher for presenting the student text and for evaluating and recording student progress are provided in the Teacher's Edition and in various support materials. The following chart shows how these materials may be used.

Resource

Teaching Step	Student Text	Teacher's Edition	Skills Practice Book, Diagnostic and Mastery Test Booklet, Duplicating Masters
Preparing the Students 1. Pretest/Diagnosis		Diagnostic Tests	Diagnostic Tests
2. Motivation	Chapter Opener	Chapter Notes: Preparing the Students	
Teaching the Lesson 1. Basic Lesson	Part Lesson	Presenting the Lesson	

2. Individualizing		Individualizing the Lesson
		    Less-Advanced Students
		    Advanced Students	

Reinforcing the Lesson 1. Written exercises	Part Exercises	Optional Practice	SPB/DM's page(s) listed under Additional Resources
2. Review of lesson, with practice exercises			SPB, DM's
3. Group activities		Optional Practice	
Extending the Lesson		Extending the Lesson	
Applying Grammar and Other Skills to Writing		Using Grammar (or Other Skills) in Writing (listed at end of sections on Grammar, Usage, and Mechanics)	SPB, DM's
Testing the Lesson 1. Individual Part check-up	Review Exercises		
2. Mixed review check-up		Mixed Review Exercises	Chapter Review and Cumulative Review pages of SPB/DM's
3. Chapter test			Mastery Tests
Reteaching	Any unused Part Exercises	Any unused exercises in Optional Practice	Any unused worksheets in SPB, DM's
Retesting			Alternate Mastery Tests

Guidelines for Evaluating Composition

Adapted from *Teaching and Evaluating Student Writing*, copyright © 1984 by McDougal, Littell & Company

Most educators would agree that constant, helpful evaluation of student writing is the only way to help young writers develop their skills. For many teachers, however, this "helpful" feedback has come to mean endless amounts of time spent with a stack of papers and a red pencil, marking every incorrect spelling or misplaced comma. Such an evaluation is suffered through for the good of the students. Yet how much does this evaluation system aid the developing writer?

When a child is learning to talk, a parent will accept and respond to single words or incomplete phrases, recognizing that the child has a message to communicate even if the form of the message is undeveloped. Similarly, when a student is learning to write, he or she needs the encouragement of a response to a written message, no matter what the form of that message is. A teacher cannot afford to require correct sentence structure, grammar, capitalization, punctuation, and spelling before looking at the ideas in a piece of writing.

The practical classroom application of these ideas, advanced by recent research into the writing process, is that students should be given opportunities to write as frequently as possible and that they be given some evaluation of the sense and style of their writing as frequently as possible. This emphasis on quantity means that some teachers may need to rethink their evaluation procedures.

Types of Evaluation

In order to give student writers the constant practice and feedback they need, teachers must have a practical method of evaluation. Obviously, if the student will be writing constantly, a teacher cannot be expected to evaluate each piece in a line-by-line, word-by-word manner. Nor would such an evaluation necessarily be useful to the developing writer. It is therefore suggested that a teacher learn to use two different evaluation methods—the holistic method and the more detailed analytic method.

Holistic evaluation of writing is a quick, guided method of rating pieces of writing. It can best be used to evaluate daily writing samples or first drafts of more complex pieces. With holistic evaluation, an evaluator reads the written piece as a whole, considers certain features, and immediately assigns a grade. The grade may be a single rating for the entire piece of writing or a set of ratings for the different features being considered.

The evaluation form provided on page T31 of this Teacher's Edition is of this second type of holistic evaluation, but will also guide teachers who wish to use the single rating evaluation. It lists the major characteristics of content and form that can be identified in most types of writing. When the teacher desires to evaluate a certain type of writing, such as narrative composition, he or she might supplement the general questions about content with more specific guidelines.

Analytic evaluation should occur only when the student has turned in the clean, final copy of a piece of writing. In this detailed type of evaluation, the teacher analyzes each aspect of a piece of writing, including both content and mechanics. By this point, many of the student's errors will have been spotted and corrected during the revision process. Problems that remain in the final copy are likely to be indicative of where the student's real weaknesses lay, and both student and teacher can concentrate on identifying and correcting them.

Evaluators

The evaluation process can be utilized by three types of evaluators: the writer of the piece, other students, and the teacher. Each type of evaluation offers unique benefits to the developing writer.

1. Self-Evaluation. In this type of evaluation, a writer comments on his or her own work, noting which parts were successful and which unsuccessful. During self-evaluation, a student may be guided by a chart such as the one on page T31, as well as by what "feels" right.

It will not always be possible for a student to pinpoint exactly what is wrong in a piece of writing. When this occurs, the writer should be encouraged to underline any sentence or section that doesn't "feel" right, verbalize the problem as he or she perceives it, and then seek further clarification and help from the teacher. This estimation of errors will eventually become more precise as the student learns to recognize similar problems in later writing.

It is very helpful for students to be guided through the evaluation process before they attempt self-evaluation. The teacher might, for example, project a sample composition using an overhead projector, and then guide the class to an understanding of the types of questions they should ask during the revision process. Such guided evaluation helps the young writer develop a sense of when information is incomplete or ideas unclear. This knowledge can then be applied during self-evaluation.

2. Peer Evaluation. Evaluating the writing of others is often a strong learning experience. In peer evaluation, students work together in small groups to improve a piece of writing. Student evaluators should always be given a list of specific criteria that the writing is expected to meet, and should then comment on how well each paper succeeds. Peer evaluation is most effective when the writer is given time to make revisions after the group suggests ways to improve the work.

3. Teacher Evaluation. The teacher's comments and suggestions may be incorporated at any point in the writing process. Studies indicate that evaluation by the teacher is most successful when it is done in combination with self- and peer evaluation. The evaluation form on page T31, therefore, provides for such a combination of evaluation procedures.

Teacher evaluation should also involve direct communication with every student. Such help can be provided in student-teacher conferences. These conferences provide an opportunity for students to ask the questions they develop during self-evaluation. They also give teachers a chance to comment on the strong points of the paper, offer additional suggestions, provide individualized instruction when it is needed.

Teacher evaluation of a final copy should be the last step in the evaluation process. When a student turns in a clean, final copy of a paper, the teacher should require that previous drafts be turned in with it. The teacher should then provide an in-depth analysis of the final copy, judging it not only on its final content, but also on how well the student incorporated earlier suggestions.

Keeping a Record of Improvement

Both the teacher and students benefit when writing folders are maintained throughout the school year. A piece of writing from early in the year, along with its evaluations, can be compared with later pieces. Progress from one piece to the next will be erratic, as the writer takes risks using new techniques and appears to move backwards until gaining mastery of each new technique. However, over the course of the year, progress should be evident.

BIBLIOGRAPHY

Cooper, Charles R. and Lee Odell, eds. *Evaluating Writing: Describing, Measuring, Judging.* Urbana, Illinois: National Council of Teachers of English, 1977.
Evertts, Eldonna L., ed. *Explorations in Children's Writing.* Urbana, Illinois: National Council of Teachers of English, 1970.
Graves, Donald H. *Balance the Basics: Let Them Write.* New York: The Ford Foundation, 1978.
Murray, Donald M. A *Writer Teaches Writing: A Practical Method of Teaching Composition.* Boston: Houghton Mifflin, 1968.
Sager, Carol, "Improving the Quality of Written Composition in the Middle Grades," *Language Arts* 54 (1977): 760–762.

Using the Evaluation Form

The following form for composition evaluation may be used at any stage of the writing process, and may be re-used after each revision.

The form should be filled out by the student and turned in with the writing. There is also space on the form for peer evaluation, if desired. The teacher may ask students to turn in only final copies, or may ask to see work in progress. The student states whether the submitted writing is the final copy.

On the evaluation form, content may be rated at any point; mechanics should be graded only on a final copy.

Self-Evaluation: Besides the questions on the form, the student can ask himself or herself the questions concerning revising listed in the relevant composition chapter. The student may use 1, 3, and 5 subjectively.

Peer Evaluation: Members of the peer group should rate each feature as objectively as possible. In order to focus on ideas and organization, the group should evaluate content only.

Teacher Evaluation: The following standards for evaluating composition are provided to assist the teacher in rating papers with objectivity and consistency. In a conference, the teacher might discuss one or two of these areas in detail.

Standards for Holistic Evaluation

Content	1—Low	3—Average	5—High
1	Unclear, unimaginative writing.	Understandable but unimaginative writing.	Imaginative, interesting writing.
2	Boring or poorly defined topic.	Topic adequately limited and defined.	Well-chosen, precisely developed topic.
3	Purpose unclear, or not achieved in the writing.	Purpose defined adequately. Not completely achieved.	Clear, well-defined purpose. Writing achieves purpose successfully.
4	Writing so lacking in detail that topic remains undeveloped.	Incomplete development. More information needed.	Topic thoroughly covered. Writing is rich in detail and supporting information.
5	Many irrelevant sentences or details.	Few irrelevant sentences or details.	Well-chosen, relevant sentences and details.
6	Disjointed ideas. No transitional words, phrases, or ideas.	Inconsistent flow. Some transitional devices.	Ideas flow well. Good use of transitional devices.
7	Lack of any logical organization of ideas.	Some organization of ideas evident.	Well-organized ideas. Type of organization suited to topic and purpose.
8	Dull, general words, poorly chosen. Inappropriate to audience.	Suitable but unimaginative language. Generally appropriate to audience.	Specific, vivid language. Appropriate to audience.

Mechanics

1	Many fragments and run-on sentences. Frequent mistakes in the use of nouns, verbs, pronouns, and subject-verb agreement.	Few fragments and run-ons. Some mistakes in the use of nouns, verbs, pronouns, and subject-verb agreement.	No fragments or run-ons. Few mistakes in the use of nouns, verbs, pronouns, and subject-verb agreement.
2	Frequent mistakes in capitalization.	Occasional mistakes in capitalization.	Infrequent mistakes in capitalization.
3	Punctuation marks frequently misused or missing.	Punctuation marks usually used correctly.	Infrequent mistakes in punctuation.
4	Frequent mistakes in spelling, without any indication of awareness of spelling patterns.	Occasional misspellings, usually indicating an approximation of the correct spelling and an awareness of spelling patterns.	Infrequent spelling mistakes.
5	Paragraphs not indented. Writing illegible. Incorrect headings or margins.	Some carelessness or inconsistency in form. Occasionally hard to read.	Correct form. Neat, legible handwriting.

Composition Evaluation Form

Writer _____ **Date** _____

Title _____ **Circle one:** Unfinished   Final Copy

Evaluation Symbols
1   Needs a great deal of work
3   Acceptable—could be improved
5   Very good. Needs no further revision.

Content

	Writer's Opinion	Peer Group Opinion	Teacher's Evaluation	Teacher's Comments
1. **Interest.** Is the writing interesting and understandable? Does it hold the reader's attention?				
2. **Topic.** Is the topic a good one? Has it been narrowed sufficiently?				
3. **Purpose.** Is the purpose of the writing clear? Has the writer accomplished this purpose?				
4. **Development.** Has the topic been developed well? Is there sufficient information?				
5. **Unity.** Are all ideas and details related to the topic? Do they all help to develop or strengthen the main idea?				
6. **Continuity.** Do ideas flow smoothly? Has the writer avoided any breaks in thought?				
7. **Organization.** Were ideas arranged in a logical order? Does this order suit the purpose of the writing?				
8. **Language.** Is the language appropriate to the writing? Does it suit the audience? Are the words vivid?				
Additional Guidelines				

Mechanics (to be graded by teacher on final copy only)

1. **Grammar and Usage.** Are there any fragments or run-ons? Is the correct form of every pronoun or verb used? Are adjectives and adverbs used correctly?				
2. **Capitalization.** Are all first words, initials, proper nouns, proper adjectives, and titles capitalized?				
3. **Punctuation.** Does each sentence have the proper end mark? Are all punctuation marks used correctly?				
4. **Spelling.** Are all words spelled correctly? Are plurals and possessive forms spelled correctly?				
5. **Form.** Is the writing legible? Is the heading correct? Are there sufficient margins?				

Programs Correlated with *Building English Skills*

McDougal, Littell & Company provides integrated language arts programs at the elementary level. While each of these programs is designed to stand alone, together they produce highly effective results in the classroom. For students, skill-learning is enhanced . . . with the consistent treatment of topics, and the reinforcement of common terms and concepts from one series to another. For teachers, instruction is easier: each series features the same clarity of organization and presentation, and a logical, one-step-at-a-time approach to learning.

The *McDougal, Littell Literature* Series

The *McDougal, Littell Literature* Series for grades 7-8 provides an in-depth presentation of literary types at each level to give students a strong grasp of the possibilities of each genre. Carefully-chosen selections illustrate the concepts, skills, and literary techniques students need in order to understand and appreciate literature. For each selection, a useful list cross-references writing skills to specific lessons in *Building English Skills*.

Building Reading Skills

This basal reading series is specifically designed to teach reading skills to middle and junior high school students. While most reading programs shift the emphasis from skill *development* to skill *application* in the middle grades, *Building Reading Skills* continues the emphasis on skill development. A three-part instructional plan teaches the skills, then leads students to a guided application of the skills, and finally to independent reading.

Building Spelling Skills

This unique spelling series for grades 1–8 offers instruction geared to three types of learner: the visual learner, the auditory learner, and the kinesthetic learner. Based on years of spelling research, the program groups words by structural patterns to give students a framework for learning and remembering the spelling.

Building English Skills

Purple Level

Yellow Level

Blue Level

Orange Level

GREEN LEVEL

Red Level

Gold Level

Silver Level

Aqua Level

Brown Level

Plum Level

Pink Level

Kindergarten Level

THE McDOUGAL, LITTELL ENGLISH PROGRAM

Building English Skills

Green Level

Joy Littell, EDITORIAL DIRECTOR

McDougal, Littell & Company
Evanston, Illinois
New York   Dallas   Sacramento

Prepared by the Staff of
THE WRITING IMPROVEMENT PROJECT

Joy Littell, Editorial Director, McDougal, Littell & Company

Donna Rae Blackall, Chairperson, English Department, Miner Junior High School, Arlington Heights, Illinois

J. A. Christensen, East High School, Salt Lake City, Utah

William H. Horst, Henrico County Schools, Virginia

Eric L. Kraft, Writer and Editor, Stow, Massachusetts

Carolyn McConnell, Former Language Arts Teacher, West Haven, Connecticut

Debbie Rosenberger, formerly, Henrico County Schools, Virginia

Kathleen Bell, Department of English, University of Miami, Coral Gables, Florida

Consultants

H. Kaye Griffin, Ed. D., Language Arts Coordinator, Klein Independent School District, Spring, Texas

Thomas C. Holland, Ed. D., Assistant Superintendent, Curriculum and Instruction, McKinney Independent School District, McKinney, Texas

Marilyn Sherman, Specialist in Curriculum Development, Wilmette, Illinois

Edmund Sullivan, Supervisor of Language Arts, Evansville-Vanderburgh School Corporation, Evansville, Indiana

Cathy Zollars, Director of Instruction, Grand Prairie Schools, Grand Prairie, Texas

Acknowledgments: See page 618

The twelve sections on grammar, usage, and mechanics contain, in revised form, some materials that appeared originally in *The Macmillan English Series, Grade 8,* by Thomas Clark Pollock et al., copyright © 1963, 1960, 1954 by The Macmillan Company. Used by arrangement.

ISBN: 0-86609-084-3   TE ISBN: 0-86609-085-1

Contents

Grammar, Usage, and Mechanics

SPECIAL FEATURES OF THIS TEXT

In order to achieve a logical, developmental presentation of skills, this book divides language concepts into two main sections. The first half of the text concerns composition and related skills. The second half of the book consists of fourteen numbered sections that deal with grammar, usage and mechanics.

The Composition Chapters (First half of text)

Developing Your Vocabulary. Chapter 1 emphasizes procedures for learning word meanings from context: definition, restatement, examples, comparison, and contrast.

Using the Dictionary. Chapter 2 shows students how to use the dictionary: how to locate words; how to divide, pronounce, and define them; and how to select precise synonyms.

Sentence Combining. Chapter 3 presents a basic introduction to sentence combining. Its purpose is to help students create mature sentences and to help them become aware of the choices they have in combining ideas. This chapter has been designed so that a knowledge of grammar terms is not necessary to understand the concepts involved.

The Process of Writing. Chapter 4 introduces and begins analysis of the three major steps in writing: *pre-writing, writing the first draft,* and *rewriting or revising,* which includes proofreading. This process is the basis of all good writing, and is used and reinforced throughout all of the composition chapters.

The Paragraph. Chapters 5, 6, and 7 comprise an intensive study of the paragraph. Chapter 5 introduces the form of the structured paragraph and explains the function of a topic sentence. Chapter 6 treats in detail several ways of developing paragraphs: using specific sensory details, using facts or figures, using examples and incidents, and using a definition. Chapter 7 provides a working explanation of three kinds of paragraphs: narrative, descriptive, and explanatory. Each chapter provides a wealth of first-rate models, along with helpful analysis.

Writing Compositions. Chapter 8 begins by analyzing the structure of a composition. It then provides a clear, workable blueprint for writing a composition. It once again leads students through the process of writing, expanding on the information they received in Chapter 4. Models are provided to clarify each step, and one sample composition is used to show all the steps in the process of planning, writing, and revising. Chapter 9 demonstrates how the techniques from the previous chapter can be applied to narrative compositions, descriptive compositions, explanatory compositions, and persuasive compositions.

Writing Reports. Chapter 10 applies the process of writing to the specific requirements of a report. In addition to reviewing the basic steps of pre-writing, writing a first draft, and revising, this chapter teaches students how to work with facts and opinions, how to take notes using note cards, how to use an outline, and how to operate a bibliography.

Thinking Clearly. Chapter 11 helps students understand the process of clarifying their thinking by separating fact from opinion, checking facts, making facts clear, and reasoning logically.

Using the Library. Chapter 12 helps students understand the classification and arrangement of books, the use of the card catalog, and reference materials.

Study and Research Skills. Chapter 13 provides students with valuable keys to improving all areas of their schoolwork. The chapter presents information to help students understand an assignment, listen to directions, use an assignment book, set long- and short-term goals, design a study plan, take notes, learn to skim and scan, understand graphic aids, and take tests more effectively. The chapter also introduces the SQ3R method of study, which provides students with a technique for approaching reading and study assignments across the curriculum.

Writing Letters. Chapter 14 shows in detail how to go about writing friendly and business letters. The chapter contains a wide variety of model letters.

Interviews and Group Discussions. Chapter 15 provides guidelines for conducting interviews and helps students feel comfortable about talking before a group.

Literature. Chapter 16 is an introduction to four main types of literature: oral literature, poetry, nonfiction, and fiction. Students study such genres as the legend, tall tale, ballad, poem, ancedote, essay, satire, short story, and play. Important literary terms are also introduced. In addition, students are made aware of how the techniques they learned in their study of composition are demonstrated in the literature they are reading. In the exercises, they are given many opportunities to do creative writing of their own.

Grammar, Usage, and Mechanics (Second half of text)

The Simple Sentence. Section 1 presents the simple sentence and its parts.

The Parts of Speech. Sections 2-6 introduce the parts of speech. Throughout, the emphasis is on usage. Students are urged to "say it right, hear it right, and write it right."

Sentence Patterns. Section 7 analyzes word order and meaning and introduces five basic sentence patterns.

Compound and Complex Sentences. Section 8 helps the students understand and use compound and complex sentences.

Making Subjects and Verbs Agree. Section 9 helps students acquire an ear for subject/verb agreement.

Verbals. Section 10 introduces students to verbals and verbal phrases.

Capitalization, Punctuation, and Spelling. Sections 11-13 deal with the mechanics of writing in an orderly, easy-to-use form.

Outlining. Section 14 provides guidelines for preparing a topic outline.

Chapter 1

Developing Your Vocabulary

You have a group of words that you know well, use well, and feel comfortable with. These are the words that you use from day to day. You use them when you talk with friends, and your friends use them when they talk with you. This group of words that you use so comfortably in speaking is your **speaking vocabulary.**

When you sit down to write a letter or a composition, you have more time to think about the words you will use. In fact, when you are writing, you may use some words that you would not use when you are speaking. You may not feel as sure of these words as you do of the words in your speaking vocabulary. You do understand them, however, and you use them when you think about them. These words, in addition to

1. To use these five context clues to learn the meanings of unfamiliar words:

  a. definition
  b. restatement
  c. examples
  d. comparison
  e. contrast

2. To use synonyms and antonyms to express precise meanings

Preparing the Students

Read and discuss the introduction on pages 1 and 2. Draw a diagram on the chalkboard to help the students understand the concept of the three vocabularies. Draw a small circle and label it *speaking vocabulary*. Then draw a larger circle around the first and label it *writing vocabulary*. Explain that all of the words from the speaking vocabulary are included. Lastly, draw a still larger circle around the two inner circles and label it *reading vocabulary*. Explain that all of the words in a person's speaking and writing vocabularies are included in this category.

Tell the students that the purpose of this chapter is to show them how to increase their reading and writing vocabularies.

Additional Resources

Mastery Test—See pages 9–10 in the test booklet. Recommended for use after teaching the chapter.

Reinforcement Exercises—See pages 12–13 in the student text.

Skills Practice Book—pages 1–8.

Duplicating Masters—pages 1–8.

1

the words in your speaking vocabulary, make up your **writing vocabulary.**

There is another group of words that you understand when you read them. You do not know these words well enough to feel comfortable about using them in speaking or in writing. But you do understand them when you come across them in your reading. These words, added to all the words in your writing vocabulary, equal your **reading vocabulary.**

The larger your reading vocabulary is, the better you will understand what you read. The larger your writing and speaking vocabularies are, the better you will be able to make people understand you. In this chapter you will learn how to make your reading vocabulary larger. You will also learn how to use words to say exactly what you mean in writing or speaking.

Part 1 Learning Word Meanings from Context

Many words have more than one meaning. For example, the word *sink* has a different meaning in each of these sentences.

> If we don't plug that leak, this boat will *sink*.
> The *sink* is full of dishes.

In one sentence, *sink* means "to go under water." In the other, it means "a tub or basin." You can easily tell which meaning fits which sentence. You can tell from the other words in each sentence.

The meaning of a word depends on its **context,** the words that come before or after it. Often the context makes the meaning clear, as it did in the two sentences above. Sometimes it does not, as in this sentence.

> We waited to see if Donna would *sink* it.

Here the context does not tell you whether Donna is playing golf or trying to sink a boat.

Part **1**

Objective

To use these five context clues to learn the meanings of unfamiliar words:

   a. definition
   b. restatement
   c. examples
   d. comparison
   e. contrast

Presenting the Lesson

1. Read the introduction on pages 2 and 3. Write the word *context* on the chalkboard and define it. Have the students define the word *calf* in each of the following sentences.

The cow fed her *calf*.

The dog bit the mailman's *calf*.

Explain that the students probably already knew each of those defini-

Context can tell you which meaning of a word fits what you are reading. It can also help you decide the meaning of a word you do not know. As you have seen, context will not always tell you enough to let you decide. But if you learn to look for certain clues, context can be a great help.

In this chapter you will learn how to use five kinds of context clues that will help you in your reading.

Context Clue 1: Definition

Sometimes a writer knows that a word will be unfamiliar to many readers. To make the word easier to understand, the writer may include a definition of the word in a sentence. It is as if the writer were saying to the reader, "I know you won't know the meaning of this word, so I am going to tell it to you." This context clue is the easiest one to spot, and it is the easiest to understand. Look at the following examples.

> At the zoo we saw a *gnu*, which is a large African antelope.
> Helium makes the balloon *buoyant*; in other words, it floats.
> The harbor is protected by a *jetty*. A jetty is a wall built out into the water.

In the first example, the writer tells you that a gnu is a large African antelope. The key words *which is* signal the definition. In the second example, the writer tells you that to be buoyant means to float. The key words *in other words* signal this definition. In the third example, the definition of *jetty* is given in a sentence of its own. The key word in this example is *is*. Watch for the key words *which is* (or *that is*), *in other words*, and *is* when you read. These key words often signal a definition.

Exercise Definition

Number a sheet of paper from 1 to 10. Read each of the following sentences. Each sentence includes a definition for the

tions of *calf*; the context showed them which meaning was appropriate. Tell the students that context clues can also help them determine the meanings of words that they do not know. On the chalkboard, write the names of the five context clues that will be studied: definition, restatement, examples, comparison, and contrast.

2. Read and discuss **Context Clue 1: Definition** on page 3. Have the students study the following additional examples. Point out the key words that signal the definition in each example.

> The musketeer put away his *foil*, which is a long, thin, fencing sword.

> The pond was *stagnant*; in other words, it was dirty and smelly from lack of movement.

> Samuel Clemens's *nom de plume* was Mark Twain. A *nom de plume* is a pen name.

3. Assign and discuss the Exercise on pages 3–4.

4. Read and discuss **Context Clue 2: Restatement** on pages 4–5. Have the students study the following additional examples. Point out the key word or punctuation that signals a restatement.

> My cousin has been described as *loquacious*, or talkative.

> Chuck broke his *clavicle*—his collarbone—while playing football.

5. Assign and discuss the Exercise on page 5.

6. Read and discuss **Context Clue 3: Examples** on page 6. Discuss the following additional examples. Point out the key words that signal an example.

> The costumes were made of a silky material, like *faille*.

Succulents, such as jade plants and aloe plants, are easy to care for.

7. Assign and discuss the Exercise on page 6.

8. Read and discuss **Context Clue 4: Comparison** on pages 7 and 8. Discuss the following additional examples.

Their singing voices were as *raucous* as crows' caws.

The *geodesic dome* was like a glass-and-metal igloo.

9. Read and discuss **Context Clue 5: Contrast** on page 8. Note the key words that signal contrast as a context clue. Discuss the following additional examples.

Grant is *lethargic* today; Gloria, however, is full of energy.

The climate of Florida is *balmy*, unlike that of Minnesota.

10. Assign and discuss the Exercise on page 9.

Individualizing the Lesson

Less-Advanced Students

1. Read the sentences in the Exercise beginning on page 3 aloud. Point out the key words in each sentence that signal a definition. Then have the students complete the Exercise independently.

2. Do the first half of the Exercise on page 5 orally. Point out the key or keys that signal a restatement. Then assign the remainder of the Exercise as independent work.

3. Have the students write the dictionary definition for each word in the Exercise beginning on page 6 after the inferred definition. Discuss the differences.

4. Read the sentences in the Exercise on page 9 aloud, pointing

italicized word. Write the <u>meaning</u> of each italicized word. Be ready to tell what (key words) helped you spot the definition.

1. We stayed in *youth hostels,* (which are) cheap places to stay for young people who are traveling.

2. Metal can be polished with *pumice,* (which is) rock formed from the lava of a volcano.

3. Clarice is *indecisive;* (that is), she can't make up her mind.

4. We had to *rappel* down the face of the cliff. (In other words), we had to lower ourselves on ropes.

5. I learned to use a *pantograph.* A pantograph (is) a mechanical gadget used to make a copy of a drawing.

6. The legs should be *perpendicular* to the top of the table. (That is), they should meet the top at right angles.

7. The *marimba,* (which is) a kind of xylophone, is played with mallets.

8. The crops were destroyed by *locusts.* Locusts (are) large grasshoppers.

9. The sculpture is made of *gesso,* (which is) a kind of plaster.

10. Our feet were tangled in a kind of seaweed (called) *kelp.*

Context Clue 2: Restatement

You will not always be lucky enough to find a definition for a word in its context. More often, you will find a restatement. A restatement tells you almost as much as a definition, but it is not as easy to spot. Look at the following examples.

The walls were *buttressed,* or propped up, with sturdy logs.

We need volunteers to make *hors d'oeuvres*—appetizers—for the parents' meeting.

He had a *wan* look, pale and weak.

In the first example, the writer restates *buttressed* as "propped up." The writer has not directly said that *buttressed* means "propped up." Instead, the writer has written the same idea twice. The keys to spotting "propped up" as a restatement of *buttressed* are the word *or* and the commas that separate "or propped up" from the rest of the sentence.

In the second example, *hors d'oeuvres* is restated as "appetizers." Dashes separate *appetizers* from the rest of the sentence. These dashes are a key to spotting "appetizers" as a restatement of *hors d'oeuvres*.

The words *pale and weak* restate the idea of "wan" in the third example. The only key to *pale and weak* as a restatement is the comma that separates these words from the rest of the sentence.

The examples show three keys to spotting restatement as a context clue. They are the word *or*, a dash or a pair of dashes, and a comma or a pair of commas. Parentheses can also indicate a restatement.

Exercise **Restatement**

Number a sheet of paper from 1 to 10. Read each of the following sentences. Each sentence includes a restatement of the italicized word. Write the meaning of each italicized word. Tell what key or keys helped you spot the restatement.

1. The new school seemed like a *labyrinth*—a maze—to me. dashes
2. The meeting turned into quite a *fracas*, or uproar. comma and *or*
3. My favorite spot at the zoo is the *aviary*, the building where the birds are kept. comma
4. Colonial families cleaned house with a *besom*—a broom made of twigs tied to a handle. dash
5. We have to *collate* these pages—put them in the right order—before we staple them. dashes
6. Carl led us on a *devious*, or winding, route home. commas and *or*
7. For short hikes you may want to use a *haversack*, a small bag that you can carry over one shoulder. comma
8. She has always been an *upright* person, honest and just. comma
9. We play *quoits*, a game like horseshoes. comma
10. Carbon monoxide is a *noxious* (poisonous) gas. parentheses

out the key words that signal comparisons and contrasts. Then have the students complete the Exercise independently.

Advanced Students

1. Do all the Exercises orally.
2. Have the students use each italicized word in each Exercise in an original sentence.

Reinforcement Exercise

Assign and discuss Exercise A beginning on page 12.

Optional Practice

1. Have the students follow the directions for the Exercise beginning on page 3, using these sentences:

1. Part of the necklace is made of *electrum*, which is a mixture of gold and silver.
2. The gold box was in the shape of a *cartouche*. A cartouche is an oval ring that encloses the characters expressing an Egyptian king's name.
3. The *archeologist* Howard Carter discovered Tutankhamen's tomb. An archeologist is a scientist who studies prehistoric peoples and their cultures.
4. Most of the treasures of the great *pharaohs*, who were the ancient Egyptian kings, have been lost to us.
5. The statue is *gilded*; that is, it is covered with gold.

2. Have the students follow the directions for the Exercise on page 5, using these sentences:

1. Tutankhamen's mirror case is in the shape of an *ankh*, the hieroglyphic sign for "life."

2. The *scarab*, or beetle, was a symbol of the sun god in ancient Egypt.

3. The chair was made of *ebony*—a hard, heavy, black wood.

4. The lid was made of *alabaster*—a smooth, white stone.

5. The hostages were *incarcerated*, or imprisoned, in the embassy.

3. Have the students follow the directions for the Exercise beginning on page 6, using these sentences:

1. Cathy is allergic to such *crustaceans* as shrimp, lobster, and crabs.

2. The *gemsbok* can be found with the other antelopes in the zoo.

3. The agent performed *covert* missions, like secretly bugging telephones and photographing secret papers.

4. We put *basil*, oregano, and other herbs in the casserole for flavoring.

4. Have the students follow the directions for the Exercise on page 9, using these sentences:

1. Sue's mood is *petulant* today, but usually she is easygoing.

2. *Buddhism*, like other Eastern religions, is an entire way of life.

3. The *avocado*, unlike most fruits, is not sweet.

4. Joe's supervisor is *fastidious*; Jan's, on the other hand, is careless.

5. Laura put the *conch* with the other shells in her collection.

Extending the Lesson

Have each student find a published example of each kind of context clue. Books and articles on technical and scientific subjects (a

Context Clue 3: Examples

Examples can also give you a clue to the meanings of unfamiliar words. Study the following sentences.

Kelp and other kinds of seaweed can be made into food.

Some kinds of seaweed, like *kelp*, can be made into food.

Neither sentence tells you just what kelp is, but both sentences tell you that kelp is one example of seaweed. Now that you have an idea of what kelp is, look at the following sentence.

Marine algae, such as *kelp*, can be grown in underwater farms.

In this sentence, kelp is mentioned as an example of marine algae. The sentence does not tell you what *marine algae* means. It does, however, tell you that kelp is one kind of marine algae. From that clue you should be able to figure out that *marine algae* must mean something like "seaweed."

The following key words signal an example (or examples) as a context clue. The key words are in boldface type. The sentences show how they are used to give clues to the meaning of the italicized words.

Elaine has mastered the *half gainer* **and other** difficult dives.

Tony is good at difficult dives **like** the *half gainer*.

Diane can do some difficult dives—the *half gainer*, **for instance.**

Phil is no good at difficult dives **such as** the *half gainer*.

Martha did some difficult dives—**for example,** the *half gainer*.

Kurt is good at all difficult dives, **especially** the *half gainer*.

Exercise Examples

Write definitions for the italicized words in the following sentences. Use context clues alone to write your definitions. Check your definitions in a dictionary.

1. The forest was made up of pine, fir, and other *conifers*.

trees like pine and fir

2. A good camper knows how to tie a *half hitch*, a *bowline*, a *clove hitch*, and other useful knots. useful knots

3. *Perishable* foods, like milk and butter, vegetables, and meats, should be kept refrigerated. foods that spoil if not kept cold

4. I like all kinds of sausage, but especially *knockwurst*. kind of sausage

5. In this chapter you will read about such ancient heroes as *Ulysses* and *Hercules*. ancient heroes

6. *Mollusks*, especially clams, oysters, and snails, may be grown on "sea farms" in the future. sea animals with shells like clams, oysters, snails

7. She's studying *glaucoma* and other diseases of the eye. disease of the eye

8. In this display you'll find *hedgehogs* and other animals that eat insects. animal that eats insects

9. We're learning how to make some fancy desserts—*chocolate mousse*, for example. fancy dessert

10. If you're serious about mountain climbing, you'll need *crampons* and other special climbing equipment. mountain climbing equipment

Context Clue 4: Comparison

When you compare things, you see how they are like each other. You usually compare things that are not much alike in order to point out one important way that they are alike.

Comparisons in writing can give you clues to the meanings of unfamiliar words. Look at the following examples to see if you can get an idea of the meaning of each italicized word.

> The hot-air balloon tugged at its *tether* like a dog tugging at its leash.
>
> At last the balloon took off. It was as *buoyant* in the air as a cork is in water.

In the first example, the writer compares a balloon on a tether to a dog on a leash. Both are tugging, trying to get free. The balloon is like a dog. The tether is like a leash. From the comparison you should be able to see that a tether must be something like a leash.

science textbook, for example) are good hunting grounds for sentences with context clues, especially if they are written for young people or another audience that the writer assumes is ignorant of the vocabulary necessary to understand the subject. Have the students read their sentences in class. Discuss the clues, the meanings of the unfamiliar words, and the key words that signal each clue.

7

In the second example, the writer compares a balloon in air to a cork in water. You know that a cork floats in water, and that it may bob a bit while it floats. The writer says that a balloon is buoyant in air. The writer says that a cork is buoyant in water. The buoyant balloon is compared to the buoyant cork. From the comparison you should be able to see that something buoyant is something that floats.

Key words that help you spot comparison as a context clue include *like*, *as*, and *similar to*.

Context Clue 5: Contrast

When you contrast things, you look at them to see how they are different from each other. You often contrast things that are alike in many ways in order to point out one important way that they are different. You don't usually contrast trees and rocks or buses and pickles, because you already know that these things are quite different from each other. Instead, you contrast things that are similar to show an important way in which they are different.

A contrast between two things can give you a clue to the meaning of an unfamiliar word. Look at the following examples to see if you can get an idea of the meaning of the italicized words.

> Unlike most other rats, the *bandicoot* carries its young in a pouch.
> *Rodents*, unlike most other animals, have teeth that keep growing throughout their lives.
> Tony was *reticent*, but Phyllis spoke right up.

In the first example, the bandicoot is contrasted with "most other rats." The writer points out one way in which the bandicoot is different from most other rats. Because the writer makes this contrast, you can be reasonably sure that except for this difference the bandicoot is like most other rats. A bandicoot, then, must be a kind of rat.

In the second example, the writer contrasts rodents with "most other animals." The writer points out one way in which rodents are different from most other animals. Because the writer makes this contrast, you can be reasonably sure that rodents are like most animals in other ways. Therefore, rodents must be animals.

In the third example, Tony is contrasted with Phyllis. Tony was reticent. Phyllis spoke right up. This was something that made Tony different from Phyllis. Therefore, being reticent must be different from speaking right up. Being reticent must mean something like "not speaking right up."

Key words that signal contrast as a context clue include *unlike, but, on the contrary,* and *on the other hand.*

Exercise Comparison and Contrast

Write definitions for the italicized words in the following sentences. Use context clues alone to write your definitions. Check your definitions in a dictionary.

1. Anna, unlike most *ailurophobes,* can at least stand to be in the same room with a cat. someone with a fear of cats

2. Like other *marsupials,* a kangaroo carries its young in a pouch. a class of animal that carries its young in a pouch

3. The museum has many examples of early bicycles, such as the *ordinary* and the *high wheeler.* early bicycles

4. Laura spends her time reading about *griffins, unicorns,* and other imaginary beasts. imaginary beasts

5. Some people think Paul is *irrational,* but he has always seemed reasonable to me. not reasonable

6. I was *anxious,* but everyone else seemed calm and relaxed. tense and worried

7. Pull the taffy until it is as *elastic* as a rubber band. stretchy

8. When you hit the bar, it will make a *plangent* sound like a bell. loud, ringing

9. Most of us agreed. However, Cheryl *dissented.* disagreed

10. *Stalactites* hung from the roof of the cave like icicles. icicle-shaped formations

9

Objective

To use synonyms and antonyms to express precise meanings

Presenting the Lesson

1. Read and discuss pages 10 and 11. Write the word *synonym* on the chalkboard and define it. Have the students suggest synonyms for the following words:

old   ate   saw
happy big little

Discuss differences in the meanings of the synonyms they suggest.

2. Assign and discuss Exercises A and B on page 11.

3. Read and discuss page 12. Write the word *antonym* on the chalkboard and define it. Have the students suggest pairs of antonyms.

4. Assign and discuss Exercises A and B on page 12.

Individualizing the Lesson

Less-Advanced Students

1. Before the students begin Exercise A on page 11, read the list of synonyms for *said* aloud. Define any unfamiliar ones. Then have the students complete the Exercise independently.

2. Before the students begin Exercise B on page 11, review the use of a synonymy in a dictionary.

3. Work with the students to complete Exercise A on page 12 orally. Help them find antonyms in a dictionary.

4. Compare the first two items in Exercise B on page 12 orally to

Part 2 Gaining Precision in the Use of Words

When you have something to say to someone, you want to say it in such a way that it can be understood. You don't want people to misunderstand you. Neither do you want them to only half-understand you. You can help people understand you by using words that make your meaning clear.

If your speaking and writing vocabularies are small, you won't have many words to choose from. You will not be able to say exactly what you mean.

To help people understand exactly what you mean, you must say exactly what you mean. You must choose the best words to express your meaning.

Using Synonyms

In order to be able to say exactly what you mean, you will need to know the synonyms for many words. **Synonyms** are words that have nearly the same meanings. However, they do not have exactly the same meanings. When you use a word from a group of synonyms, you must pick the one that is closest in meaning to what you want to say.

Think about the word *run*. It has many synonyms. They include *trot*, *dash*, *flee*, *scamper*, and *sprint*. Each of these synonyms has a slightly different meaning. If you want to describe a squirrel running across a park, you might use *scamper*. However, if you want to describe the finish of the Kentucky Derby, *scamper* would be the wrong word.

If you look at passages of dialogue in stories, you will find many synonyms for the word *said*. You may find some or all of the synonyms shown here and in Exercise A.

shouted	bellowed	exclaimed
whispered	declared	muttered

Which of these synonyms would you use for someone speaking in a loud voice? Which would you use for an excited person? You can see that there are important differences among these words.

Exercises Using Synonyms

A. Following is a list of synonyms for *said* that might be used in sentences 1 through 10. Choose the word that best fits each sentence.

whispered	chanted	screamed
called	cried	growled
announced	muttered	
explained	declared	

1. "I am the best violinist in class," ___declared___ Mark.
2. "Don't look now, but someone's watching us," ___whispered___ Nancy.
3. "There will be a quiz on Friday," ___announced___ Mr. Hunt.
4. "Wait! You forgot your notebook, hat, and pencil," ___called___ Madeline.
5. "I can't make this problem work out," ___muttered___ Sam.
6. "You have to multiply, not divide," ___explained___ Mr. Crandall.
7. "Stay in line. Stay in line. Stay in line," ___chanted___ Ms. Donovan.
8. "You always get more than I do," ___cried___ Lucy.
9. "If I get any trouble from you, you'll get plenty of trouble from me," ___growled___ Rafferty.
10. "A giant clam has me by the foot," ___screamed___ Louise.

B. List as many synonyms as you can for the following words. Use a dictionary for help. Answers will vary.

pull	break	hard	dull	intelligent
funny	fast	angry	tired	

demonstrate what the students are to do. Then have the students complete the Exercise independently.

Advanced Students

1. After the students have completed Exercise A on page 11, challenge them to think of five additional ways to say *said*. Discuss whether their synonyms can be used appropriately in any of the sentences.

2. After the students have completed Exercise B on page 11, have them write sentences using the synonyms they found. Tell the students to make their sentences illustrate the shades of difference among the synonyms.

3. After the students have completed Exercise A on page 12, have them write sentences using each pair of antonyms.

4. For Exercise B on page 12, have the students use two antonym pairs in each comparison.

Reinforcement Exercise

Assign and discuss Exercise B on page 13.

Optional Practice

1. Have the students follow the instructions for Exercise B on page 11, using these words:

dry	leave	touch
know	sad	weak

2. Have the students complete each sentence with an antonym for the italicized word.

1. Marc was *careless*; Morton, on the other hand, was _____.
2. The *aroma* of bread filled the bakery; the _____ of garbage filled the alley behind it.

3. The *exterior* of the building was brick; the _____ was wooden.
4. "This scalpel is *dull*; hand me a _____ one," said the surgeon.
5. This photograph is *clear*; that one is _____ .

Extending the Lesson

Introduce the students to *Roget's Thesaurus*. If possible, borrow a classroom set and review Exercise B on page 11, having the students look up each word. Explain that a thesaurus only lists synonyms; it does not define them. Therefore, the students should check the definition of an unfamiliar synonym in a dictionary before using it, to make sure that it conveys the desired meaning.

Reinforcement Exercises

These Reinforcement Exercises may be used for additional practice as needed.

Review

If you have not assigned the Reinforcement Exercises before this time, you can use them as an excellent Chapter Review.

Using Antonyms

Antonyms are words that are nearly opposite each other in meaning. The words *light* and *dark* are antonyms. So are *old* and *new*. So are *wide* and *narrow*.

Notice that a word may have more than one antonym. The word *old* is an antonym for *new*, but so is *ancient*. The word *new* is an antonym for old, but so are *recent* and *modern*.

You can use antonyms to clarify your ideas by making comparisons. If you are comparing two buildings, you could say that one is tall and the other is short. You could say that one is lofty and the other is squat. You could say that one is towering and the other is stumpy. Each comparison creates a different picture. You must decide which words are the best for the picture you want to create.

Exercises Using Antonyms

A. Write an antonym for each word listed in Exercise B under Using Synonyms on page 11. Answers will vary.

B. Use antonyms to compare each of the following: Answers will vary.

1. two people   5. two athletes   9. two places
2. two books   6. two buildings   10. two cars
3. two pets   7. two metals
4. two moods   8. two seasons

Reinforcement Exercises Putting Your Vocabulary Skills Together

A. Use context clues to decide the meaning of each italicized word in the following sentences. Write a definition for each word. Then be ready to tell what clue and what keys helped you decide the meaning.

1. (Like) all *carnivores*, wolves prefer to eat meat. comparison

2. The design was made of three *concentric* circles; (that is), three circles with the same center. definition

3. The new government was extremely *fragile*; (in other words), it could easily fall apart. restatement

4. You have to *interlace* the two colors of wool—weave one over and under the other. restatement

5. For weeks the hunters lived on nothing but *pemmican*, dried meat pressed into cakes. restatement

6. I gathered my spade, rake, hoe, (and other) gardening *implements*. examples of garden tools

7. If you're going to spend the night, you'll have to put up with the creatures that haunt this castle, (including) *ghouls*, *poltergeists*, and *bogies*. examples of scary creatures

8. Joan's ideas seemed *incontestable* to me, (but) Frank went ahead and argued with her anyway. contrast, not arguable

9. She used to be a *retiring* type, (but) now she's the life of the party. contrast, shy, quiet

10. The disease became *pandemic*; (that is), it spread through the entire country. definition

B. Read each of the following sentences. Try to think of a more precise synonym for each italicized word. If you need help, use a dictionary. Answers will vary.

1. That was a really *good* dinner.
2. There's a *cold* wind blowing from the north.
3. Elaine *said* that she could beat any of us at ping-pong.
4. I *jumped* over the fence and ran for my life.
5. The quake *moved* the buildings as if they were toys.
6. She *moved* quickly across the floor.
7. Cars *moved* along the highway at rush hour.
8. It was a *bad* place to be.
9. The elephant *walked* slowly down the ramp.
10. The boy *walked* aimlessly down the street.

Chapter 2

Using the Dictionary

How many words are there in the English language? Would you guess 100,000? 200,000? 500,000? A good guess would be more than 500,000, but no one is really sure how many words there are. Old words die out and new ones are born all the time. Some words have short lives. Some live on and on. Some are used often by nearly everyone. Some are not used much at all. No one can know the meanings of so many words. That is why everyone runs into an unfamiliar word now and then. When that happens, a person turns to a dictionary.

Just what is a dictionary? How can a dictionary help you? A dictionary is a list of words, with information about each word. It will divide the words into syllables and tell you how to pronounce them. It will tell you the meanings of the words. It will tell you what words are related in meaning. Finally, it will tell you the history of each word. This chapter will show you how to get the most out of a dictionary.

Chapter Objectives

1. To use alphabetical order to locate words in a dictionary

2. To use guide words to locate words in a dictionary

3. To locate words with unfamiliar spellings in a dictionary

4. To use a dictionary to find syllabification and word division

5. To use phonetic respellings and a pronunciation key to learn the pronunciations of unfamiliar words

6. To choose the correct definition of a word for a given context

7. To use a synonymy

Preparing the Students

Read page 15. Have the students suggest words that have puzzled them when they came upon them while reading or when they heard them used in speech. Write these words on the chalkboard or write them on a large sheet of paper and post them for reference during the students' study of this chapter. Encourage the students to add other words as time goes by. Explain that this chapter will show them how to use a dictionary well, and that they will learn how to find the meanings of words and a great deal more information about words as well.

Additional Resources

Mastery Test—See pages 11–12 in the test booklet. Recommended for use after teaching the chapter.

Reinforcement Exercises—See page 27 in the student text.

Skills Practice Book—pages 9–14.

Duplicating Masters—pages 9–14.

Part 1

Objective

To use alphabetical order to locate words in a dictionary

Presenting the Lesson

1. Read page 16. Have the students alphabetize the class list of unfamiliar words.

2. Assign and discuss Exercises A and B on page 16.

Individualizing the Lesson

Less-Advanced Students

1. Before the students begin Exercise A, show them how to alphabetize systematically.

2. Before the students begin Exercise B, have them check their dictionaries to see where letters fall.

Advanced Students

When the students have completed Exercise A, have them combine all the lists into one alphabetical listing.

Reinforcement Exercise

Assign and discuss Exercise A on page 27.

Optional Practice

Have the students alphabetize the last names of everyone in the class.

Extending the Lesson

Challenge the students to list as many titles of books as they can and arrange them alphabetically.

The words in a dictionary are listed in alphabetical order. All words that begin with *a* come first. All words that begin with *b* come next. Words that begin with *s* come before words that begin with *t*, and so on. When words begin with the same letter, they are alphabetized according to the second letter. If the second letter is the same, the words are alphabetized according to the third letter, and so on.

The words in these columns are in alphabetical order.

anteater	a**a**rdvark	gr**a**sshopper
groundhog	a**l**batross	gr**e**yhound
hedgehog	a**n**teater	gr**i**ffin
mole	a**r**madillo	gr**o**undhog

To find words quickly, learn to open the dictionary at the right spot. With practice, you will be able to find words quickly.

Exercises Alphabetical Order

A. Arrange each group of words in alphabetical order.

1	**2**	**3**	**4**
2 franc	2 elm	4 Sun	5 neck
3 peso	5 walnut	3 Mercury	1 arm
1 dollar	1 beech	5 Venus	3 head
5 rupee	4 pine	1 Earth	2 hand
4 pound	3 fir	2 Mars	4 heart

B. Working with a classmate, practice opening the dictionary as close as you can to a particular letter. Have your classmate say a letter. Try to open your dictionary to that letter. Then switch roles and say a letter for your classmate. Continue until you can open the dictionary close to a specific letter most of the time.

Part 2   Guide Words

In most dictionaries you will find **guide words** at the top of each page. These help you find a word more quickly. The guide word on the left tells you the first word on the page. The guide word on the right tells you the last word on the page.

On pages 18 and 19 you will find a reproduction of a dictionary page. The guide words for this page are *ridgepole* and *righteous*. Notice that all the other words on the page fall between these two in alphabetical order.

After you have opened to the right section of the dictionary for the word you want to find, you can find the exact page by following the guide words. Flip pages quickly until the guide words tell you that you are getting close. In your mind, compare the guide words and the word you are looking for.

Exercises   Using Guide Words

A.   Write the numbers 1 through 5 on a sheet of paper. Beside each of the following numerals you will find the guide words for a dictionary page. After the guide words is another word. Decide whether you would find that word on a page *before* the given one, *on* it, or *after* it. Write *before, on,* or *after* on your paper.

1.	**bloodhound**	**blubber**	blowout on
2.	**career**	**caribou**	careful on
3.	**contact**	**content**	contest after
4.	**endive**	**engage**	endow on
5.	**frazzle**	**free lance**	freedom on

B.   See how quickly you can find these words in your dictionary. Copy the guide words from the page where you find each one.
Answers will vary with the dictionary used.

eggplant	trampoline	shuffleboard	vulture
iguana	dolphin	emu	yak
moose	newt	anaconda	woodchuck

Part 2

Objective

To use guide words to locate words in a dictionary

Presenting the Lesson

1. Read page 17. Have the students study the sample dictionary page on pages 18 and 19. Ask the students which of these words fall between the guide words *ridgepole* and *righteous*: *ridge, right, ride, riding, rifle,* and *riddle.* Explain that they should not have to search the page to see if the word is included or not. They should use alphabetical order to see if the word falls between the two guide words.

2. Assign and discuss Exercises A and B on page 17.

Individualizing the Lesson

Less-Advanced Students

Work with the students to complete Exercise A. Help them see that a word must fall alphabetically between guide words to appear on a page.

Advanced Students

1. Add the following words to Exercise B on page 17.

mischief   ruffian
lathe   pancreas

Reinforcement Exercise

Assign and discuss Exercise B on page 27.

Optional Practice

Have the students follow the directions for Exercise A on page 17, using these words:

1. **obtain ocean**
   occur
2. **pleasing plier**
   please
3. **Schubert scoop**
   scoopful
4. **fed feint**
   fedora
5. **mildew miller**
   mild

Extending the Lesson

Introduce the students to an unabridged dictionary. Explain that an unabridged dictionary is the largest and most complete dictionary. Since there are so many entries, usually over 250,000, it is particularly important for the students to use their dictionary skills of alphabetizing and using guide words to locate words. Then repeat Exercise B on page 17, using the unabridged dictionary.

ridge·pole (rij′pōl′) *n.* the horizontal timber or beam at the ridge of a roof; also **ridge′piece′**

rid·i·cule (rid′i kyōōl′) *n.* [Fr. < L. *ridiculum*, a jest, ult. < *ridere*, to laugh: for IE. base see VERSE] **1.** the act of making a person or thing seem foolish, as by making fun, mocking, laughing, etc. **2.** words or actions used in doing this —*vt.* -**culed**′, -**cul**′**ing** to make fun of or make others laugh at; deride; mock

SYN.—**ridicule** implies a making fun of a person or thing by way of showing disapproval [*he ridiculed her new hat*]; **deride** suggests contempt for or a strong dislike of what is being made fun of [*to deride another's beliefs*]; **mock** suggests a ridiculing by the unkind imitation of another's manner-isms or habits [*it is cruel to mock his lisp*]; **taunt** implies insulting ridicule, esp. as shown by jeering at another and harping on something that makes him feel ashamed [*they taunted him about his failure*]

ri·dic·u·lous (ri dik′ye les) *adj.* deserving ridicule; absurd —see SYN. at ABSURD —**ri·dic′u·lous·ly** *adv.* —**ri·dic′u·lous·ness** *n.*

rid·ing[1] (rid′ing) *adj.* **1.** that rides **2.** of or for riders on horseback [*jodhpurs and boots are parts of a riding habit*] ☆**3.** designed to be worked by a rider [*a riding mower*] —*n.* the act of one that rides

rid·ing[2] (rid′in) *n.* [OE. -*thrithing*, a third part] any of the three administrative divisions of Yorkshire, England

ri·el (rē el′, rēl) *n.* [see RIAL, REAL[2]] *see* MONETARY UNITS, table (Cambodia)

Rif (rif) mountain range along the Mediterranean coast of Morocco: also **Er Rif** (er)

rife (rif) *adj.* [OE. *ryfe*] **1.** happening frequently or commonly; widespread [*gossip was rife*] **2.** *a*) abundant *b*) abounding; filled [*rife with error*] —see SYN. at PREVAILING —**rife′ness** *n.*

Riff (rif) *same as* RIF —*n., pl.* **Riffs, Riff′i** (-ē) a member of a Ber-ber people living in or near the Rif

RIDGEPOLE

to dress; clothe (usually with *out*) [*all rigged out in a cowboy suit*] —*n.* **1.** the arrangement of sails, masts, etc. on a vessel ☆**2.** equipment for a special purpose; gear [*a ham radio opera-tor's rig*] ☆**3.** equipment for drilling an oil well ☆**4.** *a*) a car-riage, etc. with its horse or horses *b*) a tractor-trailer or, sometimes, the tractor alone **5.** [Colloq.] dress or costume, esp. if odd or showy —**rig′ger** *n.*

Ri·ga (rē′gə) capital of the Latvian S.S.R.; seaport on the Baltic Sea: pop. 733,000

ri·ga·to·ni (rig′ə tō′nē; *It.* rē′gä tô′nē) *n.* [It., pl. < pp. of *rigare*, to mark with lines] short, ridged casings of pasta, often stuffed with ground meat, cheese, etc.

Ri·gel (rī′j′l, -g′l) [Ar. *rijl*, foot: in the left foot of Orion] a bright, bluish star, brightest in the constellation Orion

rig·ging (rig′iŋ) *n.* **1.** the chains, ropes, etc. used for support-ing and working the masts, sails, etc. of a vessel ☆**2.** equip-ment; gear

right (rīt) *adj.* [OE. *riht*: for IE. base see REGAL] **1.** orig., straight: now only in mathematics [*a right line*] **2.** *a*) formed by a straight line perpendicular to a base [*a right angle*] *b*) having the axis perpendicular to the base [*a right cylinder*] **3.** in accordance with justice, law, morality, etc.; virtuous [*right conduct*] **4.** in accordance with fact, reason, etc.; correct; true [*the right answer*] **5.** fitting; suitable [*the right dress for a dance*] **6.** designating the side meant to be seen [*the right side of cloth*] **7.** *a*) physically or mentally healthy [*he doesn't look right*] *b*) in a satisfactory condition; in good order [*to make things right again*] **8.** *a*) designating or of that side of one's body which is toward the east when one faces north, the side of the more-used hand in most people *b*) designating or of the corresponding side of anything *c*) closer to the right side of a person facing the thing mentioned [*the top right drawer*] **9.** of or at the right of a river on the right of a person facing downstream of the bank of a river on the right of a person facing downstream **10.** of the political right; conservative or reactionary —*n.* **1.** what is right, or just, lawful, proper, etc. [*to know right from wrong*] **2.** *a*) a power, privilege, etc. that a person has or gets

side [the first door on the *right*] *b)* a turn toward the right side [take a *right* at the corner] **5.** *Boxing a)* the right hand *b)* a blow delivered with the right hand **6.** [*often* **R-**] *Politics* a conservative or reactionary position, party, etc. (often with *the*): from the seating (on the right) of conservatives in some European legislatures —*adv.* **1.** in a straight line; directly [go *right* home] **2.** in a way that is correct, proper, just, favorable, etc.; well [do it *right*] **3.** completely [soaked *right* through his coat] **4.** exactly [*right* here] ☆**5.** immediately [come *right* down] **6.** on or toward the right hand or side **7.** very [he knows *right* well]: colloquial except in certain titles [the *right* reverend] —*interj.* agreed! I understand! —*vt.* **1.** to put in or restore to an upright position [to *right* a capsized boat] **2.** to correct [to *right* an error] **3.** to put in order [she *righted* the room] **4.** to make amends for [to *right* a wrong] —*vi.* to regain an upright position —**by right** (or **rights**) in justice; properly —**in one's own right** through one's own status, ability, etc. —**in the right** on the side supported by truth, justice, etc. —**right away** (or **off**) without delay; at once —**to rights** [Colloq.] in or into proper condition or order —**right′er** *n.* —**right′ness** *n.*

right·a·bout (rīt′ə bout′) *n. same as* RIGHTABOUT-FACE —*adv., adj.* with, in, or by a rightabout-face

right·a·bout-face (-fās′) *n.* **1.** a turning directly about so as to face in the opposite direction **2.** a complete turnabout, as of belief —*interj.* a military command to do a rightabout-face

right angle an angle of 90 degrees, made by the meeting of two straight lines perpendicular to each other

right-an·gled (rīt′aŋ′g'ld) *adj.* having or forming one or more right angles; rectangular: also **right′-an′gle**

right·eous (rī′chəs) *adj.* [altered < OE. *rihtwis:* see RIGHT & -WISE] **1.** acting justly; doing what is right; upright; virtuous [a *righteous* man] **2.** morally right or having a sound moral basis [*righteous* anger] —see SYN. at MORAL —**right′eous·ly** *adv.* —**right′eous·ness** *n.*

RIGHT ANGLE

---

see ROW] ☆**1.** *a)* a shoal, reef, etc. in a stream, producing a stretch of ruffled or choppy water *b)* a stretch of such water, or a ripple on it **2.** the act or a method of riffling cards —*vt., vi.* **-fled, -fling 1.** to ruffle or ripple **2.** to leaf rapidly through (a book, etc.) by letting the edges of the pages slip lightly across the thumb **3.** to shuffle (playing cards) in a way like this by holding part of the deck in each hand

riff·raff (rif′raf′) *n.* [< OFr. *rif et raf* < *rifler*, to scrape + *rafle*, a raking in] **1.** those people regarded as worthless, low, coarse, etc.; rabble **2.** [Dial.] trash

ri·fle1 (rī′f'l) *vt.* **-fled, -fling** [Fr. *rifler*, to scrape < OFr. < MHG. *riffeln*, to scratch] **1.** to cut spiral grooves on the inside of (a gun barrel, etc.) ☆**2.** to hurl or throw with great speed —*n.* ☆**1.** a shoulder gun with spiral grooves cut into the inner surface of the barrel: see RIFLING **2.** [*pl.*] troops armed with rifles

ri·fle2 (rī′f'l) *vt.* **-fled, -fling** [< OFr. *rifler*, to plunder, orig. to scratch: see prec.] **1.** to ransack in order to rob; pillage; plunder [to *rifle* a safe] **2.** to take as plunder; steal —**ri′fler** *n.*

ri·fle·man (-mən) *n., pl.* **-men 1.** a soldier armed with a rifle **2.** a man who uses, or is skilled in using, a rifle

rifle range a place for target practice with a rifle

☆**ri·fle·ry** (-rē) *n.* the skill or practice of shooting at targets with rifles

ri·fling (rī′fliŋ) *n.* **1.** the cutting of spiral grooves within a gun barrel, to make the projectile spin when fired **2.** a system of such grooves

rift (rift) *n.* [Dan., a fissure < *rive*, to tear: see RIVE] **1.** an opening caused by splitting; fissure; cleft **2.** an open break in friendly relations —*vt., vi.* to burst open; split

rig (rig) *vt.* **rigged, rig′ging** [< Scand.] **1.** *a)* to fit (a ship, mast, etc.) with sails, shrouds, etc. *b)* to fit (a ship's sails, shrouds, etc.) to the masts, yards, etc. **2.** to fit (*out*); equip **3.** to put together or prepare for use, esp. in a makeshift or hasty way (often with *up*) [to *rig* up a table out of old boxes] **4.** to arrange in a dishonest way; fix [to *rig* an election] **5.** [Colloq.]

fat, āpe, cär; ten, ēven; is, bīte; gō, hôrn, tōōl, look; oil, out; up, fur; get; joy; yet; chin; she; thin, *th*en; zh, leisure; ŋ, ring; ə for *a* in *ago, e* in *agent, i* in *sanity, o* in *comply, u* in *focus;* ' as in *able* (ā′b'l); Fr. bal; ë, Fr. coeur; ö, Fr. feu; Fr. mon; ô, Fr. coq; ü, Fr. duc; r, Fr. cri; H, G. ich; kh, G. doch; ‡ foreign; ☆ Americanism; < derived from. See inside front cover.

Objective

To locate words with unfamiliar spellings in a dictionary

Presenting the Lesson

1. Read page 20. Pronounce the following words: *gypsum, physique, psoriasis*. Have the students use the Word-Finder Table and a dictionary to find the correct spelling of each.

2. Assign and discuss the Exercise at the top of page 21.

3. Emphasize that the Word-Finder Table is a simplified guide for initial sounds only.

Individualizing the Lesson

Less-Advanced Students

Work with the students to find the first word described in the Exercise.

Advanced Students

Add the following item to the Exercise.

5. what Little Miss Muffet ate with her curds that sounds similar to *way*

Optional Practice

Pronounce the following words: *ghastly, gist, rhesus, sieve, wholesale, quoits, scythe*. Have the students locate each in a dictionary.

Extending the Lesson

Have the students survey dictionaries and write the title of each that has a word-finder chart.

Part 3 Finding a Word

You may have asked this question before: "How can I look up a word in a dictionary if I'm not sure how to spell it?" You can find a word even if you are not sure of the spelling. It will take you more time than it would if you knew the spelling, but you can do it.

Below you will find a "Word-Finder Table." This table shows many ways to spell the sounds you may hear at the beginnings of words. To use the table, first find the spellings for the sound you hear. Then check the dictionary under those spellings until you find the word you want.

Word-Finder Table

If the word begins with a sound like . . .	then also try the spellings . . .	as in the words . . .
a in care	ai	air
e in get	a	any
e in here	ea, ee	ear, eerie
f in fine	ph	phrase
g in go	gh, gu	ghoul, guard
h in hat	wh	who
j in jam	g	gym
k in keep	c, ch, q	can, chorus, quick
n in no	gn, kn	gnu, kneel
o in long	a, ou	all, ought
r in red	rh	rhyme
s in sew	c, ps, sc	cent, psychology, scene
sh in ship	s	sure
t in top	th	thyme
u in under	a, o	ago, onion
u in use	you, yu	youth, yule
ur in fur	ear	earn
w in will	wh	wheat
z in zero	x	xylophone

Exercise Using the Word-Finder Table

Use the Word-Finder Table to find each of the words described below. When you find the word, write its correct spelling.

1. the name for a small glass bottle that sounds like *file* phial
2. the name of an herb that sounds like *time* thyme
3. the name for a wharf or dock that sounds like *key* quay
4. the name for an African antelope that sounds like *new* gnu

Part 4 Word Division

The spelling of a word in the dictionary shows how the word is divided into syllables. Some dictionaries use space to show this. Others use a centered dot.

bub ble   bub·ble

Sometimes, when you are writing or typing a paper, you may find that a long word will not fit at the end of a line. Part of the word will have to run on to the next line. When that happens you should divide the word between syllables. Use a hyphen to show that the word continues on the next line.

RIGHT: bub-ble   WRONG: bu-bble, bubb-le

Exercises Word Division

A. Rewrite each of the following words. Show the syllables just as your dictionary does.

jel·ly·fish
jellyfish
hel·i·cop·ter
helicopter
name·less
nameless
con·nec·tion
connection
ham·mer
hammer
bot·tle
bottle
na·tion·al
national
pa·rade
parade

B. Use a hyphen to show how you could divide each word.

gear-shift
gearshift
hack-saw
hacksaw
mal-let
mallet
crick-et
cricket
han-dle-bars
handlebars
chis-el
chisel
but-ter-fly
butterfly
lo-cust
locust

Objective

To use a dictionary to find syllabification and word division

Presenting the Lesson

1. Read page 21. Have the students refer to pages 18 and 19 to divide the words *riffling*, *ridiculous*, and *rigatoni*.

2. Assign and discuss Exercises A and B on page 21.

Individualizing the Lesson

Less-Advanced Students

Work with the students on the first item in each Exercise. Then have them work independently.

Advanced Students

1. Add to the list for Exercise A: *differentiate, panorama*.

2. Add these words to the list for Exercise B: *itinerary, rehabilitate,* and *prevaricate*.

Reinforcement Exercise

Assign and discuss Exercise C on page 27.

Optional Practice

Have the students divide the words in Exercise B on page 17.

Extending the Lesson

Have the students use a dictionary to check word division in a short newspaper article.

Objective

To use phonetic respellings and a pronunciation key to learn the pronunciations of unfamiliar words

Presenting the Lesson

1. Read pages 22 and 23. Have the students use the key at the bottom of the sample dictionary page shown on pages 18 and 19 to pronounce the words on the sample page. Then have the students find the pronunciations of the words on the class list in the classroom dictionary.

2. Have the students refer to pages 18 and 19 to tell which syllable is emphasized most strongly in the words *ridicule, ridiculous, rigatoni,* and *righteous.*

3. Have the students compare the chart of respellings on page 24 with the pronunciation key in the classroom dictionary.

4. Assign and discuss the Exercise on page 23.

Individualizing the Lesson

Less-Advanced Students

Have each student look up the words in only one of the columns in the Exercise.

Advanced Students

Add these words to the Exercise on page 23: *neurology, phosphorescence, gnome, cellophane, surveillance.*

Part 5   Pronunciation

Sometimes you will use a dictionary to find out how to pronounce a word. Most dictionaries give the pronunciation in parentheses. The pronunciation follows the word itself. As you read the explanation that follows, refer to the dictionary page reproduced on pages 18 and 19.

Accent Marks

In two-syllable words, one syllable gets a stronger emphasis than the other when the word is pronounced. You say **RID**ing and **RI**fle, putting a heavier emphasis on the first syllable in each word. Dictionaries show you where to put this heavier emphasis by using accent marks.

> rid·ing (rīd′iŋ)
> ri·fle (rī′f'l)

The mark (′) following a syllable tells you that the syllable is emphasized, or accented.

In words of more than two syllables, usually two syllables are emphasized. One of the two gets a stronger emphasis than the other. Dictionaries show the two emphasized syllables by using two accent marks. One accent mark is larger and heavier than the other. The syllable with the heavier accent mark gets the heavier emphasis.

> rid·i·cule (rid′i kyool′)

Respellings

Notice that the respellings of the words on pages 18 and 19 are not exactly the same as the normal spellings. The spelling of the pronunciation is a way of showing the sounds in the word. In the word *right*, the letters *igh* stand for the long *i* sound. The dictionary shows this sound as *ī*. In the word *ridgepole*, the letters *dge* stand for the same sound as *j* in *jam*. The dictionary shows this sound as *j*.

Most dictionaries use letters of the alphabet in respellings wherever possible. For instance, the letter *b* stands for the first sound in *bat*. Sometimes letters are used in pairs. Many dictionaries use *sh* for the first sound in *sure*.

Some sounds are shown by letters with special marks above them. These marks are called **diacritical marks.** A diacritical mark above a letter shows that it stands for a particular sound. The letter *a* with a short line above it, *ā*, stands for the long *a* sound. This is the sound you hear at the end of the word *pay*. The short line above *a* is a diacritical mark called a **macron.**

A few sounds are shown by special symbols. These symbols are not letters. They are used only to stand for sounds in dictionary respellings.

On page 24 is a chart showing respellings that most dictionaries use. After each respelling is a word that shows the sound that the respelling stands for.

Not all dictionaries use the same system for respelling words. Your dictionary will have a chart called a **pronunciation key.** This chart will show you the system that your dictionary uses. Most dictionaries print a short version of the pronunciation key at the bottom of every right-hand page. You should study the pronunciation key for your dictionary.

Exercise Pronunciation

Look up each of the following words in your dictionary. Copy the respelling. Be sure to copy the accent marks and diacritical marks and any special symbols that your dictionary uses. Pronounce each of the words.

bucket	difficult	foreign	(buk′ it)	(dif′ i kəlt)	(fôr′ in)
jewel	masonry	oblique	(joo′ əl)	(mā′ s'n rē)	(ə blēk′)
phonograph	profession	rustle	(fō′ nə graf′)	(prə fesh′ ən)	(rus′ 'l)
slight	strawberry	thermometer	(slīt)	(strô′ ber′ ē)	(thər mäm′ ə ter)
turmoil	vacant	weave	(tur′ moil)	(vā′ kənt)	(wēv)

Reinforcement Exercise

Assign and discuss Exercise D on page 27.

Optional Practice

Have the students follow the directions for the Exercise on page 23, using these words:

bracket	fuel
chronic	freight
poise	physics
mission	profit
slight	sleight

Extending the Lesson

Bring to class several foreign language dictionaries that give English translations. Explain that the students will be able to pronounce most of the foreign words properly by following the respellings. Read the pronunciation key in each dictionary to determine whether any sounds are included that are not on the chart on page 24. After discussing any differences, have each student select a word and pronounce it.

Respellings Used in Most Dictionaries

Sounds Shown by Letters of the Alphabet

a	ask	b	bat	n	not
e	ten	d	dip	p	put
i	it	f	fall	r	red
u	up	g	get	s	sell
		h	hat	t	top
		j	jump	v	van
		k	kick	w	wish
		l	let	y	yet
		m	met	z	zip

Sounds Shown by Letters in Pairs

oo	look	ch	chip
oi	oil	sh	she
ou	out	th	thin
		th	then
		zh	garage

Sounds Shown by Letters with Diacritical Marks

ā	ate	ō	go
ä	hot	ô	law
ē	meet	o͞o	who
ī	bite	yo͞o	use

Sounds Shown by Special Symbols

ə	ago	ŋ	sing

'l (shows the sound between *b* and *l* in *bubble*: bub''l)

Part 6 Definitions

Most often, you will look up a word to find out what it means. Many words in English have more than one meaning. After you find your word, you will have to find the meaning that fits what you are reading.

Look at the definitions for the word *right* on pages 18 and 19. Notice that each different definition has a number. For most of the definitions a phrase or a sentence is given as an example. These examples show how the word is used with a particular definition.

Exercise Definitions

Refer to the dictionary entry for *land* below. On your paper, write the number of the definition that fits each sentence.

1. Flight 703 will arrive at 6 o'clock and land on runway 24. vi., 3
2. She hopes to travel to a foreign land. n., 2, a)
3. A peninsula is land bordered on three sides by water. n., 1
4. I want to leave the city and live out on the land. n., 5
5. Ogilvy Construction landed that big contract. vt., 5
6. The package landed right side up. vi., 4

> **land** (land) **n.** [OE. < IE. base *lendh-*, heath] **1.** the solid part of the earth's surface not covered by water **2.** *a)* a country, region, etc. [a distant *land*, one's native *land*] *b)* a country's people **3.** ground or soil [rich *land*, high *land*] **4.** ground thought of as property [to invest in *land*] **5.** rural or farming regions [to return to the *land*] **6.** *Econ.* natural resources —**vt. 1.** to put on shore from a ship [the ship *landed* its cargo] **2.** to cause to end up in a particular place or condition [a fight *landed* him in jail] **3.** to set (an aircraft) down on land or water **4.** to catch [to *land* a fish] **5.** [Colloq.] to get or win [to *land* a job] **6.** [Colloq.] to deliver (a blow) —**vi. 1.** to leave a ship and go on shore [the tourists *landed*] **2.** to come to a port or to shore: said of a ship **3.** to arrive at a specified place [he *landed* in Phoenix after a long bus ride] **4.** to alight or come to rest, as after a flight, jump, or fall [the cat *landed* on its feet]

Objective

To choose the correct definition of a word for a given context

Presenting the Lesson

1. Read this page and the definitions of *right* on pages 18 and 19. Work with the students to compose sentences using each definition of *right* correctly.

2. Assign and discuss the Exercise on page 25.

Individualizing the Lesson

Less-Advanced Students

Work with the students on the first sentence, then have them complete the Exercise independently.

Advanced Students

Have the students write original sentences for definitions of *land* not included in the Exercise on page 25.

Reinforcement Exercise

Assign and discuss Exercise E on page 27.

Extending the Lesson

Have each student find one of these words in a classroom dictionary and write a sentence for each of its definitions.

sound   stock   pull

Part 7

Objective

To use a synonymy

Presenting the Lesson

1. Read page 26. Review the definition of *synonym*. Have the students find the word on pages 18 and 19 for which a synonymy is given *(ridicule)*. Discuss the differences among the synonyms, and have the students use each word in a sentence.

2. Assign and discuss the Exercise on page 27.

3. Review the dictionary skills learned in this chapter.

Individualizing the Lesson

Less-Advanced Students

Have the students find only one synonym for each word in the Exercise on the top of page 27.

Advanced Students

Challenge the students to find three synonyms for each word in the Exercise.

Optional Practice

Add these words to the Exercise on page 27:

see   think
tell   confusion

Extending the Lesson

Have the students make synonym crossword puzzles with the help of

Part 7   Synonyms

As you learned in Chapter 1, **synonyms** are words that have similar meanings. The words *big* and *large* are synonyms. *Happy* and *glad* are also synonyms.

Look at the following dictionary entry for the word *story*. After the definitions you will find the abbreviation SYN. This abbreviation stands for the word *synonym*. A **synonymy** is a list of synonyms for a word.

Dictionary Entry for Story

sto•ry (stôr•e) **n.,** *pl.* **-ries** [< OFr. < L. < Gr. *historia:* see HIS-TORY] **1.** the telling of an event or series of events, whether true or made-up; account; narration **2.** an anecdote or joke **3.** a piece of fictional writing shorter than a novel; narrative; tale; specif., *same as* SHORT STORY **4.** the plot of a novel, play, etc. **5.** *a)* a report or rumor *b)* [Colloq.] a falsehood or fib **6.** romantic legend or history ☆**7.** a news event or a report of it, as in the newspapers —**vt. -ried, -ry•ing** to decorate with paintings, etc. of scenes from history or legend
SYN.—story is a general term for any informative or entertaining account, either oral or written, of something that really happened or that is partly or wholly made-up; **narrative,** a more formal term, is typically a prose account of a happening or series of happenings, either real or fictional; **tale** usually means a simple, leisurely story, more or less loosely organized, esp. one that is made-up or legendary; **anecdote** is a term applied to a short, entertaining, often instructive account of a single incident, usually personal or biographical

---

Notice that the synonymy for *story* does more than just list synonyms. Three words are given with meanings close to *story*. They are *narrative, tale,* and *anecdote*. The synonymy explains the special meaning and use of each of these words. Sometimes a synonymy will also give sample phrases or sentences to show how each synonym is used.

A synonymy can help you choose the best word for what you want to say. Did that disaster movie *scare, frighten,* or *terrify* the audience? A synonymy will tell you just what the differences among the three words are. Then you can choose the best one.

Exercise Synonyms

Find two synonyms for each of these words. Use each synonym in a sentence to show its specific meaning. <small>Answers will vary.</small>

strong	neat	praise	sloppy	beautiful
mystery	talk	lean	impolite	support

Reinforcement Exercises Putting Your Dictionary Skills Together

A. Arrange the following words in alphabetical order.

11 shout	4 cry	8 murmur	2 call
12 whisper	5 declare	6 grumble	3 chatter
1 announce	10 say	9 mutter	7 mumble

B. Below are the guide words for four dictionary pages. Write a word that you would find on each page. <small>Answers will vary.</small>

cannon - - - - - - cantaloupe   himself - - - - - - - - - - - - hire
elephant - - - - - - - - - ellipse   mariachi - - - - - - - - - market

C. Divide each of the following words into syllables.

sal|mon	dachs|hund	mum|my	non|res|i|dent
cal|a|bash	des|ig|nate	glut|ton|y	spe|cif|ic

D. Write the pronunciation for each of the following words.

mountain <small>moun' t'n</small>   valley <small>val' ē</small>   desert <small>di zurt' or dez',ert</small>   tundra <small>tun' drə</small>
demonstrate <small>dem' ən strāt'</small>   prevention <small>pri ven' shen</small>   freight <small>frāt</small>   ladle <small>lā' d'l</small>

E. Use your dictionary to find the meaning of each italicized word.

1. He didn't win, but we all admired his *pluck*. <small>courage to meet danger or difficulty; fortitude</small>
2. Fred's Diner isn't one of my favorite *haunts*. <small>a place often visited</small>
3. The edges of a quarter are *milled*. <small>raised and ridged</small>
4. No *nostrum* will cure this disease. <small>a medicine made by the person selling it</small>
5. The cows were *lowing* in the meadow. <small>mooing</small>

the classroom dictionary. Collect the puzzles, reproduce them, and use them for additional practice in finding synonyms in a dictionary.

Reinforcement Exercises

These Reinforcement Exercises may be used for additional practice as needed.

Review

If you have not assigned the Reinforcement Exercises before this time, you can use them as an excellent Chapter Review.

Chapter 3

Sentence Combining

A sentence is a group of words that states a single main idea. However, some main ideas are made up of smaller ideas. If each smaller idea is stated in a sentence of its own, the result is often choppy. The writing may give the reader only a vague idea of how the smaller ideas are related. Study the following group of sentences:

> Phil sat in the dining room. He shredded his napkin. He was nervous.

The ideas can be combined in one sentence.

> Phil sat in the dining room, nervously shredding his napkin.

The new sentence has only one main idea, but that main idea has several parts. The new sentence flows smoothly and shows how the ideas are related. It is much more effective than the group of sentences. This chapter will give you practice in writing sentences that express ideas clearly and precisely.

29

Chapter Objectives

1. To join sentences that express ideas of equal importance

2. To join related sentence parts

3. To add single words to one sentence from another without changes in form

4. To add words to one sentence from another one, making changes in form where necessary

5. To add groups of words to one sentence from another.

6. To combine sentences by substitution

7. To use the word *who* to combine sentences

8. To use the words *which* and *that* to combine sentences

9. To combine sentences to show causes and effects

10. To eliminate choppiness and vagueness by combining sentences

Preparing the Students

Read page 29 and discuss the examples. Have the students tell how the two versions differ. Explain that a good writer is able to find more than one way to express an idea and then to choose the best of several ways. Tell the students that this chapter will help them achieve a similar flexibility in their writing.

Additional Resources

Mastery Test—See page 13 in the test booklet. Recommended for use after teaching the chapter.

Reinforcement Exercises—See pages 48-49 in the student text.

Skills Practice Book—pages 15-16.

Duplicating Masters—pages 15-16.

Sentence Combining—Use this separate booklet on sentence combining as a supplement to the text.

Objective

To join sentences that express ideas of equal importance

Presenting the Lesson

1. Read and discuss this page, emphasizing the critical effect that the choice of *and, but,* or *or* to join the sentences has on the meaning.

2. Assign and discuss the Exercise on this page.

Individualizing the Lesson

Less-Advanced Students

Before the students begin the Exercise, discuss how the sentences in each pair are related.

Advanced Students

Have the students replace the second sentence in each pair in the Exercise with another sentence that can be combined with the first.

Reinforcement Exercise

Assign and discuss Exercise A on page 48.

Optional Practice

Have the students find sentences of their own that could be combined.

Extending the Lesson

Have each student find one published sentence that combines related ideas. Have the students tell what ideas have been combined.

Two sentences may state similar ideas that are equally important.

Libby fed the animals. Sam cleaned all the animals' cages.

These sentences can be joined by a comma and the word *and*. Here is the combined sentence. It states both ideas.

Libby fed the animals, and Sam cleaned all the animals' cages.

The sentences could also be joined by a semicolon.

Libby fed the animals; Sam cleaned all the animals' cages.

Two sentences may state contrasting ideas of equal importance. The sentences usually can be joined by a comma and the word *but*.

The sound on this TV set is not working. The picture is clear.
The sound on this TV set is not working, but the picture is clear.

A pair of sentences may express a choice between ideas of equal importance. The sentences usually can be joined by a comma and the word *or*.

Should we go skating? Should we go for a bike ride?
Should we go skating, or should we go for a bike ride?

Exercise Joining Sentences

Join each pair of sentences. Follow the directions given.

1. The door was locked. The windows were boarded shut. (Join with **, and.**) [*, and the*]

2. Shall we go by train? Would you rather take the bus? (Join with **, or.**) [*, or would*]

3. The lights grew dim. The curtains parted. (Join with **;**) [*; the*]

4. Amy offered to lend me her running shoes. They didn't fit. (Join with **, but.**) [*, but they*]

30

Part 2 Joining Sentence Parts

The ideas expressed by two sentences may be so closely related that words are repeated in the sentences. The ideas may be combined in one sentence, using only the important parts of each sentence. The repeated words can be eliminated.

When the sentence parts express similar ideas that are equally important, they usually can be joined by *and*. (The words in italics can be eliminated.)

>   Anna designed the posters. *She designed* the pennants.
>   Anna designed the posters and the pennants.

When the sentence parts express contrasting ideas, they usually can be joined by *but*.

>   I burned the rolls. *I* made a delicious salad.
>   I burned the rolls but made a delicious salad.

When the sentence parts express a choice between ideas, they usually can be joined by *or*.

>   Shall we rake the leaves today? *Shall we rake the leaves* Thursday?
>   Shall we rake the leaves today or Thursday?

Exercise Joining Sentence Parts

Join the related parts in each pair of sentences by following the directions in parentheses. Eliminate the italicized words.

1. Lisa worried. <del>Jon worried.</del> (Join related parts with **and.**)
2. The dog may have eaten the steak. <del>The dog may have</del> buried it. (Join related parts with **or.**)
3. The conductor was busy. <del>He was</del> friendly<del>, though</del>. (Join related parts with **but.**)
4. The ball rolled around the rim once. <del>It</del> fell through the net. (Join related parts with **and.**)
5. Sherry lost the letter I sent her. <del>Sherry lost the</del> map <del>I sent her.</del> (Join related parts with **and.**)

Part 2

Objective

To join related sentence parts

Presenting the Lesson

1. Read and discuss page 31. Have the students explain how the ideas in each pair of example sentences are related. Stress the idea that only sentence parts that express related ideas of equal importance should be joined by *and, but* or *or*.

2. Assign the Exercise on this page.

Individualizing the Lesson

Less-Advanced Students

Work with the students to complete the Exercise.

Advanced Students

Have the students explain the difference in meaning that would result if the fourth pair of sentences in the Exercise were combined with *but*.

Reinforcement Exercise

Assign and discuss Exercise B on page 48.

Optional Practice

Have students look through previous writing assignments for sentences that could be combined

Objective

To add single words to one sentence from another without changes in form

Presenting the Lesson

1. Read and discuss page 32. Point out to the students that each of the words added in the examples describes a word in the first sentence. Be sure that they understand that the italicized words are to be eliminated even though they are not always repeated words. Help the students see how little meaning these words add to the uncombined sentences.

2. Emphasize that the main idea of the sentences should not be changed when they are combined. Have the students explain how each of the details is related to the main idea in the sample sentences.

3. Complete the first half of Exercise A on page 33 as a class activity. Ask volunteers to write the revised sentences on the chalkboard and to circle the word or words that have been added to each. Assign the remaining sentences as individual work. Then assign and discuss Exercise B.

Individualizing the Lesson

Less-Advanced Students

Provide small group help for students having trouble completing the combinations.

The ideas in a pair of sentences may not be equally important. Perhaps only one word in the second sentence is really important to the main idea expressed by the pair of sentences. The one important word can be added to the first sentence. The new sentence will be a tighter and more effective way of expressing the idea.

> Carol is an illustrator. *She's* good.
> Carol is a good illustrator.
>
> Benjamin arranged the wrenches. *He did it* carefully.
> Benjamin arranged the wrenches carefully.
>
> We couldn't help admiring the team. *The team was* losing.
> We couldn't help admiring the losing team.

You may be able to add several single words to a sentence. Adding several words will allow you to combine more than two sentences. You can combine more than two sentences if one of the sentences states a main idea, and each of the others adds only one important detail to the main idea.

> A book rested on the table. *The book was* heavy. *The table was* wobbly.
> A heavy book rested on the wobbly table.

Be careful to choose the right location in the first sentence for each word that you add.

You may have to use a comma when you add more than one word to a sentence.

> Sludge washed up on shore after the oil spill. *The sludge was* thick. *The sludge was* sticky.
> Thick, sticky sludge washed up on shore after the oil spill.

Sometimes you can join the words with *and*.

> Diana received a message. *It was* long. *It was* complicated.
> Diana received a long and complicated message.

Exercises Adding Single Words

A. Combine each of the following groups of sentences by adding the important words. Eliminate the italicized words and follow any special directions given in parentheses.

1. John had a parrot. *The parrot was* talkative.
2. Katy set the lamp on the table. *The lamp was* polished.
3. Lois slipped into the room. *She came in* silently. *The room was* darkened.
4. I realized I was standing in cement. *The cement was* wet.
5. The audience burst into applause after the finale. *The audience was* delighted. *The applause was* enthusiastic. *The finale was* rousing.
6. Paul spread a glaze over the ham. *The glaze was* thin. *The glaze was made of* apricot. (Do not use a comma.)
7. The book is in a drawer in the kitchen. *It is a* telephone *book. It is* new. (Do not use a comma.)
8. The starship sped through the asteroid belt. *The starship was* battered. *The asteroid belt was* dangerous.
9. The most popular performer was a juggler. *He was* Canadian.
10. Rose placed the coins in a box. *The coins were* shiny. *The box was* purple.

B. Combine each of the following groups of sentences by adding important words to the first sentence. Decide on your own how the sentences should be combined.

1. The experiment was a success. The success was complete.
2. Ellen adjusted the sails. The sails were flapping.
3. The curtains faded in the sunlight. The sunlight was dazzling.
4. The puppies scampered across the floor. The puppies were muddy. The floor was shiny.
5. The cyclists displayed a map of their trip. The map was hand-made. They displayed it proudly.

Objective

To add words to one sentence from another, making changes in form where necessary

Presenting the Lesson

1. Read and discuss page 34. Emphasize again that the main idea of the sentences should not be changed when they are combined.

2. Have students explain how each of the details is related to the main idea in the sample sentences.

3. Have students describe the changes in form that occurred in each of the added words.

4. Do Exercise A in class. Work with any students who have difficulty. Then assign Exercise B on page 35.

Individualizing the Lesson

Less-Advanced Students

Help the students decide what words to eliminate and what changes of form are necessary. Have students suggest combinings orally before writing out answers independently.

Advanced Students

Have students add further details to the sentences by using any combining techniques suggested so far.

Reinforcement Exercise

Assign and discuss Exercise C on page 48.

Part 4 Adding Words That Change Form

Before you add an important word to a sentence, you may have to change the form of the word. You may have to add *-y*.

Don't sit on that chair. *It* wobbles.
Don't sit on that wobbly chair.

Sometimes you will have to add *-ing* or *-ed*.

Nate and I set up the chairs. *They would* fold.
Nate and I set up the folding chairs.

Trish smoothed the paper. *It had a* crease.
Trish smoothed the creased paper.

At other times you will have to add *-ly*.

Alan solved our electrical problems. *He was* quick.
Alan quickly solved our electrical problems.

Often, the word ending in *-ly* can be placed in any of several positions in the sentence.

Jean remarked that she had not seen Eve in years. Jean was sad.

Sadly, Jean remarked that she had not seen Eve in years.
Jean remarked sadly that she had not seen Eve in years.

Exercises Adding Words That Change Form

A. Combine each pair of sentences by adding the important word. Follow the directions given. Eliminate the italicized words.

1. Luis backed away from the snake. *The snake* hissed. (End the important word with **-ing.**) Luis backed away from the hissing snake.

2. I cleaned the shelves. *They were covered with* dust. (End the important word with **-y.**) I cleaned the dusty shelves.

3. We arranged the turkey on a platter. *The turkey was in* slices. (End the important word with **-ed.**) We arranged the sliced turkey on a platter.

4. Alec whistled to tell us that he'd spotted the hawk. *His whistling was* soft. (End the important word with **-ly**.)

Alec whistled softly to tell us that he'd spotted the hawk.

5. The cat stalked the chipmunk. *The cat's movements were* slow. (End the important word with **-ly**.)

The cat slowly stalked the chipmunk.

B. Choose the important word from the second sentence in each pair. Add it to the first sentence. Decide on your own how to change its form.

1. That stack of dishes may fall. The stack leans.

That leaning stack of dishes may fall.

2. Rob scrubbed the tub. The tub had dirt in it.

Rob scrubbed the dirty tub.

3. Charlie made a banner. The banner had stripes.

Charlie made a striped banner.

4. Michelle called my name. Her voice was loud.

Michelle called my name loudly.

5. We had to wash the rags. The rags had oil on them.

We had to wash the oily rags.

Part 5   Adding Groups of Words

You may find that one sentence contains a group of words that can add important information to another sentence.

> Dad is fixing dinner. Dad is in the kitchen.
> Dad is fixing dinner in the kitchen.

This part will show you ways to add groups of words from one sentence to another to create a tighter expression of an idea.

Adding Groups of Words Without Changes in Form

You may be able to add a group of words to a sentence without making any other changes. When the group of words gives more information about someone or something, add it near the words that name the person or thing.

> The noise was startling. *The noise was* in the basement.
> The noise in the basement was startling.

Have the students review an earlier writing to find sentences that can be combined in this way.

Extending the Lesson

Have the students find sentences reflecting this type of combination in their school newspaper or in a popular magazine.

Objective

To add groups of words to one sentence from another

Presenting the Lesson

1. Read and discuss the introduction and **Adding Groups of Words Without Changes in Form**, pages 35 and 36. Point out that the added group of words in each example describes a word in the first sentence.

2. Emphasize that the group of words should be placed as close as possible to the word it describes. To illustrate the confusion that can result if the group of words is misplaced, write the following sentences on the chalkboard and have the students explain how their meanings differ.

A sudden crash in the attic startled everyone.

A sudden crash startled everyone in the attic.

3. Do Exercise A on page 36 orally, and have volunteers write the responses on the chalkboard.

4. Assign Exercise B on page 36 for students to complete independently. Mention that more than one combination is possible and "right" for some of the groups of sentences. The students should try to decide which is best for the meaning intended.

5. Read and discuss **Adding Groups of Words with Commas** on page 37. In explaining this combination, show the steps by writing the two sentences to be combined on the chalkboard, crossing out the words to be omitted, drawing an arrow from the group of words to the word described, and then writing out the combination.

6. Do Exercise A on page 37 orally or at the chalkboard.

7. Assign Exercise B as independent work.

8. Read and discuss **Adding Groups of Words with -ing and -ed**, pages 38 and 39. Students will be helped to understand the steps

1. Mount Fuji is a volcano in Japan.

2. The blister on my heel began to hurt.

3. Joy and Jeff stood poised on the tightrope.

4. Tom stood at the center of the stage.

5. Becky will mail the package at noon.

When the group of words describes an action, add it near the words that name the action.

Don was waiting. *He was* at the door.
Don was waiting at the door.

When the group of words adds more information to the entire main idea of the other sentence, you may add it at the beginning or at the end.

Mr. Yamada always sends his mother flowers. *He sends them* on his birthday.
Mr. Yamada always sends his mother flowers on his birthday.
On his birthday, Mr. Yamada always sends his mother flowers.

Exercises Adding Groups of Words Without Changes in Form

A. Combine each of the following pairs of sentences by adding a group of words to the first sentence. Eliminate the italicized words.

You will be sleeping in a bed with a canopy.

1. You will be sleeping in a bed. *The bed is one* with a canopy.

The red coat in the lost-and-found is mine.

2. The red coat is mine. *The coat is* in the lost-and-found.

3. The pastries look delicious. *The pastries were* at Henson's Bakery. The pastries at Henson's Bakery look delicious.

4. Ms. Foster will be flying a red biplane. *She will be* in the air show. Ms. Foster will be flying a red biplane in the air show.

5. My brother loves to talk. *He talks* about his archaeological studies. My brother loves to talk about his archaeological studies.

B. Combine each group of sentences.

1. Mount Fuji is a volcano. The volcano is in Japan.
2. The blister began to hurt. The blister was on my heel.
3. Joy and Jeff stood poised. They were on the tightrope.
4. Tom stood. He was at the center of the stage.
5. Becky will mail the package. She'll mail it at noon.

Adding Groups of Words with Commas

In some cases, when you add a group of words to a sentence, you will have to separate it from the rest of the sentence with a comma or a pair of commas.

> My favorite bread is challah. *Challah is* a soft yeast bread.
> My favorite bread is challah, a soft yeast bread.

> "Alligator on the Escalator" was written by Eve Merriam.
> *"Alligator on the Escalator" is* a humorous poem.
> "Alligator on the Escalator," a humorous poem, was written by Eve Merriam.

Exercises Adding Groups of Words with Commas

A. Combine each of the following pairs of sentences by adding a group of words to the first sentence. Follow the instructions given in parentheses. Eliminate the italicized words. Answers may vary.

1. My dog is the world's worst watchdog. *My dog is* a dachshund. (Use a pair of commas.) My dog, a dachshund, is the world's worst watchdog.

2. The man in the gorilla suit is George Appleby. *He is* our neighbor. (Use a comma.) The man in the gorilla suit is George Appleby, our neighbor.

3. Stacy's alarm clock is loud enough to wake the whole household. *Stacy's alarm clock is* a small portable one. (Use a pair of commas.) Stacy's alarm clock, a small portable one, is loud enough to wake the whole household.

4. Neighbors of ours celebrate Bastille Day. *They are* the Legers. (Use a pair of commas.) Neighbors of ours, the Legers, celebrate Bastille Day.

5. Patty Benoit is the only person I know who has made a parachute jump. *She is* my sister's roommate. (Use a pair of commas.) Patty Benoit, my sister's roommate, is the only person I know who has made a parachute jump.

B. Combine each of the following pairs of sentences.

1. On the table was my father's most famous creation. It was an artificial grapefruit. On the table was my father's most famous creation, an artificial grapefruit.

2. Marilyn couldn't open the register. Marilyn was the substitute cashier. Marilyn, the substitute cashier, couldn't open the register.

involved if the combining is performed on the chalkboard.

9. Have the students complete Exercise A on page 39 orally or as a chalkboard activity. Then assign Exercise B as independent work.

Individualizing the Lesson

Less-Advanced Students

The students may have difficulty with the Exercises on page 39. Have them explain orally what each detail describes. Then have them find the key words and give help in finding the location for placing the detail in the other sentence.

Advanced Students

Have the students find other possible combinations for the sentences in the Exercises, using alternative combining techniques.

Reinforcement Exercise

Assign and discuss Exercise D on page 48.

Optional Practice

Have the students revise a previously written assignment, looking for combinations covered in this part.

Extending the Lesson

Have each student find a strong, well-written sentence in a short story. Have the students discuss how each detail in the sentence is related to its main idea. If possible, have the students rewrite the sentence as it would have appeared if each detail had been expressed in a sentence of its own.

3. We had cannoli for dessert. Cannoli is an Italian pastry.

We had cannoli, an Italian pastry, for dessert.

4. Ms. Lorenzo organized our school's first science fair. She is our science teacher.

Ms. Lorenzo, our science teacher, organized our school's first science fair.

5. I saw Charles A. Lindbergh's plane in Washington. Charles A. Lindbergh's plane was the *Spirit of St. Louis*.

I saw Charles A. Lindbergh's plane, the Spirit of St. Louis, in Washington.

Adding Groups of Words with *-ing* and *-ed*

Sometimes when you add a group of words to a sentence, you will have to change the form of one of them. In its new form, the word will often end with *-ing* or *-ed*.

> The man must have been a spy. *The man* stood under the street lamp.
> The man standing under the street lamp must have been a spy.

> We keep the octopus in a tank. *We* fill *the tank* with salt water.
> We keep the octopus in a tank filled with salt water.

Occasionally, a group of words will already contain a word ending in *-ing, -ed,* or another appropriate ending. Then you can add the entire group to the other sentence without changes.

> The crow must have been injured. *The crow was* dragging its left wing.
> The crow dragging its left wing must have been injured.

> The lobsters were great. *The lobsters were* flown in from Maine.
> The lobsters flown in from Maine were great.

> Inspector Hale stared at the mattress. *The mattress was* filled with money.
> Inspector Hale stared at the mattress filled with money.

When the words add information about someone or something, be sure to place the group next to the words naming the person or thing.

38

Ashley thought she saw her missing neighbor. *Ashley was* peering through the bookstore window.

Peering through the bookstore window, Ashley thought she saw her missing neighbor.

Ashley thought she saw her missing neighbor. *Her missing neighbor was* peering through the bookstore window.

Ashley thought she saw her missing neighbor peering through the bookstore window.

Exercises Adding Groups of Words with *-ing* and *-ed*

A. Combine each pair of sentences by adding a group of words to the first sentence. Follow any directions given.

1. The woman is my aunt. *The woman is* weaving a rug. The woman weaving a rug is my aunt.

2. A man has left a large donation for the relief fund. *The man* calls himself "a friend." (Use **-ing.**) A man calling himself "a friend" has left a large donation for the relief fund.

3. The singers were nervous. *They were* going on stage. The singers going on stage were nervous.

4. My sister gives her baby a vitamin supplement. *She dissolves it* in orange juice. (Use **-ed.**) My sister gives her baby a vitamin supplement dissolved in orange juice.

5. P. J. was surprised to see hundreds of people. *They were* waiting outside the theater. P.J. was surprised to see hundreds of people waiting outside the theater.

B. Combine each pair of sentences by adding an important group of words to the first sentence. Decide how the sentences should be combined and what changes may have to be made.

1. The people could barely breathe. The people were packed into the tiny elevator. The people packed into the tiny elevator could barely breathe.

2. Connie searched through the photographs. The photographs were spread out on the table. Connie searched through the photographs spread out on the table.

3. The library doesn't have the book. The book was reviewed in yesterday's paper. The library doesn't have the book reviewed in yesterday's paper.

4. The library is holding an exhibit of pottery. People make the pottery in the local area. The library is holding an exhibit of locally made pottery.

Objective

To combine sentences by substitution

Presenting the Lesson

1. Read and discuss page 40. To illustrate the mechanics of this method of combining, write the first two sample sentences on the chalkboard. Draw a box around the word *something*. Erase the word *I*. Change the verb *memorized* to *memorizing*. Circle what is left of the second sentence, and draw an arrow from the circle to the box containing the word *something*.

2. Do Exercise A on page 40 orally or at the chalkboard.

3. Assign Exercise B on page 41 as independent work.

Individualizing the Lesson

Less-Advanced Students

Have the students first read the sentences in the Exercises aloud and explain the meaning of the pair. Then have them find the word that will be replaced (*that* or *something*). Finally, have them change the form of the verb and make the appropriate substitution.

Advanced Students

Have the students write five pairs of sentences of their own that could be combined by substitution (using Exercise B as a model). Have students exchange papers and complete each other's exercise.

Part 6 Combining Sentences by Substitution

You may be able to put a complete idea expressed by one sentence into another sentence. The *-ing* form of a verb can be used when substituting the idea of one sentence for the word *something* or the word *that* in another sentence.

> *Something* improved my grade in spelling. *I* memorized the word list.
> Memorizing the word list improved my grade in spelling.

Notice that the idea in the second sentence explains the word *something* in the first. The word *memorized* was changed to *memorizing*. Then *memorizing the word list* was substituted for *something* in the first sentence.

> *We* pounded the clay on the table. *That* helped us soften it.
> Pounding the clay on the table helped us soften it.

The word *pounded* was changed to *pounding*. Then *Pounding the clay on the table* was substituted for *That* in the first sentence.

Exercises Substitutions with *-ing*

A. Combine each of the following pairs of sentences by substituting with *-ing*. Eliminate the italicized words.

1. *People* water cactus plants too much. *That* can harm them. Watering cactus plants too much can harm them.

2. Betty has always enjoyed *something*. *She* exercises as soon as she wakes up. Betty has always enjoyed exercising as soon as she wakes up.

3. I wait in line for lunch. *That* makes me impatient. Waiting in line for lunch makes me impatient.

4. *Jeff* started a quilting business. *That* was Jeff's best idea. Starting a quilting business was Jeff's best idea.

5. *Tony* practices the piano. *That* is Tony's favorite after-school activity. Practicing the piano is Tony's favorite after-school activity.

B. Combine each of the following groups of sentences by substituting the idea in one sentence for the word *something* or the word *that* in the other sentence. Decide on your own what changes may have to be made.

1. Jack and Juanita began something. They mixed the pancake batter. Jack and Juanita began mixing the pancake batter.

2. I wrote a report about the Middle East. That took a lot of work. Writing a report about the Middle East took a lot of work.

3. I ran for the presidency of the student council. That was not as easy as I had thought it would be. Running for the presidency of the student council was not as easy as I had thought it would be.

4. Paul planned on something. He would join us after the game. Paul planned on joining us after the game.

5. I said goodbye to Sol. That made me sad. Saying goodbye to Sol made me sad.

Part 7 Combining with *who*

A group of words that gives information about a person can sometimes be added to a sentence by using the word *who.*

> The people are planning another trip for next year. *The people* organized the trip to St. Louis.
>
> The people who organized the trip to St. Louis are planning another trip for next year.

In the example above, the group of words added to the first sentence is necessary to make it clear which people are meant. In some sentences, the added group of words is not absolutely necessary. The words merely add additional information. When the group of words merely adds additional information, combine with **, who.**

Reinforcement Exercise

Assign and discuss Exercise E on page 49.

Optional Practice

Have the students follow the directions for Exercise B on page 41.

1. People run water until it is cold. That wastes water.
2. Something made me late for school. I missed the bus.
3. We heard about Jan's trip to Florida. That made us want to go, too.
4. I have always disliked something. I wait for a bus in the rain.

Extending the Lesson

Have each student find a published example of a sentence that illustrates this type of combining.

Part 7

Objective

To use the word *who* to combine sentences

Presenting the Lesson

1. Read and discuss pages 41–42. Illustrate the mechanics of the combination by writing the two sentences in the example on the chalkboard. Cross out the word or words to be omitted, draw an arrow to the word described, and then write the combined version.

2. Do Exercise A on page 42 orally. Assign Exercise B as independent work.

Individualizing the Lesson

Less-Advanced Students

These students may have difficulty deciding if the information to be added to each sentence in the Exercises is necessary for clarity. Help them decide this issue first; then have them write the combination.

Advanced Students

Have these students add details to the sentences by using combinations already covered in the chapter.

Reinforcement Exercise

Assign and discuss Exercise F on page 49.

Optional Practice

Have the students follow the directions for Exercise B on page 42.

1. My father pitched in the parent-faculty game. My father once played professional baseball.
2. Cathy Lester sent me a post card. Cathy is on vacation in Canada.
3. The man is our new math teacher. The man is sitting beside Mr. Harper.
4. Students should report to Ms. Harvey. They want to join the bowling club.

Extending the Lesson

Have the students replace the second sentence in each pair in Exercise A with an alternative sentence and write the new combinations.

Mr. Stanley and Ms. Wilson are planning another trip for next year. *Mr. Stanley and Ms. Wilson* organized the trip to St. Louis.

Mr. Stanley and Ms. Wilson, **who** organized the trip to St. Louis, are planning another trip for next year.

Exercises Combining with *who*   Answers may vary.

A. Combine each of the following pairs of sentences by following the directions in parentheses. Eliminate the italicized words.

Julie Grimes, who came into the game as a pinch-hitter, hit the only home run.

1. Julie Grimes hit the only home run. *She* came into the game as a pinch-hitter. (Combine with **, who.**) , who

2. Dulcie (entertained my parents for hours.) *Dulcie* really knows how to tell a story. (Combine with **, who.**)

3. Steve Adler directed this movie. *Steve Adler* is my second cousin. (Combine with **, who.**)

4. Mr. Goodwin has a huge collection of campaign buttons. *Mr. Goodwin* enjoys politics. (Combine with **, who.**)

5. The girl is Terry Jackson. *The girl* offered to fix your bike. (Combine with **who.**) The girl who offered to fix your bike is Terry Jackson.

B. Combine each of the following pairs of sentences. Decide on your own whether to combine with **who** or **, who.**

1. Ed couldn't remember where he had put the masking tape. Ed likes to have a place for everything and everything in its place. Ed, who likes to have a place for everything and everything in its place, couldn't remember where he had put the masking tape.

2. I called Frank. Frank is at home with a cold. I called Frank, who is at home with a cold.

3. Sandy Miller does volunteer work at the animal shelter. Sandy wants to be a veterinarian. Sandy Miller, who wants to be a veterinarian, does volunteer work at the animal shelter.

4. The girl is visiting from Finland. The girl is standing beside Jack. The girl who is standing beside Jack is visiting from Finland.

5. People should sign up before the end of the day. They want to try out for the variety show. People who want to try out for the variety show should sign up before the end of the day.

Part 8 Combining with *which* and *that*

At times, the information added to a sentence is joined to it by the word *which* or the word *that*. When the group of words added to the first sentence is necessary to make the meaning clear, combine with **that.**

> This is the record. I wanted you to hear *the record*.
> This is the record that I wanted you to hear.

When the group of words is not absolutely necessary, but just adds additional information, combine with **, which.**

> Lentil soup is not hard to make. *Lentil soup* is high in protein.
> Lentil soup, **which** is high in protein, is not hard to make.

The word *that* can sometimes be omitted without changing the meaning of the sentence.

> This is the record I wanted you to hear.

Exercises Combining with *which* and *that*

A. Combine each of the following pairs of sentences by following the directions in parentheses. Eliminate the italicized words.

1. These bricks came from the old city hall. ~~The city plans to recycle~~ *these bricks*. (Combine with **, which.**)
   , which the city plans to recycle,

2. Steve repaired Lucy's pocket watch. *It* was given to her by her grandfather. (Combine with **, which.**)
   , which

3. I was upset because I had lost the new scarf. I had crocheted ~~it~~ myself. (Combine with **that.**)
   that

4. Carrie fixed the radio. I found ~~it~~ in the attic. (Combine with **that.**)
   that

5. The newspaper has just won a Pulitzer Prize. ~~I read~~ *that newspaper*. (Combine with **that.**)
   that I read

43

Part 8

Objective

To use the words *which* and *that* to combine sentences

Presenting the Lesson

1. Read this page. Discuss the examples. If students have difficulty understanding the difference between groups of words that are essential to the meaning and those that merely add additional information, explain that in the first example *that I wanted you to hear* must be added to specify which record is meant, but in the second example *lentil soup* already specifies exactly what is "not hard to make."

2. Do Exercise A on page 43 orally, and then assign Exercise B on page 44 to be completed independently.

Individualizing the Lesson

Less-Advanced Students

For both Exercises, have the students decide whether the additional information is necessary before performing the combination.

Advanced Students

Have these students further expand their combinations with details of their own.

Reinforcement Exercise

Assign and discuss Exercise G on page 49.

Optional Practice

Have each student edit another student's previous draft of a paper, looking for sentences that could be combined with *which* or *that*.

Extending the Lesson

Have each student find, in a textbook or magazine, a sentence that illustrates combining with *which* and *that*. Have the student copy the original and then write the uncombined version.

Part 9

Objective

To combine sentences to show causes and effects

Presenting the Lesson

1. Read and discuss pages 44 and 45.

2. Many students have difficulty stating cause and effect relationships clearly. When discussing the examples, point out that the uncombined sentences hint at a cause and effect relationship, but that the reader must decide that one exists. Emphasize that the uncombined sentences leave no doubt that one event caused another, and that they clearly identify the cause and the effect. To demonstrate how important the choice of a single word can be, compare the combined sentences

B. Combine each of the following pairs of sentences. Decide on your own whether to combine **, which** or **that.**

The map that Kent drew helped us find the fairgrounds.

1. The map helped us find the fairgrounds. Kent drew the map.

The typewriters that we use for the school paper were donated by local businesses.

2. The typewriters were donated by local businesses. We use the typewriters for the school paper.

that I bought on sale

3. The shoes turned my feet red. I bought the shoes on sale.

4. Ingrid's shin guards fit me perfectly. They no longer fit her. Ingrid's shin guards, which no longer fit her, fit me perfectly.

5. Have you ever eaten in the restaurant? Your sister recommended the restaurant.

Have you ever eaten in the restaurant that your sister recommended?

Part 9 Combining To Show Causes and Effects

Often in your writing you will want to explain to your readers that something happened because of something else. If you do not make it clear that one thing caused another, your reader may not realize that one event was a cause and the other, an effect. The following example uses the word *because* to make the relationship clear.

We moved closer to town.
I can walk to the movie theater now. (**because**)

Because we moved closer to town, I can walk to the movie theater now.

Notice that a comma separates the two sentences. The sentences might be combined in another order. Then the comma would not be needed.

I can walk to the movie theater now because we moved closer to town.

The word *since* can also be used to show a cause-and-effect relationship.

44

We'll be having sandwiches for dinner.
The stove is broken. (**since**)

Since the stove is broken, we'll be having sandwiches for dinner.
We'll be having sandwiches for dinner since the stove is broken.

There is another way to combine sentences to show a cause-and-effect relationship. Words can be added before the effect, or result. If you use this method, you will also have to use a semicolon **(;).**

We moved closer to town.
I can walk to the movie theater now. (**; as a result,**)
We moved closer to town; as a result, I can walk to the movie theater now.

The stove is broken.
We'll be having sandwiches for dinner. (**; therefore,**)
The stove is broken; therefore, we'll be having sandwiches for dinner.

You will find the following words useful for indicating causes in your combined sentences.

because   since   for

You will find these words useful for indicating results in your combined sentences.

so   as a result   thus   therefore   consequently

Exercise Combining To Show Causes and Effects

Combine each of the following pairs of sentences by using the key words given in parentheses. First decide which sentence states the cause, and which states the effect. Answers may vary.

1. These shoes hurt my feet. (**since**)
   I don't wear them. Since these shoes hurt my feet, I don't wear them.

with the following inadequate sentences.

We moved closer to town, and I can walk to the movie theater now.

The stove is broken, and we will be having sandwiches for dinner.

3. Assign and discuss the Exercise on page 45.

Individualizing the Lesson

Less-Advanced Students

Urge the students to try their combinations on scrap paper before writing their final answers.

Advanced Students

Do the Exercise orally.

Reinforcement Exercise

Assign and discuss Exercise H on page 49.

Optional Practice

Challenge the students to try using each key word or phrase to combine each pair of sentences in the Exercise.

Extending the Lesson

Have students find, in their science textbooks, examples of sentences expressing cause-and-effect relationships. Have the students copy the originals and then write the uncombined versions.

2. These shoes hurt my feet.

I don't wear them. **(; so,)**

These shoes hurt my feet; so, I don't wear them.

3. Dan has a wonderful voice. **(because)**

He won the lead role in the musical.

Because Dan has a wonderful voice, he won the lead role in the musical.

4. Dan has a wonderful voice.

He won the lead role in the musical. **(; therefore,)**

Dan has a wonderful voice; therefore, he won the lead role in the musical.

5. Eric lost his watch. **(because)**

He has been asking me for the time all day.

Because Eric lost his watch, he has been asking me for the time all day.

Objective

To eliminate choppiness and vagueness by combining sentences

Presenting the Lesson

1. Have the students reread the introduction to this chapter on page 29 and discuss the ideas presented there in the light of the combining techniques they have learned.

2. Have the students read pages 46 and 47 and compare the sample paragraphs sentence by sentence, describing the kinds of combining that have been used in the second paragraph. Emphasize the clarity of the combined sentences, and point out their compactness.

3. Have the students read all the sentences in the Exercise on page 47 at least twice before they begin to combine them and write them as a paragraph. Emphasize that the meaning of the group of sentences

Part 10   Applying Combining Skills

As you have learned, there are several ways to combine related ideas in your sentences. Your next step is to use these combining skills to eliminate choppiness and vagueness from your writing.

Notice how the following paragraph has been revised.

Some sports require team play. Other sports depend on individual effort. Success in a team sport depends on something. Each player works for the good of the team. Success in an individual sport depends on one person alone. Some people prefer team sports. They are in a group of people. The people share a common goal. They enjoy that. Some people prefer individual sports. They like to be on their own. They rely only on themselves.

Some sports require team play, but other sports depend on individual effort. Success in a team sport depends on each player's working for the good of the team, but success in an individual sport depends on one person alone. Some people prefer team sports because they enjoy being in a group of people who share a common goal. Some people prefer individual sports because they like to be on their own, relying only on themselves.

Read something that you have written. Think about how it might be improved. Remember that there are many ways to express any idea; one way may be more effective than another. Good writers choose the way that communicates an idea most clearly.

Exercise Applying Combining Skills

Combine the sentences in each of these groups into a single sentence. Write the combined sentences as a paragraph. Then, in your own words, complete the story.

1. I was sitting in a room.
   I was sitting alone.
   The room was dimly lit.
   I was watching the news.
   The news was on TV.
   I was sitting alone in a dimly lit room watching the news on TV.
2. The newscaster was talking about a gorilla.
   The newscaster was Bobby Bunt.
   The gorilla was huge.
   The gorilla was kept at the zoo.
   The zoo was nearby.
   The newscaster, Bobby Bunt, was talking about a huge gorilla kept at the nearby zoo.
3. The gorilla weighed four hundred pounds.
   The gorilla was so strong.
   It could pick up a car.
   The gorilla, who weighed four hundred pounds, was so strong that it could pick up a car.
4. The zoo-keepers were worried.
   The gorilla could rip open its cage.
   The gorilla could escape.
   The escape would be easy.
   The zoo-keepers were worried that the gorilla could rip open its cage and escape easily.
5. I turned suddenly.
   I saw a hand.
   The hand was reaching through the window.
   The hand was large.
   The hand was hairy.
   I turned suddenly and saw a large, hairy hand reaching through the window.

must not be changed in the revision. Urge the students to try several versions before settling on one.

4. Before they can continue the story begun in the Exercise, the students will have to add details from their knowledge and imagination. Brainstorm possible details orally before the students begin to write.

Individualizing the Lesson

Less-Advanced Students

These students may have difficulty with the length of some of the combinations in the Exercise. Have them try to combine in stages. For example, number 2 has five sentences. Have the students first combine the first and second sentences. Then have them combine the new sentence and the third sentence, and so on.

Advanced Students

Have these students write a more involved narrative, using dialogue and other characters, based on the idea suggested in the Exercise.

Optional Practice

Have students revise a previous writing assignment, looking for sentence structures covered in this chapter.

Extending the Lesson

Challenge the students to find one example of each type of combining in a single issue of a local newspaper.

Reinforcement Exercises

These Reinforcement Exercises may be used for additional practice as needed.

Review

If you have not assigned the Reinforcement Exercises before this time, you can use them as an excellent Chapter Review.

Reinforcement Exercises **Sentence Combining** Answers may vary.

A. Join each pair of sentences by using **, and** or **, or** or **, but.**

1. Yesterday I flew in a plane. I saw five states in an hour.
Yesterday I flew in a plane, and I saw five states in an hour.

2. The tickets went on sale this morning. By the time we got to the theater, they were all gone.
The tickets went on sale this morning, but by the time we got to the theater, they were all gone.

3. Pets are fun. They require care and attention.
Pets are fun, but they require care and attention.

B. Join the related parts of each pair of sentences by using **and** or **or** or **but.** Eliminate the italicized words.

1. Sir Gawain buckled his armor. *He* rode after the dragon.
Sir Gawain buckled his armor and rode after the dragon.

2. Next summer, I may get a job as a paper carrier. *I may babysit.*
Next summer, I may get a job as a paper carrier or a babysitter.

3. I saw Sam standing at the end of the hall. *I saw Harry standing at the end of the hall.*
I saw Sam and Harry standing at the end of the hall.

C. Combine each group of sentences by adding important words. Follow the directions given in parentheses. Eliminate the italicized words.

1. Ron looked for the election results in the paper. *He was* anxious. (End the important word with **-ly.**)
Ron anxiously looked for the election results in the paper.

2. My sweater shrank in the dryer. *My sweater was* wool.
My wool sweater shrank in the dryer.

3. A rainbow arched across the bay. *The rainbow was* pale. *The rainbow was* shimmering. (Use a comma.)
A pale, shimmering rainbow arched across the bay.

D. Combine each of the following pairs of sentences by adding an important group of words to the first sentence. Follow the directions given in parentheses. Eliminate the italicized words.

1. A local police officer taught the first-aid course. *The officer was* Mr. George Garcia. (Use a pair of commas.)
A local police officer, Mr. George Garcia, taught the first-aid course.

2. Two statues guarded the entrance. *The statues were* of monkeys. *It was the entrance* to the temple.
Two statues of monkeys guarded the entrance to the temple.

3. Did you see the recipe for fudge? *The recipe was* in Tuesday's paper.
Did you see the recipe for fudge in Tuesday's paper?

48

E. Combine each of the following pairs of sentences by substituting with *-ing*. Eliminate the italicized words.

1. Dr. Hendricks is very good at *something*. *She* puts her patients at ease. Dr. Hendricks is very good at putting her patients at ease.

2. *I* comb my cat's long fur. *That* can be tedious. Combing my cat's long fur can be tedious.

3. *Something* became Judy's passion. *She* practiced tennis. Practicing tennis became Judy's passion.

4. *People* parachute from planes. *That* requires training. Parachuting from planes requires training.

F. Combine each pair of sentences by following the directions in parentheses. Eliminate the italicized words.

1. Tracy Kidder has now joined a troupe of jugglers. *He* used to be very clumsy. (Combine with **, who.**) Tracy Kidder, who used to be very clumsy, has now joined a troupe of jugglers.

2. The boy saved four families. *The boy* spotted the smoke. (Combine with **who.**) The boy who spotted the smoke saved four families.

3. Students limit their career choices. *Students* don't explore many areas of study. (Combine with **who.**) Students who don't explore many areas of study limit their career choices.

G. Combine each of the following pairs of sentences by following the directions in parentheses. Eliminate the italicized words.

1. I can fix the lamp. *It* fell off the table. (Combine with **that.**) I can fix the lamp that fell off the table.

2. I wanted someone to invent a pen. I would never be able to lose *it*. (Combine with **that.**) I wanted someone to invent a pen that I would never be able to lose.

3. This building was once a customs house. *The building* is now a museum. (Combine with **, which.**) This building, which is now a museum, was once a customs house.

H. Combine each of the following pairs of sentences by using the key words given in parentheses.

1. Claire overslept. Claire overslept; as a result, she missed the bus for the class picnic.
   She missed the bus for the class picnic. **(; as a result.)**

2. Arthur's car ran out of gas. **(because)** Because Arthur's car ran out of gas, we missed the first half of the movie.
   We missed the first half of the movie.

3. Arthur's car ran out of gas. Arthur's car ran out of gas; so, we missed the first half of the movie.
   We missed the first half of the movie. **(; so,)**

49

Chapter 4

The Process of Writing

Chapter Objectives

1. To understand how to choose and limit a subject
2. To understand how to plan pre-writing notes
3. To understand how to write a first draft
4. To understand how to revise a draft
5. To know how to prepare a final copy

Preparing the Students

To clarify the difference between process and product, use the example of sculpting. Show pictures of many different kinds of statues, and talk about the creation process that resulted in each of these different pieces of art. Discuss the fact that the tools, material, and basic process remained the same for all of these statues, but that the final products varied greatly due to the technique of the artist, and depending on what he or she wanted to create.

Read page 51. Discuss briefly the different types of writing familiar to the students. These might include newspaper articles, class reports, essay tests, textbook chapters, and TV scripts. Explain that, despite the differences among these types of writing, the process of writing each is basically the same. Explain that this writing process is the focus of Chapter 4.

Think for a moment about all the types of writing you do. Sometimes you write reports, at other times you create stories, and at still other times you write letters or make entries in a journal. Each piece of writing has its own specific purpose and its own special style. In addition, each one reflects your particular thoughts, feelings, and experiences.

Although every finished piece of writing is unique, there will always be something that remains the same: the process of writing. There are certain steps you should always follow: pre-writing, writing a first draft, and rewriting, or revising. These steps are important. They help you decide what to write about, how to organize what you write, and how to rewrite, or revise, what you have written. You will learn how to follow these necessary steps in this chapter.

Part 1

Objectives

1. To understand how to choose and limit a subject
2. To learn how to plan pre-writing notes
3. To understand the terms *audience*, *purpose*, and *formal* and *informal* writing

Presenting the Lesson

1. As the students read through this chapter, focus on one step at a time, using the Guidelines on page 59 to show that the process is broken down into small steps. Assure the students that difficult skills, such as narrowing a topic, will be taught in more detail later in this book.

2. Read and discuss the explanation of the five pre-writing steps on pages 52-53. Stress that in the planning or pre-writing stage the writer seeks ideas, decides on a purpose and audience for the writing, and tentatively organizes ideas.

In your discussion of audience, point out that level of language must be adapted to suit an audience. Discuss formal and informal English, and the types of writing in which each is appropriate. Put several examples on the board, such as the following:

I was feeling wiped out.
I was exhausted.

3. You may wish to introduce the students to the following activities that can help a writer at the pre-writing stage to generate or focus on ideas:

Part 1   Pre-Writing

The success of a piece of writing often depends on the time you take before you ever begin to write. This time is needed for the **pre-writing,** or planning stage. At this point in the process of writing you will do two basic things:

1. Decide exactly what you will be writing about
2. Find the best way to present your ideas

To accomplish these two important goals of pre-writing, make the following steps a part of the planning process.

1. Choose and limit a topic.

To find a topic that you will enjoy and which will fit the assignment, ask yourself these questions:

What are the subjects that interest me? Sometimes your subject will be assigned, but often you will be given the chance to select your own topic. Make a list of things that have happened to you, or of subjects you would be interested in finding out more information about. Select one idea to be your topic.

Have I narrowed my topic to the proper size? The writing you do may be as short as a paragraph or as long as a report. Limit your topic to an idea that can be handled within the specified length.

2. Decide on your purpose.

After you have selected a topic, ask yourself these questions to determine exactly what you want to accomplish.

What do I want to say about my topic? Do you want to describe it, analyze it, criticize it, or explain it? Knowing your purpose will help you select supporting details later on.

What effect do I want my writing to have? A piece of writing can do many things for your reader. It can entertain, inform, explain, or persuade. Make sure you know which of these purposes you are trying to accomplish with your writing.

3. Identify your audience.

Another question you should ask yourself is "Who will read my writing?" The answer will help you decide many things. First of all, your audience will determine the type of language you will use. If you are writing a report for a teacher or a letter to a newspaper, for example, you would use **formal** English. Formal English follows all rules of grammar and usage and contains no slang or colloquial expressions. **Informal** English, however, may occasionally depart from such strict guidelines. It can be used in letters, stories, or other less formal situations.

Knowing your audience also tells you how much information to include. If your audience is unfamiliar with your subject, you will have to discuss it in more detail than if they knew more about it.

4. Gather supporting information.

Once you have decided on your topic, purpose, and audience, make a list of the specific details you could use to develop your topic. Sometimes the details will be from your own knowledge or experience. At other times, you may need to use sources of information that can be found in your library. List as many details or pieces of information as you can think of.

5. Strengthen and organize your ideas.

With your topic, audience, and purpose in mind, look through your list of specific details. Ask yourself these questions:

Are all of the details related to my topic and purpose?

Can any details be added that would make my purpose clearer or my writing more interesting?

Adjust your list as necessary. You may change one idea or several. You may even revise or change your topic.

Brainstorming — talking freely as a class or a group, sharing general ideas for topics or working on solutions for solving a particular problem.

Journal-writing — diary-like jottings about interesting ideas, sense impressions, and descriptions of feelings. Such a book can become a source of topics and ideas for writing.

Idea starters — exposure to new situations or new ways of looking at ordinary situations that can provide material for writing. These include film, art, poetry, photography, and speakers.

Discussion — talking about an assignment or debating ideas to clarify thoughts and opinions.

Studying models—analysis of prose writing with a purpose and audience similar to the assigned writing.

Interviewing — seeking opinions or information from others, especially experts on a topic.

Preliminary reading — skimming informative books and articles to become familiar with a topic or to discover starting points.

4. Discuss the sample pre-writing notes on page 54. Point out how the purpose and audience of the writing affect the selection of details. Stress the importance of keeping the audience and purpose in mind during the planning of any writing.

5. Note that the Parts in this chapter are not followed by Exercises. Students will be expected to apply the process of writing when completing assignments for the chapters on writing paragraphs and compositions.

Individualizing the Lesson

Less-Advanced Students

Have the students plan a paragraph to be developed by the group as each Part is discussed.

Advanced Students

These students may be tempted to skip some of the pre-writing steps. Emphasize that each step contributes in some way to an improved final product.

Optional Practice

1. Have the students keep a journal to practice recording observations and experiences.

2. Practice brainstorming on the topic "When a Family Moves." Then take the students through the five steps in the pre-writing process.

3. Have students consider the effect of audience on a piece of writing by explaining how a letter would be written differently to the following: an aunt, a friend who moved, the principal, the School Board.

4. Have the students take notes on the physical appearance of the classroom. Have the students save their notes for use in the Optional Practice for Part 2.

Extending the Lesson

Have students seek publications that address the same topic, but which are written for different audiences or purposes. For example, students might explore magazines about computers, such as *CompuKids*, *Personal Computing*, *Byte*, and *Office Management Systems*.

Once you have completed your list, try putting the details into a logical order. If you are telling a story, you would probably want to present your details in the order they occurred. If you are describing a scene or an object, you might want to arrange your details in the order in which a viewer would notice them. If you are presenting an argument, you might decide to organize your facts from least important to most important.

Study this example of pre-writing notes.

1. Possible topics
   the balloon man
   my TV hero
   the county fair *
   my friend's party

2. Narrowed topic
   arriving at the fair

3. Purpose
   to describe the excitement we felt
   when we arrived

4. Audience
   my classmates

5. Specific details
   hot and dusty   sword swallower
   crowds   tattooed man
   smells of food   ~~penny arcade~~
   games of chance   loud music
   ~~craft exhibit~~   rides

6. Order of details
   spatial

54

Part 2 Writing the First Draft

If you have taken time with the pre-writing steps, you are now ready to put your ideas together in a paragraph. As you write, leave space between the lines of writing to enable you to make corrections later. Remember that this is only a rough version, so don't be too concerned with details such as spelling and punctuation. Instead, concentrate on getting your ideas on paper and making them flow together smoothly. Keep your purpose and audience in mind at all times, but don't be afraid to depart somewhat from your original plan. You will find you often have new ideas as you write.

> The smell of peanuts was in the air as we waited in line at the gate of the county fair. We were listening to the noise and excitment around us. On our right, a red shirted man was telling everyone to come to see the sword swallower. On our left was a yellow tent with a colored poster of a tatooed man. Soon we could hear the sound of the Roller Coaster. The poeple in it were screaming. Jan and I didn't know what to do first. The loud music of the merry-go-round, the smell of popcorn, and the crowds of people made us a little dizzy.

Part 2

Objective

To understand how to write a first draft

Presenting the Lesson

1. Read the opening paragraph.
2. Direct students' attention to the sample first draft. Guide students to an understanding of how the writer's audience and purpose affected the content and language.
3. Have students find ideas the writer added to the first draft that were not in the pre-writing notes. Stress that writing should involve continuous reassessments.

Individualizing the Lesson

Less-Advanced Students

From their pre-writing notes, have the students write a first draft of their group paragraph.

Advanced Students

Encourage students to add several new ideas to their draft that were not in their notes.

Optional Practice

Have the students write a first draft using the notes they made in Part 1. (See Optional Practice 4)

Extending the Lesson

Invite a professional writer to your class. Ask the writer to explain and perhaps demonstrate the process he or she follows when writing.

To learn how to revise a draft

Presenting the Lesson

1. Read the explanation of the revising process, including **Proofreading,** on this page. Make sure students understand the six questions and how they are used to evaluate drafts.

Stress that the revising process involves both content and mechanics. Demonstrate the use of proofreading symbols on the chalkboard.

2. Ask volunteers to read and explain the Guidelines for the Process of Writing on page 59.

3. Have students point out differences between the revision and the first draft of the sample paragraph. Ask students how the paragraph has been improved.

4. You may want to introduce students to the following techniques for revising their work:

Peer evaluation — In pairs or small groups, students critique each other's writing.

Conference — Oral evaluations by the teacher concentrate on both strengths and problems, while the student asks questions.

Editorial group — Students assigned the roles of author, editor, and proofreader work together on an assignment and later change roles.

Group questioning — After one student in a group reads a piece of writing aloud, the other students ask questions focusing on what they still want to know about the subject.

Part 3   Rewriting, or Revising

At this point in the process of writing, fine tune your work. Read what you have written, and ask yourself these questions.

1. Did I stick to my topic?
2. Are there any unnecessary details?
3. Could any points be added that would clarify or improve my writing?
4. Do the ideas flow together smoothly?
5. Would a different organization of ideas be better?
6. Are there more precise or vivid words I could use?

As you answer these questions, make corrections and notes on your rough draft. You may even want to begin all over again, rearranging your ideas or improving the way you say them. Writers often make several drafts of a piece of writing before they are satisfied.

Proofreading

After you make your content changes, proofread your writing for incorrect grammar, capitalization, punctuation, and spelling. Correct any errors on your draft. The following symbols may be useful.

SYMBOL	MEANING	EXAMPLE
$\wedge$	insert	would have gone
$\equiv$	capitalize	United states
/	make lower case	our club President
$\sim$	transpose	t h i e r
$\mathcal{e}$	delete	finished the the race
¶	make new paragraph	. . . be complete. ¶ Another one . . .
$\cup$	close up space	head line

Now look at this draft, which is in the process of being revised. Notice how precise language was substituted for vague words and phrases. Look at the way an idea was moved to make the paragraph flow better. Finally, notice how the writer corrected all errors in grammar, capitalization, punctuation, and spelling. Examine these changes carefully. Then read the final draft on the next page to see how much the paragraph was improved by these changes. Revise your own writing just as thoroughly.

> *(handwritten draft with revision marks)*
>
> The [tantalizing] smell of peanuts [roasting] was in the air [hung over us] as we
> waited in [the hot, dusty] line at the gate of [entrance to] the county
> fair. [Once inside,] We were listening to [caught up in] the noise and ex-
> citment around us. On our right, a [fat] red-shirted
> man was telling [calling] everyone to come to see the
> [amazing] sword swallower. On our left [stood] was a [bright] yellow
> tent with a [vividly] colored poster of a tatooed man [in front of it].
> [As we moved on,] Soon we could hear the [roar] sound of the Roller
> Coaster. The [and screams of the] people in it were screaming.
> Jan and I didn't know what to do first [where to begin.] The
> [high-pitched] loud music of the merry-go-round, the
> smell of [freshly popped corn] popcorn, and the crowds of people [swarms, around us]
> made us a little [bit giddy.] dizzy.

Clinics — In workshops, students with similar writing problems receive instruction from the teacher. This may involve completing prepared material, or working together to solve common problems.

Tutoring — A student who is weak in some area is paired with a student who is stronger in the same area.

Individualizing the Lesson

Less-Advanced Students

Work with the students to revise the group paragraph. Make the use of proofreading marks optional.

Advanced Students

Have the students revise a paragraph written for an earlier assignment. As a further challenge, you might instruct students to change the audience for the paragraph.

Optional Practice

Provide specific revising exercises for students to work on. For example:

a. Ask students to make these words more precise: *hit, hold, smile, unhappy, calm, noisy, stone, container, bird.*

b. Ask students to think of more details to add to this paragraph:

Learning how to swim is important for everyone . . . .

Extending the Lesson

Use several samples of unrevised writing, such as student essay tests, to demonstrate the revising and proofreading processes. Project the samples, using an overhead projector, or duplicate them and distribute them to the class.

Objective

To know how to prepare a final copy

Presenting the Lesson

1. Read and discuss the introductory paragraph. If necessary, explain the meaning of *indentations, margins,* and *heading.* Emphasize the value of reading one's writing aloud.

2. Direct students' attention to the final copy of the sample paragraph. Ask students how it differs from the two preceding versions.

3. Review the entire Guidelines for the Process of Writing on page 59. Urge students to refer to these Guidelines often as they write.

Individualizing the Lesson

Less-Advanced Students

Have the students make final copies of their group paragraphs after reading them aloud to the group and incorporating suggestions and corrections.

Advanced Students

1. Have students make final copies of one of the paragraphs they revised for Part 3.

2. Ask several students to explain to small groups the steps they followed in the process of writing a paragraph, from how they got their topic idea to writing the final copy.

Part 4   Preparing the Final Copy

Finally, when you are satisfied that your writing is clear and correct, write your final copy. Write carefully. Make your copy as neat as possible. Make correct paragraph indentations. Leave good margins around your writing. Use whatever headings your teacher requires.

When you have finished your final copy, proofread your work again. Read it aloud. Sometimes your ears catch errors your eyes have missed.

Here is the final copy of the paragraph. Compare it with the two preceding paragraphs.

> The tantalizing smell of roasting peanuts hung over us as we waited in the hot, dusty line at the entrance to the county fair. Once inside, we were caught up in the noise and excitement around us. On our right, a fat red-shirted man was calling everyone to come see the amazing sword swallower. On our left stood a bright yellow tent with a vividly colored poster of a tattooed man in front of it. As we moved on, we could hear the roar of the roller coaster and the screams of the people in it. The high-pitched music of the merry-go-round, the smell of freshly popped corn, and the swarms of people around us made us a bit giddy. Jan and I didn't know where to begin.

Guidelines for the Process of Writing

Pre-Writing

1. Select a topic and narrow it.
2. Decide on your purpose and audience.
3. Gather details to help you develop your topic.
4. Organize and strengthen your list of details.

Writing the First Draft

1. With your purpose and audience in mind, begin to write.
2. Do not be concerned with grammar or mechanics at this stage.

Rewriting, or Revising

1. Did you stick to your topic? Does your writing have unity?
2. Have all important details been included?
3. Are the topic sentences strong and interesting?
4. Do the ideas flow smoothly? Are ideas in a logical order?
5. Is the language vivid and precise?
6. Have you accomplished your purpose?

Proofreading Additional instruction on these concepts may be found in the indicated sections.

Grammar and Usage
Are there any sentence fragments or run-ons? (Sect. 1)
Do all verbs agree with their subjects? (Sect. 9)
Have you used the correct form of each pronoun? (Sect. 3)
Have you used adjectives and adverbs correctly? (Sect. 5)

Punctuation
Does each sentence have the proper end mark? (Sect. 12)
Are marks such as colons, semicolons, apostrophes, hyphens, and quotation marks used correctly? (Sect. 12)

Capitalization
Did you capitalize first words and all proper nouns and adjectives? (Sect. 11)

Spelling
Did you check all unfamiliar words in the dictionary? (Sect. 13)
Are plurals and possessive forms spelled correctly? (Sect. 2, 3)

Form
In your final copy, is the writing legible?
Have you used the proper heading and margins?

Optional Practice

Have students make final copies of the paragraphs they revised for Optional Practice, Part 3.

Extending the Lesson

Invite a newspaper, magazine, or book editor to class to explain the importance of the editing process that takes place after an author submits an article or a manuscript. Perhaps the editor might show samples of edited manuscripts, including proofreading symbols and changes.

Chapter 5

Writing the Paragraph

Chapter Objectives

1. To understand the importance of unity in a paragraph
2. To understand that a paragraph must provide enough information to support or explain the main idea
3. To understand that a topic sentence states the main idea of a paragraph
4. To write effective topic sentences

Preparing the Students

Read and discuss the Chapter introduction.

Emphasize the idea that the paragraph is a basic unit for organizing ideas in writing. Point out the paragraphs in a magazine article or book. Note that generally the beginning of a paragraph is signaled by an indentation of the first line.

Tell the students that a person must be able to organize ideas logically and effectively to make the ideas understood. As the students study this chapter and the two succeeding chapters, they will learn about this most important and basic form for organizing ideas—the paragraph.

Additional Resources

Mastery Test—pages 14-15 in the test booklet. Recommended for use after teaching the chapter.

Skills Practice Book—pages 17-20.
Duplicating Masters—pages 17-20.

The paragraph is the basic tool for organizing ideas in any kind of writing. If you can write a good paragraph, you can write a good composition, a good report, or a good letter. In this chapter, you will review the main parts of a paragraph. You will study the way that sentences are put together into well written paragraphs.

Objectives

1. To understand the importance of unity in a paragraph

2. To understand that a paragraph must provide enough information to support or explain the main idea

Presenting the Lesson

1. The composition chapters in this book present a highly structured type of paragraph, a basic model that consists of a topic sentence developed by several additional sentences. This model is useful in getting students to discipline their thinking and their writing. However, it should not be presented as the only way to organize a paragraph. Therefore, you may want to mention occasionally that the sample paragraphs represent one way to write a paragraph.

2. Read and discuss the definition of *paragraph* at the top of page 62. Point out that each supporting sentence in the sample paragraph tells something about how soundly Tom slept.

3. Read and discuss **Paragraph Unity** on pages 62 and 63. Have the students suggest sentences that could be used to support the idea stated in the first sentence of the sample paragraph on the bottom of page 62.

Tell the students that they can assess the unity of paragraphs they develop by reading each supporting sentence and asking themselves how it supports or explains the main idea.

A **paragraph** is a group of sentences that work together to explain or support one main idea. That idea usually is stated in the first sentence. The rest of the paragraph contains several sentences that develop the main idea more fully. Following is an example of a well written paragraph.

> *Tom slept more soundly that night than he had in a long time.* His dreams were of the new friend he had found. He dreamed of the deer and himself running over the green meadows and up the gentle slopes of the hills. He dreamed beautiful dreams like these until the morning when the sun came through his window and woke him.—JENNY DEBOUZEK

The first sentence tells you that the paragraph is going to be about Tom's sound sleep. This is the one main idea of the paragraph. The rest of the sentences develop that idea. They give you a sense of Tom's long and peaceful rest.

Paragraph Unity

When all of the sentences in a paragraph relate to one main idea, the paragraph has **unity.** Sometimes a paragraph contains sentences that stray from the main idea. These "extra" sentences can be removed easily to create a unified paragraph.

Other paragraphs, like this one, have more serious problems.

> Driver's training should be a required course in every high school in the United States. Defensive driving means anticipating the actions of other drivers. Millions of people are killed in automobile accidents every year. Insurance statistics have not proved that teen-agers are unsafe drivers. Many insurance companies offer lower insurance rates to students who have completed driver's training courses.

The first sentence in this paragraph is about the need for a driver's training course in every high school. Each of the next three sentences introduces a different idea. The second sentence defines defensive driving. The third sentence makes a statement about automobile accidents. The fourth sentence gives a fact about insurance statistics. Only the last sentence relates directly to the opening sentence in the paragraph. It begins to explain why driver's training should be required.

The sentences in this paragraph do not develop one main idea. They are, therefore, a series of unrelated sentences, not a unified paragraph.

Paragraph Length

"How long does a paragraph have to be?" is a question asked by many beginning writers. The answer is easier than you might suppose: *A paragraph should be long enough to develop a main idea.* For example, the following paragraph is too short to explain the topic sentence clearly:

> Almost all of us agreed that Jack was the luckiest boy in town. To our envious eyes, he had everything a boy could ever wish for.

Why was Jack lucky? What did he have? The question can be answered only by adding more sentences.

> Almost all of us agreed that Jack was the luckiest boy in town. He had his own minibike and lots of space to ride it in. When he was tired of that, Fallah, his black mare, stood waiting patiently in the stable. No matter what he asked his dad for, it miraculously appeared the next day. He even had his own pool table. Furthermore, he didn't have to do chores like the rest of us. The gardener and the stable hand took care of the chores. To our envious eyes, he had everything a boy could ever wish for.

The detailed information in the longer paragraph explains clearly and completely why Jack was considered the luckiest boy in town.

4. Read and discuss **Paragraph Length** on page 63.

Tell students that the best way to decide whether they have included enough information in a paragraph is to have someone else read the paragraph and decide whether it is clear. The next-best way is to try to read the paragraph as such a reader would read it.

5. Assign and discuss the Exercise on page 64.

Individualizing the Lesson

Less-Advanced Students

Do the Exercise orally. First have the students read all the sentences in each paragraph. Then help the students determine the main idea of the paragraph. Next help them determine whether each sentence explains or supports the idea.

Advanced Students

Challenge the students to replace the unrelated sentence or sentences in each group in the Exercise. For example, the second and third sentences in paragraph 1 could be replaced by the following sentences:

> No one should attempt a deep-sea dive without training and practice. Deep-sea divers must know how to avoid dangerous fish.

Optional Practice

Have the students follow the directions for the Exercise on page 64, using this paragraph:

> Claudia had never experienced such a dreadful day in her entire life. Her father had stormed out of the

house after breakfast, furious at everyone. Her favorite uncle had missed his plane and wouldn't arrive in time for the special family dinner. To the family, Uncle Harold was affectionately known as "Racks." She argued with her sister about a sweater her sister had borrowed. When dinner was finally served, no one felt much like eating. She ruined the dessert she had wanted to be perfect.

Extending the Lesson

1. Have the students begin a collection of paragraphs that appeal strongly to them as readers. Explain that content, vivid language, and good organization should be the criteria for choosing a paragraph. Set a goal of five paragraphs to be collected by each student during the study of this chapter. Direct the students to copy each paragraph on a clean sheet of notebook paper. Above each paragraph, the student should write one sentence explaining what he or she liked about that paragraph. Under the paragraph, the student should record the author and source.

2. Have each student choose one paragraph from a magazine article and state the main idea of the paragraph in a single sentence.

Exercise Studying Paragraph Unity

In each of the following paragraphs, one or more sentences do not relate to the main idea of the paragraph. Pick out the ("extra") sentences. Then decide whether the remaining sentences give enough information about the main idea to make a fully developed paragraph.

1

Deep-sea diving requires more than putting on a wet suit and an iron mask. (Treasures lie buried at the bottom of the sea.) (Jacques Cousteau has spent most of his life filming undersea life.) Divers must be knowledgeable about their equipment.

2

All animals have senses, but not all animals use them in the same way. (Many people have lost their sense of hearing.) A frog, for instance, does not see a fly as we see it—in terms of legs, shape of wings, and number of eyes. In fact, a frog won't spot a fly at all unless the fly moves. (Frogs are amphibious animals.) Put a frog into a cage with freshly killed insects, and it will starve.

3

My cousin and I learned most of our family's history by playing in Grandmother's attic. (Grandmother lived in a little town in Ohio.) In one corner stood a brass-bound trunk, filled with forgotten dolls once treasured by aunts and mothers. Grandfather's World War I uniform hung proudly on a metal rack, along with once-stylish dresses. (The clothing now is much more comfortable than it was thirty years ago.) When we dressed up in the old-fashioned clothes, we felt that the past was truly part of our lives.

4

Jeff Daniels is deaf, yet he knows when his telephone rings or his alarm clock goes off. His "hearing ear" dog, Rags, tells him. Rags, who was trained by the American Humane Association, alerts his master whenever there is a knock on the door or a phone call and leads Jeff to the source of the sound. (Seeing-eye dogs are used by blind people.)

Part 2   The Topic Sentence

The topic sentence is usually the first sentence in a paragraph. It tells what the rest of the paragraph is going to be about. The topic sentence is the key to paragraph unity. It states the one main idea that must be developed by the other sentences. If a sentence relates directly to the topic sentence, it belongs in the paragraph. If it relates only indirectly or not at all, it does not fit and should be removed.

The topic sentence is important from the point of view of both the writer and the reader. It helps the writer to focus on the one idea that gives direction to the paragraph. It helps the writer to stay on the track so that he or she does not bring in ideas that are unrelated to the main idea. For the reader, the topic sentence acts as a guide by letting him or her know immediately what the entire paragraph is going to be about.

To understand more clearly what a topic sentence does, look at the following paragraph.

> My husband had very definite opinions about raising children. He believed that parents should provide proper models for their children and should give them guidelines as to what they can and cannot do. He thought that children should be taught to face reality, to accept themselves, to be able to function under supervision, to seek some formal training and education, and to realize that it was their duty to help oppressed people. He believed that children should have a belief in a tradition and that this should come originally from the home. He did not believe in spoiling children.
>
> —BETTY SHABAZZ

The topic sentence says: "My husband had very definite opinions about raising children." This is the main idea of the paragraph. The sentences that follow describe the opinions. These sentences relate directly to the topic sentence. The paragraph, therefore, has unity.

Part 2

Objective

To understand that a topic sentence states the main idea of a paragraph

Presenting the Lesson

1. Read and discuss pages 65 and 66. Have the students explain how each supporting sentence in the sample paragraph is related to the topic sentence.
2. Assign and discuss Exercise A beginning on page 66.
3. Assign Exercise B on page 67. Have volunteers read their paragraphs aloud.

Individualizing the Lesson

Less-Advanced Students

Work with the students to complete Exercise A. First read all the sentences in a group. Then have the students determine the general topic of the group of sentences. Finally, have them decide which sentence states a main idea about the topic.

Advanced Students

Have each student bring a short newspaper article to class. Have students read their articles aloud and discuss how well the headline states the main idea of the article.

Have the students follow the directions for Exercises A and B on pages 66–67, using this set of sentences:

a. His watch was found at the scene of the crime.

b. He cannot account for his whereabouts during the time of the robbery.

c. The evidence points to Ed Jackson as the thief who robbed Jones's jewelry store.

d. He shook and stuttered when he was brought in for questioning.

e. A check made out to Mr. Jones was found in his apartment.

Extending the Lesson

Divide the class into two teams. Write one of the topic sentences from Exercise A on page 66 on the chalkboard. Then have each student write an original sentence that will support the topic sentence. Collect the sentences and read them, alternating between teams. Have the students discuss whether each sentence supports the topic sentence. The team with the greatest number of sentences that do support the topic sentence wins.

The topic sentence of the paragraph is a general statement. It presents the idea of definite opinions without giving any specific information about them. The other sentences in the paragraph explain the opinions in some detail. The same arrangement can be found in most paragraphs. The topic sentence gives an idea that covers, or takes in, the specific ideas in the rest of the paragraph.

Exercises Working with Topic Sentences

A. Each of the following groups has five sentences about one topic. Choose the one sentence in the group that would work best as the topic sentence.

1. a. Living things are organic matter.

b. Things that were never alive, such as minerals and glass, are inorganic matter.

c. Lumber, wood, and cotton were once alive, so they are organic matter.

d. Anything that takes up space is called "matter."

e. Matter can't be destroyed, but it can be changed into energy.

2. a. Jack drinks so much milk that Dad jokes about buying a cow.

b. Jack's standard question after school is, "What's for dinner?"

c. When Jack packs his school lunch, it looks like a grocery bag.

d. My brother Jack claims that his hobby is eating.

e. Mom is threatening to put a padlock on the refrigerator.

3. a. The bare branches of the maple trees were outlined in shimmering white.

b. Our yard looked magically different after the heavy winter snow.

c. The bushes in front of the garage drooped, heavy with snow blossoms.

d. The old garage wore a fresh white coat of snow-paint.

e. The bird bath near the house had become a frosty snow-cone.

4. a. Sometimes a giraffe's height can lead to its death.

b. Every time a giraffe takes a drink of water, it is in danger.

c. A giraffe can't drink easily because it can't kneel down.

d. A giraffe takes a long time to bend its legs apart.

e. While a giraffe is drinking, it is helpless if a lion or tiger attacks.

5. a. When my little brother had the measles, Mrs. Paulson played checkers with him every day.

b. Mrs. Paulson often bakes cookies for us.

c. Mrs. Paulson bandages our scraped knees without scolding us for being careless.

d. I guess every child on the block has had her for a babysitter at one time or another.

e. Bespectacled Mrs. Paulson is like a grandmother to everyone in the neighborhood.

B. Select one of the groups of sentences from Exercise A, and work the sentences into a paragraph. Begin the paragraph with the topic sentence. Arrange the rest of the sentences in the order you think is best. If necessary, revise the sentences or add words and phrases so that your finished paragraph reads smoothly.

Objective

To write effective topic sentences

Presenting the Lesson

1. Read and discuss pages 68-70. Emphasize the two functions of a topic sentence: (1) to state the main idea of a paragraph and (2) to catch the reader's attention.

To illustrate these concepts, review the sample paragraphs on pages 62, 63, and 65. Discuss the topic sentences in these paragraphs, showing that each states a main idea and catches a reader's attention.

2. Have the students use the guidelines on page 70 to evaluate the topic sentences in the paragraphs in the Exercise beginning on page 66.

3. Assign and discuss Exercises A and B on pages 70 and 71.

Individualizing the Lesson

Less-Advanced Students

1. Work with the students to revise the topic sentences in Exercise A on page 70. Help students choose specific verbs, nouns, adjectives, and adverbs that will make each sentence more interesting.

2. Simplify Exercise B by having the students improve the following topic sentences instead of creating entirely original ones.

1. Horses were important to transportation.
2. I saw a man.
3. Some dynamite was in a box.

Part 3   Writing Topic Sentences

The topic sentence of a paragraph has two main jobs:

1. It must state the main idea of the paragraph, which is the idea developed by the rest of the sentences.
2. It must capture the reader's attention so that he or she wants to find out more about the main idea.

Stating the Main Idea

In Part 2 you learned that a topic sentence is a general statement. It presents an idea that can be developed with details.

Sometimes, in writing a topic sentence, a writer may express an idea that is *too general* to be developed in a single paragraph. Following is an example of such a sentence:

There are many kinds of dogs.

This subject is so broad that about all the writer could do is list the different dog breeds. The paragraph would probably be as dull to write as it would be to read.

Suppose the topic sentence were revised like this:

The poodle has played a starring role in the history of dogdom.

The writer narrowed her main idea so that it could be developed in one paragraph. She went on to supply more details.

> *The poodle has played a starring role in the history of dogdom.* The breed is believed to have originated in Russia, where black standard-sized poodles were used as water retrievers for bird hunters. The Russians called the dog "pudel," which literally means "splashing in water." The breed spread to northern Germany, where the brown color was introduced. German artists as early as the fifteenth century depicted the poodle, and the great Spanish artist, Goya, used this breed in several of his paintings. The first evidence of a toy poodle's existence came from England, where the "White Cuban" breed,

said to have begun in Cuba, became an English favorite. Queen Anne had several poodles during her reign in the early eighteenth century.—EVELYN MILLER

The writer was able to explain her main idea in one paragraph. She gave sufficient details within that paragraph to leave the reader feeling satisfied.

Writing Interesting Topic Sentences

Any writer who puts time and effort into a paragraph wants it to be read. If the topic sentence is dull and uninteresting, however, the reader may not read the entire paragraph.

Look at the following topic sentence:

I'd like to tell you about the use of teaching machines in the schools of the future.

This sentence makes clear what the rest of the paragraph is going to be about. It is a general statement that is narrow enough to be developed in one paragraph. The sentence, though, is flat and unimaginative.

Now, look at this topic sentence:

In the world of tomorrow, teaching machines will take into account different learning rates, working as fast (or as slowly) as the students using them.

Your response to the sentence might be, "Gee, that sounds interesting. Tell me more." The writer has caught your attention. You want to find out more about teaching machines.

In the world of tomorrow, teaching machines will take into account different learning rates, working only as fast (or as slowly) as the students using them. They will offer the child individual attention. They will possibly offer more patience than could be expected from the average teacher. They will offer immediate feedback so that the children know how well they are doing and can take pride in their progress. More than that, the machines will help make learning fun.

69

Writing a Topic Sentence

When writing a paragraph, begin by jotting down some ideas about what you might want to say. Study your notes and cross out those ideas that do not seem to fit well with the others. Then write a topic sentence.

Guidelines for Writing Topic Sentences

1. Does the sentence clearly state the main idea that you plan to develop in the paragraph?
2. Does the sentence present an idea that is narrow enough to be explained or supported in a single paragraph?
3. Does the sentence express the main idea in such a way that the reader will want to read the entire paragraph?

Exercises Writing Good Topic Sentences

A. Here is a list of poorly written topic sentences. They are either too broad, too uninteresting, or both. Decide what is wrong with each sentence. Then rewrite the sentence so that it would be an effective topic sentence for a paragraph.

1. In this paragraph I am going to explain several ways of conserving energy.
2. Summer is the best time of the year.
3. Each year Mother invites my teacher to dinner.
4. This story about a blind deer made me very sad.
5. There are many ways to raise money when you need it.
6. Younger brothers take advantage of their sisters.
7. My favorite sports are basketball and soccer.
8. This literary masterpiece is going to be about someone I've known for years—me.
9. I like all kinds of music.
10. America's history is filled with heroes.

B. In the following paragraphs, the topic sentences have been removed. Read each paragraph carefully. Then write a good topic sentence. Be sure that it does the things listed on page 70.

1. _____(topic sentence)_____. In cities, all deliveries were by horse and wagon. Horses moved urban local passengers by carriage, omnibus, and horse-drawn streetcars. Stagecoaches bore passengers, mail, and baggage across rough and dusty Western roads, negotiating steep grades and fording unbridged streams. After 1840, teams of fast trotting horses for light coaches became popular in the East.

2. _____(topic sentence)_____. He was a husky, long-legged chap, to me a perfect physical specimen. I asked him where he'd been, and he replied that he had been climbing the foothills north of town. I asked him why he did it. He told me that his doctor had advised it; that he was trying to correct certain difficulties following an illness. He was climbing the foothills every day to develop his lungs and legs.

3. _____(topic sentence)_____. The dynamite had been frozen and thawed many times. Its paper covering had absorbed the nitroglycerine, making it dangerous no matter how carefully it was handled. In fact, dynamite like that sometimes explodes when two sticks of it are pulled apart, as the ghosts of a good many miners could tell you.

4. _____(topic sentence)_____. There they were—thirty-six whales pulled up on the shore. Every one of them weighed up to 4,000 pounds and measured nearly twenty feet long. They were the true monsters of the deep, the "black-fish" in Melville's famous story, *Moby Dick*.

5. _____(topic sentence)_____. They took him into a room where there were only some boxes and three bananas hanging from the ceiling. They wanted to see how long it would take the chimp to pile up the boxes and climb on them. The chimp did not touch the boxes. He pushed one of the men under the bananas, crawled up on his back, and brought the bananas down in two minutes.

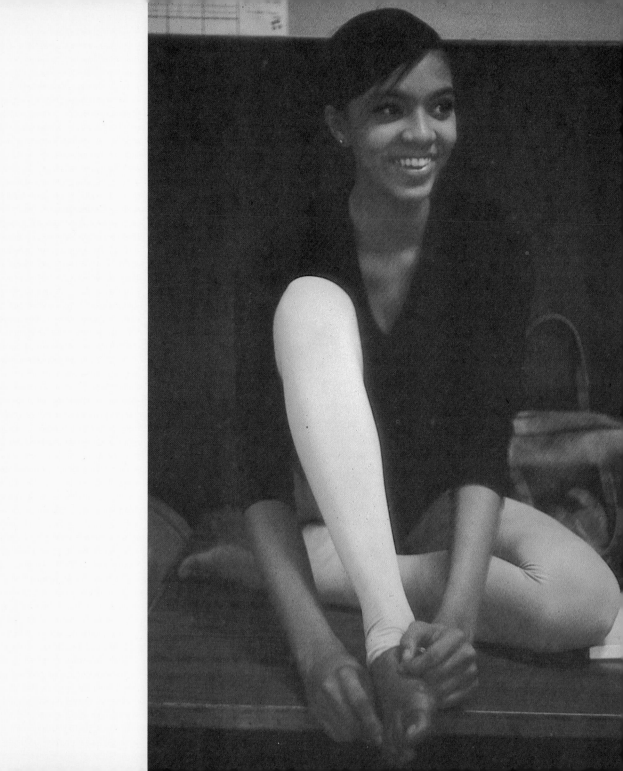

Chapter 6

Developing the Paragraph

Chapter Objectives

1. To develop paragraphs using specific details
2. To develop paragraphs using facts or figures
3. To develop paragraphs using examples
4. To develop paragraphs using incidents
5. To develop paragraphs using definitions

Preparing the Students

Read and discuss the chapter introduction.

Tell the students to suppose that they were going to write a paragraph about the classroom that they are now in. (If the students did write paragraphs on this topic as part of the Optional Practice in Chapter 4, remind them of the paragraphs they wrote.) On the chalkboard, write the headings DETAILS, FACTS, FIGURES. Have the students suggest specific information about the classroom that could be included under each heading.

Explain that this chapter will teach the students how to develop paragraphs with such information and also by using examples, incidents, and definitions.

Additional Resources

Mastery Test—See pages 16-17 in the test booklet. Recommended for use after teaching the chapter.
Skills Practice Book—pages 21-25.
Duplicating Masters—pages 21-25.

In writing, just as cooking, you may have available all the ingredients for a good product. The trick lies in selecting the right ingredients from those on hand and in putting them together correctly and creatively.

For a paragraph, the "right ingredients" are ideas that develop the main idea. Supporting ideas can take a variety of forms. They might be details that appeal to the senses. They might be facts, figures, or examples. They might be definitions of things or concepts. This chapter discusses how different kinds of supporting ideas can be used to develop paragraphs.

Part 1 Using Specific Details

Objective

To develop paragraphs using specific details

Presenting the Lesson

1. Read and discuss the introduction on page 74. Ask the students to close their eyes and try to picture the character described in the Chaucer passage as you read the lines aloud. Emphasize the fact that specific details help a reader "see" what a writer describes.

2. Read and discuss **Using Visual Details** on pages 74 and 75. Have the students compare the sample paragraph with the following paragraph:

That summer we camped on the outskirts of a village. Our tent was in a row of several others just like it. The floor was set up on bricks. The roof was held down by ropes. Between the tents there were lean-tos. There was a swamp nearby, and a ditch separated the camp from some railroad tracks.

2. Read and discuss **Writing About a Person** on pages 75 and 76. Have the students identify details in the sample paragraph that describe the girl's physical appearance and details that describe her behavior, moods, and outlook on life.

3. Read **Developing a Paragraph** on page 76. Discuss each of the five steps for writing a paragraph, referring to the paragraphs on pages 74 and 75 as examples of implementing the five steps.

4. Before assigning the Exercise on pages 76-77, work with the stu-

Part 1 Using Specific Details

Details are items of information that work together to create a clear impression in a reader's mind. To better understand the nature of details, let's examine five lines written by Geoffrey Chaucer, an early English poet.

> His beard was broader than a shovel, and red
> As a fat sow or fox. A wart stood clear
> Atop his nose, and red as a pig's ear
> A tuft of bristles on it. Black and wide
> His nostrils were.

The details in these lines of poetry are visual details. They appeal to the reader's sense of sight, with phrases such as these:

broader than a shovel	red as a pig's ear
red as a fat sow or fox	tuft of bristles
atop his nose	black and wide

By choosing such vivid details, Chaucer succeeds in communicating a clear picture of a person's appearance in just a few lines.

Using Visual Details

Visual details can be used to build a paragraph that describes a place or a thing. In the following example, the writer tells about a camp on the outskirts of a village.

> That summer we camped along the railroad tracks on the outskirts of a village. Our tent was next to the last in a row of several others just like it—a square of brown canvas curtains with a roof sloped like a pyramid, held up by a pole that peeped through a vent at the top. The plank floor of the tent was set up on bricks, the ends of the timbers sticking out in front, making a shelf that we used for a porch. The roof was held down by ropes staked down at the four corners and along the sides. Between the tents there were lean-to's where the women cooked and washed clothes in iron tubs, heating

the water over stone fire pits. The swamp came up close in back, and in front spilled into a ditch, making a moat that separated the camp from the tracks just beyond. Over this ditch there was a catwalk of planks leading to the tracks, the main street of the neighborhood.—ERNESTO GALARZA

The writer opens the paragraph with a general statement about the camp. He then expands this idea with details about the location of his family's tent, about the way the tent was constructed, about the lean-to's between the tents, about the swamp behind and in front of the campsite, and about the tracks beyond the ditch. Each detail is carefully selected to give the reader a good idea of what the camp looked like.

Writing About a Person

Suppose you want to describe a person. Each person has some special distinction—something in the way he or she looks, or dresses, or acts—which makes that person an individual. These are the specific details you would include in your description of that person. Some of the details would be visual details about the person's appearance. Others might be details about the person's behavior, moods, and outlook on life.

Notice, in the following paragraph, how the writer combines different kinds of details.

> She was a black child, with huge green eyes that seemed to glow in the dark. From the age of four on she had a look of being full-grown. The look was in her muscular, well-defined limbs that seemed as though they could do a woman's work and in her way of seeing everything around her. Most times she was alive and happy. The only thing wrong with her was that she got hurt so easily. The slightest rebuke sent her crying; the least hint of disapproval left her moody and depressed for hours. But the other side of it was that she had a way of springing back from pain. No matter how hurt she had been, she would be her old self by the next day.—JEAN WHEELER SMITH

dents to develop a paragraph from the first sentence. Follow the steps listed on page 76. Then have the students work independently to develop paragraphs of their own. Review students' paragraphs with them, and have volunteers read their paragraphs to the class.

Individualizing the Lesson

Less-Advanced Students

Discuss each of the topic sentences in class before the students begin independent work on the Exercise. Help the students list details that might be included in each paragraph.

Advanced Students

In addition to the paragraphs required by the Exercise, have each student write a paragraph on an original topic, developing the paragraph with specific details. Have the students follow the steps listed on page 76.

Optional Practice

Have each student use specific details to develop a paragraph about the classroom, following the steps listed on page 76.

Extending the Lesson

1. Display a photograph of an interesting individual or scene. Have each student write a paragraph about the subject of the picture, developed through visual details. Have the students refer to the five steps listed on page 76.

2. For each of the following topics, have the students list specific

details that appeal to senses other than sight:

My Favorite Food
A Visit to the Seashore
Stranded in the Desert
The Haunted Tunnel

Have the students try writing paragraphs on these topics that are developed with specific details that appeal only to the senses of hearing, touch, smell, and taste.

The writer first gives specific details about the child's outward appearance; for example: "a black child," "huge green eyes," and "muscular, well defined limbs." She then describes the child's sensitivity and resilience. The writer develops the paragraph with details that help us to see a unique individual.

Developing a Paragraph

When you sit down to write a paragraph that is to be developed with many details, keep these five steps in mind.

Five Steps for Writing a Paragraph

1. Decide on a topic that lends itself to this method of development.

2. List details that you might possibly include in the paragraph.

3. Choose the details that you will include in the paragraph.

4. Write a good topic sentence that states the main idea of the paragraph.

5. Add supporting sentences that develop the main idea.

Exercise Developing a Paragraph with Details

Each of these topic sentences may be expanded into a paragraph by using specific details. Choose two sentences. Use your imagination to develop each into a well written paragraph. Follow the Guidelines for the Process of Writing on page 59.

1. Old Rob was certainly an unusual dog.

2. Not a breath stirred over the open prairie.

3. Walking from the marble terrace, we entered the central hall of the mansion.

4. The visitor from Neptune looked nothing like a human.

5. Sam was in his early fifties, and the hair that showed under his hat was iron gray.

6. The old peddler's cart was piled high with fruit.

7. The landlord had moved enough stuff into the room to furnish three rooms its size.

8. The bird watcher waited patiently on the park bench.

9. The first light of dawn glowed faintly on the horizon.

10. Every day I explored a little more of the river.

11. At night I dreamed of nothing but the cat.

12. I shall never forget the guest who arrived at our house one afternoon last September.

Part 2 Using Facts or Figures

A topic sentence sometimes makes a statement that is best supported with facts or figures. Following is an example of this method of paragraph development. Notice that the writer has used a few figures along with many facts.

A most enchanting part of Puerto Rico is El Yunque Rain Forest, named after the 3496-foot-high mountain El Yunque. This 28,000-acre stretch of jungles, hills, streams, and waterfalls, a bare hour's drive from San Juan, is the only rain forest in the West Indies and the only tropical preserve of the United States National Park Service. Here, giant ferns unfurl feathery branches up to 30 feet. Orchids in pastel shades cling to their host trees. Among the 200 species of trees are hardwoods which, elsewhere, were cut down centuries before to build Spanish cathedrals, forts, monasteries, and homes. One of these is the mighty *ausubo*, called the bullet wood tree because of the toughness of its wood.—ROBIN MCKOWN

77

Part 2

Objective

To develop paragraphs using facts or figures

Presenting the Lesson

1. Read and discuss pages 77 and 78. Emphasize that the main idea in the sample paragraph on this page is an opinion. An opinion must be supported with factual information to convince a reader that it is correct. In the paragraph, the writer has used facts and figures to support an opinion.

Point out that in the example on page 78 the writer has used figures to explain why something is so.

2. Assign the Exercise on page 79. Before the students begin inde-

pendent work, have them suggest possible sources for information on each topic. Tell the students to take notes when gathering information from outside sources, summarizing and paraphrasing rather than copying information. Review students' paragraphs with them, and have volunteers read theirs to the class.

Individualizing the Lesson

Less-Advanced Students

Before the students begin independent work on the Exercise, work with them to develop one of the topics into a paragraph, following this procedure. First, have the students vote on the topic to be developed. Then have each student find and read aloud two relevant facts or figures from outside sources. On the chalkboard, list, or have volunteers list, the factual information students have found. Discuss which of the listed facts would be best for the paragraph. Discuss possibilities for an effective topic sentence. Finally, have the students write their paragraphs independently.

Advanced Students

In addition to the paragraphs required by the Exercise, have each student write a paragraph on an original topic, developing the paragraph with facts and figures.

Optional Practice

Have the students decide which of the following topics would best be developed by facts and figures and which would best be developed with visual details.

1. Baseball is America's most popular sport.

In the opening sentence, the writer introduces the subject of the paragraph—the El Yunque Rain Forest. She follows with facts and figures about the forest.

1. It is a 28,000-acre stretch of jungles, hills, streams, and waterfalls.
2. It is an hour's drive from San Juan.
3. It is the only rain forest in the West Indies.
4. It is the only tropical preserve of the National Park Service.
5. Giant ferns there grow up to 30 feet.
6. Orchids grow there also.
7. In the forest are 200 species of trees.
8. Some of the forest's trees are hardwoods.
9. The *ausubo* is called the bullet wood tree because of its hard wood.

Together, these facts and figures develop the idea that the El Yunque Rain Forest is an enchanting part of Puerto Rico.

Using Figures

In some paragraphs, like the following, figures are used to give weight to the main idea.

> Until the 1930's, many Americans believed that anyone who couldn't find work was lazy and shouldn't be helped by the government. The experience of the Great Depression (1929–1939) changed that. From 1931 to 1940, the unemployment rate was never less than 14 percent of the total work force. In 1933, the worst year of the Depression, 25 percent (one out of every four persons) couldn't find a job—any job.
> —MARC ROSENBLUM

The writer tells us in his topic sentence that "Until the 1930's, many Americans believed that anyone who couldn't find work was lazy. . . ." He then explains that the Great Depression changed that idea and presents dates and unemployment statistics. The figures in this paragraph emphasize the idea that there can be reasons other than laziness for a person's not working.

78

Developing a Paragraph with Facts or Figures

Develop two of these topic sentences into well written paragraphs using facts and figures. You may have to do some outside reading. Be sure, though, that your paragraphs are your own work. Do not copy them from other sources. Refer to the Guidelines for the Process of Writing on page 59.

1. The 55 m.p.h. speed limit saves lives.
2. Our wild animals are disappearing rapidly.
3. The (*name of team*) is made up of individual champions.
4. The future looks bright for careers in technical fields.
5. Father penguin "babysits" with his children.
6. Each year, fires destroy great tracts of valuable land.
7. The Catskill Mountains are a popular vacation area.
8. It's easy to spot poison ivy if you know what to look for.
9. The platypus is one of the world's oldest animals.
10. George Washington Carver helped to make peanuts big business.

Part 3   Using Examples

A topic sentence may express an idea that is best developed through the use of examples. Following is such a sentence.

> Poverty can be measured by more than income.

The writer could have supported this idea with facts and figures like the following:

1. The percentage of American families whose income falls below the official poverty line
2. The percentage of American families that do not have indoor plumbing
3. The number of complaints received each winter from tenants who do not have sufficient heat in their apartments
4. The number of rat bites treated each year at one hospital

2. The sunset was magnificent.
3. The streets in the game of Monopoly are named for real streets in Atlantic City, New Jersey.

Extending the Lesson

Have students anonymously develop paragraphs giving facts and figures about themselves. Remind students that their paragraphs must include a topic sentence. Post the paragraphs, and challenge the students to see how many of their classmates they can identify from data supplied in the paragraphs.

Part 3

Objective

To develop paragraphs using examples

Presenting the Lesson

1. Read and discuss pages 79 and 80. Emphasize that the situation of one particular family supports the topic sentence in the sample paragraph. Help students see that this kind of development often makes a topic more personal—its impact is stronger because facts are given about one group of people in one situation.

2. Assign the Exercise on page 80. The students may have to consult outside sources to get information they need to develop their paragraphs. Review the students' paragraphs with them, and have volunteers read theirs aloud.

Individualizing the Lesson

Less-Advanced Students

Work with the students to list examples that could be used to develop each topic sentence in the Exercise. Then have each student choose only one topic sentence to develop in a paragraph.

Advanced Students

In addition to the paragraphs required by the Exercise, have each student write a paragraph on an original topic, developing the paragraph with examples.

Optional Practice

1. Have the students suggest examples that could be used to develop each of the following topic sentences:

Haste makes waste.
When it rains, it pours.
A bird in the hand is worth two in the bush.

2. Have students decide which of the topic sentences in the Exercise on page 79 could be developed with examples. Students should determine that all but sentences 5, 7, and 8 could reasonably use examples. Then have the students suggest examples that could be used in paragraphs developing the topics.

Instead, the writer gave several examples from the experience of one family. The facts and figures in the paragraph relate to that family rather than to poor people in general.

> Poverty can be measured by more than income. There are five people in Cass Tanner's family. They live in a one-bedroom apartment. The building they live in violates at least fifteen city building-code regulations. It has exposed electrical wiring. The plumbing does not work properly. In January, during five days of subfreezing weather, the heat did not go above fifty-five degrees. Cass wakes up each night to make sure that his brothers and sisters are not bothered by rats. Mr. Tanner's take-home pay from a part-time job is $380 per month. The rent is $165 per month.—WILLIAM F. SAALBACH

In this paragraph, the idea that "Poverty can be measured by more than income" becomes drastically clear through a series of examples. By focusing on the living conditions of one poor family, the examples make a stronger emotional impact on the reader than impersonal facts and figures would have done.

Exercise Developing a Paragraph with Examples

Each of the following topic sentences can be developed into a paragraph by using examples. Choose two of the sentences. Then support each main idea with several specific examples. Follow the Guidelines for the Process of Writing on page 59.

1. Many American Presidents have served only one term.
2. Violence has increased both on and off the playing field.
3. You can add just about anything to a basic hot dog.
4. Not everything that glitters is as valuable as gold.
5. Clothing that looks stylish may feel far from comfortable.
6. Some healing drugs come from unlikely sources.
7. Young animals play in ways similar to human children.
8. (*Name of town or city*) has interesting museums.
9. Life in the wilderness was hard for the pioneers.
10. Some animals make better pets than others.

Part 4   Using an Incident

A topic sentence might lend itself to development with an incident. Following is an example of such a sentence:

> Life in this electronic age is tough on kids.

The writer could have supported this topic sentence with several examples of how the electronic age is "tough on kids." Instead, he related an incident that illustrates the main idea.

> Life in this electronic age is tough on kids. Two sixth-graders felt the call of the fishpole one afternoon and took along their walkie-talkies. Word of this got to the teacher, who borrowed a walkie-talkie from another student. The teacher tuned in and, sure enough, heard the truants. He promptly cut in to suggest that they appear in the classroom post-haste. They did.—JOHN BROWN

An incident, like the one in this paragraph, can be drawn from personal experience or from a writer's imagination. Whatever its source, though, the characteristics and function of an incident remain the same. It is a brief "story" that illustrates the general idea in the topic sentence.

Exercise Developing a Paragraph with an Incident

Each of the following topic sentences may be expanded into a paragraph by using an incident. Choose two of the sentences and develop each into a well written paragraph. Refer to the Guidelines for the Process of Writing on page 59.

1. A practical joke can backfire.
2. You're never too old to learn to ride a bike.
3. I never believed in ghosts.
4. My dog taught me the meaning of loyalty.
5. One today is worth two tomorrows.
6. Running away never solved a problem.
7. You're never too old to cry.

81

Objective

To develop paragraphs using incidents

Presenting the Lesson

1. Read and discuss page 81. Have the students identify the events described in the sample paragraph. Note the time sequence in which the events are organized.

2. Assign the Exercise. Have volunteers read their paragraphs.

Individualizing the Lesson

Less-Advanced Students

Before the students begin independent work, discuss incidents that could be used to illustrate the idea in each topic sentence.

Advanced Students

Have each student write a paragraph on an original topic, developing the paragraph with an incident.

Optional Practice

Have the students suggest incidents that could be used to develop the following topic sentence:

Breakfast can make a day a success.

Extending the Lesson

Have the students review the paragraphs they have written and find one that could have been developed with an incident. Have the students write new paragraphs, developing their topics with incidents.

Part 5

Objective

To develop paragraphs using definitions

Presenting the Lesson

1. Read and discuss page 82. Tell the students that a definition must be clear and specific and must not repeat itself.

2. Read and discuss **Avoiding Errors** on page 83. Have the students restate each of the poorly phrased definitions to make it conform to the model definitions.

3. Read and discuss **Expanding a Definition** on pages 83-84. Have the students suggest details, examples, facts and figures, or incidents that could be used to expand each of the model definitions.

4. Assign and discuss Exercise A on page 85.

5. Assign and discuss Exercise B on page 85.

Individualizing the Lesson

Less-Advanced Students

1. Work with the students to develop a correct three-part definition for each the first five items in Exercise A. Have the students complete the Exercise independently.

2. Have each student write only one paragraph, defining one of the following words: *motorcycle, rectangle, minnow, elevator, carburetor, helicopter*.

Part 5   Using a Definition

When developing a paragraph, a composition, or a report, a writer may wish to use a word or phrase in a very specific way or to use a term that may be unfamiliar to the reader. To make certain that the term will not be misunderstood, the writer will provide a definition.

Every good definition has three parts:

1. The term to be defined
2. The general class to which the term belongs
3. The particular characteristic that sets the term apart from the other members of the general class

Study the following examples:

Term To Be Defined	General Class	Particular Characteristic
Hypnotism is	a kind of sleep	induced by motions of the hands or other suggestions.
A tariff is	a tax	placed on certain goods brought into a country.
A pilgrim is	a person	who travels to a sacred place.
A quarterback is	a football player	who directs the team
Sorrow is	a feeling of grief	that comes from suffering, loss, or regret.
Geography is	a science	dealing with the earth and its life.
A granary is	a building	in which grain is stored.

Avoiding Errors

In defining a term, a writer must be careful not to make the following errors:

1. Defining the word or phrase by using *where* or *when*. For example:

   "Sorrow is when a person feels grief," or "A granary is where grain is stored." *Sorrow* is not a "when"; it is a feeling. A *granary* is not a "where"; it is a building.

2. Defining the term with the same word or a variation of the same word. For example:

   "Hypnotism is the process of hypnotizing."

3. Putting the term into too large a general class. For example:

   "A granary is a place where grain is stored."

Expanding a Definition

A basic definition can be accompanied by an explanation, an illustration, or both. The definition then becomes a paragraph, as in the following examples.

1

Water that is fit to drink is called *potable water*. It must be clear and colorless, pleasant-tasting, free of harmful bacteria, and fairly free of dissolved solids. Although distilled water is pure, it does not make the best drinking water. Small amounts of mineral matter and air in the water make it taste better, unlike distilled water which has a "flat" taste.—TRACY, TROPP, AND FRIEDL

2

Empathy is a feeling of positive regard for others—being able to sense how the other person is feeling and the emotion

Advanced Students

In addition to the paragraphs required by Exercise B, have each student write an original definition of a word not included in the list and develop the definition in a paragraph.

Optional Practice

Have the students find dictionary definitions for five of the words listed in Exercise B. Have them use the column headings suggested in Exercise A to write the parts of each definition.

Extending the Lesson

Have the students invent words for the following imaginary things:

an animal that is part parrot, part mule
a tree that bears money
a talking plant
a robot housekeeper
a pizza-flavored frankfurter

Then have the students write definitions of their terms and develop them into paragraphs.

taking place. It also takes in the ability to communicate the feeling back to that person in the receiver's own words. It means "the ability to walk in another person's moccasins."
—GWEN MOJADO

3

A pueblo was a type of village built by the Indians of the Southwest. Its buildings were placed in a receding terrace formation and each one housed a number of families. The houses were flat-roofed and built of stone or clay. They were America's first apartment houses. Some of the houses were four stories high, and some had over five hundred rooms. The people reached their homes by climbing up ladders placed on the outside of the larger buildings. When other tribes raided a village, the Pueblo Indians pulled up the ladders and the enemy had a hard time getting in. A room below the ground was special. It was called a kiva and was used for religious ceremonies and social meetings.—ROSEBUD YELLOW ROBE

In these three paragraphs, the basic definitions function as topic sentences. Each sentence contains the three necessary parts of a definition.

Term To Be Defined	General Class	Particular Characteristic
Potable water is	water	that is fit to drink.
Empathy is	a feeling	of positive regard for others.
A pueblo was	a village	built by the Indians of the Southwest.

The other sentences in each paragraph give additional details about the word or phrase being defined. The reader comes away with a clear understanding of what the term means.

Exercises Developing a Paragraph with a Definition

A. Each of the following sentences presents a faulty definition. A part of the definition may be missing. The general class may be too large. The term may have been defined by using *where* or *when*. The word may have been defined with the same word.

Divide a sheet of paper into three columns. Head the columns "Term To Be Defined," "General Class," and "Particular Characteristics." Then write the correct three-part definition for each.

Answers will vary.

1. A good friend is a special person.
2. Play is activity.
3. A novel is written in prose.
4. Studying is when you read and think.
5. A dog is a kind of animal.
6. A fly has two wings.
7. A bicycle is a machine with two wheels.
8. Quarantine is where you're isolated because you're sick.
9. The sun is something that gives off light and heat.
10. Anthropology is all about people.
11. A lyric is a song.
12. Graduation is the act of being graduated.
13. R.S.V.P. is when you must answer someone's invitation.
14. A hat is a thing people wear on their heads.
15. Passing a course is when you get above a certain grade.

B. Following is a list of words that may be defined in paragraph form. Choose two of the words. Write a topic sentence containing a three-part definition for each word. Then expand the topic sentences into well written paragraphs. Follow the Guidelines for the Process of Writing on page 59.

motorcycle	snob	carburetor
sorceress	elevator	friend
honor	energy	helicopter
minnow	conservation	nitrogen
loyalty	fad	love

Chapter 7

Different Kinds of Paragraphs

Chapter Objectives

1. To write first-person and third-person narrative paragraphs developed in chronological order

2. To write descriptive paragraphs using specific sensory details

3. To recognize and write four types of explanatory paragraphs: the paragraph that gives instructions, the paragraph that defines, the paragraph that gives reasons, and the paragraph that persuades

Preparing the Students

Review with the students what they have learned about writing paragraphs in Chapters 5 and 6.

Read this page. If necessary, clarify the idea of *purpose*. Then have students recall paragraphs they have written and their purposes for writing them. Discuss these purposes.

Tell the students that this chapter will show them how to organize a paragraph to accomplish a specific purpose.

Additional Resources

Mastery Test — See pages 18-19 in the test booklet. Recommended for use after teaching the chapter.

Skills Practice Book — pages 26-34.

Duplicating Masters — pages 26-34.

Before you begin to make a cake, you must decide on the kind of cake you want to produce. Your choice will determine the ingredients you use and the way you blend those ingredients together.

Similarly, when you are going to write a paragraph, you must first decide on your purpose for writing. Do you want to tell a story? Do you want to describe something? Do you want to explain an opinion or an idea? Your answers to these questions will determine the kind of paragraph you will write.

Three major kinds of paragraphs are examined in this chapter: the narrative paragraph, the descriptive paragraph, and the explanatory paragraph. Each has a different purpose and is, therefore, put together in a slightly different way.

Objective

To write first-person narrative paragraphs developed through specific details

Presenting the Lesson

1. Read and discuss the introduction and **The First-Person Narrative Paragraph** on page 88. Emphasize the importance of organizing details in chronological order. Have volunteers name events that have occurred so far during the school day. Write these on the chalkboard as they are suggested, then work with the students to rearrange them in chronological order.

Call attention to the pronouns that signal a first-person narrative. Have students use each of the pronouns in an original sentence.

2. Read and discuss **Studying an Example,** pages 88-89. Have students point out vivid words and phrases.

3. Assign and discuss the Exercise on page 89. If students have been keeping journals, these journals may provide subjects and ideas for the paragraphs they write. Once students have decided on an incident to narrate, you may want to help them to select details by guiding them through a visualization of the experience. Have them close their eyes and

   a. Picture the setting
   b. Relive the central event and the events leading up to it
   c. Remember how they felt

Part 1   The Narrative Paragraph

When you tell a friend what happened on the way to school, or about a program you saw on television, or about your friend's experience at camp, you are telling, or narrating, a story. A paragraph that does the same thing is called a narrative paragraph. Narrative paragraphs relate events in the order in which they took place. This type of organization is called time sequence or chronological order.

The First-Person Narrative Paragraph

Your first reaction to an assignment requiring you to write a narrative paragraph might be, "What can I possibly write about?" Think for a minute about all the things that have happened to you—funny things, serious things, exciting things. Then think about the things you imagine happening, either in the future or in a made-up world where anything is possible.

As you do your preliminary thinking, you will most likely discover several possible subjects for your paragraph. All of these subjects relate to your own real and imagined experiences. Each idea could be developed as a first-person narrative. This is the kind of paragraph in which a writer tells a story using first-person pronouns such as *I*, *we*, *us*, *me*, *my*, *mine*, and *our*.

Studying an Example

One writer chose as a subject her first ride on a motorcycle. Before she began to write, she took a few minutes to plan her paragraph. First she asked herself the following questions: How did I feel about taking the ride? Was I enthusiastic? Was I frightened? Whose motorcycle was it? How did I get the chance for a ride? She wrote down the answers to these questions so that she would remember to include the ideas in the opening of her paragraph.

Next she thought about how she felt when she was actually on the motorcycle. She asked herself these questions: Was it like riding a roller coaster? a fast bicycle? How did I feel at the beginning of the ride? Did my feelings change? How did I behave during the ride? She added these ideas to her list. Then she wrote the following paragraph:

> I was torn between panic and pleasure when Pete offered to drive me to school on his new motorcycle. Suppose I fell off? My hands felt clammy-cold at the thought. Bravely, I managed a weak smile. With fingers shaking, I buckled on the helmet Pete offered and hoisted myself behind him. With a roar like a jet, we took off down the street. Gradually, I relaxed my knuckle-white grip and looked around. It was like skimming over the streets on a sleek, two-wheeled space ship. By the time we reached school, all my fears had been blown away by the force of the wind around us. The motorcycle seemed like an old friend, and I had been the first girl in school to ride on it.

From the first sentence on, the writer involves the reader in her experience. She vividly describes her reactions with phrases such as "torn between panic and pleasure," "hands felt clammy-cold," and "my knuckle-white grip." By doing so, she allows the reader to see life, for a few minutes, through her eyes.

Exercise Writing a First-Person Narrative Paragraph

Following is a list of topic sentences that may be developed into first-person narrative paragraphs. Choose one of these sentences, or write one of your own. Then develop the sentence into a well written paragraph that relates a real or imaginary experience. Refer to the Guidelines for the Process of Writing on page 59.

1. Something exciting happened when I least expected it.
2. I still blush when I think of my most embarrassing experience.

Encourage students to search for specific words that precisely describe the scene and their feelings.

Introduce students to the Guidelines for Writing and Revising Paragraphs on page 107. Suggest that they use this as a supplement to the Guidelines for the Process of Writing.

4. Read and discuss **The Third-Person Narrative Paragraph,** pages 90-91. Call attention to the pronouns that signal a third-person narrative. Have students use each of the pronouns in a sentence.

5. Assign and discuss the Exercise on page 91. You may want to divide the class into small groups to discuss each of the topics and the kinds of details that might logically follow each topic sentence. Then have each student select a topic and make pre-writing notes. After the students have written their paragraphs, have them work with a partner to improve the paragraphs.

Individualizing the Lesson

Less-Advanced Students

1. Display a photograph or drawing that depicts action. Have the students discuss what is happening *now,* what may have happened *before,* and what may happen *later.* Use the students' suggestions to reinforce the idea of chronological order.

2. Have the students base narrative paragraphs on comic strips. Remind the students that they can become a part of the action and write in the first person, or step back from the action and describe it in the third person.

3. Before the students begin independent work on either of the Exercises, work with them to list details that might be used to develop each topic sentence. Urge the students to follow the steps they learned in Chapter 4, "The Process of Writing."

Advanced Students

1. If possible, have the students view a film or filmstrip without the sound. Have them write a narrative paragraph (or two) describing what they saw. Later, students can compare what they wrote to the sound provided for the film or filmstrip.

2. After the students write first drafts of their Exercise paragraphs, have them work together in small groups to evaluate each other's work. These comments will give the students direction for their revisions.

3. After the students have completed the Exercises, challenge them to list two synonyms for each verb they used. Have the students decide whether any of the synonyms they listed would be a better choice than the original verb.

Optional Practice

1. Have each student choose a great moment in history — a moment he or she would like to have witnessed. Have the student gather details about the event and then narrate it either in the first person (as if he or she were taking part) or in the third person (as if he or she were witnessing it). Students' paragraphs might be displayed as an arrangement titled, "We Were There."

2. To demonstrate the importance of point of view in a narration, have the students write paragraphs

3. It was the funniest April Fool trick I had ever played.

4. I knew something was going to happen the moment I woke up.

5. It was a baby-sitting job I'll never forget.

6. It was my first speech, and I tried not to show how nervous I felt.

7. I learned to like being the _____ child in the family.

8. Last summer, I did something I've never done before.

9. I was determined to succeed at _____.

10. The day I broke my arm began like any other day.

The Third-Person Narrative Paragraph

In a first-person narrative, the writer has a part in the action. In a third-person narrative, the writer mentally steps back from the action and relates something that happened to someone else. The subject of a third-person narrative can be a real or an imaginary event. As in all narrative paragraphs, the story in a third-person narrative unfolds in chronological order, the order in which it happened.

Following is an example of a third-person narrative paragraph. Notice the use of the third-person pronouns *he, she, his, her,* and *him.*

> Grace watched the cobra, waiting for a chance to master the deadly snake. Suddenly the cobra's head hit Grace's hand, but he did not bite. He struck with his mouth closed. As rapidly as an expert boxer drumming on a punching bag, the snake struck three times against Grace's palm, always for some incredible reason with his mouth shut. Then Grace slid her open hand over his head and stroked his hood. The snake hissed again and struggled violently under her touch. Grace continued to caress him. Suddenly the snake went limp and his hood began to close. Grace slipped her other hand under

the snake's body and lifted him out of the cage. She held the reptile in her arms as though he were a baby. The cobra raised his head to look Grace in the face; his dancing tongue was less than a foot from her mouth. Grace braced her hand against the curve of his body and talked calmly to him until he folded his hood. He curled up in her arms quietly.—DANIEL MANNIX

The writer of this paragraph uses strong, specific verbs throughout the paragraph; for example: *hit, bite, struck, slid, stroked, hissed, struggled, caress, slipped, lifted, raised, braced, folded,* and *curled.* These action words help the reader to visualize the encounter between Grace and the cobra. The reader "sees" the events as they were seen by the writer.

Exercise Writing a Third-Person Narrative Paragraph

Choose one of the sentences suggested below, or write a topic sentence of your own. Then use your imagination to develop the sentence into a third-person narrative paragraph. Refer to the Guidelines for the Process of Writing on page 59.

1. When Jack awoke, he found that he had become invisible.
2. Gloria tried to run, but her legs had turned to water.
3. The two boys had been marooned on the island for a month.
4. Jenny was determined to win first prize.
5. Steve was in the bank when the robbers entered.
6. The bicycle lay upside down, its wheels still turning.
7. The search for the lost child continued all night.
8. When Tom learned that his uncle had left him a million dollars, he began to make plans.
9. Jean had always wanted to be an actress.
10. Darlene's childhood had been filled with hardships.

in first person from the point of view of a non-human, such as one of the following:

a family pet
a computer
a video game
a baseball bat
a television set

Have students share their paragraphs with the class.

3. Duplicate two paragraphs written by students for the Exercises on pages 89 and 91, and give copies to each student. Have the students analyze each paragraph by doing the following:

1. Circle all pronouns that indicate point of view.
2. Underline the topic sentence.
3. Number the events covered in the paragraph.
4. Checkmark the five most colorful phrases in the paragraph.

4. Hold clinics for small groups on the following narrative techniques:

using chronological order
leading up to a climax
conveying subtle details
focusing on a single event
deciding on the most effective point of view

Extending the Lesson

Have each student find and read to the class a narrative paragraph from a short story. Tell the students to be prepared to tell whether the paragraph was a first-person or third-person narrative. Then ask the students to comment on why that viewpoint was chosen and how a different one would affect the narrative.

Part 2

Objective

To write descriptive paragraphs using specific sensory details

Presenting the Lesson

1. Read and discuss the introduction and **Choosing Words and Details Carefully.** Remind students that to create clear mental images they should choose words and phrases that are colorful, specific, and precise and that have connotations that convey their feelings about the subject.

Write the following sentences on the chalkboard:

1. The man walked along the street.
2. The night was windy and dark.
3. A piece of newspaper blew along the street.
4. Somewhere a dog howled.
5. The smell of the harbor filled the air.

Have the students revise the sentences to make them more specific and to help create a clear picture in a reader's mind.

2. Read and discuss **Appealing to the Sense of Sight** on pages 93-94.

3. Have each student bring to mind a local scene that is familiar to most of the students. Give the students time to write sentences that describe the scene's visual appearance vividly without naming the location. Then have each student read his or her word picture to the class, and have the other students try to identify the scene.

Part 2　The Descriptive Paragraph

The purpose of a descriptive paragraph is to paint a picture with words. A description appeals to one or more of the five senses—sight, hearing, smell, taste, or touch. Of these senses, sight and hearing are the most highly developed. Therefore, most descriptive paragraphs appeal mainly to either sight or hearing or to a combination of the two.

Choosing Words and Details Carefully

The success of a descriptive paragraph is judged by the clarity of the picture created in the reader's mind. This picture depends on the specific words and details used by the writer.

Suppose, for example, that a writer described a new girl in class as "pretty." The reader would have only a vague idea of what the girl looks like. On the other hand, if the writer used details such as "curly jet-black hair," "creamy skin," and "clear blue eyes with long black lashes," the reader would have a good mental image of the girl.

Specific nouns, strong verbs, adjectives, adverbs, and descriptive phrases all help to create a clear picture in a reader's mind. Without them, descriptive writing is lifeless and ineffective. Read, for example, this sentence: "The bird sang in the tree." The nouns *bird* and *tree* are general. The verb *sang* does not give the reader a clue about how the bird sounded. The sentence lacks adjectives, adverbs, and descriptive phrases.

Compare the sample sentence in the preceding paragraph with this revised version: "The fat old bluejay chattered angrily in the blackened pine tree." In place of the general noun *bird* is the specific noun *bluejay*. The general verb *sang* has been replaced with the specific verb *chattered*. The adjectives *fat, old, blackened,* and *pine* and the adverb *angrily* have been added to the sentence. The reader can now see and hear the bluejay in the same way that the writer did.

Appealing to the Sense of Sight

Many descriptions appeal to the sense of sight. The details in these paragraphs describe size, shape, color, appearance, position, and movement. Together, they create a visual image in the mind of the reader.

Following is an example of a descriptive paragraph that includes many sight details.

> By the time the boy had got to the house, the walking man was only halfway down the road, a lean man, very straight in the shoulders. Jody could tell he was old only because his heels struck the ground with hard jerks. As he approached nearer, Jody saw that he was dressed in blue jeans and a coat of the same material. He wore clodhopper shoes and an old, flat-brimmed Stetson hat. Over his shoulder he carried a gunny sack, lumpy and full. In a few minutes he had trudged close enough so that his face could be seen. And his face was as dark as dried beef. A mustache, blue-white against the dark skin, hovered over his mouth; and his hair was white, too, where it showed at his neck. The skin of his face had shrunk back against the skull until it defined bone, not flesh, and made the nose and chin seem sharp and fragile. The eyes were large and deep and dark, with eyelids stretched tightly over them. Irises and pupils were one, and very black, but the eyeballs were brown. There were no wrinkles in the face at all.—JOHN STEINBECK

The paragraph is a vivid and interesting word picture of an old man. The writer carefully painted the picture with specific words and details, such as "heels struck the ground with hard jerks," "dressed in blue jeans and in a coat of the same material," "clodhopper shoes and an old, flat-brimmed Stetson hat," "a gunny sack, lumpy and full," "a mustache, blue-white against the dark skin," "shrunk back against the skull," and "sharp and fragile." In addition, he drew the comparison that "his face was as dark as dried beef." Comparisons like this help to create a clear image in the reader's mind.

4. Read and discuss **Following Spatial Order** on page 95. Have the students suggest other direction words and phrases that can help a reader picture a scene. List these on the chalkboard as they are suggested, and have the students copy them for use when they write descriptive paragraphs.

5. Read and discuss **Appealing to the Sense of Hearing** on page 96. Ask students to suggest words and phrases that appeal to the sense of hearing. Have the students close their eyes for a moment and attempt to describe the sounds around them.

6. Read and discuss **Combining Sense Details.** Have the students tell how they would feel if they were in the kitchen described in the example paragraph. Have them find the details that contribute to a feeling of warmth and coziness. Tell the students that, in writing a descriptive paragraph, they should focus on the thing they want to describe and the feeling they want to convey about it. They should think about the subject's unique qualities and the specific words needed to describe them. Important questions students might ask themselves before writing a descriptive paragraph include the following:

1. What information do I need to give a reader who may be totally unfamiliar with this subject?

2. What details can I use to involve the reader's sense of sight, sound, and perhaps even smell, touch, and taste?

3. How do I want the reader to feel about this subject? What words and phrases can I use to convey this feeling?

By changing specific details, a writer can change completely the picture drawn in a paragraph. The following paragraph is basically the same as the first paragraph about a walking man. The details, though, are different.

> By the time the boy had got to the house, the walking man was only halfway down the road, a short, fat man, very round-shouldered. Jody could tell he was young only because his heels struck the ground with short, quick jerks. As he approached nearer, Jody saw that he was dressed in white duck pants and a coat of the same material. He wore dusty white shoes and a new black derby hat. In his right hand he clutched a bright red and black carpetbag, plump and full. In a few minutes he had walked close enough so that his face could be seen. And his face was as white as blackboard chalk. A thin mustache, black against the white skin, drooped over his mouth, and his hair was black, too, where it showed at his neck. The skin of his face was puffed out so that it was difficult to define bone, and the nose and chin seemed lost in rolls of flesh. The eyes were small and pale blue, with thin black eyebrows arched above them. There were no wrinkles in the face at all.

Now, rather than seeing a lean, hard old man, the reader sees a short, fat young man.

To better understand the importance of details in descriptions, study the following paragraph. In it, an unskilled writer attempts to describe an old man.

> By the time the boy had got to the house, the walking man was only halfway down the road. Jody could tell he was old; and, as he approached nearer, Jody saw that he was dressed in old jeans and a coat. He wore old shoes and an old hat. Over his shoulder he carried a sack. In a few minutes he had walked close enough so that his face could be seen. His face was very dark. He had a white mustache and white hair, dark eyes, and thin nose. There were no wrinkles in the face at all.

The paragraph is dull, uninteresting, and too general to evoke much of a picture in a reader's mind.

Following Spatial Order

The ideas in a descriptive paragraph must be arranged in some kind of logical order. In paragraphs that appeal to the sense of sight, the order usually is spatial order. Things are described in relation to other things in the same area or space.

Some descriptions are organized in loose spatial order. The first paragraph about the old man, for example, presents details in three groups: 1. the details noticed from a distance; 2. the details Jody noticed as the man approached; and 3. the details Jody saw at close range. Within these groups, the details are given in the order that they caught Jody's attention. The writer does not bother to explain that the shoes are on the man's feet or that the hat is on top of his head. The space relationships are clear.

In some descriptions, particularly in descriptions of places, information about space relationships is essential. The following paragraph describes a scene at the edge of a river.

> The river ran smooth and shallow at our feet, and beyond it a wide sandy beach sloped upward gently to the edge of the forest, against which the rocks shone as white as weathered bones. The red soil bank on our side of the river, the silver sheet of water in front of us, the wet browns and greys of the sandbars, the whitewashed ramp of rocks on the opposite shore, the green forest front and the pale purple of the Sierra Madre were like stripes of water colors. Across them strings of mules and donkeys moved with their loads, fording the river with their bellies awash. The drivers followed, their white *calzones* rolled above their thighs and the water up to their waists.—ERNESTO GALARZA

In this paragraph the writer uses specific space, or direction, words to show the relationship of one thing to another. The words and phrases are: "at our feet," "beyond," "upward," "to the edge," "on our side," "in front of," "on the opposite shore," "across," "above," and "up to." These direction words allow the reader to picture the scene.

3. Work with the students to develop good topic sentences for each of the topics in Exercise C before the students complete the Exercise independently.

Advanced Students

1. Have the students do Exercise A orally.

2. Require the students to develop one original paragraph for Exercise B on page 98.

3. After the students have completed their paragraphs for Exercise C on page 98, have them write second versions, changing the details to create a different word picture. For example, a student might describe a garden in spring and in winter.

Optional Practice

1. Reinforce students' understanding of spatial order by having them suggest a list of details that describe the arrangement and appearance of the classroom. As students respond, have them suggest specific space or direction words that state the relationships of items to one another.

2. Choose a common paragraph topic, such as "The First Snowfall." Ask the students to suggest descriptive phrases, and write these on the chalkboard. Then, to challenge the students to find fresh, original phrases, tell them to write paragraphs on the topic without using any of the listed phrases. Remind students to follow the steps outlined in The Guidelines for the Process of Writing on page 59.

3. Show the students the following foods, and ask them to write down precise descriptions of smell, appearance, feel, and taste, as well as any sounds associated with eating the food.

celery   pickle
peppermint   potato chip

Then have the students organize and develop their notes for a paragraph. During the revising process, you may want to have small groups work together to point out where each paragraph could be more specific.

Extending the Lesson

1. Show the class slides or large photographs of three or four scenes, some including people and some without people. As a slide is projected, have students suggest specific sensory descriptions. Discuss with the students how they would organize details for a descriptive paragraph on the picture.

2. Have the students work in pairs to develop a display of word portraits. Each member of a pair should write phrases and sentences that describe his or her partner. Then have the students write paragraphs based on their notes. Later the descriptions can be "framed" and displayed as a "Word-Picture Gallery."

Appealing to the Sense of Hearing

The second most common kind of description appeals to the sense of hearing. The details in these paragraphs describe sounds rather than sight, as in the following example.

> The sound of a strange song floated in the air and seemed to be coming right out of the trunk of the tree. I stood there, turning my ears around in search of the source. The voice was light and unstrained, like some bird, and with a melancholy, human note. The sounds of the frantic children screaming for me to hurry with the ball faded into the background. My heart drummed fiercely, as I felt the presence of an unknown force.—J. E. FRANKLIN

The writer of this paragraph captures the quality of a sound with words such as "strange," "floated," "light," "unstrained," "melancholy," and "human." He also describes the screaming of the children and the drumming of his own heart, sounds whose sharpness and realism contrast with the strange sound. These details help the reader to share the writer's uneasiness.

Paragraphs that appeal to the sense of hearing are not necessarily organized in spatial order. The details, however, must be arranged in some logical order that is easy to follow.

Combining Sense Details

The word picture created in this paragraph makes you feel that you are actually in the kitchen described by the writer.

> I close my eyes and remember my mother's kitchen. The cocoa steamed fragrantly in the saucepan. Geraniums bloomed on the window sills, and a bouquet of tiny yellow chrysanthemums brightened the center of the table. The curtains, red with a blue and green geometrical pattern, were drawn, and seemed to reflect the cheerfulness throughout the room. The furnace purred like a great sleepy animal; the lights glowed with steady radiance. Outside, alone in the dark, the wind battered against the house.

Most of the details in the paragraph appeal to the sense of sight; for example: "tiny yellow chrysanthemums brightened," "red with a blue and green geometrical pattern," and "lights glowed." Two details appeal to the sense of hearing: "purred like a great sleepy animal" and "battered against the house." One phrase, "cocoa steamed fragrantly," appeals to a third sense, the sense of smell. The writer weaves these details together to recreate a scene from her past.

Exercises Writing Descriptions

A. In each pair of sentences, choose the sentence that creates a more vivid image in your mind. Then write a sentence that gives different details about the same subject. Answers will vary.

1. a. The branch clicked against the window with the sound of snapping fingers.
   b. The branch made little noises as it hit the window.

2. a. My mother made a delicious dessert last night.
   b. My mother baked a juicy apple pie last night.

3. a. Tom's sunburn felt as though his back were on fire.
   b. Tom's sunburn was painful.

4. a. Dad gave Mother some beautiful flowers.
   b. Dad gave Mother a dozen long-stemmed red roses for her birthday.

5. a. The steak was as tough as shoe leather.
   b. The steak was not as good as I had expected.

6. a. She had a voice that sounded like chalk squeaking against a blackboard.
   b. She had an unpleasant voice.

7. a. The night wrapped us in black velvet.
   b. The night was extremely dark.

8. a. The sandwich filling tasted like old library paste.
   b. The sandwich filling tasted awful.

B. Following is a list of topic sentences. Choose two—one describing sight, and one describing sound—or write sentences of your own. Then, using either your personal experience or your imagination (or both), develop the two sentences into descriptive paragraphs. In the paragraph that appeals to the sense of sight, arrange the details in spatial order. Be sure to use specific details in both paragraphs. Also refer to the Guidelines for the Process of Writing on page 59.

1. On Sundays, I hear the peal of church bells.
2. My room was on the second story above the garage.
3. After the storm, a rainbow appeared.
4. From the sound of her voice, I knew she was frightened.
5. In the distance, cars rumbled over the bridge.
6. My aunt gave me a lovely Japanese doll for my birthday.
7. My favorite painting is _____.
8. At sunup, construction on the building across the street began again.
9. The sounds of the awakening city intruded on the pre-dawn stillness.
10. The Golden Gate Bridge is beautiful at sunset.
11. Overhead, geese flew south for the winter.
12. The rock group seemed more concerned with quantity of sound than with quality of sound.
13. He was the oldest man I had ever seen.
14. I awoke at midnight to the sound of a fire engine.
15. Nefertiti was a gorgeous Siamese cat.

C. Choose one of the ideas below, or use an idea of your own. Develop a one-paragraph description of at least six sentences that appeals to two or more senses.

1. A garden
2. The kitchen before dinner
3. A laundromat
4. A barbecue or picnic
5. Your street at night
6. A hospital room
7. Cows grazing in a pasture
8. A circus or carnival
9. A gas station
10. A busy shopping center

Part 3   The Explanatory Paragraph

The explanatory paragraph is one of the most important kinds of paragraphs that you must learn to write. This is because you will probably do more explanatory writing throughout your life than any other kind. In an explanatory paragraph, you explain, as clearly as possible, *how, what,* or *why.*

Paragraphs That Give Instructions

Imagine this situation. You are standing on the corner of 5th South and State Street. A stranger asks you for directions to the VA Hospital. You give the person these instructions.

> We're on the corner of 5th Street and Lincoln Avenue, about a half-hour walk from the VA Hospital. Fifth Street isn't a through street, so to get to the hospital the easiest way, you'll first have to go south one block to 6th Street. At 6th Street, turn to your left and go east. Go straight east until you reach 13th Street, then turn north. Go north on 13th Street for one block until you reach Foothill Drive. Turn right, or east, on Foothill Drive and continue going east for about a mile. You'll see the hospital on the south side of the street.

These directions, written as they are in paragraph form, are an example of one type of explanatory paragraph. In this kind of paragraph, a writer explains, in chronological order, how something is done. He or she tells what to do first, what to do next, and so on.

After reading a paragraph that gives instructions, the reader should be able to do or make something. Consider, for example, the following situation. You have been invited to a Chinese banquet, where you will be expected to eat with chopsticks. A friend who is experienced in using chopsticks gives you these written directions.

Objective

To recognize and write four types of explanatory paragraphs: the paragraph that gives instructions, the paragraph that defines, the paragraph that gives reasons, and the paragraph that persuades

Presenting the Lesson

1. Read and discuss the introduction and the explanation of **Paragraphs That Give Instructions** on pages 99-100. Emphasize that the purpose of this type of paragraph is to explain how to do or make something and that the ideas are arranged in chronological order. Work with the class to develop a paragraph that gives directions for walking from one local landmark to another, and another paragraph that explains how to use a pencil sharpener or another simple tool.

2. Assign and discuss the Exercise on page 100. Have the students use the Guidelines for Writing and Revising Paragraphs on page 107 to review their paragraphs before they revise them. Have students exchange paragraphs and evaluate how clear, specific, and easy to follow the directions are. Partners may suggest further revisions in the paragraphs.

3. Read and discuss **Paragraphs That Define** on pages 101-102. Have the students suggest supporting details that could be used in a paragraph defining a zebra and in one defining a snorkel.

4. Assign and discuss the Exercise on page 102. Have the students use the Guidelines on page 107 to review their first drafts before they revise them. During the revision process, you may want to have students work in editing groups, alternating roles of author, editor, and proofreader.

5. Read and discuss **Paragraphs That Give Reasons** on pages 102-104. Emphasize that although the topic sentences of these paragraphs can take different forms, the supporting sentences always give reasons. When discussing topic sentences that state opinions, check to make sure that the students know the difference between a fact and an opinion. For more information on facts and opinions, you may refer students to Chapter 11, "Clear Thinking."

6. Assign and discuss the Exercise on page 104. As a pre-writing activity, you might have small groups of students debate the statements or, as an alternative, interview other students about the topics.

As students plan and write their paragraphs, have them follow the steps outlined in The Guidelines for the Process of Writing on page 59. Then have them use the Guidelines on page 107 to review their paragraphs before they revise them.

7. Read and discuss **Paragraphs That Persuade** on pages 105-106. Make sure that students understand that a persuasive paragraph differs from the other two kinds of explanatory paragraphs in that the writer is attempting to persuade others to adopt a view or opinion.

Review the use of organization by

Eating with chopsticks adds an extra something to any Chinese meal. Learning to use chopsticks properly is not hard; after all, even a Chinese toddler can do it. First, hold the sticks in your right hand, one on top of the other. Grip them about a third of the way from the ends. Next, place the lower stick at the base of your thumb. Rest it also on the tip of your fourth (or ring) finger. Then, place the second stick between the tip of your thumb and the tips of your index and middle finger. Hold the lower stick steady, but move the upper stick so that together they act like "tongs." Remember to keep your hand relaxed and to hold the chopsticks lightly but firmly.

These instructions are detailed and well organized. They tell you exactly what to do and how to do it. After practice, you will be able to eat with chopsticks at the banquet.

Exercise Writing a Paragraph That Gives Instructions

Following is a list of topic sentences. Choose one of the sentences, or write one of your own about something that you do well. Then expand your topic sentence into a well written paragraph that gives clear instructions. Refer to the Guidelines for the Process of Writing on page 59.

1. One of the first things you have to learn in archery is how to string the bow.

2. How do you get a cranky two-year-old to take a nap?

3. Changing a bike tire is easy.

4. Finger painting can be taught to a three-year-old.

5. You, too, can make ice cream the old-fashioned way—in a crank freezer.

6. Housebreaking a puppy requires a week of hard work.

7. To pass a test, you first have to learn how to study.

8. Water conservation begins at home.

9. Hiking is fun—if you know how to do it right.

10. Do you know the easiest way to learn to play the guitar?
11. Taking good photographs is fun.
12. You can teach your parakeet to talk.
13. Part of the fun of swimming is learning how to dive.
14. Learning to dance the _____ is a real challenge.
15. Tying a shoelace is as easy as one, two, three.

Paragraphs That Define

A second type of explanatory paragraph tells what something is and what it does. In other words, it defines a word or phrase.

In Chapter 6, Part 5, you studied paragraphs developed by expanding a definition. You learned that the topic sentence of this kind of paragraph contains three parts: the term to be defined, the general class to which the term belongs, and the particular characteristic that sets the term apart from the other members of the general class. Together these three parts form the basic definition of the term. Study the following examples.

Term To Be Defined	General Class	Particular Characteristic
A zebra is	an animal like a horse	with wide black-and-white stripes.
A snorkel is	a breathing tube	that can be used only on the surface of the water.
A hurricane is	a strong, swirling storm	that usually measures several hundred miles in diameter.

In Chapter 6 you also learned that the remainder of this kind of paragraph is made up of supporting details. The details further explain the basic definition, as in the example on the next page.

order of importance in persuasive paragraphs. Stress the importance of a strong topic sentence and convincing facts, reasons, or examples.

Work with the class to list reasons that would persuade school officials to make a needed change. Then have students explain how the list could be developed into a paragraph.

8. Assign the Exercise on page 106. As a pre-writing activity, you may want to allow the students to discuss the topics and share their opinions within small groups. Students may also need to do some preliminary reading to find out about their topics. Remind students that they should always keep their audience and purpose in mind.

Hold conferences with students before they revise their paragraphs. Check to make sure they have used logical reasons as well as relevant facts, figures, or examples.

During the revising process, have students work in groups of three, alternating the roles of author, editor, and proofreader.

Individualizing the Lesson

Less-Advanced Students

1. For each of the Exercises, have the students first choose the topics that interest them most. Then work with the students to plan how these topics can be developed as paragraphs. Urge the students to take notes during the discussion and to use their classmates' suggestions in their paragraphs. Finally, have the students write the paragraphs independently.

2. To make sure that the students fully develop their paragraphs that define, set the number of details that they should include in the paragraphs at four or five. During the revision process, pair students to question each other about missing details or incomplete support.

3. Have the students work together on a group paragraph that attempts to persuade students to join an extra-curricular organization.

Advanced Students

1. Have each student find, in a local newspaper, an editorial that focuses on an issue that interests him or her. Have the student respond to the editorial with a persuasive paragraph.

2. After students have written paragraphs that persuade and paragraphs that support opinions, ask them to rewrite one of their topic sentences to say the opposite. Then have them support these new topic sentences with reasons in a paragraph.

Optional Practice

1. Have each student write one paragraph that defines and describes a favorite food, a paragraph that explains how to prepare the food, and a paragraph that gives reasons to support the preference.

2. Have a student explain how to draw a certain geometric shape, such as a parallelogram or a star. The student should use no hand movements. The rest of the class should follow the student's directions and then evaluate how clear the explanation was by how easily they were able to draw the shape.

A hurricane is a strong, swirling storm that usually measures several hundred miles in diameter. The eye of the hurricane, often measuring 20 miles wide, is usually calm and has no clouds. Around the eye, winds blow at 75 miles an hour or more. Death and destruction, unfortunately, are too often part of the hurricane's story.

This paragraph, developed by definition, explains what a hurricane is and what it does.

Exercise Writing a Paragraph That Defines

Choose one of the following topics. Write a topic sentence that gives a three-part definition of the term. Then expand the topic sentence into a well written paragraph. Refer to the Guidelines for the Process of Writing on page 59.

1. hang-glider	5. celebrity	9. hockey
2. gossip	6. popularity	10. civil war
3. tadpole	7. battery	11. loneliness
4. courage	8. giraffe	12. lizard

Paragraphs That Give Reasons

This kind of explanatory paragraph gives reasons to explain the idea in the topic sentence. The idea is usually one of three basic types.

Sometimes the idea in the topic sentence is simply a statement about something that happened; for example:

I didn't do my homework last night.

The reader most likely would respond to this sentence by asking, "Why didn't you do your homework?" The rest of the paragraph answers that question.

I didn't do my homework last night. Right after school, I had softball practice, and we practiced for about two hours. Just before we finished the last inning, I was playing catcher.

John threw a fast ball. I tried to jump aside, but the ball hit me in the stomach and knocked all the wind out of me. When I got home, I was so tired and so sick to my stomach, I just didn't feel like doing homework.

The writer of this paragraph relates an incident that explains why she didn't do her homework. She presents one detailed reason to explain her opening statement. Another writer might have developed the same idea by giving several individual reasons. Either approach works, as long as the body of the paragraph explains why the event described in the topic sentence happened.

The idea presented in the topic sentence might also be a statement of fact; for example:

Beavers do a lot of good when they build their dams in the right places.

This sentence raises the questions: What good do beavers do? Why can the writer make this statement? The rest of the paragraph answers these questions.

Beavers do a lot of good when they build their dams in the right places. Beaver dams slow down the rush of water in brooks and streams. Brooks that otherwise would dry up in the summer flow all year 'round if a beaver dam is built across them. The trees and bushes near the brooks have enough moisture to grow well. Their roots hold the soil so that it does not wash away. Also, wells that usually go dry in summer hold water all year when beavers are put to work on nearby streams.

The writer gives three reasons to support his topic sentence.

1. Beaver dams slow down the flow of water.
2. Trees and bushes near beaver dams grow well; they prevent soil from being washed away.
3. Wells near beaver dams do not go dry in the summer.

These three reasons are specific facts that explain the more general fact stated in the topic sentence.

3. Ask the students to choose one favorite possession. In a paragraph that is supported by reasons, have students state what that possession is and why it is their favorite.

4. Require students to write paragraphs explaining how to get from the school to any local spot. Have partners check each other's explanations with a map before offering suggestions for revision.

5. As a pre-writing activity, have students debate in small groups the changes needed in grading, course offerings, or scheduling at your school. Then ask students to choose one priority for the subject of a persuasive paragraph.

Extending the Lesson

1. Have the students find published examples of each kind of paragraph discussed in this chapter. Use these paragraphs to create a bulletin board display summarizing the key points in the Guidelines on page 107.

2. Publish at least one paragraph by each student at some point during the study of this chapter. This publication may occur as part of a class journal or magazine, as part of a bulletin board display on the different types of paragraphs, or as an oral reading during class.

The third type of idea that may begin a paragraph that gives reasons is an opinion. Following is an example of this type of topic sentence.

The frontier woman was, indeed, a special breed.

The writer develops this idea with strong supporting reasons.

The frontier woman was, indeed, a special breed. She proved her ability to uphold her end of the load even where physical endurance was required. She bore the children, cared for them when they were sick, and often taught them to read and write. She tended the garden, cooked the family's food, and preserved what she could for the winter. And when danger from wild beasts threatened, she proved herself capable of defending her family.—JANET HARRIS

In this paragraph, the writer explains why she thinks the frontier woman was a special breed. She presents these reasons:

1. The frontier woman held up her end of the load.
2. She bore and cared for the children.
3. She often taught the children to read and write.
4. She grew, cooked, and preserved the food.
5. She defended her family from wild beasts.

These facts support the opinion in the topic sentence.

Exercise Writing a Paragraph That Gives Reasons

Following is a list of topic sentences that can be expanded into paragraphs. Choose one of these sentences or write one of your own. Then develop the sentence with reasons. Refer to the Guidelines for the Process of Writing on page 59.

1. Physical training is more important than mental training.
2. Older citizens are one of our most valuable resources.
3. Everyone should have a hobby.
4. Music synthesizers will never replace musicians.
5. Baby-sitting is a job that requires training.

Paragraphs That Persuade

Sometimes you will want to do more than simply express an opinion and tell your reasons for it. You may also want to persuade someone else to share that opinion as well, or to take action on an issue. In this case, you would write a special kind of explanatory paragraph called a **persuasive** paragraph.

To be convincing, a persuasive paragraph must be supported by more than your feelings on a subject. It must also be supported by specific information. This information can include facts and figures, examples, and incidents.

Your supporting material must be organized so that it is most effective. Usually, arranging your facts from least important to most important is the best way to organize them. That way, your best reason is the last one your readers will be presented with, and the one they will be most likely to remember. Good organization is often the key to a successful persuasive paragraph.

Look at the following example. Find the reasons used to support the opinion and notice the order in which they are presented.

> The use of stereo headsets in our community should be limited. First of all, the headsets weaken communication between people. The listener is cut off from the conversation of others, and no one else can share in the music. Secondly, the use of these headsets can actually result in hearing loss. Many users keep the volume of their units turned up quite high. This magnified sound goes directly into the ear, and can affect the listener's hearing. The most frightening aspect of the headsets, however, is that they have become traffic safety hazards. When worn by drivers or pedestrians, the headsets block out the sounds of sirens, horns, and approaching vehicles. This situation has already resulted in several bad accidents and one traffic fatality in our town. For this reason alone, we must find a way to control the use of headsets.

In this paragraph, the writer is hoping to persuade his readers to do something about the use of headsets in his community. He gives three reasons for his view.

1. The use of headsets weakens communication.
2. Constant use can harm hearing.
3. Headsets are traffic safety hazards.

The most powerful reason is presented last, where it will have the most impact on the reader.

Exercise Writing a Persuasive Paragraph

The following list of topic sentences can be expanded into persuasive paragraphs. Choose one sentence, or write one of your own, and develop it with facts and figures, examples, or incidents. Refer to the Guidelines for the Process of Writing on page 59.

1. A course on emergency first aid should be required in every school.
2. The age at which it is legal to drive should be raised/lowered.
3. The tradition of trick-or-treating on Halloween is too dangerous to continue.
4. Any student should be allowed to join school sports teams.
5. The present school year is too long/not long enough.
6. Children's television programing must be improved.

Guidelines for Writing and Revising Paragraphs

These Guidelines will help to remind you of the qualities necessary for good paragraphs. You should also follow the steps in the Guidelines for the Process of Writing on page 59.

1. Does the paragraph have unity? Do the sentences work together to explain or support one main idea?

2. Does the paragraph have a topic sentence? Does the topic sentence capture the reader's interest?

3. If the paragraph is developed by using specific details, do the details create a clear impression for the reader?

4. If the paragraph is developed by facts or figures, are they accurate? Do they fully develop the main idea?

5. If the paragraph is developed by examples, are there enough examples to develop the paragraph fully? Do they all relate to the main idea?

6. If the paragraph is developed by using an incident, does the incident help the reader understand the main idea?

7. If it is a paragraph of definition, are the three basic parts of a definition expanded by explanation or illustration?

8. If it is a narrative paragraph, is it developed in chronological order?

9. If it is a descriptive paragraph, does it use vivid sensory details? Does it use space words to describe its subject in a logical order?

10. If it is a paragraph that gives instructions, does it present the steps in logical order? If it is a paragraph that defines, does it use supporting details to expand the basic three-part definition? If it is a paragraph that gives reasons, are the reasons arranged in an effective order?

Grammar and Usage

Are there any sentence fragments or run-ons?
Do all verbs agree with their subjects?
Have you used the correct form of every pronoun?

Chapter 8

Writing the Composition

Chapter Objectives

1. To understand the function and organization of a five-paragraph composition

2. To develop methods for finding a subject for a composition

3. To recognize how to narrow a subject and record details for a composition

4. To understand how to gather and organize details for a composition

5. To recognize and write a good introduction, body paragraphs, and a conclusion for a composition

6. To understand how to revise a first draft and make a final copy of a composition

Preparing the Students

Look over sample paragraphs that students have studied in the two preceding chapters, and discuss the limitations of paragraphs. Guide students to the understanding that for broader topics, paragraphs must be coordinated into a composition.

Read the introduction on this page. Emphasize that the paragraph is the basic unit of the composition.

Additional Resources

Mastery Test — See pages 20-21 in the test booklet. Recommended for use after teaching the chapter.

Skills Practice Book — pages 35-40.

Duplicating Masters — pages 35-40.

In the preceding three chapters, you have spent time mastering paragraphs. First you studied the structure of paragraphs. You then learned to develop them in a variety of ways and for a number of different purposes. You saw how a paragraph can be used to communicate your thoughts effectively.

Because a paragraph is so short, however, it often takes several paragraphs to explain an idea thoroughly. In this chapter, you will study and write **compositions**, groups of paragraphs that communicate a writer's ideas and feelings.

Part 1

Objective

To understand the function and organization of a five-paragraph composition

Presenting the Lesson

1. Read and discuss the sample composition and related discussion on pages 110-112. Define a composition as a group of paragraphs that work together to explain or support one main idea.

2. Have the students identify the topic sentence of each component paragraph in the sample composition. Explain briefly how the supporting sentences in the paragraph develop the idea in the topic sentence.

Individualizing the Lesson

Less-Advanced Students

Tell the students that, as they work through this chapter, they will develop a composition as a group. They will complete each step in the process in class and then apply these steps in writing compositions of their own.

Advanced Students

Have the students classify paragraphs in the sample composition as narrative paragraphs. In groups, students might discuss clues that lead up to the conclusion in the final paragraph. Have students list details for the body paragraphs that would lead to a different conclusion.

Part 1 Parts of the Composition

A composition is a group of closely related paragraphs that develop a single idea. Like a paragraph, a composition may be narrative, descriptive, or explanatory. Usually, a composition begins with an **introductory paragraph** that tells the reader what the composition will be about. This opening paragraph introduces the main idea of the composition, just as the topic sentence of a paragraph introduces its main idea.

The **body paragraphs** of a composition develop the idea introduced in the first paragraph. For example, if a student wrote a composition about why he or she loves Phoenix, Arizona, the first paragraph might tell about the climate, the second about the scenery, and the third paragraph about the lifestyle. Together, these paragraphs would develop the main idea of the composition.

The final paragraph, or **conclusion,** of a composition signals "the end" to the reader. The conclusion might restate the main idea of the composition, summarize the supporting ideas, or present one last thought on the subject.

Following is an example of a five-paragraph narrative composition with a well developed introduction, body, and conclusion.

THE PERFECT DAY

Introduction   July 27th was no ordinary summer Saturday. After a week of cloudy, rainy weather, the day was absolutely perfect. I didn't even mind cleaning my room that morning because it gave me a chance to plan my afternoon. After considering options such as swimming and baseball, I decided that the day was made for bike riding on the beautiful trails a few miles away. I called my friend Ron and asked him to join me.

Body   Ron said he'd like to go, but explained that he had to deliver some cookies to his uncle first. He suggested that I come with him so we could start our ride immediately afterwards. We were halfway there when Ron told me that we were on our way to a nursing home. With visions of gloomy sick people clouding my perfect day, I was ready to head for home. Inside a nursing home was the last place I wanted to spend such a glorious day.

I was still protesting when Ron steered me up the steps, through a hallway, and into an old-fashioned living room. Ron's uncle was sitting in a wheelchair by the window. A half dozen other patients sat around the room. It smelled like cough medicine, and the sight of wheelchairs made me uncomfortable. I could feel my precious day slipping away. As I edged toward the door, I tripped over someone's feet. A quiet old man murmured apologies. I noticed then an unusual set of wooden chess figures on the table beside the man. He invited me to examine a piece. He explained that he had carved the complete set by hand and that he had never played with it because he had no visitors and no one at the home played chess.

I couldn't believe it when I heard myself offering to play chess with him. I could see that Ron was still talking to his uncle, so I planned to play a quick game before setting off for the bike trails. Three hours later I was still playing chess! Mr. Watson was the best player I had ever seen. He beat me seven straight times. Then we took a break, and he showed me how to begin carving. I became disgusted when I found I was no better at carving than at chess. Mr. Watson explained that both take patience and practice. We laughed when he reminded me that he had several years' head start.

Conclusion It was almost supper time when Ron and I finally left. Ron was shocked that we had stayed so long. He apologized for causing me to miss my afternoon of biking and asked if we could go the next Saturday. I suggested that, since we couldn't really depend on the weather to be fine enough for biking, we should plan to visit his uncle again. After all, the weather is always perfect for chess!

Optional Practice

Project the sample composition that appears on pages 110 and 111, using an overhead projector. Have the students state the main idea of the composition in one sentence. Then have them explain briefly how each paragraph develops that main idea. In addition, have students consider the purpose and audience of the composition, and how they may have affected the author's choice of details.

Extending the Lesson

Ask each student to find a short magazine article or newspaper feature story. As students share these, ask them to point out the following:

1. the introduction, body, and conclusion
2. paragraph development with specific facts or details
3. the main idea
4. the intended audience

111

This composition, like the other sample compositions you will study in this chapter, is made up of five paragraphs. Notice how they work together to tell the story.

- The **introductory paragraph** of this composition introduces the topic "no ordinary summer Saturday."

- The three **body paragraphs** develop this idea. The second paragraph discusses Ron's errand and the writer's reaction to it. The third paragraph relates what happened inside the nursing home. The fourth paragraph describes the experience of playing chess and of taking time out to try carving.

- The **conclusion** of the composition shows the result of that one summer afternoon. It suggests that the writer discovered a new enthusiasm and a new friend.

Part 2 Pre-Writing: Finding a Subject

When you talk with your friends, you probably have no problems deciding what to say. Words almost trip over one another in your haste to communicate your ideas. However, when you are faced with a blank sheet of paper, you may feel that you have absolutely nothing to write about.

When you are in this situation, try using yourself as a subject. Imagine that a good friend asks you what has been happening lately. What would you tell him or her? Maybe you would describe the spaghetti dinner that your class sponsored. Perhaps you would share a funny or frightening experience. You might want to tell about a trip you have taken. The stories you could tell would probably make good subjects for narrative compositions. Something you saw on your trip might become the subject for a descriptive composition.

Part 2

Objective

To develop methods for finding a subject for a composition

Presenting the Lesson

1. Read and discuss pages 112-113. Remind students that finding a subject is the initial pre-writing step in the process of writing. If students are keeping journals, remind them that these records may provide ideas for subjects.

2. Assign the Exercise on page 113. Encourage students to use different pre-writing techniques to help them find possible subjects. (See the Teaching Suggestions for Chapter 4.)

Now think a little more. Do you have any opinions about which you feel strongly? Are there ideas or feelings you would like to share? Perhaps you have some special skill or area of knowledge in which you think others might be interested? Any of these could be the focus of an explanatory composition.

All of the subjects mentioned above come from personal experience or knowledge. They are developed with ideas drawn from your own mind. Whether your purpose in writing is to entertain, inform, or persuade, you will write best about a subject that you know well.

Exercise Listing Possible Subjects

Study the following list of subjects. Choose five that you think might be interesting subjects for a composition and write them on a sheet of paper. Then add five more subjects that are based on your own experience. *Keep your list for future reference.*

1. A perfect party
2. Adjusting to a change
3. How to budget your allowance—sort of
4. My awkward age
5. Pet peeves
6. When my mother/father went to school
7. The night I told my little brother/sister a ghost story
8. How my dog trained me
9. Being different
10. Why I'll never go camping again
11. My collection of _____
12. My least favorite chore and ways to avoid it
13. The strangest place
14. Teen-age blues
15. How to sail a boat
16. When I found out parents are people
17. Building models
18. Learning to accept others

Individualizing the Lesson

Less-Advanced Students

1. After assigning the Exercise, help the students make their lists of possible subjects by encouraging them to think about questions such as these:

a. Who would you like to be like?
b. What is your hobby, and what makes it interesting to you?
c. What was the funniest situation you've ever been in?
d. Who are the most memorable characters you've ever met?

2. Help students to choose a topic for the group composition.

Advanced Students

Challenge the students to broaden their thinking about composition topics by requiring them to write a subject for each of the following areas:

cities	fads
modern music	television
computers	movies

Remind students that the subjects should be based on experience.

Optional Practice

Provide the students with a stimulating idea-starter to serve as a springboard for a composition. A trip to a museum or a nature preserve, for example, might spark many ideas for topics.

Extending the Lesson

Have the students spend part of a class period in the school library looking through books and magazines for subject ideas. Before the visit, have the students suggest subject areas that interest them.

Part 3

Objectives

1. To recognize how to narrow a subject
2. To plan details for a composition

Presenting the Lesson

1. Read and discuss the introduction and **Narrowing the Subject** on pages 114 and 115. Suggest that one way to narrow a topic is to look for a fresh or unusual angle on it. To demonstrate this, you might have students brainstorm for unusual viewpoints on a single topic, such as "Weather." Such viewpoints could include "Why I Love a Blizzard" or "How To Ignore a Heat Wave."

2. Assign the Exercise on page 115. Remind students that as they narrow any topic they should begin to consider the purpose and audience of their composition. Check each student's final subject before proceeding.

3. Read and discuss **Putting Down Ideas** and the sample list of details on page 116. Point out that success at this stage in the process of writing depends on the writer's ability to observe closely, remember clearly, visualize vividly, or reason logically, depending on the purpose of the composition. Remind students that knowing their purpose and audience will help them write down only the details that will best suit their composition.

Part 3 Pre-Writing: Planning the Composition

The process of writing begins when a writer finds a general idea for a subject. Too often, though, inexperienced writers think that this is all there is to the pre-writing stage. They begin to write immediately. Very soon they find that they have no idea what they want to say or how they want to say it. The problem is that they did not first work out a plan for writing.

Planning takes time, but the time spent is worthwhile. The end product is a clear, well organized composition that communicates ideas effectively from writer to reader.

Narrowing the Subject

The first thing you must do when planning a composition is to decide on a general subject. Then you must decide how far to narrow the subject so that it can be developed in a few paragraphs. Study the following composition ideas:

1. How to paint miniatures
2. Jobs

The first subject—how to paint miniatures—focuses on a specific process. A writer could easily develop this idea in a short composition. Therefore, the subject is acceptable as it is and does not have to be narrowed.

The second subject, however, would most likely present problems. There are thousands of different jobs in many different fields. The writer could give only the briefest and most general information within the limits of a few paragraphs.

The subject "Jobs" must be narrowed. To do this, the writer could limit the topic to a familiar area, such as summer jobs for young people. This subject is sufficiently narrow to be developed with enough specific information to make the composition interesting and meaningful to the reader.

Exercise Choosing and Narrowing Your Subject

From the list of subjects you made in the preceding exercise, choose the one subject you would like to write about. Study it carefully. Decide if it is narrow enough to be covered in five paragraphs. If it is too general, narrow it so that it is a workable topic. You may wish to check your final topic with your teacher.

Putting Down Ideas

You have decided on a general subject, then narrowed it to the point where it can be easily covered in a few paragraphs. If you have chosen your subject well, ideas will start to jump around in your mind. The next step is to get all of these ideas out of your head and down on paper. Do not worry about order or format at this point. Just write.

As you record your ideas, you may find that you have more thoughts than you can handle. To help you make some preliminary decisions as to which ideas will be useful and which will not, take a moment to think about these two things:

Purpose. What are you trying to accomplish with your composition? If you are telling a story, use only the ideas that will help further the action. If you are describing a person or place, stick to the details that will help your reader paint a mental picture of your subject. If you are explaining an idea or process, include only the information that will help your reader understand.

Audience. Who will read your composition? How much do your readers know about your subject? If they are familiar with your topic, leave out the more elementary ideas. If the subject is new to them, include all the background they will need to understand it completely.

The writer who chose the topic "Summer Jobs for Young People" decided that she wanted to write an informative composition directed at others of her own age group. Here is her

Exercises like the following that develop thinking skills might be helpful at this pre-writing stage:

a. Record everything you see and hear during five minutes in the cafeteria.
b. Recall your experiences on the first day of school, at a dance, or on a sports team.
c. Present arguments pro and then con the movie rating system.

Later students may develop one of these ideas into a composition.

4. Assign the Exercise on page 116. SInce this composition is to be written from personal experience, students may benefit from such pre-writing techniques as discussion, interviewing, journal-keeping, and brainstorming.

Individualizing the Lesson

Less-Advanced Students

1. Before assigning the Exercise on page 115, work with the students to narrow the subject and put down ideas for their group composition.

2. Hold conferences with each student as he or she completes the Exercise on page 115. Question students about the purpose and audience of their compositions.

3. For the Exercise on page 116, require at least ten details.

Advanced Students

Urge students to heighten their awareness of sensory details by rewriting their list of details and making several details more precise or vivid.

Optional Practice

1. Have the students narrow a second topic for the Exercise on page 115.

2. Have the students explain the process by which they arrived at their final topics. Ask them which pre-writing techniques helped them most.

Extending the Lesson

Read aloud some descriptive passages from John Steinbeck's *The Red Pony,* and ask students to state which details help to make the author's point and which make the writing have impact.

Part 4

Objectives

1. To identify main ideas

2. To understand how to organize ideas for a composition

Presenting the Lesson

1. Read and discuss the explanation of the two steps in planning a composition. Make certain that students understand the difference between a main idea and a supporting detail. Compare main ideas to "umbrellas," under which other ideas fit.

Point out that the sample notes are for an explanatory composition

list of ideas, written in the order in which they occurred to her.

Lawn care, gardening
Babysitting
Painting, cleaning
Bike repair business
After school jobs
Teenagers who succeed with their own businesses
Community service organizations
Garage sales
Services that people in the community need
Volunteering
Jobs that spring from interests or hobbies
Work permits

Exercise Writing Down Ideas

Think about the subject you have chosen for your composition. Write down all the details you can about your subject. Save this list. Add to it as more ideas occur to you.

Part 4 Pre-Writing: Organizing the Composition

Once you have written down your ideas, your next step is to organize them. Organizing notes involves these main steps:

1. Identifying your main ideas
2. Putting your ideas into logical order

Take time with these steps. They will make the actual writing of the composition much easier later on.

Finding the Main Ideas

Read over your list of details. You will find that most of the details fit under a few key ideas. Identify these key ideas and list them. The writer of the composition on jobs examined her list and came up with these three main points:

1. Old standbys
2. Volunteer work
3. A business of your own

At this point she also decided on a title: "Summer Jobs in Your Neighborhood."

Putting Your Ideas in Logical Order

You now have a list of main ideas. The final step in planning is to put these ideas and their supporting details into some kind of logical order. For compositions that give directions or tell about personal experiences, the most common order is chronological. The events are recounted in the order in which they happen. Compositions that describe places often are organized in spatial order. The writer moves smoothly from one part of the scene to another.

Compositions that present ideas or opinions are frequently organized in order of importance. Usually, the least important ideas are given first and the most important ideas are given last. The composition thus builds to a climax and holds the attention of the reader right to the end.

The writer of the composition "Summer Jobs in Your Neighborhood" arranged her ideas in order of familiarity. She began with familiar job ideas and ended with what she felt were the more unusual jobs.

SUMMER JOBS IN YOUR NEIGHBORHOOD

First Main Idea   The old standbys

Child care
Lawn care
Gardening
Painting
Cleaning

in which the ideas will be organized in order of familiarity. Make sure that students are aware of four ways of organizing details — chronological order, spatial order, order of importance, or order of familiarity. Emphasize the importance of the pre-writing steps for any type of composition.

2. Assign Exercise A on page 118. Work with the students to organize the first group of ideas before you assign the rest as independent work. As a class, discuss which order is most appropriate for each set of ideas.

3. Assign Exercise B on page 119. Remind the students to adjust details to suit their audience and purpose, as they learned in "The Process of Writing," Chapter 4. Referring to the questions on pages 52-53 will be very helpful for students at this stage of the pre-writing process. Encourage students to use the checklist and to add and delete details if necessary.

Individualizing the Lesson

Less-Advanced Students

1. Work with the students to arrange their ideas for the group composition.

2. Before assigning Exercise B on page 119, require the students to write down the main idea, purpose, and audience of their compositions. Encourage them to refer to that information constantly as they plan their compositions. Confer with the students about the most appropriate order for their compositions.

As the students make their notes for Exercise B, have them work with editorial partners to find details that are vague and to note if more details are needed. Then each student can revise his or her own list of notes.

Optional Practice

1. To give the students practice in analyzing which are main ideas, have them pick out the three main ideas from the following list of notes for a composition on dreams:

1. If I'm worried about a new class, the teacher might appear in my dream.
2. Remembering my dreams gives me a clue to what's bothering me.
3. One dream of mine recurs often.
4. In my recurring dream, I forget something important.
5. Sometimes a dream is about soccer if I've played that day.
6. Many of my dreams concern things that have happened during the day.
7. I may forget to learn lines for a play or to study for a test.

Help the student to see that the second, fourth, and sixth statements are important ideas while the other statements support one of those three.

2. On the overhead projector show a well-written student composition, and ask the class to point out the topic sentences and also the details that effectively develop each one. Ask the students to list these main ideas and supporting details.

3. Have the students view a brief film that tells a story. Discuss with the students the major events in the

Second Main Idea   A business of your own

Businesses that use special talents (growing plants, etc.)

Businesses that fill a need in the community (pet sitting)

Examples of teens who have succeeded (bike repairs, magic shows, garage sales)

Third Main Idea   Volunteer work

For a hospital
For a church
For a service organization
For a campaign

Notice that the writer has expanded her original list of ideas. She has also included examples that she thinks might be useful in her composition. On the other hand, she decided that two ideas from her original list—after school jobs and work permits—were not appropriate for her subject. These were deleted from her working list. The writer will now use this list as a guide for writing the first draft of her composition.

As you work on your own composition plan, remember that the process of writing is really just a series of changes. Never be afraid to add, delete, or rearrange ideas at any point in the process.

Exercises Organizing the Composition

A. Following are four groups of ideas. Rearrange each into logical order. Be ready to explain which order you followed—chronological, spatial, or order of importance. Answers will vary.

1 **The Value of a Good Novel**   Order of Importance

1. It sharpens understanding of human character.
2. It provides relaxation and entertainment.
3. It introduces readers to different kinds of societies.
4. It can lead to changes in law, education, politics, and social attitudes.
5. It is an aid to the study of history and geography.

2 Cleaning the Basement Chronological Order

1. I piled the giveaways into clean boxes and labeled the boxes.
2. I carried home boxes from the grocery store.
3. I swept and washed the basement floor.
4. I sorted the various stacks of junk into three piles: throwaways, giveaways, and things to keep.
5. I admired the completed job.
6. I stuffed the throwaways into large garbage bags and hauled the bags to the alley.
7. I neatly stacked the things to keep on shelves.

3 Our Rooftop Deck Spatial Order

1. Rows of tomatoes, beans, peppers, onions, and carrots grew in long planters set into the deck.
2. Scattered among the tables and chairs were trees and flowering bushes planted in large wooden pots.
3. Colorful flowers surrounded the bases of some of the trees.
4. At the other end of the deck, away from the tables and chairs, was the vegetable garden.
5. At one end of the deck were tables and chairs.
6. Redwood covered the entire rooftop.

4 How To Make Yourself Popular Order of Importance

1. Don't take offense easily.
2. Avoid arguing over differences.
3. Don't attack the beliefs and opinions of others.
4. Don't expose the weaknesses of others needlessly.
5. Follow the golden rule.
6. Don't betray secrets.

B. Organize your own list of ideas into a logical order. Save this list to use as a guide when writing the first draft of your composition.

film, and list these on the chalkboard. Then have the students suggest which details elaborate on each main event or idea.

Extending the Lesson

Invite the principal to class, and have the students interview him or her about how students' classes are scheduled or how students can prepare for high school. Require students to plan questions that will seek specific details from the principal.

Afterward, on the chalkboard, have volunteers list ideas and information that they learned from the principal on the topic. Work with the students to organize these notes into main ideas and supporting details. Develop a pre-writing plan for a composition on the topic.

Part 5

Objective

To become familiar with ways to write a good introduction, body paragraphs, and a conclusion for a composition

Presenting the Lesson

1. Read aloud and discuss the explanation of the first draft on page 120. Emphasize that the first draft is a crucial step in writing. Then read **Writing the Introduction.** Referring to the three sample paragraphs, stress the twofold function of an introductory paragraph:

1. to convey a clear idea of purpose
2. to catch the reader's attention

2. Discuss the first paragraph in Exercise A on pages 121-122 with the class before assigning the rest of the Exercise as individual work. Guide the students in understanding that the first paragraph builds the reader's curiosity and at the same time introduces the main idea that computers are useful. Ask students what they would expect the body paragraphs to explain, based on the introduction.

After the students have completed the Exercise, have them discuss what the main idea for each composition is. Then have them share ideas on how to improve the weak introductions. The students should see that each paragraph has some merits, but that the following revisions would be worthwhile:

Paragraph 2: Make the second sentence more specific.

The plan for your composition is now finished. You have chosen your topic, gathered and recorded details, grouped your ideas, and arranged the groups of ideas in logical order. You are now ready to begin writing the first draft of your composition. Remember that at this stage in the process of writing you should be concerned only with getting your ideas down on paper and making them flow smoothly. You will have time to fine-tune your writing later, in the revision process.

Writing the Introduction

As you learned earlier, the introduction of a composition or report is the paragraph that tells what the composition is going to be about. The introduction must do more than that, however. It must also catch the reader's attention so that he or she will want to finish reading what you have written.

When writing your introduction, you will certainly want to avoid such dull, uninteresting paragraphs as these:

> When my father was in the Army, we lived in Germany. Germany is a pretty neat place to live. In my composition, I will try to tell you what it's like to live in Germany, and why I think it's so neat.

> I am going to write about summer jobs. I think you will be interested in these ideas.

Both of these introductions tell the reader what the compositions are going to be about, but both of them are so boring that no one would want to read further. Compare these two paragraphs with the following example, which the writer arrived at after several revisions. Keep in mind that this is still a rough draft. The writer will make further improvements later on.

Summer is a good time to goof off. But twelve weeks without school or homework leaves a lot of free time. Much to your surprise, you may find yourself getting bored. One way to turn those long, lazy hours into a neat profit is with a neighborhood job. With a little creative thinking, you can find a job that will help to make your summer super—and maybe fill your piggybank at the same time.

This paragraph leads into the ideas listed under the first main idea of the writing plan for "Summer Jobs in Your Neighborhood." It introduces the reader to the topic of the composition and at the same time appeals to the reader with vivid language and a personal tone.

Exercises Working with Introductory Paragraphs

A. Following are five paragraphs. Read them carefully. Decide which are good introductory paragraphs. Your choices should be interesting and should tell what the composition is going to be about. Be prepared to explain why you think the others are not good. Answers will vary.

1

The first time I worked on a computer, I was shaking. The second time, I was still a bit nervous. By the third time, though, I realized that computers are not my enemy. In fact, they might be useful after all.

2

There's something about Halloween night that always frightens me, even though I'm too old to believe in ghosts and goblins. The black always seems blacker and the shadows more eerie. Even the familiar howl of a neighbor's cat sounds different, somehow.

3

I think that the government ought to make every citizen vote. If I were President, I would introduce a law stating that every citizen had to cast a ballot in every election. Voting is important, so everyone should vote.

Paragraph 3: Eliminate the repetition that weakens the strong idea stated in the first sentence. Begin with a more interesting opening.

Paragraph 5: Revise the entire paragraph to grab the reader's attention.

3. Assign Exercise B on page 122. Encourage the students to experiment with different angles and approaches as they write introductions. After each student has completed one or two introductions, you may wish to have them present their work in small groups, asking for feedback on how to improve the introductions. Remind students to make their introductions interesting as they state the main idea for the composition.

4. Read and discuss **Writing the Body** on pages 122-123, including the sample body paragraphs. Ask students to do the following in the sample composition:

find the topic sentence in each body paragraph

identify the details that support each topic sentence

notice precise words and phrases

Have the students compare the body of the sample composition with the writing plan on pages 117-118 to see how each paragraph was developed from one main idea in the notes. Remind them that this is a rough draft. *Note:* This rough draft will be shown again in the chapter part on revision. Additional errors in grammar and mechanics are shown in the second version, but are not shown here to avoid confusing the students.

5. Assign the Exercise on page 124. Emphasize that each main idea from the student's writing plan becomes the topic sentence of a paragraph in the first draft. Tell students that if their writing plans are detailed and well organized, the body paragraphs will fall into place easily.

6. Read and discuss **Writing the Conclusion** on page 124. Analyze the sample conclusion as to how it finalizes the composition. Ask the students to notice the phrase "No matter what kind of summer job you choose," and to explain how it ties the conclusion to the body paragraphs. Then have the students identify key ideas in the introduction that are repeated in the conclusion. Have students draw conclusions about what makes a good conclusion for a composition.

7. Assign the Exercises on pages 124-125.

Individualizing the Lesson

Less-Advanced Students

1. Have the students complete the Exercise on pages 121-122 orally in small groups. Work with the students to revise one of the weak introductions, such as Paragraph 3 or 5.

2. Before assigning Exercise B on page 122, have the students work together to write an introduction for the group composition.

3. Before assigning the Exercise on page 124, work together with the students to write body paragraphs for the group composition. Similarly, before assigning the Exercise on page 125, work with the students to help them write a conclusion for the group composition. At each step, remind the students that this first draft will be revised later.

4

Many of us open our ears to compliments, yet close them to criticisms. Yet, criticism can teach us more than the most well-meant compliment. It is from criticism that we learn our mistakes and how to do better next time.

5

There are many different kinds of pollution. Among them are noise pollution, water pollution, and air pollution. Pollution is a problem that we should all try to solve.

B. Write the introductory paragraph to your composition. Make it as clear and interesting as you can. Be sure that it leads into the first main idea of your writing plan. Revise when necessary.

Writing the Body

The body is the most important part of a composition. It is in these paragraphs that the main idea presented in the introduction is supported or explained. The specific ideas in the body may take the form of descriptive details, events, facts and figures, examples, incidents, or definitions.

Refer back to the writing plan for "Summer Jobs in Your Neighborhood" on pages 117 and 118. Each main group of ideas becomes a paragraph in the composition. Now look at the body paragraphs below. Notice how they follow the writing plan. Remember that this is a rough draft of the composition. Further changes will be made later.

The first jobs that come to mind are usually the old standbys like babysitting and odd jobs. Even before our parents' time, teenagers have been babysitting, delivering newspapers, and mowing lawns. These jobs should not be ignored just because they are so common. The reason they are plentiful is that so many people need these services. No matter how many of your friends are doing these chores, dozens of your neighbors will still be anxious to hire someone to wash windows, cut plants, or paint porches. You might even organize a day camp for neighborhood children. Just knock on a few doors and you'll soon have customers.

If you want to do something different, look into a business of your own. Many teenagers have been quite successful with this. For example, two twelve-year-olds I know do bike repairs. Another girl does magic shows. Three eighth graders raise and sell plants. Consider your skills and interests and try to find a way to make them profitable. Another way to get an idea is to find out what people need. If many have pets, for example, you might start a pet-sitting service for people on vacation.

Another kind of summer job is volunteer work. Such work really helps other people. One good place to do volunteer work is at a hospital, where many aides are needed. Another place is at a church or temple, which usually has service projects. You can also work for a community service organization. Finally, you might like to campaign for a cause you believe in. The rewards that come from helping in any of these jobs can far outnumber the dollars you might receive at a paying job.

This example illustrates two important points concerning the body of a composition or report.

1. **A composition is always divided into paragraphs.** These divisions relieve the monotony of the page and make the composition easier to read.

Each paragraph in a composition deals with a new idea. The indentation at the beginning of a paragraph, therefore, signals that the composition is moving from one idea to another. The indentation acts like a rest stop on a road. Notice, however, how the writer uses words and phrases such as "The first," and "Another," to bridge his ideas from one paragraph to another.

2. **Each paragraph in a composition begins with a topic sentence.** The topic sentence tells what the paragraph is about. The supporting details in the paragraph relate to the topic sentence. Each paragraph in turn relates to the introductory paragraph. Thus, the composition has *unity*. All of the sentences within it support the same main idea.

4. Help the students translate their main ideas into composition paragraphs. Provide individual and small-group help as needed, guiding students in rephrasing and expanding ideas, as well as in supporting them with relevant details.

Advanced Students

1. Challenge students to find additional samples of well-written introductory paragraphs in magazines and books.

2. Encourage the students to rewrite weak introductory paragraphs in Exercise A on pages 121-122.

3. Ask each student to prepare a critique of another student's first draft. The student may then use these comments as he or she revises the composition.

Optional Practice

1. Select several student-written introductory paragraphs and project them on a screen for class analysis. Focus class attention on the structure of each paragraph and on how well it fulfills the two purposes of an introductory paragraph. Then ask the students for specific suggestions about ways to improve the paragraph or ways to better relate it to the intended audience. Be sure to protect the anonymity of the students whose paragraphs are displayed.

2. Have the students underline the topic sentences in the bodies of their compositions and check carefully to make sure that each sentence in the paragraph develops the idea in that topic sentence.

3. Read aloud the conclusions of several student compositions. See if students can identify the purpose and main idea of the compositions.

Extending the Lesson

1. Have the students reread the composition "The Perfect Day" on pages 110-111. Have the students do the following:

decide how the introduction catches a reader's attention

list the adjectives and adverbs that help to make the introduction interesting to read

list the topic sentence of each body paragraph

identify details that develop the main event of each body paragraph

note how the conclusion follows logically from the events narrated in the body paragraphs

list key ideas and phrases from the introduction that are repeated in the body

2. To provide a transition between Parts 5 and 6, have each student read the first draft of his or her introduction to a partner. Ask the partners to suggest possible improvements.

Exercise **Writing Your Body Paragraphs**

Write the three body paragraphs of your composition, following your writing plan. Begin each paragraph with a topic sentence.

Writing the Conclusion

You have almost finished the first draft of your composition. One step remains—writing the conclusion.

The conclusion presents the last idea the reader will take away from your composition. Therefore, it should be as clear and interesting as the introductory paragraph. The final paragraph should tie everything together in a way that clearly indicates "The End" to a reader.

A conclusion can be a sentence that makes a final comment:

I vowed never again to go near a cemetery at night.

A conclusion can also be a paragraph that summarizes the ideas in the composition, as in this example:

Whatever kind of summer job you choose, you will be sure to get good experience if you do it well. A job well done not only pleases the people you work for, but it also introduces you to the pride of accomplishment. That's a very special way to make sure that your summer doesn't just slide away.

Exercise **Writing Your Conclusion**

A. Read the following paragraphs. Decide which ones would make good conclusions, and why. Be prepared to discuss why the remaining paragraphs are weak.

1

We stood at the edge of the marsh long after the last of the geese had disappeared from view. Now the water was still, and the sky showed nothing more than an ordinary fall sunset. Yet we knew that the picture that would remain in our minds

124

would be that of a cyclone of Canadian geese whirling across the marsh, trumpeting their eerie cries to the wind, the clouds, and the water.

2

Some of Ted's friends are still kidding him about trying to change the world. After all, they say, being a Big Brother to Jimmy is not going to have too much of an impact on anything. Somehow, though, Ted doesn't believe them. I don't think Jimmy does, either.

3

My coach told me to keep on practicing. She said that was the only way to get better. I'll take her advice, and see what happens. I hope she's right.

4

I tried to persuade my folks to look at the disassembled lawn mower as a giant jigsaw puzzle that the whole family could have fun putting together again. They responded with a look that indicated that I might be the next thing to need reassembling. I discreetly left them to survey the damage, and went into the house to find a good place to hide for a few days. Somehow, I don't think I'll be doing too many more repairs around the house.

5

Painting miniatures can be a fascinating and extremely satisfying hobby. Once you have mastered the basic techniques, there will be no limit to what you and your paintbrush can do.

6

These were my reasons for feeling that movie producers should come out with more family films. Perhaps not everyone agrees with me, but I think they should. Everyone would benefit, so why not?

B. Write the conclusion of your composition. Make sure it makes a statement that ties it into the rest of your composition and signals "The End" to the reader.

Part 6

Objective

To understand how to revise a first draft and make a final copy of a composition

Presenting the Lesson

1. Read and discuss pages 126-128, including the sample revision of "Summer Jobs In Your Neighborhood." Stress the importance of the revising steps in the process of writing that the students learned in Chapter 4. Review the Guidelines for the Process of Writing on page 59, as well as the Guidelines for Writing and Revising Compositions on page 131. Note that revising means improving both content and form and that the two checklists will give students direction during this process.

As the class studies the sample revision, ask students to review why the various changes were made. Stress to students that during the revising process they should try to look at their work with a fresh viewpoint and be willing to make whatever changes are needed. The purpose and audience of the composition must always be kept in mind.

2. Assign the Exercise on page 128. As a peer evaluation activity, have groups of three students alternate as author, editor, and proofreader to work on revisions. Urge them to use the Guidelines for Writing and Revising Compositions on page 131.

Part 6   Revising Your Composition

A piece of writing is never perfect after the first draft. It needs to be reworked—polished into a good final product.

Read through your composition. Check to see that your ideas flow well. Reorganize them if you have to. Delete unnecessary information and add needed details. Replace dull words and phrases with lively, colorful ones. Check for errors in grammar, capitalization, punctuation, and spelling. See the Guidelines on pages 59 and 131 for more help with revising.

The writer of "Summer Jobs in Your Neighborhood" knew that her composition could be improved. Look at this version of her rough draft. It shows some of the changes she made during the revision process.

SUMMER JOBS IN YOUR NEIGHBORHOOD

Summer is a good time to ~~goof off.~~ _relax and have fun._ But twelve weeks without school or homework leaves a lot of free time. Much to your surprise, you may find your self getting bored. One way to ~~turn~~ _fill_ those long lazy hours ~~into a neat profit~~ is with a neighborhood job. With a little creative thinking, you can find a job that will help to make your summer super—and maybe ~~fill your~~ _increase your bank account_ ~~piggybank~~ at the same time.

The first jobs that come to mind are usually the ~~old stand-bys like~~ _familiar ones, such as_ babysitting, _mowing lawns,_ and ~~odd~~ _other_ jobs. ~~Even before our parents time, teenagers have been babysitting, delivering newspapers, and mowing lawns.~~ These jobs should not be ~~ignored~~ _overlooked_ just because they are so ~~common,~~ _ordinary_ the reason they are plentiful is that so many people need these services. No matter how many

---

126

of your freinds are doing these chores, dozens of your neigh-

bors will still be ~~anxious~~ *eager* to hire someone to wash windows,

prune ~~cut~~ plants, or paint porches. You might even organize a day

camp for neighborhood children. Just knock on a few doors

and you'll soon have *several* customers. *[Move to next paragraph]*

If you want to do something diffrent, *a little* look into *e* *try starting* a business

of your own. Many teenagers have been quite successful with

this *approach.* For example, two twelve year olds I know do bike repairs.

Another girl does magic shows *at children's parties.* Three eighth graders raise

and sell plants. Consider your skills and interests and try to

find a way to make them profitable. Another way to get an

idea is to find out what people need. If many have pets, for

example, you might start *consider* a *the* pet-sitting service *in your neighborhood* for people on

vacation. *There is another type of summer job that may be more satisfying than any of the others. This*

~~Another kind of summer job~~ is volunteer work. Such work

really helps other people. One good place to do volunteer work *and also gives you a worthwhile experience.*

is at a hospital, where many aides are needed. Another place

to volunteer is at a church or temple, which usually has service projects.

A third possibility is to ~~You can also~~ work for a Community Service Organization, *such as an ecology group.*

Finally, you might like to campaign for a cause you believe in.

The rewards that come from helping in any of these *volunteer* jobs can

far outnumber the dollars you might receive at a paying job.

Whatever kind of summer job you choose, you will be sure

to ~~get a good experience~~ *benefit from it* if you do it well. A job well done not

only pleases the people you work for, but it also introduces you

to the pride of accomplishment. That's a very special way to

make sure that your summer doesn't just ~~slide~~ *slip* away.

3. Read and discuss **Making a Final Copy** on pages 129-130. Remind students that Chapter 4, "The Process of Writing," encourages them to read their final copies aloud to check for errors. In addition, you may want to confer with students about problems before they make their final copies.

4. Assign the Exercise on page 130.

Individualizing the Lesson

Less-Advanced Students

1. Help the students to revise their group composition. Guide them to see weaknesses in organization, unity, or development that need to be changed. In addition, point out vague wording, needed transitions, and problems in usage or mechanics. Work together to correct these problems.

2. Work with the students on revising their own compositions. Methods such as peer evaluation and group questioning may help the students to improve their first drafts. Be sure to have the students read their compositions aloud, both to themselves and also to a partner. Point out items in the Guidelines for Writing and Revising Compositions on page 131 that students need to work on in their revisions.

3. If possible, have the students bring in samples of writing done earlier in the school year. Use these samples to point out improvements that have been made in each student's writing.

Advanced Students

1. Ask the students to review the paragraphs that they wrote for preceding chapters, and to list usage and mechanics errors that recur in their writing. Then assign the students to study the Sections in the second half of this book that teach how to avoid these particular errors.

2. Pair each student with a student who has an opposite style (terseness — wordiness, overelaboration — leanness, etc.) to discuss problems in revising.

Optional Practice

1. Hold grammar and mechanics clinics in specific problem areas, and assign students to the clinics that they will profit from most. Some examples of clinic concerns might be as follows:

1. subject–verb agreement
2. avoiding sentence fragments
3. pronouns and antecedents
4. uses of commas

Supply the clinic participants with prepared exercises. Provide additional instruction as necessary, using appropriate sections from the back of this book.

Extending the Lesson

1. Have students seek information on how many drafts professional writers write and how they revise their work. You might instruct students to look in books about writers and writing to find out information on how their favorite authors write and rewrite.

Analyzing the Revision

Now examine the revised draft again. Look for the following changes, which the writer felt would improve her composition:

1. Vague language was replaced by precise words and phrases. For example, the word "prune" was substituted for the word "cut," and "ordinary" replaced "common." In addition, words and phrases were added to clarify or modify other words.
2. Formal language was substituted for informal language. Phrases such as "goof off" and "old standbys" were replaced.
3. Ideas were rearranged. The writer decided that the idea of day camps in paragraph two worked better in paragraph three, so she moved it. She also moved another sentence in that paragraph. These changes made the paragraph flow more smoothly.
4. Errors in grammar and mechanics were spotted and corrected. An error in subject-verb agreement was corrected in paragraph two, as was a run-on sentence. Mistakes in grammar, capitalization, punctuation, and spelling were corrected throughout the composition.
5. The audience was considered, and changes were made to make the language more suitable for the readers. In the introductory paragraph, for example, the writer decided that "fill your piggybank" sounded too young for people her age. She changed it to a more adult phrase.

Work through your own composition just as carefully. The changes you make could improve your composition a great deal.

Exercise Revising the Rough Draft

Read through your rough draft. Indicate any changes you think will improve your composition. Use proofreader's marks to help make your corrections clear.

Making a Final Copy

When you are satisfied with your story, make a final, neat copy. Use whatever heading your teacher directs. Make sure you leave sufficient margins at the top, bottom, and sides of your paper.

When you have completed your final copy, proofread it one more time. Check for errors in grammar, capitalization, punctuation, and spelling.

Read through the corrected copy of "Summer Jobs in Your Neighborhood." Notice how all the changes from the rough draft have been used in the final paper.

SUMMER JOBS IN YOUR NEIGHBORHOOD

Summer is a good time to relax and have fun. But twelve weeks without school or homework leaves a lot of free time. Much to your surprise, you may find yourself getting bored. One way to fill those long, lazy hours is with a neighborhood job. With a little creative thinking, you can find a job that will help to make your summer super—and maybe increase your bank account at the same time.

The first summer jobs that come to mind are usually the familiar ones, such as babysitting, mowing lawns, and other odd jobs. These jobs should not be overlooked just because they are so ordinary. The reason they are plentiful is that so many people need these services. No matter how many of your friends are doing these chores, dozens of your neighbors will still be eager to hire someone to wash windows, prune plants, or paint porches. Just knock on a few doors and you'll soon have several customers.

If you want to do something a little different, try starting a business of your own. Many teenagers have been quite successful with this approach. Consider your skills and interests and try to make them profitable. For example, two twelve-year-olds I know do bike repairs. Another girl does magic shows at children's parties. Three eighth-graders raise and sell plants.

2. Ask the students to relate to the class which specific activities or techniques helped them most during each stage of the process of writing a composition.

3. Appoint a student committee to put together booklets made up of the students' final compositions. Other students in the class can design covers, duplicate and collate the publications, or distribute them to classmates.

Another way to get an idea for starting a business is to consider what the people in your neighborhood need. If many have pets, for example, you might start a pet-sitting service for people on vacation. You might even organize a day camp for neighborhood children.

There is one other type of summer job that may be more satisfying than any of the others. This is volunteer work. Such work really helps other people, and also gives you a worthwhile experience. One good place to do volunteer work is at a hospital, where many aides are needed. Another place to volunteer is at a church or temple, which usually has service projects. A third possibility is to work for a community service organization, such as an ecology group. Finally, you might like to campaign for a cause you believe in. The rewards that come from helping in any of these volunteer jobs can far outnumber the dollars you might earn at a paying job.

Whatever kind of summer job you choose, you will be sure to benefit from it if you do it well. A job well done not only pleases the people you work for, but it also introduces you to the pride of accomplishment. That's a very special way to make sure that your summer doesn't just slip away.

Exercise Making the Final Copy

Rewrite your composition, making all the changes you marked in your revision. Proofread the final copy.

Guidelines for Writing and Revising Compositions

As you write a composition, follow the steps in the Guidelines for the Process of Writing on page 59. Use these additional Guidelines as you revise your first draft.

1. Has the subject been narrowed to a single topic or idea that can be covered in a few paragraphs?

2. Does the composition have an introduction, a body, and a conclusion?

3. Does the **introduction** present the main idea? Does it catch the reader's interest?

4. Does each **body** paragraph explain or support the main idea? Do the paragraphs work together to develop that idea?

5. Does each paragraph begin with a clear and interesting topic sentence? Are there sufficient details to develop each topic sentence?

6. Does the **conclusion** summarize the information or comment on it?

7. Is the composition appropriate for the audience for which it is intended? Is the purpose clear?

8. Do the paragraphs flow together smoothly?

Additional Guidelines

If it is a **narrative** composition, are the events told in the order in which they happened?

If it is a **descriptive** composition, does it use specific sensory details to paint a word-picture? Are the sight details presented in spatial order?

If it is an **explanatory** composition, does it explain how something is done or why something is believed to be so? If the composition gives instructions, are the steps organized in time sequence? In a composition that supports an idea with reasons, are the reasons organized from the least important to the most important?

Chapter 9

Kinds of Compositions

Chapter Objectives

1. To recognize and to write first-person and third-person narrative compositions
2. To understand the importance of sensory details in descriptive writing and to use such details in descriptive compositions
3. To understand the differences in purpose and organization among four kinds of explanatory compositions: the composition that gives instructions, the composition that defines, the composition that gives reasons, and the composition that persuades

Preparing the Students

Tell the students to look closely at the photograph on page 84. Ask them to do three things:

1. Tell a story about the boy in the photograph.
2. Describe the boy.
3. Explain how to prepare for a bike race like the one in the photograph, or tell why biking is a challenge.

Guide the students in drawing the conclusion that experiences can lead to three kinds of writing: narrative, descriptive, and explanatory.

Explain that Chapter 9 will broaden the students' understanding of narration, description, and explanation, concepts that they studied in Chapter 7, "Different Kinds of Paragraphs." Emphasize the parallels in purpose between the compositions students will study in this chapter and the paragraphs they studied in Chapter 7 as you review that chapter.

Before writing a composition, you must make two important decisions. First, you must decide on a subject. Second, you must decide how to treat the subject. Suppose, for example, that you know a great deal about gerbils. You select this subject for a composition. Then you ask yourself: Do I want to tell a story about an experience I had with my gerbils? Do I want to describe the way they look and act? Do I want to explain how to care for gerbils?

If you decide to tell a story about the time your gerbils were

Read the introduction on pages 133 and 134. Emphasize to the students that the process of writing a composition remains the same no matter what kind of composition is being written.

Additional Resources

Mastery Test — See pages 20-21 in the test booklet. Recommended for use after teaching the chapter.

Skills Practice Book — pages 41-53.

Duplicating Masters — pages 41-53.

lost in the classroom, you will write a narrative composition. If you want your reader to "see" your pet gerbils, you will write a descriptive composition. If you want to give instructions about how to care for gerbils, you will write an explanatory composition. These three kinds of compositions—narrative, descriptive, and explanatory—are examined in detail in this chapter.

Writing any kind of composition requires that you follow the steps described in the preceding chapter. These are the steps:

Steps for Writing a Composition

Pre-Writing

1. Choose a subject.
2. Narrow the subject.
3. Think or read about the subject.
4. Make a list of details.
5. Identify main ideas.
6. Arrange the ideas and details in logical order.
7. Add or delete details as necessary.

Writing the First Draft

8. Write the introductory paragraph.
9. Write the body paragraphs.
10. Write the conclusion.

Revising

11. Reread, and revise where necessary.
12. Proofread the composition.
13. Make a final copy.

Part 1 The Narrative Composition

Narrative compositions tell stories. These stories differ widely in their content, yet they have several things in common. First of all, they relate events in chronological order; that is, the time sequence in which the events took place. Each story has a beginning, a middle, and an end. As a rule, the beginning leads up to the main events in the story, the middle describes the events, and the end tells what happened as a result of the events.

The purpose of a narrative composition is to interest and entertain the reader. Specific details are essential, for they help the reader to become involved in the action of the story.

Narrative compositions fall into two basic categories. They are first-person narratives in which the writers relate events that happen to them or that they imagine happening to them. Or they are third-person narratives in which the writers recount events that happened or might have happened to others. In the following sections are examples of a first-person and a third-person narrative.

First-Person Narrative

I WASHED THE DISHES

When my brother enlisted in the Navy, I inherited his record player, his lower bunk on the bed we shared—and his job of doing the dishes. Now, I don't mind taking out the trash or raking leaves, but I hate doing dishes. A gloomy future of dishpan hands stretched before me unless I could convince Mom that I was the wrong person for the job.

The day after Will left for boot camp, Mom handed me a bottle of detergent. She pointed to the dirty dishes waiting on the side of the sink and ordered me to get busy.

I moaned and complained and offered to mow the lawn or to shovel the walks instead. (I was pretty safe in doing this because there was snow on the ground and the walks had al-

To recognize and to write first-person and third-person narrative compositions

Presenting the Lesson

1. Read and discuss the introduction and **First-Person Narrative** on pages 135 to 137. Explain that, in first-person narration, the writer relates events from "inside" the action; he or she is not merely an observer but a participant in what happens. Ask students how they can tell that the composition is a narrative one.

2. Review the basic structure of a composition, using the sample on pages 135 and 136. Ask volunteers to identify the introductory paragraph, body paragraphs, and conclusion; to read the topic sentence of each body paragraph; and to explain how each body paragraph develops the main idea of the composition.

3. Read and discuss **Third-Person Narrative** on pages 137-138. Have the students identify the pronouns that refer to the king. Work with the students to retell the story from the point of view of the king. Discuss the changes in the plot that would be necessary; for example, some way would have to be found for the king to discover or deduce that a witch had put drops into the well.

Similarly, discuss how the sample composition "I Washed the Dishes" would change if it were written in the third person.

4. Assign and discuss the Exercise on page 138. Hold a brainstorming session in class to discuss how each idea might be developed. Emphasize that students will write more effective compositions by choosing topics that interest them and about which they have some knowledge.

Have the students follow the prewriting, writing, and revising steps outlined in the Guidelines for the Process of Writing and the Steps for Writing a Composition on page 134. Check students' work at each stage in the process. You may decide to hold peer evaluations and conferences as well. Require students to submit their first drafts for comments before they proceed with final copies.

Individualizing the Lesson

Less-Advanced Students

1. Work with the students to develop a writing plan for one of the ideas listed in the Exercise. Then either have each student write a composition based on the group writing plan or have each student write a composition entirely independently. If the students write compositions based on the group writing plan, discuss the different details that each student provided.

2. Prepare copies of a narrative composition. Have the students identify whether the composition is written in first person or third person and circle the pronouns that indicate first person or third person. Have the students explain how the composition would be different if it were written from a different point of view.

ready been shoveled.) Next I tried appealing to Mom's reason. I pointed out that school work is far more important than dishes and that, unless I got busy *immediately*, I couldn't possibly finish my homework before midnight. Mom's resolve didn't waver. She explained coolly that washing the dishes would take only a few minutes.

I realized that I was getting nowhere fast, so I decided to try a new angle. I filled the sink with cold water, squirted in a splash of detergent, and began to wash dishes. I put all the plates, glasses, silverware, and utensils into the sink at the same time. I didn't bother to scrape the plates beforehand, and bones, scraps of meat and vegetables, and soggy bread crusts floated to the top of the water like survivors of a miniature shipwreck. I rescued a few plates from the murky water and set them on the drainboard. Small flecks of food still clung to them. Then I took a misfit glass that wasn't too important, and dropped it on the floor. It broke with a crash that brought Mom directly to the kitchen. Right away she noticed the dishes on the drainboard and the mess in the sink. From the look on her face, I could tell my scheme was working.

With a pained smile, Mom urged me to run along and do my homework. As I left the room, I commented innocently, "Why thanks, Mom. I'm glad you'd rather have a scholarly son than a dumb one with dishpan hands."—ALLAN SMART

The first paragraph of the composition introduces the problem: how to avoid doing the dishes. In the body paragraphs, the writer relates, in chronological order, the steps he took to accomplish his goal. He first describes his unsuccessful attempts:

1. He offered to do other chores.
2. He tried to use homework as an excuse.

Then he tells how he carried out his successful plan.

1. He filled the sink with cold water and added detergent.
2. He put all the plates, glasses, silverware, and utensils in the sink together.

3. He didn't bother to scrape the dishes.
4. He stacked plates that were still dirty on the drainboard.
5. He dropped a glass on the floor.

As a conclusion, the writer tells us the "clever" remark he made to his mother after winning his battle.

Third-Person Narrative

THE WISE KING

Once there ruled in the distant city of Wirani a king who was both mighty and wise. He was feared for his might and loved for his wisdom.

Now, in the heart of that city was a well, whose water was cool and crystalline, from which all the inhabitants drank. Even the king and his courtiers drank from this well, for there was no other.

One night when all were asleep, a witch entered the city, and poured seven drops of strange liquid into the well, and said, "From this hour he who drinks this water shall become mad."

Next morning all the inhabitants, save the king and his lord chamberlain, drank from the well and became mad, even as the witch had foretold. During that day the people in the narrow streets and in the market place did naught but whisper to one another, "The king is mad. Our king and his lord chamberlain have lost their reason. Surely we cannot be ruled by a mad king. We must dethrone him."

That evening the king ordered a golden goblet to be filled from the well. When it was brought to him he drank deeply and gave it to his lord chamberlain to drink. There was great rejoicing in that distant city of Wirani, because its king and its lord chamberlain had regained their reason.—KAHLIL GIBRAN

In the opening paragraph, the writer introduces his main character, a wise and mighty king. In the next paragraph, he

1. Have each student find a short news article about a sporting event. Explain that the writers of the articles related the events as observers. Have the students rewrite the accounts, using the facts but writing from a first-person point of view.

2. Have students work in pairs or groups of three to develop a script for a play based on one of their narratives.

Optional Practice

1. After the students have completed the Exercise, ask them to exchange compositions with a partner. Have each student list the main events covered in the partner's composition.

2. Select a short narrative to read aloud to the class, or choose a volunteer to do so. Have students note the order of details and identify the three main parts.

3. Have the students identify transitional words that indicate chronological order and the passage of time in the sample compositions.

Extending the Lesson

1. Have the students study several short stories by famous writers as models of narrative compositions. Discuss what makes the stories have impact.

2. Select several of the students' narratives to be used in a mock "radio" dramatization. Students might tape their narratives or present them by reading aloud behind a screen. Suggest that students put together an entire radio show, including sound effects and commercials between stories.

draws you a little farther into the story by telling you about the city's only well. You begin to wonder what is going to happen to the king and what it has to do with the well. The writer then tells you, in chronological order, what happened.

1. A witch put into the well a strange liquid that would make people go mad.
2. All the people except the king and the lord chamberlain drank from the well.
3. The people went mad and decided that the king and the lord chamberlain should be dethroned because *they* were mad.
4. The king and the lord chamberlain drank water from the well and became mad.

The writer gives an interesting twist to the ending by telling you that in the eyes of the people the king and the lord chamberlain "had regained their reason."

Exercise Writing a Narrative Composition

Following are two lists of ideas for narrative compositions. Choose one, or use an idea of your own, and write either a first-person or a third-person narrative. In writing the composition, be sure to follow the steps presented in the preceding chapter.

FIRST-PERSON NARRATIVE

1. The Day I Broke the Neighbor's Window
2. My New Job
3. When My Mother Visited School
4. The Experiment That Failed
5. My Shopping Spree
6. One Day I Would Like To Forget
7. I Lost My Temper
8. My Secret Ambition

THIRD-PERSON NARRATIVE

1. Crisis at the Zoo
2. Sam Makes Breakfast
3. Some People Were Born To Make Trouble
4. A Dog That Loves Everybody
5. She Didn't See the "Wet Paint" Sign
6. The Sad Clown
7. The Creature Appeared Unexpectedly
8. He Took the Wrong Road

Part 2   The Descriptive Composition

No two people experience things in exactly the same way. When you write a descriptive composition, you share a little of your own way of perceiving reality with your reader. For a short time, your reader sees, hears, touches, tastes, and smells through your senses.

Like the descriptive paragraph, the descriptive composition relies on specific details to communicate mental images to the reader. These details can be organized in spatial order. This arrangement is common for compositions that appeal mainly to the sense of sight. Compositions that appeal to one of the other senses or to a combination of senses are organized in a variety of ways, depending on content and on the writer's approach.

Following is an example of a descriptive composition that appeals to three senses—sight, hearing, and smell.

BY DAWN'S EARLY LIGHT

The dawn is the freshest, most beautiful part of the day. The traffic has just started. One car at a time goes by, the tires humming almost like the sound of the brook behind the hill. The sound carries not because it is sound, but because everything else is still.

It isn't exactly a mist that hangs over the thickets, but more nearly the ghost of a mist. It will be gone three minutes after the sun comes over the treetops. The lawns shine with a dew not exactly dew. There is a rabbit bobbing about on the lawn. If it were truly a dew, his tracks would shine black on the grass, and he leaves no visible track. Yet there is something on the grass that makes it glow a depth of green it will not show again all day. Or is it something in the dawn air?

And now the sun is shining in full. The leaves of the Japanese red maple seem a transparent red-bronze when the tree is between me and the light. This is the only tree I know

Part 2

Objective

To understand the importance of sensory details in descriptive writing and to use such details in descriptive compositions

Presenting the Lesson

1. Read and discuss pages 139 and 140. Compare the descriptive paragraph and the descriptive composition, having students refer to pages 92-97 to review what they have learned about descriptive paragraphs.

2. Have the students close their eyes and picture the scene described as you reread the sample composition. Ask them what makes the portrayal of morning come alive.

3. Assign the Exercise on page 141. Encourage the students to choose experiences that they remember vividly. Direct the students, as part of their pre-writing activities, to list as many sensory details as possible related to their subjects. Have the students follow the Guidelines for the Process of Writing on page 59 and the Steps for Writing and Revising Compositions on page 131. Before students revise their compositions, have them exchange papers and suggest revisions for one another's work.

Individualizing the Lesson

Less-Advanced Students

1. Hold a brainstorming session to help the students begin work on their compositions. Have each student tell the class what topics he or she has been considering, and have the others ask questions to help the student recall the details that are needed.

2. Check the development of the students' writing at several stages: after they have chosen subjects, after they have completed their writing plan, and after they have written first drafts.

Advanced Students

Have the students collect and study travel folders and travel advertisements. Then have each student select a favorite place, imagine himself or herself there, and complete the six pre-writing steps outlined in the Guidelines for the Process of Writing on page 59 for a descriptive composition about the visit.

Optional Practice

1. Have the students keep journals and use them as a source for ideas during descriptive writing.

2. Have the students consider what their topics for the Exercise on page 141 would be like under different conditions. For example, if a student wrote about a storm, he or she should imagine the setting after the storm had passed. Have each student complete pre-writing steps for a second composition about the same topic under different conditions.

3. Have students write a descriptive composition set in a familiar place. Ask students to choose one of the following moods to create in their descriptions:

excitement	disgust
anger	happiness
calm	

whose leaves let the sun through in this way—except when the fall colors start. Green takes sunlight and holds it; red and yellow let it through.

I hear a brake squeak and know that the newspaper has arrived. I sit on the patio and read until the sun grows too bright on the page. Suddenly a hummingbird the color of green crushed-velvet hovers in the throat of my favorite lily, a lovely high-bloomer. The lily is a crest of white horns with red dots and red-velvet tongues along the inside of the petals and with a fragrance that drowns the patio. The hummingbird darts in and out of each horn, then hovers an instant and disappears.

Even without the sun's glare, I have had enough of the paper. I'll take the hummingbird as my news for this dawn. It is over now. It's time to call it a day.—JOHN CIARDI

The writer of this composition has chosen an unusual arrangement for a description. He moves in chronological order from just before dawn, to dawn, to after dawn. The details that recreate each specific time for the reader appeal to the different senses; for example:

sight	the ghost of a mist
	shine with a dew not exactly dew
	glow a depth of green
	transparent red-bronze
	the color of green crushed-velvet
	a crest of white horns with red dots and red-velvet tongues along the inside of the petals
	the sun's glare
hearing	tires humming . . . like the sound of the brook
	everything else is still
	a brake squeak
smell	a fragrance that drowns the patio

Indirectly, the composition also appeals to a fourth sense, the sense of touch. The reader can almost feel the cool pre-dawn mist and the growing warmth of the sun. This careful choice of words and details enables the author to share his favorite time of day.

Exercise Writing a Descriptive Composition

Have you ever seen storm clouds forming or a cat sleeping peacefully under a porch? Perhaps you remember an especially beautiful sunset or your back yard after a violent rainstorm. Maybe you know an interesting-looking person. Choose a topic from your own experience that you think you can describe for your classmates. Then write a five-paragraph descriptive composition, following the steps summarized on page 134. Try to use details that appeal to two or more senses. Consider arranging the details in spatial order, especially if your details appeal mainly to the sense of sight.

Part 3   The Explanatory Composition

The explanatory composition, like the explanatory paragraph, explains something to the reader. It may explain *how* something is done, *what* something is, or *why* something is so or is believed to be so.

Compositions That Give Instructions

This type of explanatory composition explains how something is done. These compositions are usually written in a direct, straightforward style. The instructions are presented in chronological order, telling the reader what should be done first, what should be done next, and so on. Compositions explaining how to construct a tree house, how to modify a pattern, or how to use a potter's wheel are examples of this kind of composition. The model on the next page is also an example of a composition with a step-by-step instructional approach.

Extending the Lesson

1. Create a still-life setting in the classroom. Have the students write descriptions of the setting. Later have students read and compare their descriptions, paying particular attention to their choices of spatial order and physical point of view.

2. Select the best examples of compositions written for the Exercise, and read them aloud to the class. Ask students to comment on specific sensory details that create a marked impression on them.

Part 3

Objectives

1. To understand the differences in purpose and organization among four kinds of explanatory compositions: the composition that gives instructions, the composition that defines, the composition that gives reasons, and the composition that persuades.
2. To know how to write each kind of explanatory composition

Presenting the Lesson

1. Read and discuss the introduction and **Compositions That Give Instructions** on pages 141-144. Compare the explanatory paragraph and the explanatory composition, having students refer to pages 99-106 to review what they have learned about explanatory paragraphs.

Have the students point out words that reinforce the chronological order of the composition "Kefta: A Burger with a Difference"; *first, then,* and *after about ten minutes* are some examples. Have the students read aloud the topic sentences of the body paragraphs, as you stress that these paragraphs are organized around major steps in a process.

Have the students find each specific suggestion given in "Reading the Water." List these on the chalkboard as students read them. Have the students notice how each suggestion is developed into a well-supported paragraph.

2. Assign and discuss the Exercise on page 144. You may wish to brainstorm as a class for additional topics for this assignment. Then have the students follow the Guidelines for the Process of Writing on page 59 and the Guidelines for Writing and Revising Compositions on page 131. Remind students to keep their audience and their purpose in mind. Before students revise their compositions, have them exchange papers and suggest revisions for one another's work.

3. Read and discuss **Compositions That Define** on pages 145-146. Have the students review the requirements for a good definition, explained on pages 101-102.

Referring to the sample composition, ask students to identify the topic sentence of each body paragraph and to explain how it represents a major element in defining Hanukkah.

KEFTA: A BURGER WITH A DIFFERENCE

America is the hamburger capital of the world. Yet the hamburger was not an American invention, nor is America the only place where this food is served. Although their burgers may not always look like a ground meat patty on a bun, people in Asia, Africa, and Europe have enjoyed their own versions of hamburgers for many years. People in the land of the Sahara, for example, eat a kind of round burger called Kefta.

To make Kefta, first get your ingredients and equipment ready. You'll need one pound of ground lamb or ground beef, one egg, one quarter cup of chopped onion, a dash of pepper, and a dash of salt. You'll also need a skillet or outdoor grill, a spatula, a large mixing bowl, and a pot holder.

Using your clean hands, mix and shape the ingredients. First mix the meat, egg, onions, and seasonings thoroughly. Then, if you wish, add any or all of the following: chopped cucumbers, chopped tomatoes, or chopped green peppers. Roll the meat mixture into seven or eight balls, each about the size of a golf ball.

Fry the Kefta in a skillet or barbeque it on an outdoor grill. If you use a skillet, adjust the flame of the stove to medium high. After about ten minutes, turn the meat over and cook it another ten minutes. On an outdoor grill, the cooking time probably will be shorter. You'll want to watch the meat closely and turn it often to prevent burning.

Kefta is delicious alone or served with rice. Try it the next time you're bored with the same old burger on a bun—it's an African treat that's great to eat!—GAY SELTZER

Sometimes, instructions may be presented in a less direct manner. They often include general "hints" and suggestions about ways to apply a technique in different situations. As a rule, the subjects of these compositions are not developed in chronological order, because the steps involved do not necessarily follow one after another. In the following composition, for example, the writer describes clues that do not have to be noted in any particular order.

READING THE WATER

If you want to catch more fish, learn how to read the water. Your favorite lake, pond, or stream is full of clues that point to fish. If you look for the clues before you start casting, your chances of catching fish are sure to improve.

Anglers who like to wade streams for bass or trout read the water carefully. Riffles where water bubbles over the rocks and flows into a quiet pool are good fishing places. Especially during the mornings and evenings, fish gather around riffles to feed. They lie pointed upstream, waiting for the current to carry food to them. Cast a bait or lure above the riffles, and let the current carry it into the pool with the natural foods. Do this carefully at the right time of day, with the right bait, and you'll learn that reading the water means more fish.

In the warmer, brighter times of day the fish, especially the bigger ones, may be hiding in deep holes. Fish like to rest in shady places. This may be beside a rock or beneath a half-sunken log. It may be along a rocky ledge dropping off into the stream or lake. It may even be a hole so deep that the light is dim near the bottom. Also, watch for weedy places. Fish may be resting under submerged weeds, and a spinner or plastic worm worked along the edge of a weed bed can bring them out. Find where the smaller streams feed into a river, and you have located another fishing spot worth exploring.

Lakes, like fishing streams, can also be read by the fisherman who knows what to look for. Every lake has some fishing spots that are better than others. You can learn a lot just by looking at the surface of the lake. Are logs lying partly submerged on the edge of the lake? These are good hiding places for bass and other fish. Look around for other signs. The mouths of streams emptying into the lake, rocky ledges reaching into the water, old roads buried when the lake was filled, and fields of stumps sticking from the water are all good places to fish.

The more you study a lake or stream, the more fish you are going to catch. That is the best reason for learning to read the water.—GEORGE LAYCOCK

4. Assign and discuss the Exercise on page 146. Remind the students to keep their audience in mind at all times as they plan and write. Have the students follow the Guidelines for the Process of Writing on page 59 and the Guidelines for Writing and Revising Compositions on page 131. Before students revise their compositions, have them form small groups to read each composition and question the writer about further distinctions or explanations that are needed in the composition.

5. Read and discuss **Compositions That Give Reasons** on pages 146-147, including the sample composition. In this kind of composition, students should be aware, the topic sentences of the body paragraphs are the main reasons why something is so. Stress the need for ample support for each topic sentence. Ask students to point out the following in the sample composition "One Family's Failure":

the statement of the composition's main idea

reasons to support the thesis

facts and examples that support the reasons

6. Assign and discuss the Exercise on page 147. Have the students debate several current events topics and school-related issues before students choose and limit their subjects. Confer with students about their planning notes. Before students revise their compositions, have them work with an editing partner to suggest revisions for one another's work.

7. Read and discuss **Compositions That Persuade,** including the sample persuasive composition, on pages 148-151. Ask students to distinguish the differences in purpose between the two sample compositions, "One Family's Failure" and "Readin', Writin', and Computin'." Then discuss the steps students should follow when writing a persuasive composition.

Ask students if they can determine the audience for the composition on computer literacy, and then have students point out the following in that composition:

the main idea

topic sentences that give reasons in support of the main idea

examples that develop an argument

facts or figures that develop an argument

conclusions of experts that develop an argument

8. Assign the Exercise on page 151. As a pre-writing activity, have students browse through newspaper editorial pages and news magazines to find current, controversial topics. Then have the students discuss or debate these topics in small groups to clarify their opinions.

Make sure that students follow the pre-writing, first draft, and revising steps of writing as they carry out this assignment.

Individualizing the Lesson

Less-Advanced Students

1. Have the students as a group choose one topic to write about for each of the Exercises. For each

In the opening paragraph, the writer tells you that you can "read" clues in the water that will help you catch more fish. The three body paragraphs describe in a clear, interesting way the signs to look for. The paragraphs contain traces of chronological order. However, the structure of the entire composition is tailored to its content, not to strict time sequence. The last paragraph of the composition restates the idea that reading the water will result in catching more fish. This conclusion lets you know that the writer has finished what he had to say.

Exercise Writing a Composition That Gives Instructions

Think of something you know how to do well, something your classmates might enjoy learning about. Then write a five-paragraph composition that clearly explains how to do it. Arrange your ideas in chronological order, if this order fits the content of your composition. Be sure to follow the Steps for Writing a Composition summarized on page 134, and the Guidelines for the Process of Writing on page 59.

Ten suggested topics are given here, in case you have trouble thinking of a topic of your own.

1. How to win at _____ (game) _____
2. How to build a birdhouse
3. How to budget your time
4. How to paint a bicycle
5. How to make bread
6. How to drive a minibike
7. How to stretch your money
8. How put up a tent
9. How to plan a party
10. How to raise bees successfully

Compositions That Define

A composition of this type defines a word or phrase. The definition in the composition has the same three parts as does the paragraph that defines: (1) the term to be defined, (2) the general class to which the term belongs, and (3) the particular characteristic that sets the term apart from the other members of the general class.

The remainder of the composition is made up of supporting ideas, usually arranged from the least to the most important, that further explain the definition. Following is an example of this type of composition.

THE FEAST OF LIGHTS

For most Americans, the big winter festival is Christmas, but for American Jews, this season is the time for an important winter festival called Hanukkah. Hanukkah is also called the Feast of Lights because it is observed by lighting candles each day for eight days. Hanukkah also is observed by religious services in the temple, by parties at home, and by gift giving. Like Christmas, Hanukkah is a joyful family holiday.

Hanukkah celebrates an event that took place more than 2,100 years ago. Then, the land that is now Israel was ruled by the Seleucid Empire. The Seleucids worshipped the gods of ancient Greece and insisted that the Jews worship their gods too. For nearly twenty years, the Maccabees, or Jewish soldiers, fought for freedom and independence. The decisive battle occurred in 165 B.C., when the Maccabees returned to Jerusalem and destroyed the Greek statues. Then they repurified the temple and dedicated it to their God. In Hebrew Hanukkah means dedication.

A legend explains that, when the Maccabees were ready to light the oil lamps in the temple, they found enough oil for only one day. By a miracle, however, the lamps burned for eight days, and that is why Hanukkah lasts for eight days.

In Jewish homes today, the main feature of the Hanukkah

topic, guide them through the pre-writing steps of narrowing their topics, gathering details, and organizing details. When those steps have been completed, either have each student write a composition on the topic you have just discussed, or encourage them to develop a composition on another topic by following the same steps.

2. Provide the students with several student-written explanatory compositions, and ask them to identify them as compositions that give instructions, compositions that define, compositions that give reasons, or compositions that persuade. Have the students summarize what each composition explains.

Advanced Students

1. Require students to make notes for a second explanatory composition. Two possibilities are a response to the composition on computer literacy or an evaluation of some situation, similar to the composition "One Family's Failure."

2. After the students have completed the Exercises, help them develop a list of topics appropriate for a debate. Then have the group choose one topic. Divide the students into two groups, each supporting one side of the issue. Hold a debate. Then have the students, or the entire class, write persuasive papers on the topic, using the insights they gained from the debate.

Optional Practice

1. Have the students tell which kind of explanatory composition would best be used in each of the following situations:

1. You want to explain the playing of the game "Dungeons and Dragons."
2. You want to express your opinions about rules in the school that you feel are outdated.
3. You want to tell what the art of origami is.
4. You want to give instructions for building a model.
5. You want to convince a State Senator to vote for a certain bill.
6. You want to express your support for the new program developed by your student council.
7. You want to change students' attitudes toward the defeated soccer team.

2. Have each student create a one-page advertisement for a product, real or imaginary, presenting at least three reasons for the product's superiority over its competitors. The advertisement may be realistic or humorous.

As an alternative, students might develop scripts for 30-second television or radio commercials that give convincing reasons that will persuade consumers to buy the product.

3. Have students make pre-writing notes for a composition on one of the following topics:

how to do aerobic dance
what a dulcimer is
how to bathe a dog
why students should attend _____
how families can stay close
why TV news programs should be changed

Extending the Lesson

1. Have the students review copies of local newspapers to find

celebration is the lighting of the candles at dusk each evening. On the first night, one candle is lighted. The number of candles lighted is increased by one each succeeding evening until all eight candles are lighted. These candles are kindled each night by another candle, popularly known as the "shamos." A special blessing is said before each lighting and gifts are exchanged.

However it is celebrated, Hanukkah is a time of joy for every Jew.

In the first paragraph, you learn that Hanukkah is a Jewish family holiday, observed by candle lighting, religious services, parties, and gift giving. The body of the composition explains why Hanukkah is celebrated and more about the lighting of the Hanukkah candles. The ideas are organized from past to present, the order of importance for the writer. The conclusion restates the idea of Hanukkah as "a time of joy."

Exercise Writing a Composition That Defines

Suppose that an amazing time machine has carried you back to the days before the Revolutionary War. Write a five-paragraph composition that describes a modern-day invention for a man or woman living in the days of George Washington. Remember to include the general class to which your subject belongs and its special qualities. Be sure to follow the Steps for Writing a Composition and the Guidelines for the Process of Writing.

Compositions That Give Reasons

The composition that gives reasons explains why something is so, why something happened, or why the writer believes a certain way. The opening paragraph states a fact or an opinion. The body paragraphs give reasons to explain why the fact stated is true or why the writer holds that particular opinion. Generally, the reasons are presented in their order of importance.

Following is a composition in which the writer tells why her family deserved a "failing grade" in energy conservation.

ONE FAMILY'S FAILURE

Last night I told the family the bad news. I had monitored and graded our use of energy for a week. Our family got an F.

Every day Mom drove twenty-eight miles back and forth to work alone, though two co-workers live nearby. So far, all three of them have ignored the chance to carpool. I was guilty of wasting gas, too. I had pestered Dad to pick me up after baseball practice on three afternoons, although I could easily have ridden the bus home.

Tuesday night was a disaster. My brother watched the same movie on the basement TV set that the rest of us watched in the den. Dad ran a dishwashing cycle for three cups, six glasses, four plates, and three little spoons. Also, several lights burned all evening without anyone's being in the rooms.

We wasted heat. The thermostat was lowered only three nights out of seven. We left the front door open much longer than necessary when coming and going. Wednesday afternoon, Mom even left the door ajar while she searched for change to pay for a postage-due letter. The furnace worked overtime for the next half hour to warm the house.

This country is consuming energy at a shocking rate. Unless every person cuts down on energy use, the future looks dim.

In the opening paragraph, the writer states that she gave her family an F for their use of energy. She then describes some of the activities that led her to this conclusion. She gives two examples of gas wasting, focuses on one wasteful night, and mentions an area in which the family is especially careless. These reasons explain why the family received a failing grade. The writer concludes by emphasizing the importance of conserving energy. She thus leaves the reader with a strong final comment on the problem.

Exercise Writing a Composition That Gives Reasons

Choose a subject that you feel strongly about. Write a composition in which you state an opinion about the subject and then explain why you think the way you do.

examples of each kind of explanatory composition. Mention that editorials are frequently, if not usually, compositions that persuade. Articles on gardening, home repairs, and household hints are usually compositions that give instructions. Articles that give background explanations for scientific and technical developments are often compositions that define. Tell students to label each article they choose. Display the articles for students' reference.

2. Using the example on page 142 as a guide, have the students develop similar compositions about favorite or special recipes. Remind them that each composition should also include some background information about the dish.

3. In the journals that students keep, have them jot down ideas and opinions that may be developed into persuasive compositions. Urge students to react to the programs that they see on television, the events that they hear about in the news, and the personal experiences that affect them deeply.

4. Have each student analyze one letter to the editor in a local newspaper. Ask the students to identify the topic of the letter, the writer's opinion on the topic, and the reasons given by the writer in support of the opinion.

Compositions That Persuade

Sometimes you do not simply want to state an opinion. Sometimes you also want to persuade readers to share that view, or possibly to take some sort of action on it. When writing for this purpose, use a special type of explanatory composition called a **persuasive** composition.

To write a persuasive composition, follow these five steps:

1. Present your opinion. Use the introduction of a persuasive composition to present the opinion or issue that you want your readers to adopt. You may also want to present some background on the subject or mention an opposing view.

   Sometimes presenting the opposing view is a good way to begin a persuasive composition. An opening sentence that begins with a phrase such as "Many people believe that . . ." serves two purposes. First of all, it gives you a springboard for your own ideas. Secondly, it can attract the readers who might otherwise disagree with what you have to say.

2. Select reasons that support the opinion. Develop each of the reasons in one of the body paragraphs. When selecting the reasons, keep your audience in mind. Reasons that would be convincing to adults, for example, might not be as convincing to students.

3. Further develop each reason with carefully chosen details that illustrate the reason or help make it clearer. These details can include facts and figures, examples, and incidents. The thoughtful selection of details can make a good reason even stronger.

4. Put the reasons and their supporting details in some sort of logical order. Organizing reasons from least important to most important is usually most effective, but once again you must consider the audience that will read the

composition. A reason that is important to one type of reader might not be as important to another.

There is also another method of organization that you can consider. If your view is one you know that your readers are strongly opposed to, you might first present the ideas and reasons with which they would be most likely to agree. Then you would proceed to ideas that would be more difficult for them to accept.

5. Write a conclusion. This conclusion may be a restatement of your opinion, a summary of the reasons you presented, or a request for some action to be taken on the issue.

As you begin to write, use language carefully. Some writers make the mistake of thinking that they must attack the opposing view or use strong or slanted language in order to prove their point. Such tactics, however, often make a bad impression on the reader. Let your facts argue for you. Keep your presentation logical and your tone reasonable.

Now look at the composition that begins on this page. The writer hopes to persuade readers to make computer literacy courses a part of the school curriculum. As you read, try to decide what audience the writer was directing the composition at. Also identify the reasons that are given, and the order in which they are presented.

READIN', WRITIN', AND COMPUTIN'

One summer activity that is surging in popularity is not swimming or boating, but computing. Young people spend hours in front of display screens at home, in summer classes, and even in camps. The attraction that computers hold for students is clear. It is time schools recognized this attraction and began to teach students what they want and need to know—computer literacy.

One advantage of courses on computer skills would be that they would help students become comfortable with what is quickly becoming an important teaching tool. Computer lessons on every subject are being written and can be individualized so that the student can go at his or her own pace. Furthermore, experts feel that computers can also motivate students and help make ideas easier to understand. The sooner students are comfortable with computers, the sooner they will be able to take advantage of this wonderful learning resource.

Computer courses can also develop a student's creativity and logic. Using a computer, a student can compose music, write poems, or make drawings. He or she can also become skilled at the complicated logic needed to program games and lessons. But these challenging and creative uses of the computer await only those who are computer literate.

Finally a course on computers may soon be necessary to teach students what they need to know simply to get along in the "outside world." Computers have become an important part of that world. Today's consumers use computers to locate books in a library, to store data, to get airline reservations, and to run businesses. In the future, computers will be used even more widely. In fact, many experts are beginning to call computer literacy a "survival skill." If this is so, learning about computers should be a basic concern of modern-day education.

To aid in education, to stimulate creativity, and to enable students to function in the world of the future—all are goals of the computer literacy course. Such a course should become as much a part of the school day as math or English. It is as important as any "traditional" subject ever was.

This composition appears to have been directed at the teachers, parents, and administrators who have the means of adding a new course to the school curriculum. The three reasons were organized from least important to most important. They were supported by facts, examples, and the conclusions of experts in the field.

Now read the conclusion once more. Notice how it restates each of the main reasons that the writer had presented in the composition. The final sentences then repeat writer's opinion. Such a conclusion acts as a concise summary of the entire composition.

Exercise Writing a Persuasive Composition

Choose an issue or problem about which you feel strongly. Write a persuasive composition in which you state your opinion on the subject. Try to persuade your readers to agree with you or take some action on your idea. Direct your writing at a specific audience. If you cannot think of a subject, use one of those listed below.

1. Violence in movies must be controlled.
2. Our school needs _____.
3. Professional athletes must find a better way to settle contract disputes.
4. We must put meaning back in our holidays.
5. Students should/should not be able to select their own classes.

Chapter 10

Writing the Report

Chapter Objectives

1. To develop techniques for selecting and limiting a subject for a report

2. To prepare for research by posing questions to answer

3. To understand how to gather information for a report

4. To understand how to organize notes and make an outline

5. To understand how to write a report from an outline

6. To name sources in a bibliography

7. To improve a report by revising, proofreading, and making a final copy

Preparing the Students

Play a tape of a radio newscast. Then display a business report, club minutes, and several school reports. Discuss the characteristics of reports, as well as when reports are written, both in school and in the world of work. Ask students what all reports have in common. Then read the introduction on this page. Stress that while other compositions are based on personal knowledge or opinion, reports are factual and are based on research from outside sources. Point out that the purpose of a report is always to inform.

Explain that in this chapter, students will study how to write reports.

Additional Resources

Mastery Test — See page 22 in the test booklet. Recommended for use after teaching the chapter.

Skills Practice Book — pages 54-56.

Duplicating Masters — pages 54-56.

In Chapters 8 and 9, you learned that there are several different kinds of compositions. Each kind has its own purpose, and its own distinct type of content. However, you also learned that no matter what kind of composition you write, the basic steps of pre-writing and development remain the same.

Now you will study another type of composition—the **report.** The purpose of writing a report is to gather material from a number of sources and to present the material clearly and accurately. Reports differ from the other compositions you have studied in that all of the material in a report comes from outside sources. You do not simply write from your own knowledge or experience. In this chapter, you will learn a practical method of writing this kind of composition.

Part 1

Objective

To develop techniques for selecting and limiting a subject for a report

Presenting the Lesson

1. Read and discuss pages 154-155. Once again, stress that reports are based on outside information, not personal experience or opinion. Note that preliminary reading on a subject is a good way to determine how to limit it.

2. Have the students point out why each topic in Exercise A on page 155 is appropriate for a report.

3. Assign Exercises A and B on page 155. These Exercises require library time.

Individualizing the Lesson

Less-Advanced Students

Work with the students to limit several of the topics in Exercise A on page 155 before you assign the rest of the Exercise as independent work.

Advanced Students

1. To broaden the students' thinking about possible topics for reports, have them suggest questions that they would like to have answered in the areas of science, history, and current events. Urge the students to consider these questions as subjects when they are completing the Exercise.

Part 1   Pre-Writing: Choosing and Limiting a Subject

You may be assigned reports in any of your subjects—science, English, social studies, math, art, or music. It is important that you know how to prepare these reports on your own. As with any composition, your first step is to choose and limit a subject.

Begin by making a list of subjects that interest you and that you feel would be of interest to your readers. Next, make certain that these subjects do not involve you personally and can be developed from outside sources of information. Subjects such as Navajo sand painting, ocean farming, or termites would meet these requirements. If you find that the topic you selected would have *you* as its main source of information, you have made an inappropriate choice. Begin again.

Once you have found a general subject, you must then narrow it to an idea that can be developed within the specified length of the report. Which of these subjects do you think would make a good five-paragraph report?

1. The geography of Latin America
2. The Viking spacecraft's pictures of Mars

The second topic, of course, is the correct choice. It concerns one particular space flight. The topic is specific enough to be explained in a short, informative report. The first subject, however, needs to be narrowed.

In order to limit a subject, consider how much information is available on it and how long the report is that you are writing. Narrow the subject accordingly. You may have to do a little preliminary reading on the subject to make this decision. Try looking at a general encyclopedia article. It will give you an idea of just how large your subject is, and may also provide possibilities for limiting it.

One way a writer could limit the broad subject "The Geography of Latin America" would be to concentrate on one particular country. The topic "The Geography of Mexico," for example, might be a good choice for a five-paragraph composition.

Guidelines for Choosing a Report Topic

- The subject should require information from outside sources.
- The subject should be of interest to both you and your audience.
- The subject should be narrow enough to be developed within a specified length.

Exercises Choosing and Narrowing a Report Topic

A. The following topics are too general to be covered in a short report. Narrow each one so that it is suitable for a five-paragraph paper.

1. bicycles	11. the F.B.I.
2. Thomas Edison	12. dinosaurs
3. the Civil War	13. the mail service
4. pioneers	14. exotic plants
5. the Mississippi River	15. Alaska
6. Mars	16. endangered species
7. Japan	17. space flight
8. computers	18. American songwriters
9. the Presidency	19. the desert
10. painting	20. science fiction

B. From the list of topics you made in Exercise A, choose five topics that you might like to gather information on. Then add five more topics of your own. Be sure to narrow each one so that it is appropriate for a five-paragraph report. Keep this list.

2. Some students may wish to explore topics that would require more than a five-paragraph report. Allow them to determine their own length for the report, and to choose their own topic accordingly.

Optional Practice

Challenge the students to think of three alternate report topics for each of the following general subjects. Remind students to narrow the topics so that they would be manageable in five paragraphs.

railroads	energy conservation
Olympics	wildlife
photography	holidays
motion pictures	U.S. economy
federal agencies	computers

Extending the Lesson

1. If the students are keeping journals, have them read through their entries for ideas that could be used as report topics. Point out that they may have to take a more technical view of what may be very personal entries.

2. Introduce students to the basics of journalistic news reporting as an adjunct to the report writing skills they learn in this chapter. Have them analyze several newspaper reports. Make sure that they identify these characteristics of news reporting:

the summary of *who, what, where, when, why,* and *how* of a story
objectivity
use of facts
organization by order of importance
conciseness of news style
information-gathering through interviews and research

Objectives

1. To identify purpose and audience for a report
2. To understand how to separate fact from opinion
3. To prepare for research by planning questions to answer in a report

Presenting the Lesson

1. Read and discuss the introduction and **Identifying Your Purpose** on page 156. Make sure that students understand these different purposes: to inform, to compare or contrast, to analyze. Ask them to suggest more report topics with each kind of purpose under the general subject of "government." Ask students to identify the purposes of reports with these titles:

Christmas Customs in England
Why People Dream
The Video Revolution
Early American Crafts
Pros and Cons of Nuclear Energy
How Records Are Made

2. Read and discuss **Identifying Your Audience** on page 157. Review the ways that the audience affects a report.
3. Read and discuss **Understanding Facts and Opinions.** Note that the writer of a report seeks facts and therefore must be able to distinguish them from opinions. Review the definitions of *fact* and *opinion,* and ask students to explain why the first three sample statements on page 157 are facts and the second three opinions. Ask students to de-

Part 2 Pre-Writing: Preparing To Do Research

Depending on your topic, there may be a great deal of information for you to read, sort through, and record. To make this job easier, take some time before you begin to think through a few key points. They will help you pinpoint the specific kind of information you should look for.

Identifying Your Purpose

The first thing you should consider is exactly what you want to accomplish with your report. In most cases, your purpose will simply be to **inform** your readers. For informative reports, look for facts and details that will provide your readers with whatever information they need to understand your subject. Here are topics for some reports whose purpose would be primarily to inform:

> F.D.R.'s New Deal
> Why stars shine
> Hydroponic gardening

Another purpose of a report is to **compare** or **contrast** one thing with another. Here are some topics that have this purpose:

> Galesburg in 1800 and today
> Private schools and public schools
> The Australian Outback and the American Wild West

For this sort of report, begin your research by reading about both topics individually. Look for details that they have in common. Your report will then be based on these similarities and differences.

A third purpose of a report is to **analyze.** For this sort of report, search for material that will help your reader to draw conclusions about the benefits or disadvantages of the topic.

Look for details that discuss trends, causes and effects, benefits, and drawbacks. The following topics fit in this category:

> The use of solar energy
> Reasons for food labeling
> How computers are changing our schools

Knowing the purpose of your report will make your research easier.

Identifying Your Audience

Whom are you writing for? Will your report be read by other students or is it directed at a different group? Are your readers familiar with the subject, or is it new to them?

The answers to these questions will help you decide how much background you will need to provide on your subject. They will also tell you how detailed and technical you can get in the main body of the report. Your purpose and your audience are two of the most important things to remember throughout the writing process.

Understanding Facts and Opinions

A report is made up of facts. A fact is a piece of information that can be shown to be true. Here are some examples of facts:

> The Grand Canyon is in Arizona.
> The city of New York contains eight million people.
> Saturn has nine known satellites.

An opinion cannot be shown to be true. It is a statement of how someone *feels* about a subject. Compare these opinions to the facts above.

> The Grand Canyon has the best scenery in the country.
> The city of New York is too crowded.
> Saturn is a beautiful planet.

cide whether the following are facts or opinions:

> A newborn baby sleeps approximately eighteen hours a day.
> Cable TV will never be as successful as network TV.
> The table of contents is located at the front of a book.
> Analyzing dreams is a waste of time.
> Gray is not a flattering color.

4. Assign the Exercise on page 158. Discuss the first statement by asking students:

> Is it a fact?
> Is it relevant to the topic?
> Is it appropriate for the purpose and audience of the report?
> Then does it belong in the report?

Write these questions on the chalkboard for students to ask themselves as they complete the Exercise independently. Afterward, have students compare their decisions. They should come to the conclusion that statements 2, 4, 6, 8, 11, 14, and 15 are not appropriate for this report.

5. Read and discuss **Making a List of Questions** on page 159. Stress that questions will give direction to research and that preliminary reading will help in planning the questions. Note that audience and purpose also help to determine the right questions to pose. Have students read the sample questions for the report on Mexican geography and explain why each is appropriate.

6. Assign the Exercises on page 159. Remind students to consider what questions their specific audience would have about this subject and which questions would help them to achieve the purpose of the report.

To help students direct their research, you may want to check their questions for Exercise B and ask for revisions when necessary.

Individualizing the Lesson

Less-Advanced Students

Help the students to find basic articles for preliminary reading on their subjects. You may need to teach them some basic library skills. See Chapter 12 for additional information on using the library.

Ask the students what questions they have about the subject, both before and after they do the preliminary reading.

Advanced Students

Have the students develop a checklist for evaluating their questions. These items might be included:

Do the questions stick to the narrowed topic?
Are the questions interesting?
Are the questions worded precisely?

Then, using the checklist, ask the students to evaluate the six lists of questions that they wrote for Exercises A and B on page 159.

Optional Practice

1. To give the students further information on identifying and checking facts, you may wish to have the class study Chapter 11, "Clear Thinking."

2. Ask students to pick five of the narrowed subjects they wrote for Exercise A on page 155 and to write five questions that would need to be answered in each report. Have students evaluate each other's questions.

When you do your research, be sure to avoid including opinions in your notes. See Chapter 11 for more information on facts and opinions.

Exercise Learning To Work with Facts

Assume that you are writing a report on "Early Photography." The purpose of the report is to inform people of your age who are unfamiliar with the topic. Look at the list of statements below. Keeping your subject, purpose, and audience in mind, find seven statements that are not appropriate for your report. Write them on your paper and be ready to tell why you would not use them. Remember that opinions should not be part of a report.

1. Early photographs were not permanent.
2. Early photography was too difficult and complicated to be enjoyable.
3. The first camera was a boxlike device as big as a closet.
4. Color photos are more interesting than black-and-white.
5. The first camera was used in about 1500.
6. Sodium thiosulfate (hypo) was used as a fixative agent.
7. The first popular form of photography was called the daguerreotype.
8. George Eastman had one of the most amazing inventions ever seen.
9. Lighting affects photographs.
10. Two British scientists produced the first photographic images on paper.
11. In the twentieth century, photography is regarded as a special kind of art.
12. Originally, images were projected onto a metal plate.
13. It took eight hours for Joseph Niépce to make the first permanent photograph in 1826.
14. The history of photography is an interesting topic.
15. Today photography is widely used in industry.

Making a List of Questions

The final step in preparing to do research is to make a list of the questions that you have about your topic, or that you think your readers would want answered. Such questions will help you make sure that you gather all necessary information as you read.

The writer who decided on the topic "The Geography of Mexico" listed these five questions:

1. Does Mexico have seasons like the United States?
2. Does Mexico's climate differ among its many regions?
3. What is the overall shape of the country?
4. Does the country have mountains?
5. Does Mexico have any unusual features?

Similar questions will serve as a guide to your own research. Of course, you may find facts as you read that are not covered by these questions. If they fit your subject, purpose, and audience, do not hesitate to use them.

Exercises Planning Questions for a Report

A. Assume that the following are topics for a report. For each, write five questions that need to be answered by outside sources. You may want to read a brief encyclopedia article on each topic.

1. TV viewing in the average family
2. Sun spots
3. The training of an Olympic gymnast
4. The first World's Fair
5. Energy sources of the future
6. Making pottery

B. Choose a topic from the list you made in Part 1. You will use this as the topic for your own report. Write five to ten questions about your topic that you can use as a reading guide.

Extending the Lesson

1. Have each student find a factual news story in a newspaper and rewrite it, adding several opinions and slanted words. Then, using the overhead projector, show the altered news stories, and have the class locate facts and opinions.

2. Duplicate and distribute a brief informative magazine article. Have the students list the questions that it answers.

3. Invite a news reporter to class to explain how he or she plans questions for an interview. Afterward, ask students what tips from the reporter could be applied to report writing.

1. To understand how to gather information for a report

2. To understand how to use note cards

Presenting the Lesson

1. Read and discuss the introductory paragraph on page 160, as well as **Taking Notes.** Carefully review Guidelines for Sources on Note Cards, and ask students to point out how these Guidelines are followed on the sample note cards.

Use a sample book, magazine, and reference book to demonstrate to the class how to locate the source information needed for note cards.

Give each student three blank note cards. Read brief passages from the book, magazine, and reference book, and have the students fill out cards for each source, using the sample note cards on page 162 as models. Discuss the results.

Emphasize that note cards *must* use the students' own wording, and not the phrasing of the source. Refer to the sample note card based on an encyclopedia excerpt on page 161, noting the difference in wording. Review how direct quotations are handled, and why.

2. Assign Exercise A on page 163. Have students exchange note cards to check for completeness of source information, form, accuracy, and rewording.

3. After students have successfully completed Exercise A, assign Exercise B. As students gather in-

Part 3 Pre-Writing: Gathering Information

In order to collect all the material you need to write a thorough report, read as much as you can about your subject. You will find most of what you need in the library.

Begin by reading a general encyclopedia article. Then check the card catalog and the *Readers' Guide to Periodical Literature*. These sources will direct you to books and magazine articles on your subject. Also consult reference books. See Chapter 12 for more guidance in using the library.

Taking Notes

As you look up information on your topic, record the facts you want to use on 3″ x 5″ note cards. Write only one piece of information on each card. Also record your source.

Guidelines for Sources on Note Cards

1. For books, give the title of the book, the name of the author, and the page number of the information.

2. For magazines, give the name and date of the magazine, the title of the article, the name of the author, and the page numbers of the article.

3. For encyclopedias, give the name of the set, the title of the entry, the volume number where the entry appears, and the page numbers of the entry.

4. For other reference books, give the name of the book or set of books, the title of the entry, the volume number, and the page numbers.

As you take notes, be sure that you record the information in your own words and not those of the source. Then the report that you write from the cards will be original. Notice how this writer summarized a fact about the space shuttle:

The concept of the space shuttle is that it will be used again and again, as many as one hundred times. Projections for the mid-1980's are that an earth-orbiting space shuttle will carry a manned space station.

U. S. Space Missions

by Marsha Black, page 67

U. S. scientists plan to use a space shuttle to keep a space station in orbit.

Occasionally, you may want to copy a direct quotation from an expert. If you do, be sure to put quotation marks around it on your note card. Do the same in the report itself and give the source.

The writer of a report on solar energy searched the card catalog and the *Readers' Guide to Periodical Literature*. There he found the titles of books and articles on energy and energy sources. He also looked over the reference shelves for books that might contain useful information. He read about his subject in several sources. As he read, he wrote facts on note cards, putting only one fact on each card. He was careful to record each fact accurately and completely and to write it in his own words.

formation for their own reports, emphasize that they should keep their narrowed topic, purpose, and audience in mind. The questions that they planned for Part 2 will help them focus their research.

Individualizing the Lesson

Less-Advanced Students

1. Work with these students to help them become familiar with the library research tools explained in Chapter 12. Help students to determine appropriate sources, and work with the students in the library as they gather information on their topics.

2. Explain the ideas of skimming and scanning, which are further discussed in Chapter 13. Emphasize that students should not try to read every article on their subject word for word.

Advanced Students

Assign Chapter 12, "The Library and How To Use It," to these students as independent reading in preparation for researching their topics.

Optional Practice

Ask volunteers to make two note cards on the chalkboard from this book's information for a report on William Tell:

"William Tell was a legendary hero of Switzerland. His story, though not verified by history, represents the spirit of the Swiss movement for independence from the Austrian Hapsburgs in the 1300's."

— *The World Book Encyclopedia*, page 103, Volume 19

Extending the Lesson

1. Have each student find two statements of factual information in a textbook and verify them in other sources.

2. Assign Chapter 13, "Study and Research Skills," as a way to prepare students for research.

3. Have groups of students discuss or demonstrate the pitfalls of poor research skills, including the following:

haste
reading every piece of information word for word instead of scanning
not using indexes and tables of contents to aid in scanning
not being familiar with the card catalog
not using the *Readers' Guide*
not taking notes; trusting one's memory
not using note cards

Here are some sample note cards for the report on "Using Solar Energy":

Book

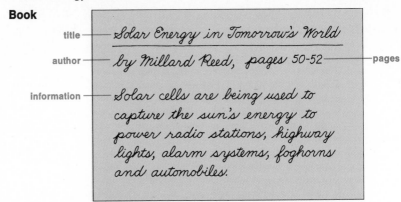

title — *Solar Energy in Tomorrow's World*
author — by Millard Reed, pages 50-52 — pages
information — Solar cells are being used to capture the sun's energy to power radio stations, highway lights, alarm systems, foghorns and automobiles.

Magazine

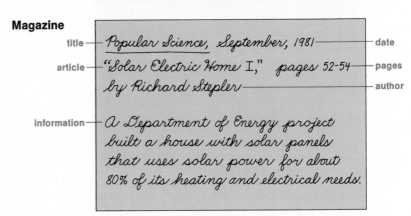

title — *Popular Science*, September, 1981 — date
article — "Solar Electric Home I," pages 52-54 — pages
by Richard Stepler — author
information — A Department of Energy project built a house with solar panels that uses solar power for about 80% of its heating and electrical needs.

Encyclopedia

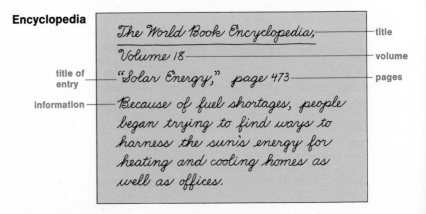

The World Book Encyclopedia, — title
Volume 18 — volume
title of entry — "Solar Energy," page 473 — pages
information — Because of fuel shortages, people began trying to find ways to harness the sun's energy for heating and cooling homes as well as offices.

Exercises Taking Notes

A. Assume that you are writing a report on the Ganges River. Write five note cards from this article in the *World Book Encyclopedia,* Volume 8, page 28. Make sure that you put the information into your own words.

> **GANGES RIVER,** *GAN jeez,* is the greatest waterway in India and one of the largest in the world. Hindus consider it the most sacred river in India. Each year, thousands of Hindu pilgrims visit such holy cities as Banaras and Allahabad along the banks of the Ganges to bathe in the river and to take home some of its water. Some pilgrims come to bathe in the water only to cleanse and purify themselves. The sick and crippled come hoping that the touch of the water will cure their ailments.
>
> The river is an important trade area. Its valley is fertile and densely populated. Some of India's largest cities, such as Calcutta, Howrah, Patna, Banaras, and Kanpur stand on its banks.

B. Take notes for your report on 3″ x 5″ cards (or on pieces of paper cut into 3″ x 5″ rectangles). Follow the guidelines given in this lesson for recording information and sources. Save your notes to use when you plan and write your report.

Part 4 Pre-Writing: Organizing a Report

Once you have gathered all the information you need, you are ready to organize your notes. You will probably notice that most of your information seems to fall under certain key ideas. One good organizational technique is to divide your note cards into groups. Each group should contain only the cards related to one of the key ideas. You may want to begin separating your cards this way while you are still taking notes.

163

Part 4

Objective

To understand how to organize notes and make an outline for a report

Presenting the Lesson

1. Read and discuss the explanation of organizing notes on pages 163-165. Tell students that they must look for common ideas in their notes, as did the writer of the report on Mexican geography. Emphasize that gathering information and organizing a report are two complementary processes: often, as students are organizing a report they will find that they need more information on an idea, or that some of the facts they have gathered are not suitable to their purpose or audience. Refer students to the questions on pages 52-53 in Chapter 4, which remind students to continually evaluate their factual details during all phases of their writing.

2. Read and discuss **The Order of Information** on page 165. Review spatial order, chronological order, and order of importance as these terms apply to organizing report facts. Have students suggest topics that will be organized in these ways.

3. Read and discuss **Making an Outline** and the sample outlines on pages 165-167. Discuss the value of outlining as a means of organizing a report. You may wish to assign Section 14 as required or optional reading at this point. Use the sample outline to review the following elements of outline form:

1. Roman numerals followed by periods for main heads
2. Capital letters followed by periods for subheads
3. Arabic numerals followed by periods for lesser subheads
4. Alignment of main heads over the letters for the subheads
5. Initial capital letter for each main head and subhead
6. Parallel construction

Point out that the first sample outline has four main heads, which correspond to the introduction and three body paragraphs of the report. Have students notice that the main headings I, II, III, and IV in the

The writer of the report on "The Geography of Mexico" had note cards with these facts:

Mexico is a long triangle pointing to South America.
Cold mountain roads
Warm, humid valleys with groves of bananas, guavas, mangoes, mameys, and sapotes
The mountains are breathtakingly steep and high.
Mexico is wide at the top and narrow at the bottom.
Paricutin, a new volcano
Mexican culture is rich and varied.
Strange plants and fruits in the lowlands; hedges of cactus
Some peaks are wild and rugged.
Wet season in summer; dry season in winter
In the dry months, no rain falls.
In the wet months, the rain is so heavy that it carries the soil from the mountains.
The first Europeans in Mexico were the Spaniards.
One village now lies at the bottom of a lake.
Some mountains are planted in orderly plots.
Mexico is a land of beauty, violence, and the unexpected.

The writer found that she could sort her note cards into four piles. One group concerned shape, another climate, a third contained information about mountains and lowlands, and a final group told of the unexpected. Here are her four groups of note cards:

Shape
1. Mexico is a long triangle pointing to South America.
2. Mexico is wide at the top and narrow at the bottom.

Climate
1. Cold mountain roads
2. Warm, humid valleys with groves of bananas, guavas, mangoes, mameys, and sapotes
3. Wet season in summer; dry season in winter
4. In the dry months, no rain falls.
5. In the wet months, the rain is so heavy that it carries the soil from the mountains.

Mountains and Lowlands

1. The mountains are breathtakingly steep and high.
2. Some peaks are wild and rugged.
3. Some mountains are planted in orderly plots.
4. Strange plants and fruits in the lowlands; hedges of cactus

The Unexpected

1. Mexico is a land of beauty, violence, and the unexpected.
2. Paricutin, a new volcano
3. One village now lies at the bottom of a lake.

In sorting her note cards, the writer also noticed two facts that were not related to her topic. She set these aside because they had nothing to do with geography:

Mexican culture is rich and varied.
The first Europeans in Mexico were the Spaniards.

The Order of Information

Once you have sorted your facts, arrange them into a logical order. Many reports are organized in order of importance. Starting with the most familiar information and ending with the least familiar material is another good way to organize. Other reports are best suited to chronological order or spatial order. For example, facts in a report on "The Growth of the Railroads" would be most logical in chronological order.

Making an Outline

Outlining is a good way to organize your notes into a working plan for your report. An outline lays out a framework for a report, showing how the facts should be arranged.

Each group of note cards becomes a major division in an outline. The key idea of the group becomes the division's main heading. It is labeled with a Roman numeral. For more information about outlines, see Section 14 in this book.

outline are based on the four groups of note cards on pages 164-165.

Discuss how the factual details under each main heading logically support and develop it. Stress that outlining is a process of discovering the best organization for a report and that outlining may well highlight the need for further research.

Have students notice the form and organization in the outline for the report "Gliders." Point out that each of the three main headings would be developed into a body paragraph in the report.

4. Assign Exercise A on page 167. When students have shown that they are familiar with outline form, assign Exercise B. Confer with each student about his or her outline, and require students to revise their outlines if necessary.

Individualizing the Lesson

Less-Advanced Students

As students group their note cards, help them to identify the common concept that ties the ideas in each group together.

Advanced Students

Have students comment on each other's outlines, checking for logical order, depth of support, and parallelism of construction.

Optional Practice

1. Have the students outline the sample composition "The Feast of Lights" on page 145.

2. To give the students practice at organizing notes, give them the following headings to arrange for a report about Elizabeth Blackwell,

America's first woman doctor. Encourage them to put the main heads and details in logical order.

Blinded while working with a patient
Elizabeth Blackwell's accomplishments
At first, denied entrance to medical school
Born in 1821 in Bristol, England
Wrote about medicine and influenced reforms
Hardships Elizabeth Blackwell overcame
Founded a hospital
Graduated from medical school
Came to the U.S. in 1832
Elizabeth Blackwell's background
Founded a medical college
Taught school before becoming interested in medicine

Extending the Lesson

With the help of students, create a checklist, similar to the Guidelines for the Process of Writing on page 59, to use specifically for the process of organizing a report. The list might include the following:

Reread note cards.
Group notes by common ideas.
List one main idea for each group of notes.
Check to see if facts are relevant and complete.
Do more research, if necessary.
Choose a logical order for development.
Organize an outline using main ideas as major headings.
Check for completeness and relevance of subheadings.
Revise the outline, if necessary.

Duplicate the checklist for all students to use when they write reports.

Example 1. Notice how the writer of "The Geography of Mexico" used an outline to structure the report.

THE GEOGRAPHY OF MEXICO

I. Shape
   A. Mexico is a long triangle pointing to South America.
   B. Mexico is wide at the top and narrow at the bottom.

II. Mountains and lowlands
   A. The mountains are breathtakingly steep and high.
   B. Some peaks are wild and rugged.
   C. Some mountains are planted in orderly plots.
   D. Strange plants and fruits grow in the lowlands.
   E. Hedges of round cactus appear in the lowlands.

III. Climate
   A. Cold mountain roads rise above warm, humid valleys.
   B. Groves of bananas, guavas, mangoes, mameys, and sapotes grow in the valleys.
   C. Summer is the wet season; winter is the dry season.
   D. In the dry months, no rain falls.
   E. In the wet months, the rain is so heavy that it carries the soil from the mountains.

IV. The unexpected
   A. Mexico is a land of beauty and violence.
   B. Paricutin is a new volcano.
   C. One village now lies at the bottom of a lake.

Did you notice that the writer arranged her facts in order of familiarity? She began with commonly known information about the shape of the country and ended with more colorful facts about the unexpected in Mexico.

Sometimes after making an outline you will see that you need more facts under a certain heading. Then it's time to return to the library to seek out new sources of information. Also check to see that the order you have chosen works well for your topic. You may want to rework your outline several times.

Example 2. Here is another outline. Notice how the facts were grouped, and the order in which they were arranged.

GLIDERS

I. Parts of a glider
   A. Wings
   B. Body
   C. Tail assembly

II. Flying a glider
   A. Launching
   B. Soaring
   C. Landing

III. History of gliders
   A. First gliders
   B. Gliding after World War I
   C. Use of gliders in World War II
   D. Gliding as a sport today
      1. Soaring contests
      2. Hang gliding

Exercises Making Outlines for Reports

A. Sort these facts into three groups under the key ideas of *awards, education,* and *achievements.* Try to decide on the order that would be best for the report. Finally, make an outline.

BEN FRANKLIN, SCIENTIST

Invented the lightning rod
Had only two years of schooling
Honorary degrees from two colleges
Invented the fuel-efficient Franklin stove
Given Copley Medal for scientific achievement
Read extensively on many subjects
Made a Fellow of the Royal Society of London
Proposed several new theories of electricity

B. Put the note cards for your own report into three or four related groups. Set aside any unrelated ideas. After you decide on the most logical order, make an outline for your report.

Objectives

1. To become familiar with the process of writing a report from an outline

2. To name sources in a bibliography

Presenting the Lesson

1. Read and discuss the introductory paragraph and **The Introduction** on page 168. Emphasize the two functions of a report's introduction, which are to tell the topic of the report and to arouse interest. Have students explain why the second sample introduction is more interesting than the first.

2. Discuss the first two paragraphs in Exercise A on pages 169 and 170 before assigning the rest of the Exercise as individual work. Point out that the first introduction, while highlighting the topic of the report, is dull and lifeless. Note that the second introduction begins with a catchy opening and then leads in to the topic of the report. Then help students to see that

  a. Paragraph three is extremely uninteresting and unimaginative. It needs an appealing opening and a less direct approach.

  b. Paragraph four is appealing because it builds suspense, uses sensory details, and then introduces the topic with a rhetorical question.

  c. Paragraph five uses captivating facts to lead into the topic of the report. The background information will help a reader to understand the report.

Part 5 First Draft: Writing from an Outline

In Chapter 8, you learned about writing a composition with an introduction, body, and conclusion. A report, like any composition, has three parts.

The Introduction

In the introduction of a report, you want to capture your audience's attention. You also want to tell what your topic is. How well do you think this paragraph introduces the report about Mexican geography?

> I'd like to tell you about the geography of Mexico. Mexico is a very interesting country. Its geography is very interesting, too, because it's so different.

The paragraph is dull and lifeless. While it introduces the topic, it doesn't catch a reader's attention as this one does:

> Mexico is a long triangle, pointing to South America. In the North it is a wide land, with many miles of cactus country between the Gulf of Mexico and the Pacific Ocean. In the South the country narrows as it meets the Central American states.

The above paragraph not only introduces the topic of the report, it also treats the factual material with a fresh approach. For example, instead of merely stating that Mexico is wide at the top, the writer notes the "many miles of cactus country between the Gulf of Mexico and the Pacific Ocean." With details such as these, she captures the reader's interest in the geography of Mexico.

You probably noticed that the introduction about Mexico uses the first group of facts from the outline. Another way of introducing a topic is with an interesting idea or a general definition.

Exercises Understanding Introductory Paragraphs

A. Decide which of the following are good introductory paragraphs. Then rewrite the other paragraphs to make them interesting introductions to the topic.

1

The first English settlers arrived in India in the early 1600's. They immediately set up colonies. Those long-ago settlements were very interesting.

2

It isn't common for a person to succeed at five careers. But back in the eighteenth century, Benjamin Franklin was respected as an author, statesman, printer, and philosopher. This brilliant man was also a scientist. His scientific inventions astounded people of his time and gave him a special place in history.

3

I'm going to write a report about solar energy. Most people don't know how it works. This report will explain it and tell what it can be used for.

4

For millions of years it glows brightly in the evening sky. Then suddenly, without warning, it fades or falls and disappears. What makes a star die? The answer is in the composition of these heavenly bodies.

5

High above the towns in western Italy sits an active volcano, Vesuvius. Over 1900 years ago that volcano erupted and buried the town of Pompeii. When scientists dug out the ruins of Pompeii, they discovered what everyday Roman life was like in A.D. 79. The frozen town of Pompeii tells the story of Roman family life, housing, and business.

6

Vitamin C is good for you. Your body needs it. You should know about how Vitamin C helps your body and makes it grow.

d. Paragraph six is terse and lifeless. It needs a more interesting opening sentence and development.

After students have completed the Exercise, have them compare their revisions in small groups and continue revising if necessary.

3. Assign Exercise B on page 170. Urge students to continue revising until their introductions are appealing.

4. Read and discuss **The Body** on pages 170-171, as well as the sample body paragraphs on these pages. Point out how each body paragraph was developed from a section of the outline on page 166. Have students identify the topic sentence and supporting facts in each paragraph.

5. Assign the Exercise on page 171. Refer students to the Guidelines for the Process of Writing on page 59, as well as the Guidelines for Writing and Revising Compositions on page 131.

6. Read and discuss **The Conclusion** on page 172. Have students compare the sample conclusion for the report on Mexican geography with the introduction. Ask students how the conclusion summarizes in a fresh way the body of the report.

7. Assign the Exercise on page 172. Remind students that a concluding paragraph should have more than one sentence.

8. Read and discuss **The Bibliography** on 172-173. Emphasize that each fact in a report must be backed up by a reliable source. Point out the following elements of form for entries for books, magazine articles, and encyclopedia articles:

1. author's name with last name first
2. period after author's name
3. comma between article name and name of reference work or magazine
4. more commas before both the volume or date and the page number, if applicable
5. period at the end of each source entry
6. underlining of book titles
7. quotation marks for article titles
8. each entry indented

9. Assign the Exercise on page 173. Tell students to consult their note cards for source information.

Individualizing the Lesson

Less-Advanced Students

Provide individual help, guiding students in developing outlined ideas into smoothly written paragraphs. Have conferences with each student to answer questions or help solve writing problems.

Students may find it helpful to write source information in the correct form on separate note cards that may be easily alphabetized before they make their final copy.

Advanced Students

Provide instruction in using transitions since a common problem in report writing is the monotonous stringing together of facts. Have students list transitional words and phrases, and require them to incorporate some in their first drafts.

B. Write the introductory paragraph to your report. Either cover point I in your outline, or write a paragraph that uses a new idea to lead into the facts in your outline.

The Body

The body of the report follows the writing plan presented in the outline. Each main division in the outline becomes a paragraph in the body. As in any paragraph, each report paragraph has a topic sentence and contains facts or details that support it. If your outline was well thought out, then each paragraph will be tightly organized.

In the report on Mexico, the introduction covered the first grouping of facts. The body paragraphs will cover the information listed under these three headings:

II. Mountains and lowlands
III. Climate
IV. The unexpected

Now read the introduction and body of the report on Mexico. The version you see is the result of several earlier drafts. Notice, too, the new, catchier title.

MEXICO: A LAND OF CONTRASTS

Mexico is a long triangle, pointing to South America. In the North it is a wide land, with many miles of cactus country between the Gulf of Mexico and the Pacific Ocean. In the South the country narrows as it meets the Central American States.

Mexico is a country of ups and downs. The mountains are breathtakingly steep and high. Some of the great peaks are wild and rugged, while others are planted in orderly plots so far up that they look like patchwork patterns against the sky. Along the lowlands, the earth grows strange plants and fruits. The cactus appears as round as a barrel, in great, fierce hedges.

The climate is up and down, too. From a cold mountain road, where pines recall Canadian forests, one may look down on warm, humid groves of bananas, guavas, mangoes, and soft mameys and sapotes, sweet and sticky. Mexico has a wet season in summer and a dry season in winter. In the dry months no rain falls, and the steep slopes become brown and gray. When the rains come, water pounds the roofs of mud huts like drumbeats and washes down the mountainsides through deep ravines in a rushing roar. The high slopes grow green, and flowers spring out all over them. The rains carry away soil from the mountains, however, and run so fast through the ravines that they do the lower slopes little good.

Mexico is a land of beauty and violence. It is a land of flowers and color, of song and brilliant birds. Snow-topped volcanoes glitter against a sky of vivid blue. Mexico is serene and beautiful, but it can also be unexpectedly violent. Only a few years ago a volcano, called Paricutin, thrust up abruptly through a farmer's field. It quickly buried a village under lava and ashes. A lake once covered a town, and the church spire may be seen by looking straight down into the water from a boat. Mexico is a land where anything can happen.

You can see that each paragraph explains a different aspect of the topic. Look back at the outline on page 166 to see how the body paragraphs follow the outline.

As you write your report, you may find yourself wanting to add, delete, or reorganize information. Do not be afraid to depart somewhat from your outline. Just make certain that the ideas are all related to your subject, and that the order of their presentation makes sense.

Exercise Writing the Body Paragraphs of a Report

Write the three body paragraphs of your report, following your outline. Make sure that each paragraph has a topic sentence.

Optional Practice

1. Have the students exchange rough drafts and try to make an outline of each other's reports. This exercise will help point out any weaknesses in content or organization.

2. Have students make bibliographies for a report on Elizabeth Cady Stanton that uses these sources:

The World Book Encyclopedia, page 659, "Elizabeth Cady Stanton," Volume 18; Ms magazine, January, 1982, pages 8-11, "Elizabeth Cady Stanton: The Freedom That Comes with Age," by Elizabeth Griffith; Elizabeth Cady Stanton, a book by Mary Ann B. Oakley.

Extending the Lesson

1. Have students find and analyze brief textbook chapters or encyclopedia articles as examples of reports. Noting that encyclopedia articles are condensed and often do not have introductions or conclusions, ask students to notice the paragraph organization and factual development of topic sentences.

Show one of the reports on the overhead projector for analysis.

2. Have the students find books that contain bibliographies. Discuss the functions of these bibliographies: to document sources of information, to lend credence to the book, and to direct interested readers to further information on the book's topic.

The Conclusion

A report, like any other composition, ends with a concluding paragraph. Even though it may not add new information, a conclusion is necessary. It not only ties the report together, but it also tells the reader "The End."

Often the conclusion of a report summarizes the ideas of the report in a new way. Because it is the last thing a reader remembers about a report, the conclusion should be fresh and vivid. The writer of "Mexico: A Land of Contrasts" ends her report this way:

> Mexico is truly a land of contrasts. It is a land of mountains and valleys, of hot and cold, of droughts and drenching rains. It is a land of bright green mountains and gray-brown deserts. Above all else, Mexico is a land where one learns to expect the unexpected.—MAY McNEER

Exercise Concluding Your Report

Write the concluding paragraph of your report. Make sure it ties the report together and provides a definite finish.

The Bibliography

In a report, you must give credit to the outside sources you used. The usual method is to name the sources at the end of the report in a section called the **bibliography.** Use the source information on your note cards.

Here is the bibliography for the report on solar energy.

Bibliography

Reed, Millard. *Solar Energy in Tomorrow's World.* 1980.
"Solar Energy," *The World Book Encyclopedia*, Volume 18, pp. 471–473.
Stepler, Richard. "Solar Electric Home I," *Popular Science*, September, 1981, pp. 52–54.

The sources listed on page 172 are a book, an encyclopedia article, and a magazine article. You can see that they are listed in alphabetical order, according to the authors' last names or the name of the article when there is no author. When you make bibliographies, follow this form.

Exercise Making a Bibliography

List sources you used in your report under the heading *Bibliography*. Use the examples on page 172 as guides. Be sure to underline the titles of books and magazines. List your sources at the end of your report, or on a separate sheet of paper, as your teacher directs.

Part 6   Revising a Report

When you have finished writing the first draft of the report, study your work carefully. Use the Guidelines on pages 59 and 131 to help you find ways to improve your writing. Make sure that you have covered your topic thoroughly and presented the information in a clear and lively manner. Rewrite the sections that need work.

Because this is a report, you must add one more step to the revision process. *Check your facts.* Make sure all dates, statistics, and other information are correct. Check to see that you have listed your sources accurately. One error of fact could make a reader question your whole report.

Once you are finished revising, make your final clean copy. Follow the form your teacher gives you. Use correct grammar, capitalization, punctuation, and spelling. Proofread this copy for errors.

Exercise Revising a Report

Read, revise, and proofread your report. Make a final copy.

Part 6

Objective

To improve a report by revising and making a final copy

Presenting the Lesson

1. Read **Revising a Report** on page 173. Show students how the Guidelines on pages 59 and 131 can help them in revising.
2. Assign the Exercise on page 173. Comment on each student's first draft after it has been proofread.

Individualizing the Lesson

Less-Advanced Students

Allow time for individual conferences during which students can ask for special help.

Advanced Students

Encourage the students to go through their report and make their word choice more precise and interesting. Introduce them to the thesaurus for help.

Optional Practice

As an exercise in fact-checking, take the students to the library. Have them check each other's accuracy.

Extending the Lesson

Have students find articles in *Time, Newsweek,* or *U.S. News & World Report* that present factual reports in an interesting way. Analyze what makes the articles effective.

Chapter 11

Clear Thinking

Chapter Objectives

1. To differentiate between statements of fact and statements of opinion
2. To recognize judgment words
3. To recognize the connotations of words
4. To recognize slanted writing
5. To check facts for accuracy
6. To make facts clear by using specific language and by citing sources
7. To avoid errors in generalization by using qualifiers and by giving evidence

Preparing the Students

Read the introduction on this page. Point out that the students are bombarded with messages daily—from newspapers, television, and radio—that attempt to persuade them to think or act in a certain way—to support a political point of view, for example, or to buy a product. How can they know what to believe? Explain that this chapter will help them recognize clear and faulty thinking in what others say and write. Then they will be able to make intelligent judgments about the accuracy of information. Also, they will be able to apply those thinking skills to their writing so that it, too, will be clear.

Additional Resources

Mastery Test—See pages 23-24 in the test booklet. Recommended for use after teaching the chapter.

Reinforcement Exercises—See page 191 in the student text.

Clear writing begins with clear thinking. Think about your ideas carefully. Be sure that they are clear and make sense. Then you will be well on your way to making yourself understood.

When you can recognize faulty thinking in yourself, you will be better able to recognize it in others. You will be able to spot faulty thinking behind what others say and write.

In this chapter you will learn how to recognize clear and faulty thinking. You will learn how to correct faulty thinking in yourself, so that it does not weaken what you say or write.

Part 1

Objective

To differentiate between statements of fact and statements of opinion

Presenting the Lesson

1. Read **What Is a Fact?** on this page. Write the definition of *fact* on the chalkboard for emphasis. Discuss the two ways facts may be true, by definition or by observation. Then ask the students if the following sentences are statements of fact. If they are facts, are they true by definition or by observation?

Horses eat oats.
Kangaroos are marsupials.

2. Read **What Is an Opinion?** on pages 176 and 177. Write the definition of *opinion* on the chalkboard. Emphasize that an opinion is a statement about the way someone *feels* about something. Give the students some additional examples of opinions:

Avocados taste great.
That dress is gorgeous!

3. Read **Examples of Facts and Opinions** on page 177. Then have each student write one statement of fact and one statement of opinion. Discuss them in class.

4. Assign and discuss the Exercise on pages 177-178.

Individualizing the Lesson

Less-Advanced Students

Do the first half of the Exercise orally.

Part 1   Fact or Opinion?

What Is a Fact?

A fact is a piece of information that can be shown to be true. The following sentence is a statement of fact.

> The Lincoln Memorial is in Washington, D.C.

A person who reads the statement can check to see if it is true. The reader could go to Washington to find out if the Lincoln Memorial is there. The reader could also find an encyclopedia article on Washington or on the Lincoln Memorial.

A fact may be true in one of two ways:

1. A fact may be true by definition, as the following sentence is.

> Trout are fish.

That sentence is a statement of fact. You can check it in a dictionary. You will find that the word *trout* is the name given to one kind of fish. Therefore, the statement "Trout are fish" is true by definition.

2. A fact may be true by observation, as this sentence is.

> Trout cannot live out of water.

You can check that statement by performing an experiment. You can get a trout, keep it out of water, and observe it to see if it lives. Scientists have already made this observation, so you don't have to make it yourself. You can look in an encyclopedia or in a book about fish to find out if the statement is true. The statement is true by observation.

What Is an Opinion?

An opinion cannot be shown to be true. The following sentence is a statement of opinion.

> Fried trout is delicious.

That statement is not a statement of fact. You may agree with it. You may not. If you were to ask everyone in your neighborhood whether fried trout is delicious, some would say that it is. Some would say that it is not. The statement cannot be proven. It cannot be checked, either by definition or by observation. It is a statement about the way someone *feels* about fried trout, not a statement of a fact about fried trout.

Examples of Facts and Opinions

Following are two sets of statements. In each set, the first two statements are statements of fact. The third is a statement of opinion.

> The moon is a satellite of the earth.
> The moon takes more than twenty-seven days to orbit the earth.
> The full moon is a beautiful sight.

> Spinach is a vegetable.
> Spinach contains Vitamin A.
> Spinach makes a tasty salad.

We all have opinions. Some of us like city life, others prefer the country or the suburbs. Some of us like to eat fish. Some don't. Our opinions are some of the things that make us different from each other. You are entitled to your opinions, but don't try to make people think that your opinions are facts.

Exercise Fact or Opinion?

Read each of the following pairs of statements. Identify each statement as *fact* or *opinion*.

1. Children spend too much time watching television. opinion
   The average child between the ages of two and five spends more than thirty-one hours a week watching television. fact

2. Franklin D. Roosevelt was elected to four terms as President of the United States. fact
   Franklin D. Roosevelt was an outstanding President. opinion

Advanced Students

Add these items to the Exercise.

9. Linda likes chocolate bars. Chocolate bars are delicious.
10. Deep-sea fishing is exciting. John prefers fishing from a pier to fishing from a boat.

Optional Practice

Have the students identify each of these statements as fact or opinion:

1. Cotton is a cooler fabric than nylon.
2. The Indy 500 is a boring race.
3. The average temperature in San Francisco is 48°.
4. College costs are rising annually.
5. Golf is an exciting sport to watch.
6. John prefers chocolate ice cream to vanilla.
7. United States senators run for six-year terms of office.
8. The average work week should be shortened from 40 to 30 hours.

Extending the Lesson

Study a newspaper with the students. Have each student find three statements of fact and three statements of opinion. Point out that statements of opinion should be more difficult to find because newspaper articles are supposed to be objective and report only facts. Explain that statements of opinion are reserved for the editorial page. An exception, of course, is a statement of opinion made by someone and quoted in a news article.

3. The average humidity in Phoenix, Arizona, is 37 percent. fact
Phoenix, Arizona, has a dry, uncomfortable climate. opinion

4. In 1976, doctors in the United States earned an average of $62,799. fact
Doctors are overpaid. opinion

5. Americans conduct more than 633 million telephone conversations every day. fact
People waste money on telephone calls when they could write letters. opinion

6. One American in ten lives in a big city with a population of a million or more. fact
Big cities are exciting places to live. opinion

7. Ty Cobb was the greatest hitter in baseball. opinion
Ty Cobb had a lifetime batting average of .367. fact

8. More than forty million foreign tourists visited the United States last year. fact
We should be doing more to attract foreign tourists. opinion

Part 2

Objective

To recognize judgment words

Presenting the Lesson

1. Read and discuss pages 178 and 179. Write the definition of *judgment words* on the chalkboard. Have the students list synonyms for the judgment words listed on page 179.
2. Assign the Exercise on page 179.

Individualizing the Lesson

Less-Advanced Students

Do the Exercise orally.

Part 2   Judgment Words

Judgment words are words that express opinions rather than give facts. Often they are adjectives, as in the following examples.

a *lazy* person   a *luxurious* home   a *clever* idea

The words *lazy*, *luxurious*, and *clever* are all judgment words. They give us someone's opinion of the person, the home, and the idea. They do not tell us facts about them.

Watch and listen for judgment words. Ask yourself whether the facts would support the opinions that the judgment words express. In your writing, be careful of the adjectives you use. Ask yourself whether your facts can be checked.

Following is a list of judgment words. Be especially careful of these words and their synonyms.

sensible	foolish	valuable	worthless
beautiful	ugly	good	bad

Exercise Judgment Words

Find the judgment word in each of the following statements.

1. Test-drive the beautiful new Hurricane Six.
2. Senator Hearst is doing an excellent job.
3. Dan wastes his allowance playing electronic games.
4. Sudsy Satin gives your hair a lovely shine.
5. Here's the tastiest coffee money can buy!

Part 3 Connotations of Words

Many words have two kinds of meanings. One kind of meaning is clear-cut and direct. This kind of meaning is given in a dictionary. It is called a word's **denotation** or **denotative meaning.** The other kind of meaning is not clear-cut. It is a meaning that is only suggested by the word. This kind of meaning comes from the ideas or feelings that a word brings to a person's mind. This suggested meaning is called a word's **connotation** or **connotative meaning.** The following pairs of examples show how important connotation can be to meaning.

fortified with essential nutrients
vitamins added

passenger-restraint system
seatbelt

living room with view
living room with one window

The connotations of words can make them work like judgment words. If vitamins are added to a cereal, the cereal has

Advanced Students

Have the students substitute another word for each judgment word in the Exercise.

Optional Practice

Have the students find each judgment word in the Exercise beginning on page 177.

Extending the Lesson

Have the students underline the judgment words used in a theater, movie, or restaurant review.

Part 3

Objective

To recognize the connotations of words

Presenting the Lesson

1. Read and discuss pages 179 and 180. Write denotation and connotation and their definitions on the chalkboard for emphasis. Explain that some words have positive, or good, connotations for most people and some have negative, or bad, connotations for most people. For each of the following neutral words, have the students suggest synonymous words or phrases with positive and negative connotations: house, thin, said, overweight.

2. Assign Exercises A and B on page 180.

Individualizing the Lesson

Less-Advanced Students

1. Discuss with the students the connotations of each name in Exercise A.

2. For Exercise B, first work with the students to find the words with strong connotations, then have them complete the Exercise independently.

Advanced Students

After the students have completed exercise A, have them think of teams, clubs, or other organizations for which the rejected names would be appropriate. For example, "The Guppies," would be appropriate for a pre-schoolers' swimming class because it suggests small fry, baby fish.

Optional Practice

Explain the meaning of *euphemism,* an expression with mild, vague connotations substituted for one thought to have offensive, harsh, or blunt connotations. Have the students substitute a euphemism for each of the underlined words or phrases.

1. Mr. Santori <u>died</u> last night.
2. The <u>garbage men</u> in our neighborhood make pick-ups twice a week.
3. Lily told a <u>lie</u> to her mother.
4. The <u>undertaker</u> led the family to the chapel.

Extending the Lesson

Have the students bring to class advertisements from magazines and discuss them. Have them point

been fortified with essential nutrients. However, the word *fortified* suggests strength and well-being, and the words *essential nutrients* emphasize the idea of good health and nutrition.

A seatbelt is a passenger-restraint system. It is something that holds a passenger in place. However, the phrase *passenger-restraint system* sounds very technical, suggesting that a lot of engineering research went into development of the product.

If you were looking for an apartment, would you be more attracted by one that was described as having a *living room with view* or one that had a living room with one window?

Exercises Connotations of Words

A. Football teams are often named for animals. Following are twelve possible names for football teams. Think about the connotations of each name. Explain why the connotations of each make it a good or bad choice as a name for a football team.

Answers may vary.

The Poodles	The Mice	The Guppies
The Hawks	The Stallions	The Mammoths
The Sharks	The Panthers	The Goats
The Hippos	The Pigeons	The Grizzlies

B. Each of these statements contains at least one word or phrase with strong connotations. Find them. Replace them with words or phrases that do not have strong connotations.

Answers will vary.

1. Johnson admitted that he had not attended last week's meeting.

2. Neighborhood residents begged to be heard.

3. Are you ready to put up with Governor Nelson for four more years?

4. Let's stop giving handouts to people who don't work.

5. Nancy boasted that she had finished in twenty minutes.

6. With this policy you will feel secure in knowing that your loved ones will never lose their home.

7. Dallas crushed the Eagles, 24–10.

8. Supporters of the tax cut have spread this propaganda all over the state.

9. We'll help you find a rewarding position with a good firm.

10. At The Country Shoppe you will find selected antique furnishings for gracious living.

Part 4   Slanting

Writing that uses the power of connotation and judgment words to influence a reader's opinions is called **slanted writing.** The term *slanting* comes from the idea that the writer "leans" toward one side of an issue. Read the following sentences. Notice that the first one states facts. The second and third are slanted in different directions.

1

A hundred people tried Sunburst toothpaste and Mintgreen toothpaste. Sixty-six thought that Sunburst tasted better. Sixty-four thought that Mintgreen cleaned teeth better.

2

A hundred people tried Sunburst toothpaste and Mintgreen toothpaste. An overwhelming majority praised new Sunburst's fresh, bright, wake-up flavor. Of course, we knew that new Sunburst had great taste. What made us especially proud was the number of people who said that Sunburst cleaned their teeth better.

3

Let's talk about Mintgreen, the toothpaste for people who really care about their teeth. In a recent test, a hundred people tried Sunburst toothpaste and Mintgreen toothpaste. An overwhelming majority thought that Mintgreen really did the job, leaving their teeth truly clean and germ-free.

out words with strong connotations. Then have the students pick a product, name it, and write an ad describing it.

Part 4

Objective

To recognize slanted writing

Presenting the Lesson

1. Read pages 181 and 182. Write the definition of *slanted writing* on the chalkboard for emphasis. Discuss the three sample paragraphs and note the use of judgment words and words chosen for their connotations. Explain that a reader must be able to recognize slanted writing in order to evaluate an issue fairly.

2. Assign the Exercise on page 182.

Individualizing the Lesson

Less-Advanced Students

Read the three reports in the Exercise aloud. Help the students see which is neutral and which are slanted. Find the examples of slanting in one of the reports together. Have the students find the examples of slanting in the remaining report independently.

Advanced Students

After the students complete the Exercise, have the students choose partners. Give each pair of students a neutral newspaper article. Have one student rewrite it with a positive slant and the other rewrite it with a negative slant. Compare the new versions. Discuss how each is slanted.

Optional Practice

Have each student write a slanted paragraph on one of the following topics. Then discuss the paragraphs in class. Find the judgment words and words with strong connotations.

1. Describe the classroom so that it seems beautiful.
2. Describe the classroom so that it seems ugly.
3. Describe a bicycle so that everyone will want to buy it.
4. Describe a bicycle so that no one will want to buy it.

Extending the Lesson

Have the students search local newspapers for examples of slanted writing. Have them consider editorials, letters to the editor, columns, and advertisements. Discuss how each item is slanted.

If you come across such statements in reading—or if you write them yourself—ask yourself which words are judgment words and which words have been chosen for their connotations. In the examples, *overwhelming*, *great*, *really*, and *truly* are judgment words. The words *fresh*, *bright*, *wake-up*, and *germ-free* have been chosen for their connotations.

Exercise Slanting

Following are three reports. Two are slanted. One is neutral. It is not slanted; it reports only the facts. Find every example of slanting in the two slanted reports. Explain how each is an attempt to influence the reader.

1

Striking school bus drivers met with the school committee today to discuss two issues. First, the drivers say that twelve buses should be replaced. Each of these buses is more than ten years old. Second, bus drivers would like to be covered by the retirement plan for other city workers. School attendance was off by 50 percent in this fourth day of the strike. Neutral

2

Striking school bus drivers hit the school committee with their demands today. First, they want the committee to spend your tax dollars on twelve luxurious new buses. Second, the drivers are calling for an enormous increase in their retirement benefits. For four long days now, they have brought education in this community to a virtual standstill. Slanted against bus drivers.

3

Striking school bus drivers today asked the school committee to consider two proposals. First, twelve old buses that need frequent repair should be replaced with newer models, which feature improved safety devices. Second, the drivers asked that they be covered by the city retirement plan, so that they will be able to enjoy their golden years without undue financial worry. School attendance has declined somewhat during the brief strike. Slanted toward bus drivers.

Part 5   Checking the Facts

Facts can be checked. As a writer and speaker, you owe it to your reader or listener to check your facts before you present them as true. An incorrect fact can embarrass you as a writer. You may base an opinion on an incorrect fact, only to have someone point out to you that your information is wrong.

Most readers are willing to give a writer the benefit of the doubt. They accept the writer's information as it is presented— as true information. An honest and careful writer makes certain that it *is* true.

Do not take facts for granted. Let's suppose that you are going to write about transportation needs in your city. You are about to write that bus fares have doubled in the last five years. Where did you get that information? Did you read it in a newspaper? Did a friend mention it to you? Do not assume that the information is correct. If you are going to state it as a fact, check it.

Before accepting information as true, ask yourself:

What is the source of this information?
Is the source reliable?

If you cannot remember the source for some information, do not think of it as a fact.

A reliable source is one that is widely recognized, qualified, and unbiased.

1. A source will be widely recognized if many people have used its information and found it to be correct. Which is likely to be a better source of information about a local election—a newspaper or a conversation you overhear while riding on a bus?
2. A source is qualified if care has been taken to learn about the subject in depth and check the facts in advance. Which is likely to be a better source of information about nutrition —a booklet written by a dietitian or a book written by a movie star?

Part 5

Objective

To check facts for accuracy

Presenting the Lesson

1. Read and discuss pages 183-184. On the chalkboard, write the two questions students should always have in their minds when writing factual material:

What is the source of this information?
Is the source reliable?

2. Carefully review the definition of a *reliable source*—one that is widely recognized, qualified, and unbiased. Discuss the three examples. Then have the students tell which source in each of the following pairs would be more reliable and why.

1. For information about a city—a chamber of commerce brochure or an article in *National Geographic*
2. For information about careers in the airline industry—a booklet published by the personnel department of an airline or an article in a newspaper
3. For information on skydiving—a person who has done it once or a book published by the National Skydiving Association

3. Assign the Exercise on page 184.

Individualizing the Lesson

Less-Advanced Students

Divide the class into two groups. Have the students in the first group check the first five statements, and

183

have the students in the second group check the second five statements.

Advanced Students

Have the students check each statement in two sources.

Reinforcement Exercise

Assign and discuss Exercise A on page 191.

Optional Practice

Have the students follow the directions for the Exercise on page 184.

1. The first shot of the Civil War was fired at Fort Sumter.
2. Abraham Lincoln was assassinated by John Wilkes Booth on April 14, 1866.
3. John Adams was George Washington's Vice-President.
4. Spirit Lake is in the state of Oregon.
5. Henry David Thoreau wrote *Walden*.

Extending the Lesson

Have each student find one statement of fact in a magazine article and check it in two sources.

3. A source is unbiased if it has nothing to gain from presenting inaccurate facts. Which is likely to be the less biased source of information about a new car—a road test in a consumer magazine or a television advertisement for the car?

As a reader or listener, you owe it to yourself to check the facts in what you read or hear before you accept them as true.

You can check facts in two ways. One way is to collect first-hand information. If someone says "Snow is falling," you can check the statement by stepping outside. Another way to check a fact is to collect second-hand information from reliable sources. If someone says, "The Indian elephant has smaller ears than the African elephant," you don't have to go to India and Africa to check the statement. You can go to the reference section of your local library. There you will find encyclopedias, almanacs, atlases, and dictionaries that will answer most of your needs in checking facts.

Exercise Checking the Facts

Following are ten statements. Check the facts in each statement. Use reliable sources. Tell what source you used to check each. Correct the statements that are incorrect.

1. Benjamin Franklin was born in Philadelphia in 1706. Boston
2. Philadelphia lies on the Delaware River. Correct
3. The Delaware River forms the border between Pennsylvania and New Jersey. Correct
4. Pittsburgh is the capital of Pennsylvania. Harrisburg
5. The population of Pittsburgh in 1970 was 1,000,000. 520,000
6. The United States Bureau of the Census was established in 1902. Correct
7. In 1902, the Wright Brothers made the first successful airplane flight. December 17, 1903
8. The Wright brothers made their first flights at Kitty Hawk, Georgia. North Carolina
9. Georgia is bordered on the east by the Atlantic Ocean. Correct
10. The Atlantic is the largest of the world's oceans. Pacific

Part 6   Making the Facts Clear

The work that goes into checking your facts will be wasted if your reader can't understand the facts you write. To make them clear, choose the most specific words you can. However, choose your words carefully. Do not choose words that say more than you can prove.

Be Specific

Words refer to people and things. A general word refers to a great number of things. A specific word refers to a small number of things. A general word may mean different things to different people. A specific word is more likely to be clear to most readers. Think about the following pairs of sentences.

> Last year Bay City grew enormously.
> Last year the population of Bay City increased by 20 percent.

> Executive suitcases have sturdy handles.
> Executive suitcases have handles that can support six times the weight of the suitcase.

In each pair of sentences, the second is more specific than the first. The phrase *grew enormously* leaves the reader wondering how much the city grew. Did it double in size? Writing that the population increased by 20 percent tells the reader just how much the city grew. The word *sturdy* may mean one thing to a person who packs shirts and socks in a suitcase. It may mean something else to a traveling salesperson who packs a suitcase with samples of plumbing supplies.

A general statement may be much like a judgment. Compare the following sentences.

> The mayor announced some small budget cuts.
> The mayor announced that the salaries of all city employees would be cut by 10 percent.

A 10-percent cut in the salaries of all city workers may be

Objective

To make facts clear by using specific language and by citing sources

Presenting the Lesson

1. Read the introduction and **Be Specific** on pages 185-186. On the chalkboard, list statistics about the class; for example, number of boys, number of girls, age range, number of people of each age, height range, number of people at each height. Then have the students write specific statements about the information. Discuss their statements.
2. Read **Give Your Source** on pages 186-187. Then pass out newspaper articles. Instruct the students to find examples of reporters' citing of specific sources.
3. Assign the Exercise on page 187.

Individualizing the Lesson

Less-Advanced Students

Do the first three items in the Exercise orally.

Advanced Students

In addition to the requirements of the Exercise, have the students cite sources that they would use to check the facts in the statements.

185

Have each student write one factual statement about one of the following topics. Remind them to be specific and to cite sources.

unemployment
rapid transit systems
inflation
nutrition
tourism
politics

small in the opinion of the writer. However, it is not likely to seem small to the workers who face it.

When you use specific words to state your information, your reader will have an exact idea of what you mean. You will be sure that you have said something that you can prove. Compare the following four statements.

1. Fifty-five percent of the students who buy lunch in our school cafeteria do not eat spinach when it is served.
2. Most students in our school do not eat spinach.
3. The students in our school don't eat green vegetables.
4. Teenagers don't like vegetables.

The first statement is the most specific. It tells us about a group of students who are clearly identified and a behavior that can be observed. The statement can be proved.

Think about ways that the other statements could be challenged.

The second statement is less specific than the first. The word *most* does not tell us how many as specifically as *fifty-five percent* does. The statement does not limit the student's behavior to the school cafeteria. Perhaps some of the students like to eat spinach at home. This statement would be harder to prove.

The third statement is still more general and would be even harder to prove. First, it suggests that all students in the school do not eat green vegetables. Second, *green vegetables* includes everything from lettuce to pickles.

The last statement would be hardest to prove. The word *vegetables* names a great many foods. Entire cookbooks have been devoted to vegetables. The word *teenagers* names more than twenty million people in the United States alone.

Give Your Source

Tell your reader where you got your information. If you do, you will show that you have gone to the trouble of checking your facts. Your reader will be able to judge whether your information is from a reliable source. Your reader will also be able to check your facts.

Each of the following statements gives a source for the information it contains.

> According to the Bureau of the Census, the population of Bay City increased by 20 percent last year.

> The school dietitian has reported that 55 percent of the students who buy lunch in our school cafeteria do not eat spinach when it is served.

Exercise Making the Facts Clear

Choose the more specific statement from each pair.

1. Phoenix, Arizona, has a dry climate.
On the average, only fifteen inches of rain falls in Phoenix in a year. more specific

2. Nature Bread contains flour, water, yeast, and salt. more specific
Nature Bread contains only natural ingredients.

3. Hernandez's campaign has received frequent coverage in the media recently.
The local paper has run stories about Hernandez's campaign for five days in a row. more specific

4. The new four-cylinder Chipmunk will save you money.
The new four-cylinder Chipmunk uses less gas than last year's model. more specific

5. The average salary for a professional football player is over 55,000 dollars. more specific
Professional athletes earn more money than most people.

6. A person can learn useful information from television.
Last night I saw a television show about whales, and learned that some whales can hold their breath for an hour. more specific

7. Foreign travel in the United States is increasing.
The number of foreign visitors to the United States doubled from 1977 to 1978. more specific

Objective

To avoid errors in generalization by using qualifiers and by giving evidence

Presenting the Lesson

1. Read the introduction on page 188. Write the definition of *generalizing* on the chalkboard for emphasis. Then have the students make generalizations about the following classroom occurrences:

> frequency of homework
> volume of homework
> frequency of tests

2. Read **Errors in Generalizing** on pages 188-189. As an example of the first type of error—not enough cases for a true pattern to show up—mention the "person on the street" interviews so common on television news shows. Usually not enough people are questioned nor are the people who are questioned representative of the entire population.

After discussing the second error in generalizing—making generalizations that are too broad—have the students correct the two example generalizations.

3. Read **Qualifying Generalizations** on page 189. After discussing qualifying words and the examples on page 189, have the students use qualifying words to correct the overgeneralizations.

4. Read **Giving Evidence for a Generalization** on pages 189-190. After reading the example, discuss

Part 7   Generalizing

When you see something happen many times, you may find a pattern. Finding a pattern in what you observe is called **generalizing.** Once you spot the pattern, you have made a **generalization.**

Public opinion polls depend on generalizing. A pollster may ask questions of a thousand people in a city of a million. The answers that the thousand people give will be taken to represent the answers that all the people would have given if they had been asked.

Suppose that you have started a small business of your own. You sell T-shirts that you have designed and made. You have two designs. One has a cartoon of a smiling cat; that other has a cartoon of a smiling dog. In the first week of selling, you sell twice as many cat shirts as dog shirts. In the second week of selling, you again sell twice as many cat shirts. The results for the third week are the same. When it is time to make some new shirts, will you make more cat shirts or more dog shirts? You will make more cat shirts, of course. You have made a generalization: "Cat shirts are twice as popular as dog shirts."

Errors in Generalizing

Mistakes in generalizing usually occur in one of two ways.

1. There may not have been enough cases for a true pattern to show up. Suppose that the public opinion poll had been based on only ten people. Would that have been enough to predict what the other 999,990 thought? Probably not.

2. The generalization may be too broad. It may try to take in more occurrences than the facts will support. Think about each of the following generalizations.

> Everybody loves a parade.
>
> April is always rainy.

These generalizations are too broad. There are people who don't like parades. There is a possibility that an area will have a very dry April. Farmers and fruit growers know that they have to be prepared for dry weather that may come when they least expect it.

Qualifying Generalizations

Generalizations become too broad when you try to make them cover *all* cases. The following words can push your generalizations too far.

always	never	nobody	all the time
everyone	every	everybody	no one

Qualifying a generalization means telling how many cases it applies to. You might qualify a generalization with words like:

sometimes	some	a few	frequently	many
rarely	most	often	infrequently	

If you do not use a qualifying word, your generalization may seem too broad even if you don't use words like *always* and *never*. Compare the sentences in each of the following pairs. Which one is an accurate generalization?

Lefty Cortez never bunts.
Lefty Cortez has tried to bunt only three times this season.

People like to drive big cars.
Some people like to drive big cars.

Jill visits her grandmother every Friday.
Jill visits her grandmother on Friday whenever she can.

Giving Evidence for a Generalization

Generalizations are useful. Without them we would see only details. We wouldn't see the patterns in life and in the way people behave. However, generalizations can be dangerous if

how the students would go about supporting this generalization: "Professional women athletes earn less than professional men athletes." Ask what kinds of facts they would look for. Also, ask if a qualifier should be added to the statement.

5. Assign the Exercise on page 190.

Individualizing the Lesson

Less-Advanced Students

Do the Exercise orally.

Advanced Students

After the students have completed the Exercise, have each student write one accurate generalization about the school.

Reinforcement Exercise

Assign and discuss Exercise B on page 191.

Optional Practice

Review the qualifying words on page 189. Also look at the words that can push a generalization too far. Then have the students add or change words in the following sentences to make each generalization accurate.

1. It never rains in California in the summer.
2. Students enjoy physical education classes.
3. Kirsten always takes the bus.
4. Everybody likes ice cream.
5. Babies like to play with their toes.

Have the students write a generalization for each of the following topics. Instruct them to avoid generalizations that are too broad.

tests	carnivals
watermelon	rainy days
clowns	medicine

we think of them as rules or as true statements that apply to every case. You can avoid this danger by telling your reader how you made your generalization. Consider the following:

> Most students in our school prefer salad to cooked vegetables at lunch. I have worked in the school cafeteria for six weeks. During that time, salads were served on twelve days. Cooked vegetables were served on eighteen days. As students turned in their dishes, I counted the number of salads that were completely eaten and the number of servings of vegetables that were completely eaten. More than 83 percent of the salads, but only 46 percent of the servings of vegetables, were eaten.

The statement "Most students in our school prefer salad to cooked vegetables at lunch" is a generalization that the reader can accept. The facts support the generalization.

Exercise Generalizing

Read each pair of statements below. Decide which of the two statements is better. Explain what is wrong with the other.

1. The average child between the ages of two and five spends more than thirty-one hours a week watching television. no evidence
   According to the 1980 *Information Please Almanac*, the average child between two and five in America spent more than thirty-one hours a week watching television during 1978. better

2. We observed pedestrians on High Street between Summer and Court Streets for six hours last Friday. Ninety-seven people crossed High Street in that area during that time. Only thirty-nine crossed within the crosswalks. We concluded that most pedestrians do not use the crosswalks on High Street. better
   Pedestrians do not use the crosswalks on High Street. no evidence

3. Americans are more concerned about inflation than any other problem. no evidence
   In yesterday's paper I read the result of a poll showing that most people think inflation is America's biggest problem. better

4. The voters of South Hargrove want Connolly for Mayor. no evidence

A majority of the voters of South Hargrove want Connolly for Mayor. better

5. In last night's game, Jackson struck out three times. better
Jackson can't hit. no evidence

Reinforcement Exercises Putting Your Thinking Skills Together

A. Tell which of the following are statements of fact and which are opinions. Tell how you would check each fact.

1. Businesses spend too much money on advertising. opinion
2. Television networks sell advertising time. fact
3. Advertising time on a popular show can be outrageously expensive. opinion
4. More than forty-three billion dollars was spent on advertising in the United States during 1978. fact
5. Approximately twenty-eight billion dollars was spent on advertising in 1975. fact
6. The increase from 1975 to 1978 was huge. opinion
7. About 27 percent of the money is spent on radio and television advertising. fact
8. Most of the rest is spent on newspapers and magazines. fact

B. Following are examples of faulty generalizing. Use a qualifying word or phrase to make each generalization accurate. Answers will vary.

1. People are interested only in their own problems.
2. Old people do not drive well.
3. People in Maine love snowy winters.
4. Everybody loves a sunny day.
5. No one in this city wants to see taxes go up.
6. Left-handed people are generous.
7. Young people do not like hard work.
8. Commuters would rather ride in private cars than use public transportation.

Chapter 12

The Library and How To Use It

Chapter Objectives

1. To understand the classification of books as fiction or nonfiction

2. To become familiar with the Dewey Decimal System of classifying nonfiction books

3. To understand the function of call numbers

4. To use the card catalog to locate books

5. To become familiar with and to use efficiently basic reference works: dictionaries; encyclopedias; almanacs and yearbooks; atlases; biographical references; the vertical file; the *Readers' Guide to Periodical Literature*

Preparing the Students

Read and discuss the introduction on page 193. If possible, arrange to begin the chapter with a trip to the school library. The librarian can review the locations of fiction books, nonfiction books, and reference books. Distribute unlabeled floor plans of the library, and have the students label the shelves and reference areas. If a trip to the school library is impossible, bring as many of the materials to the classroom as possible.

Additional Resources

Mastery Test—See pages 25-26 in the test booklet. Recommended for use after teaching the chapter.

Skills Practice Book—pages 57-62.

Duplicating Masters—pages 57-62.

Each year that you are in school, the building, your teachers, and the courses you take may change, but the uses of a library and the organization of a library will not. Each year you will be expected to be able to work more independently in the library.

The books in every library are organized by the same basic system. Of course, not all libraries have exactly the same books. For that reason it is important for you to become familiar with all of the materials offered in the library that you use.

Just how well do you know the library that you use? This chapter will help you to review what you already know about the library. The chapter will also help you make better use of the library than ever before.

Part 1

Objectives

1. To understand the classification of books as fiction or nonfiction
2. To become familiar with the Dewey Decimal System of classifying nonfiction books
3. To understand the function of call numbers

Presenting the Lesson

1. Read the introduction and **Fiction** on this page. Review the definition of *fiction*. Show the students the markings on the spines of several fiction books. Point out that if an author has written more than one book, the books are arranged alphabetically by title. Have the students arrange the following books correctly:

Charmed Life, Diana Wynne Jones
The Silver Sun, Nancy Springer
Tell Me No Lies, Hila Colman
The Spellcoats, Diana Wynne Jones
The Grey King, Susan Cooper

2. Read **Nonfiction** on pages 194-195. Review the definition of *nonfiction*. Discuss the breakdown of the Dewey Decimal System. Have the students use the chart on page 195 to answer the following questions:

In what category would you find a book about eliminating garden pests?
In what category would you find a book about mental health?
In what category would you find a book about styles of painting?

3. Read **Call Numbers** on pages 195-197. Discuss the example on

Part 1 The Classification and Arrangement of Books

Books are classified into two major groups: **fiction** and **nonfiction** books. Each group is classified in a different way.

Fiction

Fiction books contain stories that an author has imagined or invented. These books are arranged on the shelves alphabetically by the author's last name and are usually marked with an *F* for fiction on the spine.

Nonfiction

Nonfiction books are books that are true and factual. They can help you to learn about any subject. Nonfiction books are classified according to the Dewey Decimal System. This system was originated by the famed American librarian, Melvil Dewey. The Dewey Decimal System classifies all books by number in one of ten major categories:

	The Dewey Decimal System
000–099	**General Works** (encyclopedias, almanacs, etc.)
100–199	**Philosophy** (conduct, personality, psychology, etc.)
200–299	**Religion** (the Bible, mythology, theology)
300–399	**Social Science** (economics, law, education, government)
400–499	**Language** (languages, grammars, dictionaries)
500–599	**Science** (mathematics, chemistry, physics, biology, etc.)
600–699	**Useful Arts** (farming, cooking, sewing, nursing, radio, television, business, gardening)
700–799	**Fine Arts** (music, painting, acting, photography, sports)
800–899	**Literature** (poetry, plays, essays)—not fiction
900–999	**History** (biography, travel, geography)

The Dewey Decimal System is a highly organized system for classifying books. Each major section is divided into smaller categories. By looking at the list on the left below, you can see how the 900–999 History section is further divided. Each of the divisions within the 900 History category is then subdivided to become even more detailed, as in the list on the right.

900	History		970	North America
910	Geography, travel, description		971	Canada
920	Biography		972	Middle America
930	Ancient history		973	United States
940	Europe		974	Northeastern states
950	Asia		975	Southeastern states
960	Africa		976	South central states
970	North America		977	North central states
980	South America		978	Western states
990	Other places		979	States of the Great Basin and Pacific Slope

These divisions and subdivisions of the Dewey Decimal System make it possible for all of the books on one subject to be put on the library shelves together so that you can find them easily.

Call Numbers

The **call number** is an organized sequence of numbers and letters printed on the spine of a book. The call number helps you to identify a book. Books are arranged on the shelves according to the details included in their call numbers. This arrangement makes it easier for you to find the book you need. The following example identifies the parts of a call number.

Book: *Bicycling*   Call number: **796.6**
Author: Nancy Neiman Baranet   **B 225 b**

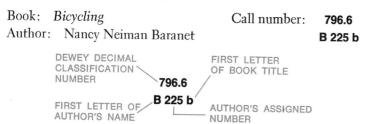

DEWEY DECIMAL
CLASSIFICATION
NUMBER ⟍ **796.6**   FIRST LETTER
                         OF BOOK TITLE
              B 225 b
FIRST LETTER OF ⟋
AUTHOR'S NAME   AUTHOR'S ASSIGNED
                     NUMBER

page 195. Have the students arrange the following call numbers in proper order.

610.73   599.03
S192f   S641z
604.2   610.73
C121d   N221b

List the special classifications on the chalkboard for emphasis.

4. Assign Exercises A, B, and C on pages 197 and 198.

Individualizing the Lesson

Less-Advanced Students

1. Read the titles in Exercise A and identify the general topic of each book. Then have the students complete the Exercise independently.

2. For Exercise B, read the titles and identify each as a biography, collective biography, or short story collection. Have the students write the call numbers independently.

3. For Exercise C, have the students find only two titles of each type.

Advanced Students

1. After the students have assigned the correct classification number to each title in Exercise A, have them arrange the titles of the books in the proper shelf order.

2. Add the following titles to Exercise B.

   9. *The Firebringer and Other Great Stories*, Louis Untermeyer
   10. *Ten Brave Women*, Sonia Daugherty

3. For Exercise C, have the students write a brief explanation of the

kind of information available in each item they select.

Optional Practice

Have the students arrange the following titles of fiction books in proper shelf order.

The Great Gilly Hopkins, Katherine Paterson
Home Before Dark, Sue Ellen Bridgers
The Slave Dancer, Paula Fox
Bridge to Terabithia, Katherine Paterson
Deenie, Judy Blume
All Together Now, Sue Ellen Bridgers
The Chocolate War, Robert Cormier
A Hero Ain't Nothin' But a Sandwich, Alice Childress

3. Have the students follow the instructions for Exercise A on page 197.

1. *The Story of a Painting,* H. W. Janson and Dora Jane Janson
2. *America,* Alistair Cooke
3. *Inside the Atom,* Isaac Asimov
4. *A History of the English Language,* G. L. Brook
5. *Africa Is People,* Barbara Nolen
6. *Shreiks at Midnight: Macabre Poems, Eerie and Humorous,* Sara and John Brewster
7. *Essays in the History of Economics,* George J. Stigler
8. *House Plants for the Purple Thumb,* Maggie Baylis

4. Have the students follow the instructions for Exercise B on page 198.

1. *The Life and Words of Martin Luther King, Jr.,* Ira Peck
2. *Score: A Baker's Dozen Sports Stories,* William MacKellar
3. *Jack London: The Pursuit of a Dream,* Ruth Franchere
4. *The Linebackers: The Tough Ones of Pro Football,* Paul Zimmerman
5. *Phineas: Six Stories,* John Knowles
6. *Bob Dylan,* Daniel Kramer

Books are first arranged by the Dewey Decimal number on the top line of the call number. Then, within each classification number, the books are arranged by the first letter of the author's last name.

Both the Dewey Decimal number and the call number identify books as precisely as possible in order to make it easier for you to find them. Within this system, there are three sections that deserve special mention:

Biography. Biographies and autobiographies are nonfiction books classified together and shelved in a special section of the library. The class numbers reserved for biography are 920 and 921.

> **920** This class number is reserved for collective biographies. These are books that contain the life stories of more than one person. The call number for a collective biography is 920, plus the initial of the author's or editor's last name.

For example: *Five Artists of the Old West* by Clide Hollmann

Call number: 920
H

> **921** This class number is used for individual biographies and autobiographies. These books are arranged differently on the shelves. They are arranged alphabetically by the last name of the *person written about.* For this reason, the call number is composed of 921 and the initial of the last name of the person the book is about. For example, the call number for a biography about Benjamin Franklin would be: 921
F

Reference Books. Reference books of particular types or on specific subjects are also shelved together, with the letter R above the classification number:
R
423.1
D56

Fiction. Fiction books are arranged on the shelves alphabetically by the author's last name. For this reason, fiction books are labeled with an *F* on the top line and the first initial of the author's last name on the second line along with the author number and the initial of the first word of the title. This is especially important when the author has written more than one book.

The Outsiders   **F**
by S. E. Hinton   **H666O**

Short Story Collections. Most libraries keep the fiction books that contain several short stories in a separate section. They are usually marked with *SC*, which stands for "Story Collection." The initial of the author's or editor's last name is placed below the SC. The books are arranged alphabetically by the author's or editor's name. Here is an example:

SC   *Journey to Another Star and Other Stories*
E   by Roger Elwood

Exercises The Classification and Arrangement of Books

A. Using the Dewey Decimal System on page 194, assign the correct classification number to each of the following.

1. *Skylab, Pioneer Space Station*, Wm. G. Helder   500–599
2. *You and Your Feelings*, Eda J. LeShan   100–199
3. *Inside Jazz*, James Lincoln Collier   700–799
4. *The Right To Remain Silent*, Milton Meltzer   300–399
5. *Understanding Photography*, George Sullivan   700–799
6. *Plays for Great Occasions*, Graham DuBois   800–899
7. *Hieroglyphs for Fun*, Joseph and Lenore Scott   400–499
8. *Insects as Pets*, Paul Villiard   500–599
9. *Dictionary of Mis-information*, Tom Beunaur   000–099
10. *We, the Chinese*, Deirdre Hunter   900–999

Extending the Lesson

1. Divide the class into ten groups, one for each Dewey Decimal category. Have each student find the titles and authors of ten books in his or her category.

2. Have the students refine the library maps they started at the beginning of the chapter by labeling each nonfiction shelf with the first and last Dewey Decimal number included in it.

B. Each of these books belongs in one of the special categories of *biography, collective biography,* or *short story collection.* After reading each title, assign it the proper call number code.

1. *Record-Breakers of the Major Leagues,* Lou Sabin
2. *Carly Simon,* Charles and Ann Morse
3. *Masters of Modern Music,* Melvin Berger
4. *The Phantom Cyclist and Other Short Stories,* Ruth Ainsworth
5. *Driven to Win: A. J. Foyt,* Mike Kupper
6. *Americans in Space,* Ross Olney
7. *Annie Sullivan, A Portrait,* Terry Dunnahoo
8. *Men and Machines; Ten Stories of Science Fiction,* Robert Silverberg

C. Go to your school library. List these headings on your paper: *Fiction, Nonfiction, Biography, Reference,* and *Magazines.* Under each heading, list three titles and authors of books and materials that you would be interested in using. Answers will vary.

Part 2 Using the Card Catalog

The **card catalog** is a cabinet of small drawers in which a card for each book is filed alphabetically in the library. In the card catalog, there are usually three cards for each book in the library: the *author card,* the *title card,* and the *subject card.* Each of these cards has the same information. However, each would be found in a different section of the card catalog. Look carefully at the following examples for the book *A Special Kind of Courage* by Geraldo Rivera.

The Author Card

If you happen to know only the name of the author and not the title of the book, you should use the card catalog to look

---

Part 2

Objective

To use the card catalog to locate books

Presenting the Lesson

1. Read the introduction on page 198. Write the names of the three kinds of cards on the chalkboard, the author card, the title card, and the subject card. Remind students of the location of the card catalog in the school library.

2. Read **The Author Card** on pages 198 and 199. Discuss the sample author card on page 199. Point out that the first line of the

up the name of the author. The author card will tell you the call number of the book you want to read. Also, the titles of all of the other books that the author has written and that are in that library will be listed on a separate card and filed alphabetically by the first word in each title. Cards for books *about* the author are filed *behind* his or her author cards. Here is an example of an author card for the book A *Special Kind of Courage:*

```
920      Rivera, Geraldo
R621

         A special kind of courage; profiles
         of young Americans.
         Illus. by Edith Vonnegut.
         Simon 1976.
                319p., illus.
            1. Courage    2. Youth—Case Studies
                          ○
```

The Title Card

When looking up the title of a book in the card catalog, remember that *A, An* and *The* do not count as first words in a title. Here is the title card for A *Special Kind of Courage:*

```
920          A special kind of courage
R621
          Rivera, Geraldo
             A special kind of courage;
             profiles of young Americans.
             Illus. by Edith Vonnegut.
             Simon 1976.
                   319p., illus.
               1. Courage    2. Youth—Case Studies
                            ○
```

card, the author's name, is in boldface type. Also note that the title of the book is not underlined or italicized and only the first word is capitalized.

3. Read **The Title Card** on page 199. Discuss the sample title card. Point out that the first line, the title, is in boldface type.

4. Read **The Subject Card** on page 200. Discuss the sample subject card. Point out the use of boldface type and capital letters for *courage* as a subject. Then have the students review all three cards. Impress on them that all of the cards include the same information; they differ only in the organization of the information.

5. Read **Cross-Reference Cards** on page 201. Discuss the example *See* and *See Also* cards. Explain that these cards do not give specific titles; they only refer the user to other subject cards.

6. Read **Guide Cards** on page 202. Explain that guide cards are like guide words in a dictionary. Only titles, authors, or subjects beginning with words that fall alphabetically between the two guide card words will be filed between the cards.

7. Assign Exercises A, B, and C on page 202.

Individualizing the Lesson

Less-Advanced Students

1. Work with the students to complete the first half of Exercise A.

2. Have each student find four of the books described in Exercise B.

3. Have each student choose only one topic in Exercise C.

The Subject Card

When you want to find resources on a particular subject, the best approach is to look up the subject in the card catalog. A subject card for the book A *Special Kind of Courage* will be found under the heading *Courage*, as in the following example:

```
920     COURAGE
R621
              Rivera, Geraldo
                   A special kind of courage;
              profiles of young Americans.
              Illus. by Edith Vonnegut.
              Simon 1976.
                   319p., illus.
              1. Courage    2. Youth—Case Studies
                        ◯
```

Notice that all three types of catalog cards (author, title, subject) give the same information. This information includes the following:

1. The call number.

2. The title, author, publisher, and date of publication.

3. The number of pages and a listing of special features, such as illustrations, index, maps, etc.

Often the card will also provide a brief description of the material in the book and a listing of other catalog cards for the book. Pay particular attention to the use of capitalization on the catalog cards. Only proper names and the first word of the title are capitalized. To find the title, look at the entry immediately following the author's name.

Cross-Reference Cards

When you look up a subject you will sometimes find a card that reads *See* or *See also*. The "See" card refers you to another subject heading in the catalog that has the information you want. For example, this "See" card tells you that the library catalogs all books on cars under the subject heading of *transportation*.

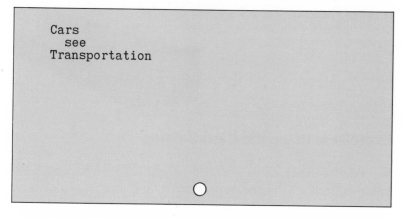

```
Cars
    see
Transportation
```

The "See also" card refers you to other subjects closely related to the one you are interested in. This card will help you to find a variety of information on the topic. A "See also" card will look like this:

```
        COOKING
            see also
    Appetizers
    Barbecue cookery
    Casserole cookery
    Food as gifts
    Frying
    Microwave cookery
    Salads
    Sandwiches
    Soups
    also names of individual foods, e.g., Rice
```

Guide Cards

Guide cards are placed in the card catalog to help guide you to the correct place in the alphabet for the word you are looking for. These cards extend above the other cards, and they have letters or general headings on them. For example, if you were looking up *housing* in the catalog drawer, you would look between the guide cards *Hob* and *How*.

Exercises Using the Card Catalog

A. What subject cards would give you information about the following topics? Discuss your answers in class. Answers will vary.

1. How to make a film
2. Backpacking in Maine
3. Records of the Super Bowl
4. Careers in medicine
5. How to play tennis
6. Designing stained glass
7. The early history of soccer
8. How to refinish furniture

B. Use the card catalog to find the title, author, call number, and publication date of each of the following books. Answers will vary.

1. A book about rock music
2. A book of detective stories
3. A book about Pelé
4. A book about astronomy
5. A book on flags
6. A book of Christmas plays
7. A book about aquariums
8. A book about newspapers

C. Using the card catalog, list the title, author, call number, and publication date of all resources about two of the following:
Answers will vary.

1. Babe Didrikson
2. A career as a cartoonist
3. Hank Aaron
4. Franklin D. Roosevelt
5. Space exploration
6. A career as a dentist

Part 3 Using Reference Materials

Every library has either a reference room or a reference section. It is here that you will find a variety of reference materials, including dictionaries; encyclopedias; pamphlets, handbooks, and catalogs; almanacs and yearbooks; atlases; biographical reference books; and magazines. Each of these reference books is used for a certain purpose, and each has its own particular organization. Some offer you very general information about a topic while others are very specific and detailed.

Learning to use the many different reference books that are available will enable you to find the detailed, up-to-date information you need for a thorough report on any subject.

Dictionaries

General Dictionaries. The dictionary is one of the best and most convenient general references you can use. A dictionary gives you the spelling, pronunciation, and meanings of a word, as well as brief information about such subjects as people, places, abbreviations, and foreign terms.

Unabridged Dictionaries. These are the largest and most complete dictionaries. They contain well over 250,000 words, and give the complete history of each word and every definition and use for that word.

Abridged Dictionaries. These dictionaries are often called "desk" or "collegiate" dictionaries. They contain about 130,000 to 150,000 words. They contain the information you would normally need about spellings, pronunciations, definitions, and matters of usage. In addition, they usually provide special sections that contain such information as biographical and geographical references.

On the next page is a list of frequently used abridged dictionaries.

Part 3

energy, ballooning, cartooning, dinosaurs, England, Formosa, gnu, helium, Iceland, judo, karate, lace, Monroe Doctrine, neon, oil, protozoa, quicksand, railroads, skiing, Tolstoy, uranium, volcanoes, weasels, X-rays, yucca plants, zoology.

4. Assign Exercises A and B on page 206.

5. Read **Almanacs and Yearbooks** on page 207. Distribute several for the students to examine.

6. Read **Atlases** on pages 207-208. Distribute several for the students to examine.

7. Read **Biographical References** on page 208. Distribute several for the students to examine. Read a sample entry.

8. Assign Exercises A and B on pages 208-209.

9. Read **The Vertical File** on page 209. Show the students a sample folder and discuss the information it contains.

10. Read **Readers' Guide to Periodical Literature** on page 210. Then discuss the excerpt from the *Readers' Guide* on page 211.

11. Assign Exercises A and B on page 210.

Individualizing the Lesson

Less-Advanced Students

1. For Exercise A on page 206, read each question aloud and discuss whether the students should use a dictionary or an encyclopedia to find the answer. Have the students complete the exercise independently.

2. Read the questions in Exercise B on pages 206 and 207 aloud.

General Dictionaries

The American Heritage Dictionary of the English Language
The Random House Dictionary of the English Language
Thorndike-Barnhart Dictionary
Webster's New World Dictionary of the American Language

Pocket Dictionaries. These dictionaries are very limited in the number of words they contain. They should be used mainly to check the spelling of ordinary words or to give you a quick definition of an unfamiliar word.

Dictionaries About Your Language. Another group of dictionaries contains information about specific aspects of the English language, such as synonyms, antonyms, rhymes, and slang. These dictionaries have limited but specific uses.

Abbreviations Dictionary
Brewer's Dictionary of Phrase and Fable
A Dictionary of Slang and Unconventional English
A Dictionary of Word and Phrase Origins (3 volumes)
Mathew's Dictionary of Americanisms
The New Roget's Thesaurus in Dictionary Form
The Oxford Dictionary of English Etymology
Roget's International Thesaurus
Wood's Unabridged Rhyming Dictionary

The *thesauruses* that are included in the language dictionary list above serve a special purpose. A **thesaurus** is a dictionary of words that have similar meanings. It is sometimes called a dictionary of synonyms. By using a thesaurus when you write, you will be able to use words that convey the exact meaning you need, and you will avoid repeating already overused words.

Dictionaries on Specific Subjects. There are also many dictionaries that deal with specific subjects, such as music, geography, medicine, and science. The following list includes the names of many of these dictionaries. There are far too many to list here, so check to see what your library offers.

Specific-Subject Dictionaries

Compton's Illustrated Science Dictionary
Dictionary of American History (5 volumes)
Dictionary of Sports
Harvard Dictionary of Music
An Illustrated Dictionary of Art and Archaeology
Mathematical Dictionary
Webster's Biographical Dictionary

Encyclopedias

An encyclopedia contains general articles on nearly every known subject. This information is organized alphabetically into volumes. There are guide words at the top of each page to help you find information. Each set of encyclopedias also has an index, which you should check before looking for your information. The index is usually in the last volume of the encyclopedia. The following encyclopedias are used frequently by young people.

General Encyclopedias

Collier's Encyclopedia (24 volumes)
Compton's Encyclopedia (26 volumes)
Encyclopaedia Britannica (29 volumes)
Encyclopedia Americana (30 volumes)
World Book Encyclopedia (22 volumes)

The library also has many encyclopedias that contain information on specific subjects. Here are some of them:

Encyclopedias on Specific Subjects

The Baseball Encyclopedia
Better Homes and Gardens Encyclopedia of Cooking

Have each student choose five of the questions to answer.

3. Have each student answer five of the questions in Exercise A on pages 208 and 209.

4. Assign each student two of the questions in Exercise B on page 209.

5. Do Exercise A on page 210 in class. Have a volume of the *Readers' Guide* on hand for the students to consult.

6. Do Exercise B on page 210 in class.

Advanced Students

1. Add these questions to Exercise A on page 206.

11. What is the history of the word *sabotage*?
12. What incident started the First World War?

2. After the students have answered the questions in Exercise B on pages 206 and 207, have them use each italicized word in sentences 1, 5, and 7 in an original sentence.

3. Add these questions to Exercise A on pages 208 and 209.

11. Who won the World Series in 1969?
12. What is the highest mountain in the world?
13. What is the population of Liverpool, England?
14. What film won the Academy Award for best picture in 1957?

4. After the students have completed Exercise B on page 209, have them write questions of their own that can be answered by using a biographical reference. Collect the students' questions and distribute them at random. Have each student answer the question he or she receives.

5. After the students have completed Exercises A and B on page 210, have each student use the *Readers' Guide* to find two articles on a topic that interests him or her.

Optional Practice

1. Have the students follow the instructions for Exercise B on page 206.

1. Where would a person search for an *ibex*?
2. Name five synonyms for *silent*.
3. If your home has a *riparian* setting, what is it near?
4. Use the word *onus* in a sentence.
5. What is the origin of the word *lacrosse*?
6. Would you find a *felucca* in the air, on land, or in the water?
7. Does *queue* sound like *cue* or *key*?
8. Name four synonyms for *importance*.

2. Have the students use an almanac to answer the following questions:

1. How many times has Miss Illinois won the Miss America contest?
2. How many immigrants were admitted to the United States from 1881–1890?
3. In what conference is the San Francisco 49'ers football team?
4. What was the U.S.S.R.'s best year for wheat and rice production?
5. How many Democrats were in the House of Representatives during the 96th Congress?
6. What is the name of the Stanford University football team?
7. Who won the 1978 Indianapolis 500 auto race?
8. What is the population of the country of Liechtenstein?

The Encyclopedia of American Facts and Dates
Encyclopedia of Animal Care
Encyclopedia of Careers and Vocational Guidance
Encyclopedia of World Art (15 volumes)
Family Life and Health Encyclopedia (22 volumes)
The Illustrated Encyclopedia of Aviation and Space
The Mammals of America
Popular Mechanics Do-It-Yourself Encyclopedia
     (16 volumes)

This list is by no means complete. You should check your library to see the many kinds of encyclopedias that are available.

Exercises Using the Dictionary and the Encyclopedia

A. To answer the following questions, first determine whether you should use a dictionary or an encyclopedia. Then answer each question, and list the title of the reference book you used. Answers not given will vary.

1. How many different kinds of rhinoceroses are there? five
2. Where are these three colleges: *Monmouth,* Illinois, 1853 *Hollins,* Virginia, 1842 *Simpson?* Iowa, 1860 Which is the oldest? Hollins
3. How many different methods of gold mining are there? three
4. When was the French painter Henri Matisse born? 1869
5. Where exactly is the Mason-Dixon line? boundary between Pennsylvania and Maryland
6. How are diamonds mined?
7. What are the chief events in the life of Neil Armstrong?
8. What are four synonyms for the word *meager*? scanty, scant, spare, sparse
9. How do you draw the symbol for the Greek word *delta*? Δ
10. Who discovered the Hawaiian Islands? Captain James Cook

B. Using either your dictionary or thesaurus, answer the following questions. Write the name of the resource you used after each answer. Answers will vary. Examples are provided.

1. Would you use a *serigraph* to cook dinner, or would you hang it on your wall? silk screen

2. What are five synonyms for the word *serious?* grave, solemn, sedate, earnest, sober

3. From what language is the word *aardvark* derived? What does the translation of the word mean? Afrikaans, earth pig

4. What are four synonyms for the word *wet?* What is an appropriate noun for each synonym to describe? damp room, dank fog, moist air, humid day

5. Do you have a *palaestra* at your school? gymnasium

6. What are five antonyms for the word *noisy?* quiet, silent, still, hushed, noiseless

7. If you were a *plebe,* what would you be? a member of the freshman class

8. Does *quay* rhyme with *day, me,* or *buoy?* me

9. What is the monetary value of a *krone?* .177 in U.S. currency

10. What words could replace the italicized words to make the following sentence more interesting? Answers will vary.

He put on his *hat* and walked away *quickly.*

He put on his beret and walked away jauntily.

Almanacs and Yearbooks

Almanacs and yearbooks are published annually. They are most useful sources of information, facts, and statistics on current events and historical records of government, sports, entertainment, population, and many other subjects. The information in an almanac is not arranged in any particular order, so you will have to consult the index and the table of contents to find the location of the information you need. Here is a partial list of the most widely used almanacs and yearbooks:

Guinness Book of World Records
Information Please Almanac, Atlas, and Yearbook
World Almanac and Book of Facts
World Book Yearbook of Events

Atlases

An atlas is a reference book that contains many large, detailed maps of the world. It also contains other geographical information, such as statistics about population, temperatures, oceans, and rainfall. Some atlases publish other information,

3. Have the students use an atlas to answer the following questions:

1. Where is Aruba?
2. What is the longest river in the world? Where is it located?
3. What is the highest mountain in North America?
4. What countries border Colombia, South America?
5. What desert is on the border of Mongolia and China?
6. What is the capital of Iceland?
7. What states border Kentucky?
8. In what body of water is the island of Madagascar located?

4. Have the students use biographical references to identify each of the following people:

Margaret Mead
Chuck Yeager
Milton Friedman
Jane Goodall
Edward R. Murrow
Nancy Lopez

Extending the Lesson

1. Have the students make an annotated catalog of all of the reference materials in the library. Divide the class into groups, one for dictionaries, one for encyclopedias, one for almanacs and yearbooks, one for atlases, one for biographical references, and one for magazines. Have each group list the title of each book or other resource, tell how the resource is arranged, and briefly describe the type of information each includes. Compile the information, reproduce it, and give a copy to each student.

2. Teach the students the proper form for a bibliography. Then explain that they are going to put all of the skills they have learned about the library to work. Have each student choose a topic and find five books, five reference works, and five magazine articles that contain information on the topic. The product of each student's research will be a bibliography including these sources.

so it is a good idea to study the table of contents and any directions given to the reader before you try to use an atlas. The following is a list of reliable atlases:

Atlas of World History
The Britannica Atlas
Collier's World Atlas and Gazetteer
Goode's World Atlas
National Geographic Atlas of the World
Webster's Atlas with Zip Code Directory

Biographical References

Both a dictionary and an encyclopedia will give you information about people. However, the best references to use when you need detailed information about a person are biographical references. They are specific subject books that deal only with information about people. Here are a few.

Contemporary Authors
Current Biography
Dictionary of American Biography
The International Who's Who
Who's Who
Who's Who in America
Who's Who in the West
Who's Who of American Women

Exercises Using Almanacs, Atlases, and Biographical References

A. Use both an almanac and an atlas to answer the following questions. List the reference you used after your answer.

Caspian Sea   1. What is the largest lake in the world?

"What hath God wrought!"   2. What were the first words sent over the telegraph?

Francis Bellamy   3. Who wrote the Pledge of Allegiance to the flag?

1,315 feet   4. What is the depth of the Dead Sea?

5. What are the three largest islands in the Mediterranean Sea? Sicily, Sardinia, Cyprus

6. What is the address for the League of Women Voters? 1720 M Street, N.W., Washington, D.C. 20036

7. How long is a day on the planet Jupiter? ten years

8. What are the world's highest and lowest elevations? Mt. Everest, 29,028 feet; Dead Sea, 1,286 feet below sea level

9. What is the most popular breed of dog in the United States? Answers will vary by year. 1982-poodles.

10. What is the distance from the earth to the moon? 238,857 miles

B. Using a biographical reference, answer the following questions. After each answer, list the title of the reference you used to answer the question.

1. For what two things was Philip K. Wrigley famous? Owner of chewing gum business and of Chicago Cubs baseball team.

2. For what is Bruce Jenner famous? Where and when was he born? Won the Olympic decathlon in 1976; October 28, 1944; Mt. Kisco, New York.

3. What well-known book did Harper Lee write? Who starred in the movie version? To Kill a Mockingbird; Gregory Peck

4. For what newspaper does Bob Woodward write? In what historical event was he involved? Washington Post; Watergate

5. Jacques Cousteau is the co-inventor of what device? Aqua-lung

6. What are the titles of three books written by Ray Bradbury? Answers will vary.

7. How old was Dorothy Hamill when she won her Olympic Gold Medal? nineteen

8. Where and when was Bessie Smith born? 1895; Chattanooga, Tennessee

9. What is the name of a play written by Paul Zindel? The Effects of Gamma Rays on Man-in-the-Moon Marigolds or And Miss Reardon Drinks a Little

10. Who is Robyn Smith? a woman jockey

The Vertical File

Many libraries have a file cabinet in which they keep an alphabetical file of pamphlets, catalogs, handbooks, booklets, and clippings about a variety of subjects. Always check this vertical file when you are writing a report or looking for information, especially on careers.

Readers' Guide to Periodical Literature

The *Readers' Guide to Periodical Literature* is a monthly index of magazine articles listed alphabetically by subject and author. It is issued twice a month from September to June, and once a month in July and August. An entire year's issues are bound in one volume at the end of the year. There are two forms of the *Readers' Guide*. The unabridged edition indexes over 135 magazines and is used in high school and public libraries. The abridged edition of the *Readers' Guide* indexes 45 magazines and is generally used in junior high school libraries.

The *Readers' Guide* is a valuable source of information. It is important to read the abbreviation guide in the preface so that you will understand how to read each entry.

Exercises Using the *Readers' Guide*

A. Write the meanings of the following abbreviations used in the *Readers' Guide*:

Lib J	no	Je	Spr	bi-w	bibl	w
abr	m	cont	+	tr	il	supp

B. Use the excerpt from the *Readers' Guide* on page 211 to answer the following questions:

1. What magazines have articles on the subject of salt?
2. What issue of *Antiques* carried an article on the Boston Museum of Fine Arts? Was the article illustrated?
3. On what page of *Glamour* did the article "How to Ask for—and Get—a Raise" appear? In what issue did the article appear?
4. Who wrote an article on "How Not to Crumble under Criticism"? In what magazine did the article appear?
5. Give the complete magazine title for the following abbreviations:

> N Y Times Book R   Field & S   Good H

A.

Row 1:	Row 2:
Library Journal	abridged
number	monthly
June	continued
Spring	continued on later pages of same issue
bi-weekly	
bibliography	translated
weekly	illustrated
	supplement

B.

1. *Good Housekeeping, Seventeen, Science*
2. August, 1980. Yes.
3. 98. July, 1980.
4. Carol Saline. *Redbook*.
5. *New York Times Book Review*
   Field & Stream
   Good Housekeeping

Excerpt from the *Readers' Guide*

SALARIES

How to ask for—and get—a raise [women's salaries] — name of article
S. S. Fader. il. Glamour 78:98 Jl '80

SALES promotion

See also — "see also" cross-reference
Trading stamps

SALESMEN and salesmanship

Boss as pitchman (chief executives appearing in commercials) A. M. Morrison. il. Fortune 102: 66-70+ — volume number
Ag 25 '80

New life of a salesman [L. J. Manara of American Cyanamid Company] H. D. Menzies. il por Fortune 102: — name of magazine
172-4+ Ag 11 '80

On the road with a book salesman. N. R. Kleinfield. il
N. Y. Times Bk R 86:3+ Ag 24 '80

SALESWOMEN

Cashing in on your spare time. G. L. Wohlner. McCalls
107:32+ Ag '80

SALINE, Carol — author entry

How not to crumble under criticism. il Redbook
155:19+ Ag '80

SALISBURY, Harrison E.

Code the Times can't crack [excerpt from Without fear or favor] Wash M 12:20-7 Jl/Ag '80 — page reference

SALMON, Larry

Textiles at the Museum of Fine Arts, Boston. bibl il
Antiques 118:278-84 Ag '80

SALMON

Is capelin key to salmon problems? [Atlantic salmon]
J. Gibbs. il Outdoor Life 166:38 Ag '80

SALMON fishing — subject entry

Coho caper [stocking New Hampshire's Great Bay] S. J.
Bodio. il por Outdoor Life 166:54-7 Ag '80

Dreamer. G. Hill. il Field & S 85:20+ Ag '80

SALT

Food-lover's guide to salt. Good H 191:164+ Ag '80 — date of magazine

SALT in the body

Go easy on sugar and salt! E. Scott. Seventeen 39:26+ — author of article
Ag '80

Sodium-induced elevation of blood pressure in the anephric state. P. Hatzinikolaou and others. bibl f il — illustrated article
Science 209:935-6 Ag 22 '80

SALT water fishing

Salt water. L. Kreh. See issues of Outdoor life — "see" cross-reference

Chapter 13

Study and Research Skills

How many times have you wished that there were more hours in a day? Sometimes it seems impossible to fit school, homework, special projects, and other activities into twenty-four hours and still have time to eat and sleep.

There is little you can do about the length of the day or the number of hours you need to sleep. There are, however, some special skills you can learn that can help you make the most of the time that you have left. By learning to use study and research time efficiently, you can soon be working more quickly, and with better results.

In this chapter, you will learn how to study, how to organize your work time, and how to approach different assignments most effectively. These study and research skills will be useful to you in all phases of your school work, and in several other areas as well.

Chapter Objectives

1. To understand and record assignments and directions
2. To choose a study area
3. To learn to organize study time
4. To become familiar with the SQ3R study method
5. To know how to take notes for research, on reading assignments, and in class
6. To know how to use three different types of reading
7. To understand how to read and interpret graphic aids
8. To recognize and prepare for different kinds of tests

Preparing the Students

Ask the students to name several problems they encounter when completing assignments or taking tests. Such problems may include difficulty in recording or following directions, problems with planning time, poor study habits, or nervousness. Tell students that Chapter 13 will help them to learn methods for overcoming these problems, and will help them improve their work on assignments and tests.

Read and discuss this page. Stress the benefits of good study skills and point out that they can apply to all school subjects.

Additional Resources

Mastery Test — See page 27 in the test booklet. Recommended for use after teaching the chapter.

Skills Practice Book — pages 63-65.
Duplicating Masters — pages 63-65.

Part 1

Objective

To understand and record assignments and directions

Presenting the Lesson

1. Read and discuss pages 214-216. Stress the importance of understanding an assignment and of learning to ask clarifying questions when necessary. Review the four questions on page 214.

Ask students for examples of directions they follow each day that are not related to school. Then have them explain the special skills needed for following oral directions and written directions successfully.

2. Assign the Exercise on page 215. If students are using the guidelines **How To Follow Written Directions,** they will soon realize that no writing is called for.

3. Read **Keeping An Assignment Book** on page 216. Stress the importance of recording assignments accurately.

Have students examine the sample assignment notebook on page 216. Point out that such a book would enable the student to do his or her work correctly and on time. If students do not already have assignment books, encourage them to begin using them.

4. Assign the Exercise on page 216. Read aloud each set of directions, and have the students record the assignment on a mock assignment book page. Have the students exchange papers to check for the following: subject, assignment details, date given, and due date.

Part 1 Understanding the Assignment

Before you begin any assignment, make certain that you know the answers to these four questions:

1. *What kind of assignment is it?* Should you be writing, reading, sorting, constructing, observing, or reviewing?
2. *What should my final product be?* Should the end result be a report, a speech, or answers to questions?
3. *What resources will I need?* Is the textbook sufficient? Will you need to go to the library? Are there any special supplies or equipment that you need?
4. *When is the assignment due?* How long will it take to complete? How will you organize the work in order to complete it on time?

Following Directions

The answers to the questions listed above can usually be found in the directions you are given for the assignment. The directions may be oral or written. If they are oral, use the following guidelines:

How To Listen to Directions

1. Concentrate only on what is being said.
2. Notice how many steps are involved.
3. Associate a key word with each step, such as *Read, Answer,* or *Write.*
4. Ask questions to clarify any step you do not understand.
5. Repeat the directions and then write them down.

You must learn to follow other kinds of directions as well. Suppose, for example, that you are following a recipe in a cookbook, or reading the steps of a laboratory experiment. In each case you would need the skill of following written directions. You can improve your ability to follow written directions by remembering the following steps:

How To Follow Written Directions

1. Read all the directions completely before you start to carry any out.
2. Ask questions to clarify any points not covered in the directions.
3. See what materials you will need, and assemble them before you begin.
4. Look over any diagrams or illustrations that go with the directions.
5. Decide on the best order in which to proceed.
6. Notice any special information.
7. Reread each step before you actually do it.

Exercise Reading Directions

Use the steps you have learned to follow this set of directions.

1. Write down the number of letters in your first name.
2. Add to that the number of letters in your last name.
3. Double the result and add your age to it.
4. Omit step three if you are left-handed. Instead, add 25 to the result of step two.
5. Subtract the answer to step three from the current year if you are right-handed.
6. Remember, if you are reading the directions correctly, you should be reading all six before you begin following them. Now, write your name and ignore directions 1–5.

Individualizing the Lesson

Less-Advanced Students

1. Review the definitions of *resources* and *final product*. Have the students write answers to the four questions on page 214 for each assignment in the Exercise on page 216.

2. Give the students practice in following directions. Have the students bring several textbooks to class, or use assignments they have recorded in other classes. Go over directions to various activities and exercises, stressing the following:

the kind of assignment
the final product called for
the resources needed to complete
the assignment

Advanced Students

1. Ask the students to define each of these key words often used in assignments: *analyze, evaluate, interpret, review, identify, compare, contrast, diagram, report, record, summarize,* and *outline.* Have them compile these and any other words they think of into an assignment glossary. These glossaries may be prepared for distribution to the entire class.

2. Point out that the clearer directions are, the easier it is for someone to follow them. Have students write directions for some simple activity. Refer them to **Paragraphs That Give Instructions** on page 99.

Optional Practice

1. Ask the students to record all the directions they are given in one day, both in and out of school. Tell them not to overlook directions from

parents or in materials such as game booklets or computer instructions.

2. Ask the students to record the following sample assignments in a mock assignment book and to write one clarifying question for each:

1. "For tomorrow, answer the Review questions at the end of Chapter 5 in your social studies book."
2. "On Thursday, bring to class a picture or photograph of a healthful meal."
3. "Make an outline of Chapter 4 in the science book for Friday."
4. "Write a paragraph describing your morning activities. Turn in your final copy on Wednesday."

3. Have the students practice listening to oral directions by first reviewing **How To Listen to Directions** and then following these three-step directions after you read them aloud. Do not repeat an instruction.

Write down your age, add 8, and divide the sum by 3.

Draw a tree, in it draw a bird, and above it make a star.

Write your name, cross out the first letter, and add that letter plus -ay to the end of your name.

You might have students make up their own three-step directions and present them to the class.

Extending the Lesson

Have the students find and bring to class magazine articles that tell how to do something, such as make a sand sculpture, change a tire, or create a submarine sandwich. Ask them to identify the materials needed and the key steps. Then have the students present their information to the class.

Keeping an Assignment Book

Most of your assignments will be given orally in class. You won't be able to remember every detail of every assignment you are given. Therefore, get in the habit of writing down each one immediately. Record the information in a separate assignment book or in a special section of your notebook.

Include the following details about each assignment:

1. The name of the subject
2. The details of the assignment
3. The date the assignment was given
4. The date the assignment should be completed

You might want to divide each page of your assignment book into columns and use headings such as those shown below.

	Subject	Assignment	Date Given	Date Due
◯	History	① Read pp. 210-217	11-8	11-9
		② Book report - Civil War content 300 words. Include summary of story and opinion on how facts are presented.	11-8	11-24

Exercise Recording Directions

Prepare a sample page of an assignment book. Record the necessary details from these directions.

1. "Complete the activities on page 56 of your math book by tomorrow. Your test will be the day after tomorrow."

2. "Tonight read the story by Ruth Ainsworth in your literature book. Write the answers to the questions at the end of the story. Be prepared to discuss your answers tomorrow."

3. "Beginning today, keep a list of the fruits and vegetables you eat daily. Bring your list to class a week from today when we will begin the unit on food in our health books."

Part 2 Developing Good Study Habits

You will find that you can complete your assignments much more quickly and easily if you learn how to study effectively. This involves learning how to make the most efficient use of your time and skills.

Finding a Place To Work

You will find that you work much better if you have a regular place to use for a study area. If you work at home, use the following guidelines to set up your work area.

1. Choose a quiet location. Avoid such distractions as the telephone, radio, and TV.
2. Make sure your work area is well lit and comfortable. It should not be so comfortable, however, that you will find it easier to daydream than to concentrate.
3. Keep such tools as a dictionary, paper, notebook, and pens close at hand so that you can work without interruption.

If you cannot find such a space at home, you may want to get into the habit of working in school or at the library.

Learning To Set Goals

You will continually be balancing daily assignments with more involved, long-term projects. If you organize your time well, however, you will have no trouble completing all of your assignments by their due date. The key to planning your time is learning to set long- and short-term goals.

At the end of each day, look over your assignment book. Determine which assignments have to be completed overnight. Make these your **short-term goals.** Establish a regular block of time each day for completing these assignments.

Objectives

1. To plan a study area
2. To understand how to organize time

Presenting the Lesson

1. Read and discuss pages 217-219. Ask the students to think of the places in their homes and in school that are best for study.

2. Have the students distinguish between short-term goals and long-term goals and to give examples of each. Then present this long-term project: Make a notebook that summarizes and illustrates ten Greek myths.

Ask the students to break this project into smaller tasks. Help them to see that they would have to read myths, select ten, write summaries, revise and make final copies of their summaries, search for photographs or draw pictures, and compile all their work in a notebook. Discuss the amount of time they would need to allot for each step.

Have students examine the sample schedule on page 219. Point out that it accommodates the long-term report assignment, as well as regular activities. Have students explain why such schedules are beneficial.

3. Assign Exercise A on page 219. Discuss the answers afterwards with the class.

4. Assign Exercise B. Tell the students to use the two-week schedule on page 219 as a model. After the students have completed their schedules, write these steps on the board. See if the students have also

217

identified these tasks and allowed enough time for each.

Find a novel.
Read the book.
Plan and organize the report.
Write a first draft.
Revise and proofread the draft.
Make a final copy.

Individualizing the Lesson

Less-Advanced Students

1. Help the students to plan schedules that show their regular activities and daily homework time. Help the students to identify the steps involved in the assignment explained in Exercise B before they complete the Exercise independently.

2. Discuss the first two sample assignments of Exercise A with the students before they complete the rest independently. Make sure they can identify the following:

the kind of assignment
the final product called for
the resources needed

Advanced Students

Have the students make study plans for the next two weeks that incorporate all their regular activities, homework time, and the steps involved in long-term projects that have been assigned in class.

Optional Practice

After the students are certain that they understand the following assignments, have them identify the steps involved in each and incorporate them into a study plan.

1. Choose ten poems on the same topic and compile them in a notebook together with illustrations and biographies of the poets. The notebooks are due in two weeks.

Some types of assignment cannot be completed overnight. You must approach these differently. First, recognize that each long project is made up of several steps. Each one of these steps may take a few days to complete. With such an assignment, finishing the entire project by the due date is your **long-term goal.** Each of the steps you must complete to finish the project becomes a short-term goal.

It is up to you to identify the smaller steps, or tasks, and decide how much time is needed to complete each one. For instance, suppose you are writing a report on hummingbirds. Your first step will be getting to the library to begin your research. Once you find your research sources, you must read and take notes. This step alone may take several days. Next, you must organize your notes and put them in outline form. After that, you will work on your first draft, and then spend time revising it. Finally, you will write your final, clean copy. Obviously, you must plan ahead to allow yourself time to complete each step.

Making a Study Plan

In order to organize your time so that you can achieve both your long- and short-term goals, learn to make study plans. A study plan is simply a means of scheduling the various tasks you have to complete.

To meet your short-term goals, establish a regular block of study time. Begin by examining your daily schedule. What regular chores and activities occupy your time after school each day? When is the best time for you to study? Is there time during the school day when you can work? It may take you a few weeks to set up a workable, practical study schedule. But once you do, keep the schedule until it becomes a habit.

The smaller tasks for a long-term assignment must fit into this schedule, too. Look once more at the steps that would be required for the report discussed on page 218. Notice how one student fit these tasks into a two-week schedule, making sure that there was also time for other homework.

Monday	Tuesday	Wednesday	Thursday	Friday	Saturday	Sunday
Go to library Begin research	Committee meeting	Research	Write up science experiment	Basketball game	Finish research	Organize notes
Begin rough draft	Rough draft	Study for history test	Revise	Sharon's party!	All day trip	Make final copy

Exercise **Organizing Your Work**

A. Decide which of these assignments should become short-term goals and which should be long-term goals. Then break each of the long-term assignments into four or five smaller steps.

1. Reading two pages of the science textbook short term
2. Writing a six-page composition long term
3. Studying fifteen words for a spelling test short term
4. Completing ten math problems due tomorrow short term
5. Studying for an exam on eight chapters of the history book long term
6. Keeping a journal for one month long term
7. Answering five questions at the end of a health lesson short term
8. Preparing a five-minute speech on flower arranging long term
9. Collecting a set of articles on a recent political issue long term
10. Taking notes on a textbook reading assignment short term

B. Assume that your assignment is to read a novel and write a book report. You have fourteen days to complete the assignment. List the steps involved. Then draw up a schedule to show how you might plan your time for the next two weeks to complete each step of the assignment.

2. Review Chapters 2-9 in the science text. Write answers to all eight sets of Unit Review questions. You will be tested on the material in one week.
3. With three other students, choose a one-act play to dramatize for the class. Use costumes and props, and have it ready in two weeks.
4. Read a biography of a historical figure you admire. Prepare a brief informative speech on that person for class next Tuesday.

Extending the Lesson

Have the students keep logs of what, when, and where they study each day. At the end of a week, have the students draw conclusions about how to improve their study habits.

Part 3

Objective

To become familiar with the SQ3R study method

Presenting the Lesson

1. Read and discuss page 220. Stress that the SQ3R method can help students to better understand and remember what they study. Make sure that students can define these key terms: *headings, introduction,* and *recite.* Write the five steps of the SQ3R method on the board, and review what each one involves.

Discuss how students can identify the main ideas in a chapter. Help them see that topic sentences, headings, boldface or italic print, and repetition provide clues to an idea's importance.

2. With the overhead projector, show a sample textbook lesson and demonstrate the SQ3R procedure. Try to find a lesson that can be projected in one or two sections.

3. Assign the Exercise on pages 221-222. Afterward, discuss the main points in the selection and how SQ3R helps students to identify and remember them. The following questions are similar to those the students may prepare for this Exercise.

What are the sources of history?
What is oral history?
How did the Indians arrive in North America?
What records show the existence of big-game hunters?
What is meant by a food-gathering culture? An agricultural society?

Remind students that the study questions must also be answered.

Part 3 Studying an Assignment

Most of your daily assignments involve reading and studying information. You can do this most efficiently if you use an organized method of study. One such method is called the **SQ3R method.** It consists of these five steps: **S**urvey, **Q**uestion, **R**ead, **R**ecite, and **R**eview. Now study these steps in detail.

Using SQ3R

1. **Survey** the material. Look over the entire article or selection to get a general idea of what you will be reading. Read the introduction and also the summary, if there is one. Check the titles and headings and look at any illustrations.

2. **Question.** Prepare a set of questions. Decide what questions you should be able to answer at the end of your reading. Use any study questions presented in the book or provided by your teacher. You can also make up your own questions by turning each title and heading into a question. Pictures, maps, or charts can also be used to make up questions.

3. **Read** the selection. Look for the answers to the questions as you read. Also identify the central thoughts in each section.

4. **Recite** the answers. After you finish your careful reading, recite in your own words the answers to your prepared questions. Make notes on the answers. In addition, make sure you have grasped any other important points of the selection and record those, too.

5. **Review** the selection. Quickly read over your notes and look over the main points in the book to impress them on your memory. Look up the answers to any questions you are still not sure of.

Exercise Practicing Using SQ3R

Use the SQ3R method to read this selection on Indian history from the social studies textbook *A Proud Nation.* Follow the directions that precede the selection as you study it.

1. Survey the selection. What titles and subtitles do you notice? What is the general topic of the selection?

2. Prepare a set of questions. Are study questions included with the selection? If so, preview them.

3. Now read the selection. Find answers to your questions.

4. Recite the answers to your own study questions and those at the end of the selection. Write these answers.

5. Record other important points from the selection.

A LONG HISTORY

Oral History. The many groups of Indians living in America knew they had a long past. They told of their beginnings and their history in song and story. Theirs was an oral tradition; the elders in each Indian group passed on the ancient stories to the next generation.

Sources of History. All peoples record the events of their past, their *history.* Some records are spoken, and some records are written. Still other records are the tools and buildings that have survived the passage of time. In all cases, however, what has survived does not tell the whole story. We have to rely on *theory*, a guess based on limited evidence.

Theory Explains the Indian Arrival. Many years ago glaciers covered most of North America. This ice expanded and melted many times before it finally withdrew from the continent. Scientists have developed a theory that animals and people walked from Asia into what is now Alaska during a time when an ice bridge connected

Individualizing the Lesson

Less-Advanced Students

Help the students with each step of the SQ3R method in the Exercise on pages 221-222.

Advanced Students

Have the students bring to class a reading assignment for another class and use the SQ3R method to study the material. Check to see that they complete each step.

Optional Practice

Provide the students with a brief textbook excerpt for additional SQ3R practice. Give students both a pre-test and a post-test over the material to demonstrate how well SQ3R helps them learn.

Extending the Lesson

1. Have the students work on a bulletin board display illustrating the five steps in the SQ3R study method.

2. Have the students prepare a TV script for a brief show presenting and demonstrating the SQ3R method to other junior high school students.

Asia and North America. Over many years, these early peoples wandered southward and fanned into eastern areas of both North and South America.

Records of Big-Game Hunters. The first Americans hunted large animals called big game. Records of these early life-styles exist in the form of stones and bones. Carved bones of now extinct animals have been found in central Mexico. Remains of a bison killed thirty thousand years ago by early Americans have been found in Idaho. The search for more knowledge continues.

Food-Gathering Cultures. When big-game hunting declined, early Americans had to find other food sources to survive. The shift from big-game hunting to the use of plants and small animals for food was an important step in the history of early Americans. A new culture based on food gathering reached its broadest development about seven thousand years ago.

Agricultural Societies. Over five thousand years ago maize (corn) was first grown from wild plants. In 1948 tiny cobs of domesticated maize were found in caves in New Mexico and Mexico. Also domesticated were beans, chili peppers, sweet potatoes, and other crops. After farming became possible, many American cultures changed from food-gathering to farming societies.

As people began to rely on farming, they had to settle down and live in one place, at least during the planting and harvesting seasons. The settlements around farmlands became villages. Some villages grew to be cities with streets, plazas, and temples.

For Review

1. What is history? How can people learn about the past?
2. Identify three significant changes that occurred in early American history.
3. Why was the domestication of maize important?

Part 4   Taking Notes

Whether you are doing research for a report, using the SQ3R method of study or listening to a lecture in class, you should get in the habit of taking notes. Note-taking helps you in four ways:

1. It helps you understand and remember what you read or hear by forcing you to concentrate.
2. It helps you identify the main points of the material.
3. It helps you understand how facts are related.
4. It provides a handy reference source and a concise study guide for later review.

Taking Notes as You Read

You have already learned in Chapter 11 to take notes on index cards when you are doing research for a report. These notes provide a concise record of information, and can be easily arranged when you organize the report. Remember that these notes should be brief and written in your own words. If you include a direct quotation, be sure to use quotation marks and put the source of the information on each card.

When you are taking notes in class or while reading your daily assignments, use a notebook. Divide your notebook into sections for each subject you study. Keep all notes for the same subject in one section. Put the subject and the date at the top of each page of notes. If you keep an organized notebook, you will have a concise summary of all the materials you study. You will also have the tools you need to review for a test.

When you take notes on your reading assignments, use your own words. Develop a set of abbreviations you can use to save time, such as ✛ for *and* and *w/* for *with*. Make sure your notes include all the important points, key words, and definitions you identify as you read.

Part 4

Objective

To know how to take notes for research, on reading assignments, and in class

Presenting the Lesson

1. Read and discuss pages 223-224. Ask students who take notes in class or on their reading how it helps them. Review the four reasons for taking notes.

2. Discuss the function of an organized notebook and require students to keep one if they don't have one already. Stress that in taking notes, students should record only the main points.

3. Call students' attention to the sample modified outline on page 224. Then demonstrate the use of a modified outline on the board, using this chapter part as the source material.

4. Assign the Exercise on page 224. You might pair students working on the same assignments to check each other's work or discuss which points should be recorded.

Individualizing the Lesson

Less-Advanced Students

Provide reading assignments and work with the students as a group to do the Exercise on page 224. Help the students to recognize important ideas. Teach them to be aware of the following:

ideas that are general rather than specific

ideas highlighted in boldface or italics

ideas presented in topic sentences or
  headings
terms defined in context
ideas that follow signal words, such
  as *consequently* or *first*
ideas that are repeated

Advanced Students

Have students take notes on an
article you have selected from a
magazine. Then collect the articles
and ask students questions on the
material. They may refer to their
notes for answers.

Optional Practice

1. Show a filmstrip, and ask the
students to take notes. Afterward,
guide the students to agreement on
the main points that would be important to record in notes.

2. Have several students give
brief informative talks from outlined
notes on articles they have read.
Have the class take notes on each
speech. Afterward, ask each speaker to display his or her outlined
speech notes, and have the students compare them with their own
notes on the speech.

Extending the Lesson

1. Use the overhead projector to
display an encyclopedia article. See
if the students can agree on the
most important information, and
have volunteers make modified outlines on the chalkboard. Finally, ask
the students how their notes would
differ if they were taking notes for
research on a report topic.

2. Invite a news reporter to class
to explain how he or she takes notes
on interviews and events.

Taking Notes as You Listen

There are times when you will want to record notes on a
class lecture. You will not be able to write down every word
you hear. Therefore, take notes only on major points and the
key details that explain these points. You do not need to write
in complete sentences. Just make sure that you will be able to
understand your notes when you read them later.

Be alert for clues that tell you what is important and how
your information should be organized. Listen for key phrases
such as "The main point is . . ." or "What you should remember is . . ." Also listen for clues such as *first, also, furthermore,
for these reasons,* and *the following causes.* The key to note-
taking is learning to recognize the important information.

Using a Modified Outline

One way to take notes quickly and skillfully as you listen is
to use a modified outline. A modified outline is a simplified
version of the formal outline you use to write a report.

A modified outline breaks information into main headings
and related details. Underline each main heading and list the
related details beneath it. Use numbers, letters, or dashes to
indicate the details. Look at this example:

Points that affect consumer choices
—Personal taste
—Cost
—Safety
—Health

Exercises Taking Notes

Look through your assignment book and select two reading
assignments. Take notes on both selections. One set of notes
should be in modified outline form.

Part 5   Types of Reading

The way you read changes with your purpose for reading. For example, when you flip through a magazine, you read differently than when you read a chapter of a textbook. Different types of reading are appropriate for different situations.

Fast Reading

There are two types of fast reading that you should become familiar with. These are **skimming** and **scanning.**

When you survey written material to get a general impression of its content, you are using the skill of **skimming.** Skimming is useful when you are surveying in the SQ3R method, when you are selecting a book to read, or when you are trying to determine whether a book would be a good resource for a report.

To skim, move your eyes quickly over the entire page or selection. Look for guides such as titles, chapter headings, italicized words, and any pictures, charts, or graphs. When you are trying to decide if a book would be useful for your research, you should also skim the table of contents and the index.

Scanning is another type of fast reading. The purpose of scanning is to quickly locate a particular piece of information, such as a fact or definition. To scan, move your eyes quickly over the page until you find the information you want. Do not read every word. Look only for key words or phrases that will help you locate the detail you need.

In-Depth Reading

When you want to get the full benefit of a piece of writing, you must use in-depth reading. This type of reading is different from skimming and scanning. It calls for careful, thoughtful reading and rereading of paragraphs.

Objective

To know when to use the three types of reading

Presenting the Lesson

1. Read and discuss pages 225-226. Write the terms *scanning, skimming,* and *in-depth reading* on the chalkboard. Ask students to define each type of reading and explain when it is used.

2. Assign the Exercise on page 226. Remind the students that skimming will help them to quickly identify the subject of the article and then in-depth reading will provide them with understanding of the main ideas and details. Point out that they will probably scan the article to locate the answers to the questions in the Exercise.

Individualizing the Lesson

Less-Advanced Students

1. Help the students to read the Exercise paragraphs in depth by asking them to find specific details that explain the main ideas.

2. Instruct the students on using the table of contents, index, and headings to help them in skimming.

Advanced Students

Provide students with an article from a magazine and a list of questions to be answered. Plan the questions so that students will be able to answer the first few after skimming and the rest only with in-depth reading. Encourage students to use SQ3R as they study the article.

Optional Practice

Take the students to the library. Take the students to the library. Have the librarian introduce them to the various types of reference books. Have students skim each reference work to see what information it contains. Then have them scan the information in the books to find the following data:

a. the year of the launching of the first space shuttle
b. the average family income in the U.S.
c. the two ways to release atomic energy
d. the location of the National Baseball Hall of Fame
e. the name of the head of the Spanish government
f. the name of a sculpture by Rodin
g. the date when postage stamps were first issued

You may continue this scanning activity by having groups of students make up "treasure hunt" lists of facts for other groups to find.

Extending the Lesson

Have each student bring a newspaper to class. Ask the students to practice different types of reading by:

a. skimming the front page for an understanding of the day's top news
b. scanning the newspaper for this information: the previous day's sports scores, the following day's weather prediction, and a news article relating to the President
c. finding two articles of special interest to them and reading them in depth

After students complete these activities, discuss how they can use their reading skills to become better newspaper readers.

The key to in-depth reading is to look for the topic sentence or main idea of each paragraph. Then notice what method is used to develop that main idea. Did the writer use examples, reasons, details, or comparisons?

Finally, train yourself to notice how the paragraphs relate to each other and to the entire selection. You must be able to isolate the paragraphs that present main ideas from those that contain less important details.

Exercise Practicing Different Types of Reading

Follow these directions.

1. Skim the paragraph below to see what the topic is.
2. Read the paragraph in depth.
3. Scan to find the answers to these questions.
    What is a microbe?
    What are types of microbes?
    What is known about viruses? What information is uncertain?

WHAT CAUSES DISEASE?

Except for accidental injuries, health problems that prevent parts of the body from working properly are called diseases.

Many diseases are caused by **microbes. These are different forms of life too small to be seen without a microscope. Viruses are the smallest known microbes. All known viruses cause disease, but there is some question as to whether or not a virus is a living cell. This is because viruses seem to reproduce only when inside a cell that is living. Bacteria, fungi, rickettsiae, and protozoans are** also different kinds of microbes. They are larger than viruses, and they are known to be living—most often as single cells. Most bacteria, fungi, rickettsiae, and protozoans are harmless. Some of these one-celled creatures cause disease by releasing poisonous waste products in the body in which they are living and multiplying.

Part 6 Using Graphic Aids

Quickly skim a few of your textbooks. Most of the content will be organized into paragraphs. But what else do you notice besides sentences and paragraphs? Are there any pictures, charts, tables, diagrams, maps, or graphs? Most of the material you study will include some or all of these types of **graphic aids.**

1. **Pictures and illustrations** allow a reader to see clearly and instantly what might take several paragraphs to describe. Always read the captions that accompany the pictures.
2. **Sketches and diagrams** are usually accompanied by labels that show the parts or workings of the subject. They enable the reader to identify each part and see its relationship to all the others.
3. **Maps** display geographical areas. They can show not only the physical characteristics of the land, but also such things as climate and population. Look for a title to see what the purpose of the map is. Also look for the legend, or key, which will list symbols and abbreviations.
4. **Tables and charts** may list many pieces of information. This information is often set up in columns. First check to see if there is a key that explains how the information is organized. Always read the key first. Then use your skimming skills to look for the information you need.

Reading Graphs

One of the most common graphic aids is the graph itself. A graph is a special type of chart that shows a relationship between sets of facts. To understand any graph, first read the title. Then read all the material outside the frame of the graph. If there is a key to any symbols or abbreviations used, read it carefully. Then proceed within the frame of the graph to locate specific information or comparisons.

Objective

To understand how to read and interpret graphic aids

Presenting the Lesson

1. Read and discuss the introduction on page 227. Review the four main types of graphic aids and the kind of information each can convey. Discuss why and when certain information is conveyed better through visuals than through words.

2. Read and discuss **Reading Graphs** and **Types of Graphs** on pages 227-229. Stress that in reading any graph, students should be aware of the title, heading, and key to symbols as they attempt to read the graph.

Review the four types of graphs — bar, picture, circle, and line — as you direct students' attention to the samples. Have students explain what each sample graph tells.

3. Assign the Exercise on page 230. Remind students to use the headings, titles, and keys. After students have completed the Exercise, discuss the answers as a class. Have students describe how they read the graphs.

4. Read and discuss **Drawing Conclusions.** Review the sample graphs on pages 228-229, and discuss possible conclusions that might be drawn from each set of facts. Caution students about drawing conclusions without sufficient information.

5. Assign the Exercise on page 231. After students have completed the Exercise, discuss their conclusions and what facts lead them to those conclusions. The following are the most likely answers:

a. Posters and newspaper ads are the best types of publicity.
b. WFL's rating dipped again because they were showing the re-runs too often.

Individualizing the Lesson

Less-Advanced Students

1. Help the students to find answers to the questions in the Exercise on page 230. Then have students answer three additional questions independently:

a. In what type of work are most of the people in Hamilton employed, according to the bar graph? the least?
b. According to the picture graph, how many people are employed in transportation in Hamilton? in construction?
c. According to the line graph, what was the highest attendance at the sports banquet? the least?

2. Have the students decide which type of graphic aid would be most appropriate for presenting the following facts: the location of the five time zones, the parts of a telescope, how consumers spend each dollar, the surface of Mars, and daily TV viewing habits according to age.

Advanced Students

1. Require the students to draw three alternate conclusions from each set of facts in the Exercise on page 231 and to decide which conclusion is most feasible and why.
2. Have the students find graphs in their textbooks and work together in small groups to draw possible conclusions from the facts presented.

Types of Graphs

To read graphs skillfully, you should recognize the four basic types: circle graphs, bar graphs, picture graphs, and line graphs.

A **circle graph** is always drawn inside a circle. The circle represents 100%, or the whole, of something. Each wedge or pie-shaped piece represents a part of the whole. When you look at a circle graph, you can easily see the relationship of these parts to the whole and to each other.

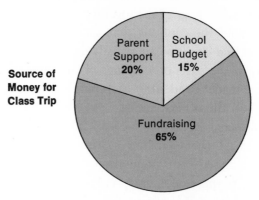

Source of Money for Class Trip

Parent Support 20%

School Budget 15%

Fundraising 65%

A **bar graph** uses the length of separate bars to show relationships. First, read the information at the top, bottom, and sides of a bar graph. Find specific information by locating the point where the end of a bar meets a column.

Employment in Hamilton

Type of Work

Manufacturing
Construction
Transportation
Trade
Social and Personal Services

Number of People · 100 · 200 · 300 · 400 · 500 · 600 · 700

A **picture graph** uses symbols in place of bars to present information. Read the key to learn the meaning of each symbol.

Employment in Hamilton

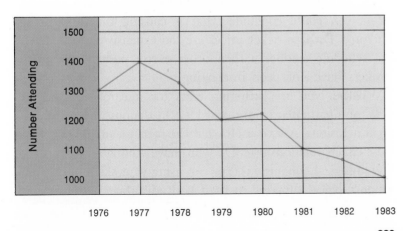

Manufacturing	🧍 🧍 🧍 🧍 🧍 🧍
Construction	🧍 🧍
Transportation	🧍
Trade	🧍 🧍 🧍 🧍
Social and Personal Services	🧍 🧍 🧍 🧍 🧍 🧍 🧍

Each 🧍 = 100 people

A **line graph** can show changes in relationships over a period of time. Follow the line to see a pattern of change or a trend in a certain direction. Get specific information by finding the spot where the two columns (across and down) meet.

Attendance at the Sports Banquet

1. Provide the students with copies of the text of a magazine article, and ask them to plan graphic aids that would add information visually. Remind them to consider which type of graphic aid would best display the information. You may want to have students actually create the graphics.

2. Have the students examine the photographs in a magazine such as *Time* or *Newsweek*. Have them explain how the pictures aid their understanding of the articles.

3. Have the students skim an almanac to find two diagrams, two tables or charts, and two maps. Ask the students to explain why that type of graphic aid was chosen for presenting the information.

4. Have the students clip examples of the different types of graphic aids used in one day's newspaper.

5. To help students become familiar with different types of graphic aids, work together in class to construct a line graph showing changes in enrollment at your school over the past eight years. Then have the students make any two of the following graphic aids:

a. a bar graph showing the number of school days in each month
b. a circle graph showing the number of hours the student spends in one day on the following: sleep, school, study, chores, and personal time.
c. a picture graph showing the number of students in each of the student's classes
d. a diagram picturing and labeling the components of a fire extinguisher
e. a map showing the fire exits nearest the classroom

229

Extending the Lesson

1. Bring to class a collection of famous news photographs, such as *The Best of Life.* Show the photographs to the class, and ask what stories they tell. Discuss how outstanding photographs communicate with great impact.

2. Ask the students to consider how graphic aids could add to the reports they wrote for Chapter 10. Encourage the students to think about using graphic aids for reports they write in the future.

Exercise Reading Graphs

Use the information from the graphs on pages 228 and 229 to answer these questions.

1. Which is the biggest source of income for the class trip, according to the circle graph?

2. What is the title of the bar graph? According to it, how many people are employed in Social and Personal Services?

3. What does each 👤 stand for in the picture graph?

4. In what year was attendance at the Sports Banquet the highest? the lowest?

5. What type of graph would you use to show how your class's yearly budget is divided? What kind of graph might best display the change in temperature in your town over a two-week period?

Drawing Conclusions

Graphs can present you with a set of facts. It is up to you to decide the implications of those facts. For instance, after looking at the graph entitled "Attendance at the Sports Banquet," what can you conclude about the trend in popularity of the event? Does the graph indicate any reasons for the steady decline in attendance? You would have to do further research before you could conclude what is causing the drop in attendance. Perhaps ticket prices are too expensive; maybe there is a schedule conflict with another event; perhaps the guest speakers have not been interesting.

Whether you are gathering facts for research or studying facts for a particular course, stay alert to the possibility of drawing conclusions. Ask yourself what the facts mean. Do you see a cause-effect relationship? Do you have enough evidence to draw a logical conclusion? You are using your skills of organizing and logical thinking to their best advantage when you are able to draw meaningful conclusions.

Exercise Drawing Conclusions

Look at the following information. Write a conclusion that could be drawn from each set of facts.

1. The following graph was put together by the publicity committee for the school carnival. They wanted to figure out what kind of publicity was most effective.

Number of people responding

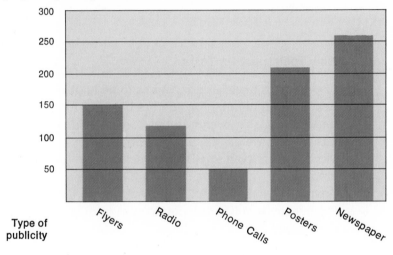

Type of publicity

If you were a member of this committee, what would your suggestions be for next year?

2. WFL, a small, independent TV station, has been trying to improve its ratings. Recently, it acquired reruns of a popular comedy series that had always ranked in the top ten. Confident that this show would improve the station's ratings, WFL management began offering the show at 6:00 and 10:00, opposite news programs on other stations. For the first few weeks, the ratings were very high. Then they began to drop, as viewers switched back to the news shows. New episodes of the series that were playing on the networks, however, were still in the top ten. Why were the reruns not popular?

Part 7 Taking Tests

Objective

To recognize and prepare for different kinds of tests

Presenting the Lesson

1. Read and discuss the introduction and **Preparing for Test Questions** on pages 232-233. Stress that the student who has been taking notes and using the SQ3R method has already begun to prepare for tests. Discuss how students should schedule time for test study. Emphasize the four points listed under **How To Prepare for Tests,** and give illustrations if possible.

2. Review the six types of test questions and the tips for completing each kind. Point out that for essay tests, students follow pre-writing steps similar to those learned in Chapter 4 "The Process of Writing."

3. Read and discuss **Taking the Test** on page 234. Compare the process of test-taking to the steps in the SQ3R study method.

4. Assign the Exercise on pages 234-235. After students have completed the Exercise, discuss why each statement is false and how it should be corrected.

Individualizing the Lesson

Less-Advanced Students

Give the students a sample test, and have them do the following:

scan the test to see what it covers

Part 7 Taking Tests

The thought of a test often makes students nervous. With the proper preparation, however, you should be able to be as comfortable with tests as with any other assignment. The key to taking tests successfully is being prepared. By taking notes as you read and by keeping an organized notebook, you have already begun to prepare yourself for testing. Here are some further suggestions.

How To Prepare for Tests

1. Listen in class and ask questions to find out exactly what information you are being tested on. Will the test cover material from class discussions as well as portions of the textbook?

2. Make a study plan to allow yourself time to review. Avoid last-minute, late-night cramming.

3. Review the subject matter. Use your notes and the questions you developed as part of the SQ3R method.

4. Get a good night's sleep the night before the test.

Preparing for Test Questions

Learn to recognize the different kinds of test questions and the best way to approach them. The following information may help you.

1. **True-False.** You are given several statements, and are asked to decide whether each one is true or false. Read such questions carefully. Watch out for words like "always," "never," "all," or "none," which often make a statement false.

_____F_____ The human heart has three chambers.

2. **Multiple Choice.** Here, you are provided with several possible answers for one question. Sometimes it may seem as though more than one answer is correct. Read all the choices carefully and select the *best* answer.

Which of the following are characteristics of folklore?
A. written by author   C. has different versions
B. oral   D. both B and C

3. **Matching.** You are given two lists and are directed to match items in one with those from the other. Begin these questions by matching up the items you are certain of. This will limit the choices for those that are left.

Match each type of poetic foot with the word that demonstrates it.
1. iamb   1. uninspired
2. trochee   2. forest
3. anapest   3. lovingly
4. dactyl   4. enjoy

4. **Completion.** You are given an incomplete sentence and must finish it with the proper word or phrase. Do not spend too much time on questions you are unsure of. Sometimes the answer will occur to you as you continue with the test.

A triangle with three equal sides is an *equilateral* triangle.

5. **Short Answer.** Here, you provide a short answer to each question. Always answer in complete sentences.

What are the two types of musical clefs? *The two types are bass clef and treble clef.*

6. **Essay.** In this case, you must write out a complete answer to a question. These answers can be as long as a paragraph or longer. Plan them as you would any piece of writing. First, identify your purpose. Words in the directions such as "explain" or "describe" are clues. Write a topic sentence. Then list and organize your ideas on a piece of scratch paper.

tell how they would have prepared for the test using SQ3R

identify types of questions and how to approach them

explain how they would plan their time

define the terms in the directions

tell why reviewing answers would be important

Advanced Students

Have students prepare a humorous skit that shows one group of students that does not prepare for a test correctly, and another that does.

Optional Practice

Divide the class into six groups, assigning each group a type of test question: true/false, matching, short answer, multiple choice, completion, or essay. Then give each group copies of the same brief textbook chapter to study. Have students make up several of their type of questions using the material in the chapter. Ask each group to present their questions for the rest of the class to answer.

Extending the Lesson

1. Encourage the students to use the study skills and test-taking strategies they have learned in all their classes.

2. Have the students outline a script for a "How To Study" filmstrip. Make sure that they pay attention to visual devices.

3. Prepare a test over Chapter 13 or one of the other chapters in this book. Encourage students to use the guidelines given in Part 7 to prepare for the test.

Taking the Test

Taking a test calls for the same type of study and organizing skills you have already learned about. Follow these steps whenever you take a test.

1. **Survey the test.** Look it over completely to see what type of test it is and how long it is.
2. **Plan your time.** Read all of the directions and decide in what order you will begin answering questions. Also decide how much time you will need for each portion of the test. Allow more time for sections that require planning, such as essay questions.
3. **Read each test item carefully.** Make sure you understand the questions and directions completely. If there are several essay questions, read all of them before you begin so that you don't repeat yourself in several answers. Also make sure you are following the directions. For example, are you supposed to answer only one of the essay questions or all of them? Where answers are provided, read through all the choices before deciding on the correct one.
4. **Save time at the end to review the test.** Scan to make sure you have not accidentally omitted any answers. Try to answer those questions you skipped. Reread any answers you are unsure of. Do not change answers too often, however. Your first ideas are usually the correct ones.

Exercise Using Test-Taking Skills

Correct and rewrite each of these statements about preparing for and taking tests.

1. In true-false questions, words like "all" or "none" do not affect the answer.
2. Plan to stay up studying most of the night before a test.

1. In true-false questions, words like "all" or "none" often mean the statement is false.
2. Get a good night's sleep the night before a test.

234

3. Review by rereading all of the material you have studied.

4. Don't worry about how much time you have to finish the test.

5. Begin writing the first answer as soon as you are handed the test.

6. Hand in your paper as soon as you finish. Don't bother to look it over first.

7. Don't worry about topic sentences when you write your answers in paragraph form.

3. Review by rereading your notes.
4. Plan your time before beginning a test.
5. Survey the test before you begin writing.
6. Review the test before handing it in.
7. Write essay answers as you would write any good paragraph.

Chapter 14

Writing Social and Business Letters

Chapter Objectives

1. To write interesting friendly letters in the proper style and form

2. To use the proper style and form for thank-you notes and notes of invitation, acceptance, and regret

3. To use the proper style and form for a business letter

4. To write three types of business letters: letters of request, order letters, letters of complaint or adjustment

5. To fold letters properly and address envelopes properly for mailing

Preparing the Students

Read the introduction on page 237. Discuss with the students letters they have written recently and their reasons for writing them. Have the students suggest reasons for writing each type of letter mentioned in the introduction.

End the discussion by pointing out that all written communication is a reflection of the writer. Letters written in the proper style and form that express a message clearly and concisely are likely to make favorable impressions on readers.

Additional Resources

Skills Practice Book—pages 66-74.
Duplicating Masters—pages 66-74.

Writing letters is a good way to keep friendships alive. It is also a good way to obtain information, to order products, and to express your opinions. If you are like most people, you enjoy receiving letters. In order to receive them, however, you must also write them yourself.

There are three basic types of letters: friendly letters, social notes, and business letters. Each type has its own form. Having a form to follow can make letter writing a much easier and more pleasant task, because each form is a guide to what to say.

Part 1

Objective

To write interesting friendly letters in the proper style and form

Presenting the Lesson

1. Read **Writing Friendly Letters** on pages 238 and 239. Have the students study the illustration on page 238. List the five parts of a friendly letter (heading, salutation, body, closing, signature) on the chalkboard. Draw a rectangle to represent a piece of stationery on the chalkboard and have students fill in the parts. Then refer the students to the sample letter on page 241 and have them identify the five parts. Point out that each new paragraph is indented, and that there is a new paragraph for each new idea.

2. Read **Guidelines for Writing Friendly Letters** on page 240. Then turn each of the six guidelines into a question and lead the students in an analysis of the sample letter on page 241. (Example: Did the writer make comments about the last letter she received from her friend?)

3. Assign Exercise A, page 240. Have students read their revisions aloud. Discuss which are the most interesting and why.

4. Assign Exercise B on page 242. Have the students use the guidelines for friendly letters on page 240 to review their letters, and then have them revise as necessary.

Individualizing the Lesson

Less-Advanced Students

1. Work with the class to write a

Part 1 Writing Friendly Letters

In a friendly letter, your writing can be casual, just as if you were talking. The purpose of a friendly letter is to let your friend know what you have been doing and how you feel about what has been happening. Letter writing is an enjoyable sharing of experiences between friends, but even casual letters need a standard form to keep them organized and easy to read. The following example of the form for a friendly letter will help you review the five parts of a friendly letter.

Heading
267 Palm Drive
Cruz, California 95063
July 18, 1984

Salutation
Dear Terry,

Body
_____

_____

_____

_____

_____

Love, Closing
Beth Signature

The **heading** is written in the top right-hand corner. It consists of three lines. The first line is your street address. The second line is your city, state, and ZIP code. The third line is the date of the letter. In the heading, pay particular attention to punctuation and do not abbreviate, especially on the date line.

The **salutation,** or greeting, is the way you say "hello" to your friend. It can be as casual or personal as you wish. Here are some examples:

Dear Todd, *Greetings Pal,*
Hi Manuel, *Hello Good Buddy,*

The salutation begins at the left margin. The first word and all other nouns are capitalized, and the last word in the salutation is followed by a comma.

The **body** of a friendly letter is where you communicate your message. Since you are writing to someone you know well, your writing can be conversational, just as if you were talking. In this way, your personality will show through, and your writing will be more interesting. Remember to indent each paragraph in the body.

The **closing** is a simple way of saying "goodbye" to your friend. Capitalize only the first word of the closing and use a comma at the end of the closing. Usually the closing lines up with the first word in the heading. Some closings are common, and some are more personal. Here are some suggestions for closings:

Love, *Your friend,* *Missing you,*
Sincerely, *Still waiting,* *Confused,*

The **signature** in a friendly letter is written below the closing. Only your first name is needed. Keep your letter personal by always writing your signature by hand, even if you have typed the rest of the letter.

friendly letter based on one of the topics in Exercise A on page 240. Follow the guidelines for friendly letters on page 240. Then have the students complete the Exercise independently.

2. For Exercise B, have the students write rough drafts of their letters. Have them work in groups to check the letters for proper content and form, using the guidelines for friendly letters on page 240 as a checklist. Then have the students rewrite their letters, incorporating any suggested improvements.

Advanced Students

1. For Exercise A, have the students write a complete letter. Refer them to page 238 for an example of standard form.

2. For Exercise B, discuss a sample of the completed letters in class. Select well written and poorly written letters. Make copies or display them on an overhead projector, allowing the authors to remain anonymous. Discuss the style, form, and appearance of each. Ask the class to suggest improvements.

Optional Practice

Have the students exchange the letters they wrote for Exercise B and write letters replying to the letters they receive.

Extending the Lesson

1. Arrange an exchange of letters with another school. Have each student write a friendly letter to a student in the other school. Before mailing the letters, have the students check one another's letters in class for form and content. Then have the

students rewrite their letters, making any necessary improvements.

When the letters from the other school arrive, select a sample of them, make copies, and discuss how well they follow the guidelines for friendly letters.

2. Have the students make a bulletin board display of friendly letters. Tell them to include the guidelines for friendly letters in the display.

Guidelines for Writing Friendly Letters

What you do every day may not seem particularly interesting to you, but remember that a friend enjoys just keeping in touch. A friendly letter gives you the chance to write about events and feelings that are meaningful to you and interesting to your friend. The following guidelines will help you.

Guidelines for Friendly Letters

1. In the first paragraph, make comments about the last letter you received from your friend.

2. Write one or more paragraphs about people and events that interest both you and your friends.

3. Use specific words for descriptions and action.

4. Ask questions so that your friend has something to write back about.

5. Make your handwriting neat and legible.

6. Use the proper letter form.

Read the sample of a friendly letter on page 241. See how each part is developed.

Exercises Writing Friendly Letters

A. Choose one of the following ideas and rewrite it. Develop each situation more specifically, and use vivid details.

1. We bought a puppy last week. It's really cute, but it's always getting into trouble, and it's very hard to train.

2. When my brother left for college, he said I could use his CB. I have set it up in my room. It's a lot of fun.

3. Last weekend I babysat for a family of six kids. You wouldn't believe how busy they kept me. What a mess!

318 Laurel Road
Bexley, Ohio 43209
October 28, 1984

Dear Julie,

I was so glad to get your letter at last. I guess I just couldn't wait to see the pictures. Boy, are they fantastic! I especially like the one of you and Andy in the sailboat. Of course, Jim's favorite is the one where we're all standing there like drowned rats holding up our fish. That's just like a brother, especially since he caught the biggest fish. Anyway, it was a great family reunion, and already I can't wait until the next one.

You'll never guess what I'm doing in school. I actually tried out for the girl's basketball team and made it! Our first game is next week so I'll be writing again soon to let you know how it went. I'm really excited.

I really have to get to my homework now. Say "hi" to your family for me and write soon.

Miss you,
Suzanne

B.   Write a friendly letter to one of your best friends. You may write about events that have actually happened to you, or you may want to use some of those suggested in the following list. Follow the guidelines on page 240. Use your best handwriting.

> Student Council elections at school
> How your cat destroyed your science project
> The movie you saw last weekend
> How you redecorated your bedroom
> Your friend's surprise birthday party
> Your recent camping trip

Part 2   Social Notes

Social notes are written for a specific purpose, such as to invite someone to a party, to thank someone, or to accept an invitation. Social notes have the same form as a friendly letter, but they are much shorter. Sometimes only the date is used in the heading instead of the writer's whole address.

Social notes are a form of courtesy that people appreciate. The following kinds of social notes are the ones you will write most often.

The Thank-You Note

Usually a thank-you note is written after you have received a gift. Even if you don't particularly like the gift, it is still important to thank the person for thinking of you.

Another form of thank-you note is called a "bread-and-butter" note. You write this note when you have stayed overnight at someone's house.

Both forms of thank-you notes express your appreciation for someone else's thoughtfulness toward you. On the next page are samples of the two types of thank-you notes.

242

Part 2

Objective

To use the proper style and form for thank-you notes and notes of invitation, acceptance, and regret

Presenting the Lesson

1. Read the introductory paragraph on this page. Emphasize the similarities between friendly letters and social notes. Then list on the chalkboard the four types of notes that will be studied: thank-you notes, invitations, notes of acceptance, and notes of regret.

2. Read **The Thank-You Note** on page 242. Ask the students to name recent occasions when it would have been appropriate for them to write thank-you notes. Then read and discuss the sample thank-you notes on page 243. Point out that the form is the same as that of a friendly letter.

3. Read and discuss **Notes of Invitation, Acceptance, and Regret** on page 244. Tell the students

A Thank-You Note

2217 Massachusetts Avenue
Lawrence, Kansas 66044
June 5, 1984

Dear Aunt Alice,

The sweater you knitted for me for graduation is soft and warm and beautiful. It matches perfectly the skirt Mother made for me. How thoughtful both of you were. Thank you so much.

Mother and Dad and Grandmother were able to come to the ceremony, and we went out to dinner afterwards. I wish you and Uncle Fred could have been there too.

Love,
Cindy

A Bread-and-Butter Note

4950 North Marine Drive
Chicago, Illinois 60640
April 14, 1984

Dear Mr. and Mrs. Pacini,

Thank you very much for letting me spend last weekend at your house while my parents were out of town. I had a great time at the baseball game.

I really enjoyed myself. I hope that Tom can spend a weekend with me soon.

Sincerely,
Matt Brendan

that an easy way to remember what should be included in an invitation is to remember *Who, What, When, Where, Why,* and *How. Who* is giving the party? *What* type of activity is planned? *Why* is the party being held? *Where* is it? *When* is it? *How* should the guest reply to the invitation? Also point out that a note of acceptance means that the writer can attend a party; a note of regret means that the writer cannot attend. Read and discuss the sample invitation, note of acceptance, and note of regret.

4. Assign the Exercise on page 246.

Individualizing the Lesson

Less-Advanced Students

Divide the students into six groups, and assign one of the situations in the Exercise to each group. Have the students compose the body of the note as a group. Then have each student write a final copy independently, using his or her address for the heading.

Advanced Students

Have each student select three situations for the Exercise: one that calls for a thank-you note, one that calls for an invitation, and one that calls for a note of acceptance or regret.

Optional Practice

1. Have each student write an appropriate thank-you note for one of the following situations:

1. Your uncle took you to an amusement park.

2. A neighbor took care of your dog while you were on vacation.
3. Your grandmother sent you a birthday gift.
4. You spent the weekend at your aunt's summer cottage.

2. Have each student write an invitation to one of the following events:

1. a birthday party to be held at a beach or swimming pool
2. a farewell party for a teacher
3. a bon voyage party for a friend leaving on an extended trip
4. a surprise birthday party
5. a lunch before a football game

3. Have the students exchange the invitations they wrote for the activity suggested above and write notes of acceptance or regret replying to the invitations they receive.

Extending the Lesson

1. Have the students make a bulletin board display of social notes. Tell them it must include a definition of each type of note, guidelines for writing it, and well-written examples.

2. Have the students research the subject of social notes in several etiquette books and report their findings to the class.

Notes of Invitation, Acceptance, and Regret

Invitations have to be written carefully to make sure that all the necessary details are included. Use the following checklist:

Guidelines for Writing Invitations

1. Specify the type of the activity.
2. Tell the purpose of the activity.
3. Give the address of the place where the activity will be held.
4. Give the day, date, and time of the activity.
5. Tell how the person should reply to the invitation.

Include directions or transportation suggestions if needed.

The abbreviation R.S.V.P. stands for a French phrase that means "please respond." The person sending the invitation would like to know how many people are going to attend the party. Sometimes there will be a phone number next to the R.S.V.P. so that all you have to do is call. Usually, however,

> 417 Monroe Avenue
> Mapleton, Iowa 51034
> June 1, 1984
>
> Dear Juanita,
> You are invited to attend a graduation party at my house on Friday, June 14. The party will start immediately following our graduation ceremony, at approximately 10:00. Your parents are welcome, too.
> I sure hope you can be there.
>
> Sincerely,
> Carla
>
> R.S.V.P

you should send a note of acceptance or regret. Always answer an invitation as soon as possible.

A Note of Acceptance

June 5, 1984

Dear Carla,

After graduation is a great time to have a party. Being at your house is always lots of fun. My parents will be coming, too.

Thanks for the invitation.

Your friend,
Juanita

A Note of Regret

June 5, 1984

Dear Carla,

I wish I could attend your graduation party. I know it will be lots of fun. Unfortunately my parents have already invited several of our relatives over for a celebration.

Ask if you can spend the night on Saturday so you can tell me all about the party.

Your friend,
Juanita

Exercise Writing Social Notes

Choose two of the following situations and write the appropriate notes on plain paper.

1. Write a note to your uncle thanking him for helping you with a project. You select the project.
2. Write an invitation to a surprise birthday party.
3. Write a note thanking a friend's parents for taking you on vacation with them.
4. Write a note to a neighbor apologizing for crushing her flowers. You decide how it happened.
5. Write a note accepting an invitation to join a club.
6. Write a note of regret for a barbecue you are unable to attend.

Part 3

Objective

To use the proper style and form for a business letter

Presenting the Lesson

1. Read the introductory paragraph on page 246. Ask the students if they have ever written business letters. If they have, discuss the occasions for their letters. Then emphasize the fact that the style of a business letter should be more formal than that of a friendly letter. A business letter should be brief, clear, and to the point.
2. Read **Business Letter Form** on pages 246-248.
3. Write the names of the two letter forms on the chalkboard, *modified block* and *block*. Point out that modified block is the same form that

Part 3   Writing Business Letters

When you want to request information, or order a product, or even complain about a product, you will need to write a business letter. A business letter is written for a specific purpose and requires a different style of writing from that of a friendly letter. A business letter should be brief, clear, and to the point. It should follow the required form.

Business Letter Form

When writing a business letter, always use 8½″ × 11″ unruled white paper. If possible, type your letter. If you do not type well, write your letter with blue or black ink. Leave equal margins on both sides, and at the top and bottom of the paper, and use only one side of the paper.

The form for a business letter is similar in many ways to the form for a friendly letter. There are two types of business letter forms: **block form** and **modified block form.**

246

The block form for a business letter is to be used only when the letter is typewritten. Notice that all parts of the letter begin at the left margin. There is a double space between paragraphs, and the paragraphs are not indented.

Block Form

Heading
920 South Lake Avenue
Greenville, South Carolina   29602
November 23, 1984

Inside Address
The Danbury Mint
47 Richards Avenue
Norwalk, Connecticut   06856

Dear Sir or Madam: Salutation

Body
_____
_____
_____
_____

_____
_____
_____
_____

Sincerely,   Closing

Valerie Hayward   Signature
Valerie Hayward

is used in a friendly letter. Write the characteristics of each form below its name. Alternatively, make line illustrations. Point out that most business letters are typewritten. Block form is used only for typewritten letters. Modified block form is always used for handwritten letters.

4. Read **Parts of a Business Letter** on page 249. Compare this list with the list of parts of a friendly letter on page 239. Note the similarities and differences.

Discuss the importance of keeping a copy of a business letter.

Individualizing the Lesson

Less-Advanced Students

Have a student copy the illustrations on page 247 and 248 on large poster paper. Post these in the classroom for reference.

Advanced Students

Have the students design letterheads for themselves. They can use the designs they create on the stationery they use for writing business letters.

Optional Practice

Display a business letter with obvious mistakes (colored stationery, uneven margins, cross-outs, red ink, grease stains, writing on both sides of the paper). Have the students identify the problems and tell how to correct them.

Extending the Lesson

Using an opaque or overhead projector, display a number of busi-

The modified block form is always used when the letter is handwritten. In this form, the heading remains in the upper right-hand corner, as in a friendly letter. Notice that in this form the paragraphs are indented, and the closing and signature line up with the heading.

Modified Block Form

Heading

920 South Lake Avenue
Greenville, South Carolina 29602
November 23, 1984

Inside Address

The Danbury Mint
47 Richards Avenue
Norwalk, Connecticut 06856

Dear Sir or Madam: Salutation

Body

_____

_____

_____

_____

_____

Yours truly,   Closing
Valerie Hayward   Signature
Valerie Hayward

Parts of a Business Letter

The parts of a business letter are similar to the parts of a friendly letter except that they are written more formally. Follow these suggestions for writing the parts of a business letter:

1. **Heading.** The heading of a business letter is the same as the heading for a friendly letter. Check capitalization and punctuation and do not abbreviate.

2. **Inside Address.** The inside address consists of the name and address of the firm or organization to which you are writing. This address follows the same capitalization and punctuation rules as the heading. The inside address always begins at the left margin.

3. **Salutation.** The salutation begins two lines after the inside address and ends with a colon (:). If you are writing to a specific person, use *Dear* and then the person's name, such as *Dear Mr. Reed:*. If you do not know the name of the person to whom you are writing, use a general greeting, such as *Dear Sir or Madam:* or *Ladies and Gentlemen:*.

4. **Body.** The body of a business letter is brief, courteous, and to the point. State clearly the purpose of your letter.

5. **Closing.** The closing appears on the first line below the body. Here are common closings for a business letter:

    Sincerely yours,   Yours truly,   Respectfully yours,

    Notice that *only* the first word of the closing is capitalized and that the closing is followed by a comma.

6. **Signature.** Type or print your name four spaces below the closing; then write your signature in the space between. Even if your signature is not clear, your name can be clearly read.

Make a copy of each of your business letters so you will have a record of what you wrote and when you wrote it. You can do this by using carbon paper. Always mail the original.

Part 4

Objective

To write three types of business letters: letters of request, order letters, letters of complaint or adjustment

Presenting the Lesson

1. Read the introduction on page 250. List the three types of letters on the chalkboard: letter of request, order letter, and letter of complaint or adjustment. Emphasize that each type of letter is written in the same form; only the information included in the body is different.

2. Read **The Letter of Request** on page 250. Turn the guidelines for letters of request into questions and analyze the sample letter of request on page 251. (1. Who is the writer? 2. Why is he writing to Action for Children's Television? 3. What specific information does he need? 4. Why does he need the information?)

3. Assign the Exercise on the top of page 252.

4. Read **The Order Letter** on page 252. Turn the guidelines for order letters into questions and analyze the sample letter on page 253. (1. What is the product and how many does the writer want? 2. In what publication did the writer see the ad? 3. Is a catalog number, size, or color necessary? 4. What is the cost of the item? 5. What is the cost of postage and handling? 6. What is the total cost? 7. Are any items enclosed? 8. What important

There are three basic types of business letters, each with its own specific purpose: the letter of request, the order letter, and the letter of complaint or adjustment. Each of these business letters follows the same basic business letter form and includes the same parts of a letter. The only differences appear in the information you include in the body of the letter.

The Letter of Request

This type of business letter is particularly useful for getting first-hand information for reports, for receiving catalogs and pamphlets, and for researching a product before you buy it. In a letter of request, be sure to include the following information:

Guidelines for Letters of Request

1. Identify yourself.

2. Tell why you are contacting the person or company.

3. Tell what specific information you need.

4. Tell why you need the information.

Notice how these guidelines are followed in the letter of request on the next page.

58 Eagle Road
La Crosse, Wisconsin 54601
February 10, 1984

Action for Children's Television
46 Austin Street
Newtonville, Massachusetts

Dear Sir or Madam:

Our language arts class at Winston Junior High School is studying television and advertising. Our teacher listed your organization as a good resource for information on this subject. My particular report concerns advertising for Saturday morning programs. I would appreciate your sending me any information you have on this subject. It is necessary that I receive this information by March 1 for my report.

Yours truly,
David Stewart
David Stewart

terms of the ad are restated?)

5. Assign the Exercise on page 254.

6. Read **The Letter of Complaint or Adjustment** on page 254. Turn the guidelines for letters of complaint or adjustment into questions and analyze the sample letter on page 255. (1. What is the specific name of the product? 2. When and where was the item purchased? 3. What is the nature of the problem? 4. How does the writer want the problem corrected?)

7. Assign the Exercise on page 256.

Individualizing the Lesson

Less-Advanced Students

1. For the Exercise on page 252, work with the students to write each address on the chalkboard in the correct form for an inside address. Have the students complete the Exercise independently.

2. For the exercise on page 254, have the students choose only one situation.

3. Break the Exercise on page 256 into smaller tasks. First have each student find an address for the situation he or she has chosen. Then have each student write a draft of the body of the letter. Discuss the drafts in class, and suggest revisions. Finally, have the students write clean copies of their letters.

Advanced Students

1. For the Exercise on page 252, have the students choose two topics. Ask them to arrange one letter in block form and one in modified block. (If they cannot type the block form letter, have them write "Typed"

251

on the bottom of the page to remind them that only typed letters should be in block form.)

2. For the Exercise on page 254, break the class into small groups after the students have written their letters. Have them use the guidelines for order letters on page 252 to criticize the letters. Instruct the students to rewrite their letters making any necessary corrections.

3. For the Exercise on page 256, have the students select more than one situation.

Optional Practice

1. Have each student select a city in the United States that he or she would like to visit. Then have him or her write a letter to the department of tourism or chamber of commerce requesting information about local tourist attractions. (Tell students that most public libraries have a collection of telephone books, in which they should be able to find the correct address.)

2. Bring a collection of magazines and catalogs to class. Have the students select items to order and then write order letters.

3. Have the students follow the instructions for the Exercise on page 256.

1. A book club mailed you the wrong book. Send it back and request the correct one.
2. The photo lab where you left a roll of film to be developed and printed has not returned your pictures after six weeks.
3. Write to your school board about an issue in your school that you feel needs attention.

Exercise Writing Letters of Request

Write a letter of request dealing with one of these situations. Use correct business letter form. (Do not send the letter.)

1. You have just started backpacking as a hobby and would like to join a group or club. Write to International Backpackers Association, P.O. Box 85, Lincoln Center, ME 04458.

2. Your uncle has given you his stamp collection. You would like to add to it, but you need more information. Write to *National Stamp News,* Box 4066, Anderson, SC 29622.

3. Your family is moving to Texas, and you want to learn all you can about the state. Write to Texas Tourist Development Agency, Box 12008, Dept. NW, Austin, TX 78711.

The Order Letter

In the order letter, you must include many specific details to make sure you receive the exact merchandise you want to buy.

Guidelines for Order Letters

1. Give the name of the product and how many you want.

2. Give the name of the publication in which you saw the ad.

3. Give the catalog number, size, and/or color.

4. Compute the price of the item(s).

5. Include the cost of the postage and handling.

6. Compute the price of the total order.

7. State any item you are enclosing, such as a check or money order, or a picture, etc.

8. Restate any important terms that are a part of the ad, such as delivery time.

The following is a sample of an order letter.

163 Poinsettia Drive
Tampa, Florida 33684
October 14, 1984

Masterwork
1708 17th Street
Santa Monica, California 90404

Dear Sir or Madam:
　　Please send me the photo belt buckle advertised in the September issue of Better Homes and Gardens. I am enclosing $7.95, plus $1.00 postage.
　　I am enclosing the black and white photo to be used. I understand that my photo will be returned and that delivery will take four to six weeks.

Yours truly,
Robert Takamoto
Robert Takamoto

253

Exercise Writing Order Letters

Choose two of the following situations. Write an order letter for each. Include all of the necessary information. Use correct business letter form. (Do not send the letter.)

1. Order one sports equipment caddy, Style Q–56, $8.50 ppd., from Spear Engineering Company, Dept. 3053, Box 7025, Colorado Springs, CO 80933, as seen in the September issue of *Better Homes and Gardens*.

2. Order two sets of 14 personalized pencils, each with your full name. $1.00 per set with 25¢ handling per set, from Atlas Pencil Co., Dept. BHG, Hallandale, Florida 33009, as seen in the July issue of *Boys' Life*.

3. Order the following plans as seen in *Popular Mechanics*: PL–1715, $5.95; PL–1406, $14.95; PL–1401, $6.95; PM Catalog, 50¢; ppd. from Popular Mechanics Plans Library, Box 1014, Radio City Station, New York, NY 10019.

The Letter of Complaint or Adjustment

When you have spent time and money ordering or buying a product, you naturally want to be a satisfied customer. The manufacturer of the product usually wants you to be a satisfied customer. If you are not totally satisfied, write directly to the company and courteously state your problem.

Guidelines for Letters of Complaint or Adjustment

1. Give the specific name of the product.

2. Tell when and where the item was purchased.

3. Describe the specific nature of the problem.

4. Tell how you want to have the problem corrected or state that you are returning the merchandise either to be fixed or for a refund.

---

557 Lindal Avenue
Seattle, Washington 98124
August 18, 1984

Holiday Gifts
Department 409-8H
Rock Ridge, Colorado 80034

Dear Sir or Madam:

When I received my personalized sweat-shirt in the mail, I noticed that my name was misspelled.

I have already waited four weeks and I am very disappointed.

I am returning the sweatshirt to you and would like to have the mistake corrected as soon as possible. If delivery will take another four weeks, please refund the $14.95 that I have already paid.

Respectfully,
Frank Steiner
Frank Steiner

Exercise Writing Letters of Complaint or Adjustment

Choose one of the following situations and write an appropriate letter of complaint. Use correct business letter form. Use your local telephone directory or a product you own as a resource for an appropriate address.

1. Write to a candy company complaining about the freshness of a candy bar you bought.

2. The magazine subscription you ordered cost $8.00 for a year's subscription. When you received the bill, it read $80.00.

3. The catalog you ordered still has not arrived. The ad stated 3–4 weeks' delivery. It has now been 6 weeks and you have already paid $3.00 for the catalog.

4. The new 10-speed bike you bought is missing a part. The store can't replace it, so you must write to the company.

5. Write to your local city or village government complaining about a particularly dangerous intersection.

Part 5

Objective

To fold letters properly and address envelopes properly for mailing

Presenting the Lesson

1. Read and discuss the introduction and **Folding Your Letter** on pages 256 and 257.
2. Give each of the students a piece of 6″ x 8″ paper. Have them fold the paper as shown in the instructions for folding a friendly letter on this page. Check their folds.

Part 5 Preparing Your Letter for the Mail

Once you have taken the time to write a friendly letter or a business letter, it is important to fold the letter correctly so that it can be read easily. It is also important to address the envelope carefully so that the letter will reach its destination.

Folding Your Letter

If your friendly letter is written on writing tablet paper, which is generally 6″ × 8″, you should first fold the paper in half. If the letter is still too large for the envelope, fold it in thirds beginning from each side, as shown in the following diagram.

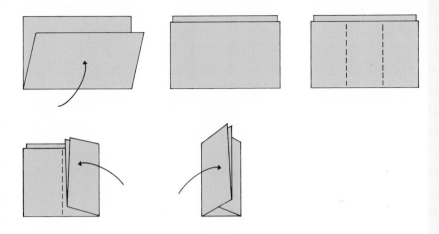

A business letter that is written on standard 8½″ × 11″ paper should be folded into thirds. First, fold from the bottom up and then fold the top third down, as shown below.

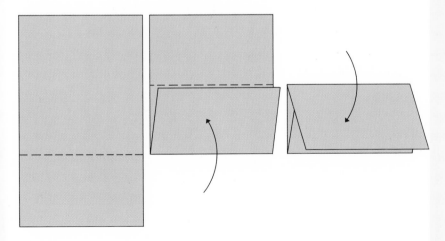

Then have the students fold one of their business letters, following the instructions for folding a business letter on this page. Check their work.

3. Read and discuss **Addressing the Envelope** on page 258. Have the students write the following address as you dictate it:

Mr. Paul Pomeroy
17672 S. E. 147th Street
Clayton, Illinois 64253

Reread the address slowly, and have the students check their work. Emphasize the importance of accuracy.

4. Read **Addressing Envelopes for Friendly Letters** on page 258. Then have each student draw a small "envelope" on a piece of paper. Have the students address their envelopes to their parents.

5. Read **Addressing Envelopes for Business Letters** on page 259. Have each student draw a business "envelope" on a piece of paper. Have the students address their envelopes to the school principal at the school address. Check the students' work.

6. Assign the Exercise on page 259.

Individualizing the Lesson

Less-Advanced Students

Read the addresses in the Exercise orally. Discuss which are for friendly letters and which are for business letters. Have the students complete the Exercise independently.

Advanced Students

Add the following items to the Exercise on page 259.

5. Mr. Samuel Weston, President, Weston Industries, Inc., 15 Long-valley Road, Vail, CO 81657
6. National Geographic Society, 17th and M Streets N.W., Washington, D.C. 20036

Optional Practice

Have the students address envelopes for each of the three business letters they wrote in class.

Extending the Lesson

Explain that most businesses use letterhead stationery and printed envelopes. Bring in an assortment to show the students. Explain that many times a company or institution will have a logo, a trademark, company name, or device. Show examples.

After the students have studied the examples, tell them to imagine that they have formed their own companies, and have them design appropriate logos and letterhead stationery. You might even bring in a chart of type faces for students to choose from.

Addressing the Envelope

The following steps should be taken when addressing your envelope:

Guidelines for Addressing Envelopes

1. Make sure the envelope is right-side up.

2. Always put your return address on the envelope.

3. Double-check all numbers to make sure they are in the proper order.

4. Include the correct zip code.

Addressing Envelopes for Friendly Letters

Envelopes for friendly letters are usually small, such as 6½" × 3½" or 5" × 5":

Miss Annette Johnson
7562 North Hoyne
Chicago, Illinois 60645

Mr. James Speare
2013 St. James Street
Philadelphia, Pennsylvania 19111

When you write out the name of the state, you must place a comma between the city and the state. When you use the two-letter abbreviation for the state, capitalize both letters in the abbreviation.

Addressing Envelopes for Business Letters

When addressing a business envelope, follow the same procedure you did for a friendly letter, but always include your return address on the front of the 9½″ × 4″ envelope that is used for business letters. In addressing a business envelope, you may need an additional line if you are writing to a particular person in the company or if you want the letter to go to a specific department in the company.

Mrs. Joan Caedmon
856 Burke Avenue
Mission, KS 66202

       Mr. Lawrence Laski, Sales Manager
       Heraldica Imports, Inc.
       21 West 46th Street
       New York, NY 10036

Exercise Addressing Envelopes

Address an envelope for each of the following addresses. Use your own address as the return address. Draw a 9½″ × 4″ space on your paper for a business envelope and a 5″ × 5″ space for a friendly letter or invitation.

1. Ms. Maria Talbot, Personnel Director, Ventura Industries, Inc., 1700 4th Ave., Portland, Oregon 97201

2. Mr. W. L. Young, 2600 Vista Blvd., Fresno, CA 93717

3. Casual Designs, 325 S. Washington, Dept. BHG 9, Royal Oak, MI 48067

4. Ms. Caroline Bexley, 2308 Algonquin Rd., Bay Minette, Alabama 36507

Chapter 15

Interviews and Group Discussion

Chapter Objectives

1. To know how to plan and conduct an interview

2. To know how to conduct formal and informal group discussions

3. To know the purposes of five roles of responsibility in a group discussion: the chairperson, the initiator, the clarifier, the summarizer, and the evaluator

Preparing the Students

Read the introduction on this page. Then have the students discuss interviews they have seen on television. Point out that the best interviews are usually those that are well prepared.

Then have the students suggest occasions when they would find themselves in a discussion—a conversation with specific purposes. These situations might include classroom discussions, a planning session for a club activity, or as informal a discussion as that held by a group of friends planning a party.

Explain that this chapter will teach the students the purposes and procedures for conducting interviews and informal and formal group discussions.

Part 1

Objective

To know how to plan and conduct an interview

Most of us enjoy talking with other people. You talk to your friends because you have something to tell them or because they have something to tell you. This kind of talking you call *conversation*. Conversation plays an important part in your daily social life. It helps you to know people better.

Conversations can also have more specific purposes. You may need to interview someone in order to obtain new information for a report you are writing. You and several others may need to have a group discussion to plan a project you are working on. Both interviewing and group discussion are forms of conversation with specific purposes.

This chapter will help you improve your interviewing skills and your group discussion skills.

Presenting the Lesson

1. Read and discuss page 262 and Guidelines for Conducting Interviews on page 263.
2. Assign Exercises A and B on this page.

Individualizing the Lesson

Less-Advanced Students

Work with the students to complete the Exercises in class.

Advanced Students

Have the students actually conduct the interviews they plan.

Optional Practice

Have the students use the Guidelines for Conducting Interviews on page 263 to evaluate a television interview.

Extending the Lesson

Have each student write an article based on an interview. Include the articles in a class newspaper.

Part **2**

Objective

To know how to conduct formal and informal group discussions

Presenting the Lesson

1. Read the introduction on page 262.

Part 1   Interviewing Others

An interview is a special kind of conversation in which the purpose is either to *gather information* or to *supply information.* An interview gives people the opportunity to exchange questions and answers for a specific purpose. At times when you need to gather information for a report, interviewing a knowledgeable person will be very helpful. At other times, such as when you are applying for a job, you will be the one supplying most of the information.

Although an interview is basically conversational, it is more tightly organized than a casual conversation because it has a specific purpose. In order to make your interview a successful one, follow the guidelines on page 263.

Exercises   Planning an Interview

A. List five purposes for which you might conduct interviews in connection with your classwork or extracurricular activities. Name an appropriate person to be interviewed for each purpose.

B. Choose one of the interviews you selected in the first exercise and make a list of ten questions as a guide for an interview.

Part 2   Group Discussion

Group discussion is an easy way to find an answer to a problem, to come up with a new idea, or simply to exchange information. This discussion can be either formal or informal, depending on the subject and purpose of the discussion.

There are two basic types of group discussion: **informal group discussion** and **formal group discussion.** It is important that you know which kind of discussion you are involved in because each has a specific purpose and a certain procedure to follow.

Guidelines for Conducting Interviews

1. Plan the interview carefully.

   a. Choose a person who has special knowledge or interesting opinions about the subject on which you are reporting.
   b. Make a definite appointment by arranging a time and date that is convenient for the person being interviewed. When you request an interview, be sure to identify yourself and explain why you want the interview.
   c. Do some basic research about the subject so you can ask intelligent questions.
   d. Prepare clear, specific questions in advance so that you are sure to get the information you need.

2. Make a good impression.

   a. Arrive for your interview on time.
   b. Introduce yourself and restate your purpose for the interview.
   c. Be ready to ask your questions, one at a time. If the person being interviewed wants to just talk about the subject, you may need to save your questions until the end, unless the person has already answered them.
   d. Be a good listener. Keep your attention on the speaker and what he or she is saying. The person may add some information that you hadn't thought of before.
   e. At the end of the interview, be sure to thank the person.

3. Get the correct facts.

   a. Take notes, especially on names and figures. Make the notes brief so that you are not writing continually while the person is talking.
   b. If you want to quote the person, be sure to ask permission.
   c. Go over your notes as soon as possible after the interview and write your report while the information is still fresh in your mind.

2. Read **Informal Group Discussion** on page 264. Emphasize the purpose of informal discussion, "to exchange ideas in order to make a group decision or plan of action." Then tell the students that they are going to participate in an informal discussion. Divide the class into small groups and have each group agree upon three topics that they would like the entire class to discuss.

3. Read **Formal Group Discussion** on page 265. Compare a formal discussion and an informal discussion by comparing the summaries on pages 264 and 265. Then discuss the topics that the students listed during their informal discussions. Decide which of the suggested topics would be appropriate for a formal discussion.

4. Assign Exercises A and B on page 266.

Individualizing the Lesson

Less-Advanced Students

1. Do Exercise A on page 266 orally.

2. For Exercise B, have the students calculate the average weight of the members of the group in order to simplify the mathematics.

Advanced Students

1. For Exercise A, have the students add three topics for informal discussion and three topics for formal discussion to the list.

2. After the students have completed Exercise B, have them return to their groups and have each group select one of the topics for informal discussion from Exercise A. Remind the students to try to improve their discussions by avoiding the mistakes they made during the first discussion.

Optional Practice

Have the students follow the instructions for Exercise A on page 266.

- Where should the Christmas dance be held?
- Should schools be open 12 months a year?
- Should mass transit systems be funded by the federal government?
- What is a good idea for a summer party?
- Should advertising be banned from children's television?
- Should volunteer fire fighters be covered by a city's insurance program?
- What activities should be included in a school Olympics?

Extending the Lesson

Divide the class into small groups. Assign each group a topic for an informal discussion. If possible, record each group's discussion on tape, and play the tapes to the entire class. Have the class use the questions in Exercise B to analyze the discussions. If it is not possible to record the discussions, have each group hold its discussion at the front of the classroom.

Informal Group Discussion

An informal group discussion usually takes place as soon as a problem or the need for a decision arises. Consider the following situations.

> What would you do if your family has decided to go on a vacation, but you all want to go to different places?

> What would you do if your intramural team has to decide on the best day and time to practice together?

The best solution to these problems is to have an informal discussion. Why? Because you need to exchange your ideas and talk about the pros and cons of each idea for the purpose of arriving at a decision or plan of action that satisfies the group.

Most discussions in which you participate are informal. They usually occur spontaneously, so you don't have to prepare for them. The subjects you discuss are usually those that members of the group know something about from their common knowledge or experience. This is why informal discussions are often organized by the people involved in them.

Sometimes a class or club will break into small informal groups so that everyone will have a chance to express his or her ideas in a shorter period of time. When this method is used, you may need to select a temporary leader to help keep the discussion organized so that your purpose is accomplished.

Even though informal discussion may seem like a friendly conversation, it is more organized and has a specific purpose.

Informal Discussion	
Subjects	General knowledge
Preparation	Not required
Organization	Small groups with no audience; a temporary leader may be selected.
Purpose	To exchange ideas in order to make a group decision or plan of action.

Formal Group Discussion

A formal discussion requires more preparation and organization than an informal discussion does. Consider these topics:

Should space exploration be continued?

Is a college education necessary to achieve success?

You may know something about each of the preceding topics, but how much of what you know is only opinion and how much is fact? If you were asked to discuss one of these topics, you would first have to do some research. A formal discussion requires preparation.

Another major difference between the informal and the formal discussion is the subject to be discussed. Generally, the subject of a formal discussion is either assigned to you or is selected by your group according to the needs or interests of the audience. It is important to be prepared.

The formal discussion is highly organized. First, one person is selected to be chairperson. The chairperson states the problem or subject, directs the discussion, makes sure that everyone has a chance to speak, and keeps the discussion moving.

Each member of the group must present his or her information. Use the many references that are available in your library. The members of your group should freely exchange ideas based on the information you have prepared. In this way, both the members of the group and the audience will learn more.

Formal Discussion

Subjects	Assigned or determined by the needs or interests of the audience.
Preparation	Very important; researched facts are needed.
Organization	A chairperson is selected; discussion is presented in front of an audience.
Purpose	To exchange ideas and information in order to inform the audience.

Exercises Informal and Formal Group Discussion

A. Look at the following list of subjects. Tell which you think should be discussed formally, and which should be discussed informally. Then explain the reasons for your decision.

informal   Which team will win the Super Bowl or World Series?

formal   Should schools be air-conditioned?

formal   Should people use seat belts?

formal   What is approximately the average time per day that teenagers spend watching TV?

informal   What should be the theme for the spring dance?

informal   What are some suggestions for a new school mascot?

formal   What are the best ways of conserving energy?

formal   How does Edgar Allan Poe create suspense in his short stories?

B. Try the following informal discussion. First, divide the class into three groups. Then follow these directions:

Calculate the average height in feet and inches of the members of your group. If you don't know your exact height, you may estimate. The group must agree on the answer and submit it to the teacher.

Once you have finished your calculations and the exercise, discuss the following questions about the exercise. This will help you to understand how a group is organized.

Did anyone take over leadership?
Was he or she elected by the group?
Was a leader needed? Why or why not?
What responsibility did each member have?
Did anything slow down the group?
How could the group solve the problem faster or better next time?

Part 3   Roles of Responsibility

From your own experience in different classes and organizations, you've probably noticed that when one person talks too much, nothing ever gets accomplished. Sometimes a simple discussion turns into an argument and still nothing gets accomplished. For a group discussion to be successful, everyone in the group must accept some responsibility.

When you are a member of either an informal discussion or a formal discussion, you will find that it will be much easier to achieve the purpose of the discussion if the following five roles of responsibility are accepted by members of the group. Each of these roles has a specific purpose.

The Chairperson or Temporary Leader

The role of chairperson or temporary leader carries a lot of responsibility. Each member of the group looks to the chairperson for guidance. The leader must know the subject well, be fair with all members, and see that the purpose of the discussion is accomplished. The chairperson:

1. Starts the discussion by defining the problem or by offering the first bit of information. For example:

> "The purpose of our discussion is to decide the importance of using seat belts. There are many areas to consider in this issue, including safety, insurance benefits, government standards, and the results of manufacturers' tests. Barry, will you tell us what information you have found about this issue?"

> "If we're going to discuss what gift the student council should buy the school, let's first make a list of things that are needed. I would like to suggest a new and larger trophy case."

2. Organizes the group into task forces if the subject involves a lot of material or if more than one decision is needed.

> "Andrea will discuss the insurance benefits of using seat

To know the purposes of five roles of responsibility in a group discussion: the chairperson, the initiator, the clarifier, the summarizer, and the evaluator

Presenting the Lesson

1. Read the introduction on this page. Outline the section by writing the five roles of responsibility on the chalkboard: the chairperson, the initiator, the clarifier, the summarizer, and the evaluator.

2. Read **The Chairperson or Temporary Leader** on pages 267-268. Explain that the chairperson must give the discussion some direction and keep the speakers focused on the topic. The chairperson's job requires knowledge of the subject under discussion and skill in handling people.

Have each student prepare and present an opener for a discussion on one of the topics for a formal discussion in Exercise A on page 266. Tell the students to refer to the examples on this page.

3. Read **The Initiator** on pages 268-269. Have each student prepare and present two initiating statements for his or her topic.

4. Read **The Clarifier** on page 269. Have the students discuss the situations in the sample discussions that led to the sample clarifying questions.

5. Read **The Summarizer** on pages 269-270. Have each student write a summarizing statement about his or her topic.

6. Read **The Evaluator** on pages 270-271. Explain that members of a formal discussion may perform more than one role during the course of the discussion; for example, a person may initiate one idea and evaluate another.

7. Assign Exercises A and B on page 271.

Individualizing the Lesson

Less-Advanced Students

1. Do Exercise A orally.

2. For Exercise B, assist the chairperson in assigning research duties. Then, with the entire group, make a general outline of the topics to be covered in the discussion. Remind the students that each of them will act as an initiator. Then help each student write initiating statements. Remind the students that members of a discussion perform more than one role; each of them may be a clarifier or a summarizer at some point in the discussion.

Advanced Students

Before the students complete Exercise B, have the class discuss standards for the presentations. Duplicate the list of standards in the form of a checklist for evaluating the presentations. Have the students in the audience for each presentation evaluate it and discuss its strengths and weaknesses.

Optional Practice

Have the students repeat Exercise B on page 271 for another topic.

belts, Paul will tell us about government standards that are required, and David and Sharon will discuss the results of the manufacturers' testing to provide safety precautions."

"Since we have enough money to buy two gifts and since our ideas fall into two main categories, let's divide into two groups to make our final decision."

3. Keeps the discussion on the subject so that time and ideas won't be wasted.

"I think we're talking too much about the performance of individual cars rather than the use of seat belts in those cars. Let's get back to the importance of using seat belts."

"Instead of complaining about what's wrong with the gym, how about some good suggestions for gifts to make it better?"

4. Makes sure that everyone has a chance to talk so that all information and ideas are exchanged.

"Andrea, I think now would be a good time for you to tell us about the insurance benefits people receive when they use seat belts."

"Ed, we haven't heard your ideas yet about what we should buy as a gift. What is your suggestion?"

The Initiator

In an active discussion, everyone should "initiate" new ideas and facts. However, some people will serve only as initiators, while others choose to serve in other roles. The initiator:

1. Offers new ideas for discussion.

"I think we should also consider the safety of a small child in a car seat that has a seat belt."

"My idea is that the student council should buy more typewriters for the library. Everyone could benefit from that gift."

2. Gives additional information to support someone else's idea.

"The *Newsweek* article I read agrees with your statement that it's just as important for people in the back seat to use seat belts as for those in the front seat."

"I agree with Ann. The library needs more typewriters. It seems they are always taken when my friends and I need to type a report."

The Clarifier

As the clarifier, you help other group members to support their information and to think of new ideas. The responsibility of the clarifier is to stimulate thought, help others to make their ideas and information clear, and to initiate new ideas. The clarifier:

1. **Asks questions about other people's information.**

   "Sharon, how do we know that the test results for that manufacturer are true for all cars?"

   "A new trophy case might be a good idea, but do you really think it's something the whole school would care about?"

2. **Asks for additional information.**

   "Paul, do you have more current statistics to prove that the majority of people seriously hurt in car accidents were not wearing seat belts?"

   "We have a lot of good ideas, but do we have to spend all of the money?"

The Summarizer

The summarizer keeps everyone in touch with what's happening during the discussion. It is important for you to listen carefully in order to keep track of the main points that have been made. Take notes during the discussion in order to keep the group informed of its progress. The summarizer:

Extending the Lesson

If possible, videotape a television discussion program and watch it in class. Alternatively, record only the audio portion of the program and listen to the discussion in class. Discuss the purpose of the discussion, who took on the various roles of responsibility, and the conclusion of the discussion.

If recording is not possible at all, have the students watch a discussion program on television at home. Tell the students to take notes on the purpose of the discussion, the roles assumed by the people in the discussion, and the conclusion of the discussion. Discuss the program in class.

1. States the main points that have been made so that the group is aware of its progress and what it still has to cover.

"So far we have discussed the government regulations for seat belts and the manufacturers' testing results showing why people should use seat belts. Who has some accident statistics that will bring us closer to our goal?"

"We know that we have enough money to buy more than one gift, and that we have several good ideas and the approximate price of each. Now we need to make a final decision about what to buy."

2. Points out areas of disagreement based on information from different sources or different group members. This helps to prevent arguments and helps the group to remember what is really important about the information.

"Government regulations state that there should be enough seat belts in every car for the number of people it can hold. But David's research shows us that several manufacturers put only two seat belts in the back seat."

"Joe says that a new trophy case is a good idea because the whole school is proud of its winning teams. But Ann says that the hall is always so crowded near the trophy case that most people don't ever bother to look at it."

The Evaluator

The evaluator states the conclusions of the group at the end of the discussion. During the discussion, the evaluator can choose another role and express his or her opinions.

The evaluator:

States the conclusions of the group at the end of the discussion.

"The information presented by this group shows that the government, car manufacturers, and insurance agencies are all interested in the safety that seat belts give. The information also proves that you are less likely to be hurt seriously in an accident and that your insurance is cheaper if you use seat belts. Therefore, it is important for you to use seat belts for your own safety."

"We have enough money to buy two gifts. Since most of the gifts were suggested for the gym and the library, our final decision is to buy six new gymnastic mats for the gym and two new typewriters for the library."

The more group discussion you participate in, the easier it will be to see the importance of the five roles of responsibility. You may find that you are especially good at one role, or you may want to change roles in different discussions. The five different roles help the group to achieve the purpose of the discussion.

Exercises Roles of Responsibility

A. Read each of the following statements and identify who is speaking: the chairperson or temporary leader, the initiator, the clarifier, the summarizer, or the evaluator.

1. "What we need to do is to divide into groups to get each part of this problem solved." chairperson

2. "Do you have more facts to prove that point?" clarifier

3. "Our final decision is to hold the Christmas dance on Friday, December 18, from 7:30 to 10:00 in the gym." evaluator

4. "I would recommend any of Jack London's books for good reading, especially *Call of the Wild*." initiator

5. "So far we have three books that we all agree to recommend, but we still need two more titles." summarizer

B. With four or five other people, plan a formal discussion to present to your class. Choose a topic that interests all of you and that can be easily researched in your school library. Elect a chairperson and decide what information each person will be responsible for. Do your research carefully and keep accurate records of your sources. Present your discussion to the class.

Chapter 16

Enjoying Literature

Chapter Objectives

1. To recognize kinds and characteristics of oral literature

2. To appreciate how sound and figurative language contribute to meaning in poetry

3. To recognize types of nonfiction, including anecdotes, essays, and satires

4. To recognize elements of fiction in the short story and drama

Preparing the Students

Before the students begin this chapter, read aloud these lines from Emily Dickinson's poem:

There is no frigate like a book
To take us lands away,
Nor any coursers like a page
Of prancing poetry.

Ask the students for Emily Dickinson's reasons for liking literature. Discuss how literature can entertain, amuse, inform, enlighten, and inspire. Ask the students to name their favorite works of literature and to explain what makes them enjoyable.

Have the students read the introduction to the chapter. Explain that understanding literature makes it more enjoyable, and that this chapter will give students insight into some different forms of literature.

Additional Resources

Skills Practice Book—pages 75-78.
Duplicating Masters—pages 75-78.

Have you ever noticed that two people can look at the same object and yet see it very differently? For example, one person might find an old carpet and see no more than a floor covering. Another person might look at the same carpet, notice its beautiful colors and design, and display it on a wall.

Talented writers and gifted storytellers have this same ability to find what is special in the world. Through the skillful use of language, they create stories, poems, and plays that allow the rest of us to appreciate what they have found. In this chapter, you will learn about some of the types of literature that have developed since people first put experiences and ideas into words.

1. To become familiar with the role of the oral tradition in literature

2. To recognize different kinds of oral literature

Presenting the Lesson

1. Read and discuss the introduction to Part 1. Stress that the earliest literature was oral, and that oral literature becomes part of a culture's heritage.

Read **Legends** on pages 274-277. Emphasize that legends combine fact and fiction. Give examples of real people who have inspired legends, such as John Chapman, who became the legendary Johnny Appleseed.

Refer students to the excerpt from Arthurian legend, "The Sword in the Stone." Introduce the following vocabulary words for students to look up in a dictionary:

ordained	hilt
squire	bidden
jousting	despairing
pavilion	anvil

Tell the students that Merlin was a magician and seer who helped King Arthur, according to legend.

Discuss why people may have found this legend appealing enough to pass down for generations. Help the students to see that it idealizes the values of honor, devotion, loyalty, and peace.

Discuss the legend of John Henry, and ask the students why people might have enjoyed hearing and retelling this legend. Ask these questions to get students to compare

Part 1   Oral Tradition

Storytelling has existed almost as long as people have. Even before writing was invented, people made up stories to entertain each other, to introduce or explain new ideas, to recall important events, and to teach the values of their groups. These stories became part of an **oral tradition,** the information passed by word of mouth from generation to generation. Included in the oral tradition are legends, tall tales, and ballads.

Legends

Almost every great leader or famous person becomes the focus of many stories. These stories usually begin as accounts of the actual background and life of the person. As the stories are handed down from one generation to another, however, made-up characters, events, and details are added until the stories are as much fiction as fact. Such tales are called **legends.**

One historical character around whom many legends grew was King Arthur. The most famous portion of the Arthurian legend tells how young Arthur became King of England. At this time, England's king had recently died. The only sign as to the identity of the next ruler was a sword that had mysteriously appeared in an anvil outside a church. The sword bore the inscription, "He who draws forth this sword is the rightful King of Britain." Arthur, accompanying his foster brother and foster father to a great tournament, had never heard of the sword or of the mystery surrounding it.

THE SWORD IN THE STONE

Now Kay, Sir Ector's son, had but lately been ordained knight. He was eager to show his skill before strangers and wished to test his courage, so he begged that his father might permit him to travel to London and take part in the great tournament. To this Sir Ector agreed, and one morning he and Kay set forth. With them went Arthur as squire.

On the first day of the jousting, the three of them rode to the place where the contests were to be held. When they were in sight of the gay-colored pavilions in the tourney-field, Kay suddenly exclaimed in annoyance.

"What has happened?" asked Arthur.

"I have forgotten my sword," said Kay. "Ride back to the inn and fetch it for me."

Arthur did as he was bidden. When he came to the inn, however, he found the door locked and the windows shuttered fast. Just as Arthur was despairing, he saw before him the great church, and there, in front of it, the stone with the anvil and the sword.

"I will try to draw out the sword from the anvil," he thought, "for my brother Kay shall not lack a sword this day."

He took hold of the hilt of the sword and made to give it a mighty pull, but to his surprise the sword came out of the anvil easily, as though it had never been held fast. Yet Arthur wasted no time wondering at this; he mounted his horse and galloped back to where Kay waited for him. "Here is a sword for you, brother," he said.

Kay and Sir Ector looked at him with wonder. "How did you come by it?" asked Sir Ector.

Arthur said, "I drew it out from the anvil that my brother might not lack a sword. Have I done wrong?"

Marveling, Sir Ector said, "You shall be King of Britain, Arthur." And he and Kay knelt before Arthur.

"Do not kneel to me, father," pleaded Arthur with distress.

"I am not your father, lord," said Ector. And he told Arthur of how Merlin had brought a little child to him, wrapped in cloth of gold. "And I thought then, and have thought ever since, that you came of nobler blood than I."

Afterwards, Arthur had to replace the sword in the anvil, and then once again, in full sight of all the people gathered there, he had to draw it forth; and with one accord they called to him as their rightful king. And all the lords swore to follow Arthur, so that all the land was his.

and contrast the legendary heroes King Arthur and John Henry:

   a. What character traits do King Arthur and John Henry share?

   b. How do the men differ in social standing?

   c. How does each man represent ideals of his culture?

2. Assign and discuss the Exercise on page 277. Make sure that students cover the following points:

   Question 1— Details that are not historical include Arthur's mysterious past, Arthur's drawing the sword from the stone, and the happily-ever-after ending of peace and harmony throughout the land.

   Question 2—That John Henry lived and was a fine steel driver is probably fact. The details of the contest between John Henry and the steam drill, as well as the circumstances of his death, are probably fictional or greatly exaggerated.

   Question 3—Arthur possesses the admirable qualities of loyalty and devotion (to his brother and father), along with modesty and innocence. John Henry is admired for his strength, courage, determination, and pride.

   Question 4—Arthur is shown respect and reverence by people who become his followers. People view John Henry with respect, admiration, and later sympathy.

3. Read and discuss **Tall Tales** on pages 277-278. Stress that tall tales are stories marked by great— and often humorous—exaggeration. Ask the students how both the description of John Henry's birth and "The Largest Mosquito Ever Seen" demonstrate the characteristics of tall tales. Invite students to tell any tall tales they know.

4. Assign and discuss Exercise A on page 278. Make sure that students can explain the following:

Question 1—Exaggerations in the John Henry tale are the Mississippi running the wrong way, John Henry's weight and abilities at birth, and nature's supposed reactions to John Henry's birth. Exaggerations in the mosquito tale are the mosquito's size, the way it terrorizes a village and its ability to eat farm animals and people.

Question 2—The purpose of the tall tale is overwhelmingly to entertain. In contrast, the purpose of a legend is to communicate the ideas, events, and values of a group of people, or to be a tribute to a great figure.

5. Assign Exercise B on page 278. Remind the students of the characteristics of a tall tale. Then have students choose their own characters to base tall tales on.

6. Read and discuss **Ballads** on pages 279-280. Stress that the ballad was a verse song, and ask the students why they think ballads have been popular for preserving and passing on stories.

Before the students read "The Ballad of Casey Jones," write these railroad terms on the chalkboard and explain them:

rounder—a person who makes rounds, such as a watchman

wheeler—a railroad car having a specified number of wheels

fireman—a man who tends a fire in a locomotive engine

After a volunteer reads the ballad aloud, ask students what happened on Casey's last run. Tell students that legend also says that Casey died with one hand on the whistle and the other on the brake lever. Ask them why his actions would have inspired ballads and legends about him.

7. Assign and discuss the Exercise on page 280. Help students to understand the following:

Every country has legendary heroes. Some of these heroes were kings, queens, and nobles. Others rose from the ranks of the working classes. Such a man was the American legendary hero, John Henry. John Henry was a steel driver at a time when hammering steel into rock was still the most common type of drilling. He became a symbol of the struggle between worker and machine in his famous race with a steam drill.

JOHN HENRY

John Henry was the best steel driver anyone had ever seen. He was a big man who liked to say that his strength, like his family, had come from Africa. John Henry could drive steel all day and never miss a stroke. People came from miles around to watch him swing his two twenty-pound hammers, one in each hand. When John Henry's name was mentioned, folks would say, "Now there's a steel drivin' man."

When John Henry was thirty-four years old, his company went to work on the Big Bend tunnel. Another company had also been contracted for the same job. The workers from that company used steam drills, and claimed that these machines were the greatest of all inventions. John Henry heard the boast and laughed.

"Machines are just machines. They'll never be better than a man. I can sink more steel than any steam drill can."

A contest was arranged. John Henry had his foreman buy him two new twenty-pound hammers for the race. He and his opponent were to drill for thirty-five minutes. The race began, and every driver in the crowd was cheering for John Henry. When the contest was over, John Henry had drilled two holes seven feet deep, and the steam drill had drilled one hole nine feet deep. John Henry was declared the winner.

John Henry grinned, but to his surprise he felt weak and tired. He lay down to rest, and he never got up again. Folks mourned him a long time. To this day, when John Henry's name is mentioned, people say "Now *there* was a steel drivin' man!"

Exercise Understanding Legends

Answer the following questions about the two legends.

1. What details in the legend about King Arthur show that the account is not purely historical?

2. What parts of "John Henry" might be factual? What parts of the selection probably are more fiction than fact?

3. Legendary heroes often display qualities that are admired in their societies. What admirable qualities does Arthur possess? What admirable qualities does John Henry possess?

4. What attitude toward Arthur is shown by the other people in "The Sword in the Stone"? What attitude is shown toward John Henry?

Tall Tales

As storytellers sat around their campfires, they often tried to outdo each other's tales. To do this, they deliberately exaggerated events and details until the stories became wildly unreal. Such inventions are called tall tales. A **tall tale** is a brief story that contains obvious exaggeration.

Sometimes tall tales developed around the same characters who had been the focus of legends. For example, one tall tale about the birth of John Henry began this way:

> The night John Henry was born the stars wouldn't shine, the rain fell hard, and the earth trembled like a leaf. The panthers squalled in the woods like babies, and the Mississippi River ran upstream a thousand miles. At birth, John Henry weighed forty-four pounds. He arrived in the world with a song on his lips and his hand reaching for a hammer.

At other times, tall tales were told about familiar people, places, or situations. The following tale concerns a mosquito. These insects are always annoying, but this storyteller made certain that no one's mosquitos were worse than this one!

277

Question 1—The ballad describes Casey Jones's determination in trying to get the mail through, and his courage in sacrificing his life to save the passenger train.

Question 2—Like a legend or a tall tale, a ballad centers on either a famous person or an ordinary person who does something extraordinary. It also combines fact with fiction. Ballads are different in form from legends and tall tales since ballads have a definite form and lines that rhyme.

Question 3—Ballads can be easily passed on as songs. They are easy to remember because of their catchy rhythms and rhymes. They entertain at the same time as they enlighten.

Individualizing the Lesson

Less-Advanced Students

1. Have the students work together on a tall tale for Exercise B on page 278. After the students agree on a subject, encourage all of them to make suggestions and then incorporate the best ones.

2. Help the students to see the similarities and differences between tall tales, legends, and ballads. Read aloud several of each, and have students categorize them.

Advanced Students

1. Have the students research historical information about Casey Jones and compare the facts with the ballad's story. They may also find other versions of the ballad to present to the class.

2. Ask the students to find out about these legendary heroes: Johnny Appleseed, William Tell, Annie Oakley, Mike Fink, Joan of Arc, and Davy Crockett. Have them do short oral presentations on these characters.

Optional Practice

1. Encourage the students to predict which of today's famous people might become legendary heroes. Assign students to write a modern-day legend by adding imaginary events to the basic facts. Remind the students to follow the Guidelines for the Process of Writing on page 59 as they plan and write their narratives.

2. Have the students research and compare two heroes of oral literature, such as Robin Hood and William Tell. Once again, review with the students the Guidelines for the Process of Writing.

3. Have the students research what is known about the real King Arthur and write reports. Refer students to Chapter 10, "Writing the Report."

4. Have each student begin a tall tale, then pass it on to be continued by a second student and finally completed by a third student. Have volunteers read the tales aloud.

Extending the Lesson

1. Play records of ballads or of folksongs derived from old ballads. "Barbara Allan," "Sir Patrick Spens," and "Robin Hood and the Three Squires" are three English ballads that students might enjoy analyzing.

2. Encourage the students to find examples of other forms of oral literature, such as myths, folk tales, and fables. Point out how they are characteristic of the oral tradition in literature.

3. Assign students to find legends, ballads, or tall tales that

THE LARGEST MOSQUITO EVER SEEN

One time, the largest mosquito anyone had ever seen threatened to destroy my village. Because of a long drought there were few animals left in the marsh where this mosquito lived, and the blood he needed for food was almost gone.

Close to starvation, he headed for the village, eating almost every living thing in his path—horses, cows, goats, pigs, chickens, people.

As he approached, the villagers began to flee. Meanwhile, the leading citizens debated over what to do.

Our local doctor proposed that we feed an old, sick cow all the poison she would eat, then leave her in the road as bait for the oncoming monster. If he ate her, he would die, the doctor said.

The cow was fed the poison. A short while later the mosquito arrived and ate her, but he was so strong that the poison did not have the slightest effect on him. In fact, when he had finished with the cow, he saw a tough old mule grazing nearby and he ate him, too.

The mule didn't take kindly to this treatment. He kicked so hard on the way down that he broke the mosquito's neck, and the village was saved. So was the mule.

Exercises Understanding the Tall Tale

A. Answer the following questions about the two tall tales.

1. Give five examples of exaggeration in each tall tale.

2. Reread the first paragraph in Part 1. Then answer these two questions: What seems to be the purpose of a tall tale? How does this purpose differ from the purpose of a legend?

B. Write your own tall tale about something you have done, seen, or heard about.

Ballads

The oral tradition also includes stories that once were sung by traveling poets. Such songs that tell stories in verse are called **ballads.** Ballads usually recount the adventures of traditional heroes or of ordinary people who performed heroic deeds. To this day, the ballad remains a favorite way of preserving a legend.

Read the following ballad, which retells the legend of Casey Jones, an engineer on the Central Railroad in the early 1900's.

come from different cultures, perhaps their own ethnic or cultural groups. Have students share these during a literary festival.

THE BALLAD OF CASEY JONES

Come all you rounders for I want you to hear
The story told of a brave engineer;
Casey Jones was the rounder's name
On a heavy six-eight wheeler he rode to fame.

It had been raining for more than a week,
The railroad track was like the bed of a creek.
They rated him down to a thirty mile gait,
Threw the south-bound mail about eight hours late.

Jones says, "Fireman, don't you fret,
Keep knockin' at the firedoor, don't give up yet;
I'm goin' to run her till she leaves the rail
Or makes it on time with the south-bound mail."

Around the curve and a-down the dump
Two locomotives were a-bound to bump.
Fireman hollered, "Jones, it's just ahead,
We've got to jump and make it or we'll all be dead."

'Twas around this curve he saw a passenger train,
Casey knew he couldn't cause them misery and pain,
Fireman jumped off, but Casey stayed on,
He's a good engineer but he's dead and gone—

Headaches and heartaches and all kinds of pain
Are not apart from the railroad train,
Tales that are earnest, noble and gran'
Belong to the life of a railroad man.

279

Exercise Understanding the Ballad

Answer the following questions.

1. What brave deed is described in this ballad?
2. How is a ballad like a legend or tall tale? How is it different?
3. Why do you think ballads are such a popular way of preserving a story?

Part 2   Poetry

Look back over the ballad on page 279. When you contrasted the ballad with the tall tale and the legend, did you mention its form, the way it appears on the page? Did you point out the pairs of rhyming lines in the ballad?

A ballad is a type of poetry. **Poetry** is a form of literature that is arranged in lines and usually expresses its meaning in a tight, compact structure. A poet uses language in special ways to express an emotion, tell a story, dramatize a situation, or share a thought. The poet's ideas are presented through the **speaker,** the voice in a poem that addresses the reader.

The Form of Poetry

There are no definite rules concerning the form of poetry. A poet is free to express ideas in any form that helps to convey meaning. Sometimes poets choose **traditional** forms. In traditional poetry, each line begins with a capital letter and follows formal rules of punctuation and spelling. In addition, the lines usually share a pattern of sound and rhythm. They are grouped into units of equal length called **stanzas.**

Look at this example of traditional poetry. What patterns do you see?

Part 2

Objectives

1. To understand the different forms of poetry
2. To become familiar with different literary devices
3. To appreciate how sound and figures of speech contribute to meaning in poetry

Presenting the Lesson

1. Begin by asking students to define *poetry,* writing their definitions on the chalkboard. Stress the definition of poetry as language that expresses ideas and feelings in a more condensed and intense way than ordinary language. Introduce the term *speaker,* and ask why the speaker of the poem may not be the same as the poet.

Provide students with these guidelines for reading poetry:

a. Always try to read a poem aloud. Listen for patterns of sound and rhythm.
b. Do not automatically pause at the end of a line of poetry. Watch for punctuation or shifts in thought instead.

YOUR WORLD

Your world is as big as you make it.
I know, for I used to abide
In the narrowest nest in a corner,
My wings pressing close to my side.

But I sighted the distant horizon
Where the sky line encircled the sea
And I throbbed with a burning desire
To travel this immensity.

I battered the cordons around me
And cradled my wings on the breeze
Then soared to the uttermost reaches
With rapture, with power, with ease!

—GEORGIA DOUGLAS JOHNSON

Another kind of poetry lacks regular, predictable patterns. The writers of these non-traditional poems vary line lengths. They group lines into units that reflect thoughts rather than a pattern. These poets may even ignore or change the rules of capitalization, punctuation, and spelling in order to enrich the meaning of the poem.

Notice how the writer of the following poem plays with language. What additional meaning is conveyed by the unusual spacing and arrangement of words? How does this device help you picture this springtime scene?

281

c. Think about what you're reading. Poetry is language of emotion and ideas, and needs to be read with feeling.

Make sure that all the poems in this chapter are read aloud as the class studies them.

2. Read and discuss **The Form of Poetry** on pages 280-282, and give examples of poems that demonstrate traditional patterns in poetry, such as stanzas and rhymes. Have a student read "Your World" aloud. Make sure that students can point out how the stanzas, capitalization, rhymes, and punctuation make this poem traditional in form. Ask students about the speaker of "Your World" and the advice the speaker gives.

Have students contrast the traditional form of "Your World" with the nontraditional form of "In Just--." Have them point out unconventional capitalization, varying line lengths, and unusual spacing. Discuss the poem by asking these questions:

a. What is "just-spring"?
b. What emotions do the balloonman, puddles, and children playing convey?
c. What does the spacing in "eddieandbill" and "bettyandisbel" tell about the children?
d. Why is the balloonman "goat-footed"? (Tell students about the Greek god Pan, who was half goat and played the pipes.)
e. What does the sound and spacing of "far and wee" suggest?
f. How does the speaker of the poem feel about early spring?

3. Read and discuss **The Sound of Poetry** on pages 282-287. Help the students to recognize alliteration by having them repeat alliterative tongue twisters, such as "rubber baby buggy bumpers" and "Peter

Piper." Then ask the students to make up examples of assonance and consonance, such as "d<u>a</u>y's w<u>a</u>it" and "dar<u>k</u> bla<u>ck</u> oa<u>k</u>." Read "Alarm Clock" aloud, and review with students how and why these three sound techniques are used in the poem.

Introduce students to the concept of onomatopoeia by asking them to imitate and then write down the sound of a cow, a fly-swatter, a doorbell, and thunder. Make sure that the students recognize the words *shushes, hushes, flitter-twitters,* and *whirs* in "Cynthia in the Snow" as onomatopoeia. Also point out the alliteration of "whitely whirs away."

4. Discuss the terms *rhyme* and *rhyme scheme,* and have students practice stringing together rhyming words into sentences, as in "A lark named Clark hit its mark—a shark!" Use the overhead projector to point out the rhyme scheme of "Your World" (abcb defe eghg) on page 281. See if the students understand the concept of rhyme scheme by having them predict the pattern for four more lines of "Advice to Travelers" (efef).

Ask the students to describe the speaker of "Lone Dog." Have students point out examples of internal rhyme (lean/keen, rough/tough, mad/bad) in the poem.

5. Talk about the rhythm of music and why rhythm helps to make poetry appealing. Help the student to find key words to use for remembering the four types of poetic feet, such as

return	family
tiny	interrupt

"IN JUST—"

in Just—
spring   when the world is mud-
luscious the little
lame balloonman

whistles   far   and wee

and eddieandbill come
running from marbles and
piracies and it's
spring

when the world is puddle-wonderful

the queer
old balloonman whistles
far   and   wee
and bettyandisbel come dancing

from hop-scotch and jump-rope and

it's
spring
and
    the
       goat-footed

balloonMan   whistles
far
and
wee
         —e. e. cummings

The Sound of Poetry

When you read a poem, you respond to sound as well as meaning. Poets create sound patterns with a variety of techniques. These techniques can help extend the meaning of the poem.

Alliteration. Poets often repeat the same consonant sound at the beginnings of words. This technique is called **alliteration.** Notice how the repetition of the *f* sound in this poem helps create a quiet, restful feeling—until the buzz of the alarm intrudes!

ALARM CLOCK

in the deep sleep forest
there were ferns
there were feathers
there was fur
and a soft ripe peach
on a branch within my
r-r-r-r-r-r-r-r-r-r-r-r-r-r-r-r-r-r-r-r-r-r-r-r-r-r-r-r-r-r-r
—EVE MERRIAM

Assonance and Consonance. When a vowel sound is repeated within words, the technique is called **assonance.** When consonant sounds are repeated, the technique is called **consonance.** Reread "Alarm Clock." Listen for the long *e* sound and for the consonant sounds of *p, r,* and *ch.* Why might the poet have chosen to repeat these sounds?

Onomatopoeia. When poets use words that imitate real-life sounds the technique is called **onomatopoeia.** In this poem, find words that help you hear as well as see the snow.

CYNTHIA IN THE SNOW

It SHUSHES.
It hushes
The loudness in the road.
It flitter-twitters,
And laughs away from me.
It laughs a lovely whiteness,
And whitely whirs away,
To be
Somewhere otherwhere,
Still white as milk or shirts.
So beautiful it hurts.
—GWENDOLYN BROOKS

Read "Song of the Truck" aloud and have the students tap their pencils to the beat. Talk about the monotonous traveling sound that the regular /◡◡ meter gives the poem, and have students contrast that regular rhythm with the free verse of "Inside a Poem." Help the students to see how Merriam illustrates the sense of her poem with the sounds in it.

6. Read aloud "African Dance," and ask students about the feelings repetition creates. In addition, have students explain the effect of assonance using the long *o* sound.

7. Assign and discuss Exercise A on page 287. After the students read "Where Would You Be?" aloud, ask them about the speaker of the poem and the two choices the speaker offers for how to live. Let students respond to the questions in the poem. Make sure they understand that the speaker is not necessarily advocating the "comfortable" choice.

During discussion of the Exercise, be sure to cover these points:

Question 1—The poem has traditional stanza and line patterns, as well as traditional capitalization and punctuation. Lines of the poem rhyme.

Question 2—The rhyme scheme is abccb cdeed fghiiig. The rhythm shows a fairly regular pattern with /◡◡ feet dominant.

Question 3—There are many examples of *w* alliteration, as well as the sounds in "searching for stars" and "twisting trees are tossed." There are many examples of assonance with the long *i* sound *(whine, wild, night).*

Question 4—Each stanza repeats "Where would you . . ." and "Or . . ."

283

8. Assign Exercise B on page 287. Suggest that students jot down ideas for poetic devices before combining them in a poem. Work with the students individually.

9. Read and discuss **The Language of Poetry** on pages 288-290. Help the students to understand imagery by having them describe the sound, appearance, smell, taste, and feel of a marshmallow by comparing these characteristics with something similar. Talk about details that appeal to each sense.

Stress the definitions of *simile, metaphor,* and *personification,* and discuss why these techniques are used widely in poetry. Ask students to give examples from their experience of two things that could be compared, such as a rooster and an alarm clock. Help them to create their own similes, metaphors, or personifications. Go over the definition of *cliché,* and discourage the use of such overworked similes as "busy as a bee" and "hungry as a bear."

Read aloud "The Base Stealer." Have students find the three similes in this excerpt and tell why each is appropriate.

Before the students read "Rain," introduce these words for them to define:

soprano
bass
attentively

Have students find the three main metaphors in the poem (old man, harp strings, the soft weary music) and explain why each is a good comparison. Then ask how the sound techniques of repetition, alliteration, assonance, and onomatopoeia contribute to the poem?

Rhyme. When the same syllable sound occurs at the ends of two or more lines of poetry, the poet is using the familiar technique of **rhyme.** The pattern of end rhyme in a poem is called the **rhyme scheme.** This pattern can be identified by marking the end of each line with a letter of the alphabet, beginning with *a.* Lines that rhyme are marked with the same letter. Notice the rhyme scheme in the following poem.

ADVICE TO TRAVELERS

A burro once, sent by express,	**a**
His shipping ticket on his bridle,	**b**
Ate up his name and his address,	**a**
And in some warehouse, standing idle,	**b**
He waited till he like to died.	**c**
The moral hardly needs the showing:	**d**
Don't keep things locked up deep inside—	**c**
Say who you are and where you're going.	**d**

—WALKER GIBSON

Poets sometimes include rhyming words within lines. Such rhyme is called **internal rhyme.** Notice the use of both internal and end rhyme in the following lines. The rhyme helps to emphasize the harsh adjectives describing the dog.

from LONE DOG

I'm a lean dog, a keen dog, a wild dog, and lone;
I'm a rough dog, a tough dog, hunting on my own;
I'm a bad dog, a mad dog, teasing silly sheep;
I love to sit and bay the moon, to keep fat souls from sleep.

—IRENE RUTHERFORD MC LEOD

Rhythm. Rhythm is the pattern of stressed and unstressed syllables in a line of poetry. Rhythm helps to create the mood experienced by the reader. Rhythm also emphasizes important words and ideas and brings out the musical quality of the language.

In poetry, the basic unit of rhythm is called a **foot.** Each foot represents a pattern of stressed (/) and unstressed ($\smile$) syllables. Usually a foot has either two or three syllables. If a foot has two syllables, it might have one of the following patterns: / $\smile$, $\smile$ /. If a foot has three syllables, it probably follows one of these patterns: / $\smile$ $\smile$, $\smile$ $\smile$ /.

The pattern of feet in a poem, along with the number of times that each foot is repeated in a line, is the **meter** of a poem. The following poem has a regular meter. Read the poem aloud, tapping out the strong, accented beats.

from SONG OF THE TRUCK

This is the song that the truck drivers hear
In the grinding of brake and the shifting of gear,
From the noise of the wheel and the clarion horn,
From the freight and the weight—
      a song has been born.
      —DORIS FRANKEL

What poetic foot seems to dominate the poem? Why do you think the poet chose to use it? The steady rhythm is interrupted in the last line. What effect does that have on the reader?

Many poems, especially those by more modern writers, have no regular patterns of rhyme or meter. Such poetry is called **free verse.** The rhythm in free verse reflects the natural rise and fall of everyday patterns of speech. The following example of free verse explains this kind of poetry.

To illustrate personification, ask students to make up sentences giving trees human qualities. Read aloud "Surf." Ask which human qualities the speaker gives waves. Discuss the appropriateness of the figures of speech comparing waves to wheels and pole vaulters. Ask what the alliterative sound of "foam fingers" suggests.

10. Assign and discuss Exercise A on page 290. Make sure that students identify the following:

> **Question 1**—simile comparing skydiver to a frog; metaphor comparing parachute to a flower
> **Question 2**—metaphors comparing wind with an accordian, a hurricane with a dancer, the sea with a carpet, and palm with a broom; the personification of the hurricane as a musician and as a dancer that whirls on its toes

11. Assign Exercise B. Work with the students individually on poems. During the revision process, allow students to work with editing partners.

Individualizing the Lesson

Less-Advanced Students

1. Ask the students to make dictionaries of these poetic terms: *alliteration, assonance, consonance, rhyme, free verse, meter, foot, onomatopoeia, internal rhyme, traditional poetry, imagery, simile, metaphor, personification,* and *figure of speech.* Have students include definitions as well as examples from poems they read.

2. Direct the students in working together on a group poem for the Exercises on pages 287 and 290. Then have the students work on poems individually.

3. Have the students complete the following sentences to make similes and metaphors:

a. Morning is like a _____.
b. The water was as cool as _____.
c. Her hair glistened like _____.
d. Stars are the night's _____.
e. Leaves fell onto the _____ of grass.
f. His moustache was a _____ of hair.

4. Work with the students on reading poems aloud. As they read, emphasize the sounds and rhythms that are important to a poem's meaning.

Advanced Students

1. Have the students choose poems that illustrate each of the figures of speech. Ask the students to read these aloud and present several questions for class discussion.

2. Ask students to choose a poem and write a composition analyzing its meaning, form, or use of sound and imagery.

Optional Practice

1. Modeling their poems after "In Just--," have the students write free verse about "just-fall" or "just-winter."

2. Pass out copies of poems, and have the students identify the imagery and figurative language used.

3. Read these phrases, and ask the students to identify the poetic techniques used:

a. "with a whoop it swooped"
b. "a rag of a tail"
c. "a beak like scissors"
d. "the kettle hummed and danced"
e. "as magical as music"

4. Have students listen to recordings of poems, paying close atten-

INSIDE A POEM

It doesn't always have to rhyme,
but there's the repeat of a beat, somewhere
an inner chime that makes you want to
tap your feet or swerve in a curve;
a lilt, a leap, a lightning-split:—
thunderstruck the consonants jut,
while the vowels open wide as waves in the moon-
   blue sea.

—EVE MERRIAM

Repetition. The repetition of words, phrases, and lines is a technique common to both patterned poetry and free verse. Notice how the repetitions in the following poem emphasize ideas and create a highly rhythmic effect. You can almost feel the beat of the drums.

AFRICAN DANCE

The low beating of the tom-toms,
   The slow beating of the tom-toms,
   Low . . . slow
   Slow . . . low—
Stirs your blood.

            Dance!
A night-veiled girl
   Whirls softly into a
   Circle of light.
Whirls softly . . . slowly,
Like a wisp of smoke around the fire—
   And the tom-toms beat,
   And the tom-toms beat,
And the low beating of the tom-toms
   Stirs your blood.

—LANGSTON HUGHES

Exercises Understanding Form and Sound in Poetry

A. Read the following poem. Then answer the questions.

WHERE WOULD YOU BE?

Where would you be on a night like this
With the wind so dark and howling?
Close to the light
Wrapped warm and tight
Or there where the cats are prowling?

Where would you wish you on such a night
When the twisting trees are tossed?
Safe in a chair
In the lamp-lit air
Or out where the moon is lost?

Where would you be when the white waves roar
On the tumbling storm-torn sea?
Tucked inside
Where it's calm and dry
Or searching for stars in the furious sky
Whipped by the whine of the gale's wild cry
Out in the night with me?

—KARLA KUSKIN

1. In what ways is this poem traditional in form?

2. Does this poem have a rhyme scheme? A regular meter? Explain your answer.

3. Find three examples of alliteration. Fine one example of assonance.

4. Find an example of repetition.

B. Write a poem on the subject of animals or a particular animal. You may write free verse or stanzas with regular patterns of end rhyme and meter. Use at least two of these poetic devices: alliteration, assonance, consonance, onomatopoeia, internal rhyme, or repetition.

tion to how sound contributes to meaning.

5. Have each student find a poem and write a composition analyzing how poetic techniques contribute to its meaning.

Extending the Lesson

1. Assign students to write reports on poets. Review biographical resources, as well as Chapter 10, "Writing the Report."

2. Assign the students to write their own ballads modeled on "The Ballad of Casey Jones," memorializing a brave deed from history.

3. Compile a literary magazine that includes each student's best poem.

The Language of Poetry

How are poets able to get so much meaning into so few words? Poets rely on **imagery;** that is, they use concrete words and phrases that appeal to the five senses. Notice how the poet's selection of just the right words helps the reader of the following poem to picture and hear the movements of a cat. The writer obviously knows cats well—but does she *trust* them?

from CATALOGUE

Cats sleep fat and walk thin.
Cats, when they sleep, slump;
When they wake, stretch and begin
Over, pulling their ribs in.
Cats walk thin.

Cats wait in a lump,
Jump in a streak.
Cats, when they jump, are sleek
As a grape slipping its skin—
They have technique.
Oh, cats don't creak.
They sneak.

—ROSALIE MOORE

Poets also create images through **figures of speech,** expressions that are not literally true. A poet uses figures of speech to change abstract ideas into vivid word pictures. Common figures of speech include **simile, metaphor,** and **personification.**

Simile. A **simile** is a figure of speech that compares two things that are basically unlike but that have something in common. The comparison includes the word *like* or *as*. Some similes, such as "strong as a horse," have been used so much that they have become *clichés*—overworked expressions. A poet, however, will create sharp, fresh similes that allow the reader to see familiar things in new ways. Notice how this poet uses similes to vividly describe the movements of the baseball player.

from THE BASE STEALER

Poised between going on and back, pulled
Both ways taut like a tightrope-walker,
Fingertips pointing the opposites,
Now bouncing tiptoe like a dropped ball
Or a kid skipping rope, come on, come on . . .
—ROBERT FRANCIS

Metaphor. Often poets make comparisons without using *like* or *as*. The result is the figure of speech known as **metaphor.** Like a simile, the metaphor allows the reader to see something familiar in a new way. In the following poem, the speaker compares rain with an old man, and houses with harp strings. With what does he compare the sound of rain?

RAIN

Today the rain
is an aged man
a gray old man
in a music store

Today houses
are strings of a harp
soprano harp strings
bass harp strings
in a music store

The ancient man
strums the harp
with thin long fingers
attentively picking
a weary jingle
a soft jazzy jangle
then hurries away
before the boss comes 'round. . . .
—FRANK MARSHALL DAVIS

Personification. Another way of creating a vivid image is to give human qualities to an animal, object, or idea. This figure of speech is called **personification.** Notice how the use of personification in this poem brings the waves to life:

SURF

Waves want
to be wheels,
They jump for it
and fail
fall flat
like pole vaulters
and sprawl
arms outstretched
foam fingers
reaching.
—LILLIAN MORRISON

Exercises Understanding the Language of Poetry

A. Identify one or more of the following techniques in each excerpt: simile, metaphor, personification.

1. Grotesque, jumping out
   like a clothed frog, helmet and glasses,
   arms and legs wading the sky,
   feet flapping before the cloth flower opens:

   from "Sky Diver" by ADRIEN STOUTENBURG

2. When the hurricane unfolds
   Its fierce accordion of winds,
   On the tip of its toes,
   Agile dancer, it sweeps whirling
   Over the carpeted surface of the sea
   With the scattered branches of the palm.

   "The Hurricane" by PALES MATOS

B. Write a short poem that includes two figures of speech.

Part 3   Nonfiction

Any writing that is not poetry is known as **prose.** When prose deals with real people, places, and events, the writing is a work of **nonfiction.** Nonfiction literature includes journals, biographies, narrative stories, and essays. The purpose of this type of writing is usually to inform or persuade the reader, or to examine and record experiences and events.

Anecdotes

You may have heard the phrase "stranger than fiction." It means that sometimes the people and situations in the real world are as odd, exciting, or humorous as anything that could be invented in the imagination. Because this is so, writers often record favorite stories, or **anecdotes,** that they hope will amuse others. The following anecdote recounts an episode that involved the author's mother and their dog, an unusually self-assured animal named Mutt.

from THE DOG WHO WOULDN'T BE

Mutt had a disconcerting effect upon strangers. So strong was his belief that he was not simply "dog" that he was somehow able to convey this conviction to human onlookers.

One bitterly cold day in January, Mother went downtown to do some post-Christmas shopping and Mutt accompanied her. She parted from him outside the Hudson Bay Department Store, for Mutt had strong prejudices, and one of these was directed against any type of shopping. Mother was inside the store for almost an hour, while Mutt was left to shiver on the wind-swept pavement.

When Mother emerged at last, Mutt had forgotten that he had voluntarily elected to remain outside. Instead he was

Part 3

Objectives

1. To recognize types of nonfiction
2. To understand the techniques used in nonfiction

Presenting the Lesson

1. Read and discuss the introduction and **Anecdotes** on pages 291-293. Stress that nonfiction recounts actual events or describes actual people, places, and things.

To reinforce the definition of *anecdote,* ask the students to share some amusing anecdotes with the class. Before the students read the anecdote from *The Dog Who Wouldn't Be,* have them look up definitions for these words:

disconcerting	*sotto voce*
prejudice	adamantly
grievance	exasperated
calculated	reproachfully
indifference	guttural
sulk	disdain
frigid	dispatch
	linger

Tell the students that Dukhobors are members of a Canadian Christian sect.

Lead a discussion of the anecdote with these questions:

  a. How does the author think his dog is different from others?
  b. What is the author's attitude toward the incident?
  c. What makes the anecdote humorous?

2. Assign and discuss Exercise A on page 293. Prepare the students by discussing the definition of *tone.* In discussing the Exercise, be sure to cover these points:

Question 2—Examples of personification are that Mutt was prejudiced against shopping, that he held a grievance against Mother, and that he responded with varying degrees of indifference to all of the humans. Descriptions of the police officer "wagging" a "paw" compare him to a dog.

3. Assign Exercise B on page 293. Point out that the anecdotes will most likely be in the form of a narrative composition.

4. Read and discuss **Essay** on pages 293-295. Contrast the purpose of an essay with that of an anecdote. Ask the students to point out all first-person pronouns.

Before the students read this essay, have them close their eyes and try to describe the room they are in. Ask them how observant they think they are of sights and sounds in their environment.

Then introduce these words for students to look up in a dictionary:

incredulous   panorama
symmetry   stricken

After the students read Helen Keller's essay, see if their attitude toward seeing and observing has changed. Ask the students to summarize the main point of Helen Keller's essay and to point out five examples of vivid language that help to make that point. Help the students to appreciate that these beautiful descriptions were written by a woman who had never seen or heard the things she described.

5. Assign Exercise A on page 294. Be sure that the students understand the following:

nursing a grievance at what seemed to him to be a calculated indifference to his comfort on my mother's part. He had decided to sulk, and when he sulked he became stubborn. Nothing that Mother would say could persuade him to get up off the frigid concrete and accompany her home. Mother pleaded. Mutt ignored her and fixed his gaze upon the steamed-up windows of the Star Cafe across the street.

Neither of them was aware of the small audience that had formed around them. There were three Dukhobors in their quaint winter costumes, a police officer enveloped in a buffalo-skin coat, and a dentist from the nearby Medical Arts Building. Despite the cold, these strangers stood and watched with growing fascination as Mother ordered and Mutt, with slightly lifted lip and *sotto-voce* mutters, adamantly refused to heed. Both of them were becoming exasperated, and the tone of their voices grew increasingly violent.

It was at this point that the dentist lost touch with reality. He stepped forward and addressed Mutt in man-to-man tones.

"Oh, I say, old boy, be reasonable!" he said reproachfully.

Mutt replied with a murmur of guttural disdain, and this was too much for the police officer.

"What seems to be the matter here?" he asked.

Mother explained. "He won't go home. He just won't go!"

The officer was a man of action. He wagged his mittened paw under Mutt's nose. "Can't you see the lady's cold?" he asked sternly.

Mutt rolled his eyes and yawned and the police officer lost his temper. "Now, see here," he cried, "you just move along or, by the gods, I'll run you in!"

It was fortunate that my father and the car came by at this moment. Father had seen Mutt and Mother in arguments before, and he acted with dispatch, picking them both up almost bodily and pushing them into the front seat. He did not linger, for he had no desire to be a witness to the reactions of the big police officer and of the dentist when they became aware of the fact that they had been arguing with a dog upon a public street.

—FARLEY MOWAT

Exercises Understanding Anecdotes

A. Answer the following questions.

1. The attitude that a speaker takes toward a subject is called the **tone.** For example, the tone might be serious, sad, or humorous. What is the tone of this anecdote?

2. Much of the comedy in this piece comes from the writer's personification of Mutt. Find three examples where Mutt is given human characteristics. Can you find an example where a human is given the characteristics of a dog?

B. Think of an incident in your life that made a strong impression on you. Write it in the form of an anecdote.

Essay

In the excerpt about Mutt, the writer's primary purpose was to tell a story. Sometimes, though, a writer wants to share beliefs or feelings on a subject rather than relate experiences.

An **essay** is a kind of nonfiction writing in which a writer shares thoughts with the reader. The writer's purpose might be to comment on a situation or to persuade the reader to agree with his or her ideas. An essay may be humorous, or it may be straightforward and serious. It is usually written from the **first-person point of view,** using pronouns such as *I* or *we.* **Third-person point of view** uses pronouns such as *he, she,* and *they.*

Following is an essay written by Helen Keller, a woman left blind and deaf at a young age. As you read, think about the purpose of this essay and about the opinions expressed.

THE SEEING SEE LITTLE

Now and then I have tested my seeing friends to discover what they see. Recently I was visited by a very good friend who had just returned from a long walk in the woods, and I asked her what she had observed. "Nothing in particular,"

Question 1—Helen Keller's basic idea is summarized in the title. She claims that sighted people take their senses for granted and do not use them fully.

Question 2—Helen Keller's purpose is to inspire sighted people to take advantage of their senses and experience the world more deeply and fully.

Question 3—The tone is serious, even passionate.

Question 4—An author might write objectively when she or he wants to allow the readers to make up their own minds, as in a factual news account. An author usually writes subjectively when she or he wants to sway or persuade readers.

6. Read and discuss **Satire** on pages 295-296. Emphasize the purpose of satire, and ask students to mention examples of satire they have read. Before the students read "Is There Life on Earth?" have them look up these words in a dictionary:

light-year	stalagmite
feasibility	granite

After the students read "Is There Life on Earth?" ask them which elements are fictional and what Buchwald satirizes. Discuss the tone of this satire, explaining that satire can be bitter, angry, or playful.

7. Assign and discuss the Exercise on page 296. Make sure that the students recognize these points:

Question 1—Because of the masses of concrete, as well as the air and water pollution, Venusian scientists conclude that Earth cannot sustain life.

Question 2—The dense network of highways, sidewalks, and buildings in Manhattan give the appearance from a distance of solid concrete. The metal particles are cars, and the stalagmites are skyscrapers.

Individualizing the Lesson

Less-Advanced Students

1. Have the students keep lists of these literary terms and their definitions: *prose, nonfiction, first-person point of view, essay, anecdote, satire, tone, objectivity, subjectivity.* Urge students to find examples of each.

2. For Exercise B on page 295, help the students to work together to brainstorm for a subject and then make notes for the essay. From that point on, assist the students individually with their essays.

Advanced Students

1. Have the students work with editing partners to make improvements in the first drafts of essays for Exercise B on page 295.

2. Ask the students to debate these two issues: Do sighted people misuse their faculties? For what purpose should sight and hearing be used?

3. Introduce students to other forms of satire, such as the *parody.* Have them compose their own examples.

Optional Practice

1. Assign the students to talk over favorite family anecdotes with their families and then to write one, following the Guidelines for the Process of Writing on page 59.

she replied. I might have been incredulous had I not been accustomed to such responses, for long ago I became convinced that the seeing see little.

How was it possible, I asked myself, to walk for an hour through the woods and see nothing worthy of note? I who cannot see find hundreds of things to interest me through mere touch. I feel the delicate symmetry of a leaf. I pass my hands lovingly about the smooth skin of a silver birch or the rough shaggy bark of a pine. In spring I touch the branches of trees hopefully in search of a bud, the first sign of awakening Nature after her winter's sleep. Occasionally, if I am very fortunate, I place my hand gently on a small tree and feel the happy quiver of a bird in full song.

At times my heart cries out with longing to see all these things. If I can get so much pleasure from mere touch, how much more beauty must be revealed by sight. Yet, those who have eyes apparently see little. The panorama of color and action that fills the world is taken for granted. It is human, perhaps, to appreciate little that which we have and to long for that which we have not, but it is a great pity that in the world of light the gift of sight is used only as a mere convenience rather than as a means of adding fullness to life.

I who am blind can give one hint to those who see: Use your eyes as if tomorrow you would be stricken blind. The same method can be applied to the other senses. Hear the music of voices, the song of a bird, the mighty strains of an orchestra, as if you would be stricken deaf tomorrow. Make the most of every sense; glory in all of the pleasure and beauty which the world reveals to you through the several means of contact that Nature provides. —HELEN KELLER

Exercises Understanding the Essay

A. Answer these questions about the essay.

1. Summarize in two or three sentences the writer's opinions about how well people use or appreciate the five senses.

2. What is the author's purpose in writing this essay?

3. What is the tone of the essay?

4. In **objective** writing, an author does not include any personal opinions or reactions. In **subjective** writing, the author does just the opposite. When might an author want to write objectively? When would he or she want to write subjectively, as in this essay?

B. Write an essay expressing your beliefs on some subject.

Satire

The previous essay is an example of one way a writer can express an opinion or deliver a message. Occasionally, however, a writer will choose to communicate an idea in a less direct manner, through the use of satire.

Satire is a special type of writing used to criticize or show the foolishness of some ideas, customs, or situations. The author makes a point through the use of humor or exaggeration.

Satire often contains fictional elements. That is, the author might use imaginary characters or situations to convey the message, as in the following satirical article.

IS THERE LIFE ON EARTH?

There was great excitement on the planet of Venus this week. For the first time Venusian scientists managed to land a satellite on the planet Earth, and it has been sending back signals, as well as photographs, ever since.

The satellite was directed into an area known as Manhattan (named after the great Venusian astronomer Professor Manhattan, who first discovered it with his telescope 200,000 light-years ago). Because of excellent weather conditions and extremely strong signals, Venusian scientists were able to get valuable information on the feasibility of a manned flying saucer's landing on Earth. A press conference was held at the Venus Institute of Technology.

2. Assign the students to write either an anecdote, an essay, or a satire on the subject of sports.

3. As an extension of Helen Keller's essay, show the students slides, and ask them to observe and record minute details. After this pre-writing activity, have the students observe and write descriptions of a favorite place.

4. Read excerpts from James Thurber's and Mark Twain's satirical essays, and have the students comment on the objects and techniques of these satires.

Extending the Lesson

1. Have the students bring newspapers to class, and discuss the various kinds and purposes of the nonfiction there. Ask students to write comparisons of two nonfiction articles.

2. Encourage students to keep journals for recording humorous, dramatic, or interesting anecdotes from their daily experiences. You might allow several minutes of class time each day for journal writing.

3. Assign the students to write reports on Helen Keller or her teacher, Annie Sullivan. Review Chapter 10 and the process of writing a report.

4. Have the students collect examples of satire from magazines and newspaper columns. Have each student read an example aloud and then explain the author's purpose.

2. Assign and discuss Exercise A on page 301. Help students to understand the following:

Question 1—The time of the story is the early 1900's, a time when following social customs was important. Custom led Nuttel to visit the Sappleton family with a letter of introduction, and so set up the plot of the story. The country surroundings provide the plot details about hunting.

Question 2—The characters are Mrs. Sappleton, her self-possessed and imaginative niece, and the nervous Mr. Nuttel. The reader learns about the characters primarily through the dialogue, but also through the narrator's description of Mr. Nuttel's thoughts.

Question 3—Mr. Nuttel's reaction is foreshadowed by the references to his nervous condition.

Question 4—The climax of the story occurs when Nuttel sees the three men returning.

Question 5—The story is told in the third person by a narrator outside the story. With Nuttel as narrator, the reader would not get the insight at the end of the story or the humorous view of Nuttel. With the niece as narrator, the ending would not be as great a surprise.

3. Assign Exercise B. Review the character traits and perspective Nuttel would bring to his narration.

4. Read and discuss **Drama** on pages 301-305. Review the definitions of the terms *act* and *scene*. Ask the students how drama differs from fiction, helping them to see that in drama character, plot, and conflict must be developed largely through dialogue. Discuss these reasons for stage directions: to indicate a character's mood or emotions, to provide actions and gestures that advance the plot, and to assist actors in delivering their lines. Have the students point out

THE OPEN WINDOW

"My aunt will be down presently, Mr. Nuttel," said a very self-possessed young lady of fifteen; "in the meantime you must try and put up with me."

Framton Nuttel attempted to say the correct something which should duly flatter the niece without discounting the aunt. Privately he doubted more than ever whether these formal visits to total strangers would do much towards helping the nerve cure which he was supposed to be undergoing.

"Do you know many of the people round here?" asked the niece.

"Hardly a soul," said Framton. "My sister was staying here some four years ago, and she gave me letters of introduction to some of the people here."

He made the last statement in a tone of distinct regret.

"Then you know practically nothing about my aunt?" pursued the self-possessed young lady.

"Only her name and address," admitted the caller. He was wondering whether Mrs. Sappleton was in the married or widowed state. An undefinable something about the room seemed to suggest masculine habitation.

"Her great tragedy happened just three years ago," said the girl; "that would be since your sister's time."

"Her tragedy?" asked Framton; somehow in this restful country spot tragedies seemed out of place.

"You may wonder why we keep that window wide open on an October afternoon," said the niece, indicating a large French window that opened on to a lawn.

"It is quite warm for the time of the year," said Framton; "but has that window got anything to do with the tragedy?"

"Out through that window, three years ago to a day, her husband and her two young brothers went off for their day's shooting. They never came back. In crossing the moor to their favorite snipe-shooting ground they were all three engulfed by a treacherous piece of bog. It had been that dreadful wet summer, you know, and places that were safe in other years gave way suddenly without warning. Their bodies were never recovered. That was the dreadful part of it." Here the child's voice lost its self-possessed note and became falteringly human. "Poor aunt always thinks that they will come back some day, they and the little brown spaniel that was lost with them, and walk in that window just as they used to do. That is why the window is kept open every evening till it is quite dusk. Poor dear aunt, she has often told me how they went out, her husband with his white waterproof coat over his arm, and Ronnie, her youngest brother, singing 'Bertie, why do you bound?' as he always did to tease her, because she said it got on her nerves. Do you know, sometimes on still, quiet evenings like this, I almost get a creepy feeling that they will all walk in through that window—"

She broke off with a little shudder. It was a relief to Framton when the aunt bustled into the room with a whirl of apologies for being late in making her appearance.

"I hope Vera has been amusing you?" she said.

"She has been very interesting," said Framton.

"I hope you don't mind the open window," said Mrs. Sappleton briskly; "my husband and brothers will be home directly from shooting, and they always come in this way. They've been out for snipe in the marshes today, so they'll make a fine mess over my poor carpets. So like you menfolk, isn't it?"

She rattled on cheerfully about the shooting and the scarcity of birds, and the prospects for duck in the winter. To Framton it was all purely horrible. He made a desperate but only partially successful effort to turn the talk on to a less ghastly topic; he was conscious that his hostess was giving him only a fragment of her attention, and her eyes were constantly straying past him to the open window and the lawn beyond. It was certainly an unfortunate coincidence that he should have paid his visit on this tragic anniversary.

"The doctors agree in ordering me complete rest, an absence of mental excitement, and avoidance of anything in the nature of violent physical exercise," announced Framton, who labored under the widespread delusion that total strangers and chance acquaintances are hungry for the least detail of one's ailments. "On the matter of diet they are not so much in agreement," he continued.

stage directions in the scene from *Harvey* and explain how they affect the way the play is enacted. You might demonstrate by reading lines in different moods and with different gestures.

5. Assign parts and have students enact the scene after they have read it at least once silently. Discuss these aspects of the play.

a. How do sister Veta and Myrtle Mae feel about Elwood? How do you know?

b. Describe each of the three women in one or two sentences. How did you form your opinions of them?

c. What is Elwood's attitude toward his family? How does he seem to react to most of the people he meets?

d. Elwood explains later in the play that Harvey is a Pooka—a Celtic spirit he met while out walking one day. What personality does Harvey seem to have? How does the reader learn about Harvey?

6. Assign the Exercise on page 305. Go over the following points with the students.

Question 1—Elwood, the main character, is a gentle, soft-spoken, agreeable man. This character is developed through Elwood's treatment of the women, his politeness toward Harvey, and his remarks to his Aunt Ethel and his sister.

Question 2—Stage directions describe movements, give suggestions of how lines are to be delivered, and provide descriptions of the scenery and setting. Stage directions are especially important in this play if the audience is to "see" Harvey through Elwood's actions.

Question 3—Conflicts might develop between Elwood and his family, and perhaps between Elwood and a world that might not consider him normal.

Individualizing the Lesson

Less-Advanced Students

1. Work with the students on reading and analyzing the short story. You may wish to read the entire story aloud. Provide the students with study questions to answer as they read.

2. As a visual reinforcement, have students diagram the interest level and excitement of "The Open Window," showing how the plot builds to a climax when the men appear and then drops off as the conflict unravels.

3. Allow the students to work on the Exercises on pages 301 and 305 in pairs or small groups. Encourage discussion of students' interpretations of character, plot, and conflict.

Advanced Students

1. Give students a list of short stories. Have them choose one and analyze the plot, character, or setting in a composition.

2. Encourage students to find and perform short plays for the rest of the class. Some students may even wish to write original plays.

Optional Practice

1. Have the students rewrite "The Open Window" as a play, complete with stage directions. Have groups of four students choose one of their plays to act out, using three students as the characters and one as the director.

2. Based on their reading of "The Open Window," assign the students to write paragraphs analyzing one of the following:

"No?" said Mrs. Sappleton, in a voice which only replaced a yawn at the last moment. Then she suddenly brightened into alert attention—but not to what Framton was saying.

"Here they are at last!" she cried. "Just in time for tea, and don't they look as if they were muddy up to the eyes!"

Framton shivered slightly, and turned towards the niece with a look intended to convey sympathetic comprehension. The child was staring out through the open window with dazed horror in her eyes. In a chill shock of nameless fear Framton swung round in his seat and looked in the same direction.

In the deepening twilight three figures were walking across the lawn towards the window; they all carried guns under their arms, and one of them was additionally burdened with a white coat hung over his shoulders. A tired brown spaniel kept close at their heels. Noiselessly they neared the house, and then a hoarse young voice chanted out of the dusk:

"I said, Bertie, why do you bound?"

Framton grabbed wildly at his stick and hat; the hall-door, the gravel-drive, and the front gate were dimly-noted stages in his headlong retreat. A cyclist coming along the road had to run into the hedge to avoid imminent collision.

"Here we are, my dear," said the bearer of the white mackintosh, coming in through the window; "fairly muddy, but most of it's dry. Who was that who bolted out as we came up?"

"A most extraordinary man, a Mr. Nuttel," said Mrs. Sappleton; "could only talk about illnesses, and dashed off without a word of good-bye or apology when you arrived. One would think he had seen a ghost."

"I expect it was the spaniel," said the niece calmly; "he told me he had a horror of dogs. He was once hunted into a cemetery somewhere on the banks of the Ganges by a pack of pariah dogs, and had to spend the night in a newly dug grave with the creatures snarling and grinning and foaming just above him. Enough to make anyone lose their nerve."

Romance at short notice was her specialty.

—SAKI

Exercises Understanding the Short Story

A. Answer these questions about the sample short story.

1. What is the setting of this story? Is the setting important to the development of the action?

2. Who are the characters in the story? How do you learn about each character?

3. **Foreshadowing** is the writer's use of hints or clues to indicate events that will occur later in the story. What details foreshadow Mr. Nuttel's reaction to the appearance of the hunters?

4. What event is the climax, or turning point, of the story?

5. What kind of narrator is used in this story? Is the narration in first or third person? How would the story change if Mr. Nuttel were the narrator? The girl?

B. Rewrite a section of the story from Mr. Nuttel's point of view.

Drama

The elements of setting, character, and plot also are found in drama. **Drama** is fiction written to be acted out before an audience. In a play, the story is told through the **dialogue,** or words spoken by the characters. A written play includes all the dialogue. It also includes instructions from the writer about the setting and about the actions of the actors. These instructions are called **stage directions.**

Most plays are made up of units called **acts.** A play usually consists of from one to five acts. The acts might be further divided into **scenes,** with each new scene representing a change in time or place.

The following excerpt is from the play *Harvey* by Mary Chase. The play tells the story of Elwood P. Dowd, a quiet, gentle, extremely pleasant middle-aged man. Mr. Dowd is very content with his life and thoroughly enjoys everyone he meets.

a. mood in "The Open Window"
b. the niece's character
c. Nuttel's character
d. the most sympathetic character in the story and why

3. Have students listen to a recording of a short play while reading the script. Analyze how the actors followed, added to, or departed from the play directions.

Extending the Lesson

1. Assign more reading and analysis of short stories with surprise endings. Introduce the students to stories by the master of the surprise ending, O. Henry, as well as stories by Edgar Allan Poe, Saki, Guy de Maupassant, and Joan Aiken.

2. Have the students listen to recordings of short stories, paying attention to the stories' characters and settings.

3. Ask students to write and perform one-act parodies of TV dramas.

4. Prepare questions about characterization, setting, plot, and conflict for the students to answer.

He especially enjoys Harvey, a six foot, one-and-a-half inch invisible white rabbit who is his closest friend and constant companion.

This scene introduces Elwood's sister Veta and his niece Myrtle, who live with him. The two are attempting to give an afternoon party for some friends. As they greet a new arrival, Mrs. Chauvenet, they are dreading the possible arrival of Elwood and his invisible friend.

MRS. CHAUVENET: Veta Louise Simmons! I thought you were dead. (*Gets to her and takes hold of her.*)

VETA (*rushing to her, they kiss*): Aunt Ethel! (*Motioning to* MYRTLE *to come forward and meet the great lady.*) Oh, no—I'm very much alive—thank you—

MRS. CHAUVENET: (*turning to* MYRTLE): —and this full-grown girl is your daughter—I've known you since you were a baby.

MYRTLE: I know.

MRS. CHAUVENET: What's your name, dear?

VETA (*proudly*): This is Myrtle—Aunt Ethel. Myrtle Mae— for the two sisters of her father. He's dead. That's what confused you.

MRS. CHAUVENET: Where's Elwood?

VETA (*with a nervous glance at* MYRTLE MAE): He couldn't be here, Aunt Ethel—now let me get you some tea.

MRS. CHAUVENET: Elwood isn't here?

VETA: No—

MRS. CHAUVENET: Oh, shame on him. That was the main reason I came. (*Takes off scarf—puts it on chair.*) I want to see Elwood.

VETA: Come—there are loads of people anxious to speak to you.

MRS. CHAUVENET: Do you realize, Veta, it's been years since I've seen Elwood?

VETA: No—where does the time go?

MRS. CHAUVENET: But I don't understand it. I was saying to Mr. Chauvenet only the other night—what on earth do you suppose has happened to Elwood Dowd? He never comes to dances anymore. I haven't seen him at a horse show in years. Does Elwood see anybody these days?

VETA (*and* MYRTLE *glance at each other*): Oh, yes—Aunt Ethel. Elwood sees somebody.

MYRTLE: Oh, yes.

MRS. CHAUVENET (*to* MYRTLE): Your Uncle Elwood, child, is one of my favorite people. (VETA *rises and crosses around chair.*) Always has been.

VETA: Yes, I remember.

MRS. CHAUVENET: Is Elwood happy, Veta?

VETA: Elwood's very happy, Aunt Ethel. You don't need to worry about Elwood——(*Looks through doorway. She is anxious to get the subject on something else.*) Why, there's Mrs. Frank Cummings—just came in. Don't you want to speak to her?

MRS. CHAUVENET: (*crosses above chair to peer out*): My—but she looks ghastly! Hasn't she failed though?

VETA: If you think she looks badly—you should see him!

MRS. CHAUVENET: Is that so? I must have them over. (*Looks again.*) She looks frightful. I thought she was dead.

VETA: Oh, no.

MRS. CHAUVENET: Now—what about tea, Veta?

VETA: Certainly—(*Starts forward to lead the way.*) If you will forgive me, I will precede you——(ELWOOD *enters.* MRS. CHAUVENET *turns back to pick up her scarf from chair, and sees him.*)

MRS. CHAUVENET (*rushing forward*): Elwood! Elwood Dowd! Bless your heart.

ELWOOD (*coming forward and bowing as he takes her hand*): Aunt Ethel! What a pleasure to come in and find a beautiful woman waiting for me!

MRS. CHAUVENET (*looking at him fondly*): Elwood—you haven't changed.

VETA: (*moves forward quickly, takes hold of her*): Come along, Aunt Ethel—you mustn't miss the party.

MYRTLE: There's punch if you don't like tea.

MRS. CHAUVENET: But I do like tea. Stop pulling at me, you two. Elwood, what night next week can you come to dinner?

ELWOOD: Any night. Any night at all, Aunt Ethel—I would be delighted.

VETA: Elwood, there's some mail for you today. I took it up to your room.

ELWOOD: Did you Veta? That was nice of you. Aunt Ethel —I want you to meet Harvey. As you can see, he's a Pooka. (*Turns toward air beside him.*) Harvey, you've heard me speak of Mrs. Chauvenet? We always called her Aunt Ethel. She is one of my oldest and dearest friends. (*Inclines head toward space and goes "Hmm!" and then listens as though not hearing first time. Nods as though having heard someone next to him speak.*) Yes—yes— that's right. She's the one. This is the one. (*To* MRS. CHAUVENET.) He says he would have known you anywhere. (*Then as a confused, bewildered look comes over* MRS. CHAUVENET's *face and as she looks to left and right of* ELWOOD *and cranes her neck to see behind him—*ELWOOD, *not seeing her expression, crosses her toward* VETA *and* MYRTLE MAE.) You both look lovely. (*Turns to the air next to him.*) Come in with me, Harvey—We must say hello to all of our friends—(*Bows to* MRS. CHAUVENET.) I beg your pardon, Aunt Ethel. If you'll excuse me for one moment—(*Puts his hand gently on her arm, trying to turn her.*)

MRS. CHAUVENET: What?

ELWOOD: You are standing in his way—(*she gives a little— her eyes wide on him.*) Come along, Harvey. (*He watches the invisible Harvey cross to door, then stops him.*) Uh-uh! (ELWOOD *goes over to door. He turns and pantomimes as he arranges the tie and brushes off the head of the invisible Harvey. Then he does the same thing to his own tie. They are all watching him,* MRS. CHAUVENET *in horrified fascination. The heads of* VETA *and* MYRTLE *are bowed in agony.*) Go right on in, Harvey. I'll join you in a minute. (*He pantomimes as though slapping him on the back, and ushers him out. Then turns and comes back to* MRS. CHAUVENET.) Aunt Ethel, I can see you are disturbed about Harvey. Please don't be. He stares like that at everybody. It's his way. But he liked you. I could tell. He liked you very much. (*Pats her arm reassuringly, smiles at her, then calmly and confidently goes on out. After his exit,* MRS. CHAUVENET, MYRTLE, *and* VETA *are silent. Finally* VETA—*with a resigned tone—clears her throat.*)

VETA (*looking at* MRS. CHAUVENET): Some tea—perhaps—?

MRS. CHAUVENET: Why, I—not right now—I—well—I think I'll be running along.

Exercise Understanding Drama

1. Describe Elwood P. Dowd. Give examples of lines of dialogue or description that help to develop the character.

2. Review the stage directions. Describe briefly the type of information they include. Why would the stage directions be especially important to this play?

3. Based on the excerpt, what conflicts might develop?

Grammar and Usage

The Mechanics of Writing

A detailed Table of Contents of Sections 1–14 appears in the front of this book.

Section 1

The Simple Sentence

Section Objectives

1. To distinguish between sentences and sentence fragments

2. To recognize the subject and predicate of a sentence

3. To identify the verb and its simple subject in a sentence

4. To identify main verbs and helping verbs in sentences

5. To identify the subject and verb in sentences with unusual word order

6. To recognize direct and indirect objects in sentences

7. To identify predicate words and linking verbs

8. To identify compound parts in simple sentences

9. To correct run-on sentences

Preparing the Students

Have the students read the introduction. Remind them that a sentence is a group of words that expresses a complete thought. Explain that this section will help them to understand the structure of good sentences.

Additional Resources

Diagnostic Test—See page 1 in the test booklet. Recommended for use before teaching the section.

Mastery Test—See pages 30-33 in the test booklet. Recommended for use after teaching the section.

Reinforcement Exercises — See pages 333-337 in the student text.

Skills Practice Book—pages 81-92.

Duplicating Masters—pages 81-92.

In conversation, you do not always have to use complete sentences. For example, you can answer a question with a word or two:

Yes.　　No.　　My sister.

You can even ask a question without using what are usually considered complete sentences:

Whose car?　　Which girl?　　What building?

In writing, you must use complete sentences to make your meaning clear, because the reader is not at hand to ask you to repeat, to explain, or to fill in words you have left out.

Sentences are clear when all the parts are properly put together. In this section you will study the different parts of sentences. You will also learn how to put these parts together most effectively.

Part 1 Sentences and Sentence Fragments

The surest way to get your meaning across is to use complete sentences.

A sentence is a group of words that expresses a complete thought.

By "complete thought" we mean the clear and entire expression of whatever you want to say. Which of the following groups of words expresses a complete thought?

1. Karen
2. Found a kitten
3. Karen found a kitten.

The third group of words expresses a complete thought. It is a complete sentence.

Sentence fragments do not express a complete thought. They are usually the result of carelessness. The writer's thoughts come faster than he or she can write them. The writer goes on to a new sentence without finishing the sentence he or she has started. The effect is something like this:

1. Last night a funny thing   2. We were sitting around the dinner table   3. Suddenly, a loud bang

The first and third groups of words above are sentence fragments.

Other fragments are the result of incorrect punctuation. Parts of sentences are written as if they were whole sentences:

1. About 3,300 feet down   2. In one of the world's deepest mines in Idaho   3. In the warmth and dampness 4. The miners have grown a lemon tree   5. About seven feet tall   6. Under light bulbs

Which of these six groups of words are sentences and which are fragments?

You can usually understand sentence fragments if they fit in with what a speaker has already said. You often use fragments in spoken conversation. You also use them in written conversation. In other writing, however, you should avoid sentence fragments.

Exercises   Recognize sentences and fragments.

A. Number your paper from 1–10. For each group of words that is a sentence, write **S.** For each sentence fragment, write **F.** In class be ready to add words to change the fragments into sentences.

s 1. I saw a TV show last Sunday afternoon
s 2. The show was about dolphins
f 3. Actually a kind of small whale
s 4. Dolphins are very intelligent
f 5. Playful animals
f 6. Under the water in the big tank
s 7. It is very entertaining to watch the dolphins
f 8. Just for fun
s 9. Dolphins can hear very well
f 10. Because dolphins breathe air

B. Follow the directions for Exercise A.

f 1. During the relay race
f 2. A very high wind and then some flashes of lightning
s 3. Tracy Austin is one of several good young tennis players
f 4. A report about car fumes in an underground parking lot
f 5. Mr. Troy, owner of Troy and Brown Sports Shop
f 6. Whose work on the blackboard
f 7. Eddie Murphy, a gifted young comedian
s 8. Martha Jane Canary was better known as "Calamity Jane"
s 9. The fire engines rushed down the street
s 10. No one else gave a report on solar energy

Extending the Lesson

Explain that writers often use fragments in dialogue to capture the flavor of casual speech. Have each student find two examples of sentence fragments in dialogue, copy them, and complete them.

311

Objective

To recognize the subject and predicate of a sentence

Presenting the Lesson

1. Read and discuss pages 312-313. Have the students suggest alternate subjects and predicates for the sentences shown in the charts on this page.

2. Assign and discuss Exercises A and B on page 313.

Individualizing the Lesson

Less-Advanced Students

Do the first five sentences of Exercise A at the chalkboard. For both Exercises, have the students add the label "Who or What" to the subject column and the label "Did or Happened" to the predicate column.

Advanced Students

Have the students write five new sentences by substituting alternative subjects in five of the sentences in Exercise A. Then have them write five more new sentences by substituting alternative predicates in five of the sentences in Exercise B.

Reinforcement Exercise

Assign and discuss Exercise B on page 333.

Part 2   Subjects and Predicates

Every sentence has two basic parts: the subject and the predicate. The **subject** tells whom or what the sentence is about. The **predicate** tells something about the subject.

SUBJECT *(Who or what)*	PREDICATE *(What is said about the subject)*
Hungry dogs	bark constantly.
A cold rain	fell all through the night.
My brother	laughed at his own mistake.

Each of these sentences expresses a complete thought. Each of them tells something (**predicate**) about a person, place, or thing (**subject**).

An easy way to understand the parts of a sentence is to think of the sentence as telling who did something, or what happened. The subject tells *who* or *what*. The predicate tells *did* or *happened*. You can divide sentences, then, in this way:

WHO OR WHAT	DID OR HAPPENED
The runner	crossed the finish line.
My parents	planted a garden.
The car	skidded on the wet pavement.
The bike	needs air in its tires.

The subject of the sentence names someone or something about which a statement is to be made.

The predicate of the sentence tells what is done or what happens.

Exercises Find the subjects and predicates.

A. Label two columns on your paper *Subject* and *Predicate*. Write the proper words from each sentence in the columns.

EXAMPLE: My sister | is fixing her bicycle.

SUBJECT   PREDICATE

My sister   is fixing her bicycle.

1. Gayle | made limeade.
2. The Packers | will play the Bears on Sunday.
3. Beth | went bowling with Jenny.
4. My parents | were fishing in Maine.
5. Heavy white smoke | came out of the chimney.
6. Calligraphy | is the art of fine handwriting.
7. I | like short stories.
8. Rebecca | sailed the boat on the pond.
9. Several passengers | stood in the aisle.
10. Rugby | is a British sport similar to our football.

B. Follow the directions for Exercise A.

1. Monarch butterflies | migrate every year.
2. Sugar cane | is the chief product of Hawaii.
3. North Dakota | produces barley, wheat, and flaxseed.
4. Kathy | ate all the brownies.
5. The bike-a-thon | raised money for muscular dystrophy.
6. Our homeroom | will play intramural hockey tomorrow.
7. *Gone with the Wind* | is the best movie I have ever seen on television.
8. Tim | built a rock garden.
9. Photography | is Elizabeth's main interest.
10. Our 4-H Club | showed Black Angus cattle at the Ohio State Fair.

Optional Practice

Have the students combine the following subjects and predicates to form ten different sentences.

Subjects

I
a stray cat
the people next door
a group of runners
a woman wearing a raincoat

Predicates

ran down the street
watched the fireworks display
sat on the lawn
performed in the talent show
called me

Extending the Lesson

Provide the students with copies of the day's school announcements. Have them find subjects and predicates in simple sentences.

To identify the verb and its simple subject in a sentence

Presenting the Lesson

1. Read and discuss pages 314-316. Make sure that the students understand the difference between the terms *subject* and *simple subject, predicate* and *simple predicate* (verb). Remind the students that they can divide all sentences into a subject and a predicate to help them find the simple subject and the verb.

Diagraming may help some students to see the relationship between subjects and predicates in sentences. Use diagraming to the extent that it clarifies sentence structure for the students.

2. Assign and discuss Exercises A and B on page 316. Do sentence 1 orally, making sure students realize that the subject is not in an intervening phrase like "of oranges."

Individualizing the Lesson

Less-Advanced Students

Do Exercise A orally. First have the students find the complete subject and predicate in each sentence; then have them find the verb and its simple subject. Have the students complete Exercise B independently.

Part 3 Simple Subjects and Predicates

In every sentence there are a few words that are more important than the rest. These key words make the basic framework of the sentence. Study these examples.

Hungry **dogs**   **bark** constantly.
A large **truck**   **rumbled** down the street.
My **brother**   **laughed** at his own mistake.

The subject of the first sentence is *Hungry dogs*. The key word in this subject is *dogs*. You can say *dogs bark constantly*. You cannot say *hungry bark constantly*.

The predicate in the first sentence is *bark constantly*. The key word is *bark*. Without this word you would not have a sentence.

The key word in the subject of a sentence is called the simple subject. It is the subject of the verb.

The key word in the predicate is called the simple predicate. The simple predicate is the **verb.** Hereafter we will use the word *verb* rather than the phrase *simple predicate*.

Finding the Verb and Its Subject

The verb and its subject are the basic framework of every sentence. All the rest of the sentence is built around them. To find this framework, first find the verb. Then ask *who* or *what* before the verb. This will give you the subject.

My brother's cookies melt in your mouth.
Verb: melt
What melts? cookies
Simple subject: cookies

You will be able to tell a fragment from a sentence easily if you keep your eye on subjects and verbs.

A group of words without a subject makes you ask *Who did? What did? Who was? What was?* A group of words without a verb makes you ask *What about it? What happened?*

Fragment   Ran down the street (Who ran down the street?)
Sentence   *The child* ran down the street.

Fragment   A cold rain (What about it? What happened?)
Sentence   A cold rain *fell all day.*

Looking at the Sentence as a Whole

The **complete subject** is the simple subject plus any words that modify or describe it.

EXAMPLE: Hungry dogs bark constantly.

Hungry dogs is the complete subject. What is the simple subject?

The **complete predicate** is the verb plus any words that modify or complete its meaning. What is the complete predicate in the sentence above? What is the simple predicate, or verb?

Diagraming Subjects and Predicates

Below is the basic structure of a sentence diagram.

Subject	Predicate
Hungry dogs	**bark constantly.**

The subject and verb are placed on the main horizontal line. Modifiers go on slanted lines below the words they modify.

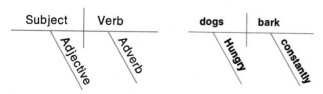

315

Remember that adverbs may modify adjectives or other adverbs. Here is how they appear in a diagram.

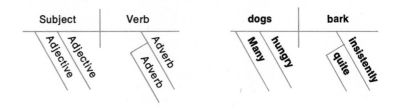

Exercises Find the verb and its subject.

A. Label two columns *Verb* and *Simple Subject*. Number your paper from 1–10. For each sentence, write the <u>verb</u> and its simple <u>subject</u>.

1. A <u>crate</u> of oranges <u>arrived</u> from Florida.
2. The new IBM <u>computer</u> <u>printed</u> our class schedules.
3. A tiny, gray <u>kitten</u> <u>perched</u> itself on our windowsill.
4. The <u>bike</u> in the garage <u>has</u> a flat tire.
5. The jubilant, cheering <u>crowd</u> <u>rose</u> to its feet.
6. The tall, wiry <u>center</u> <u>sank</u> the winning basket.
7. The <u>locker</u> next to the library <u>belongs</u> to Miki and me.
8. My <u>sister</u> <u>won</u> an award at the art fair.
9. The <u>woman</u> in the pin-striped suit <u>is</u> my math teacher.
10. The aluminum <u>cans</u> in those plastic bags <u>go</u> to the recycling center.

B. Follow the directions for Exercise A.

1. The chestnut-brown <u>thoroughbred</u> <u>trotted</u> victoriously around the track.
2. An abandoned <u>nest</u> in the old oak tree <u>became</u> home for three little sparrows.
3. The <u>corridor</u> outside the cafeteria <u>leads</u> to the music room.

4. A shaggy white puppy wandered aimlessly into the gym.

5. The new booklet on bicycle rules explains the need for safety in cycling.

6. A tiny, tiger-striped kitten chased playfully after the huge ball of yarn.

7. The sound-slide show on energy conservation explained the importance of natural resources.

8. The friendly driver assisted the passenger off the bus.

9. A continuous, heavy snow delighted the skiers.

10. The drought reduced the waterfall to a trickle.

Part 4   The Parts of a Verb

A verb may consist of one word or of several words. It may be made up of a **main verb** and **helping verbs.** In naming the verb of any sentence, be sure to name all the words that it is made of.

HELPING VERBS	+	MAIN VERB	=	VERB
might have		gone		might have gone
will		see		will see
are		driving		are driving
could		go		could go

Sometimes the parts of a verb are separated from each other by words that are not part of the verb. In each of the following sentences, the verb is printed in red. The words in between are not part of the verb.

> I **have** never **been** to Disney World.
> We **did** not **see** the accident.
> The bus **has** often **been** late.

Some verbs are joined with other words to make contractions. In naming verbs that appear in contractions, name only the verb. The word *not* is an adverb. It is never part of a verb.

317

Part 4

Objective

To identify main verbs and helping verbs in sentences

Presenting the Lesson

1. Read and discuss pages 317-318. Explain that the words between the verb parts in the sample sentences at the bottom of page 317 are not part of the verb because they do not tell what was done or what happened. Read the example sentences without the words that separate the parts of the verb, and help the students understand that a complete sentence remains although the meaning has changed.

2. Assign and discuss Exercises A and B on page 318.

Individualizing the Lesson

Less-Advanced Students

Tell the students to first divide the sentences in the Exercises into subjects and predicates, then to look for simple subjects and verbs. Do the first five sentences in Exercise A in class. Then have the students complete the Exercises independently.

Advanced Students

Have the students suggest alternative verbs and helping verbs for each sentence in the Exercises.

Optional Practice

Have the students write sentences using the helping verbs *was*, *were*, *have*, *had*, *does*, and *would*.

Extending the Lesson

Have each student underline every verb in a brief newspaper article.

CONTRACTION	VERB
hasn't (*has not*)	*has*
weren't (*were not*)	*were*
I've (*I have*)	*have*
we'd (*we had* or *would*)	*had* or *would*

Exercises Find the verb.

A. Number your paper from 1–10. List the <u>verbs</u> in the following sentences.

1. We <u>have</u> not <u>gone</u> to the lake once this summer.
2. This report <u>has</u> not <u>been completed</u>.
3. The buses often <u>arrive</u> late.
4. I <u>have</u> never <u>been</u> to Martha's Vineyard in Massachusetts.
5. Cheryl <u>did</u> not <u>see</u> *Rocky* or *Star Wars*.
6. The 747 <u>will arrive</u> at midnight.
7. The hockey team <u>is practicing</u> on the ice until 6 P.M.
8. Our class <u>is going</u> on a field trip next week.
9. The package <u>may have been delivered</u> to the wrong house.
10. I <u>am going</u> to a ski lodge next weekend.

B. Follow the directions for Exercise A.

1. We aren't <u>giving</u> our panel discussion today.
2. I <u>don't</u> really <u>like</u> Barry Manilow or Linda Ronstadt.
3. The ambulance <u>had</u> cautiously <u>approached</u> every intersection.
4. Jim and I <u>will finish</u> this job later.
5. It hasn't <u>rained</u> for a month.
6. Our play rehearsal <u>wasn't</u> very successful.
7. Raul <u>was</u> carefully <u>walking</u> around the fountain.
8. We haven't <u>planted</u> a flower garden this year.
9. My sister and I <u>have</u> already <u>made</u> a rock garden, however.
10. The counselors <u>had</u> quickly <u>collected</u> the test booklets.

318

Part 5   Subjects in Unusual Positions

Sentences Beginning with *There*

Many sentences begin with the word *there*. Sometimes *there* is used as an adverb modifying the verb to tell *where* something is or happens.

> There stood the boy. (The boy stood *there*.)
> There is our bus. (Our bus is *there*.)

In other sentences, *there* is only an introductory word to help get the sentence started.

> There is no candy in the machine. (No candy is in the machine.)
> There are some mistakes here. (Some mistakes are here.)

In diagraming sentences that begin with *there*, it is necessary to decide whether *there* is used as an adverb or whether it is simply an introductory word. When *there* modifies the verb, it is placed on a slant line below the verb. When *there* is an introductory word, it is placed on a straight line above the sentence line.

In most sentences beginning with *there*, the subject comes after the verb. To find the subject, first find the verb. Then ask *who* or *what*.

319

Objective

To identify the subject and verb in sentences with unusual order

Presenting the Lesson

1. Read and discuss this page. Work with the students to rewrite the following sentences in usual order:

> There are the scissors.
> There are some people waiting outside.

Have the students identify the subject and verb in each sentence.

2. Do Exercise A on page 320 orally. Assign and discuss Exercise B on page 320.

3. Read and discuss pages 320-322.

Work with the students to rewrite the following sentences in usual order:

> Here is the path.
> Here's a clue.

Show the students how to rearrange questions beginning with helping verbs into declarative sentences, as in the following:

> Did you see that shot?
> You did see that shot.

After forming a statement, the students will be able to find the subject and all verb parts more easily.

Work with the students to rewrite the sentence *From somewhere in the darkness came a deep voice* in usual order as *A deep voice came from somewhere in the darkness.*

To impress upon the students that the subject of a command is understood to be *you*, issue commands to the class. Point out that it is clear who would be doing the action in commands such as "Raise your hand."

Remind the students that even in sentences written in unusual order the subject still tells *who or what* and the verb still tells *did or happened*.

4. Assign and discuss Exercises A and B on page 322.

Individualizing the Lesson

Less-Advanced Students

1. Work with the students to find the subject and verb in each sentence in Exercise A on page 320. Have the students complete Exercise B independently.

2. Work with the students to find the subject and verb in each sentence in Exercise A on page 322. Have the students complete Exercise B independently.

Advanced Students

Have the students diagram the subjects and verbs in the sentences in Exercise B on page 320 and Exercise B on page 322.

Reinforcement Exercises

Assign and discuss Exercises C and D on pages 334 and 335.

Optional Practice

Have students rearrange the sentences in the Exercises on pages 320 and 322 to put the subjects and verbs in the usual order.

Exercises Find the verb and its subject.

A. Write down the simple subject and the verb in each sentence. Tell whether *There* is used as an adverb or as an introductory word.

1. There he goes. adverb
2. There stood the trophy. adverb
3. There they are. adverb
4. There will be basketball practice tomorrow. introductory word
5. There go the runners. adverb
6. There I sat. adverb
7. There I waited in line for over an hour. adverb
8. There will be a picnic tomorrow. introductory word
9. There was a sudden pause. introductory word
10. There will be pony races. introductory word

B. Follow the directions for Exercise A.

1. There goes the bus. adverb
2. There is cheesecake for dessert. introductory word
3. There will be no school on Monday. introductory word
4. There is the lock for your bicycle. adverb
5. There are plenty of napkins. introductory word
6. There might be a thunderstorm later tonight. introductory word
7. There is a swimming meet on Friday. introductory word
8. There came a chilly wind. introductory word
9. There will be an assembly at noon. introductory word
10. There are several students in line. introductory word

Other Sentences with Unusual Word Order

The usual order of words in a sentence is *subject–verb*. In many sentences, however, the subject comes after the verb or between parts of the verb. You have seen one example of this arrangement in sentences beginning with *there*. Here are some others.

1. Sentences beginning with *here*

Here is your hat. (Your hat is here.)
Here are the keys. (The keys are here.)

Unlike *there*, the word *here* is always an adverb telling *where* about the verb.

2. Questions

Are you leaving? (You are leaving?)
Has the mail come? (The mail has come?)

3. Sentences beginning with phrases or adverbs

Onto the field dashed the team. (The team dashed onto the field.)
Finally came the signal. (The signal finally came.)

To find the subject in a sentence with unusual word order, first find the verb. Then ask *who* or *what*.

EXAMPLE: Here comes the parade.

Verb: comes
Who or *what comes?* the parade
Subject: parade

To diagram sentences with unusual word order, find the verb and its subject. Place them in their proper positions. Then place the modifiers where they belong.

Imperative Sentences

In imperative sentences, which state commands or requests, the subject is usually not given. Since commands and requests are always given to the person spoken to, the subject is *you*. Since the *you* is not given, we say that it is *understood*.

(*You*) Bring me the newspaper.
(*You*) Wipe your feet.

In the diagram of an imperative sentence, the subject is written in parentheses.

(You)	Wait

Exercises **Find the verb and its subject.**

A. Label two columns *Subject* and *Verb*. Number your paper from 1–10 and write down the subject and verb for each sentence.

(You) 1. Hang on!
2. Are there two minutes left?
3. Did you read the article about bicycles?
4. Economy is one advantage of the bicycle.
5. Down the slopes raced the skiers.
6. Down came the rain.
7. Is our team in the play-offs?
8. There comes the bus.
9. On the porch hung several plants.
10. Have you seen that movie?

B. Follow the directions for Exercise A.

1. Are these books due today?
2. Out came the sun.
3. Here are the T-shirts for the Pep Club.
4. Have you heard the new Fleetwood Mac album?
5. All along the shoreline swimmers basked in the sun.
6. After the storm a beautiful rainbow appeared.
7. Over the phone came the reply.
(You) 8. Don't just stand there.
9. Here comes the mail.
10. Do you like frozen yogurt?

Part 6   Objects of Verbs

Some verbs complete the meaning of a sentence without the help of other words. The action that they describe is complete.

> The boys *came*.   We *are going*.

Some verbs, however, do not express a complete meaning by themselves. They need other words to complete the meaning of a sentence.

> Sue hit _____. (Hit what? Sue hit the *ball*.)
> Jane raised _____. (Raised what? Jane raised the *window*.)

Direct Objects

The word that receives the action of a verb is called the **direct object** of the verb. In the sentences above, *ball* receives the action of *hit*. *Window* receives the action of *raised*.

Sometimes the direct object tells the *result* of an action.

> We dug a *hole*.
> Edison invented electric *lights*.

To find the direct object, first find the verb. Then ask *whom* or *what* after it.

Carlos saw the President.
  Verb: saw
  Saw whom? President
  Direct object: President

Anne painted a picture.
  Verb: painted
  Painted what? picture
  Direct object: picture

A verb that has a direct object is called a **transitive verb.** A verb that does not have an object is called an **intransitive verb.** A verb may be intransitive in one sentence and transitive in another.

Intransitive   We were watching.
Transitive   We were watching the race.

Objective

To recognize direct and indirect objects in sentences

Presenting the Lesson

1. Read and discuss page 323 and the top of page 324. Help the students to see the relationship between verbs and direct objects. Stress that a direct object answers the question *what?* or *whom?* after the verb.

2. Assign and discuss the Exercise on page 324. Remind students that a transitive verb will have a direct object.

3. Read and discuss pages 324 and 325. Show the students how to find an indirect object by first finding the direct object and then asking *for whom?* or *for what?* or *to whom?* or *to what?* after the verb and the direct object.

4. Do Exercise A on page 325 orally. Assign and discuss Exercises B and C on page 326.

Individualizing the Lesson

Less-Advanced Students

1. For the Exercise on page 324, have the students first find the verb in each sentence. Then have them find the subject. Finally, have them ask *who?* or *what?* to find the direct object if there is one.

2. For Exercises A and B on pages 325 and 326, have the students find the verb and its subject in each sentence. Then have them find the direct objects in the sentences that have them. Finally, have them ask *for whom?* or *for what?* or *to whom?* or *to what?* after the verb and the direct object to find the indirect objects.

3. Omit Exercise C on page 326.

Advanced Students

Have the students diagram the subjects, verbs, and objects for the sentences in Exercise B on page 326.

Reinforcement Exercises

Assign and discuss Exercises E and F on page 335.

Optional Practice

Have the students decide which sentences in Exercise A on page 316 have direct objects.

Extending the Lesson

Have each student find one sentence with a direct object and one sentence with an indirect object in a front-page news story.

Direct Object or Adverb?

Many verbs used without objects are followed by adverbs that tell *how, where, when,* or *to what extent*. These words are adverbs that go with or modify the verb. Do not confuse them with direct objects. The direct object tells *what* or *whom*.

To decide whether a word is a direct object or a modifier of the verb, decide first what it tells about the verb. If it tells *how, where, when,* or *to what extent*, it is an adverb. If it tells *what* or *whom*, it is a direct object.

> Don worked *quickly*. (*quickly* is an adverb telling *how*.)
> Sue worked the *problem*. (*problem* is a direct object.)

Exercise Recognize transitive and intransitive verbs.

Number your paper from 1–10. Find the verb in each sentence. Decide whether each verb is *Transitive* or *Intransitive*. To do so, you should first decide whether the word in italics is a direct object or an adverb.

1. Several guests left *early*. intransitive
2. Someone left a red *sweater*. transitive
3. The band plays *often*. intransitive
4. The band plays good *music*. transitive
5. I enjoyed *that*. transitive
6. I enjoyed that delicious *pie*. transitive
7. Please return *soon*. intransitive
8. Please return my *camera*. transitive
9. Michele tried *again*. intransitive
10. Mark tried the *door* again. transitive

Indirect Objects

Some words tell *to whom* or *for whom* something is done. Other words tell *to what* or *for what* something is done. These words are called the **indirect objects** of the verb.

> Anne knitted **Kim** a *sweater*. (knitted *for* Kim)
> We gave the **boat** a *coat* of paint. (gave *to* the boat)

In these sentences, the words in red type are the indirect objects. The words in italics are the direct objects.

The words *to* and *for* are never used with the indirect object. The words *to* and *for* are prepositions. Any noun or pronoun following *to* or *for* is the object of the preposition.

> They baked *me* a cake. (*me* is the indirect object of *baked*.)
> They baked a cake for *me*. (*me* is the object of *for*.)

Diagraming Objects

In a diagram, the direct object is placed on the main line after the verb. Notice that the line between verb and object does not go below the main line.

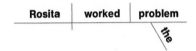

The indirect object is placed below the main line.

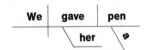

Exercises Find the sentence parts.

A. Number your paper from 1–10. Label three columns *Verb, Indirect Object,* and *Direct Object.* Fill in the parts that you find for each sentence. After each verb write *Transitive* or *Intransitive.*

> EXAMPLE: Todd drew us a very rough map.
>   V   IO   DO

VERB	INDIRECT OBJECT	DIRECT OBJECT
drew (transitive)	us	map

1. I brought Cindy her scarf. transitive
2. We gave our dog a good bath. transitive
3. Maria made us a Mexican dinner. transitive

4. Paul waited for me in the park. *intransitive*
5. I hooked Mom a rug for her birthday. *transitive*
6. The principal gave the co-captains the trophy. *transitive*
7. Will you bring me some ice? *transitive*
8. The sun sparkled on the waves. *intransitive*
9. Brenda must have hoed the garden. *transitive*
10. Pat got a digital watch for Christmas. *transitive*

B. Follow the directions for Exercise A.

1. Our class cleaned the courtyard. *transitive*
2. Jill loaned me her thesaurus. *transitive*
3. The captain spoke to his crew. *intransitive*
4. Judy was whistling an old Beatles' song. *transitive*
5. Uncle Don gave the cactus to me. *transitive*
6. Did you buy me some more film? *transitive*
7. Liz shouted down the stairs. *intransitive*
8. Did you adjust the thermostat? *transitive*
9. Please get me some stamps. *transitive*
10. We fixed the antenna for my CB. *transitive*

C. Look at the verbs in the following sentences. If the verb has no object, write another sentence using the same verb and an object. If the verb already has an object, write a sentence with the same verb but no object. Answers will vary.

> EXAMPLE: An old highway looped around the mining town.
>
> > Verb: *looped* (no object)
> > Bob looped the rope twice.

1. Dad had already packed. no object
2. We reached the airport about 2 o'clock. object
3. I ran without stopping. no object
4. The plane climbed another 2000 feet. object
5. Elizabeth painted the garage door. object

Part 7 Predicate Words and Linking Verbs

Some verbs do not express action. They tell of a state of being. These verbs link the subject of a sentence with a word or group of words in the predicate. Because they link the subject with some other word or words, they are often called **linking verbs.**

He *is* a doctor.
They *are* good swimmers.

The most common linking verb is the verb *be*. The verb can have many forms. Study these forms of *be* to make sure you recognize them:

be	been	is	was
being	am	are	were

The verbs *be*, *being*, and *been* can also be used with helping verbs. Here are some examples:

might be	is being	have been
could be	are being	might have been
will be	was being	would have been

The words linked to the subject by a linking verb like *be* are called **predicate words.** There are **predicate nouns, predicate pronouns,** and **predicate adjectives.**

Renee is *president*. (predicate noun)

This is *she*. (predicate pronoun)

Bill was *happy*. (predicate adjective)

Notice how the subjects and the predicate words in the above sentences are linked by *is* or *was*.

Part 7

Objective

To identify predicate words and linking verbs

Presenting the Lesson

1. Read and discuss pages 327 and 328. Point out that linking verbs always connect two words that refer to the same thing. If students are confused by linking verbs, tell them to imagine linking verbs as equal signs. Write the following on the chalkboard:

```
he = doctor
they= swimmers
Renée = president
this = she
Bill = happy
```

Point out that each sentence that uses a linking verb says that the subject and a word in the predicate are equal or similar.

2. Assign and discuss Exercises A and B on pages 328 and 329.

Individualizing the Lesson

Less-Advanced Students

1. Have the students label three columns *Subject*, *Linking Verb*, and *Predicate Word*. Have them write the appropriate parts of each sentence in Exercise A on page 328 in the columns.

2. Work with the students to find the verb in each sentence in Exercise B. Then have them complete the Exercise independently.

Advanced Students

1. Have the students diagram the sentences in Exercise A.

2. Have the students rewrite the sentences in Exercise A, using alternate predicate words.

Reinforcement Exercise

Assign and discuss Exercise G on page 336.

Optional Practice

Have the students find and copy the sentences with linking verbs and predicate words in the Exercises on page 313. Have them underline each predicate word.

Extending the Lesson

Have each student find a sentence with a linking verb and a predicate word in a biographical article in an encyclopedia. Discuss how these sentences help define their subjects.

Here are some other common linking verbs:

seem	feel	become	look
appear	taste	grow	sound

Like *be,* these verbs can have various forms (*seems, appears, felt*), or they can be used with helping verbs (*will appear, could feel, might have become*).

The *music* sounded *beautiful.* (predicate adjective)

The *plants* grew *taller.* (predicate adjective)

I have become an *expert.* (predicate noun)

In diagrams, the predicate words appear on the main line with subjects and verbs. Note that the line between the verb and the predicate word slants back toward the subject.

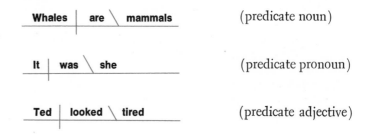

Whales	**are** \ **mammals**	(predicate noun)
It	**was** \ **she**	(predicate pronoun)
Ted	**looked** \ **tired**	(predicate adjective)

Exercises Find predicate words and linking verbs.

A. As your teacher directs, point out the subject, linking verb, and predicate word in each sentence.

    1. Snakes are reptiles.
    2. The singing sounded good.
    3. This is he.
    4. The flowers looked wilted.
    5. Has Kathy been sick?

328

6. The driver was angry.
   <small>S LV PW</small>
7. The house seemed empty.
   <small>S LV PW</small>
8. Karen felt lonesome.
   <small>S LV PW</small>
9. Was it she?
   <small>LV S PW</small>
10. Sue became chairperson.
    <small>S LV PW</small>

B. Make four columns on your paper. Number from 1–12 down the columns. Label the columns *Subject*, *Verb*, *Direct Object*, and *Predicate Word*. Fill in the parts that you find in each sentence.

1. Our new puppy has behaved badly.
2. We left him in his pen today.
3. We left him some water.
4. He looked miserable.
5. On returning we were angry.
6. The puppy had spilled the water.
7. He had escaped from the pen.
8. He had chewed the sofa pillow.
9. Feathers covered the floor.
10. The puppy looked very happy.
11. He had taught us a lesson.
12. We will never leave him inside alone again.

Part 8   Compound Sentence Parts

The word *compound* means "having two or more parts."

Every part of the sentences we have studied in this chapter can be compound—subjects, verbs, direct objects, indirect objects, and predicate words.

If the compound form has only two parts, there is usually a conjunction (*and, or, but*) between them. If there are three or more parts, the conjunction usually comes between the last two.

Part 8

Objective

To identify compound parts in simple sentences

Presenting the Lesson

1. Read and discuss pages 329 and 330. Point out that both parts of a compound serve the same function in a sentence.

2. Have the students suggest alternative compounds for each of the examples on page 330.

3. Assign and discuss Exercises A and B on page 331.

Individualizing the Lesson

Less-Advanced Students

1. Have the students work in pairs to complete Exercise A on page 331.

2. Work with the students to find the required sentence part in each sentence in Exercise B. Then have them complete the Exercise independently.

Advanced Students

Have the students diagram sentences in Exercise A to highlight compound parts.

Reinforcement Exercise

Assign and discuss Exercise H on page 336.

Optional Practice

Have the students find the sentences in the Exercises on page 318 that have compound sentence parts. Then have them make one part compound in five of the remaining sentences.

Extending the Lesson

Display a picture of a group of people engaged in a vigorous activity. Have the students suggest sentences with compound parts to describe the action in the picture.

Compound Subjects

Posters, streamers, and *balloons* decorated the room.

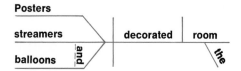

Compound Verbs

The crowd *cheered* and *applauded.*

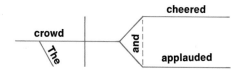

Compound Objects of Verbs

We saw the *President* and his *family.* (direct objects)
The boss showed *Nancy* and *me* the shop. (indirect objects)

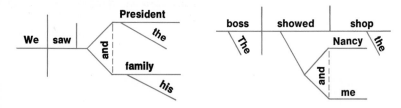

Compound Predicate Words

The winners were *Rebecca* and *Sherry.* (predicate nouns)

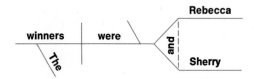

Exercises Find the compound sentence parts.

A. As your teacher directs, show the compound parts in the following sentences. Tell whether they are compound subjects, verbs, objects, or predicate words.

1. The water was cool and refreshing. *compound predicate words*
2. Last weekend we skated and skied. *compound verbs*
3. The engine hesitated and then purred. *compound verbs*
4. Tara and Charlene painted the scenery. *compound subjects*
5. Jeff and I washed and waxed the car. *compound subjects, compound verbs*
6. We brought chicken and fruit to the picnic. *compound objects*
7. Did you give Cindy the posters and the flyers? *compound objects*
8. Marla and Robin made hanging planters in shop class. *compound subjects*
9. We suspended the balloons and the prizes from the ceiling. *compound objects*
10. The gymnasts looked strong but graceful. *compound predicate words*

B. In each of the following sentences, make a compound of the part noted in parentheses. *Answers will vary.*

EXAMPLE: We unpacked the crates. (*direct object*)
We unpacked the crates and the cartons.

1. Jon carried the groceries into the house. (*direct object*)
2. The spaghetti was spicy! (*predicate word*)
3. Did you remember the Kleenex? (*direct object*)
4. There are pickles over here. (*subject*)
5. The hypnotist's performance was fascinating. (*predicate word*)
6. Mrs. Lopez gave Janelle a bracelet. (*direct object*)
7. Next came the President's car. (*subject*)
8. Linda fixed the handlebars. (*direct object*)
9. Mr. and Mrs. Karnatz gave Meredith a job at the store. (*indirect object*)
10. There are ten divers competing. (*subject*)

Part 9   Avoiding Run-on Sentences

Objective

To correct run-on sentences

Presenting the Lesson

1. Read and discuss page 332. Exaggerate your reading of run-ons to stress the confusion they can' create.

2. Assign and discuss the Exercise on this page.

Individualizing the Lesson

Less-Advanced Students

Ask the students to underline the subjects and verbs in the sentences they write for the Exercise.

Advanced Students

Discuss with the students the possibility of revising some of the run-on sentences in the Exercise by joining related sentences with conjunctions. Briefly review Chapter 3, "Sentence Combining." Discuss the differences in meaning that result from different revisions.

Reinforcement Exercise

Assign and discuss Exercise I on page 337.

Extending the Lesson

Have the students correct the following run-on sentence and develop it into a paragraph of complete sentences:

People in a family have individual tastes, the people in my family like different styles of music and different foods.

Part 9   Avoiding Run-on Sentences

A **run-on sentence** is two or more sentences written incorrectly as one. Sometimes no punctuation mark at all is used between the sentences. At other times, a comma is incorrectly used.

Incorrect *(run-on)*   Tony made a pie it tasted great.
Correct   Tony made a pie. It tasted great.

Incorrect *(run-on)*   Tia went to the fair, her sister did not.
Correct   Tia went to the fair. Her sister did not.

As you can see, a run-on confuses readers. It doesn't show clearly where one idea ends and another one begins. You can avoid run-ons by using a period or other end mark to show the reader where each complete thought ends.

Exercise   Correct the run-on sentences.

All but two of the following sentences are run-ons. Rewrite the run-on sentences correctly.

1. Laurie sings with the chorus, she is an alto.
2. Britt rides horses, she entered a show.
3. I answered the phone, somebody laughed and hung up.
4. Did you see that TV program, wasn't it good?
5. Marissa plays flute in the orchestra and the band. Correct
6. I like science fiction movies, *Alien* was my favorite.
7. The helicopter landed, four men stepped onto the field.
8. Loggers cut down trees, then the logs are sent to the mill.
9. Marcus races on his ten-speed, he works out every day.
10. Jenny joined the hockey team, she is a good forward.
11. The Bombers have two outs, Beth is at bat.
12. The sailors and their captain were worried by the storm. Correct
13. Sit in the balcony, you'll see best there.
14. Our class studied pollution, we cleaned up the pond.
15. Look for a green Chevy, that's my mom's car.

Reinforcement Exercises — Review

The Simple Sentence

A. Recognize sentences and sentence fragments.
(Use after page 311.)

Number your paper from 1–10. For each group of words that is a sentence, write **S.** For each sentence fragment, write **F.** In class, be ready to add words to change the fragments into sentences.

1. Because of the driving snow F
2. A special track was designed and built for the skateboard races s
3. A big wave broke over the side of the boat s
4. Thousands of people along the parade route F
5. Bill's new yellow car out in the driveway F
6. A heavy gray sky over the lake F
7. The coach explained the basic rules s
8. A cheer from the grandstand F
9. A helicopter over the traffic jam F
10. Brownies and Dutch chocolate ice cream for dessert F

B. Find complete subjects and complete predicates.
(Use after page 315.)

Copy each sentence. Draw a line between the complete subject and complete predicate.

1. Rick | caught the ball easily.
2. The atomic submarine | surfaced before dawn.
3. A red-tailed hawk | circled the field.
4. My uncle | uses mulch on his tomato plants.
5. Our janitor | was cleaning the basement.

Mixed Review

The following exercises provide review of the concepts and skills presented in this chapter.

A. Find subjects and verbs in different kinds of sentences. Write the subject and verb from each sentence. Underline the subject once and the verb twice.

1. There was a huge crowd at the grand opening.
2. After the storm, Marcy shoveled and salted the driveway.
3. Did Hank really win a prize at the art fair?
4. Here is the missing puzzle piece.
5. (You) Please make a cup of herbal tea for me.
6. Finally the rain stopped.
7. There had never been a problem before.
8. (You) Follow the instructions carefully.
9. Has Craig returned your ski jacket?
10. In the morning, my sister will start her new job.

B. Find verbs and their subjects.
Copy each sentence. Underline subjects once and verbs twice. Then tell whether the verb is *Transitive* or *Intransitive*. The parts may be compound.

Tr. 1. The player in the blue shorts won the tennis tournament last year.
Int. 2. That huge dog and the Siamese cat raced through the yards.
Tr. 3. She bought and distributed the concert tickets.
Tr. 4. The waitress in the gypsy costume has taken our order.
Int. 5. Old rusty tools hung in the shed.
Tr. 6. The rangers had spotted and reported the large blaze.
Tr. 7. A severe frost had damaged the entire citrus crop.
Tr. 8. Many canned soups contain a high percentage of salt.
Int. 9. After lunch, Sarah and her brothers ride around the ranch.
Tr. 10. The driver of the van did not see the detour sign.

C. Identify action and linking verbs.
Copy the following sentences and circle the **verb** in each. If it is an action verb, put one line under its direct object. If it is a linking verb, put two lines under the predicate word.

1. The antique plate was very fragile.
2. Ben made his little brother a thick sandwich.
3. Everyone at the party wore jeans.
4. This pickle tastes sour.
5. The park seems unusually empty today.
6. The art class dyed yarn for a weaving project.
7. Brian carefully sanded the bookcase.
8. The old wooden bleachers looked uncomfortable.
9. My grandmother taught me the alphabet.
10. I oiled the wheels on the skates.

6. A new apartment building was constructed near the shopping center.
7. They unloaded the elephants in the pouring rain.
8. My sister and I went canoeing on Sunday.
9. The tall brunette in the front row spiked the ball over the net.
10. You could hear the crickets outside the cabin.

C. Find the verb and its simple subject. (Use after page 319.)

Number your paper from 1–10. Write the simple subject and the verb in each sentence. Tell whether *there* is used as an adverb or as an introductory word.

1. There is the library. adverb
2. There will be band practice in the morning. introductory word
3. There is a truck parked in the driveway. introductory word
4. There wasn't a cloud in the sky. introductory word
5. There was no play rehearsal today. introductory word
6. There was no more room in the stadium. introductory word
7. There will be a dance next Friday. introductory word
8. There sat the box by the bus stop. adverb
9. There were only two commercials during the show. introductory word
10. There will be a slight delay before take-off. introductory word

D. Find the verb and its subject in unusual kinds of sentences. (Use after page 322.)

Number your paper from 1–10. Label two columns *Subject* and *Verb*. Write down the subject and verb for each sentence.

1. Through the back door the new puppy scampered.
2. Over the hill the motorcyclists raced.
3. Did the rocket misfire?
(You) 4. Find the villain.
5. Here is the newspaper.
6. Out swarmed the bees.
7. Here are the results of the test.

334

8. Onto the field the marching band paraded.

(You) 9. Fire this ceramic vase in the kiln.

10. Did you read the editorial in the newspaper?

E. Recognize transitive and intransitive verbs.

(Use after page 324.)

Number your paper from 1–10. Find the verb in each sentence. Then tell whether it is *Transitive* or *Intransitive.*

1. The telephone rang. Intransitive
2. The lightning flashed overhead. Intransitive
3. Paulo scored the first goal. Transitive
4. The crowd cheered wildly. Intransitive
5. Paula lost her wallet. Transitive
6. The laundromat charges 50 cents. Transitive
7. My team won. Intransitive
8. The newscaster smothered a yawn. Transitive
9. Mrs. Brock checked the meter. Transitive
10. Steve rose quickly from his chair. Intransitive

F. Find the sentence parts. (Use after page 326.)

Number your paper from 1–10. Label three columns *Verb, Indirect Object,* and *Direct Object.* For each sentence below fill in those parts that you find. After each verb write *Transitive* or *Intransitive.*

1. Two tugboats were chugging through the canal. Intransitive
2. The crowd gave the coach a big hand. Transitive
3. That cub scooped a fish out of the water. Transitive
4. The fan is making a strange noise. Transitive
5. Write us a letter. Transitive
6. Sonia made Dad a lamp in shop class. Transitive
7. Mary threw the dog the Frisbee. Transitive
8. The center raced toward the net. Intransitive
9. I brought Chris her assignments from school. Transitive
10. I developed the film in the photo lab. Transitive

D. Fix run-ons and fragments.

The following paragraphs contain sentence fragments and run-on sentences. Rewrite the paragraphs, correcting the fragments and run-ons.

Now and then I get the urge to be creative. In the kitchen. Recently, I decided to make a cake. For my sister's birthday. I read the recipe quickly, then I got all the ingredients together. I separated eggs, sifted flour, and beat everything in a large bowl. I put the cake into the oven. when it was done it looked beautiful.

My sister came home, I could hardly wait to show her the surprise. The surprise was on me! Why didn't someone tell me, That an angel food cake has to cool upside down? The cake had fallen it looked more like an angel food pie.

Using Grammar in Writing

1. Have the students expand the following subject-verb sentences to make them more vivid. Have the students read their expanded sentences and identify the complete subject and complete predicate.

Rain fell.
Waves pounded.
Fans cheered.
People waved.
Girl ran.

2. List the following main verbs on the chalkboard: *left, eaten, changing, tried,* and *gone.* Have the students write sentences using a different helping verb with each main verb.

3. Have the students complete each of the following sentences:

There goes . . .
Through the crowd dashed . . .
Here are . . .
How does . . . ?
Stop . . .

Have each student develop one of the resulting sentences into a paragraph.

4. Have the students observe and report on one key play or one particularly exciting sequence of events in a sporting event. Have them underline direct and indirect objects in their accounts.

5. Have the students write paragraphs of definition, using predicate words accurately and precisely, on two of these topics: jeans, soccer, junior high, politics, common sense.

6. Have the students write sentences with compound parts to answer these questions:

What are your three favorite foods?

What three people have influenced you most?

Which three animals make the best pets?

G. Find predicate words, linking verbs, and objects.

(Use after page 329.)

Number your paper from 1–10. Label four columns *Subject, Verb, Direct Object,* and *Predicate Word.* Fill in the parts that you find for each sentence. You will find either a direct object or a predicate word in each sentence.

1. Nine men moved the piano. [DO]
2. The sky to the west looks strange. [PW]
3. The muffins in the oven smell delicious. [PW]
4. My mother canned peaches all morning. [DO]
5. The gulls on the beach faced the wind. [DO]
6. We picked apples from the orchard trees. [DO]
7. Their fishing boat weathered the storm. [DO]
8. From the airplane the toll road appeared empty. [PW]
9. The center snapped the ball to the quarterback. [DO]
10. The boughs on the mantel look lopsided. [PW]

H. Find the compound parts in a sentence. (Use after page 331.)

As your teacher directs, show the compound parts in the following sentences. Tell whether they are compound subjects, verbs, objects, or predicate words.

1. Your backstroke is better and stronger. *(compound predicate words)*
2. Three monkeys and their trainers were juggling oranges. *(compound subjects)*
3. Emily and Ken can walk on stilts. *(compound subjects)*
4. The photography club furnished the doughnuts and cider. *(compound objects)*
5. A marathon runner must have experience and determination. *(compound objects)*
6. A landslide uprooted those trees and rocks. *(compound objects)*
7. The roadrunner looked fierce and determined. *(compound predicate words)*
8. The December wind was cold and biting. *(compound predicate words)*
9. The Ford Fiesta and the Chevy Chevette are American economy cars. *(compound subjects)*
10. Laplanders and Finns traditionally hunt reindeer. *(compound subjects)*

I. Avoid run-on sentences. (Use after page 332.)

Pick out the run-on sentences in the following group and rewrite them correctly. If a sentence does not need to be rewritten, write *Correct.*

1. The train left early.^Wwe missed it by five minutes.
2. The group of girls had a picnic in the park by the fountain. Correct
3. We saw the magic show,.^Tthe magician did terrific tricks.
4. Josh lives in a high-rise,.^Hhis apartment is on the sixty-fifth floor.
5. The wind lifted my kite.^Iit stayed high for hours.
6. Lisa hung posters of Leif Garrett in her room. Correct
7. Barry rode with Judith on^Ia tandem bike. Correct
8. This is the art museum.^Iit has a special exhibit of teen-agers' art.
9. Call me tomorrow.^II'll be home all day.
10. Meredith took the bus to Yorkville with the other girls on the field hockey team. Correct

5. Some nouns ending in *f* simply add -*s*:

beliefs   chiefs   dwarfs   handkerchiefs

Many words ending in *f* or *fe* change the *f* to *v* and add -*es* or -*s*. Since there is no rule to follow, these words have to be memorized. Here are some examples of such words:

thief—thieves	leaf—leaves	life—lives
shelf—shelves	half—halves	calf—calves
loaf—loaves	wife—wives	knife—knives

6. Some nouns have the same form for both the singular and plural. Memorize these:

deer	salmon	trout	sheep	moose
tuna	cod	pike	bass	elk

7. Some nouns form their plurals in special ways:

child—children	goose—geese	man—men
mouse—mice	ox—oxen	woman—women

Here is a dictionary entry for the word *knife*. Notice that the entry shows the plural, *knives*. Most dictionaries show the plurals of nouns if the plurals are formed in an irregular way.

---

plural
knife (nīf) **n.,** *pl.* **knives** [O.E. *cnif:* for IE. base see KNEAD] **1.** a cutting or stabbing instrument with a sharp blade, single-edged or double-edged, set in a handle **2.** a cutting blade, as in a machine—**vt.** **knifed, knif'ing 1.** to cut or stab with a knife ☆**2.** [Colloq.] to use underhanded methods in order to hurt, defeat, or betray—☆**vi.** to pass into or through something quickly, like a sharp knife—☆**under the knife** [Colloq.] undergoing surgery —**knife'like'** adj.

When you are in doubt about plurals, consult a dictionary.

Exercises Form the plurals of nouns.

A. Write the plural of each of these nouns. Then use your dictionary to see if you are right.

1. church — churches
2. brush — brushes
3. elf — elves
4. wish — wishes
5. potato — potatoes
6. dish — dishes
7. elk — elk
8. sheep — sheep
9. fox — foxes
10. tooth — teeth
11. company — companies
12. watch — watches
13. bookshelf — bookshelves
14. chimney — chimneys
15. lady — ladies
16. baby — babies
17. city — cities
18. mouse — mice
19. witch — witches
20. radio — radios

B. All but one of the following sentences have at least one error in the spelling of the plural. Write the sentences correctly.

1. We placed all of the dishs on the benchs in the hallway. dishes, benches
2. Several different companys make CB radioes. companies, radios
3. The thieves took several loaves of bread. correct
4. The babys were getting new tooths. babies, teeth
5. Several companys sell frozen mashed potatos. companies, potatoes
6. First, cut the loafs in halves. loaves
7. The deers were eating the green shoots on the bushs. deer, bushes
8. Use these brushs to paint the bookshelfs. brushes, bookshelves
9. The larger boxes had scratchs on them. scratches
10. My blue jeans are covered with patchs. patches

C. Follow the directions for Exercise B.

1. Both of those churchs will have rummage sales. churches, rummage
2. The kitchen shelfs were filled with dishs and glasses. shelves, dishes
3. We sliced the tomatos in halfs. tomatoes, halves
4. Bunchs of grapes were heaped on the carts. Bunches,
5. Echos of the music could be heard in all the rooms. Echoes
6. These are photos of horses, cows, oxes, and sheeps. oxen, sheep
7. The leafs on the trees were turning brown. leaves
8. Those dictionarys are found in most librarys. dictionaries, libraries
9. What qualities must heroes have? correct
10. The fire chieves met to discuss means of fire prevention in chiefs
our citys. cities

345

Part 3

Objective

To form the possessives of nouns correctly

Presenting the Lesson

1. Read and discuss page 346. Stress that all possessive nouns have apostrophes.

2. Do Exercise A on page 346 orally. Then assign and discuss Exercises B and C on page 347.

Individualizing the Lesson

Less-Advanced Students

Have the students refer to the rules on page 346 as they work on the Exercises. Have them write the rule that applies to each word in Exercises B and C.

Advanced Students

Have the students use the possessive nouns from Exercises A and B in sentences.

Reinforcement Exercise

Assign and discuss Exercise C on page 349.

Optional Practice

1. Have the students form the possessives of *Joyce, studio, agents, Ross,* and *men* and tell which rule applies to each word.

2. Have each student write three common nouns on a piece of paper. Then have the students exchange

Part 3 The Possessive of Nouns

Most people own or possess something. We say:

Carol's coat   the doctor's bag   a lawyer's case

To show that something belongs to or is part of a person, we use the same form:

Jill's face   Ann's tooth   Bill's worries

We usually speak of ownership, belonging, or possession for people and animals. Occasionally, however, things are also used in the possessive. We speak of a *city's problems, the day's end,* or *a stone's throw.*

Forming Possessives

There are three rules for making the possessive of nouns:

1. If the noun is singular, add an apostrophe and *s:*

Bess's slicker   Mother's briefcase   Charles's bike

2. If the noun is plural and ends in *s,* add just the apostrophe:

the Hoffmans' car   students' projects   babies' toys

3. If the noun is plural but does not end in *s,* add both the apostrophe and *s.*

children's books   men's sweaters   women's jewelry

Exercises Form the possessive of nouns.

A. Write the possessive form of these nouns:

1. bee's   3. carpenter's   5. Marsha's
2. Mary's   4. child's   6. princess's

7. mouse's
8. Andrea's
9. watchman's
10. waitress's
11. Thomas's
12. Les's
13. mirror's
14. conductor's
15. Tricia's
16. winner's
17. Tracy's
18. singer's
19. lake's
20. Vince's

papers, write the plurals of the three nouns, and then write the possessives of the singular and plural of each.

Extending the Lesson

Give each student a page from a newspaper. Have the students circle any possessive nouns they find and determine whether they are formed correctly.

B. Write the possessive form of these nouns:

1. watchmen's
2. teachers'
3. women's
4. children's
5. people's
6. birds'
7. sheep's
8. schools'
9. boys'
10. ladies'
11. countries'
12. dogs'
13. socks'
14. churches'
15. dresses'
16. stereos'
17. foxes'
18. ducks'
19. engineers'
20. statues'

C. Write the possessive form for each italicized word:

1. Our *class* assignment sheets were sitting on the *teacher* desk. class's, teacher's

2. The Student *Council* decision to have a walk-a-thon was Council's supported by the *teachers* committee and the *principal* office. teachers', principal's

3. Mrs. *Thomas* car was parked in the driveway. Thomas's

4. My *brother* short story won first prize in the Young Writers Contest. brother's

5. *Maurita* and *Amy* paintings were on display in the art room. Maurita's, Amy's

6. The *farmer* newly planted field was washed out by the heavy rain. farmer's

7. The *painter* ladders were on our front porch. painter's

8. *Jonathan* bicycle needs new brakes. Jonathan's

9. Our *neighbor* treehouse is one of the best I've ever seen. neighbor's

10. *Janine* time broke the school record for the 100-yard dash. Janine's

Reinforcement Exercises

These Reinforcement Exercises may be used for additional practice as needed. Each exercise may be used after the text page indicated in parentheses.

Review

If you have not assigned these Exercises before this time, you can use them as an excellent Section Review.

Mixed Review

The following exercises provide review of the concepts and skills presented in this chapter.

A. Recognize common and proper nouns. Copy the following paragraph. Underline all nouns. Capitalize all proper nouns.

The first <u>settlement</u> in ^Aamerica was not at ^Pplymouth ^Rrock. Actually, the first <u>town</u> in what is now the <u>united</u> <u>states</u> of ^Aamerica was ^Sst. ^Aaugustine, ^Fflorida. It was settled by the ^Sspanish in 1565. In 1607, the ^Eenglish arrived and settled at ^Jjamestown, now in ^Vvirginia. It was not until 1620 that the ship ^Mmay-^Mflower brought <u>colonists</u> to ^Mmas-sachusetts. Eventually, <u>people</u> from ^Hholland, ^Ffrance, and other <u>countries</u> also came to make their <u>homes</u> in this beautiful new <u>land</u>.

B. Use plural and possessive forms correctly. Rewrite the sentences correcting the <u>errors</u> in plural and possessive forms.

1. The fishing boat brought back a good supply of <u>tunas</u>.

Reinforcement Exercises—Review

Using Nouns

A. Find the common and proper nouns. (Use after page 342.)

Label two columns *Common Nouns* and *Proper Nouns*. Decide whether the following nouns are common or proper. Place each in the right column. Capitalize the proper nouns.

1. sun valley, ravine, grand canyon, death valley, pike's peak
2. golden gate bridge, overpass, st. louis arch, brooklyn bridge
3. executive, doctor, senator rosenstein, judge, cardinal bonzano
4. musician, barry manilow, judy collins, guitar, andrés segovia
5. stream, des plaines river, niagara falls, rapids, colorado river
6. intersection, holland tunnel, haggar's corners, highway
7. nation, france, country, united states, scotland, india
8. queen, princess grace, prince charles, queen elizabeth
9. forest, yellowstone national park, westbrook park, lincoln
10. language, swahili, finnish, travel, spanish, greek

B. Form the plurals of nouns. (Use after page 345.)

Write the plural of each of these nouns.

1. tomato (tomatoes)	6. wolf (wolves)	11. radio (radios)	16. toy (toys)
2. donkey (donkeys)	7. shelf (shelves)	12. studio (studios)	17. perch (perches)
3. auto (autos)	8. party (parties)	13. scratch (scratches)	18. switch (switches)
4. track (tracks)	9. peach (peaches)	14. cry (cries)	19. leaf (leaves)
5. ditch (ditches)	10. foot (feet)	15. play (plays)	20. deer (deer)

C. Form the possessive of nouns. (Use after page 347.)

Write the possessive form in the singular or plural as indicated.

1. the horse (plural) mouths horses'
2. Lisa (singular) equipment Lisa's
3. the child (plural) beds children's
4. the cat (plural) paws cats'
5. a doctor (singular) appointment doctor's
6. the bird (plural) beaks birds'
7. one weather forecaster (singular) prediction forecaster's
8. the water (singular) edge water's
9. Ms. Marsh (singular) business Marsh's
10. the caddy (plural) hours caddies'
11. the gull (plural) cries gulls'
12. America (singular) resources America's
13. the bungalow (singular) owners bungalow's
14. a bride (singular) bouquet bride's
15. some duck (plural) backs ducks'
16. Sara (singular) singing Sara's
17. the President (singular) power President's
18. the moose (plural) antlers moose's
19. the ship (singular) captain ship's
20. Max (singular) shoes Max's

2. Ms. Andrews' Datsun looks just like that other ladies' car.
3. Henry packed sliced ham, tomatos, mustard, two loafs of bread, and some knifes.
4. The hornets nest is in the childrens' playhouse.
5. Our counties' borderes are the river, the marshs, and the state line.
6. The new babie's photoes look like the baby pictures of her mom.
7. Carls' hat and Anita's books were in the lost and found box.
8. The mens' department had a sale on bootes.
9. The factorys' employees are well-paid.
10. Dad made three batches of chili for Annies' party.

   1. tuna
   2. Andrews's, lady's
   3. tomatoes, loaves, knives
   4. hornets', children's
   5. county's, marshes
   6. baby's, photos
   7. Carl's
   8. men's, boots
   9. factory's
   10. Annie's

Using Grammar in Writing

1. Have each student define a common noun, such as *baseball,* in a paragraph.

2. Have the students write "shopping lists" for supplies needed in the classroom, such as pens, pads, passes, using plurals correctly.

3. Have each student write a description of another person's home, using possessives correctly.

Section 3

Using Pronouns

Section Objectives

1. To recognize personal pronouns, their referents, and their genders

2. To use compound personal pronouns correctly in sentences

3. To identify indefinite pronouns and to make verbs agree with them in number

4. To recognize and correctly use demonstrative pronouns

5. To recognize interrogative pronouns

6. To identify and use correctly the subject, object, and possessive forms of pronouns

7. To use pronouns correctly in compound sentence parts

8. To use the pronouns *who*, *whom*, and *whose* correctly

9. To distinguish between possessive pronouns and contractions

10. To use compound personal pronouns correctly and to avoid confusing *we* and *us*, *them* and *those*

11. To make pronouns agree with their antecedents

Preparing the Students

Read and discuss the introduction on page 351.

Additional Resources

Diagnostic Test—See page 2 in the test booklet. Recommended for use before teaching the chapter.

Mastery Test—See pages 36-37 in the test booklet. Recommended for use after teaching the chapter.

Reinforcement Exercises—See pages 371-375 in the student text.

Skills Practice Book—pages 98-109.

Duplicating Masters—pages 98-109.

Our speech and writing would be very awkward if we had only nouns to refer to persons, places, or things. We would have to talk like this:

David found David's music in David's locker.
David took David's music to the rehearsal.

Fortunately, we have words that can be used in place of nouns. These are called **pronouns.** With pronouns we can talk like this:

David found *his* music in *his* locker. *He* took *it* to the rehearsal.

The words *his* and *he* are pronouns that stand for the noun *David* and are used in place of it. The word *it* is a pronoun that stands for the word *music* and is used in its place.

351

Part 1

Objective

To recognize personal pronouns, their referents, and their genders

Presenting the Lesson

1. Read and discuss page 352. Write the following chart on the chalkboard, and encourage students to memorize it:

Singular

First:	I	me	my, mine
Second:	you	you	your, yours
Third:	he	him	his
	she	her	her, hers
	it	it	its

Plural

First:	we	us	our, ours
Second:	you	you	your, yours
Third:	they	them	their, theirs

Stress the differences among first, second, and third person, and feminine, masculine, and neuter gender.

2. Do Exercise A on page 353 orally. Then assign and discuss Exercise B.

Individualizing the Lesson

Less-Advanced Students

1. Require students to copy the chart of personal pronouns in their notebooks.

2. Encourage the students to refer to the pronoun chart as they do the Exercises.

Advanced Students

Have the students identify the number, person, and gender of each pronoun in the Exercises.

Part 1   Personal Pronouns

Personal pronouns are used to take the place of nouns that name persons.

Personal pronouns refer to persons in three ways:

1. When the pronoun refers to the person speaking, it is in the **first person:** *I, me, we, our,* and *us,* for example.

2. When the pronoun refers to the person spoken to, it is in the **second person:** *you, your, yours.*

3. When the pronoun refers to some other person or thing that is being spoken of, it is in the **third person:** *he, his, him, she, her, it, they, their, them,* for example.

EXAMPLES: The letter was addressed to *me.*
(speaker—first person)

The phone call is for *you.*
(person spoken to—second person)

The boys are looking for *him.*
(person spoken of—third person)

The word *it* is also called a personal pronoun, even though it is never used in place of a person's name.

Pronouns in the third person that refer to male persons are said to be in the **masculine gender.** Pronouns that refer to female persons are said to be in the **feminine gender.** Pronouns that refer to things are said to be in the **neuter gender.**

EXAMPLES: Bob bought *his* ticket yesterday.
(*His* is masculine in gender.)

Marie says that book is *hers.*
(*Hers* is feminine in gender.)

Jill reached for the paddle, but *it* floated out of reach.
(*It* is neuter in gender.)

Animals are often referred to by *it* or *its.* They may also be referred to by *he, his, she, her,* or *hers.*

352

Exercises   **Find the pronouns.**

A.   Number your paper from 1–10. Write the pronouns you find in the following sentences. After each pronoun, write the noun or nouns it stands for (except for first-person pronouns).

1. Sue left her math book in her locker. Sue, Sue
2. Snow was all over the ball park this morning, but it melted. snow
3. John and Ginny visited their cousins in Texas. John and Ginny
4. Ken came by and picked up his soccer ball before supper. Ken
5. The store owners said that they would sponsor our team. owners
6. The Sierra Nevadas are mountains in California. They include Mount Whitney. Sierra Nevadas
7. Dorinda lost her gloves. Dorinda
8. The cat cared for its new kittens. cat
9. Linda and her best friend are going to New York, and they will compete in a speech contest there. Linda Linda and friend
10. Jay opened the envelope, but he found nothing in it. Jay, envelope

B.   Follow the directions for Exercise A.

1. Jeff, would you like to play tennis with Carol and Sue? Jeff
2. A seismograph records earthquakes. It indicates their intensity. seismograph, earthquakes
3. Last summer, the neighbors painted their house, and Dad built a patio. neighbors
4. Joel and Jim Hertz raised tomatoes. They sold them to the neighbors and made money. Joel and Jim Hertz, tomatoes
5. The Owens parked their cars in the driveway while the workers repaired their garage roof. Owens Owens
6. Mom and Dad have their tickets for the school concert. Mom and Dad
7. Mary, have you found your umbrella? Mary, Mary
8. Bill looked for his books but couldn't find them. Bill, books
9. The sun had sundogs, circles of bright rainbow spots, around it. They are formed from ice particles. sun, sundogs
10. Did Pam and Mary find the packages they had wrapped? Pam and Mary

Reinforcement Exercise

Assign and discuss Exercise A on page 371.

Optional Practice

Have each student write one sentence using a pronoun. Collect these sentences, duplicate them, and distribute them to the class. Have the students find the pronoun in each sentence and give its person and gender.

Extending the Lesson

1. Refer students to a paragraph in their literature texts. Ask them to rewrite the paragraph, changing all pronouns to nouns. Then discuss the function of personal pronouns.

2. Have the students list all personal pronouns in a passage from a short story and determine the point of view of the author.

Part 2

Objective

To use compound personal pronouns correctly in sentences

Presenting the Lesson

1. Have students study the chart on page 354. Discuss the function of compound personal pronouns.
2. Do Exercise A on this page orally.
3. Assign and discuss Exercise B.

Individualizing the Lesson

Less-Advanced Students

1. Remind the students that compound personal pronouns must agree with the words they refer to in number and gender.
2. Encourage the students to consult the chart as they do the Exercises.

Advanced Students

Explain the terms *intensive* ("giving emphasis") and *reflexive* ("showing an action directed back upon the doer") to the students. Have them identify those two uses of compound personal pronouns in the Exercises.

Reinforcement Exercise

Assign and discuss Exercise B on page 371.

Optional Practice

Have the students revise each sentence in Exercise A so that it uses a different compound personal pronoun.

Part 2 Compound Personal Pronouns

A **compound personal pronoun** is formed by adding *-self* or *-selves* to certain personal pronouns:

First Person	myself	ourselves
Second Person	yourself	yourselves
Third Person	himself	
	herself	themselves
	itself	

Exercises Use compound personal pronouns.

A. Number your paper from 1–10. Beside each number write the correct compound personal pronoun for each of these sentences. Then write the <u>noun</u> or <u>pronoun</u> to which it refers.

EXAMPLE: He made (pronoun) a T-shirt in sewing class.
                 himself, He

(You) 1. Cut (pronoun) a bigger piece of pie. yourself
2. <u>We</u> made the loom (pronoun). ourselves
3. <u>Bret</u> let (pronoun) down by the rope. himself
4. The <u>fans</u> shouted (pronoun) hoarse. themselves
5. <u>Dan</u> could not find the answer by (pronoun). himself
6. <u>I</u> will finish washing the car by (pronoun). myself
7. Mrs. Adel suggested <u>we</u> do the painting (pronoun). ourselves
8. Nancy, Carrie, and <u>Sue</u> made the movie (pronoun). themselves
9. <u>We</u> don't weigh (pronoun) very often. ourselves
10. <u>I</u> built and stained these bookcases by (pronoun). myself

B. Follow the directions for Exercise A.

1. The <u>door</u> just locked (pronoun). itself
2. <u>Diane</u> forgot to include (pronoun) when she counted. herself
(you) 3. Jamie, don't rush (pronoun). yourself

354

4. We always can the peaches (pronoun). ourselves
5. Will you two be able to finish the job (pronoun)? yourselves
6. Bridget organized the presentation by (pronoun). herself
7. Read the article (pronoun); I think you'll find it fun. yourself
8. They just bought (pronoun) a pumpkin. themselves
9. The store more than pays for (pronoun). itself
10. He wasn't sure of (pronoun) on a high ladder. himself

Part 3 Indefinite Pronouns

Pronouns like *anyone* and *nobody* do not refer to any definite person or thing. They are called **indefinite pronouns.**

Most indefinite pronouns are singular in number. They refer to only one person or thing. Here they are:

Singular Indefinite Pronouns			
another	each	everything	one
anybody	either	neither	somebody
anyone	everybody	nobody	someone
anything	everyone	no one	

EXAMPLES: Both received *their* awards.
Few *are* really worried.

Everyone has *his or her* invitation.
(When the indefinite pronoun refers to both males and females, *his or her* is acceptable.)

A few indefinite pronouns are plural.

Plural Indefinite Pronouns			
both	many	few	several

EXAMPLES: Both received *their* awards.
Few *are* really worried.

355

Extending the Lesson

Have the students write answers to these questions, using compound personal pronouns:

Do you ever talk to yourself?
What do your friends call themselves?
What can you and your friend make by yourselves?

Part 3

Objective

To identify indefinite pronouns and to make verbs agree with them in number

Presenting the Lesson

1. Read and discuss pages 355-356. Stress the differences between the singular and plural indefinite pronouns. Encourage the students to study the charts carefully.

You may wish to point out to students that these words are pronouns only if they take the place of a noun. If they are positioned before a noun to modify it, they are adjectives.

One glass was broken. (adjective)
One was broken. (pronoun)

2. Assign and discuss Exercises A and B on pages 356-357.

Individualizing the Lesson

Less-Advanced Students

1. Allow the students to work in small groups to complete the Exercises.

2. For Exercise B, help the students identify the pronouns and determine whether each is singular or plural. Then have them complete the Exercise independently.

Have the students substitute *none* for *both, all, either,* and *each* in the Exercises, making whatever other changes are necessary. Discuss these changes.

Reinforcement Exercise

Assign and discuss Exercise C on page 372.

Optional Practice

Have the students use each of the indefinite pronouns in sentences.

Extending the Lesson

Divide the class into small groups to discuss the advantages and disadvantages of using *his or her* with singular indefinite pronouns. Ask your class to brainstorm for other words or phrases that cover both genders.

The pronouns *all, some,* and *none* may be singular or plural, depending upon their meaning in the sentence.

EXAMPLES: All of the pie *is* gone.
All of the members *are* here.

Some of the milk *is* sour.
Some of the apples *are* ripe.

None of the time *was* wasted.
None of the flowers *were* left.

Exercises Find the indefinite pronouns.

A. Number your paper from 1–10. For each sentence write down the indefinite pronoun or pronouns.

1. Is anything the matter?
2. Both of the games were postponed because of rain.
3. All of the photographs for the yearbook were too dark.
4. Somebody has left his or her jacket on the bus.
5. Either of the counselors will help you with your schedule.
6. In the spring, almost everyone rides his or her bike to school.
7. During the noon hour, anyone can go home to eat lunch.
8. All of the eighth-grade students went to the high school for orientation.
9. Each of the students filled out his or her registration cards.
10. Everyone took the high school placement test today.

B. Number your paper from 1–10. For each sentence write down the indefinite pronoun and pick the verb in the parentheses that agrees with it.

1. Neither of the keys (fits, fit) the lock.
2. Just a few of my relatives (is, are) coming.
3. Some of the band members (is, are) competing in the music contest.

4. Each of the countries (send, <u>sends</u>) two representatives.

5. <u>Neither</u> of the encyclopedias (explain, <u>explains</u>) the subject very well.

6. <u>All</u> of the runners (was, <u>were</u>) lined up for the race.

7. <u>All</u> of the bookcases (<u>have</u>, has) assembling instructions.

8. <u>Several</u> of those days last week (was, <u>were</u>) scorchers.

9. <u>Neither</u> of my shoes (is, are) wet.

10. <u>Both</u> of my brothers (works, <u>work</u>) at the ice cream parlor.

Part 4 Demonstrative Pronouns

The pronouns *this*, *that*, *these*, and *those* are used to point out which persons or things are referred to. They are called **demonstrative pronouns.**

This and *these* point to persons or things that are near. *That* and *those* point to persons or things farther away.

This is the right road.	**These** belong to Jim.
That is my camera.	**Those** are my boots.

Exercise Use demonstrative pronouns.

Number your paper from 1–10. Write the correct demonstrative pronoun for the blank space in each sentence.

1. <u>Those</u> are my boots over there.
2. <u>That</u> was Kate on the telephone.
3. <u>These, Those</u> were the books I was telling you about.
4. <u>This, That</u> is the metric table we have to learn.
5. <u>These, Those</u> are the tools you wanted to borrow.
6. <u>That</u> was my brother who read the announcements.
7. <u>These, Those</u> are the chapters I read last night.
8. <u>These</u> are probably better than those.
9. <u>That</u> is my bike parked over there.
10. <u>That</u> was Ryan in the doorway.

Part 4

Objective

To recognize and correctly use demonstrative pronouns

Presenting the Lesson

1. Read and discuss this page.
2. Assign and discuss the Exercise.

Individualizing the Lesson

Less-Advanced Students

Before they begin the Exercise, show the students how to recognize singular and plural verbs.

Advanced Students

Have each student write one sentence that clearly calls for a particular demonstrative pronoun. Use these for a class review.

Optional Practice

Have students take turns pointing to and identifying things in the classroom, using the correct demonstrative pronoun.

Part 5

Objective

To recognize interrogative pronouns

Presenting the Lesson

1. Read and discuss this page.
2. Assign and discuss the Exercise.

Individualizing the Lesson

Less-Advanced Students

Review demonstrative pronouns and indefinite pronouns before assigning the Exercise.

Advanced Students

Have the students use interrogative pronouns to write questions for the statements in the Exercise.

Reinforcement Exercise

Assign and discuss Exercise D on page 372.

Part 6

Objective

To identify and use correctly the subject, object, and possessive forms of pronouns

Presenting the Lesson

1. Read and discuss the introduction and **The Subject Form of Pronouns** on pages 358 and 359.

Part 5   Interrogative Pronouns

The pronouns *who, whose, whom, which,* and *what* are used to ask questions. They are called **interrogative pronouns.**

EXAMPLES: *Who* rang the bell?   *Which* is your paper?
Whose are those shoes?   *What* did you say?
Whom do you mean?

Exercise Find and use different kinds of pronouns.

Number your paper from 1–10. Write all the pronouns in these sentences. After each pronoun, write *Indefinite, Demonstrative,* or *Interrogative* to show what kind it is.

1. Those are the best skates to buy. Demonstrative
2. Which of the new TV shows does Rhoda enjoy? Interrogative
3. This is Jay's cassette player. Demonstrative
4. No one knew the answer to either of the questions. Indefinite, Indefinite
5. What is everybody waiting for? Interrogative, Indefinite
6. Which is the one Ann chose? Interrogative, Indefinite
7. Nobody can solve the problems. Indefinite
8. To whom did the caller wish to speak? Interrogative
9. Which of the shelves does Ernest want painted? Interrogative
10. These are the ones to be painted. Demonstrative, Indefinite

Part 6   The Forms of Pronouns

English personal pronouns have three special forms. Like nouns, they have a possessive form. In addition, they have two other forms: the **subject form** and the **object form.**

I own the book. (subject form)
The owner of the book is *I.* (subject form after linking verb)
The book belongs to *me.* (object form)
Where is *my* book? (possessive form modifying a noun)
The book is *mine.* (possessive form used as predicate adjective)

The Subject Form of Pronouns

Personal pronouns are used in the subject form (1) when they are subjects and (2) when they follow linking verbs as predicate pronouns. Here are the subject forms of each of the personal pronouns:

Subject Forms of Pronouns		
I	you	he, she, it
we	you	they

Personal pronoun used *as subject*
$\begin{cases} \textit{I} \text{ agree with you.} \\ \textit{She} \text{ is not going.} \end{cases}$

Personal pronoun used *after linking verb*
$\begin{cases} \text{This is } \textit{he.} \\ \text{It was } \textit{I.} \end{cases}$

The Object Form of Pronouns

Personal pronouns are used in the object form (1) when they are direct or indirect objects of verbs and (2) when they are objects of prepositions, which are short, connecting words such as *of, for, to, with,* and *by.* Here are the object forms of the personal pronouns:

Object Forms of Pronouns		
me	you	him, her, it
us	you	them

Direct Object
$\begin{cases} \text{The dog bit } \textit{him.} \\ \text{Jack helped } \textit{them} \text{ with the work.} \end{cases}$

Indirect Object   I gave *her* a gift.

Object of Preposition
$\begin{cases} \text{The candy is for } \textit{me.} \\ \text{Write a letter to } \textit{them.} \end{cases}$

359

Stress that subject pronouns are used only as subjects and predicate pronouns. Explain that predicate pronouns must be in the subject form because they are linked to the subject by a linking verb.

2. Read and discuss **The Object Form of Pronouns** on page 359. Have the students suggest additional examples of sentences in which pronouns are used as direct objects, indirect objects, and objects of prepositions. For more information on prepositions, see Section 6.

3. Read and discuss **The Possessive Form of Pronouns** on page 360. Have the students use each pronoun in a sentence.

4. Do Exercise A on page 360 orally.

5. Assign and discuss Exercises B and C on page 361.

Individualizing the Lesson

Less-Advanced Students

Help the students decide how each pronoun in the Exercises is used. Then have the students decide whether the subject, object, or possessive form is needed.

Advanced Students

Have the students tell how each pronoun is used in the sentences in Exercises A, B, and C.

Reinforcement Exercise

Assign and discuss Exercise E on page 373.

Optional Practice

Have the students try to replace every noun in the Exercises on pages 360 and 361 with a pronoun.

The Possessive Form of Pronouns

Personal pronouns are used in the possessive form to show ownership or possession. Personal pronouns in the possessive form consist of two groups: (1) Pronouns used, like adjectives, to modify nouns; (2) Pronouns used, like nouns, as subjects of verbs, as predicate words, or as objects of verbs or prepositions.

Possessive Forms of Pronouns Used To Modify Nouns		
my	your	his, her, its
our	your	their

EXAMPLES: *my* sister   *our* car
his book   *its* wheels
her mother   *their* money

Possessive Forms of Pronouns Used Alone		
mine	yours	his, hers, its
ours	yours	theirs

EXAMPLES: This book is *mine.* (predicate word)
Yours is on the desk. (subject of verb)
I don't see *hers.* (object of verb)
Look at the pictures in *ours.* (object of preposition)

Exercises Choose the right pronoun.

A. Choose the right pronoun from those given in parentheses. Be ready to explain how it is used in the sentence.

  1. Does this copy belong to (he, <u>him</u>)?
  2. That was (her, <u>she</u>).

3. Mrs. Walsh gave the job to (I, me).
4. Donna and I helped (they, them) with the yard work.
5. Hasn't anybody seen (he, him)?
6. It was (her, she) who answered the call.
7. Was it (they, them) who called?
8. Is there anything of (your, yours) to go home?
9. This is (he, him).
10. Will you give these books to (she, her)?

B. Follow the directions for Exercise A.

1. The principal wanted to talk to Kelly and (I, me).
2. Could it have been (they, them)?
3. I have both of (theirs, their).
4. Leave the photos with (me, I).
5. Mother asked (me, I) for the key.
6. The award was given to (she, her) for outstanding achievement.
7. Each of (us, we) had a look at it.
8. I'm sure it was (he, him) on the telephone.
9. The test results were given by (they, them) at a special meeting.
10. (Me, I) am going to the museum.

C. The personal pronouns in these sentences are in italics. Write each one. After it, write *Subject Form* or *Object Form*.

1. The puck just missed *him*. Object Form
2. Ms. Anderson gave *us* several problems for homework. Object Form
3. *I* gave *you* the schedule. Subject Form, Object Form
4. *They* were taking *her* to dinner. Subject Form, Object Form
5. *He* gave the gifts to *them*. Subject Form, Object Form
6. *We* have been waiting for *him*. Subject Form, Object Form
7. The manager sold *us* the T-shirts at a discount. Object Form
8. Carl couldn't hear *me*. Object Form
9. Did Aunt Ellen get a good picture of *us*? Object Form
10. The third one in the front row is *she*. Subject Form

Objective

To use pronouns correctly in compound sentence parts

Presenting the Lesson

1. Read and discuss this page. Have the students give additional examples of pronouns used in compound subjects, compound direct objects, compound indirect objects, and compound objects of prepositions.

2. Assign and discuss Exercises A and B on page 363.

Individualizing the Lesson

Less-Advanced Students

Remind the students to test the pronoun choice in each sentence by dropping the noun in the compound sentence part.

Advanced Students

Have the students tell how each pronoun is used in its sentence.

Reinforcement Exercise

Assign and discuss Exercise F on page 373.

Optional Practice

Have the students write sentences that contain these phrases:

my friend and I
my friend and me
Carlotta and her
Carlotta and she

Part 7 Pronouns in Compound Sentence Parts

You seldom make mistakes when you use one personal pronoun by itself. You would never say "Give *I* the pencil."

Trouble arises when two pronouns or a pronoun and a noun are used together in compound sentence parts. Would you say "Brian and me built a radio" or "Brian and I built a radio"?

Have you heard people say "between you and I"? Does this sound right? Should it be "between you and me"? How can you tell? Let's look at some sentences with pronouns correctly used in compound parts.

Compound Subject	*Terry and she* went to the rink.
Compound Direct Object	We visited the *Browns and them.*
Compound Indirect Object	Mrs. Hill gave *Sue and me* a job.
Compound Object of Preposition	The package was for *Jack and me.*

Now read the sentences above a second time. This time drop out the noun in each compound part. For example, read "*She* went to the rink." Each sentence will sound right and sensible to you.

Whenever you are in doubt about which form of the pronoun to use in a compound sentence part, drop out the noun. Read the sentence with just the pronoun, and you will usually choose the right one.

If there are two pronouns in the compound part, read the sentence for each pronoun separately.

Mrs. Huber will call for (she? her?) and (I? me?)
Mrs. Huber will call for *her.*
Mrs. Huber will call for *me.*

Caution: After forms of the verb *be,* use only *I, we, he, she,* or *they* as predicate pronouns.

Exercises Choose the correct pronoun in compound sentence parts.

A. Choose the correct pronoun from those given in parentheses in each sentence.

1. Dawn and (her, <u>she</u>) will bring the peanuts.
2. Can you give Sandy and (we, <u>us</u>) some advice?
3. Gayle and (her, <u>she</u>) are trying out for cheerleading.
4. The doorman gave Al and (I, <u>me</u>) a pass.
5. There is no difference in weight between (he, <u>him</u>) and (<u>me</u>, I).
6. Wait for Lori and (I, <u>me</u>) after school.
7. Jeff lives between (<u>them</u>, they) and (I, <u>me</u>).
8. (Her, <u>She</u>) and I are the newspaper editors.
9. The ushers were Marla and (her, <u>she</u>).
10. Just between you and (<u>me</u>, I), that speaker wasn't very good.

B. All but one of the following sentences contain a pronoun error. Write the sentences, correcting the errors.

1. My parents and me are going to the ice show tonight. ^I
2. Larry and them have gone to Detroit. ^{they}
3. The telephone must be for either you or she. ^{her}
4. Everyone had enough except Janet and she. ^{her}
5. The packages were divided evenly between Tanya and I. ^{me}
6. Judy and her just went out the back door. ^{she}
7. Mrs. McGowan made Meg and I a sandwich. ^{me}
8. The police officer gave Alex and I directions. ^{me}
9. Peggy and Linda sat next to Lauri and I at the student concert. ^{me}
10. The helicopter kept circling around Pete and me. *correct*

Tom and him
Tom and he

Extending the Lesson

Have each student find three published examples of pronouns used in compound sentence parts. Have the student copy these sentences. Discuss how the pronouns are used in the sentences.

363

Part 8

Objective

To use the pronouns *who*, *whom*, and *whose* correctly

Presenting the Lesson

1. Read and discuss this page. Have the students provide additional examples of sentences using *who*, *whom*, and *whose*.
2. Do Exercise A orally.
3. Assign and discuss Exercise B on page 365.

Individualizing the Lesson

Less-Advanced Students

Work with the students to decide how each interrogative pronoun is used in its sentence. Then have them review the explanation on this page to determine which pronoun is correct.

Advanced Students

Have the students tell how *who*, *whom*, or *whose* is used in each sentence in the Exercises.

Reinforcement Exercise

Assign and discuss Exercise G on page 374.

Extending the Lesson

Have each student compose a list of five questions to be used in an interview with a famous person. Each question must begin with *who*, *whom*, or *whose*.

Part 8   *Who* and *Whom*

The words *who*, *whose*, and *whom* are used to ask questions. When used in this way, they are called **interrogative pronouns.**

Who is the subject form. It is used as the subject of a verb.

Whom is the object form. It is used as the direct object of a verb or as the object of a preposition.

> *Who* told you that story? (*Who* is subject of *told*.)
> *Whom* did you meet? (*Whom* is object of *did meet*.)
> To *whom* did you go? (*Whom* is object of preposition *to*.)
> *Whom* did I see you with? (*Whom* is object of *with*.)

Whose is the possessive form. Like other possessives, it can be used with a noun to modify the noun: *Whose bike* is missing? When it is used without a noun, it may be the subject or object of a verb.

> *Whose* house is that? (*Whose* modifies *house*.)
> *Whose* were you using? (*Whose* is object of *were using*.)
> *Whose* are those boots? (*Whose* is subject of *are*.)

Exercises   Choose the correct pronoun.

A. Choose the correct interrogative pronoun.

1. (Who, Whose) move is it?
2. (Whose, Who) are these binoculars?
3. (Who, Whom) are these people?
4. (Whom, Who) were you thinking of?
5. (Whom, Who) do these shoes belong to?
6. (Who, Whom) swam ten lengths?
7. (Whom, Whose) speech did you like the best?
8. (Whose, Whom) is this?
9. (Whom, Whose) country has that flag?
10. For (who, whom) does the bell toll?

B. Follow the directions for Exercise A.

1. To (<u>whom</u>, who) did you give the library books?
2. (Who, <u>Whom</u>) is this letter from?
3. (Whom, <u>Who</u>) painted this picture?
4. (Who, <u>Whom</u>) do you know in Alaska?
5. (Who, <u>Whom</u>) is Randy talking to?
6. (<u>Whose</u>, Who) are these initials?
7. To (who, <u>whom</u>) should I give these letters?
8. For (who, <u>whom</u>) shall I ask?
9. (<u>Whom</u>, Who) did you ask for?
10. (<u>Who</u>, Whom) will get the MVP award in hockey?

Part 9   Possessive Pronouns and Contractions

Some contractions are formed by joining a pronoun and a verb and omitting one or more letters. The apostrophe is used to show where letters are left out.

it + is *or* has = it's   they + are = they're
you + are = you're   who + is *or* has = who's

The possessive forms of the pronouns *its, your, their,* and *whose* sound the same as these contractions: *it's, you're, they're,* and *who's.* Because they sound alike, the contractions and possessives are sometimes confused.

Wrong The groundhog saw it's shadow.
Right   The groundhog saw its shadow.

Right   You're (You are) late for your appointment.
Right   They're (They are) planning to show their slides.
Right   Who's (who is) the boy whose coat you are wearing?

Part 9

Objective

To distinguish between possessive pronouns and contractions

Presenting the Lesson

1. Read and discuss pages 365 and 366.
2. Remind students that an apostrophe indicates one or more missing letters in a contraction. Demonstrate with examples on the chalkboard.
3. Assign and discuss Exercises A and B on page 366.

Individualizing the Lesson

Less-Advanced Students

1. Allow the students to work in pairs to complete the Exercises.
2. In Exercise A, help the students determine the words each

contraction stands for and try them in the sentence. If these do not make sense in the sentence, then the contraction is the wrong choice.

Advanced Students

Have the students write rules for using *its, it's, your, you're, their,* and *they're.*

Reinforcement Exercise

Assign and discuss Exercise H on page 374.

Optional Practice

Have the students write sentences using the words *its, it's, your, you're, their,* and *they're.*

Extending the Lesson

Have the students list all the contractions and all the possessive pronouns in a newspaper editorial. Discuss whether any of the words has been used incorrectly or is likely to cause confusion.

There are two simple rules to follow to make sure that you use possessive pronouns and contractions correctly.

1. When you use one of these words that sound alike, ask yourself whether it stands for one word or two. If it stands for two words, it is a contraction and needs an apostrophe.

2. Never use an apostrophe in a possessive pronoun.

Exercises Possessive pronouns and contractions.

A. Choose the correct word from the two given in parentheses.

1. The amusement park gave free passes to (it's <u>its</u>) first 500 entrants.
2. (Whose, Who's) bike is chained to the tree?
3. (You're, <u>Your</u>) idea might work.
4. Are you sure that (<u>they're</u>, their) coming?
5. (Whose, <u>Who's</u>) going to the Ridgetown Fair?
6. (They're, Their) glad (its, <u>it's</u>) Friday.
7. (Whose, <u>Who's</u>) going to mow the lawn?
8. (Their, <u>They're</u>) going to pick up (<u>their</u>, they're) uniforms at noon.
9. Have you made up (you're, <u>your</u>) mind?
10. (<u>Who's</u>, Whose) got a dime that I can borrow?

B. Write the words each contraction below stands for.

1. <u>It's</u> twenty miles from this town to Omaha. It is
2. <u>Who's</u> next? Who is
3. <u>We've</u> walked the whole way. We have
4. <u>Who'd</u> have thought it would snow in April? Who would
5. <u>They've</u> come to repair the water main. They have
6. <u>Who's</u> been in my locker? Who has
7. <u>You've</u> got a good sense of humor. You have
8. <u>It's</u> your turn now. It is
9. The book is called <u>Who's</u> Who. Who Is
10. <u>When's</u> the pizza being delivered? When is

Part 10   Special Pronoun Problems

Compound Personal Pronouns

The compound personal pronouns (*myself*, *yourself*, etc.) must not be used in place of personal pronouns. They are used *in addition* to personal pronouns. It is a good rule to use a compound personal pronoun only when the word it refers to has been used in the same sentence.

> I saw the weather balloon *myself*. (*myself* refers to *I*.)
> You can judge for *yourself*. (*yourself* refers to *you*.)
> She *herself* knows what to do. (*herself* refers to *she*.)

We and *Us* Used with Nouns

When you use phrases like *we girls* and *us boys*, you must be sure that you are using the right form of the pronoun. You can tell which pronoun to use by dropping the noun and saying the sentence without it.

Problem	(We, Us) girls will be at Jan's house.
Correct	We will be at Jan's house.
Correct	We girls will be at Jan's house.
Problem	Will you call for (us, we) boys?
Correct	Will you call for us?
Correct	Will you call for us boys?

Them and *Those*

The word *them* is always a pronoun. It is always used as an object of a verb or preposition.

Those is sometimes a pronoun and sometimes an adjective. If a noun appears right after it, *those* is probably an adjective. Used without a noun, it is a pronoun.

> We found *them* here. (object of verb)
> We have heard from *them*. (object of preposition *from*)

367

Objective

To use compound personal pronouns correctly and to avoid confusing *we* and *us*, *them* and *those*

Presenting the Lesson

1. Read and discuss pages 367 and 368. Have the students suggest additional examples to parallel each model of correct usage.
2. Assign and discuss Exercises A and B on page 368.

Individualizing the Lesson

Less-Advanced Students

1. In Exercise A, have the students first find the referent for each compound personal pronoun.
2. In Exercise B, remind the students to test the pronoun choice by dropping the noun that follows.

Advanced Students

In Exercise B, have the students label each pronoun with its function in the sentence.

Reinforcement Exercise

Assign and discuss Exercise I on page 375.

Optional Practice

Have the students add compound personal pronouns to these sentences:

> I taught wood carving.
> Joanne went to the library.
> We cooked the roast.

Discuss how the compound personal pronouns affect meaning in the sentences.

Extending the Lesson

Have the students answer the following questions, using *we* or *us* with *students:* What subjects interest you most? What school do you attend? What plans do you have for the summer? What work do you have to do tonight?

We like *those* best. (object of verb)
Those birds are cardinals. (adjective modifying *birds*)
We will order *those* cakes. (adjective modifying *cakes*)

Exercises Use the correct form.

A. Copy these sentences. Fill in the blank with the correct compound personal pronoun.

1. I finished building the end table ___myself___.
2. You can both see for ___yourselves___ that the experiment worked.
3. We went to the movies by ___ourselves___.
4. If you jog, you compete only with ___yourself___.
5. Janelle planted the flower bed by ___herself___.
6. They can read for ___themselves___ that the track meet was cancelled.
7. I went by ___myself___ to the art exhibit.
8. We treated ___ourselves___ to hot fudge sundaes.
9. Will you take the train to St. Louis by ___yourself___?
10. David directed the play ___himself___.

B. Choose the correct word from the two words given.

1. Will you go to the beach with Diana and (me, myself)?
2. (We, Us) Scouts would like to sponsor a canoe trip.
3. (Them, Those) portraits look very old.
4. (We, Us) players are going to the Knicks-Bulls basketball game.
5. Will you call for (we, us) boys on the way to the stadium?
6. Who piled all (them, those) boards up?
7. Would you like to sit with (us, we) girls at the play?
8. Most of (us, we) boys will help paint the bleachers.
9. You won't need all of (them, those) pencils.
10. (We, Us) students held a pep rally yesterday.

Part 11   Pronouns and Antecedents

A personal pronoun, you remember, is used in place of a noun. This noun is the word to which it refers. The noun usually comes first, either in the same sentence or in the preceding sentence. The noun for which a pronoun stands is called its **antecedent.**

> We waited for Kay. *She* was making a phone call.
> (*She* stands for *Kay. Kay* is the antecedent.)

> The men had taken off *their* coats.
> (*Their* stands for *men. Men* is the antecedent.)

Pronouns themselves may be the antecedents of other pronouns:

> Does everyone have *his* books?
> (*Everyone* is the antecedent of *his*.)

> Do you have *your* music lesson today?
> (*You* is the antecedent of *your*.)

A pronoun must agree with its antecedent in number.

Here the word *agree* means that the pronoun must be the *same in number* as its antecedent. The word *number* here means *singular* or *plural*. The pronoun must be singular if the word it stands for is singular. It must be plural if the word it stands for is plural.

> The runners took *their* places.
> (*Runners* is plural; *their* is plural.)

> The scientist told of *her* early experiences.
> (*Scientist* is singular; *her* is singular.)

> Everybody brought *his* own records.
> (*Everybody* is singular; *his* is singular.)

> One of the girls left *her* project in the shop.
> (*One* is singular; *her* is singular.)

Objective

To make pronouns agree with their antecedents

Presenting the Lesson

1. Write the word *antecedent* on the chalkboard. Define it.
2. Read and discuss page 369. Stress that pronouns and their antecedents must agree in number. Demonstrate with examples.
3. Assign and discuss Exercises A and B on page 370.

Individualizing the Lesson

Less-Advanced Students

1. Allow the students to work in pairs.
2. In Exercise B, have the students identify the antecedent of each pronoun in parentheses.
3. If students are confused by indefinite pronouns, have them review pages 355 and 356.

Advanced Students

Do both Exercises orally.

Reinforcement Exercise

Assign and discuss Exercise J on page 375.

Optional Practice

Have the students find the pronoun and its antecedent in each of these sentences:

Some of the swimmers practice their strokes.

One of the trees had a fence around it.

Kay told her secret.

Hal laughed when he came in.

Extending the Lesson

Have the students list all pronouns and their antecedents in a how-to article or instructions for building something, such as a birdhouse.

Exercises Pronouns and antecedents.

A. The personal pronouns in these sentences are italicized. Find the antecedent of each pronoun. Write it.

1. One of the boys had a cast on *his* arm. One
2. You usually bring *your* own towel to the pool. You
3. The box isn't pretty, but the paper around *it* is. box
4. Everyone on the team had tears in *his* eyes. Everyone
5. Both of the owls had *their* eyes half shut. Both
6. Everyone thinks *you* can do the job, Sarah. Sarah
7. One of the glasses had a crack in *it*. One
8. Brenda bought *her* own materials. Brenda
9. The members of the cast took *their* places. members
10. One of the storm shelters had *its* entrance boarded up. One

B. Choose the correct pronoun from those given in the parentheses.

1. Has everyone taken (his, their) turn?
2. If anyone wants to go, tell (him or her, them) to see Paul.
3. Few were able to finish (his, their) work.
4. Most of the cans had lost (its, their) labels.
5. Somebody has left (his, their) wallet on my desk.
6. Everyone had an opportunity to state (their, her) opinion.
7. All of the contestants had (his, their) entries ready.
8. Nobody expected to hear (his, their) own name over the loudspeaker.
9. Neither of the actors could remember (his, their) lines at the first rehearsal.
10. Each of the students explained (his or her, their) collage to the class.

Reinforcement Exercises—Review

Using Pronouns

A. Find the pronouns. (Use after page 353.)

Number your paper from 1–10. Write the pronouns you find in each of the following sentences. After each <u>pronoun</u>, write the noun or nouns it stands for.

1. Mike said <u>he</u> would set the dinner table. Mike
2. There's no stamp on the envelope. <u>It</u> must have come off. stamp
3. One rancher drove <u>his</u> jeep ten miles out on the range. rancher
4. There's the box. <u>Its</u> lid has a picture of a cornfield. box
5. Brad and Joe said Scott could use <u>their</u> tent. Brad and Joe
6. Claire and Joy put <u>their</u> camping equipment in the car. Claire and Joy
7. Mr. Hernandez attached <u>his</u> trailer to the back of <u>his</u> van. Mr. Hernandez
8. Two archaeologists told how <u>they</u> had discovered the ruins. archaeologists
9. Sue and Wendy missed the bus, and then <u>they</u> got caught in the rain. Sue and Wendy
10. There's the tree where Megan snagged <u>her</u> kite. Megan

B. Use compound personal pronouns. (Use after page 355.)

Number your paper from 1–10. Beside each number write a correct compound personal pronoun for each of the following sentences. After it, write the noun or pronoun to which it refers.

1. The boys decorated the gym by (pronoun). (themselves) boys
2. Julie cleaned the fish (pronoun). (herself) Julie
3. I moved the plants (pronoun) so that they wouldn't get damaged. (myself) I
4. Girls, please help (pronoun) to more dessert. (yourselves) girls

---

Reinforcement Exercises

These Reinforcement Exercises may be used for additional practice as needed. Each exercise may be used after the text page indicated in parentheses.

Review

If you have not assigned these Exercises before this time, you can use them as an excellent Section Review.

Mixed Review

The following exercises provide review of the concepts and skills presented in this chapter.

A. Find the pronouns. Find all of the pronouns in the sentences below. Label each one *Personal, Indefinite, Demonstrative,* and *Interrogative.* For the personal pronouns, write the antecedent, if there is one.

1. Who painted <u>that</u>?
2. <u>Several</u> of the glasses were broken.
3. The twins loaned Joe <u>their</u> tent for <u>his</u> camping trip.
4. <u>Which</u> of <u>those</u> did <u>you</u> make <u>yourself</u>?
5. The girls said <u>they</u> loaded the photographer's equipment into <u>her</u> car.
6. <u>Both</u> of <u>them</u> know <u>her</u> and <u>me</u>.
7. Did <u>everyone</u> in the tour group see <u>these</u>?
8. <u>Each</u> of <u>us</u> wanted to win the award.
9. <u>Whom</u> would <u>you</u> choose for the job, Mr. Gordon?
10. <u>I</u> think <u>those</u> are <u>hers</u>.

1. Int. Dem.
2. Ind.
3. Per. (twins), Per. (Joe)

4. Int., Dem., Per., Per. (You)
5. Per. (girls), Per. (photographer)
6. Ind., Per., Per., Per.
7. Ind., Dem.
8. Ind., Per.
9. Int., Per. (Mr. Gordon)
10. Per., Dem., Per.

B. Use pronouns correctly. Write the correct pronoun from the two given in parentheses.

1. (Who, Whom) plays the lead role in the show?
2. (Them, Those) hockey players have new jerseys.
3. Somebody left (his, their) towel behind on the beach.
4. (Them, Those) flowering plants were presented to (her, herself).
5. To (who, whom) does this down sleeping bag belong?
6. (This, That) sweatshirt I'm wearing is mine, and (this, that) green one in the other room is yours.
7. Neither Angie nor Melissa remembered (her, their) previous plans.
8. (Who, Whom) wants to share (them, those) pistachio nuts with me?
9. Many of the villagers make (his or her, their) pottery by hand.
10. (Who, Whom) was that book about?
11. Some of (them, those) rare books have hand-inked illustrations.
12. Everyone in the office brings (his or her, their) lunch to work.
13. (Who, Whom) will go to the store for milk?
14. (These, Them) carving tools belong to (me, myself).
15. Few of the boys earned (his, their) merit badges during the first session.

5. The drum majorette usually led the parade (pronoun). (herself) majorette
6. Rob made the fudge (pronoun). (himself) Rob
7. Why doesn't Janet try out for the team (pronoun)? (herself) Janet
8. We watched (pronoun) on the TV screen. (ourselves) We
9. Ken, Rachel, and Jill painted the scenery (pronoun). (themselves) Ken, Rachel, Jill
10. A lion cub sunned (pronoun) on a rock. (itself) cub

C. Find the indefinite pronouns. (Use after page 357.)

Number your paper from 1–10. For each sentence write down the indefinite pronoun. Write the verb that agrees with it from those given in parentheses.

1. Some of the candies (taste, tastes) like strawberry.
2. Several of the foreign exchange students (come, comes) from South America.
3. Everything in the boxes (is, are) wet.
4. None of those stars to the west (set, sets) before 10 P.M.
5. Each of the divers (perform, performs) twice.
6. One of those tires (has, have) a slow leak.
7. Somebody in the prop room always (forget, forgets) the king's cushion.
8. (Are, Is) anybody coming?
9. No one in the caves (wander, wanders) away from the guide.
10. Both of us (know, knows) the way around the swamp.

D. Find different kinds of pronouns. (Use after page 358.)

Number your paper from 1–10. Write all the pronouns in each sentence. After each pronoun, write *Indefinite, Demonstrative,* or *Interrogative* to show what kind it is.

1. How did Kirk get these out of the water? Demonstrative
2. No one admitted leaving the phone off the hook. Indefinite
3. Several of the girls carried these from the station. Indefinite, Demonstrative
4. Why would anyone bring these to a picnic? Indefinite, Demonstrative

5. Everybody heckled the pitcher. Indefinite
6. Who let the cat out of the bag? Interrogative
7. Nobody knew the right answer. Indefinite
8. Pete is buying this as a present. Demonstrative
9. What's that by the rock pile? Demonstrative
10. Both of the teams had practiced vigorously. Indefinite

E. Choose the correct pronoun. (Use after page 361.)

Choose the correct pronoun from the two given in parentheses. Be ready to explain how it is used in the sentence.

1. Was it (he, him) who won the trophy?
2. It was (she, her) who painted that picture.
3. The workers demanded (their, theirs) pay immediately.
4. (We, Us) organized the pep assembly.
5. Strong winds blew the shack over on (it, its) side.
6. We thought it was (he, him) who made the announcements.
7. The manager gave Ann and (me, I) tickets to the movie.
8. Caryl and (me, I) are going to the shopping mall.
9. Jack wanted you to bring (your, yours) along.
10. Please give these music books to Darla and (she, her).

F. Use the correct pronoun in compound sentence parts. (Use after page 363.)

Choose the correct pronoun from the two given in parentheses.

1. (He, Him) and Sally set up the ping pong table.
2. Did you meet John and (they, them) at the exhibit?
3. A waiter showed Mrs. Ryan and (she, her) to a table.
4. (She, Her) and (me, I) were digging for clams.
5. They gave Ted and (we, us) just ten minutes to get ready.
6. My father packed Ken and (me, I) a lunch.

C. Use the correct form of pronouns.
Write the correct pronoun from the two given in parentheses.

1. (He, Him) and (me, I) have been friends for years.
2. It was (her, she) who called last night.
3. (They, Them) have agreed to discuss the situation with Les and (I, me).
4. Is that (your, you're) picture on the sports page?
5. (We, Us) girls do volunteer work at a nursing home on Saturdays.
6. The club members worked to clean up (their, they're) neighborhood.
7. Could someone show Kip and (I, me) how to program this computer?
8. (Its, It's) struggle over at last, the chick emerged from the shell.
9. Janice overheard (they, them) planning a surprise party for (she, her).
10. (Whose, Who's) costumes will fit (we, us) understudies?

Using Grammar in Writing

1. Have the students rewrite a paragraph from a third-person narrative in the first-person. Discuss the changes in point of view and in pronoun use.

2. Have pairs of students interview each other about favorite hobbies and write paragraphs based on their interviews. Require the students to use three compound personal pronouns in their paragraphs. Have them identify the pronouns by person, number, and gender.

3. Have the students complete this mystery plot:

All of the people in the town of Bamen awoke one morning to find their radios gone. . . .

Tell the students to include at least one indefinite pronoun in each sentence of their stories.

4. Have the students write formal introductions, using demonstrative pronouns correctly. The introductions may either be serious, as between two classmates, or humorous, as between two objects or imaginary people.

5. Have the students write questions for an interview with a famous person. Remind students to use interrogative pronouns correctly.

6. Have each student write three questions about current events. All questions must begin with the pronoun *who, whom,* or *whose.*

7. Have students write instructions for making an object, such as a paper airplane or a paper snowflake. For each pronoun they use, have them underline the antecedent.

7. Barb waited fifteen minutes for Mr. Kopp and (they, them).

8. Bob and (us, we) had to mow and rake the lawn.

9. The setter came to Greg and (he, him) right away.

10. The lifeguard warned Patty and (we, us) about the undercurrent.

G. Choose the correct interrogative pronoun.
(Use after page 365.)

Choose the correct interrogative pronoun from the two given in parentheses.

1. (Whom, Who) came in second?
2. (Who, Whose) was the best answer?
3. (Who, Whom) left her sunglasses on the counter?
4. To (whom, who) are you giving the macramé hanger?
5. (Who, Whom) did Scott give the folder to?
6. (Whom, Who) knows how to get to the airport?
7. (Whose, Whom) phone number is that?
8. (Who, Whom) did the coach choose for the starting line-up?
9. (Whom, Who) let the cats out of the house?
10. (Whose, Whom) are these cookies for?

H. Choose possessive pronouns or contractions.
(Use after page 366.)

Choose the right word from the two given in parentheses.

1. (It's, Its) too early.
2. The panther boxed (its, it's) cub's ears.
3. (Who's Whose) team do we play next week?
4. (Your, You're) appointment with the orthodontist is tomorrow.
5. Christie and Tom said (they're, their) report was on bicycle safety.
6. (Whose, Who's) got the relish?
7. (It's, Its) Monday and it's (you're, your) turn to cook.

374

8. (Their, They're) ready for take-off.
9. (It's, Its) (your, you're) turn.
10. (They're, Their) always late starting the meeting.

I. Use the correct form with special pronoun problems. (Use after page 368.)

Choose the correct word from the two given in parentheses.

1. The coach handed the trophy to (me, myself).
2. (Them, Those) are too big.
3. The principal presented (we, us) students with diplomas.
4. Please put (them, those) boxes in the trash can.
5. (Us, We) girls got special recognition for our efforts.
6. (Them, Those) posters are to be hung in the cafeteria.
7. (Them, Those) shops on Central Street are open until 9 P.M. on Thursday evening.
8. Would you like to go to the show with (us, we) girls?

J. Find the antecedent of the pronoun. (Use after page 370.)

The personal pronouns in these sentences are italicized. Write the antecedent of each pronoun.

1. The paramedics entered the fiery building carrying all of *their* equipment. paramedics
2. Chris's coat had a tear in *it*. coat
3. Phil fixed *his* back tire. Phil
4. Vicki's yard has a fence all around *it*. yard
5. Mrs. Kohl was knitting a sweater for *her* granddaughter. Mrs. Kohl
6. Bring *your* gym clothes for the intramural game tomorrow. (You)
7. Bandit looked at *his* dog dish and walked away from *it*. Bandit, dish
8. Lara and Pete told *their* parents about the band concert. Lara and Pete
9. Susie brought *her* tape recorder. Susie
10. The swallows always make *their* nests in the barn. swallows

375

Section 4

Using Verbs

Section Objectives

1. To identify action and linking verbs

2. To recognize helping verbs and main verbs

3. To identify and use verb tenses

4. To recognize and use the progressive forms of verbs

5. To form the principal parts of regular verbs

6. To use irregular verbs correctly

7. To use active and passive verb forms

8. To correctly use verbs that are often confused

Preparing the Students

Write these sentences on the chalkboard:

Jim the 40-yard pass.
Maggie to the pool.

Ask what is missing from the sentences. Note that without a verb no sentence can be complete.

Next write these sentences:

Maggie walks to the pool.
Maggie walked to the pool.

Note the differences in meaning and in form. Explain that Section 4 will help the students use the many forms of verbs correctly.

Read and discuss this page.

Additional Resources

Diagnostic Test—See page 3 in the test booklet. Recommended for use before teaching the chapter.

Mastery Test—See pages 38-41 in the test booklet. Recommended for use after teaching the chapter.

Reinforcement Exercises—See pages 407-409 in the student text.

Skills Practice Book—pages 110-126.

Duplicating Masters–pages 110-126.

Of all the parts of speech, the **verb** is the most important. It is the moving power, the motor, of a sentence.

Verbs are important because you need them for sentence building. They are important, too, because they, more than any other part of speech, help you to say exactly what you mean. See the variety of ways in which *go* can be used:

I go.	I went.
I am going.	I have gone.
I am going to go.	I had gone.
She goes.	She should have gone.

In Section 1 you studied some of the forms and uses of verbs. In this chapter you will study verbs in greater detail.

Part 1 What Are Verbs?

Objective

To identify action and linking verbs

Presenting the Lesson

1. Read and discuss page 378. Write the definition of *verb* on the chalkboard. Stress the function of verbs by reading each sample sentence aloud without its verb. Discuss what each verb shows or tells in its sentence.

2. Assign and discuss Exercises A, B, and C on page 379.

Individualizing the Lesson

Less-Advanced Students

1. Do Exercise A on page 379. orally.

2. Assign Exercise B as independent work.

3. Omit Exercise C or work with the students to complete it in class.

Advanced Students

Have the students suggest an alternative verb in each sentence in Exercises A and B.

Optional Practice

Have the students complete each of the following sentences in two ways—once using the verb as an action verb and once as a linking verb.

The gift appeared . . .

In the dark the dog looked . . .

Part 1   What Are Verbs?

A verb is a word that tells of an action or state of being.

Action Verbs

Some verbs tell of an action:

Sam *clung* to the rope.   The rain *drenched* us.

Sometimes the action is one you cannot see:

Carlos *needed* help.   Kate *had* a good idea.

Whether you can see the action or not, an **action verb** tells that something is happening, has happened, or will happen.

Linking Verbs

A few verbs do not tell of an action. They merely tell that something is. They express a state of being:

The clock *is* slow.   The sky *looks* gloomy.
The house *seems* empty.   The gloves *feel* soft.

These verbs are called **linking verbs** because they connect the subject with some other word or words in the sentence.

Here are the most common linking verbs:

be (am, are, is, was,	look	smell
were, been, being)	appear	taste
become	feel	grow
seem	sound	

Many linking verbs can also be used as action verbs.

LINKING VERB	ACTION VERB
The melon *looked* ripe.	Ann *looked* at the melon.
The melon *felt* ripe.	Ann *felt* the melon.
The night *grew* cold.	Tom *grew* tomatoes.

Exercises Find the verbs.

A. Find the verb in each sentence. Write it. After the verb write *Action* or *Linking* to show what kind it is.

1. That Dutch apple pie smells delicious. Linking
2. These candy sticks taste sour. Linking
3. The florist appeared at the door with flowers for my sister.
4. Sherry looked in the attic. Action
5. Many visitors waited in line for tickets. Action
6. The horses raced toward the finish line. Action
7. Those bananas look overripe. Linking
8. The sun broke through the smog at noon. Action
9. The sky looks ominous. Linking
10. The record sounds scratchy. Linking

B. Follow the directions for Exercise A.

1. The air smells clean and fresh after that storm. Linking
2. The first wrestler pinned his opponent in ten seconds. Action
3. A beautiful rainbow appeared across the meadow. Action
4. Our dog is a German shepherd. Linking
5. I finished my social studies assignment in class. Action
6. After dinner, Erica and I cycled to the park. Action
7. The yearbook staff sold hot dogs and soft drinks at the football games. Action
8. The speaker for the assembly sounds interesting. Linking
9. The weekend at Six Flags was fun. Linking
10. Mrs. Bauer grows cantaloupe and watermelon in her garden. Action

C. Write two sentences using each of the following words. In one sentence, use the word as an action verb. In the other sentence, use the word as a linking verb. Answers will vary.

1. tasted   2. smell   3. feel   4. looked

379

Extending the Lesson

Read a newspaper editorial, omitting all verbs. Pause after each sentence to have the students suggest verbs that would suit the sentence. Discuss how verbs add meaning to sentences.

Part 2

Objective

To recognize helping verbs and main verbs

Presenting the Lesson

1. Read and discuss this page. Most of this lesson will be review for the students.
2. Assign and discuss Exercises A and B on page 381.

Individualizing the Lesson

Less-Advanced Students

1. Work with the students to complete Exercise A on page 381.
2. Assign Exercise B as independent work.

Advanced Students

Have the students suggest alternative main verbs for each sentence. Discuss which of the suggested verbs are most vivid. The students might use a thesaurus for this activity.

Reinforcement Exercise

Assign and discuss Exercise A on page 407.

Optional Practice

Have the students use the following verbs in sentences:

were building	had built
should have built	have built
are building	

Discuss how the different helping

Part 2 Helping Verbs and Main Verbs

You will also remember that a great many verbs consist of more than one word. Verbs can be made up of a **main verb** and one or more **helping verbs.**

Verb	Helping Verbs	Main Verb
had gone	had	gone
was seen	was	seen
can go	can	go
might have gone	might have	gone
must have been caught	must have been	caught

There are three verbs that can be used either as main verbs or as helping verbs. Here are their forms:

do	has	is	was	be
does	have	am	were	been
did	had	are		

Used as Main Verb	Used as Helping Verb
Can you *do* this job?	I *do know* your sister.
Who *has* my key?	Sue *has gone* home.
Where *were* you?	The boys *were working*.

Here is a list of words frequently used as helping verbs.

can	shall	will	may	must
could	should	would	might	

Sometimes parts of a verb are separated from each other by words that are not part of the verb.

I *did* not *ask* the right question.
Mac *was* certainly *trying* hard.
Has Kim *finished* her project?

380

Exercises **Find the verbs.**

A. Find the parts of the verb in each sentence. Write them in two columns labeled *Helping Verb* and *Main Verb*.

EXAMPLE: They will deliver the packages tomorrow.
^{HV} ^{MV}

HELPING VERB	MAIN VERB
will	deliver

1. We are going to the circus tomorrow.
2. We have completed our study of the U. S. Constitution.
3. Everyone has gone home.
4. Can Manny and Liz go to the baseball game with us?
5. It must have snowed all night.
6. After the concert, we are going to a restaurant.
7. I was writing my composition during study hall.
8. My sister is running in the marathon race.
9. Colleen and I have never skated at the new roller rink.
10. The hot air balloons had landed in the stadium.

B. Follow the directions for Exercise A.

1. Mopeds have been designed for economical transportation.
2. A moped can go up to 30 miles per hour.
3. It is considered a motorized bicycle.
4. No licenses are required for moped drivers in many states.
5. Most parents are very concerned about their children's health.
6. Energy conservation has become everyone's responsibility.
7. Car pools and public transportation can help our energy resources.
8. Each of us must make individual efforts to save energy.
9. Solar energy can help us in the years ahead.
10. Some day we will probably heat our homes, schools, and offices with solar energy.

Extending the Lesson

Have each student find five sentences with helping verbs in a history textbook. Have each copy the sentences and arrange the verbs in columns as in the Exercises on page 381. Have volunteers read their sentences aloud and identify the verb parts.

Part 3

Objective

To identify and use verb tenses

Presenting the Lesson

1. Read and discuss pages 382 and 383. On the chalkboard list *present tense, past tense, future tense, present perfect tense, past perfect tense,* and *future perfect tense.* Then list the verbs *watch* and *play* in all six tenses. Discuss what time each tense indicates.

Note that the directions on forming past tense are a simplification of the real spelling rule. The ending *-ed* is always added to regular verbs. When the verb ends in silent *e,* the *e* is dropped.

2. Assign and discuss Exercises A and B on pages 383 and 384.

Individualizing the Lesson

Less-Advanced Students

Work with the students to complete the first five sentences in each Exercise. Then have them complete the Exercises independently.

Advanced Students

Have the students rewrite each sentence in the Exercises, changing the tense of the verb.

Reinforcement Exercise

Assign and discuss Exercise B on page 407.

Verbs are time-telling words. They do not only tell of an action or a state of being. They also tell when the action takes place. They tell whether the action or state of being is past, present, or future.

Verbs tell time in two ways:

1. By changing their spelling:

    walk—walked   sleep—slept

2. By using helping verbs:

    will creep   has crept   had crept

Verbs can express six different times. Each verb has a form to express each of these six different times. The forms of a verb used to indicate time are called the **tenses** of a verb.

The Simple Tenses

The **present tense** of the verb is the same as the name of the verb:

    run   go   walk

The **past tense** of regular verbs is formed by adding *-d* or *-ed* to the present tense:

    walked   placed

The past tense of irregular verbs is usually shown by a change of spelling:

    shine—shone   swing—swung

The **future tense** is formed by using *shall* or *will* with the present tense:

    shall go   will run

The three tenses just described are called the **simple tenses.** They describe:

1. What is happening now: *present tense*
2. What happened before: *past tense*
3. What will happen later: *future tense*

The Perfect Tenses

Sometimes we have to speak of two different times, one earlier than the other. To make these times clear, we can use the **perfect tenses.** The perfect tenses are formed by using *has, have,* or *had* with the past participle.

The perfect tenses are formed as follows:

Present Perfect	has run, have run
Past Perfect	had run
Future Perfect	will have run, shall have run

Exercises Recognize verb tenses.

A. Find each verb in the following sentences. Tell the tense of each.

1. What have you done with the scissors? present perfect
2. We have always enjoyed these travelogs. present perfect
3. My brother and I walk to school. present
4. Will you come to the party tonight? future
5. Have you ever gone to a volleyball game? present perfect
6. The new ice cream parlor will open in June. future
7. My parents and I have traveled to Mexico. present perfect
8. We will have eaten the cake by tomorrow. future perfect
9. When will the fair open? future
10. Lynn hasn't seen the ice show. present perfect

Optional Practice

Have the students identify the tenses of the verbs in Exercise A on page 381.

Extending the Lesson

Assign each student in the class a different verb. Have each student make a chart showing the present, past, future, present perfect, past perfect, and future perfect tenses of his or her verb. The verbs should be used in sentences that illustrate the use of each tense.

B. Write a sentence for each of the verbs below. Use the verb in the tense indicated. Sentences will vary.

1. fill (past tense) filled
2. drop (past perfect tense) had dropped
3. stay (future tense) shall stay, will stay
4. glisten (past tense) glistened
5. close (future perfect tense) shall have closed, will have closed
6. splash (present tense) splash, splashes
7. flash (present tense) is flashing
8. cause (present tense) cause, causes
9. attach (past perfect tense) had attached
10. touch (future tense) shall touch, will touch

Part 4

Objective

To recognize and use the progressive forms of verbs

Presenting the Lesson

1. Read and discuss this page. Have the students decide which of the sample sentences could be followed by *every day*, *now*, and *for an hour*. Have them discuss the differences in meaning among the new sentences.
2. Assign and discuss Exercises A and B on pages 384 and 385.

Individualizing the Lesson

Less-Advanced Students

Work with the students to complete Exercise B on page 385.

Part 4 Progressive Forms

Sometimes we tell the time of an action like this:

I *am* talking. (instead of I *talk*)
I *was* talking. (instead of I *talked*)

We use a form of the verb *be* with the form of the main verb that ends in *-ing*. We call these the **progressive forms** of the verb. Here are the **progressive forms** of *talk* that are used with *I*:

I am talking.	I have been talking.
I was talking.	I had been talking.
I shall (will) be talking.	I shall (will) have been talking.

Exercises Identify progressive forms.

A. Number your paper from 1–10. Write down the verb in each sentence.

1. The Allens <u>are raising</u> Dalmatians.
2. I <u>will be going</u> to Florida in April.

384

3. Julia was talking to Ms. O'Shea about the Science Fair.
4. I will be running for vice-president of the French Club.
5. We will be keeping in touch.
6. I was watching the "Movie of the Week" last night.
7. Bill, Tom, and Maria have been managing the pool.
8. We will be playing more soccer next year.
9. I was listening to the radio.
10. Raul and Marlene will be working at Indian Lake next July and August.

B. Copy these sentences, changing each verb to its progressive form.

1. This machine filters our drinking water. is filtering
2. From now on, the sun will set later and later. will be setting
3. The dishwater had gotten cold. had been getting
4. Kurt practiced his diving. was practicing
5. Peggy has collected information on Japan. has been collecting
6. I talked to my counselor about next year's class schedule. was talking
7. We telephoned my sister at college. were telephoning
8. Ray talked to Mrs. Pampel about his assignments. was talking
9. The audience laughed at the entertainer. was laughing
10. We waited for the bus. were waiting

Part 5 The Principal Parts of Verbs

Every verb has certain forms on which nearly all other forms of the verb are based. These essential forms of a verb are called the **principal parts** of the verb.

The principal parts of a verb are the **present tense,** the **past tense,** and the **past participle.**

PRESENT	PAST	PAST PARTICIPLE
talk	talked	(have) talked
knit	knitted	(have) knitted
add	added	(have) added
divide	divided	(have) divided

Advanced Students

Have the students suggest an alternative progressive form for each verb in Exercises A and B.

Reinforcement Exercise

Assign and discuss Exercise C on page 408.

Optional Practice

1. Have the students find each progressive verb form in the Exercises on page 381.
2. Have the students convert the verbs in sentences 2, 3, 4, 5, 9, and 10 in Exercise A on page 381 to progressive forms.

Extending the Lesson

Have the students find and copy each sentence in a newspaper sports column that uses a progressive verb form. Then discuss what meaning the sportswriter conveys with progressive verbs.

Part 5

Objective

To form the principal parts of regular verbs

Presenting the Lesson

1. Read and discuss pages 385 and 386. Review the difference between simple and perfect tenses.
2. Assign and discuss the Exercise on page 386.

Individualizing the Lesson

Less-Advanced Students

1. Have the students practice using the principal parts on page 385 in oral sentences.

2. Urge the students to check the spellings of past forms in a dictionary as they work on the Exercise.

Advanced Students

Have the students write original sentences using the present tense, past tense, and past perfect tense of each of the verbs in the Exercise.

Optional Practice

Have the students follow the directions for the Exercise on page 386.

1. hop	6. order
2. need	7. heat
3. taste	8. raise
4. spy	9. practice
5. skate	10. close

Extending the Lesson

Write these sentences on the chalkboard:

We snopped across town in an hour.

We usually snop around the park each morning.

A tall man snopped past me in a great hurry.

Ask the students to identify the principal parts of the verb *snop*. Have the students make up their own regular verbs and write sentences using the three principal parts. Ask them to share their creations with the class.

The present tense and the past tense are **simple tenses** of the verb. The past participle is used for all **perfect tenses** of the verb. It is always used with a helping verb.

As you can see, the past and the past participle forms of *talk, knit, add,* and *divide* are the same. These are **regular verbs.** In all regular verbs the past and past participle are formed by adding -d (*divided*) or -ed (*talked*) to the present form.

Many regular verbs change their spelling when -d or -ed is added to them. These changes are made in accord with regular spelling rules.

knit + -ed = knitted	hurry + -ed = hurried
fit + -ed = fitted	try + -ed = tried
rate + -d = rated	pity + -ed = pitied

Some verbs change their spelling this way:

say + -d = said   pay + -d = paid   lay + -d = laid

Exercise Principal parts of verbs.

The verbs below are regular verbs. Make three columns on your paper. Label them *Present, Past,* and *Past Participle.* Write the principal parts of each verb in the right column.

Past tense and *past participle* are the same for these regular verbs.

1. worry	worried	11. rob	robbed
2. sob	sobbed	12. like	liked
3. pay	paid	13. rap	rapped
4. carry	carried	14. hurry	hurried
5. grab	grabbed	15. rub	rubbed
6. help	helped	16. try	tried
7. pass	passed	17. flip	flipped
8. end	ended	18. push	pushed
9. slip	slipped	19. vary	varied
10. use	used	20. glow	glowed

Part 6   Irregular Verbs

There are hundreds of verbs in our language that follow the regular pattern of adding *-d* or *-ed* to the present to form the past and past participle.

Those verbs that do not follow this pattern are called **irregular verbs.** There are only about sixty irregular verbs that are frequently used. Many of these have only one change. They present few problems.

    buy   bought   (have) bought
    make   made   (have) made

A few irregular verbs do not change at all from one principal part to another. They offer no problems in usage.

    hit   let   set   shut

Most verb problems come from the irregular verbs that have three different forms:

    throw   threw   (have) thrown
    ring   rang   (have) rung

If you are not sure about a verb form, look it up in a dictionary. If the verb is regular, only one form will be listed.

If the verb is irregular, the dictionary will give the irregular forms. It may give only two forms if the past and past participle are the same: *say, said.* It will give all three principal parts if they are all different: *sing, sang, sung.* Some dictionaries will also list the present participle.

Dictionary Entry for *Begin*

present

be-gin (bi gin′), **v.** to start being, doing, acting, etc.; get under way [Work *begins* at 8:00 A.M. His cold *began* with a sore throat.] **—be-gan′**, *p.*; **be-gun′**, *p.p.*

                past participle

past

Objective

To use irregular verbs correctly

Presenting the Lesson

1. Read and discuss pages 387 and 388. Explain the difference between regular and irregular verbs. Direct the students' attention to the reference guide to irregular verbs on page 388. Remind the students that past participles are used only with helping verbs.

Review the list by asking for sample sentences using each verb. Then have the students memorize the principal parts of these verbs.

2. Read and discuss the introduction to the practice pages on irregular verbs, page 388. Assign the Exercise on page 389 to be completed independently as a diagnostic test.

3. After each student's paper has been corrected, assign him or her the practice pages on verbs that are causing difficulty. (See pages 390-401.

You might have students work in pairs. The students can take turns reading aloud and then listening to the sentences under "Say It Right Hear It Right." Emphasize the need to hear these verbs used correctly many times. Once the verbs start sounding natural, have students do the "Write It Right" exercise.

Individualizing the Lesson

Less-Advanced Students

You may want the students to complete all the practice pages. Emphasize oral practice with each verb before students try the "Write It Right" exercises. If possible, record tapes of sentences using the verbs, and have the students listen to them. Then do each "Write It Right" exercise orally before having the students write the answers independently.

Advanced Students

Have the students write original sentences using the present tense, past tense, and past perfect tense of five of the irregular verbs in the chart on this page.

Optional Practice

Have each student write original sentences using the present tense, past tense, and past perfect tense of each of the verbs that caused him or her difficulty in the Exercise on page 389.

Extending the Lesson

Have the students find and list every irregular verb on one page of a short story or magazine article. Have them write the principal parts for each verb and then check their work in a dictionary.

Common Irregular Verbs

Present	Past	Past Participle	Present	Past	Past Participle
begin	began	begun	lay	laid	laid
break	broke	broken	lie	lay	lain
bring	brought	brought	ride	rode	ridden
choose	chose	chosen	ring	rang	rung
come	came	come	rise	rose	risen
do	did	done	run	ran	run
drink	drank	drunk	see	saw	seen
eat	ate	eaten	sing	sang	sung
fall	fell	fallen	speak	spoke	spoken
freeze	froze	frozen	steal	stole	stolen
give	gave	given	swim	swam	swum
go	went	gone	take	took	taken
grow	grew	grown	throw	threw	thrown
know	knew	known	write	wrote	written

Practice Pages on Irregular Verbs

Irregular verbs can cause problems in writing as well as in speaking. Pages 390–401 provide practice in the correct use of some irregular verbs.

How well do you use these verbs? The exercise on the next page will tell you.

If the exercise shows that you need more practice with certain verbs, your teacher may ask you to turn to those verbs on the following pages. For each verb there are many sentences that will help you to "say it right," "hear it right," and "write it right."

Exercise   Use irregular verbs correctly.

Number your paper from 1–30. For each sentence, write the correct word from the two given in parentheses.

1. The party (began, begun) at about seven o'clock.
2. The gate had been (broke, broken) long ago.
3. Who (bring, brought) these posters to class?
4. Has everyone (chosen, chose) a topic for his or her report?
5. Jack (came, come) home after the debate.
6. Rob has never (did, done) such a good job.
7. At camp, we (drunk, drank) a quart of milk every day.
8. Someone had (ate, eaten) all the brownies.
9. We had never (saw, seen) such a sight.
10. The plumber (did, done) the work well.
11. Lauren has (given, gave) a good report about Presidential elections.
12. Everyone had (went, gone) home by then.
13. That tree has (grew, grown) several feet this year.
14. I wouldn't have (known, knew) what to do.
15. Our science class has (grew, grown) different plants for an experiment.
16. The team (known, knew) all of the defensive plays.
17. The alarm had (rung, rang) too soon for me.
18. The church bells (rung, rang) at seven.
19. The sun had (rose, risen) early.
20. We (run, ran) the relay races on the indoor track.
21. Bill (seen, saw) two deer.
22. The audience (sang, sung) the chorus of the song.
23. The President has (spoke, spoken) to the reporters.
24. The thief had (stole, stolen) several appliances from the shop.
25. We had never (swum, swam) as far as that.
26. We have (went, gone) skiing every winter.
27. Terry (threw, thrown) the Frisbee to Darcy.
28. Eric has (write, written) a good short story.
29. The pitcher had (threw, thrown) a curve to strike out the batter.
30. Have you (wrote, written) your report for consumer ed?

Say It Right   Hear It Right

Begin
Began
Begun

A. Say these sentences over until the correct use of *began* and *begun* sounds natural to you.

1. Have you begun yet?
2. Jill hasn't begun.
3. Bill began his job.
4. He began yesterday.
5. Mary began thinking.
6. I began to daydream.
7. I haven't begun the book.
8. Have they begun reading?

Break
Broke
Broken

B. Say these sentences over until the correct use of *broke* and *broken* sounds natural to you.

1. Pam broke the school record.
2. No one else has broken it.
3. The car broke down in Ohio.
4. Dennis broke the window.
5. Dan had broken the mug.
6. Steve broke his ankle.
7. The mirror was broken.
8. I have broken my watch.

Write It Right

Write the correct word from the two words given.

1. Has the movie (began, begun) yet?
2. Yes, it (began, begun) ten minutes ago.
3. I haven't missed that series since it (began, begun).
4. Have you (began, begun) your new book yet?
5. We (began, begun) our day playing tennis.
6. The people (began, begun) to leave the scene of the accident.
7. Jory has (began, begun) to mow the lawn.
8. I have (broke, broken) the can opener.
9. Now that it's (broke, broken), we'll need to replace it.
10. The clock is (broke, broken) beyond repair.
11. The VW had (broke, broken) down on the road.
12. Someone has (broke, broken) into the storeroom.
13. The heat wave (broke, broken) all records for July.
14. Sara (broke, broken) the record for the 100-yard dash.
15. If he has (broke, broken) the seal on that package, it can't be returned.

Say It Right   Hear It Right

A. Say these sentences over until the correct use of *bring* and *brought* sounds natural to you.

Bring
Brought
Brought

1. Did you bring the map?
2. Sam brought an atlas.
3. Did Mike bring the radio?
4. Yes, he brought it.
5. What did Suzi bring?
6. She has brought the food.
7. Claire had brought the soda.
8. I wish I'd brought some too.

B. Say these sentences over until the correct use of *chose* and *chosen* sounds natural to you.

Choose
Chose
Chosen

1. Have you chosen a book?
2. No, I haven't chosen one.
3. Bill chose his.
4. What has he chosen?
5. He chose a biography.
6. Renée had chosen a novel.
7. Ginny chose a book of poems.
8. Trina chose a book on sports.

Write It Right

Write the correct word from the two words given.

1. Patti (bring, brought) me a present for my birthday.
2. The messenger (bring, brought) good news.
3. The jury (bring, brought) in the verdict.
4. Did you (bring, brought) the book I wanted to read?
5. I have (bring, brought) candy for everyone in the class.
6. Did you (bring, brought) sleeping bags for our weekend?
7. We have (bring, brought) plenty of food, too.
8. Have you (bring, brought) all the equipment for your new experiment.
9. Our club (chose, chosen) a new treasurer.
10. Who was (chose, chosen)?
11. Have you already (chose, chosen) a new president?
12. Yes, we have (chose, chosen) our president.
13. The students (chose, chosen) good officers.
14. Which rucksack have you (chose, chosen)?
15. I (chose, chosen) this one and a down sleeping bag.

Say It Right   Hear It Right

Come
Came
Come

A. Say these sentences over until the correct use of *came* and *come* sounds natural to you.

1. Nathan came yesterday.
2. Your friends have come.
3. They all came together.
4. Janelle should have come.

5. No one came late.
6. Joe came early.
7. He has come early before.
8. Hasn't Heather come yet?

Do
Did
Done

B. Say these sentences over until the correct use of *did* and *done* sounds natural to you.

1. I did my work early.
2. Sue has not done hers yet.
3. Amy has done two sketches.
4. Did you do this diorama?

5. Doug has done his job well.
6. Tom did the dishes tonight.
7. Have you done any hiking?
8. Sue did nothing to help.

Write It Right

Write the correct word from the two words given.

1. Peter has (came, come) to the game with us.
2. He had (came, come) with us before.
3. My parents (came, come) to our play.
4. Summer has finally (came, come).
5. The coach (came, come) to see me in the hospital.
6. The sailboat (came, come) toward us.
7. We have (came, come) to the parade every Fourth of July.
8. Jonathan has (did, done) a beautiful painting.
9. Do you know how he (did, done) it?
10. He (did, done) it with oil paints.
11. Have you (did, done) your essay?
12. I (did, done) it last night.
13. We (did, done) our work and went skating.
14. Pablo had (did, done) the organizing for the program.
15. He (did, done) a better job than anyone else had ever (did, done).

Say It Right Hear It Right

A. Say these sentences over until the correct use of *drank* and *drunk* sounds natural to you.

Drink
Drank
Drunk

1. Who drank the milk?
2. Liz must have drunk it.
3. We have drunk all the tea.
4. Tom drank Squirt.
5. Sue drank all the lemonade.
6. I have never drunk Coke.
7. Al drank orange juice.
8. Who drank the soda?

B. Say these sentences over until the correct use of *eat, ate,* and *eaten* sounds natural to you.

Eat
Ate
Eaten

1. Have you eaten yet?
2. Yes, I have eaten.
3. Jenny ate quite early.
4. Did you eat at noon?
5. When did you eat dinner?
6. We ate at 6 o'clock.
7. Last night we ate outside.
8. José had eaten with us.

Write It Right

Write the correct word from the two words given.

1. The kittens (drank, drunk) all the milk.
2. We (drank, drunk) the lemonade and went back to work.
3. No, I've never (drank, drunk) one.
4. Have you ever (drank, drunk) coconut milk?
5. The patient (drank, drunk) the medicine.
6. Dad has not (drank, drunk) coffee for a month.
7. Jill (drank, drunk) all the chocolate milk.
8. The oranges have all been (ate, eaten).
9. Which one of you has (ate, eaten) all the ice cream?
10. Have you ever (ate, eaten) nectarines?
11. Yes, I have (ate, eaten) them.
12. We (ate, eaten) dinner at the Spaghetti Factory.
13. Carl and I had (ate, eaten) dinner with our grandparents.
14. Mary had (ate, eaten) before we got home.
15. Pam and Sal (ate, eaten) half the watermelon.

Say It Right   Hear It Right

Give
Gave
Given

A. Say these sentences over until the correct use of *give*, *gave*, and *given* sounds natural to you.

1. Who gave you that hat?
2. It was given to me by Amy.
3. Sue gave Al an aquarium.
4. I have given him a book.

5. Did he give his pen away?
6. I have given two pens away.
7. Dick gave me his puzzle.
8. I had given him a model.

Go
Went
Gone

B. Say these sentences over until the correct use of *went* and *gone* sounds natural to you.

1. Who went skating?
2. Pete has gone home.
3. Julie went to the park.
4. Have they gone swimming?

5. Janice went downstairs.
6. Have they gone yet?
7. They went an hour ago.
8. Everyone has gone.

Write It Right

Write the correct word from the two words given.

1. Jerry has (gave, given) up playing baseball.
2. We have always (gave, given) toys to the orphanage.
3. Maria (give, gave) me a compliment.
4. Pete has (gave, given) two recitals this year.
5. Nancy (give, gave) her brother a sweater.
6. Have you (given, gave) that album away?
7. Our team (give, gave) our rivals a beating.
8. The spacecraft (went, gone) around the earth many times.
9. Another one has (went, gone) into orbit around the moon.
10. We (went, gone) to Disneyland last summer.
11. The Petersons have (went, gone) to New York for a week.
12. My sister has (went, gone) to France to study French.
13. Have you ever (went, gone) skiing?
14. Judy has (went, gone) to Florida for spring vacation.
15. Hasn't Ellen (went, gone) to the planetarium?

Say It Right   Hear It Right

A. Say these sentences over until the correct use of *grew* and *grown* sounds natural to you.

Grow
Grew
Grown

1. The fern grew quickly.
2. The tree hasn't grown.
3. Mr. Smyth grew apples.
4. He has also grown pears.
5. The weather grew colder.
6. It has now grown warmer.
7. The child had grown tired.
8. Have you ever grown herbs?

B. Say these sentences over until the correct use of *knew* and *known* sounds natural to you.

Know
Knew
Known

1. I knew the results.
2. I have known Jim for years.
3. Who knew the answers?
4. Bret knew the answers.
5. I knew the answers, too.
6. Have you known Josh long?
7. Who knew about the race?
8. Al had not known about it.

Write It Right

Write the correct word from the two words given.

1. Les has (grew, grown) faster than his cousin has.
2. What have you (grew, grown) in your garden?
3. We've (grew, grown) lettuce and tomatoes.
4. We have also (grew, grown) beans and peppers.
5. The beans have (grew, grown) quite tall.
6. Jean (grew, grown) strawberries in her garden.
7. Alan has (grew, grown) too tall to wear his old uniform.
8. The sapling (grew, grown) into a beautiful tree.
9. How long have you (knew, known) the Bernsteins?
10. We have (knew, known) them for a long time.
11. Had you (knew, known) Christmas vacation was extended?
12. Some things are (knew, known) with certainty.
13. I (knew, known) about the airplane accident yesterday.
14. Very few others (knew, known) about it then.
15. Lou had never (knew, known) anyone from Israel before.

Say It Right   Hear It Right

Ride
Rode
Ridden

A. Say these sentences over until the correct use of *rode* and *ridden* sounds natural to you.

1. Who rode the horse?
2. The horse was ridden well.
3. Jim rode the horse.
4. I have ridden often.

5. Julie rode her bike.
6. She has ridden it often.
7. Anne rode in our new car.
8. Marla has ridden in it, too.

Ring
Rang
Rung

B. Say these sentences over until the correct use of *rang* and *rung* sounds natural to you.

1. Has the telephone rung?
2. I thought it rang.
3. It rang an hour ago.
4. It hasn't rung since.

5. The doorbell rang.
6. Who rang it?
7. I had rung it earlier.
8. The dinner bell rang.

Write It Right

Write the correct word from the two words given.

1. Have you ever (rode, ridden) a snowmobile?
2. I (rode, ridden) one several times last winter.
3. Tammy and Jill (rode, ridden) the bus to Atlanta.
4. Ron has (rode, ridden) in the Goodyear blimp.
5. Do you know anyone who has (rode, ridden) a camel?
6. We (rode, ridden) horseback in the mountains.
7. My family has (rode, ridden) on a DC-10 to Hawaii.
8. Have you (rode, ridden) on a roller coaster?
9. Sleigh bells (rang, rung) out merrily.
10. All the church bells were (rang, rung) in celebration.
11. Christmas carols (rang, rung) out everywhere.
12. The telephone has (rang, rung) several times.
13. The cries of the hounds (rang, rung) in the air.
14. We have (rang, rung) many doorbells selling magazines.
15. Has the tardy bell (rang, rung) yet?

Say It Right   Hear It Right

A. Say these sentences over until the correct use of *rose* and *risen* sounds natural to you.

Rise
Rose
Risen

1. The sun has risen.
2. It rose at 6:15.
3. The river rose rapidly.
4. It has risen before.
5. The road rose sharply.
6. The moon rose over the hill.
7. The kite rose swiftly.
8. Jo had risen from her seat.

B. Say these sentences over until the correct use of *ran* and *run* sounds natural to you.

Run
Ran
Run

1. Bill ran a race.
2. He had never run faster.
3. He ran 20 kilometers.
4. The race was run in Chicago.
5. Ed ran the race in an hour.
6. Have you run the relay?
7. I have never run in a race.
8. Sue ran the raffle.

Write It Right

Write the correct word from the two words given.

1. The audience had (rose, risen) from their seats.
2. The official has (rose, risen) to a high rank.
3. The moon (rose, risen) over the mountain.
4. Why hasn't the dough (rose, risen)?
5. The crowd had (rose, risen) to cheer the players.
6. The divers had (rose, risen) to the surface.
7. The temperature has (rose, risen) to 35 degrees C.
8. That calculator is (ran, run) by four batteries.
9. The Lions Club (ran, run) the carnival this year.
10. They had never (ran, run) it before.
11. They (ran, run) for shelter when the tornado alert sounded.
12. Have you ever (ran, run) in a relay race?
13. Our air conditioner (ran, run) for twenty-four hours.
14. Janice has (ran, run) in the Fourth of July race for two years.
15. The thieves (ran, run) when the burglar alarm went off.

Say It Right   Hear It Right

See
Saw
Seen
A.   Say these sentences over until the correct use of *saw* and *seen* sounds natural to you.

1. Have you seen Dan?
2. Yes, I saw him.
3. Ted has seen him, too.
4. Maureen saw him Sunday.
5. I saw that movie.
6. Have you seen it?
7. We saw it Saturday.
8. Bret hasn't seen it yet.

Sing
Sang
Sung
B.   Say these sentences over until the correct use of *sang* and *sung* sounds natural to you.

1. Craig sang a solo.
2. He has sung before.
3. The tenor sang softly.
4. Lori also sang a solo.
5. She had sung last year.
6. Has she sung an aria?
7. The birds sang loudly.
8. The violin had sung sadly.

Write It Right

Write the correct word from the two words given.

1. Have you ever (saw, seen) this TV program?
2. It's the best show I've ever (saw, seen).
3. Judy (saw, seen) the President at the airport.
4. Penny (saw, seen) her friends at the library.
5. I have (saw, seen) parachute jumping many times.
6. In the mountains Art (saw, seen) wild horses.
7. Jack had (saw, seen) the Bolshoi Ballet.
8. Our chorus (sang, sung) in the assembly program.
9. We (sang, sung) a medley of show tunes.
10. We had (sang, sung) them before.
11. Our quartet (sang, sung) at the state competition.
12. They had (sang, sung) last year, too.
13. Has Phil ever (sang, sung) in the choir?
14. The choir has (sang, sung) in many cities.
15. Had Jean (sang, sung) the alto or soprano part?

Say It Right Hear It Right

A. Say these sentences over until the correct use of *spoke* and *spoken* sounds natural to you.

1. Jan spoke to us yesterday.
2. She had spoken to us before.
3. Manny spoke first.
4. Has Liz spoken yet?
5. No, she hasn't spoken.
6. Terri spoke at the meeting.
7. She hadn't spoken before.
8. She spoke rather well.

B. Say these sentences over until the correct use of *stole* and *stolen* sounds natural to you.

1. Who stole the money?
2. Two gangsters stole it.
3. Why have they stolen it?
4. Had they stolen before?
5. When was it stolen?
6. It was stolen yesterday.
7. They stole it at noon.
8. They stole it wearing masks.

Write It Right

Write the correct word from the two words given.

1. Dr. Wagner has (spoke, spoken) to me about a job.
2. I have (spoke, spoken) to my parents about it.
3. Everyone in the class has (spoke, spoken) at least once.
4. Rita hasn't (spoke, spoken) to me about her plans yet.
5. Jean has not (spoke, spoken) a word.
6. Our group (spoke, spoken) on energy consumption.
7. Which person had (spoke, spoken) at the meeting?
8. Tracy Austin (spoke, spoken) at our sports banquet.
9. Someone has (stole, stolen) our spare tire.
10. Why has someone (stole, stolen) it?
11. Lou Brock has (stole, stolen) more bases than anyone else.
12. He (stole, stolen) over 800 bases in his baseball career.
13. Ty Cobb had (stole, stolen) the most bases until Brock broke his record in '77.
14. The thief (stole, stolen) three oil paintings.
15. We know why he might have (stole, stolen) them.

Say It Right   Hear It Right

Swim
Swam
Swum

A. Say these sentences over until the correct use of *swam* and *swum* sounds natural to you.

1. I swam in the pool.
2. Have you swum there?
3. Kelly swam all day.
4. We swam in the lake.
5. They had swum in the ocean.
6. Mark swam ten laps.
7. Linda had swum thirty.
8. I swam at the Y. W. C. A.

Take
Took
Taken

B. Say these sentences over until the correct use of *took* and *taken* sounds natural to you.

1. Paula took a walk.
2. Steve took one, too.
3. Lori has taken the book.
4. Craig took three cookies.
5. Who took these pictures?
6. Gene took them.
7. He has taken lots of them.
8. We took a helicopter ride.

Write It Right

Write the correct word from the two words given.

1. Beth (swam, swum) at a very early age.
2. We haven't (swam, swum) much until now.
3. Our team (swam, swum) in the state meet.
4. During vacation, Sally (swam, swum) every day.
5. Have you (swam, swum) in the new pool?
6. Tanya has (swam, swum) there many times.
7. Chuck became ill when he (swam, swum) in the icy water.
8. Our team has often (swam, swum) in the medley relay.
9. I have never (took, taken) the expressway.
10. It (took, taken) us an hour to drive downtown.
11. The troops had (took, taken) the enemy by surprise.
12. We (took, taken) our sleeping bags with us.
13. Ms. Miller has (took, taken) our guest speaker to the airport.
14. It has (took, taken) a long time to save money for the party.
15. I have never (took, taken) that kind of medicine before.

400

Say It Right   Hear It Right

A. Say these sentences over until the correct use of *threw* and *thrown* sounds natural to you.

Throw
Threw
Thrown

1. Who threw the ball?
2. Carrie threw it.
3. Have you thrown it?
4. Bruce hasn't thrown it.
5. I threw the paper away.
6. Bill threw the door open.
7. Lee has thrown the list away.
8. Chris threw a fast pitch.

B. Say these sentences over until the correct use of *wrote* and *written* sounds natural to you.

Write
Wrote
Written

1. I've written my paper.
2. Have you written one?
3. I wrote a letter.
4. Sue hasn't written yet.
5. Who has written to you?
6. Paul wrote to me.
7. Donna has written a speech.
8. They wrote the script.

Write It Right

Write the correct word from the two words given.

1. The captain had (threw, thrown) the cargo overboard.
2. The runner was (threw, thrown) out at home plate.
3. The quarterback (threw, thrown) a touchdown pass.
4. I had (threw, thrown) cold water over my face.
5. The athlete (threw, thrown) the discus expertly.
6. I have (threw, thrown) those magazines away by mistake.
7. Have you ever (threw, thrown) a horseshoe?
8. That novel was (wrote, written) by Mark Twain.
9. Jim has (wrote, written) several humorous poems.
10. Melinda (wrote, written) to her friend.
11. Have you (wrote, written) your composition?
12. I've (wrote, written) the first draft.
13. Our class has (wrote, written) letters to the governor.
14. Last year we (wrote, written) to the mayor.
15. Why haven't you (wrote, written) that letter yet?

To use active and passive verb forms

Presenting the Lesson

1. Read and discuss pages 402 and 403. Explain that people use the active voice much more often than the passive voice and that it generally seems more powerful and forceful. Students should limit their use of the passive voice to times when they do not know who performed an action or when it is not important who has performed an action. Following are examples of appropriate use of the passive voice:

All the peaches have been eaten.
The clock has been repaired.

2. Do Exercise A orally.
3. Assign and discuss Exercise B.

Individualizing the Lesson

Less-Advanced Students

1. Have the students explain what action each subject in Exercise A performs.
2. Work with the students to complete Exercise B. First have the students identify the verb in each sentence. Then have them decide whether it is active or passive. Finally, help them change it as required.

Advanced Students

Have the students decide whether active or passive is more appropriate for each sentence in Exercises A and B.

Part 7   Active and Passive Verbs

One of the interesting things about our language is the great variety of ways in which it expresses ideas. You have seen how many different times can be shown by the tenses of verbs. Now you will see another way in which verbs help you say exactly what you have in mind.

Suppose that a window has been broken. If you know who broke it, you can say something like this:

My little brother broke the window yesterday.

But suppose you don't know who broke it, or suppose you don't want to say who broke it. You might then say:

The window was broken yesterday.

In the first sentence, the subject tells who performed the action. When the subject performs the action, the verb is said to be **active.**

In the second sentence, the subject tells what received the action. When the subject tells the receiver or the result of the action, the verb is said to be **passive.** (The word *passive* means "acted upon.")

Forming the Passive

The passive form of the verb is made by using a form of *be* with the past participle.

ACTIVE

Megan has finished the project.
Chris has shown the slides.
The store will add the tax.

PASSIVE

The project has been finished by Megan.
The slides have been shown by Chris.
The tax will be added by the store.

402

Find the direct objects in the sentences labeled **Active.** What has happened to them in the sentences labeled **Passive?** Only verbs that have objects (transitive verbs) can be changed from active to passive.

A verb is active when its subject performs the action stated by the verb.

A verb is passive when its subject names the receiver or result of the action stated by the verb.

Exercises   Use active and passive forms.

A.   Change the verbs in the following sentences from active to passive. Rewrite the sentences.

1. Mr. Harvey cleaned the rug. The rug was cleaned by Mr. Harvey.
2. The digital scoreboard shows the scores and time. The scores and time are shown by the digital scoreboard.
3. Those children fed the ducks. The ducks were fed by those children.
4. The Art Club decorated the gym. The gym was decorated by the Art Club.
5. Our team had already won the trophy once before. The trophy had already been won once before by our team.
6. The fire destroyed five buildings. Five buildings were destroyed by the fire.
7. Almost everybody knows Mr. Walters. Mr. Walters is known by almost everybody.
8. Our class had written letters to our Senators. Letters to our Senators had been written by our class.
9. The lawyer will appeal the judge's decision. The judge's decision will be appealed by the lawyer.
10. Bret has found the error. The error has been found by Bret.

B.   Rewrite each sentence, changing the verb. If the verb is active, make it passive. If it is passive, make it active.

1. One of the boys baked a cake. A cake was baked by one of the boys.
2. His plans were affected by inflation. Inflation affected his plans.
3. The group discussed playground regulations. Playground regulations were discussed by the group.
4. The committee held a meeting at one o'clock. At one o'clock a meeting was held by the committee.
5. Ms. O'Brien read the class an interesting article. An interesting article was read to the class by Ms. O'Brien.
6. The tour had been planned by Aviation Travel Company. Aviation Travel Company had planned the tour.
7. Several alternatives were considered by the club. The club considered several alternatives.
8. The Potter's Wheel also sells ceramic supplies. Ceramic supplies are also sold by the Potter's Wheel.

Reinforcement Exercise

Assign and discuss Exercise D on page 408.

Extending the Lesson

Have each student bring to class a newspaper sports report of an exciting game or other event. Have the students try rewriting a paragraph or two from one of the articles entirely in the passive voice. Discuss the effect of the passive voice on the passage.

Part 8

Objective

To correctly use verbs that are often confused

Presenting the Lesson

1. Read and discuss pages 404-406. As you discuss each troublesome pair of verbs, have the students explain why the verb in each sample sentence is correct. Then have the students suggest additional sentences in which the verbs are used correctly.

2. Assign and discuss Exercises A and B on page 406.

Individualizing the Lesson

Less-Advanced Students

Have the students work in pairs to complete the Exercises, and have them write the definition of the word they choose for each sentence.

Advanced Students

Have the students identify the tense of each verb in the Exercises.

Reinforcement Exercise

Assign and discuss Exercise E on page 409.

Optional Practice

Have the students complete these sentences:

The bricklayer laid . . .
The bricklayer lay . . .

There are certain pairs of verbs that cause trouble because they are alike in meaning. They are *alike*, but they are not the same. We cannot substitute one of the pair for the other. Learn the differences so that you can use these words correctly.

Sit and *Set*

Sit means "to occupy a seat." The principal parts are *sit, sat, sat*.

Set means "to place." The principal parts are *set, set, set*.

Present	*Sit* in the car.	*Set* the box down.
Past	We *sat* in the car.	Beth *set* the box down.
Present Perfect	We *have sat* for an hour.	We *have set* the box down on the ground.

Lie and *Lay*

Lie means "to rest in a flat position" or "to be situated." The principal parts are *lie, lay, lain*.

Lay means "to place." The principal parts are *lay, laid, laid*.

Present	*Lie* down, Fido.	*Lay* the blankets here.
Past	Fido *lay* down.	We *laid* the blankets here.
Present Perfect	Fido *has lain* down.	We *have laid* the blankets on the grass.

Let and *Leave*

Let means "to allow or permit." The principal parts are *let, let, let*.

Leave means "to go away from" or "to allow something to remain where it is." The principal parts are *leave, left, left*.

Present	*Let* us help you.	*Leave* your coats here.
Past	Bill *let* us help.	The girls *left* their coats.
Present Perfect	Bill *has let* us help on other projects.	Sue *has left* her coat in the closet.

Rise and Raise

Rise means "to go upward." The principal parts are *rise, rose, risen.*

Raise means "to lift or to make something go up." The principal parts are *raise, raised, raised.*

Present	The balloon *rises* fast.	Please *raise* the flag.
Past	The balloon *rose* quickly.	Jeff *raised* the flag.
Present Perfect	The balloon *has risen* above the tree tops.	Jeff *has raised* the flag every morning.

May and Can

May refers to permission or to something that is possible. *Might* is another form of the word. There are no principal parts. *May* and *might* are used only as helping verbs.

May we go swimming?   You *might* catch cold.

Can refers to ability. *Could* is another form of the verb. There are no principal parts. *Can* and *could* are usually used as helping verbs.

Janet *can* swim beautifully because she has practiced.
You *can* catch a cold if you are tired.

Learn and Teach

Learn means "to gain knowledge or skill." The principal parts are *learn, learned, learned.*

Teach means "to help someone learn." You must be taught by someone. The principal parts are *teach, taught, taught.*

The boy sat . . .
The boy set . . .

The gardener rose . . .
The gardener raised . . .

Extending the Lesson

Have each student find, in any published work, one example of a sentence using one of the troublesome verbs correctly.

405

Present	*Learn* to swim well.	Please *teach* me the trick.
Past	Janet *learned* quickly.	My mother *taught* me the trick.
Present Perfect	We *have learned* our lesson.	Pam *has taught* us another trick.

Exercises Choose the correct verb from the pair.

A. Number your paper from 1–10. Choose the correct verb.

1. The geyser (rose, raised) at least 100 feet up in the air.
2. The sun (rises, raises) over those hills around 6 A.M.
3. (Let, Leave) your books in your locker.
4. (Let, Leave) your assignment on the desk.
5. The audience (rose, raised) and applauded the orchestra.
6. (Lie, Lay) still and listen.
7. You must have (laid, lain) your package down by the fountain.
8. A slow, cool mist had been (raising, rising) off the lagoon.
9. The dog won't (lie, lay) down.
10. They (lay, laid) the carpeting yesterday.

B. Follow the directions for Exercise A.

1. We usually (sit, set) on the porch steps and talk.
2. The moon (sat, set) well before midnight.
3. (May, Can) I use your telephone?
4. (Can, May) I go to the movie tonight?
5. I (set, sat) the box on the big chair.
6. (Teach, Learn) Ryan not to bellyflop, will you?
7. (Can, May) we borrow your tape recorder?
8. They were (sitting, setting) up waiting for Roger.
9. That's a snap. I (could, might) do that easily.
10. Marcia (learned, taught) the speech by heart.

Reinforcement Exercises—Review

Using Verbs

A. Find the verbs. (Use after page 381.)

Find the parts of the verb in each sentence. Write them in two columns labeled *Helping Verb* and *Main Verb*.

1. Where did you buy those socks?
   HV MV
2. Don't take it so hard.
   HV MV
3. Ken should have been the villain in the play.
   HV HV MV
4. Are Nancy and the others standing in line for hockey tickets?
   HV MV
5. You might have told me about the news report.
   HV HV MV
6. Can you read the sign?
   HV MV
7. He must have come down the chimney.
   HV HV MV
8. Our homeroom has decorated the school lobby for the holidays.
   HV MV
9. Do you think so?
   HV MV
10. Shall I make banana nut bread for Friday?
    HV MV

B. Recognize verb tenses. (Use after page 384.)

Find each verb in the following sentences and tell the tense of each.

1. Have you subtracted correctly? present perfect
2. The tickets for the tournament will be available in the main office. future
3. Will the new school have air-conditioning? future
4. My sister and I flew to Alaska. past
5. My sister's graduation will take place in June. future
6. Reggie Jackson is an excellent baseball player. present

407

Reinforcement Exercises

These Reinforcement Exercises may be used for additional practice as needed. Each exercise may be used after the text page indicated in parentheses.

Review

If you have not assigned these Exercises before this time, you can use them as an excellent Section Review.

Mixed Review

The following exercises provide review of the concepts and skills presented in this chapter.

A. Recognize action verbs and linking verbs. Find the verb in each sentence. State whether it is an action verb or a linking verb. Then find and label the predicate word or direct object, if there is one.

1. The head chef smelled the sauce.
   AV DO
2. The room deodorizer smelled woodsy.
   LV PW
3. The water in the pond looked stagnant.
   LV PW
4. Craig looked at the diagram carefully.
   AV
5. The crowd grew rowdier after each touchdown.
   LV PW
6. Nancy grew zinnias in the back yard.
   AV DO
7. Mr. Elwood appears uncomfortable in a suit and tie.
   LV PW
8. Laurie appeared in the local talent show.
   AV
9. The blind man felt the braille letters in the elevator.
   AV DO
10. Sam and Jake felt dizzy after their ride on the roller coaster.
    LV PW

B. Use verb forms correctly. Rewrite each sentence, putting the verb in the form asked for in parentheses.

1. The cross-country team *run* around the golf course. (past tense)
2. By tomorrow, the carpenters *complete* the job. (future perfect)
3. Cassie *paint* the walls and trim. (present perfect)
4. The repair bill *pay* by the insurance company. (passive)
5. Dad *drive* to the train in bad weather. (present)
6. The mechanic *repair* the old engine. (future)
7. The song *record* by both the Andrew Sisters and Bette Midler. (passive)
8. We *finish* the rehearsal by ten o'clock. (future perfect)
9. Special messengers *deliver* the packages. (past)
10. Several celebrities *appear* at the fundraising dinner. (present progressive)

1. ran
2. will have completed
3. has painted
4. was paid
5. drives
6. will repair
7. was recorded
8. will have finished
9. delivered
10. are appearing

C. Use the correct verb. Write the correct verb for each sentence.

1. (Sit, Set) the packages on the counter and (let, leave) me put them away.
2. Ellen (sat, set) down at the piano and waited for Mr. Jacobs to (teach, learn) the first lesson.
3. If you (lie, lay) down now, you'll never be ready on time.

7. Our music class attended an afternoon performance by the Chicago Symphony Orchestra. past

8. Liza Minnelli and Barbra Streisand are exciting performers. present

9. We had waited in line for over an hour. past perfect

10. With the help of McDonald's, we raised $1000 for the fight against muscular dystrophy. past

C. Use progressive forms. (Use after page 385.)

Copy each sentence, changing each verb to its progressive form.

1. Paul ate the melon. Paul was eating the melon.
2. Have you watched the series? Have you been watching the series?
3. We will call my grandparents tonight. We will be calling my grandparents tonight.
4. Mrs. Levy directs the junior high band. Mrs. Levy is directing the junior high band.
5. Mandy and Jenny could help us with the gardening. Mandy and Jenny could be helping us with the gardening.
6. Several volunteers will collect aluminum cans for the recycling center. Several volunteers will be collecting aluminum cans for the recycling center.
7. Jay has worked here since May. Jay has been working here since May.
8. Nancy and Marla must have fished here yesterday afternoon. Nancy and Marla must have been fishing here yesterday afternoon.
9. The choir will sing tonight. The choir will be singing tonight.
10. I had saved my money for a new ten-speed bike. I had been saving my money for a new ten-speed bike.

D. Use passive verb forms. (Use after page 403.)

Change the verbs in the following sentences from active to passive. Rewrite the sentences.

1. Tramco sponsored the program. The program was sponsored by Tramco.
2. Everybody in grade nine takes consumer education. Consumer education is taken by everybody in grade nine.
3. Stacy threw the ball out-of-bounds. The ball was thrown out-of-bounds by Stacy.
4. About fifty people called the radio station. The radio station was called by about fifty people.
5. A flat tire delayed the school bus. The school bus was delayed by a flat tire.
6. My little sister designed and painted these covers. These covers were designed and painted by my little sister.

7. This computer will record the sun-spot activity. The sun-spot activity will be recorded by this computer.
8. The Fisher Company is building a condominium on this site. A condominium is being built on this site by the Fisher Company.
9. Snow covered the ice rink. The ice rink was covered by snow.
10. Juan developed the photographs. The photographs were developed by Juan.

E. Choose the correct verb from the pair. (Use after page 406.)

Number your paper from 1–10. Choose the correct verb.

1. (Let, Leave) Craig work by himself.
2. (Raise, Rise) the shelf about another inch.
3. Dan (raised, rose) a skeptical eyebrow.
4. The tool box is (laying, lying) on the workbench.
5. I saw the shovel (lying, laying) out in the rain.
6. Cindy lost her balance and (set, sat) down hard.
7. (May, Can) I use your telephone?
8. Would you (sit, set) the groceries on the table?
9. No one (learned, taught) Laurie to roller skate.
10. How our coach can (sit, set) so calmly is beyond me!

4. Jeff (bring, bringed, brought) food that he had (growed, grown) in his garden.
5. Jenny (throwed, threw) the fris-bee, and her dog (raised, rose) from a crouch to catch it.
6. He (knew, knowed) the answer but didn't (raise, rise) his hand.
7. I have (went, gone) to the stadium several times, but I have never (saw, seen) a concert there.
8. (May, Can) we have some fruit or has it already been (ate, eaten)?
9. Has Sandy ever (gave, given) you that sweater she (begun, began) last year?
10. A valuable painting was (stole, stolen) from the museum, and no one knows who (did, done) it.

Using Grammar in Writing

1. Display a large color portrait, and ask the students to write de-scriptions of the person in the por-trait. Afterward, have the students read their descriptions aloud. Dis-cuss whether linking verbs or action verbs predominate in the descrip-tion and why.

2. Have the students write two narrative paragraphs set in a haunted house, one using only ac-tive verbs and the other using only passive verbs. Have the students decide which paragraphs are more effective and why. Have volunteers read their paragraphs to the class.

3. Have the students write para-graphs in which they explain how to do one of the following:

lie in a hammock
set a table
learn a foreign language
sit on a horse

Remind them to use the trouble-some verbs correctly.

Section 5

Using Modifiers

Section Objectives

1. To understand the functions of adjectives, and to recognize adjectives in sentences
2. To use articles correctly in sentences
3. To recognize and form adverbs
4. To use adjectives and adverbs correctly in sentences
5. To use adjectives correctly in comparisons
6. To use adverbs correctly in comparisons
7. To avoid common problems with modifiers

Preparing the Students

Write the following pair of sentences on the chalkboard:

A car drove past the house.
A long, black car drove slowly past the still, dark house.

Discuss what difference the added modifiers make. Point out how modifiers can add depth, mood, and detail to writing. Tell students that Section 5 will increase their skill in using modifiers.
Read and discuss this page.

Additional Resources

Diagnostic Test—See page 4 in the test booklet. Recommended for use before teaching the chapter.

Mastery Test—See pages 42-43 in the test booklet. Recommended for use after teaching the chapter.

Reinforcement Exercises—See pages 432-435 in the student text.

Skills Practice Book—pages 127-136.

Duplicating Masters—pages 127-136.

Nouns and pronouns help us name and identify things and people in the world about us. Verbs help us make statements and ask questions about things and people.

Modifiers—adjectives and adverbs—help us describe what we have seen and heard.

She wore a *yellow* sweater.
We heard the jet *faintly* in the distance.

In addition, modifiers help us state how we feel about things and people.

The room was *messy*.
Our new puppy was *extremely* energetic.

We have already studied nouns, pronouns, and verbs in detail. In this section we shall study modifiers closely.

Part 1

Objective

To understand the functions of adjectives and to recognize adjectives in sentences

Presenting the Lesson

1. Read and discuss the introduction on this page. Have the students give additional examples of adjectives that tell *what kind, how many*, and *which one* or *ones*.

2. Read and discuss **Predicate Adjectives** on page 412. Stress that predicate adjectives are used with linking verbs and tell about the subject. To clarify, write the following on the chalkboard:

The bird is <u>yellow</u>.
The <u>yellow</u> bird is singing.

Point out that in each sentence the adjective *yellow* describes the subject, *bird*.

3. Read and discuss **Proper Adjectives** on page 413. Have the students give additional examples of proper adjectives.

4. Read and discuss **Pronouns Used as Adjectives** on page 413. Explain that pronouns tell *which one* about the nouns they modify. Students may be confused by the idea that one word can be both a pronoun and an adjective. Tell them that a word can be both an adjective and a pronoun.

5. Assign and discuss Exercises A, B, and C on pages 413-414.

What is the difference between these sentences?

Rain fell.
A cold, hard rain fell.

The difference is in the descriptive words that tell what kind of rain fell. These words are **adjectives.** They are one of the parts of speech.

An adjective is a word that goes with, or modifies, a noun or pronoun.

Some adjectives tell *what kind* about the words they modify:

Look at the *huge, white* balloon.

Some adjectives tell *how many* or *how much* about the words they modify:

Jim found *twenty* dollars.
We have had *little* rain.

Some adjectives tell *which one* or *which ones* about the words they modify:

That door sticks.
These pens work better.

Predicate Adjectives

Sometimes an adjective is separated from the word it modifies by a linking verb:

Everyone was quiet.   Phil seemed annoyed.

An adjective that follows a linking verb and that modifies the subject is called a **predicate adjective.**

Proper Adjectives

Proper adjectives are adjectives formed from proper nouns. They are always capitalized. Here are some examples of proper adjectives:

an American dollar	the Spanish language	the French flag
a Norwegian sardine	the English custom	an Oriental rug

Pronouns Used as Adjectives

The words *this*, *that*, *these*, and *those* can be used as demonstrative pronouns. When used alone, they are pronouns. When followed by a noun, they are adjectives.

> *These* are my sunglasses. (pronoun)
> *These* problems are easy. (adjective modifying *problems*)
> *That* is the wrong answer. (pronoun)
> *That* answer is wrong. (adjective modifying *answer*)

The words *my*, *your*, *his*, *her*, *its*, *our*, and *their* are possessive pronouns, but they can also be classed as adjectives. They are modifiers that make the meaning of the nouns they modify more definite. They tell *which one* or *which ones*.

> *My* mother works at home; *your* mother commutes.
> *His* sweater is blue; *her* sweater is red.
> *Our* house is a ranch house; *their* house has two stories.

Exercises Find the adjectives.

A. Number your paper from 1–10. Write the adjectives you find in each sentence. After each adjective, write the word it modifies. Do not include *a, an,* or *the.*

1. The jockey in the blue satin shirt mounted the black racehorse.

2. Jubilant teammates carried the goalie off the muddy field.

Individualizing the Lesson

Less-Advanced Students

1. Allow the students to work in pairs.

2. For Exercise A beginning on this page, remind students to look for words that tell *what kind, how many,* and *which one.*

3. For Exercise B on page 414, have students first copy each sentence and underline the subject and verb before they look for the modifier linked to the subject.

4. For Exercise C, provide students with sentence beginnings or with sentences having blanks for adjective modifiers.

Advanced Students

1. In Exercise A, have the students label all proper adjectives and pronouns used as adjectives.

2. Show the students how to diagram adjectives on lines slanting down from the nouns they modify.

3. For Exercise C, encourage the students to use a thesaurus and a dictionary to seek precise, vivid adjectives and to build their vocabulary of adjectives.

Reinforcement Exercise

Assign and discuss Exercise A on page 432.

Optional Practice

1. Have the students combine the following pairs of sentences into

single sentences, using adjectives as modifiers:

> Al ate the pizza. It was hot and spicy.
>
> There are costumes backstage.
>
> The costumes are bright.
>
> A fish swam in the shadows.
>
> It was large and silvery.

2. Reproduce these sentences. Have the students fill the blanks with vivid adjectives:

> A _____ car rumbled up the _____ driveway.
>
> _____ boy waved to _____ girl.
>
> Dan asked for _____ _____ hamburgers.

Extending the Lesson

Have each student bring to class a travel brochure or a travel article from a newspaper or magazine. Have the students list each adjective in a descriptive paragraph from the brochure or article. Have the students label predicate adjectives, proper adjectives, and pronouns used as adjectives. Ask students to select the most colorful adjectives.

3. Two sleek, silver Mercedes were parked in the circular driveway.

4. I feel comfortable in a plaid flannel shirt, corduroy jeans, and brown suede boots.

5. Colonial costumes and decorative furniture were on display at the huge, white Georgian mansion.

6. The red, orange, yellow, and brown leaves created a beautiful scene.

7. Red and yellow flames danced on the dry logs in the fireplace.

8. Wicker baskets of white daisies and yellow roses decorated the table.

9. I have worn these old gloves for two years.

10. The small, brown puppy nestled against me as I sat on the old, rickety bench.

B. Number your paper from 1–10. Find the predicate adjectives in these sentences. Write them down.

1. The morning sun was red.
2. Over the lake the mist looked steamy and strange.
3. Gradually the air grew warm.
4. Small birds around us were busy and noisy.
5. The woods seemed full of them.
6. The woods smelled fresh and good in the sunlight.
7. Everyone appeared happy.
8. Our packs felt light.
9. Ahead of us the path was smooth and easy.
10. Life seemed great.

C. Write ten sentences of your own, using many colorful adjectives. Try to use all the different kinds of adjectives discussed on pages 412 and 413. Underline the adjectives in your sentences. Answers will vary.

Part 2   Articles

The adjectives *a, an,* and *the* are called **articles.**
The is the **definite article.**

> Please buy me *the* book (*a particular* book).

A and *an* are **indefinite articles.**

> Please bring me *a* book (*any* book).
> Please give me *an* apple (*any* apple).

Note that we use *a* before a consonant sound (*a* book, *a* cap, *a* dog). We use *an* before a vowel sound (*an* apple, *an* egg, *an* olive).

The sound, not the spelling, makes the difference. Do we say *a honest man* or *an honest man? a house* or *an house?*

Exercise   Use the correct article.

Choose the correct article in each of the following sentences.

1. (A, An) elephant supposedly has a good memory.
2. (A, The) best book on that shelf is *Treasure Island.*
3. That is (a, an) heavy chair.
4. I have (a, an) hunch you're right.
5. Joe was wearing (a, an) orange T-shirt.
6. We had (an, a) history test this week.
7. That was (a, the) best thing to do.
8. Don't use (a, an) onion in that recipe.
9. Each of us had to do a report on (a, an) event in history.
10. Tracy made (an, a) honest effort to meet the deadline for the newspaper.
11. Sheila did (a, an) excellent job as president.
12. My family took (a, an) trip through the Southwest.
13. The soldier was given (a, an) honorable discharge.
14. (A, An) gnat landed on the horns of the bull.
15. The beekeeper removed the honey from (a, an) hive.

Part 2

Objective

To use articles correctly in sentences

Presenting the Lesson

1. Read and discuss page 415.
2. Assign and discuss the Exercise.

Individualizing the Lesson

Less-Advanced Students

Allow students to work in pairs. Encourage the students to read the Exercise sentences aloud to each other.

Advanced Students

Do the Exercise orally.

Optional Practice

Have the students locate the articles and the words they modify in Exercise A on page 413.

Part 3

Objective

To recognize and form adverbs

Preparing the Students

1. Read and discuss the introduction on this page and **Adverbs Used with Verbs**. Have the students try adding adverbs to the sentence *Diane spoke to me.* Discuss the differences in meaning among the sentences they create.

2. Read and discuss **Adverbs Used with Adjectives or Other Adverbs** on pages 416-417. Have the students experiment with substituting the adverbs listed at the top of page 417 for the italicized adverbs in the sample sentences on page 416. Discuss differences in meaning.

3. Read and discuss **Forming Adverbs** on page 417. Have the students use each of the example words in sentences.

4. Assign and discuss Exercises A, B, and C on pages 417–418.

Individualizing the Lesson

Less-Advanced Students

1. Work with the students to complete Exercise A.

2. Assign Exercise B as independent work.

3. After the students have completed Exercise C, have each student use two of the adverbs in original sentences.

Part 3 Adverbs

In order to make our meaning clear, vivid, and complete, we often have to tell *how, when, where,* or *to what extent* something is true. **Adverbs** are used for this purpose.

Adverbs Used with Verbs

Adverbs are used to go with, or modify, verbs to tell *how, when, where,* or *to what extent* an action happened.

Study the following list of adverbs:

HOW?	WHEN?	WHERE?	TO WHAT EXTENT?
secretly	then	nearby	often
quickly	later	underground	deep
sorrowfully	afterwards	here	seldom
hurriedly	finally	there	always

Now use some of the above adverbs in this sentence:

The pirates buried their gold.

You can see what a great difference adverbs make. They can make the meaning of the verb *buried* clearer, and add vividness and completeness to the whole sentence.

Adverbs Used with Adjectives or Other Adverbs

Besides being used to modify verbs, adverbs are also used to modify adjectives and other adverbs. Notice the italicized adverbs in the following sentences:

Niki was happy.
Niki was *extremely* happy.

Rick spoke slowly.
Rick spoke *too* slowly.

On the next page are some more adverbs that are often used to modify adjectives or other adverbs:

very	nearly	so
just	somewhat	more
quite	rather	most

These adverbs all tell *to what extent* something is true. You can see how useful adverbs are in making clearer, more complete, or more vivid the adjectives or other adverbs that we use.

Adverbs are words that modify verbs, adjectives, and other adverbs.

Forming Adverbs

Many adverbs are made by adding *-ly* to an adjective:

secret + -ly = secretly
bright + -ly = brightly

Sometimes the addition of *-ly* involves a spelling change in the adjective:

easy + -ly = easily (*y* changed to *i*)
merry + -ly = merrily
full + -ly = fully (*-ll* changed to *-l*)

Many words, like *quite* or *so,* can be used only as adverbs:

This footprint is *quite* recent.
Sue never looked *so* happy before.

Some other words, like *early* or *fast,* can be used either as adverbs or as adjectives:

Bill arrived *early*. (adverb)
He ate an *early* breakfast. (adjective)

Dana can run *fast*. (adverb)
She is a *fast* runner. (adjective)

Exercises   Recognize adverbs.

A.   Number your paper from 1–10. Write the adverb in each sentence. After each adverb write the word it modifies. Be ready

Advanced Students

   1. Have the students tell what word each of the adverbs in Exercises A and B modifies.
   2. Have the students use each of the adverbs in Exercise C in a sentence.
   3. Show the students how to diagram adverbs on lines slanting down from the word modified.

Reinforcement Exercise

   Assign and discuss Exercise B on page 432.

Optional Practice

   1. Have the students combine the following pairs of sentences by using adverb modifiers:

   Eric played chess. He was cautious.
   Amy ate peanut butter. She was hungry and quick.
   Carlyn repaired my bike. She did it yesterday.

   2. Have the students add an adverb to each of the sentences in Exercise A, beginning on page 413.

Extending the Lesson

   1. Have the students find synonyms in a thesaurus for the *how* adverbs listed on page 416. Discuss shades of meaning. Have the students write sentences using each of the synonyms.
   2. Have each student underline every adverb in a newspaper sports report or a short article in a sports magazine.

to explain what the adverb tells about the word it modifies.

EXAMPLE: The actors usually stay here.

usually modifies *stay* (tells when)
here modifies *stay* (tells where)

1. The doctor has just left.
2. We have never studied about Greenland.
3. The runners raced vigorously around the track.
4. That movie was quite informative.
5. The newspaper was rather careful about its editorials.
6. The quarterback limped painfully off the field.
7. The runway lights shone brightly at the airport.
8. Our canoe drifted lazily down the river.
9. The summer rain fell heavily.
10. The pounding stopped immediately.

B. Follow the directions for Exercise A.

1. That pounding has started again.
2. It was nearly midnight before the train arrived.
3. The visiting football teams usually stay at the Hilton.
4. Those two cats wander aimlessly from yard to yard.
5. That pitcher seemed somewhat unsure of himself.
6. Alicia smiled weakly.
7. Because the train was ahead of schedule, we arrived early.
8. The play went smoothly until the last act.
9. Mexico City's climate is usually ideal.
10. It is extremely important that you relay the message.

C. Change the following adjectives into adverbs by adding *-ly.*
Be careful of your spelling.

surely	cruelly	terribly	grimly	sure	cruel	terrible	grim
icily	heavily	impatiently	carefully	icy	heavy	impatient	careful
fully	sadly	peacefully	happily	full	sad	peaceful	happy
loudly	beautifully	dizzily	coolly	loud	beautiful	dizzy	cool
roughly	smoothly	crazily	hopefully	rough	smooth	crazy	hopeful

An Adverb Tells	An Adjective Tells
When? Where? How? To What Extent?	Which One? What Kind? How Many?
About a Verb, Adjective, or Adverb	**About a Noun or Pronoun**

Part 4   Adjective or Adverb?

Study the following sentences. Which sentence sounds right?

Our team won *easy*.
Our team won *easily*.

The second sentence is the correct one. An adverb (*easily*) should be used, not an adjective (*easy*).

It is often difficult to decide whether an adjective or an adverb should be used in sentences like the two given above. When you are not sure which form to use, ask yourself these questions:

1. Which word does the modifier go with? If it goes with an action verb (like *won* in the sentences above), it is an adverb. It is also an adverb if it goes with an adjective or another adverb. If it goes with a noun or pronoun, it is an adjective.

2. What does the modifier tell about the word it goes with? If the modifier tells *when, where, how,* or *to what extent,* it is an adverb. If it tells *which one, what kind,* or *how many,* it is an adjective. In the sentences above, the modifier tells *how* our team won; it must therefore be an adverb: *easily.*

Part 4

Objective

To use adjectives and adverbs correctly in sentences

Presenting the Lesson

1. Read and discuss page 419. Review with the students what they have learned about adjectives and adverbs. Have the students study and memorize the chart at the top of the page.

2. Assign and discuss Exercises A and B on page 420.

3. Read and discuss page 421. Stress that the first step in choosing between an adjective and an adverb is deciding whether the verb is a linking verb or an action verb. Tell students that confusion often arises from verbs that can be either linking or action (*look, appear, smell, taste*). Give examples of these words used both with predicate adjectives and with adverbs.

4. Assign the Exercise on page 422.

5. Read and discuss *Good* and *Well* on page 422.

6. Assign and discuss the Exercise on page 423.

Individualizing the Lesson

Less-Advanced Students

Work with the students to complete the first half of Exercise B on page 420 and the Exercises on pages 422 and the top of page 423, explaining each choice. Then have the students complete each Exercise independently.

Advanced Students

Have the students suggest alternatives for each of the modifiers in Exercise A on page 420. Encourage the students to use a thesaurus and dictionary to find the most vivid and precise adjectives and adverbs.

Reinforcement Exercises

Assign and discuss Exercises C, D, and E on pages 433 and 434.

Optional Practice

1. Tell the students to divide their papers in half lengthwise, labeling one side *adjective* and the other *adverb*. Read these sentence beginnings:

The salesperson looked. . .
The St. Bernard smells. . .
The firefly appeared. . .

Have the students complete each sentence in two ways—once using the verb as a linking verb with a predicate adjective and once using

Exercises Find the adjectives and adverbs.

A. List each adjective and adverb, together with the word it modifies. (Do not list *a*, *an*, or *the*.)

EXAMPLE: The tall runner in the red shirt won easily.

tall runner   red shirt   easily won

1. Two white puppies walked carelessly through the flowers.
2. Red, white, and blue bunting was decoratively hung around the platform.
3. He paid the bill quite promptly.
4. The suspect answered the questions rather cautiously.
5. The young swimmers dived unhesitatingly into the large pool.
6. The small child cried loudly in the dentist's office.
7. The dancers moved gracefully across the tiny stage.
8. The American ambassador spoke openly and honestly about our foreign policy.
9. The commuters walked briskly toward the long, yellow train.
10. The new puppies are too big for the basket.

B. Choose the correct modifier from the two given in parentheses. Tell what word it modifies and whether it is an adjective or adverb.

1. These flowers must be kept (fresh, freshly). adj.
2. My brother drives (careful, carefully). adv.
3. Debbie's drawings were (real, really) good. adv.
4. The leaves turned very (quick, quickly) this year. adv.
5. Mrs. Watson explained the assignment (clear, clearly). adv.
6. Our dog peered (cautious, cautiously) around the sofa. adv.
7. Ted appeared at the door (prompt, promptly) at eight. adv.
8. The ice was made (rough, roughly) by the skate blades. adj.
9. Please work (quiet, quietly) during the test. adv.
10. Renee and Marsha walked (slow, slowly) to town. adv.

Adverbs and Predicate Adjectives

You will remember that a predicate adjective appears after a linking verb and modifies the subject.

> The rose is red. (*red* modifies *rose*)
>
> The sky became cloudy. (*cloudy* modifies *sky*)
>
> The pizza tastes good. (*good* modifies *pizza*)

You also remember that in addition to the forms of *be*, the following can be used as linking verbs: *become, seem, appear, look, sound, feel, taste, grow,* and *smell.*

Sometimes these verbs are action verbs. When they are action verbs, they are followed by adverbs, not adjectives. The adverbs modify the verbs and tell *how, when, where,* or *to what extent.*

Look at the following sentences to see when adjectives are used and when adverbs are used:

ACTION VERBS WITH ADVERBS	LINKING VERBS WITH ADJECTIVES
Bob *felt* his way *slowly.*	The *cloth* felt *smooth.*
We *tasted* the fudge *eagerly.*	The *fudge* tasted *good.*
A stranger *appeared suddenly.*	The *dog* appears *sick.*
Erin *looked up.*	The *water* looks *green.*
The plant *grew fast.*	The *horse* grew *tired.*
We *smelled* smoke *suddenly.*	The *flower* smells *good.*

If you are uncertain about whether to use an adverb or adjective after verbs like *sound, smell,* and *look,* try these tests:

1. Does the modifier tell *how, when, where,* or *to what extent?* If it does, the modifier is probably an adverb.

the verb as an action verb with an adverb.

2. Have students write answers to the following questions, using modifiers correctly:

> What are you good at?(Use the word *good* in your answer.)
>
> What do you do well?(Use the word *well* in your answer.)

Extending the Lesson

Have each student read a movie review in a newspaper or magazine and list every adjective and adverb. Decide whether most of the evaluative words are adjectives or adverbs.

2. Can you substitute *is* or *was* for the verb? If you can, the verb is probably a linking verb, and the modifier is probably an adjective.

Exercise Choose the correct modifier.

Choose the correct modifier for the following sentences.

1. The ice looked (thick, thickly).
2. This water tastes (bitter, bitterly).
3. Mother spoke (calmly, calm).
4. At the start of the game we played (cautiously, cautious).
5. Those people were talking rather (loud, loudly) in the library.
6. Carol's idea sounded (reasonable, reasonably).
7. Press (firm, firmly) on the button.
8. The tape stopped (abruptly, abrupt).
9. The waiter served (quick, quickly). He was (quick, quickly).
10. The music sounded (strange, strangely).

Good and *Well*

The meanings of *good* and *well* are very much alike, but they are not exactly the same. You cannot substitute one for the other in all sentences. Study the following sentences. Can you see the difference between *good* and *well?*

I feel good.	This patient is well.
I feel well.	His health is good.
Betty plays well.	

Good is always an adjective.

Well is sometimes an adjective and sometimes an adverb. In which of the previous sentences is *well* used as an adverb? In which sentences is it used as an adjective? You can see that when *well* refers to a person's health, it may be used as an adjective.

422

Exercise Use *good* and *well* correctly.

Number your paper from 1–10. Choose the correct word.

1. Shake the bottle (good, well).
2. That swim felt (good, well).
3. All of the gymnasts did quite (well, good).
4. That looks (well, good) enough to eat!
5. Both teams played (well, good) in the second half.
6. John was sick, but now he's (good, well) again.
7. The new manager has worked out quite (good, well).
8. The soup tasted (well, good).
9. Mr. Marks looks (well, good) in his new jacket.
10. Most of the performers spoke quite (well, good).

Part 5   Adjectives in Comparisons

Comparing people and things is one way of learning about the world. We say, "This new calculator is *like* a mini-computer. Of course, it is *smaller* and it is *less accurate*."

Adjectives are very useful in comparing things and people. In comparisons, adjectives have special forms or spellings.

The Comparative

If we compare one thing or person with another, we use the **comparative** form of the adjective. It is made in two ways:

1. For short adjectives like *sweet* and *happy*, add *-er*.

   sweet + -er = sweeter   happy + -er = happier

2. For longer adjectives like *beautiful*, use *more*.

   more beautiful   more capable

Most adjectives ending in *-ful* and *-ous* also form the comparative with *more*.

   more healthful   more ambitious

Part 5

Objective

To use adjectives correctly in comparisons

Presenting the Lesson

1. Read and discuss pages 423-425. Have the students give examples of comparative and superlative forms. Stress that the superlative is used only when comparing three or more things.

Call on students to use the comparative and superlative forms listed on page 425 in sentences.

2. Assign and discuss Exercises A and B on pages 425 and 426.

Individualizing the Lesson

Less-Advanced Students

Encourage the students to consult dictionaries if they are in doubt about how to form comparatives. As you discuss the Exercises, make sure that the students understand why each response is correct or incorrect.

Advanced Students

Do both Exercises orally.

Reinforcement Exercise

Assign and discuss Exercise F on page 434.

Optional Practice

1. Have the students write the comparative and superlative forms of these adjectives: *thoughtful*, *greedy*, *bad*, *fine*, *sweet*, and *terrible*.

2. Have the students insert a comparative or superlative adjective in these sentences:

My old gym shoes are _____ than my new ones.

Monday seems to be the _____ day of the week.

My home is _____ than the school building.

Extending the Lesson

Have the students write sentences about the height of members of the class, using comparative and superlative forms correctly.

The Superlative

When we compare a thing or a person with all others of its kind, we use the **superlative** form of the adjective. In fact, when we compare a thing or person with more than one other, we use the superlative.

> This is the *best* dinner I have ever tasted.
> Pat is the *smartest* person I know.
> This is the *most interesting* book I have ever read.

The superlative form of adjectives is made by adding *-est* or by using *most*. For adjectives that add *-er* to form the comparative, add *-est* for the superlative. For those that use *more* to form the comparative, use *most* for the superlative.

	COMPARATIVE	SUPERLATIVE
high	higher	highest
big	bigger	biggest
strong	stronger	strongest
agreeable	more agreeable	most agreeable
expensive	more expensive	most expensive
careful	more careful	most careful

There are three things to remember in using adjectives for comparison:

1. Use the comparative to compare two persons or things. Use the superlative to compare more than two.

> This car is *wider* than that one.
> This car is the *widest* one I have ever seen.

2. Do not leave out the word *other* when you are comparing something with everything else of its kind.

> Wrong   New York is larger than any American city.
>   (This sentence says that New York is not an American city.)
>
> Right   New York is larger than any *other* American city.

424

Wrong	Claire runs faster than any girl in her class.	
	(Is Claire a girl? Is she in her class?)	
Right	Claire runs faster than any *other* girl in her class.	

3. Do not use both *-er* and *more* or *-est* and *most* at the same time.

Wrong	Diamonds are more harder than jade.
Right	Diamonds are *harder* than jade.
Wrong	Diamonds are the most hardest of all materials.
Right	Diamonds are the *hardest* of all materials.

Irregular Comparisons

We form the comparative and superlative of some adjectives by changing the words:

	COMPARATIVE	SUPERLATIVE
good	better	best
well	better	best
bad	worse	worst
ill	worse	worst
little	less *or* lesser	least
much	more	most
many	more	most
far	farther	farthest

Exercises Use adjectives correctly in comparisons.

A. Number your paper from 1–10. Two of the comparisons in the following sentences are correct, but the others are wrong. If a sentence is correct, write *Correct*. If there is an error, write the sentence correctly.

1. These shelves are more high than those over there. higher
2. The VW Rabbit is the bigger of these three foreign cars. biggest
3. The dictionary was more helpful than the almanac. Correct
4. It was the worstest storm I had ever seen. worst

425

much friendlier	5. Our new dog is much more friendlier than the old one.
Correct	6. Of the two plants, the fern is the healthier.
warmest	7. It was the most warmest day of the summer.
any other subject	8. Math is harder than any subject in school.
more surprising	9. What happened was even surprisinger.
funniest	10. The most funniest thing happened yesterday.

B. Follow the directions for Exercise A.

worse	1. That was the worser of the two jokes.
best	2. His joke was the goodest of all.
Correct	3. Marcy felt worse than she had felt in a long time.
Correct	4. He chose the lesser of the two evils.
less	5. She had littler time than usual.
worst	6. Mine was worse, but Janet's was the worstest.
best	7. This is the most best I can do.
better	8. That was a more better game than the one last week.
least	9. At the leastest noise Prince perked up an ear.
healthier	10. Between the ivy and the fern, the ivy is the healthiest.

Part 6

Objective

To use adverbs correctly in comparisons

Presenting the Lesson

1. Read and discuss pages 426-428.

2. Have the students give examples of comparative and superlative forms. Stress that the superlative is used only when comparing three or more things.

3. Assign and discuss Exercises A and B on page 428.

Part 6   Adverbs in Comparisons

Adverbs are used to compare one action with another. We say, "This engine runs *smoothly*, but that one runs *more smoothly*."

Or we say, "Julie planned her exhibit *more carefully* than any other student in the class."

Adverbs have special forms or spellings for use in making comparisons, just as adjectives do.

The Comparative

When we compare one action with another, we use the

426

comparative form of the adverb. The comparative form is made in two ways:

1. For short adverbs like *soon* and *fast*, add *-er*.

> We arrived *sooner* than you did.
> Kim can run *faster* than Peg.

2. For most adverbs ending in *-ly*, use *more* to make the comparative.

> Bill acted *more quickly* than Jeff.
> The water flowed *more rapidly* than before.

The Superlative

When one action is compared with two or more others of the same kind, we use the **superlative** form of the adverb.

> Peg and Bill run fast, but Kim runs *fastest*.
> Of the three boys, Scott speaks Spanish the *most fluently*.

The superlative form of adverbs is formed by adding *-est* or by using *most*. Adverbs that form the comparative with *-er* form the superlative with *-est*. Those that use *more* for the comparative use *most* for the superlative.

	COMPARATIVE	SUPERLATIVE
hard	harder	hardest
long	longer	longest
rapidly	more rapidly	most rapidly
clearly	more clearly	most clearly

In using the comparative and superlative forms of adverbs, keep in mind the following three pointers:

1. Use the comparative to compare two actions and the superlative to compare more than two.

> It rained *harder* today than yesterday.
> Of all the players, Terry tries the *hardest*.

2. Do not leave out the word *other* when you are comparing one action with every other action of the same kind.

Wrong Tara runs faster than any student in our school.
Right Tara runs faster than any *other* student in our school.

3. Do not use both *-er* and *more* or *-est* and *most* at the same time.

Wrong Tara runs more faster.
Right Tara runs *faster*.

Exercises Use adverbs correctly in comparisons.

A. Write the comparative and superlative forms of these adverbs:

faster, fastest	1. fast	6. long	longer, longest
more wildly, most wildly	2. wildly	7. bravely	more bravely, most bravely
harder, hardest	3. hard	8. slowly	more slowly, most slowly
more happily, most happily	4. happily	9. recently	more recently, most recently
more closely, most closely	5. closely	10. naturally	more naturally, most naturally

B. Some of the following sentences are correct. Others contain errors in the comparative form of adverbs. Number your paper from 1–10. If the sentence is correct, write *Correct*. If there is an error, rewrite the sentence correctly.

1. We drove more carefully after seeing the collision. Correct
2. Vacation ended more soon than we had expected. sooner
3. Write the directions out more complete. completely
4. These photographs were trimmed more better than those. better
5. That fish jumped more higher than any other. higher
6. This recipe is the more consistently successful of all. most
7. Can't you walk more fast than that? faster
8. You could see the view more clearly from here. Correct
9. He tried more harder than Wayne. harder
10. Will you read that paragraph again more slower, please? slowly

428

Part 7 Special Problems with Modifiers

Them and Those

Them is always a pronoun. It is used only as the object of a verb or as the object of a preposition.

Those is an adjective if it is followed by a noun. It is a pronoun if it is used alone.

> We heard *them* in the night. (pronoun)
> *Those* bikes are too heavy. (adjective modifying *bikes*)
> *Those* are our gifts. (pronoun)

The Extra Here and There

How often have you heard someone say, "This here book" or "That there window"? The word *this* includes the meaning of *here*. The word *that* includes the meaning of *there*.

Saying *this here* is like saying, "This book is my mine," or like repeating your name every time you say *I* or *me*: "Please pass me John Jones the milk."

Kind and Sort

Kind and *sort* are singular. Use *this* or *that* with *kind* and *sort*. *Kinds* and *sorts* are plural. Use *these* or *those* with *kinds* and *sorts*.

> We like *this kind* of dessert.
> *Those kinds* of food give you energy.

Part 7

Objective

To avoid common problems with modifiers

Presenting the Lesson

1. Read and discuss pages 429 and 430. Have the students give additional examples of the correct use of each modifier.
2. Assign and discuss the Exercises on page 431.

Individualizing the Lesson

Less-Advanced Students

1. Have the students work in pairs.
2. In Exercise A, have students first find the word each modifier modifies, and then decide which form is correct.
3. In Exercise B have students write out the sentences and underline all negative words. Then have them decide whether the sentence needs rewriting.

Advanced Students

Do both Exercises orally.

Reinforcement Exercise

Assign and discuss Exercise H on page 435.

Optional Practice

Have the students write sentences using the following words: *nobody*, *them*, *kinds*, and *doesn't*.

Extending the Lesson

Have each student find one published example of the correct use of a modifier discussed in this lesson.

The Double Negative

A **double negative** is the use of two negative words together when only one is needed. Good speakers and writers take care to avoid the double negative.

Wrong   We have*n't no* more tape.
Right   We have*n't any* more tape.

Wrong   Jack did*n't* win *nothing* at the fair.
Right   Jack did*n't* win *anything* at the fair.

Wrong   She has*n't never* gone there.
Right   She has*n't ever* gone there.

The most common negative words are *no, none, not, nothing,* and *never.*

In the sentences above, the first negative is a contraction for *not.* When you use contractions like *haven't* and *didn't,* do not use negative words after them. Instead, use words such as *any, anything,* and *ever.* Do not use *no, nothing, never,* or any other negative word after such contractions.

The club *hasn't any* new members.
We *couldn't* hear *anything.*
We *haven't ever* seen an eclipse.
The band *can't* play *any* popular songs.

Hardly, barely, and *scarcely* are often used as negative words. Do not use them after contractions like *haven't* and *didn't.*

Wrong   We could*n't hardly* breathe.
Right   We *could hardly* breathe.

Wrong   They ca*n't barely* talk.
Right   They *can barely* talk.

Wrong   The cars have*n't scarcely* moved.
Right   The cars *have scarcely* moved.

Exercises Use modifiers correctly.

A. Choose the correct word in these sentences:

1. (Them, Those) are my favorite cookies.
2. Our dog won't eat (them, those) biscuits.
3. (Them, Those) gloves are too small.
4. We chose (those, those there) designs for our posters.
5. I always buy (that there, that) kind of bread.
6. (This, This here) watch needs to be fixed.
7. (Them, Those) are deer tracks.
8. These (kind, kinds) of dogs live a long time.
9. These (sort, sorts) of arguments are pointless.
10. Do you like (this, these) sort of design?

B. Number your paper from 1–10. Correct the double negatives in the following sentences. If a sentence does not contain a double negative, write *Correct* after the corresponding number.
Sentences will vary.

1. The girls couldn't scarcely believe their ears. could
2. Bryan hasn't had no piano lessons this year. any
3. We have no more time. Correct
4. The movers couldn't hardly lift the heavy box. could
5. There isn't no time for games. is
6. Marguerita couldn't find the stamps. Correct
7. Ms. Ryan won't let nobody use the power tools. anybody
8. We couldn't find the badminton net. Correct
9. Nobody could have had more fun. Correct
10. We had plenty of apples, but Ellen didn't want none. any

Reinforcement Exercises

These Reinforcement Exercises may be used for additional practice as needed. Each exercise may be used after the text page indicated in parentheses.

Review

If you have not assigned these Exercises before this time, you can use them as an excellent Section Review.

Mixed Review

The following exercises provide review of the concepts and skills presented in this chapter.

A. Find adjectives and adverbs. Copy each sentence. Underline each adjective once and each adverb twice. Then draw an arrow from each modifier to the word being modified. Do not include articles.

1. Velvety African violets completely fill the windowsill.
2. The tired referee argued wearily with the angry player.
3. The dancer looked very nervous as she moved quickly into position.
4. Those three silver trays are quite valuable.
5. The crystal vase held a single perfect rose.
6. Dad always makes a huge sandwich with several kinds of ingredients.
7. Two expensive bicycles were firmly chained to that lamppost.
8. Tiny multicolored lights decorated the long row of trees.

Reinforcement Exercises—Review

Using Modifiers

A. Find the adjectives. (Use after page 414.)

Number your paper from 1–10. Write the adjectives you find in each sentence. After each adjective, write the word it modifies. Do not include *a, an,* or *the.*

1. A blue van was parked next to the large mobile home.
2. The library has a wonderful display of old American flags.
3. A tiny gray kitten perched itself on our roof.
4. A rusty green truck clattered down the alley.
5. The narrow, rocky peninsula has a single road.
6. Tin cans and old shoes hung from the back of the black limousine.
7. Red and white geraniums filled the ceramic pots.
8. The new Japanese policy caused widespread concern.
9. Huge, white seagulls strutted across the sandy beach.
10. The automatic door was controlled by an electric eye.

B. Recognize adverbs. (Use after page 418.)

Number your page from 1–10. Write the adverbs in the following sentences. After each adverb, write the word it modifies.

1. The students walked quickly through the corridors.
2. Gretchen cautiously opened the box.
3. The two Dalmatians barked loudly.
4. Nearly forty kegs of nails split open on the highway.
5. The paramedics moved quickly through the crowd.
6. Have you ever found your odometer?
7. The toast finally popped up.

8. We arrived precisely at 8:15 P.M.
9. The children anxiously awaited the clown's arrival.
10. Many tourists strolled casually through the town square.

C. Find the adjectives and adverbs. (Use after page 420.)

Copy each sentence. Draw an arrow from the adjective or adverb to the word it modifies. Do not include *a, an* and *the*.

1. Enormous waves pounded unmercifully against the tiny boats.
2. The next lookout is the most spectacular.
3. A slight breeze danced lightly through the trees.
4. The weather was only moderately cold.
5. Gary has a very bad cold.
6. A gentle rain danced on the tin roof.
7. Four carolers in colorful costumes sang merrily in the lobby of the store.
8. A large yellow balloon drifted freely above the treetops.
9. A small cloud curled around the top of the mountain.
10. Large, white clouds were scattered across a brilliant blue sky.

D. Choose the correct modifier. (Use after page 422.)

Choose the correct modifier for the sentences.

1. The afternoon passed (slow, slowly).
2. The guards moved (quick, quickly) up the basketball court.
3. The surface of the water glistened (bright, brightly).
4. Music was playing (quiet, quietly) in the doctor's office.
5. That tar smells (awful, awfully).
6. We felt (triumphant, triumphantly) about winning the game.
7. Please walk (careful, carefully) across the wet floor.

9. The house was completely dark, and we approached it cautiously.
10. These butterscotch caramels are extremely delicious.

B. Use modifiers correctly. All of these sentences contain errors in the use of modifiers. Rewrite each sentence correctly. Sentences may vary.

1. Of the two jackets, the wool one is the *more* most expensive.
2. Michael skates *more* faster than Chris, but he also tires *more quickly* quicker.
3. They don't have *any* no extra batteries for this here calculator.
4. Brazil is the most largest country in South America.
5. Tia said she would sew that there patch on my jacket.
6. Marci doesn't feel *well* good today.
7. The boys trudged *slowly* slow through the deep snow.
8. That was the *best* bestest song you've ever written!
9. Bob chose *that* those reinforced kind of *tire* tires for his bike.
10. That there suitcase is *more* bigger than yours.

C. Choose the correct modifier. Write the correct word from the two in parentheses.

1. Jeff has a cold and can't hear (good, well).
2. (That, Those) kind of apple has a lot of seeds.
3. The band members stepped (quick, quickly) into formation.
4. A month after the fire, the house still smelled (smoky, smokily).
5. Dana hasn't received (no, any) answer to her letter.
6. The old barn looked (mysterious, mysteriously) in the thick mist.
7. Of the six cereals, this one has the (less, least) sugar.

433

8. Jana sketches (well, good), but her painting technique is (poor, poorly).
9. Which is (longer, longest), the Nile or the Mississippi?
10. Andrew looks (good, well) in that sweater.

Using Grammar in Writing

1. Have the students write a travel ad for a place in your area. Instruct them to make the description vivid by using precise adjectives.

2. Have the students use specific adverbs in a paragraph explaining how to do a dance step, how to pitch a baseball, or how to fry an egg.

3. Have the students write two paragraphs, one comparing two areas of the school building and one comparing three different buildings in the area. Remind them to use comparative and superlative adjectives correctly.

4. Have the students write brief reports comparing the way two different sports teams play. Remind students to use adverbs correctly in comparisons.

8. The desk top feels (smooth, smoothly).
9. The operator answered (angry, angrily).
10. Their change of plans seems (sudden, suddenly).

E. Use *good* and *well* correctly. (Use after page 423.)

Choose the correct word from those given in parentheses.

1. Prospects for a sunny day were (well, good).
2. You play tennis very (good, well).
3. Her word is always (good, well).
4. The practice went (well, good).
5. Almost everyone dances pretty (good, well).
6. These scissors don't cut (well, good) any more.
7. They don't feel (good, well).
8. This suit fits me (good, well).
9. Does that sewing machine work very (good, well)?
10. Clare and I did quite (good, well) on the history test.

F. Use comparisons correctly. (Use after page 426.)

Number your paper from 1–10. Two of the comparisons in the following sentences are correct, but the others are wrong. If a sentence is correct, write *Correct*. If there is an error, write the sentence correctly.

sour   1. This lemon is more sourer than others I've eaten.
better   2. This album is more better than those two.
better   3. My grandmother feels weller than usual.
smallest   4. Their kitchen is the most smallest room in the house.
Correct   5. These are the healthiest plants I've ever seen.
best   6. Always try your bestest.
Correct   7. New York is the largest American city.
better   8. This cake is more better than that one.
worst   9. That was the worstest mistake I ever made.
easier   10. This novel was more easier to read than the other one.

G. Use modifiers correctly in comparisons.

(Use after page 428.)

One of the following sentences is correct. The others contain errors in the comparative form. Number your paper from 1–10. If the sentence is correct, write *Correct.* If there is an error, write the sentence correctly.

1. Please hold the wheel more tightly. *Correct*
2. John arrived more earlier than the others. earlier
3. They weren't the carefulest house painters I've ever seen. most careful
4. That was one of the bestest programs ever shown on TV. best
5. Bill plays soccer better than any student in his class. any other student
6. The old man looked at us more thoughtful. thoughtfully
7. Lara waited patienter than Jeff. more patiently
8. May is the most nice month of the year. nicest
9. Katharine Hepburn is one of the very bestest actresses on stage or screen. best
10. The crowd greeted his next announcement more enthusiastic. enthusiastically

H. Avoid special problems with modifiers.

(Use after page 431.)

Number your paper from 1–10. If the sentence is correct, write *Correct.* If there is an error, write the sentence correctly.
Answers may vary.

1. The coaches couldn't hardly believe the final score. could
2. Them there rapids look dangerous. Those
3. I've eaten so much I can't eat no more. any
4. Them bikes belong to Roberto and Denise. Those
5. Brian never catches no fish. any
6. Them cattle haven't scarcely moved off the road. Those, have
7. That sort of behavior could get a player benched. *Correct*
8. Meredith hasn't had no pizza. any
9. Them Scouts couldn't barely finish the hike. Those, could
10. My bike doesn't need no repairs. any

Section 6

Using Prepositions and Conjunctions

Section Objectives

1. To understand the function of prepositions, and to identify prepositions in sentences

2. To differentiate between the use of a word as a preposition and its use as an adverb

3. To identify prepositional phrases and their functions

4. To identify and use conjunctions

5. To identify the eight parts of speech in sentences

Preparing the Students

Read and discuss the introduction on pages 437 and 438.

Write these words on the board:

Scott went the front the room drew his fingernails the chalkboard.

Tell the students that the words lack sense because the connectives have been omitted. Have the students try to guess which words have been omitted from the sentence:

Scott went *to* the front *of* the room *and* drew his fingernails *across* the chalkboard.

Discuss the importance of prepositions and conjunctions for making relationships clear.

Additional Resources

Diagnostic Test—See page 5 in the test booklet. Recommended for use before teaching the chapter.

Mastery Test—See pages 44-45 in the test booklet. Recommended for use after teaching the chapter.

Reinforcement Exercises—See pages 450-451 in the student text.

Skills Practice Book—pages 137-142.

Duplicating Masters—pages 137-142.

Often we can say what we mean by using short sentences:

The grocer weighed the meat.
Scott finished the painting.

Frequently, however, what we have to say is more complicated. Perhaps we want to say not merely that Scott finished the painting but also that he finished it at noon. We may want to tell someone that the grocer weighed not only the meat but also the pears and the potatoes. To express more complicated ideas like these, we use **connectives.**

Scott finished the painting *at* noon.
The grocer weighed the meat, the pears, *and* the potatoes.

This section will help you learn to use two important kinds of connectives: **prepositions** and **conjunctions.**

Part 1   Prepositions

Connectives are words that are used to join together two or more other words or groups of words. **Prepositions** are one important kind of connective.

Notice the prepositions in the following sentences:

The plane flew *into* the storm.
The plane flew *around* the storm.

In the first sentence, *into* connects *storm*, its object, with the verb *flew*. It points out the relationship between *flew* and *storm*.

In the second sentence, *around* connects *storm*, its object, with the verb *flew*. It points out the relationship between *flew* and *storm*.

You can see that *into* and *around* join parts of each sentence. Like all prepositions, they make clear a certain relationship between the words that they connect.

Now look at the prepositions in the following sentences:

My sister is the person *at* the counter.
My sister is the person *behind* the counter.

You can see that *at* and *behind* join parts of each sentence. They make clear the relationships between *person* and *counter*.

A preposition is a word used with a noun or pronoun, called its *object,* to show the relationship between the noun or pronoun and some other word in the sentence.

On the next page is a list of words often used as prepositions. Most of these prepositions tell *where*. Others show a relationship of *time*. Still others show such special relationships as *reference*,

Part 1

Objectives

1. To understand the function of prepositions, and to identify prepositions in sentences
2. To differentiate between the use of a word as a preposition and its use as an adverb

Presenting the Lesson

1. Read and discuss pages 438 and 439. Have the students study the list of prepositions on page 439. Draw a box on the chalkboard, and diagram the relationships expressed by various prepositions, such as *by*, *in*, *on*, *over*, *beside*, *around*, *under*, and *near*. Emphasize that the noun or pronoun following a preposition is its object.
2. Do Exercise A on page 439 orally. Then assign and discuss Exercise B on page 440.
3. Read and discuss **Preposition or Adverb?** on pages 440-441. Stress that prepositions are used only to relate two other words and are never used alone.
4. Assign and discuss Exercises A and B on page 441.

Individualizing the Lesson

Less-Advanced Students

1. For Exercises A and B on pages 439 and 440. remind the stu-

438

separation, and so on. Study these prepositions and see if you can tell the relationship that each of them shows between words.

Words Often Used as Prepositions

about	beneath	in	past
above	beside	inside	since
across	between	into	through
after	beyond	like	to
against	but (except)	near	toward
along	by	of	under
among	concerning	off	until
around	down	on	up
at	during	onto	upon
before	except	out	with
behind	for	outside	within
below	from	over	without

Exercises Find the prepositions.

A. Number your paper from 1–10. Label two columns *Preposition* and *Object.* Find the prepositions in the following sentences. Tell what the object of each preposition is.

EXAMPLE: On Saturday, Bret and Julie went to the beach.

PREPOSITION	OBJECT
On	Saturday
to	beach

1. The library will hold the book until tomorrow.
2. I hurried up the stairs and into the room.
3. A prop plane with several passengers made an emergency landing in a cornfield.

dents to check the list of prepositions on this page.
 2. For the Exercises on page 441, tell the students to test for an object by asking *what?* after each word that could be a preposition.

Advanced Students

 1. For Exercise B on page 440, have the students write the two words that are related by each preposition.
 2. Have the students suggest prepositional phrases to replace each italicized adverb in the Exercises on page 441.

Reinforcement Exercises

Assign and discuss Exercises A and B on page 450.

Optional Practice

Have the students find the words used as prepositions in the Exercises on page 322.

Extending the Lesson

Have the students list each preposition and its object in a short how-to or do-it-yourself article. Discuss the relationships that these prepositions express and how they clarify the instructions.

4. During the night we were awakened by thunder.

5. After the play, we're going to Mike's house.

6. The residents of Franklin Park are concerned about the pollution.

7. The football squad huddled around the coach for last-minute instructions.

8. Stack these cartons against that wall and put those books on the shelf.

9. The city was without power for several hours.

10. In the library there are several aquariums and plants on various bookshelves.

B. Follow the directions for Exercise A.

1. In July we are going to Florida for a visit to my grand-parents.

2. Student Council will meet before school on Friday.

3. Two sky-writing planes flew over the stadium during the game.

4. The bicycle shop is located on Green Bay Road.

5. On the island of Oahu we visited the Polynesian Cultural Center.

6. The dog scampered down the stairs with my glove.

7. Tony Dorsett dazzled the crowd in the Coliseum with a 93-yard run.

8. We rode the elevator to the top of the John Hancock Building.

9. Cross-country skiing through forests and across open fields is fun.

10. The pancake house near the expressway is open around the clock.

Preposition or Adverb?

Many words used as prepositions may also be used as adverbs. A preposition never appears alone. It is always followed by its object, a noun or pronoun. If the word has a noun or pronoun following it, it is probably a preposition. If it is not followed by a noun or pronoun, it is probably an adverb.

I drew a line *across* the paper. (preposition)
He dared me to jump *across*. (adverb)

Ted put his books *down*. (adverb)
He ran *down* the street. (preposition)

Exercises Recognize adverbs and prepositions.

A. Decide whether the italicized words in these sentences are adverbs or prepositions. Write *Adverb* or *Preposition* for each sentence.

1. Janice turned *around*. Adverb
2. There is a new shopping center *near* our house. Preposition
3. The committee turned our request *down*. Adverb
4. The light bulb burned *out*. Adverb
5. The horses trotted *around* the track. Preposition
6. All local traffic was allowed *through*. Adverb
7. Pete threw his old track shoes *out*. Adverb
8. The Frisbee flew *across* the picnic table. Preposition
9. The doctor is *in*. Adverb
10. We all went *inside*. Adverb

B. Follow the directions for Exercise A.

1. Come *around* four o'clock. Preposition
2. We waited *outside* the theater. Preposition
3. The chain came *off*. Adverb
4. The chain came *off* the bicycle. Preposition
5. The lion cub rolled *over*. Adverb
6. Marsha and Jory went cycling *along* the lakeshore. Preposition
7. We heard a noise *below*. Adverb
8. John, Vince, and I sat *inside* the tent. Preposition
9. That dog always stays *within* the perimeter of his yard. Preposition
10. Lew and Niki talked *with* the assistant principal. Preposition

Part 2 Prepositional Phrases as Modifiers

Objective

To identify prepositional phrases and their functions

Presenting the Lesson

1. Read and discuss pages 442-443. Stress that a prepositional phrase may include words that describe or modify the object. Have the students suggest alternatives for the italicized phrases in the examples.

2. Have the students give examples of adverb phrases and adjective phrases in sentences.

3. Read **Diagraming Prepositional Phrases** on page 443. Stress the fact that the placement of a word in a diagram mirrors its function in the sentence.

4. Assign and discuss Exercises A and B on page 444.

Individualizing the Lesson

Less-Advanced Students

1. Have the students refer to the list of prepositions on page 439 while they are doing the Exercises.

2. Simplify Exercise A by having the students simply circle the prepositional phrases after they copy the sentences. Check the students' work in class, then work with them to complete the other requirements.

3. Assign Exercise B as independent work.

Advanced Students

Have the students diagram the sentences in Exercise A.

Part 2 Prepositional Phrases as Modifiers

A modifier may be a group of words as well as a single word. A **phrase** is a group of words that belong together but do not have a subject and verb.

Notice these phrases used as modifiers:

The bears hibernated *during the long winter.*
The player *in the blue jersey* sank the next basket.
The principal's office is *on the first floor.*

The words in italics are **prepositional phrases.**

A prepositional phrase consists of a preposition, its object, and any modifiers of the object.

PREPOSITION	MODIFIERS	OBJECT
during	the long	winter
in	the blue	jersey
on	the first	floor

You remember that nouns and pronouns are modified by adjectives. Verbs are modified by adverbs.

Prepositional phrases may modify nouns, pronouns, or verbs. A phrase that modifies a noun or pronoun is an **adjective phrase.** A phrase that modifies a verb is an **adverb phrase.**

Regina found a box *of marbles.* (adjective phrase modifying the noun *box*)
Each *of us* needs a job. (adjective phrase modifying the pronoun *each*)
Mandy came *into the room.* (adverb phrase modifying the verb *came*)

Adverbs tell *how, to what extent, when,* and *where* about verbs. Adverb phrases tell the same thing about verbs.

Often you will find two prepositional phrases in a row. Sometimes the second phrase is an adjective phrase modifying the object of the first phrase.

The cat was sitting *at the top* *of the stairs*.
(*at the top* is an adverb phrase telling where about the verb *was sitting*.)
(*of the stairs* is an adjective phrase modifying *top*. It tells which *top*.)

Cory put the powder *into the can* *of paint*.
(*into the can* tells where the powder was *put*.)
(*of paint* modifies *can*. It tells *which can*.)

Diagraming Prepositional Phrases

In diagrams a prepositional phrase is placed below the word it modifies.

The girl *with the red hair* plays *in the band*.

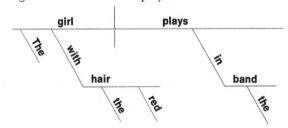

Sometimes two or more nouns or pronouns may be used as objects in a prepositional phrase.

Put butter *on the potatoes* and *squash*.

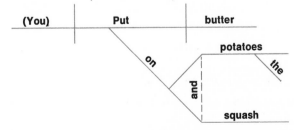

Reinforcement Exercise

Assign and discuss Exercise C on page 451.

Optional Practice

Have the students find the prepositional phrases in the sentences in Exercise A on page 316.

Extending the Lesson

1. Have the students write sentences using the following prepositional phrases, and then identify each phrase as adverb or adjective:

with a friend   on the hill
under the couch   at lunch

2. Have the students use prepositional phrases in their answers to these questions:

Where do you keep your books?
When do you get up in the morning?
Where do you live?
How do you get to the gym?

3. Use an opaque projector to project a page from a social studies textbook. Have the students list all the prepositional phrases and label each one *adjective* or *adverb*. Discuss how phrases help clarify the meaning in the text.

Exercises Use prepositional phrases as modifiers.

A. Copy these sentences. Circle each prepositional phrase. Draw an arrow from the phrase to the word it modifies. Tell whether the phrase is an adjective phrase or an adverb phrase.

EXAMPLE: He took the book with the pictures of Ireland.

with the pictures: adjective phrase modifying *book*
of Ireland: adjective phrase modifying *pictures*

adjective, adverb
1. The man in the blue coat plays for the Celtics.

adverb, adjective
2. A brown terrier sat at the bottom of the staircase.

adverb, adjective
3. We peered through the windows of the deserted mansion.

adverb, adjective
4. Patti added some ice to the pitcher of iced tea.

adjective
5. That lady in the white suit is my social studies teacher.

adjective, adjective
6. The sign over the top of the door says "No Exit."

adjective, adjective
7. The window on the east side of the garage needs repair.

adjective, adjective
8. The dancer near the back of the stage is Rudolf Nureyev.

adjective, adjective
9. The sailboat in the water near the dock has a leak.

adverb, adjective
10. The electric sander is in the cabinet near the door.

B. Follow the directions for Exercise A.

adjective
1. The passengers on the jet were served a special dinner.

adjective, adjective
2. The trees in back of the house need pruning.

adverb, adjective
3. Are you going to the shopping center down the street?

adverb
4. Jane took these pictures with a wide-angle lens.

adjective, adjective
5. The sign on the door in the office said that school will
adverb   end at 1 P.M. today.

adjective
6. The article about jogging was very informative.

adjective
7. The movie on television features Billy Dee Williams.

adverb, adjective
8. Jane Addams is well known for her contributions in social work.

adjective, adjective
9. I wrote a composition about my experiences at camp.

adjective 10. I enjoyed my work with small children last summer.

Part 3   Conjunctions

A second kind of word used to tie the parts of a sentence together is the **conjunction.**

A conjunction is a word that joins words or groups of words.

Notice the conjunctions in the following sentences:

> Lucy *and* Linda look alike. (connects subjects)
> Todd will call his father *or* mother. (connects direct objects)
> Mr. Morley hemmed *and* hawed. (connects verbs)
> The cannister smelled spicy *but* damp. (connects predicate adjectives)
> The guide book is *either* in the closet *or* on the desk. (connects prepositional phrases)

Conjunctions are unlike prepositions in that they do not have objects. They are similar to prepositions in that they do show a certain relationship between the words they connect.

Coordinating Conjunctions

To connect single words or parts of a sentence that are of the same kind, we use **coordinating conjunctions.** The most common coordinating conjunctions are *and*, *but*, and *or*.

> Maya *and* John are here. (*and* connects *Maya* and *John*.)
> We can't see, *but* we can hear. (*but* connects *we can't see* and *we can hear*.)

Correlative Conjunctions

A few conjunctions are used in pairs:

both . . . and   not only . . . but (also)
either . . . or   whether . . . or
neither . . . nor

Part 3

Objective

To identify and use conjunctions

Presenting the Lesson

1. Read and discuss pages 445-446. On the chalkboard write the definitions of *conjunction*, *coordinating conjunction*, and *correlative conjunction*.

2. Do Exercise A on page 446 orally.

3. Assign and discuss Exercises B, C, and D on page 447.

Individualizing the Lesson

Less-Advanced Students

1. For Exercise B on page 447, refer the students to the examples of conjunctions on page 445. Have the students copy the sentences and underline the words connected by the conjunctions.

2. For Exercises C and D, either provide the students with the beginnings of sentences to complete, or work with them to produce a few sentences as examples.

Advanced Students

Complete Exercise B orally. Have the students identify the sentence parts that each conjunction joins. For example, in sentence 1 *neither—nor* joins two parts of a compound subject.

Reinforcement Exercise

Assign and discuss Exercise D on page 451.

Optional Practice

Have the students complete the following sentences with conjunctions:

Andrea's birthday is in _____ June _____ July.
David _____ Renée led the singalong.
Can you play guitar _____ piano?
I heard _____ didn't answer the phone.

Have volunteers read their completed sentences. Discuss the differences in meaning their choices create.

Extending the Lesson

1. Have the students list all conjunctions and the words they connect in a brief newspaper article.

2. Have the students reread the report "Mexico: A Land of Contrasts" on pages 170 and 171. Have them find the conjunctions and the words they join. List these on the chalkboard. Discuss how the writer's frequent use of *and* and *but* emphasizes the contrasts referred to in the title.

Such conjunctions are called **correlative conjunctions.**

Both the benches *and* the tables had been painted.
Either you *or* I have made an error.
Neither football *nor* baseball can be played on that field.
We need *not only* nails *but also* a hammer.
Shall I call *whether* it rains *or* snows?

Exercises Recognize and use conjunctions.

A. Find the conjunctions in the following sentences. Be prepared to tell what words or word groups are connected by the conjunction.

EXAMPLE: The Rand Raiders and the Thomas Trojans were invited to play in the baseball tournament.

The Rand Raiders and *the Thomas Trojans* are connected by the conjunction *and.*

1. The clowns and magicians entertained the children.
2. Freezing rain and poor visibility delayed most flights.
3. Either the yearbook staff or the newspaper staff will sell refreshments at the home football games.
4. Tom and I couldn't get tickets for the match.
5. The slight breeze, pleasant temperatures, and overcast skies were assets to the marathon runners.
6. At the school picnic, we had corn on the cob and barbecued chicken.
7. Are you going to the movies or to the roller rink?
8. Marcia and I are going either to the water polo game or to the indoor tennis meet.
9. We baked an apple pie and a bundt cake in home economics.
10. The San Diego Zoo and Disneyland were the highlights of my trip to California.

B. Follow the directions for Exercise A.

1. Neither the coaches nor the timekeepers knew the final score.

2. Canoeing and backpacking are my favorite outdoor activities.

3. Either Bob or Mike will be the starting quarterback for our team.

4. You can see an opera or the Grand Kabuki by the National Theatre of Japan.

5. Both my brother and my sister are studying medicine.

6. Racquetball, tennis, and squash require speed and endurance.

7. The roadblock and the detour have delayed our trip.

8. Skateboards, painter's pants, Bubble Yum, and Frisbees are fads that characterized the mid-1970's.

9. I like neither avocados nor asparagus.

10. We not only raised enough money for the orphanage, but we also made a donation to the children's hospital.

C. Write two sentences using *and*, two sentences using *or*, and two sentences using *but.* After each sentence write the words or groups of words that are joined by the conjunctions.
Answers will vary.

D. Write one sentence for each of the following pairs of correlative conjunctions: Answers will vary.

both—and
either—or
neither—nor
not only—but (also)
whether—or

Part 4

Objective

To identify the eight parts of speech in sentences

Presenting the Lesson

1. Read and discuss pages 448-449. Emphasize the fact that many words can be used as more than one part of speech. Have the students tell what part of speech the italicized word is in each of the following sentences:

Is he driving an *orange* car?
I am eating an *orange*.

Please *wait* here.
Did you have a long *wait*?

2. Assign and discuss the Exercise on page 449.

Individualizing the Lesson

Less-Advanced Students

1. Review Sections 2–5.
2. Have the students first copy each sentence in the Exercise and then underline the subject and verb. Finally, ask them to decide the part of speech of the italicized word.

Advanced Students

1. Have the students identify the part of speech of each word in each sentence in the Exercise.
2. Have the students diagram several of the sentences in the Exercise.

Optional Practice

Have the students write sen-

Part 4   Review of Parts of Speech

As you know, there are eight parts of speech.

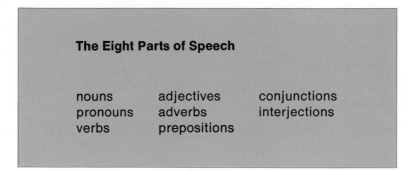

The Eight Parts of Speech

nouns	adjectives	conjunctions
pronouns	adverbs	interjections
verbs	prepositions	

Interjections

Do you remember what interjections are?

An **interjection** is a word or short group of words used to express strong feeling. It may be a real word or merely a sound. It may express surprise, joy, longing, anger, or sorrow.

An interjection is often followed by a special punctuation mark called an **exclamation mark** (!).

Hooray! We won the game.
No way! I'm not riding that roller coaster.

Words Used as Different Parts of Speech

In Part 1 of this section, you learned that words may be used as prepositions or as adverbs. Other words in our language may also be used in different ways.

Since the same word can be used in different ways as a different part of speech, how can you tell what part of speech a word is? Usually you have to see how the word is used in a sentence.

What part of speech a word is depends on how it is used in a sentence.

> Bruce moved the heavy *stone*. (*stone* is used as a noun.)
> I sat on the *stone* wall. (*stone* is used as an adjective modifying *wall*.)
>
> Don't *stand* in the doorway. (*stand* is used as a verb.)
> Bob built a *stand* for his beer can collection. (*stand* is used as a noun.)
>
> *This* book is exciting. (*This* is used as an adjective modifying *book*.)
> *This* is an interesting book. (*This* is used as a demonstrative pronoun.)

Exercise Decide the part of speech.

Number your paper from 1–12. Write the italicized word in each sentence. After it, write the part of speech that it is in that sentence.

1. Two *fence* posts were wobbly. adjective
2. Joan has gone around to the *back*. noun
3. We will *plant* a garden in the spring. verb
4. I have a couple of *stops* to make on Main Street. noun
5. The *garage* sale lasted until noon. adjective
6. The harbor is patrolled by the *port* authorities. adjective
7. Put these books *beside* the dictionaries. preposition
8. Everyone *but* Nancy stayed for the entire game. preposition
9. *Hurry!* Here's our train. interjection
10. The *door* hinge creaked. adjective
11. The *plant* shut down yesterday evening. noun
12. Tricia *backed* the car into the garage. verb

tences using each of the following words. Each word should appear in two sentences, and it should be used as a different part of speech in each.

burn   light
these   along

Extending the Lesson

Write this sentence on the chalkboard:

Did the coach time that race?

Have the students identify the part of speech of each underlined word. Then have the students use each underlined word in a different sentence as a different part of speech. Encourage them to use a dictionary to find out what other parts of speech each word can be.

Reinforcement Exercises

These Reinforcement Exercises may be used for additional practice as needed. Each exercise may be used after the text page indicated in parentheses.

Review

If you have not assigned these Exercises before this time, you can use them as an excellent Section Review.

Mixed Review

The following exercises provide review of the concepts and skills presented in this chapter.

A. Recognize adjective phrases and adverb phrases. Copy these sentences. Circle each prepositional phrase. Draw an arrow from the phrase to the word it modifies. State whether it is an adjective phrase or an adverb phrase.

adj.   1. The body of the sportscar was
adv.   constructed from fiberglass.
adj.   2. We gave the house on the corner
adj.   a fresh coat of paint.
adv.   3. Carly swept the crumbs under the
        rug.
adv.   4. Sign your name on the dotted
        line.
adj.   5. The package from my aunt was
adv.   wrapped in the comic section of
adj.   the paper.
adv.   6. The river flows into the harbor of a
adj.   large lake.
adj.   7. Ken likes spaghetti with meat-
        balls and sauce.
adj.   8. Two of the pickets in the fence
adj.   need nails.

Using Prepositions and Conjunctions

A. Find the prepositions. (Use after page 440.)

Number your paper from 1–10. Write the prepositions in the following sentences. Write the object of each preposition.

1. An account of the race will be in the newspaper.
2. Trade-ins are usually accepted at Fernstone Motors.
3. On our doorstep was a lost puppy.
4. There is a new shopping mall near the school.
5. Manny and I went to the bakery for some doughnuts.
6. We rode the subway into the city.
7. In August you can't get in without reservations.
8. The list of winners will be announced in a few minutes.
9. The photographs in the display case were taken by Sue.
10. Rafferty High is beyond the municipal building.

B. Recognize adverbs and prepositions. (Use after page 441.)

Decide whether the italicized words in these sentences are adverbs or prepositions. Write *Adverb* or *Preposition* for each sentence.

1. Dad drove twice *around* the block. Preposition
2. Think it *over*. Adverb
3. While we waited, it seemed as if days went *by*. Adverb
4. The talk show went *on* and *on*. Adverb, Adverb
5. The Statue of Liberty was a gift *from* France. Preposition
6. Try their homemade cheesecake *after* dinner. Preposition
7. We followed the Freedom Trail *through* Boston. Preposition
8. Please turn the radio *off*. Adverb

C. Use prepositional phrases as modifiers.
(Use after page 444.)

Copy these sentences. Circle each prepositional phrase. Draw an arrow from the phrase to the word it modifies.

1. Look in the drawer with the brass handle.
2. Please give me a hamburger without mustard.
3. The plants in the greenhouse need watering.
4. Some of the books on the table are Kim's.
5. The aquarium in the den needs cleaning.
6. We visited Lincoln's home in Springfield, Illinois.
7. Many French laws originated with Napoleon.
8. The elevator ride to the top of the Sears Tower takes 54 seconds.
9. Carol's expression was too funny for words.
10. Last summer I was on the swimming team with my sister.

D. Recognize and use conjunctions. (Use after page 447.)

Find the conjunctions in the following sentences. Tell what words are connected by the conjunctions.

1. Do you like Jackson Browne or Peter Frampton?
2. Last Saturday, Kathy and I went cycling and bowling.
3. Bob or Jeff can borrow this mitt.
4. "Checagou" or "land of stinking onions" is the Indian name originally given to the city of Chicago.
5. Every marathon race is 26 miles and 385 yards.
6. The origin of marathons and the Olympics can be traced back to ancient Greece.
7. Both Wisconsin and Mississippi were named by the Chippewa Indians.
8. "Ouisconsin" means "grassy place" and "mici zibi" means "great river."
9. We could go to the planetarium or to the zoo.
10. Neither the guitar nor the banjo is difficult to play.

adv 9. The majorettes marched onto the
adv. field with the band.
adj 10. Mark's room is the one at the end
adj. of the hall.

B. Recognize the parts of speech.
Write the italicized word in each sentence. After it, write its part of speech.

1. That *flower* pot is cracked. adj.
2. *Park* the bicycles in the metal stand. v.
3. *Fantastic!* The band will play another set. inter.
4. *Neither* Jerry *nor* Phil plays soccer. conj.
5. The women met in the *park* by the pond. n.
6. *Below*, we could see a reef. adv.
7. All of *those* homes were built in the 1800's. adj.
8. The officer walked *briskly* across the parade field. adv.
9. The submarine dove *below* the surface. prep.
10. Give me some of these doughnuts and some of *those*. pron.

Using Grammar in Writing

1. Have the students choose prepositions carefully as they write paragraphs explaining one of the following:

how to wrap a gift
how to bait a hook
how to plant a garden

2. Have the students use conjunctions to combine each pair of sentences into one sentence:

Kara sells newspapers. Kara delivers newspapers.

Did Ken ride his bike? Did he ride Dede's bike?

Suzanne went on the bike trip. Jenny went on the bike trip.

Kevin is a good speaker. He is a poor listener.

451

Section 7

Sentence Patterns

Section Objectives

1. To recognize the relationship between word order and meaning

2. To recognize the basic word order in the N V sentence pattern

3. To recognize the basic word order in the N V N sentence pattern

4. To recognize the basic word order in the N V N N sentence pattern

5. To recognize the basic word order in the N LV N sentence pattern

6. To recognize the basic word order in the N LV Adj sentence pattern

Preparing the Students

On the chalkboard write these lines from the poem "Jabberwocky":

'Twas brillig, and the slithy toves
Did gyre and gimble in the wabe.

Point out to the students that although most of the words are nonsense words, the lines seem to sound like English sentences. Explain that the lines follow patterns for English sentences.

Read and discuss this page.

Additional Resources

Mastery Test—See page 46 in the test booklet. Recommended for use after teaching the lesson.

Reinforcement Exercises—See pages 460-463 in the student text.

Skills Practice Book—page 143.

Duplicating Masters—page 143.

In a sentence, one word follows another. The words are arranged in order. The order in which the words are arranged is very important. If the sentence is to make sense, the word order must follow a pattern. The words cannot simply be thrown together haphazardly.

In this section, you will learn several of the patterns for English sentences. You will also see how important word order is within these patterns. Word order is so important that changing the order of the words in a sentence can change its meaning.

Objective

To recognize the relationship between word order and meaning

Presenting the Lesson

1. Read and discuss page 454.
2. Assign and discuss the Exercise.

Individualizing the Lesson

Less-Advanced Students

Have the students explain how and why the meaning changes in each sentence in the Exercise.

Advanced Students

Have the students write their own sentences that can be reversed and still make sense.

Reinforcement Exercise

Assign and discuss Exercise A on page 460.

Optional Practice

Have the students make sentences from the following word groups:

1. two has Jim brothers
2. hung we the wallpaper
3. shirt my blue is

Extending the Lesson

Challenge the students to see how many different sentences they can form from the following words:

Tom Beth Jean about told

Part 1   Word Order and Meaning

To make sense as a sentence, words must be put together in a certain logic. Read the groups of words below. Which group makes sense as a sentence?

Katie trimmed the lawn.
Lawn trimmed the Katie.

The first group makes sense. The words are in one of the patterns for an English sentence. The second group does not make sense. The words seem jumbled. Our experience tells us that the words are not in the right order for an English sentence.

Sometimes a group of words can be arranged in more than one order. Each arrangement will make sense and express a message. However, the message expressed by one arrangement is likely to be different from the message expressed by another. Read the following pair of sentences.

Jon wrote to the President.
The President wrote to Jon.

These sentences have very different meanings. What makes the meanings different? The words are the same in each sentence. The order of the words is the only thing that makes the sentences different. This difference in order makes an important difference in meaning.

Exercise   Change word order and meaning.

Read each sentence. Then change the order of the words to change the meaning. Write each new sentence on your paper.

1. Ann stopped the dog. *The dog stopped Ann.*
2. The pigeons saw the cat. *The cat saw the pigeons.*
3. Water is in the boat. *The boat is in water.*
4. Doug called the radio station. *The radio station called Doug.*
5. The ball hit Jess. *Jess hit the ball.*
6. The photograph is in the museum. *The museum is in the photograph.*
7. Tim stayed to help the teacher. *The teacher stayed to help Tim.*
8. The balloon is in the air. *The air is in the balloon.*

454

Part 2   The N V Pattern

Every sentence has a subject and a verb. The subject is usually a noun or a pronoun. The subject may have modifiers. It may be compound. The verb may also have modifiers, and it may also be compound. In this chart, N stands for the noun or pronoun in the complete subject. V stands for the verb in the complete predicate.

N	V
Christopher	cooked.
Christopher and Debbie	cooked and served.
The hungry campers	ate heartily.
We	cleaned up.

The word order in these sentences follows a pattern. That pattern is noun-verb, or N V. This pattern is called the **N V pattern.**

Exercises   Use the N V pattern.

A.   Make a chart like the one above. Label one column *N* and the other *V*. Write these sentences on the chart.

1. Everyone shouted.
2. Our team won.
3. Stan and Meg whistled loudly.
4. I slept soundly.
5. The old stove works well.
6. My science book is in the desk.

B.   Copy this chart. Complete each sentence in the N V Pattern.

Answers will vary.

N	V
1. _____	howled.
2. The refrigerator	_____.
3. _____	exploded suddenly.
4. The people in the audience	_____.
5. _____	stood and sang.

C.   Write five sentences in the N V pattern.

Answers will vary.

455

Part 2

Objective

To recognize the basic word order in the N V sentence pattern

Presenting the Lesson

1. Read and discuss this page. Point out that the N V pattern is the most basic.
2. Assign and discuss Exercises A, B, and C.

Individualizing the Lesson

Less-Advanced Students

Work with the students to complete Exercise C.

Advanced Students

Have the students expand the sentences they wrote for Exercise C, adding modifiers to the subject and verb.

Reinforcement Exercise

Assign and discuss Exercise B on page 460.

Optional Practice

Have the students find the sentences in Exercise A on page 420 that are in the N V pattern.

Extending the Lesson

1. Have the students suggest alternative verbs for the sentences in Exercise A.
2. Have each student clip a news story from the front page of a local paper and copy all N V sentences.

Objective

To recognize the basic word order in the N V N sentence pattern

Presenting the Lesson

1. Read and discuss this page. Emphasize that N V N sentences have direct objects.
2. Assign and discuss Exercises A, B, and C on this page.

Individualizing the Lesson

Less-Advanced Students

Work with the students to complete Exercise C.

Advanced Students

1. Have the students add modifiers to the sentences in Exercise A.
2. Have the students expand the sentences they wrote for Exercise C, adding modifiers to the subject, verb, and object.

Reinforcement Exercise

Assign and discuss Exercise C on page 461.

Optional Practice

Have the students find the sentences in the Exercise on page 324 that are in the N V N pattern.

Extending the Lesson

Have the students suggest alternative direct objects for the sentences in Exercise A.

Part 3   The N V N Pattern

The **N V N pattern** describes a sentence with three parts. The first N stands for the subject noun or pronoun. The V stands for the verb. The second N stands for the direct object noun or pronoun. Any of the parts may be compound. Each of the sentences in the following chart is in the N V N pattern.

N	V	N
Horses	like	apples.
Robin	will buy	that.
Two of my classmates	write and illustrate	a comic strip.
My cousin and I	collect	bottle caps.

Exercises Use the N V N Pattern.

A.   Make a chart like the one above. Label the three columns *N*, *V*, and *N*. Write these sentences on the chart.

1. Whales eat plankton.
2. The car hit the post.
3. Ellen fixed my old radio.
4. Every player scored points.
5. I ate two tacos.
6. Each one took one.
7. She buys and sells fruit.
8. Paul and I packed a bag.

B.   Copy this chart. Complete each sentence in the N V N pattern. Answers will vary.

N	V	N
1. _____	fixed	my chipped tooth.
2. Captain Elliot	studied	_____.
3. _____	wrecked	_____.
4. Ann Redsky	_____	an umbrella.
5. _____	sells and services	tape recorders.

C.   Make a chart of your own for the N V N pattern. Write five sentences in the N V N pattern. Answers will vary.

Part 4   The N V N N Pattern

The **N V N N pattern** describes a sentence with four parts. The first N stands for the subject noun or pronoun. The V stands for the verb. The second N stands for the indirect object, and the third N stands for the direct object. Any of the parts may be compound, but the verb rarely is. Each of the sentences in the following chart is in the N V N N pattern.

N	V	N	N
Tom	wrote	me	a letter.
Loud drums	give	Dad	a headache.
My mother	offered	Diane	a ride to school.
Phil and Jean	showed	Lola and me	slides and photos.

Exercises   Use the N V N N pattern.

Make a chart like the one above. Label the four columns N, V, N, and N. Write these sentences on the chart.

1. Janet threw me a curve.
2. Mr. Ortiz gave John and Louisa the job.
3. The teacher asked me the trickiest question of all.
4. Every visitor sent us a thank-you note.
5. The Paines served us homemade bread and soup.

B.   Copy and complete each sentence in the N V N N pattern. Answers will vary.

N	V	N	N
1. _____	sent	us	a bill.
2. The Senator	gave	the reporters	_____.
3. _____	offered	_____	a chance.
4. Television	_____	Phil and me	_____.
5. _____	left	_____	a message.

C.   Make a chart of your own for the N V N N pattern. Write five sentences in the N V N N pattern.   Answers will vary.

457

Objective

To recognize the basic word order in the N V N N sentence pattern

Presenting the Lesson

1. Read and discuss this page. Emphasize the pattern of direct object after indirect object.
2. Assign and discuss Exercises A, B, and C on this page.

Individualizing the Lesson

Less-Advanced Students

Work with the students to complete Exercise C.

Advanced Students

Have the students add modifiers to the sentences they wrote for Exercises B and C.

Reinforcement Exercise

Assign and discuss Exercise D on page 461.

Optional Practice

Have the students add the sentences in Exercise A on page 325 to the charts they made for Exercise A.

Extending the Lesson

1. Have each student find a sentence in the N V N N pattern in a short story.
2. Have the students suggest alternative indirect objects for the sentences in Exercise A.

Objective

To recognize the basic word order in the N LV N sentence pattern

Presenting the Lesson

1. Read and discuss this page. Point out that both the *N*'s refer to the same thing (e.g., bees and ants = social insects).

2. Assign and discuss Exercises A, B, and C on this page.

Individualizing the Lesson

Less-Advanced Students

1. Review definitions of *linking verb, predicate noun,* and *predicate pronoun.*

2. Work with the students to complete Exercise C.

Advanced Students

Have the students expand the sentences they wrote for Exercise C, adding modifiers to the subject, verb, and predicate noun.

Reinforcement Exercise

Assign and discuss Exercise E on page 462.

Optional Practice

Have the students find the sentences in Exercise A on page 328 that are in the N LV N pattern and add them to the charts they made for Exercise A.

Part 5   The N LV N Pattern

The **N LV N pattern** describes a sentence with three parts. The first N stands for the complete subject noun or pronoun. LV stands for a linking verb. The second N stands for a predicate noun or pronoun. Any part may be compound, but the verb rarely is.

N	LV	N
Bees and ants	are	social insects.
The best movie	was	the last one.
English and art	are	my best subjects.
Alexis	will be	the director of the play.

Exercises Use the N LV N pattern.

A. Make a chart like the one above. Label the three columns *N, LV,* and *N.* Write these sentences on the chart.

1. A lizard is a reptile.
2. The painting was a fake.
3. The dodo is an extinct bird.
4. Eggrolls are a great snack.
5. Jeff and I are brother and sister.
6. My entry was my stamp collection.
7. Scotty may become the new mascot.
8. The prizes are a radio and a bicycle.

B. Make a chart like the one below. Complete each sentence in the N LV N pattern. Answers will vary.

N	LV	N
1. _____	is	my favorite meal.
2. The winner	was	_____.
3. _____	may become	superstars.
4. My father and sister	_____	the family cooks.
5. _____	will be	_____.

C. Make a chart of your own. Label the columns *N, LV,* and *N.* Write five sentences in the N LV N pattern. Answers will vary.

Part 6   The N LV Adj Pattern

There are three parts to sentences that have the N LV Adj pattern. The *N* stands for the subject noun or pronoun. *LV* stands for a linking verb. *Adj* stands for a predicate adjective. Any of the parts may be compound. Each of the sentences in the following chart is in the N LV Adj pattern.

N	LV	Adj
The surprise party	was	successful.
Bob's costume	is	weird.
Bert and I	were	lost.
Katy	looks and sounds	angry.
The audience	seemed	lively and enthusiastic.

Exercises   Use the N LV Adj pattern.

A. Make a chart like the one above. Label the three columns *N*, *LV*, and *Adj.* Write these sentences on the chart.

1. You look and act happy.
2. The crust was soggy.
3. Diana sounds impatient.
4. These socks feel scratchy.
5. The cat is cozy and warm.
6. My plants look healthy.
7. Nick and I felt seasick.
8. Nan's memory is accurate.

B. Make a chart like the one below. Complete each sentence in the N LV Adj pattern. Answers will vary.

N	LV	Adj
1. _____	was	hilarious.
2. Our town	looked	_____.
3. Velvet	feels	_____.
4. Jill	_____	talented and ambitious.
5. _____	will be	_____.

C. Make a chart of your own. Label the columns *N*, *LV*, and *Adj.* Write five sentences in the N LV Adj pattern. Answers will vary.

459

Part 6

Objective

To recognize the basic word order in the N LV Adj sentence pattern

Presenting the Lesson

1. Read and discuss this page. Review linking verbs, and stress the distinction between N LV N and N LV Adj.

2. Assign and discuss Exercises A, B, and C on this page.

Individualizing the Lesson

Less-Advanced Students

Work with the students to complete Exercise C.

Advanced Students

Have the students expand the sentences they wrote for Exercise C, adding modifiers to the subject, verb, and predicate adjective.

Reinforcement Exercises

Assign and discuss Exercises F and G on pages 462 and 463.

Optional Practice

Have the students identify the pattern of each of these sentences:

The tea is ready.
Mark carried the props.
The scenery has been painted.
Sue handed her dad the keys.
That handle is the brake.

Reinforcement Exercises

These Reinforcement Exercises may be used for additional practice as needed. Each exercise may be used after the text page indicated in parentheses.

Review

If you have not assigned these Exercises before this time, you can use them as an excellent Section Review.

Mixed Review

The following exercises provide review of the concepts and skills presented in this chapter.

A. Find the sentence patterns. Write the pattern for each of the following sentences.

1. The messenger handed me the telegram. NVNN
2. Judy and Raul walked to the party. NV
3. That joke is hilarious! N LV Adj.
4. Sandra Day O'Connor is a Supreme Court Justice. N LV N
5. Larry made some popcorn. NVN
6. The store detective casually mingled with the shoppers. NV
7. The steak was hot and juicy. N LV Adj.
8. I will give Leslie the combination to my locker. NVNN
9. The skiers rode the chair lift to the top of the mountain. NVN
10. The dominant spice in that Indian dish was curry. N LV N

B. Use the sentence patterns. Write two original sentences for each of the sentence patterns.   Sentences will vary.

1. N V
2. N V N
3. N V N N
4. N LV N
5. N LV Adj.

Reinforcement Exercises—Review

Sentence Patterns

A. Put the words in order. (Use after page 454.)

Arrange each group of words to form a sentence. Some groups may be arranged in more than one way.

1. tripped Peter   Peter tripped.
2. rang the once telephone   The telephone rang once.
3. sat Elena the on cat   Elena sat on the cat.
4. fun party the was   The party was fun.
5. choice my first Lauren is   My first choice is Lauren.

B. Find the N V pattern. (Use after page 455.)

Each of the following sentences is in the N V pattern. Make a chart with two columns labeled *N* and *V*. Write each sentence on the chart.

1. Susan | called.
2. The bus | arrived on time.
3. Mr. Coe | wrote quickly.
4. The faucet | dripped constantly.
5. Ramon and his sisters | were at work.
6. The paper clips | spilled all over the floor.
7. My new sneakers | fit perfectly.
8. Every store in town | closed for the holiday.
9. The fifteen soccer players | looked at the coach.
10. Two of the presents | won't be delivered until Tuesday.

C. Find the N V N pattern. (Use after page 456.)

Each of the following sentences is in the N V N pattern. Make a chart with three columns labeled *N, V,* and *N.* Write each sentence on the chart.

1. The bell startled everyone.
2. Kim and I made breakfast.
3. She can't find any good skates.
4. Someone has bought that old theater.
5. Greg ordered a sandwich and some salad.
6. Terry and Paul use those machines.
7. We wanted one picture from each family.
8. Each animal follows a different diet.
9. The corner market sells a wide variety of magazines.
10. Everyone in the audience loved the songs and the music.

D. Find the N V N N pattern. (Use after page 457.)

Each of the following sentences is in the N V N N pattern. Make a chart with four columns labeled *N, V, N,* and *N.* Write each sentence on the chart.

1. I offered him my seat.
2. The agency sent us a typist.
3. That company gives everyone a bonus.
4. Coach Allen handed me the stopwatch.
5. The Red Cross gave the victims food and clothing.
6. No one told me anything about it.
7. Doctor Wong gave the baby two vaccination shots.
8. The people in the street gave the musician money and applause.
9. The department store sent me an application form.
10. Some movie studios will send you autographed pictures of stars.

C. Change the patterns. Rewrite each sentence so that it matches the pattern given in parentheses. You will have to add or drop words.

Sentences will vary.

1. We finally asked for directions. (N V N)
2. This dog is a champion. (N LV Adj.)
3. The opera star sang an aria. (N V)
4. Barry sent a birthday gift. (N V N N)
5. Ms. Garfield saw a local broadcaster. (N LV N)
6. The crowd watched the game intently. (N V)
7. The clock sounded the hour. (N LV Adj.)
8. The mail carrier left me a package. (N V N)
9. My older brother is very talented. (N LV N)
10. Charlene made a beautiful hanging planter. (N V N N)

Using Grammar in Writing

1. Have the students write five sentences about five different means of transportation. (Suggest planes, ships, trains, cars, trucks, space shuttles, and hot-air balloons.) Have them use only N V sentences.

2. Have the students complete these sentences in the N V pattern:

The sun . . .
Matt and Josh . . .
A patch of earth . . .
Only good friends . . .

3. Have the students write five sentences about things that they have done or that have happened to them since they left home this morning, using only N V N sentences.

4. Have the students write a fable, using at least four N V N N sentences to illustrate the saying "Good things come in small packages."

5. Have the students define the following terms by writing N LV N sentences:

leader friend
dream home

6. Have the students write N LV Adj sentences indicating their opinions of the following:

babysitting gym class
ice cream Halloween
computers rainbows

E. Find the N LV N pattern. (Use after page 458.)

Each of the following sentences is in the N LV N pattern. Make a chart with three columns labeled *N*, *LV*, and *N*. Write each sentence on the chart.

1. Amelia Earhart is my idol.
2. Their vacation was a nightmare.
3. The rainbow is a symbol of good luck.
4. Sherry will be my new boss.
5. The best candidates are Frank and Elizabeth.
6. Bowling and basketball are good sports for the winter.
7. The manager of the team is Georgia.
8. The frog is one of the most common amphibians.
9. This was their first victory in months.
10. The eruption of Mount St. Helens was front-page news.

F. Find the N LV Adj pattern. (Use after page 459.)

Each of the following sentences is in the N LV Adj pattern. Make a chart with three columns labeled *N*, *LV*, and *Adj*. Write each sentence on the chart.

1. I am chilly.
2. That bus looks crowded.
3. Their costumes were flashy.
4. Grapefruit and lemons are sour.
5. My hands feel sticky.
6. Jim's fiddle is broken.
7. Those apartments look spacious and very modern.
8. Tony is becoming famous for his salads.
9. That application blank is awfully confusing.
10. The next scene will be frightening.

462

G. Find the patterns. (Use after page 459.)

Write the pattern for each of the following sentences.

1. The dishes are dry. N – LV – Adj.
2. Everyone ran outside. N – V
3. Alan gave me an apple and half a sandwich. N – V – N – N
4. That tree is a sugar maple. N – LV – N
5. Our television was new. N – LV – Adj.
6. The lights in the auditorium flickered. N – V
7. My sister Pam can fix anything. N – V – N
8. Carlos offered me his new shinguards and face mask. N – V – N – N
9. Jeff and his family visited the Statue of Liberty in New York. N – V – N
10. The science fair will be fun. N – LV – Adj.

Section 8

Using Compound and Complex Sentences

When you were studying Section 1, you noticed that the title was "The Simple Sentence." In that section you studied about subjects, predicates, objects, predicate words, and so on.

The simple sentence has one kind of structure. There are also compound and complex sentences. They have other kinds of structure. The basis for these other kinds of sentences is the simple sentence. It is a good idea to begin your study of the more complicated kinds of sentences by reviewing the simple sentence.

1. To analyze simple sentences with compound sentence parts
2. To understand the form and function of compound sentences
3. To punctuate compound sentences correctly
4. To distinguish between compound sentences and sentences with compound verbs
5. To distinguish between clauses and phrases
6. To understand the form of subordinate clauses
7. To analyze complex sentences
8. To recognize subordinate clauses as sentence fragments
9. To identify adverb clauses
10. To identify adjective clauses
11. To use *who* and *whom* correctly in relative clauses
12. To identify noun clauses

Preparing the Students

Write these sentences on the board:

Tim was late. He woke up late. He missed the bus.

Point out that these three sentences can be combined into one. Explain that Section 8 will show how related ideas can be combined.

Additional Resources

Mastery Test—See pages 47-48 in the test booklet. Recommended for use after teaching the chapter.
Reinforcement Exercises—See pages 493-497 in the student text.
Skills Practice Book—pages 144-154.
Duplicating Masters—pages 144-154.

Part 1

Objective

To analyze simple sentences with compound sentence parts

Presenting the Lesson

1. Read and discuss pages 466-467. These pages are a review of information in Section 1.

2. Assign and discuss Exercises A and B on pages 467 and 468.

Individualizing the Lesson

Less-Advanced Students

1. For Exercise A, have the students make two columns for the subject and predicate, labeled *Who or What* and *Did or Happened*.

2. For Exercise B, have the students first copy each sentence, drawing a line between subject and predicate.

3. Review Section 1 as needed before continuing instruction in this Section.

Advanced Students

Do the Exercises orally.

Reinforcement Exercise

Assign and discuss Exercise A on page 493.

Optional Practice

Have the students identify subjects, predicates, and compound subjects, verbs, and objects in Exercises B, C, and D on pages 460 and 461.

Part 1 Review of the Simple Sentence

The **simple sentence** has two basic parts, subject and predicate.

SUBJECT	PREDICATE
Days	passed.
Time	flies.
People	asked.
Several people	asked questions.
Many people in the room	asked questions about the movie.

The **subject** of a sentence names the person or thing about which something is said. The **predicate** tells something about the subject.

The **simple predicate** is the verb. The subject of the verb is called the **simple subject.**

In the subject part of the sentence, you will find the simple subject and words that modify it. In the predicate part of the sentence, you will find verbs, objects, predicate words, and their modifiers.

Action Verbs and Linking Verbs

Some **action verbs** are complete in themselves.

Mike *was resting*.
A cold rain *fell*.

Some action verbs are followed by **direct objects,** which name the receiver of the action in the verb.

Bill *washed* the *car*.
Karen *raised* the *window*.

Some verbs do not tell of an action. They tell only that

466

something is or exists. They are called **linking verbs.** They link a predicate word to the subject.

> The horse *seems* tired.
> Dan *is* the director.

Compound Parts of the Simple Sentence

All of the parts of the simple sentence may be **compound.** That is, they may themselves have more than one part.

Compound Subject	*Bob* and *I* enjoyed the concert.
Compound Verb	The crowd *rose* and *cheered*.
Compound Object	I folded the *napkins* and the *tablecloth*.
Compound Predicate Word	The show was *long* but *interesting*. The leaders were *Ryan* and *Pam*.

Now we are ready for a definition of the simple sentence.

A simple sentence is a sentence that contains only one subject and one predicate. The subject and the predicate, or any part of the subject or predicate, may be compound.

Exercises Analyze simple sentences.

A. Copy each of the following sentences. Then draw a line between the subject and the predicate.

> EXAMPLE: Tom Mix and William S. Hart | were famous actors in old Western movies.

1. Movie-goers in the 1920's | admired such greats as Greta Garbo, Rudolph Valentino, and Douglas Fairbanks, Sr.
2. Slapstick comedy | was performed by Charlie Chaplin, Harold Lloyd, and Buster Keaton.

Extending the Lesson

Have the students look for simple sentences on one page of a short story or magazine article written for adults or young adults. Then, if possible, have them look for simple sentences on one page of a story or article written for younger children. Discuss the fact that more mature writing is characterized by more sophisticated sentence structures.

3. Movies with sound|became popular in the late 1920's.

4. The movies in the 1930's|starred such people as Shirley Temple, Mae West, and Clark Gable.

5. The city of Hollywood|was known as "the celluloid paradise."

6. One of the greatest movies|was released in 1939.

7. This particular movie|was discussed in hundreds of magazines and newspapers.

8. *Gone with the Wind*|swept movie-goers off their feet.

9. Stars Vivien Leigh and Clark Gable|were recognized by everyone.

10. Their movie|became a film classic.

B. Number your paper from 1–10. Write the compound subjects, verbs, and objects you find in these sentences.

1. Yesterday's teens and today's youth have had a variety of interests. compound subject

2. Mini-skirts, long hair, and Beatlemania were accepted by most young people in the '60's. compound subject

3. Young people have danced and have listened to all different kinds of music. compound verb

4. Big bands and rock-and-roll music characterized the 1940's and 1950's. compound subject, compound object

5. Today's youth buy albums and tapes of many different musicians. compound object

6. Some fads of the '70's included skateboards, platform shoes, Levis, and T-shirts. compound object

7. Popular music and fashion often dictate fads. compound subject

8. The Beatles and the Rolling Stones introduced a new kind of music. compound subject

9. Since then, radios and stereos have played the music of Elton John, Linda Ronstadt, Diana Ross, the Eagles, and many others. compound subject, compound object of proposition

10. In ten years, what will you and your friends be doing? compound subject

Part 2   Compound Sentences

Sometimes two sentences are so closely related in thought that we join them together. We can join them by using *and*, *but*, or *or*.

We washed the car. Mom took us for a ride.
We washed the car, *and* Mom took us for a ride.

The book was long. It was very interesting.
The book was long, *but* it was very interesting.

A compound sentence is made by joining two or more simple sentences together.

Compound sentences are useful, but they should be written with care. Two ideas should be put into one sentence only if they are closely related. If they are not closely related, the result may be confusing and hard to follow.

Wrong   Jim painted the barn, and he is nineteen.
Right   Jim painted the barn, and John repaired the roof.

Exercise   Make compound sentences.

Join each pair of sentences by using *and*, *but*, or *or*. Place a comma before *and*, *but*, or *or*. One of the pairs of sentences should not be joined because the ideas are not related.

1. I walked my bike to the garage. I filled my tires with air. *, and*
2. The car was full. They made room for one more. *, but they*
3. Look closely at the map. You will see the river. *, and you*
4. The trap was set. The fox was too crafty. *, but the*
5. You must watch carefully. You will get lost. *, or you*
6. It rained all night. The baseball game wasn't canceled. *, but the*
7. The assembly was fun. Sit in this chair. *no relationship*
8. We like Jake. We will miss him. *, and we*
9. Carl painted the picture. Suzi made the frame. *, and*
10. The girls bought Ray a sweater. He likes it very much. *, and he*

469

Part 2

Objectives

1. To understand the form and function of compound sentences
2. To punctuate compound sentences correctly

Presenting the Lesson

1. Read and discuss this page. Stress that a compound sentence is actually two complete sentences joined by *and*, *but*, or *or*.
2. Assign the Exercise on this page. Discuss why sentence pair 7 should not be joined. Have the students suggest sentences that could be combined with each of the sentences in this pair. Also discuss which conjunction is most appropriate for each pair.
3. Read **Diagraming a Compound Sentence** on page 470.
4. Assign and discuss the Exercise on page 470.
5. Read and discuss **Punctuating Compound Sentences** on pages 471–472. Demonstrate the two ways to punctuate compound sentences by writing each example on the chalkboard both ways.
6. Assign and discuss the Exercise on page 472.

Individualizing the Lesson

Less-Advanced Students

1. Work with the students to combine the first five sentences in the Exercise on page 469. Discuss the appropriateness of *and*, *but*, or *or* to join each pair. Then have the

students complete the Exercise independently. Have the students underline the subjects and verbs in their compound sentences.

2. For the Exercise on page 470, have the students copy the sentences and circle the verbs and underline the subjects. Remind them that sentence parts may be compound. The students might diagram only the subject and verb of a few sentences.

3. For the Exercise on page 472, have the students write out each sentence, underline the subjects and verbs, and then add the proper punctuation.

Advanced Students

1. After the students have completed the Exercise on page 469, have them discuss situations in which the sentences in pair 9 might be combined with *and* or *but*.

2. Have the students diagram the sentences in the Exercise on page 470.

3. After the students have finished the Exercise on page 472, have them rewrite the sentences so that those joined by a comma and a conjunction are now joined by a semicolon. Discuss which version of each sentence is more effective.

Reinforcement Exercises

Assign and discuss Exercises B and C on page 494.

Optional Practice

Have the students add to the fol-

Diagraming a Compound Sentence

The diagram of a compound sentence shows one simple sentence above the other. The two sentences are joined by a dotted line with a "step" for the coordinating conjunction. There are two main sentence lines. Each has a subject and a predicate.

The boys explored the cave, but they found nothing.

Exercise **Recognize the parts of a compound sentence.**

Show the two main parts of these compound sentences by diagraming, or as your teacher directs.

1. The football game was scheduled for TV, but the President's speech pre-empted all programing.

2. Lucinda and I cleaned the garage, and my brothers did the yardwork.

3. Babe Ruth was a leading contributor to the game of baseball, and Babe Didrikson contributed to women's participation in all sports.

4. Amelia Earhart was a school teacher, but she later became a famous pilot.

5. I enjoy reading the books of J. R. R. Tolkien, but my favorite book is *The Good Earth* by Pearl S. Buck.

6. Do you like the modern dance of Martha Graham, or do you like the ballet of Maria Tallchief?

7. We are going to the planetarium tomorrow, and we will see a slide show there.

8. Betsy Ross may have made the first flag, but little evidence of this is available.

9. Harriet Tubman was a scout for the Union army, and she was also the most celebrated "conductor" of the Underground Railroad.

10. Tanya and I were playing checkers, but I prefer chess.

Punctuating Compound Sentences

In compound sentences, a comma should be used before the conjunction.

There is a very good reason for using the comma. The comma tells you where to pause. Without a comma, a sentence can be quite confusing:

Confusing   I painted the chair and my sister painted the table.

Better   I painted the chair, and my sister painted the table.

Sometimes the parts of a compound sentence are joined by a **semicolon (;)** instead of by a conjunction and a comma.

It snowed heavily all night; classes were canceled the next day.

The whistle blew; the game was over.

Remember the two ways to join simple sentences:

1. Join them with a comma and one of the conjunctions *and, but,* or *or.* Place the comma before the conjunction.

2. Join them with a semicolon when there is no conjunction. Place the semicolon at the end of the first sentence.

---

lowing simple sentences to make them compound:

1. Whole wheat bread is nutritious.
2. Did you stay at home last night?
3. Melissa prepared the canvas.
4. Some paintings are abstract.
5. Pull up a chair.

Extending the Lesson

Have the students find five compound sentences in a magazine article. Discuss how the ideas in each sentence are related and whether the sentences are effective.

Simple sentences should not be joined by placing a comma, alone, between them. A comma is not powerful enough to hold the sentences together.

Wrong	The symphony was over**,** we went home.
Right	The symphony was over**;** we went home.
Right	The symphony was over**,** **and** we went home.

Exercise Punctuate compound sentences.

Number your paper from 1–10. Write the last word of the first part of each compound sentence. Next write the proper punctuation mark. Then write the first word of the second part of the compound sentence.

EXAMPLE: We called for Ted but he was not ready.

Ted, but

1. Nancy brought the shovel in, and she put it behind the door.
2. The new television season has started, but I don't care for any of the new shows.
3. Nobody got the answer; the problem was too difficult.
4. Clark shimmied up the rope, and Sally watched.
5. I must start now, or I will be late.
6. My favorite actress is Cicely Tyson, and my favorite singer is Dan Fogelberg.
7. Tina and Miki went to Mardi Gras, but Luanne and I went to Florida.
8. There were over eighty people in line; I counted them.
9. Our flight to San Diego was delayed, and we missed our connection to Hawaii.
10. We drove through northern Michigan last October; the fall colors were beautiful.

Part 3 Compound Sentences and Compound Verbs

A simple sentence with a compound verb looks and sounds very much like a compound sentence. It is important to know how *compound verbs* differ from *compound sentences* for two reasons: (1) They must be punctuated differently; (2) Sometimes you can improve your writing by changing a compound sentence to a simple sentence with a compound verb.

A simple sentence, you remember, has only one subject and one predicate. The subject and any part of the predicate may be compound. Here is an example:

s.   v.   v.
The students rose to their feet and applauded.

In the sentence above, there is one subject: *students*. There are two verbs: *rose* and *applauded*. Both verbs have the same subject: *students rose* and *students applauded*. In this sentence there is only one subject-verb combination. It looks like this:

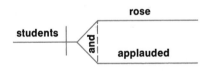

Now let's add a second subject and see what happens.

s.   v.   s.   v.
The students rose to their feet, and *they* applauded.

Now we have two subject-verb combinations. They look like this:

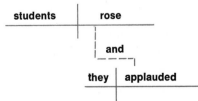

Part 3

Objective

To distinguish between compound sentences and sentences with compound verbs

Presenting the Lesson

1. Read and discuss pages 473-474. Remind the students that a compound sentence is two simple sentences, each with its own subject and verb. Explain that compound sentences in which both subjects refer to the same person or thing can be more concisely expressed as simple sentences with compound verbs.

2. Assign and discuss Exercises A, B, and C on pages 474-476.

Individualizing the Lesson

Less-Advanced Students

1. For Exercise A on page 474, have the students underline the subjects and verbs before they decide whether the sentences are compound or have compound verbs.

2. Work with the students to revise the first five sentences in Exercise C on page 476. Then have them complete the Exercise independently.

Advanced Students

1. Have the students diagram several sentences in Exercise A.

2. Complete Exercise B orally.

3. Have the students decide whether the sentences in Exercise C are more effective as simple sentences with compound verbs or as compound sentences.

Reinforcement Exercise

Assign and discuss Exercise D on page 495.

Optional Practice

Have each student write five original compound sentences.

Extending the Lesson

Have each student find one example of a compound sentence and one example of a sentence with a compound predicate in an encyclopedia entry.

You can see that the simple sentence has become a compound sentence. This has happened because of the addition of the second subject, *they*.

Now let's put the two sentences together to see the difference in the words.

Compound Sentence   The students rose to their feet, and *they* applauded.

Compound Verb   The students rose to their feet and applauded.

By dropping the second subject out of the compound sentence, we make a simple sentence that has a subject-verb combination made up of one subject and two verbs. You can do this whenever both subjects of the compound sentence refer to the same person or thing.

Sam and Andrea arrived, and *they* distributed the uniforms and the equipment.
Sam and Andrea arrived and distributed the uniforms and the equipment.

The shirt was dry, but *it* still looked dirty.
The shirt was dry but still looked dirty.

Do not place a comma between the parts of a compound verb. Study the punctuation of the sentences above.

Exercises Analyze simple and compound sentences.

A. Copy the following sentences, adding commas where necessary. After each sentence write *Compound Verb* or *Compound Sentence* to show which it is.

1. I finished my homework, and then I cleaned my room. Compound Sentence

2. I like all science fiction movies, but I really enjoy the old *Star Trek* programs. Compound Sentence

3. The dogs barked wildly and ran after the truck. Compound Verb

4. The dogs snarled at the mail carrier, but she paid no attention. Compound Sentence

5. The jet made an emergency landing, but no one on board was injured. Compound Sentence

6. The early bird gets the worm, but who wants worms? Compound Sentence

7. Has Don arrived, or has he been delayed? Compound Sentence

8. The lifeguard jumped down and dashed into the water. Compound Verb

9. For an hour we sat by the telephone and just waited. Compound Verb

10. A plane takes off or lands at O'Hare Airport every 45 seconds. Compound Verb

B. Copy these sentences. Underline each subject once and each verb twice. After each sentence write *Simple* or *Compound* to show what kind it is.

1. We saw the King Tut exhibit in New Orleans. Simple

2. The exhibit was a gesture of good will to the people of the United States from the Egyptians. Simple

3. The Wright Brothers flew their plane in Kitty Hawk, North Carolina, on December 17, 1903. Simple

4. A four-cylinder engine and two propellers gave power to their plane, and the aircraft flew a hundred feet for a total of twelve seconds. Compound

5. Queen Elizabeth II became the monarch of Britain and the Commonwealth at the age of twenty-five. Simple

6. Paper currency is printed at the Bureau of Engraving and Printing in Washington, D.C., but some coins are made at the U.S. Mint in Denver. Compound

7. Elfreth's Alley is the oldest continuously occupied residential street in America. Simple

8. It dates back to the 1690's and is one of the historic landmarks of Philadelphia. Simple

9. Jamestown, Virginia, was the first permanent English colony in the New World. Simple

10. The original Fort James was built in 1607, and today's visitors to the fort may see a full-scale reconstruction. Compound

475

C. Make a simple sentence with a compound verb from each of the following compound sentences. Be sure to use the correct punctuation in your new sentence.

1. In Acadia National Park in Maine, we built a bonfire, and we had a cookout.
2. Our 4-H Club showed black angus cattle, and we displayed home-grown vegetables.
3. In the late 1800's, immigrants flocked to the United States, and they registered with government officials at Ellis Island.
4. On our vacations, we have visited several Amish villages, and we have seen many Indian reservations.
5. A tree fell during the storm, and it landed on our carport.
6. Snow fell all night, and it buried everything in sight.
7. Our hockey team was victorious in the semifinals, and we finished second in the finals.
8. Paint dripped from the brush, and it fell onto the rug.
9. The waves pounded against the small sailboats, and they lashed against the weatherbeaten dock.
10. Vince, Maria, and Kate attended the concert, and they went out for a snack afterwards.

Part 4

Objectives

1. To distinguish between clauses and phrases
2. To understand the form of subordinate clauses
3. To analyze complex sentences

Presenting the Lesson

1. Read and discuss the introduction on pages 476-477. Write

Part 4   Complex Sentences

Before you can know what a complex sentence is, you need to know about clauses.

A clause is a group of words that contains a verb and its subject.

According to this definition, a simple sentence is a clause since it has both a verb and subject.

s.   v.

Jerry put the boxes behind the garage.

s.   v.

Sue read the announcements.

It will be easier to understand sentences, however, if we think of a clause as *part of a sentence*. We will think of a clause as *a group of words within a sentence*.

How about compound sentences? Do they contain clauses? Do they contain two or more groups of words that have a subject and a verb? Look at these examples:

s.   v.   s.   v.
Jane hit the ball, and it flew into the bleachers.

s.   v.   s.   v.
We found the box, but it was empty.

The answer is clear. Compound sentences do contain groups of words that have their own subjects and verbs.

Now, let's break up these compound sentences into their main parts and see what happens.

Jane hit the ball. It flew into the bleachers.
We found the box. It was empty.

Each of the clauses in the compound sentences can become a sentence by itself.

Phrases and Clauses

Can you tell the difference between a *phrase* and a *clause*? Look at these examples.

Phrases   of apples
          in the mountains

                  s.   v.
Clauses   that you are talking about

                  s.   v.
          who asked for you

A clause has a subject and a verb. A phrase does not.

the following sentences on the chalkboard:

> We can hike through the forest, or we can follow the river bank.
> I waited for Ralph, but he never arrived.
> The sky was gray, and the wind was brisk.

Have the students identify the clauses in each sentence.

2. Read and discuss **Phrases and Clauses** on page 477. Write the following on the chalkboard:

> when morning came
> in the morning
> because we were late
> by late afternoon

Have the students identify the clauses and tell how they were able to identify them.

3. Read and discuss **Main Clauses** and **Subordinate Clauses** on page 478. Have the students study the list of words often used as subordinating conjunctions. As an example of a word that is not always used as a subordinating conjunction, write the word *after* on the chalkboard with the following:

> after we ate dinner
> after dinner

Have the students identify the clause and tell how *after* is used in the phrase.

4. Assign and discuss the Exercise on page 479.

5. Read and discuss **Definition of the Complex Sentence** on page 479. Have the students identify the main clause and subordinate clause in each of the sample sentences.

6. Assign and discuss Exercises A and B on page 480.

1. Work with the students to make subordinate clauses from the first five sentences in the Exercise on page 479. Then have the students complete the Exercise independently.

2. For Exercise A on page 480, first have the students underline all subjects and verbs. To help them find subordinate clauses, have them check the list of subordinating conjunctions on page 478.

3. Before the students begin Exercise B, review the definitions of simple, compound, and complex sentences. Have the students copy the sentences and underline all subordinate clauses. Then have them identify sentences as simple, compound, or complex.

Advanced Students

1. Do the Exercise on page 479 orally. Have the students experiment with the subordinating conjunctions listed on page 478 to see which others can be used to make subordinate clauses from the sentences.

2. Have the students identify the subordinating conjunction in each sentence in Exercise A on page 480.

Optional Practice

Have the students write complex sentences using the clauses they wrote for the Exercise on page 479.

Main Clauses

A clause that can stand as a sentence by itself is a **main clause.** All the clauses in compound sentences are main clauses. They can all stand as simple sentences by themselves. That is why they are sometimes called **independent clauses.**

Subordinate Clauses

Now we will look at clauses of a different kind:

s.   v.   s.   v.
If the mail has come   When the door opened

Neither group of words above makes a complete thought. Each leaves you wondering, *Then what?*

Now, with your finger, cover the first word in each of these groups of words. What happens? Each group of words becomes a complete sentence. You can see, then, that the words *if* and *when* are important.

We say that these words **subordinate** the groups of words they introduce. They are called **subordinating conjunctions.** They introduce **subordinate clauses.**

Words used frequently as subordinating conjunctions are shown below:

Words Often Used as Subordinating Conjunctions

after	because	so that	whatever
although	before	than	when
as	if	though	whenever
as if	in order that	till	where
as long as	provided	unless	wherever
as though	since	until	while

Caution: These words are subordinating words only when they introduce a clause. Some can be used in other ways.

Exercise   Make subordinate clauses.

Using *if*, *because*, *when*, *after*, and *since*, make subordinate clauses out of these sentences. Answers will vary.

1. It was very foggy.
2. The window is broken.
3. The car stopped.
4. The dog howled.
5. The power went off.
6. You can go.
7. Our packages are ready.
8. The party ended.
9. The crowd had left.
10. It rained on Saturday.
11. The sun came out.
12. The book was lost.
13. She wore her red sweater.
14. The baby cried.
15. Everything had been said.

Definition of the Complex Sentence

Now that you know about main clauses and subordinate clauses, you are ready to learn what a complex sentence is.

A complex sentence is a sentence that contains one main clause and one or more subordinate clauses.

MAIN CLAUSE	SUBORDINATE CLAUSE
We left	before you came.
We'll go to the carnival	unless it rains tonight.
We were on the lake	when the storm began.

479

Exercises Analyze sentences and clauses.

A. Find the (subordinate clause) in each sentence. Copy it. Underline the subject once and the verb twice.

1. (Before basketball practice begins,) the team always runs 25 laps around the gym.
2. (Although the heat was on,) the room was still quite cold.
3. Stop and see us (when you come back.)
4. I put the books in my bag (so that I wouldn't forget them.)
5. Where were you (when I called for you?)
6. The water was colder (than I thought.)
7. Karen never speaks up, (although she usually knows the answers.)
8. (While we were in Philadelphia,) we saw Independence Hall and Betsy Ross's home.
9. (Although the land around Denver is flat,) it is almost a mile high.
10. We can't start the game (until the field is drier.)

B. Number your paper from 1–10. For each sentence, write *Simple, Compound,* or *Complex* to show what kind it is.

Simple 1. Mary and Elyse left in a hurry and forgot their tickets.

Complex 2. Close the door when you leave.

Complex 3. When the starting quarterback was injured, the substitute showed great talent.

Simple 4. Woodworking and weaving are both offered in the fall.

Compound 5. Have you finished, or may we help you?

Complex 6. Since Chicago is well known for deep dish pizza, we ordered it at a restaurant there.

Simple 7. Because of the city's drought, residents had to ration their water carefully.

Compound 8. Give us the tools, and we'll finish the job.

Simple 9. Jill and I waited in line for over two hours.

Complex 10. When we rode the Cog Railway to Pike's Peak, we saw herds of mountain sheep.

480

Part 5 More About Sentence Fragments

The sentence fragments that you studied in Section 1 were easy to spot. They were fragments because they lacked a verb or the subject of a verb.

Now we meet a new kind of sentence fragment, the subordinate clause. A subordinate clause has both a verb and a subject. It is still a fragment, however, because its meaning is not complete. Look at the groups of words below. Which is a complete sentence? Which is a subordinate clause?

It is time to leave
If it is time to leave

A subordinate clause must not be written as a complete sentence. It must always be joined to a main clause.

Fragment   If it is time to leave
Sentence   If it is time to leave, we will say good-bye.

Fragment   When you arrive
Sentence   When you arrive, come in the back door.

You can see that it is important to be able to recognize subordinating conjunctions. Study the list below so that you become familiar with words often used as subordinating conjunctions.

after	if	unless
although	in order that	until
as	provided	whatever
as if	since	when
as long as	so that	whenever
as though	than	where
because	though	wherever
before	till	while

Objective

To recognize subordinate clauses as sentence fragments

Presenting the Lesson

1. Read and discuss this page. Emphasize that, although a subordinate clause has a subject and a verb, it is not a complete thought.

2. Assign and discuss Exercises A, B, and C on page 482.

Individualizing the Lesson

Less-Advanced Students

1. Work with the students to complete Exercise A.

2. Assign Exercise B as independent work.

3. Require each student to write only three sentences for Exercise C.

Advanced Students

1. Do Exercises A and B orally.

2. Require the students to write all six of the sentences they compose for Exercise C on a single topic.

Optional Practice

Copy fifteen or twenty of the best sentences written for Exercise C on a spirit duplicating master, without underlining the subordinate clauses. Have the students underline the subordinate clause in each sentence and circle the subordinating conjunction.

Extending the Lesson

Have the students search for sentence fragments in dialogue in a short story. Have them identify any fragments that are subordinate clauses.

Exercises Recognize sentence fragments.

A. Number your paper from 1–10. Decide whether the groups of words below are sentences or fragments. Write *S* for *Sentence* or *F* for *Fragment*. Add words to make each fragment a complete sentence. Punctuate and capitalize where necessary.

Sentences will vary.

1. after the shower we saw a rainbow S
2. after the show had ended F
3. where the school always has its football games F
4. where is the box of candy S
5. since yesterday morning, the air has been clear S
6. since we have no food left F
7. because of the storm, our lights went off S
8. because the doctor advised plenty of rest F
9. when are you leaving for Europe S
10. when the old mine was closed down F

B. Follow the directions for Exercise A. Sentences will vary.

1. down the mountain rolled a boulder S
2. since the beginning of school F
3. since you agree, we can go ahead with the plans S
4. until the manager came out and stopped the noise F
5. where the car went off the road F
6. when the wind is from the south, we get rain S
7. where is the box for this puzzle S
8. before the lifeguard could reach the boat F
9. while we waited for our ride F
10. although the movie was canceled, we had a good group discussion S

C. On page 478 is a list of subordinating conjunctions. Choose six of the conjunctions that have not been used in Exercise A above. Use each conjunction in an original complex sentence. Underline the subordinate clause in each of your sentences.

Answers will vary.

482

Part 6   Adverb Clauses

An **adverb** is a word that modifies a verb, an adjective, or another adverb.

Adverb   Pam sat *down*.

An **adverb phrase** is a prepositional phrase used as an adverb. Adverb phrases usually modify verbs.

Adverb phrase   Pam sat *in the rocking chair*.

An adverb clause is a subordinate clause used as an adverb.

Adverb clause   Pam sat *where she would be comfortable*.

Adverbs and adverb phrases or clauses tell *where, when, how,* or *to what extent* about the word they modify.

Remember that a *clause* contains a subject and a verb. A *phrase* has neither a subject nor a verb.

Adverb clauses are always introduced by subordinating conjunctions:

after	because	so that	whatever
although	before	than	when
as	if	though	whenever
as if	in order that	till	where
as long as	provided	unless	wherever
as though	since	until	while

Some of the words above may also be used as prepositions. They are called subordinating conjunctions only when they introduce an adverb clause.

Preposition   *before* the game

Subordinating Conjunction   *before* the game started

Part 6

Objective

To identify adverb clauses

Presenting the Lesson

1. Read and discuss pages 483-484. Have the students use the list of subordinating conjunctions on this page to add other adverb clauses to *Pam sat*; for example:

Pam sat after she had introduced the speaker.

Pam sat, although everyone else stood.

2. Assign and discuss the Exercise on page 484.

Individualizing the Lesson

Less-Advanced Students

Have the students refer to the list on page 483 to help them find the adverb clauses in the Exercise.

Advanced Students

Have the students diagram several of the sentences in the Exercise.

Reinforcement Exercise

Assign and discuss Exercise E on page 495.

Optional Practice

Have the students use the following adverb clauses in sentences:

unless we're on time
since you're not doing anything
whenever I see Tom
as I get older

Extending the Lesson

Have each student find five sentences with adverb clauses in a story or any other narrative, for example a passage from a biographical sketch.

Preposition	*after* the party
Subordinating Conjunction	*after* the food was served
Preposition	*since* that day
Subordinating Conjunction	*since* we had already started

Diagraming Adverb Clauses

The adverb clause is placed on its own line below the main clause. A dotted line is drawn from the adverb clause to the word it modifies in the main clause. The subordinating conjunction is placed on the dotted line.

Whenever we arrive on time, we surprise her.

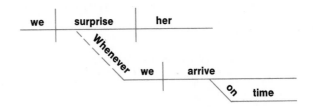

Exercise Recognize adverb clauses.

Copy the (adverb clause) from each sentence. Underline its subject once and its verb twice. Draw a circle around the subordinating conjunction.

EXAMPLE: Until I was five, I lived in New Mexico.
(Until) I was five

1. (When) we arrived in Seattle,) it was very cold.
2. (Before) we could visit the small villages,) we had to learn Japanese.
3. There was plenty of ribbon (because) we had saved it from Christmas.)
4. (Since) the mules were slow,) several tourists walked beside them.

484

5. Two partridges rose and whirred away (as we approached.)

6. (As the mist cleared,) Pike's Peak came into view.

7. (If South American mail planes are late,) search planes are alerted.

8. The geyser erupted again (before we left.)

9. (Although he had lived all his life in England,) Rick adjusted quickly to his new American lifestyle.

10. (If you had been there on Saturday,) you would have seen the precision marching.

Part 7   Adjective Clauses

An **adjective** is a word that modifies a noun or pronoun.

> *apple* box

An **adjective phrase** is a phrase that modifies a noun or pronoun:

> the box *of apples*

An **adjective clause** is a clause that modifies nouns and pronouns:

> I know the cave *that you are talking about*.

> Ms. Peters is the one *who asked about you*.

> The train, *which had been stopped*, was delayed an hour.

> Laura's the one *who telephoned us*.

An adjective clause is a subordinate clause used as an adjective to modify a noun or pronoun.

Usually, the adjective clause comes immediately after the word it modifies. Study the examples above.

Part 7

Objective

To identify adjective clauses

Presenting the Lesson

1. Read and discuss pages 485-487. Point out that all the words modified by adjective clauses are either nouns or pronouns.

2. Assign and discuss the Exercise on page 487.

Individualizing the Lesson

Less-Advanced Students

Work with the students to find and analyze the adjective clauses in the first five sentences, then have them complete the Exercise independently.

Advanced Students

Have the students diagram several sentences from the Exercise.

Reinforcement Exercise

Assign and discuss Exercise F on page 496.

Part 8

Objective

To use *who* and *whom* correctly in relative clauses

Presenting the Lesson

1. Read and discuss page 488. Stress that *who* is used as a subject in a clause while *whom* is used as an object in a clause.

2. Do Exercise A, beginning on page 488, orally. Assign and discuss Exercise B on page 489. After the Exercises have been completed correctly, have the students repeat each item several times with the relative pronoun in place so that the proper use of *who* and *whom* begins to sound natural.

Individualizing the Lesson

Less-Advanced Students

Before the students begin independent work on the Exercises, have them decide in class whether the pronoun in the blank is a subject, direct object, or object of a preposition. Help the students put the parts of the clause in natural order. For example, for the first sentence in Exercise A, rearrange the word order to read, "We spoke to _____." Then students will be more likely to see that the relative pronoun is the object of the preposition *to*.

Advanced Students

Do both Exercises orally.

The words *who, whom,* and *whose* are often used to begin adjective clauses. They tie the clause to the word it modifies in the main clause. When used in this way, *who, whom,* and *whose* are called **relative pronouns.** They relate the clause (called a **relative clause**) to the word it modifies. *That* and *which* may also be relative pronouns.

Relative Pronouns				
who	whom	whose	that	which

Relative pronouns have three jobs:

1. They begin an adjective clause.

2. They relate the adjective clause to a word in the main clause.

3. They act as subject, object, or predicate pronoun of the verb in the adjective clause. They may also be the object of a preposition in the clause.

> Kelly is the girl *who won the race.*
>   (*Who* is the subject of *won.*)
>
> Is Gayle the girl *whom you met?*
>   (*Whom* is the object of *met.*)
>
> He is the magician *of whom we were speaking.*
>   (*Whom* is the object of the preposition *of.*)

The subject form is *who.* The object form is *whom.* Which form you use depends upon how the word is used within the clause.

Exercises   Analyze relative clauses.

A.   Each relative clause is preceded by the word it modifies. Decide whether *who* or *whom* would be used in each clause. Write the pronoun. Then write its use in the clause: subject, object, or object of a preposition.

1. the guide to _____?whom_ we spoke   object of preposition
2. the doctor _____?_who_ came to see us   subject
3. the pharmacist from _____?_whom_ we got the prescription   object of preposition
4. the members _____?_who_ helped us build the float   subject
5. the teacher _____?_who_ helped us   subject
6. the family with _____?_whom_ I stayed   object of preposition
7. the runner _____?_who_ always wears a baseball cap   subject
8. the performer _____?_whom_ everyone liked best   object
9. the miners _____?_whom_ the rescue team found   object
10. the people _____?_whom_ I counted   object

B. Follow the directions for Exercise A.

1. the Indians _____?_who_ once inhabited this area   subject
2. the minister _____?_who_ performed the ceremony   subject
3. the artist _____?_who_ painted this mural   subject
4. the construction worker _____?_who_ handled the jack-hammer   subject
5. the relatives _____?_whom_ they visited   object
6. the astronauts _____?_whom_ the newscaster discussed   object
7. the journalist _____?_who_ wrote this article   subject
8. the goalie _____?_who_ wears a knit cap   subject
9. the gardener _____?_who_ grew gardenias last year.   subject
10. the grocer _____?_who_ sponsors our hockey team   subject

Part 9   Noun Clauses

You will remember that nouns can be used as subjects, as objects of verbs, as predicate words after linking verbs, and as objects of prepositions.

A **noun clause** is a clause used as a noun in a sentence. It can be used in any way that a noun is used. Noun clauses do not modify anything because nouns are not modifiers.

489

Reinforcement Exercise

Assign and discuss Exercise G on page 497.

Optional Practice

Have the students answer the following questions with sentences that use *who* or *whom* correctly in clauses:

Which of your neighbors do you know best?
Which teacher knows you best?
Which newscaster do you watch?
Which President do you admire most?

Extending the Lesson

Have the students bring newspaper sports stories to class. Ask them to find examples of *who* and *whom* in clauses and to read these aloud. Discuss whether each relative pronoun is used correctly. If the students find examples of incorrect usage, have them write letters to the writers of the stories, pointing out their errors.

Part 9

Objective

To identify noun clauses

Presenting the Lesson

1. Read and discuss pages 489-491. Emphasize the fact that a noun clause is used just as a noun is.

2. Assign and discuss Exercise A on page 491 and Exercise B on page 492.

3. Review adverb, adjective, and noun clauses.

4. Assign and discuss the Exercise at the bottom of page 492.

Individualizing the Lesson

Less-Advanced Students

1. Work with the students to complete Exercise A. Then assign Exercise B as independent work.

2. Allow the students to do the final Exercise on page 492 in pairs. Tell them to first decide whether the clause functions as a modifier or as a noun. If it is a modifier, have them determine whether it modifies a verb or a noun.

Advanced Students

1. Have the students diagram the sentences in Exercise A.

2. Have the students explain how each clause in Exercises A and B functions in its sentence.

Reinforcement Exercise

Assign and discuss Exercise H on page 497.

Optional Practice

Have the students write sentences using the following as noun clauses:

whatever you want
why he changed his mind
how blueprints are made
that the school was closed

Uses of Noun Clauses

Subject	*What we wanted* was food.
Subject	*What the magician did* astonished us.
Object	We saw *that you were in a hurry.*
Object	We know *whom you mean.*
Object of Preposition	Give the clothes to *whoever can use them.* (The clause is the object of the preposition *to*. Notice, however, that *whoever* functions as a subject within the clause.)
Object of Preposition	Jack works hard for *what he gets*. (The clause is the object of the preposition *for*.)
Predicate Noun	The answer was *what we had expected.*
Predicate Noun	The responses were *what we anticipated.*

Words That Introduce Noun Clauses

A great many noun clauses are introduced by *that* and *what*. Some are introduced by *whatever*, *whoever*, and *whomever*. Other noun clauses are introduced by *who*, *whose*, and *whom*. Still others are introduced by *where*, *when*, and *how*.

You cannot tell the kind of clause from the word that introduces it. You can tell the kind of clause only from its use in the sentence. If the clause is used as a noun, it is a noun clause. If the clause is a modifier, it is an adverb or adjective clause.

Wherever he went was a mystery. (noun clause as subject)
No one knew *where we hid*. (noun clause as object)

He left pieces of paper *wherever he went*. (adverb clause)
This is the cave *where we hid*. (adjective clause)

Diagraming Noun Clauses

A noun clause is diagramed on a bridge at the place where the clause is used in a sentence. The word that introduces the clause is placed on a horizontal line above the clause.

1. Noun clause as subject

That she wasn't coming was certain.

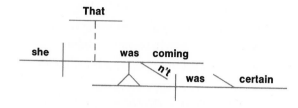

2. Noun clause as object of the verb

Donna could see *who was coming.*

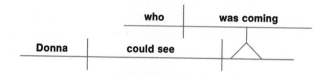

3. Noun clause as object of a preposition

We were surprised by *what happened.*

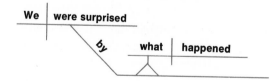

Exercises Analyze noun clauses.

A. Copy the(noun clauses) in these sentences. Underline the subject once and the verb twice. Tell how the clause is used. Your teacher may ask you to diagram the sentences.

1. I will do(whatever you decide.) object
2. (Whoever wins)gets this trophy. subject
3. Do you remember(who told you that?) object

Extending the Lesson

Have the students find an example of a sentence with a noun clause in a history or social studies textbook.

491

object   4. I don't know (where the Marcuses live.)

subject   5. (Whoever appeared) was put to work.

object of preposition   6. I was just thinking about (what you said.)

object of preposition   7. Show this card to (whoever is at the door.)

object   8. Paula didn't know (where Kevin was going.)

object   9. Our class will support (whatever candidate is chosen.)

subject   10. (Where we will go on our class trip) hasn't been decided.

B. Follow the directions for Exercise A.

subject   1. (Whoever finds Kathy's watch) will receive a reward.

subject   2. (Why they chose me) is hard to understand.

subject   3. (Whatever you decide) is all right with me.

object of preposition   4. Save these coupons for (whoever wants them.)

subject   5. (Whoever wins the tournament) deserves great recognition.

object   6. We didn't know (who was in charge of the ballot box.)

object   7. I was wondering (how you did that.)

object   8. Sally doesn't know (where the supplies are.)

object of preposition   9. Sign the papers for (whoever needs them.)

subject   10. (How you finished so quickly) is beyond me.

Exercise **Analyze clauses.**

Copy the (subordinate clauses) in these sentences. Tell whether they are adverb, adjective, or noun clauses. Underline the subject once and the verb twice.

1. We arrived (when Dr. Jordan was speaking.) adverb
2. Is this the coat (that you want?) adjective
3. Can you study (while the TV is on?) adverb
4. We did not know (who the man was.) noun
5. Jeff ducked (before the snowball hit him.) adverb
6. The plane (that leaves at 7:00 P.M.) has a feature movie. adjective
7. I don't believe (that the experiment is possible.) noun
8. Someone said (that we would have a holiday tomorrow.) noun
9. Dad lived in Colorado (when he was growing up.) adverb
10. (How the dog got out) is beyond me. noun

Reinforcement Exercises—Review

Using Compound and Complex Sentences

A. Analyze simple sentences. (Use after page 468.)

Label four columns *Subject*, *Verb*, *Object*, and *Predicate Word*. For each sentence fill in the appropriate columns. Some sentences may have compound parts.

EXAMPLE: Their confidence and determination impressed and surprised the other team.

SUBJECT	VERB	OBJECT	PREDICATE WORD
confidence	impressed	team	
determination	surprised		

1. Their supply of butane gas was low.
2. The sky looks brighter and clearer to the west.
3. The fields and meadows were covered with daisies.
4. The entire week was hot and muggy.
5. The hot sun and the humidity made football practice impossible.
6. Mariners watch the wind and clouds carefully.
7. The shutters and doors flapped and banged.
8. Darnell and I baked cookies for our picnic.
9. The books and the china were all ready for shipment.
10. The librarian ordered some new encyclopedias and a new atlas.

Reinforcement Exercises

These Reinforcement Exercises may be used for additional practice as needed. Each exercise may be used after the text page indicated in parentheses.

Review

If you have not assigned these Exercises before this time, you can use them as an excellent Section Review.

Mixed Review

The following exercises provide review of the concepts and skills presented in this chapter.

A. Recognize clauses. Copy the <u>subordinate clause</u> from each sentence. Tell whether it is an adverb, adjective, or noun clause. If it is an adverb or adjective clause, write the word or words it modifies.

1. You will not be admitted <u>unless you have a ticket</u>.
2. Chuck Yeager is the pilot <u>who broke the sound barrier</u>.
3. <u>Whoever called</u> did not leave a message.
4. The football players headed for the locker room <u>before we could ask for autographs</u>.
5. I don't know <u>what Katie is planning</u>.
6. Chess is a game <u>that requires great concentration</u>.
7. <u>Although the car was old</u>, it started faithfully every day.
8. The witnesses disagreed about <u>what happened at the scene of the accident</u>.

9. Put the receipts in the drawer where the bills are kept.
10. When the President arrived, the band played "Hail to the Chief."

1. adverb (will be admitted)
2. adjective (pilot)
3. noun
4. adverb (headed)
5. noun
6. adjective (game)
7. adverb (started)
8. noun
9. adjective (drawer)
10. adverb (played)

B. Recognize simple, compound, and complex sentences. Copy each sentence and tell whether it is simple, compound, or complex.

1. Mr. Graham buys and sells used cars.
2. The watch that Aunt Ellen gave me keeps perfect time.
3. David selected the paint color, and the salesman mixed it for him.
4. That lamp, which is an antique, is a genuine Tiffany lamp.
5. The houses on the top of that hill overlook San Francisco Bay.
6. The tigers in the zoo were sleeping, but the lions were roaring.
7. Whoever that was in the movie is a talented actor.
8. When we land in New York, we will take a cab to the hotel.
9. Lisa and Marie had cheese, fruit, and French bread for lunch.
10. Did you paint the living room, or did you wallpaper it?

1. simple
2. complex
3. compound
4. complex
5. simple

B. Make compound sentences. (Use after page 471.)

Join each pair of sentences by using *and, but,* or *or.* Place a comma before *and, but,* or *or.* One pair of sentences should not be joined because the ideas are not related. Can you find that pair?

1. Jim groomed four horses. , but he He didn't have time for the fifth.
2. Trudy went at 10 o'clock. , but the The store was still not open.
3. Do you want to make lunch? , or do Do you want to go to Burger King?
4. The short circuit in the toaster blew the fuse. The iron did it. *no relationship*
5. The tide was in. , and the The beach in the cove was covered.
6. We were going to the motocross races. , but the The heavy rain has delayed them until next week.
7. Do you enjoy ice skating? , or do Do you prefer tobogganing?
8. Our class collected aluminum cans. , and we We took them to the recycling center.
9. Marsha counted fourteen hawks. , and Sara saw eighteen.
10. The bus was full. , but the The driver was nowhere to be seen.

C. Punctuate compound sentences. (Use after page 472.)

Number your paper from 1–10. Write the last word of the *first* part of each compound sentence. Next write the proper punctuation mark. Then write the first word of the second part of the compound sentence.

1. Bill opened the door, and two dogs rushed in.
2. I like to read short stories, but I really enjoy long, detailed mysteries.
3. The helicopter flew over the park; that's its usual route.
4. Mrs. Stuart has about fifty different kinds of plants in her windows; you can hardly see out.
5. Our field trip to Knotts Berry Farm was fun, but I liked the tour at Universal Studios the best.

494

6. Should we buy Tim a birthday present, or should we make him something?

7. The great auk is a diving bird; it is almost 30 inches long.

8. Jeff stood close to the house, and Pete got on his shoulders.

9. Sandy pitches best, but Lana is the best batter.

10. I'll lend you some money; you can pay me tomorrow.

D. Analyze simple and compound sentences.
(Use after page 476.)

Copy these sentences. Underline each subject once and each verb twice. After each sentence write *Simple* or *Compound* to show what kind it is.

1. The key was on the table, and I hung it up. Compound

2. He patched and cleaned the sail of the boat. Simple

3. I threw the trash into the basket, but I didn't notice any magazines. Compound

4. The trees lined and shaded the avenue. Simple

5. Foreign newspapers come in at noon, and Lee buys one on her way home. Compound

6. A wind started about suppertime and blew hard. Simple

7. I finished quickly and went outside. Simple

8. José looked toward the noise and then pointed. Simple

9. Joan and Tom planted and fertilized each little tree. Simple

10. It rained all afternoon, and my sister and I stayed in and played chess. Compound

E. Recognize adverb clauses. (Use after page 485.)

Copy each adverb clause. Underline its subject once and its verb twice. Draw a circle around the subordinating conjunction.

1. If the shelf is too low, move it up.

2. When the alarm sounded, all classes left the building.

6. compound
7. complex
8. complex
9. simple
10. compound

C. Recognize fragments, phrases, and clauses.
Decide whether the following groups of words are sentences or fragments. Write *S* for *Sentence* or *F* for *Fragment.* Tell whether each fragment is a phrase or a clause. Then write each group of words as a complete sentence with proper capitalization and spelling.

1. where the ball was lost yesterday
2. inside the dirty, run-down shed
3. few complained about the long lines
4. because Jonathon ate all the oatmeal cookies
5. at the new art museum
6. get ready quickly
7. whatever Ben does, he does well
8. don't forget the hamburger buns
9. although every effort was made to maintain order
10. after a long, difficult climb

Sentences will vary.

1. F clause
2. F phrase
3. S
4. F clause
5. F phrase
6. S
7. S
8. S
9. F clause
10. F phrase

Using Grammar in Writing

1. Have the students write a dialogue between two students on the subject of music, using only simple sentences. Have the students discuss whether simple sentences make the speakers sound like students.

2. Have the students write a paragraph comparing two sports figures, two animals, or two vacation spots. Each sentence in the paragraph should be compound and should mention both of the subjects being compared.

3. Have the students combine the following sentence pairs into complex sentences. Remind them to choose an appropriate subordinating conjunction.

> The Superman movie was full of action. It lacked humor.
>
> I heard that song on the radio. I laughed.
>
> Do warm-up exercises. Then jog.
>
> Pollution is under control. The air will be cleaner.

4. Have the students combine the following fragments and sentences to make complex sentences.

> When it rains. I ride the bus.
>
> I spend money. Whenever I earn money.
>
> Trisha can drive. Because she's sixteen.
>
> Congress makes the laws. Although the President can veto them.

5. Have the students combine the following sentence pairs by using adverb clauses:

> There were no chairs. We sat on the floor.
>
> The cafeteria serves lunch. Some students eat lunch at home.
>
> Lightning always appears first. Then the thunder crashes.

6. Have the students write a paragraph about clouds, defining three

3. (Wherever he went,) he took his Spanish-English dictionary.

4. (Since we had lots of time,) we stayed for dessert.

5. Juanita hurt her ankle (as she was running the hurdles.)

6. (If you want my opinion,) it's available.

7. (When you go to Philadelphia,) see Independence Hall.

8. Lauren talked (as if she would run for vice-president of the French Club.)

9. (When the trumpet fanfare began,) the audience returned to their seats.

10. (When the bobsled finally stopped,) we could barely crawl out.

F. Recognize adjective clauses. (Use after page 487.)

Copy the (adjective clause) from each sentence. Underline the subject once and the verb twice. Before the clause, write the word it modifies.

1. This is the store (that I had in mind.) store

2. We enjoyed the postcards (that you wrote from South America.) postcards

3. Mount Vernon is the home (where George and Martha Washington lived.) home

4. The book (that you wanted) has been checked out. book

5. The speaker (whom they want) charges $400. speaker

6. Do you remember the time (when you fell out of the chestnut tree?) time

7. This is my friend Tracy, (whom I was telling you about.) Tracy

8. Bob, (who had just come back from the dentist,) looked rather uncomfortable. Bob

9. It was Ben Franklin (who invented bifocals, the electrical generator, and the Franklin stove.) Ben Franklin

10. This is the album (that I want.) album

G. Analyze relative clauses. (Use after page 489.)

Decide whether *who* or *whom* would be used in each clause. Write the pronoun. Then write its use in the clause: subject, object, or object of preposition.

1. the jockey _____?whom_ you picked object
2. the pilots _____?whom_ United Airlines hires object
3. the clerk _____? who_ answered your question subject
4. the sculptor _____? who_ designed this piece of art subject
5. the butcher from _____?whom_ she usually buys her meat object of preposition
6. the singer _____? who_ did that TV special subject
7. the caterers _____?whom_ the mayor hired object
8. the mail carrier _____? who_ was on duty yesterday subject
9. the police officer with _____?whom_ you were walking object of preposition
10. the teacher to _____?whom_ you talked object of preposition

H. Recognize noun clauses. (Use after page 492.)

Copy the (noun clause) in each sentence. Tell how the clause is used.

1. (Whoever wins the tennis finals) goes to the state meet. subject
2. The plaque commemorates (what she did for the school.) object
3. (How this sewing machine works) is (what I would like to know.) subject , predicate noun
4. Nancy told me (that Maurita wasn't coming.) object
5. Most of us did not agree with (what the speaker said.) object of preposition
6. Coach Larson could see (that the defense was tiring.) object
7. Zebulon Pike was ill prepared for (whatever his expedition would face.) object of preposition
8. He did not know (that his men would encounter a bitter winter.) object
9. Carol said (that her report was about Renaissance painters.) object
10. (Whoever told you that) was wrong. subject

types of clouds. Three of the sentences in the paragraph should use adjective clauses.

7. Have the students add adjective clauses to make the meanings of these sentences more specific:

> Anyone can join the photography club.

> Everyone is going on the picnic.

8. Each of the following sentences contains an adjective clause. Have the students revise the sentences, replacing the adjective clauses with noun clauses. Discuss which version of each sentence is more concise and effective.

> The archaeologists displayed things that they had discovered in Mexico.

> The newspapers didn't report the events that happened at the White House.

> The scientist showed us the way that glass is made.

Section 9

Making Subjects and Verbs Agree

Section Objectives

1. To make the verb in a sentence agree in number with its subject
2. To make the verb in a sentence agree in number with its compound subject
3. To make the verb in a sentence agree in number with an indefinite pronoun used as its subject
4. To avoid common agreement problems

Preparing the Students

Write the following sentence on the chalkboard:

The dogs next door runs loose.

Discuss the agreement error in the sentence. Help students see that, because the subject and verb should agree, *runs* is incorrect. Tell them that Section 9 will help them make the subjects and verbs of all their sentences agree.

Additional Resources

Mastery Test—See pages 49-50 in the test booklet. Recommended for use after teaching this chapter.

Reinforcement Exercises—See pages 507-509 in the student text.

Skills Practice Book—pages 155-159.

Duplicating Masters—pages 155-159.

Part 1

Objective

To make the verb in a sentence agree in number with its subject

Part 1 Making Subjects and Verbs Agree in Number

When a word refers to one thing, it is **singular.** When it refers to more than one thing, it is **plural.** When we speak of the **number** of a word, we are talking about whether it is singular or plural.

A verb must agree in number with its subject.

Presenting the Lesson

1. Read and discuss pages 499-500. Stress that the verb must agree in number with its subject, and that the subject is never part of a prepositional phrase.

2. Assign and discuss Exercises A and B on page 501.

Individualizing the Lesson

Less-Advanced Students

1. Review singular and plural forms of common irregular verbs, such as *be, have,* and *do.*

2. Have the students copy the sentences in Exercises A and B and cross out all prepositional phrases. Then have the students find the subject so that they can select the verb that agrees with it.

Advanced Students

Do the Exercises orally.

Reinforcement Exercise

Assign and discuss Exercise A on page 507.

Optional Practice

Have the students rewrite sentences 4, 5, 6, and 7 in Exercise A and sentences 2, 5, and 10 in Exercise B, making all singular subjects and verbs plural and all plural subjects and verbs singular.

Extending the Lesson

Have each student find one published sentence in which a preposi-

If the subject is singular, the verb must be singular. If the subject is plural, the verb must be plural.

SINGULAR	PLURAL
The bird *sings.*	The birds *sing.*
She *listens.*	They *listen.*
It *whistles.*	They *whistle.*

You can see that the third person singular of the verb ends in *s.* The *s* disappears in the plural.

You will have problems in agreement of subject and verb only when you are not sure what the subject is. *Remember:* To find the subject, first find the verb. Then ask *who?* or *what?* before it.

One of the players *is* my sister.

> *Verb:* is
> *Who is?* one
> *Subject:* one

The subject of the verb is never found in a prepositional phrase.

Watch for phrases that lie between the verb and the subject.

One of the eggs *was* broken.

The *pictures* on the desk *were* torn.

Phrases beginning with the words *with, together with, including, as well as,* and *in addition to* are not part of the subject.

The *principal,* in addition to the teachers, *is* here.

Mr. Bard, together with his children, *has* left.

Exercises Make verbs agree with their subjects.

A. Choose the verb that agrees with the subject.

1. One of my front teeth (are, is) loose.
2. The captain, together with his crew, (look, looks) after the ship.
3. Several pages in the book (is, are) missing.
4. The drawings on display (was, were) done by the art classes.
5. The bus with all the players (arrives, arrive) at three.
6. The schedule for all the sports events (is, are) on the bulletin board.
7. The choice of the judges (was, were) not very popular.
8. All the signs along the road (has, have) been taken down.
9. A popcorn stand in the lobby (was, were) open.
10. The new schedule for the suburbs (has, have) more trains.

B. Follow the directions for Exercise A.

1. The doctor, together with her staff, (are, is) often here.
2. The edges of the playing field (was, were) still wet.
3. My jacket, as well as my ski pants, (is, are) wet.
4. Each of the homerooms (contribute, contributes) to the Toys-for-Tots campaign.
5. Those antique cars in the driveway (belongs, belong) to the Hadleys.
6. A request for money and provisions (was, were) granted.
7. The members of the swim team (report, reports) to the pool every morning.
8. Two of my teachers (coaches, coach) the volleyball team.
9. The girls on the team (like, likes) the coach.
10. The attendants at the airport (requires, require) passengers to check their luggage.

tional phrase separates subject and verb. Use these sentences to compose an oral exercise on subject-verb agreement.

Part 2

Objective

To make the verb in a sentence agree in number with its compound subject

Presenting the Lesson

1. Read and discuss this page. Have the students explain how each sample sentence complies with the appropriate rule.

2. Do Exercise A orally. Assign and discuss Exercise B on page 503.

Individualizing the Lesson

Less-Advanced Students

1. Review the definition of *compound subject* and *conjunction* with the students.

2. Have the students copy the sentences in Exercise B, underline the subjects, and circle the conjunctions before choosing the verb.

Advanced Students

Do both Exercises orally.

Reinforcement Exercise

Assign and discuss Exercise B on page 507.

Optional Practice

Write the conjunctions *and, or, either—or,* and *neither—nor* on the chalkboard. Circulate a spirit duplicating master among the students, and have each student write

Part 2 Compound Subjects

Compound subjects joined by *and* require a plural verb.

The truck and the trailer *were* badly damaged.
The walls and the ceiling *are* soundproofed.

When the parts of a compound subject are joined by *or* or *nor*, the verb agrees with the part nearer to it.

Either Mom or the boys *have* come home.

Neither the boys nor Mom *has* been home yet.

Either the musicians or their leader *has* your music.

Exercises Make verbs agree with their subjects.

A. Choose the verb that agrees with the subject.

1. Al and Ken (hasn't, haven't) finished repairing their old car.

2. Either the coach or the co-captains (call, calls) the time-outs.

3. Both winter and summer (is, are) mild here.

4. Either a raccoon or some dogs (has, have) gotten into the garbage.

5. The evening news and the late newspaper (report, reports) the sports results of the day.

6. Neither the tent nor the sleeping bags (arrive, arrives) until tomorrow.

7. Both the tugs and the Loganville ferry (dock, docks) here.

8. Corrine and her family (is, are) arriving tomorrow.

9. Neither my gym shoes nor my uniform (need, needs) to be laundered.

10. The players and the referee (are, is) arguing about the call.

B. Follow the directions for Exercise A.

1. Either Phil or his sister (<u>is</u>, are) bringing us home.
2. Neither the cookies nor the cake (taste, <u>tastes</u>) burnt to me.
3. The water and the beach (<u>look</u>, looks) inviting.
4. Neither complaints nor threats (has, <u>have</u>) any effect on the umpire.
5. Buildings or billboards often (obscures, <u>obscure</u>) the horizon.
6. Neither fishing nor hunting (<u>is</u>, are) permitted.
7. Both the German Club and the Spanish Club (<u>help</u>, helps) decorate the lobby for Christmas.
8. Both the ordinary frogs and the bullfrog (<u>tune</u>, tunes) up at sundown.
9. Either the dog or the cat (stay, <u>stays</u>) home.
10. Either our local newspaper or our local radio stations (<u>publicize</u>, publicizes) our school's sporting events.

Part 3   Indefinite Pronouns

The indefinite pronouns in the list below are singular:

Singular Indefinite Pronouns

another	either	nobody
anybody	everybody	no one
anyone	everyone	one
anything	everything	somebody
each	neither	someone

Each of the cars *was* given a number.
Everybody *has* a job to do.
Neither of us *has* a good enough report.

a beginning for a sentence with a compound subject, omitting the predicate. Duplicate the beginnings, and have the students complete them. Discuss subject-verb agreement.

Extending the Lesson

Have each student find five sentences with compound subjects in encyclopedia articles. Have them copy the sentences, underline the compound subject, circle the conjunction, and check the subject-verb agreement.

Part 3

Objective

To make the verb in a sentence agree in number with an indefinite pronoun used as its subject

Presenting the Lesson

1. Read and discuss pages 503-504. Have the students memorize the list of singular indefinite pronouns.
2. Do Exercise A on page 504 orally. Assign and discuss Exercise B.

Individualizing the Lesson

Less-Advanced Students

Have the students copy the sentences in Exercise B and cross out all prepositional phrases. Then have the students find the subject and choose the correct verb.

Advanced Students

Do both Exercises orally.

Reinforcement Exercise

Assign and discuss Exercise C on page 508.

Optional Practice

Have the students substitute plural indefinite pronouns for the singular ones and singular indefinite pronouns for the plural ones in sentences 1, 2, 3, 5, 7, 8, 9, and 10 in Exercise B. Have them choose the verbs that agree with the new subjects.

Extending the Lesson

Have each student find an example of a sentence with an indefinite pronoun as subject in a local newspaper. Have the students check the agreement of subject and verb.

The words *both, many, few,* and *several* are plural indefinite pronouns.

> Both of the ushers *are* new.
> Several *have* already phoned.

The words *some, all,* and *most* are singular if they refer to one part of something. They are plural if they refer to several things.

SINGULAR	PLURAL
all of the paper	all of the people
most of the work	most of the books

Exercises Make verbs agree with their subjects.

A.   Choose the verb that agrees with the subject.

1. Another of those talk shows (come, <u>comes</u>) on tonight at 10 o'clock.
2. Many of Debbie's friends (<u>were</u>, was) away.
3. Most of the boathouse (need, <u>needs</u>) painting.
4. Either Michelle or Ted (<u>is</u>, are) ushering.
5. Some of the students (<u>earn</u>, earns) extra money as ushers.
6. No one told me that Mike (were, <u>was</u>) moving to South Carolina.
7. Several of her reports (<u>compare</u>, compares) prices in different cities.
8. Everyone in Rock Hill (<u>was</u>, were) here.
9. All of the books (<u>have</u>, has) been shelved in alphabetical order.
10. Each of the ensemble members (play, <u>plays</u>) at least two instruments.

B.   Follow the directions for Exercise A.

1. Few of the honeydew melons (is, <u>are</u>) ripe.

2. One of my brothers (<u>is</u>, are) in the navy.

3. Neither of the maps (show, <u>shows</u>) Rainbow Springs.

4. These bundles of newspapers (<u>go</u>, goes) to the recycling plant.

5. Neither of us (<u>is</u>, are) ready to give our speech.

6. Most of the hay (dry, <u>dries</u>) in a week.

7. Everyone in the audience (<u>was</u>, were) captivated by the performances.

8. Both of the telephones (is, <u>are</u>) busy right now.

9. Most of the players (practices, <u>practice</u>) in the morning and the afternoon.

10. Somebody (<u>is</u>, are) responsible for writing up the club's minutes.

Part 4 Other Problems of Agreement

The pronouns *he, she,* and *it* are used with *doesn't.*
All other personal pronouns are used with *don't.*

> He *doesn't* swim well enough.
> She *doesn't* need more money.
> It *doesn't* look like rain now.

> I *don't* dance.
> We *don't* dance.
> You *don't* sing.
> They *don't* know.

In sentences beginning with *Here, There,* and *Where,* the subject comes after the verb.

> Here *is* your ticket.
> Where *is* the projector?
> There *are* the keys for the cottage.

Part 4

Objective

To avoid common agreement problems

Presenting the Lesson

1. Read and discuss page 505. Have the students read the sample sentences aloud several times.
2. Do Exercise A on page 506 orally. Then assign and discuss Exercise B.

Individualizing the Lesson

Less-Advanced Students

Help the students rearrange sentences beginning with *here, there,* and *where,* putting the subject before the verb. For review, refer to pages 319–321.

Advanced Students

Do both Exercises orally.

Reinforcement Exercise

Assign and discuss Exercise D on page 509.

Optional Practice

Have the students identify the subject in each sentence in the Exercises.

Extending the Lesson

Have the students insert personal pronouns in the blanks in these sentences:

——— doesn't give up hope.
——— don't talk much.
——— doesn't embarrass me.
——— don't eat meat.

Exercises Make verbs agree with their subjects.

A. Choose the verb that agrees with the subject.

1. It (doesn't, don't) look as if the sky will clear before noon.
2. Where (was, were) she taking those packages?
3. Here (is, are) the tube socks and T-shirts the team ordered.
4. There (go, goes) the siren.
5. That idea (doesn't, don't) make any sense.
6. Where (is, are) the box for these ornaments?
7. Here (is, are) all the sheet metal that I could find.
8. Beth (don't, doesn't) want to go apple-picking with us.
9. There (are, is) several deer on the front lawn.
10. There (are, is) the new batteries for the flashlight.

B. Choose the verb that agrees with the subject.

1. There (come, comes) the other team onto the ice.
2. (Don't, Doesn't) Jennie want to ride with us?
3. There (is, are) the float we built for the parade.
4. Erica (doesn't, don't) agree with us.
5. Here (are, is) the magazine you wanted.
6. There (was, were) few skiers on the chairlift.
7. Where (do, does) these cartons go?
8. There (are, is) a fawn and its mother in our yard.
9. Where (is, are) my Disney World T-shirt?
10. Here (is, are) some of the pictures we took last winter.

Reinforcement Exercises—Review

Making Subjects and Verbs Agree

A. Make verbs agree with their subjects. (Use after page 501.)

Choose the verb that agrees with the subject.

1. The sandbars in the Mississippi (<u>cause</u>, causes) many accidents.
2. Some sections of the city (has, <u>have</u>) no bus service.
3. Three students' paintings, including mine, (was, <u>were</u>) chosen to compete in the state art fair.
4. That lady in the gray sweat suit (jog, <u>jogs</u>) five miles a day.
5. The new books in the library (is, <u>are</u>) on a special shelf.
6. The answers to the exercise (is, <u>are</u>) in the back of the textbook.
7. The evidence on these films (<u>looks</u>, look) convincing.
8. The photographers on the yearbook staff (is, <u>are</u>) Raul and Patti.
9. The price of the German binoculars (are, <u>is</u>) too high.
10. Our team, including the coach and the cheerleaders, (take, <u>takes</u>) the bus from here.

B. Choose the right verb. (Use after page 503.)

Choose the verb that agrees with the subject.

1. Neither the fenders nor the license plate (<u>was</u>, were) dented.
2. The principal and the teachers (<u>organize</u>, organizes) a student-faculty softball game every year.

507

Reinforcement Exercises

These Reinforcement Exercises may be used for additional practice as needed. Each exercise may be used after the text page indicated in parentheses.

Review

If you have not assigned these Exercises before this time, you can use them as an excellent Section Review.

Mixed Review

The following exercises provide review of the concepts and skills presented in this chapter.

A. Use the correct verb. Write the correct verb from the two given in parentheses.

1. Each of the gymnasts (<u>inspects</u>, inspect) the equipment before a meet.
2. The encyclopedia or these magazine articles (contain, <u>contains</u>) the information you need for your report.
3. All of the food (<u>was</u>, were) eaten before I arrived.
4. The director, along with the actors, (rehearse, <u>rehearses</u>) every night.
5. Aaron and Lisa (sings, <u>sing</u>) with an amateur rock group.
6. This application form (<u>doesn't</u>, don't) have enough space for my name.
7. One of the statue's arms (<u>was</u>, were) broken off.
8. We all thought you (was, <u>were</u>) gone for the weekend.
9. Here (is, <u>are</u>) the packages you were waiting for.
10. Two painters as well as a carpenter (is, <u>are</u>) working on the old house.

B. Choose the correct verb. Write the verb that agrees with the subject.

1. Sara (don't, doesn't) know how to use this typewriter.
2. Neither of the keys (fit, fits) the lock.
3. Two pages from the book (was, were) missing.
4. Where (is, are) the plastic lawn bags for the leaves?
5. Neither the train nor the buses (run, runs) on Sunday.
6. Ms. Volker and Mr. Goulet (act, acts) in television commercials.
7. Many of the students (go, goes) on to college or a trade school.
8. Bill, as well as his sister Judy, (attend, attends) these concerts every week.
9. You (was, were) the winner of the grand prize.
10. One of the maps (is, are) incomplete.

Using Grammar in Writing

1. Have each student write a paragraph about trees, birds, animals, or fish commonly seen locally. Then have the students label each subject and verb in their paragraphs *singular* or *plural*.

2. Have the students complete the following sentences:

1. The players on the team . . .
2. A carton of eggs . . .
3. They and I . . .
4. A flock of pigeons . . .
5. A few of the fans . . .

Have the students exchange papers to check for subject-verb agreement.

3. Have each student write four sentences beginning with *there*, describing the lunchroom when it is full of students. Have the students exchange papers and check for subject-verb agreement.

3. Either my alarm clock or the clock in the den (is, are) wrong.

4. If school is canceled, the principal or one of the secretaries (telephone, telephones) the radio station.

5. Both Chico and his brother (was, were) there.

6. Neither porcupine quills nor skunks (stop, stops) our dog Rusty.

7. Either Sean or his grandparents usually (pick, picks) up the mail.

8. Yogurt and frozen yogurt (come, comes) in a variety of flavors.

9. Both the Hershey Company and Sara Lee Kitchens (has, have) tours of their food processing plants.

10. Either a van or a truck (suit, suits) our purpose quite well.

C. Choose the right verb. (Use after page 505.)

Choose the verb that agrees with the subject.

1. Some of these stamps (don't, doesn't) stick.
2. Several of the entrants (wasn't, weren't) ready.
3. Not one of the newscasts (has, have) publicized our candy sale.
4. Most of the time (was, were) wasted.
5. Everything on the two bottom shelves (belong, belongs) to David.
6. All of the fenceposts (has, have) snow on them.
7. Anything made of metal (was, were) immediately magnetized.
8. Both of the gas pumps (is, are) working.
9. Nobody in the bleachers (cheer, cheers) louder than our Pep Club.
10. Most of our supplies (come, comes) from the school store.

D. Choose the right verb. (Use after page 506.)

Choose the verb that agrees with the subject.

1. Here (is, <u>are</u>) the fire trucks.
2. Here (<u>is</u>, are) what the newspaper says about the eclipse.
3. There (goes, <u>go</u>) the runners.
4. Sam (<u>doesn't</u>, don't) ever take his eyes off the TV.
5. Here (is, <u>are</u>) the photographs that Heather picked out.
6. Where (is, <u>are</u>) the envelopes for these letters?
7. There (<u>isn't</u>, aren't) any time to waste.
8. (Don't, <u>Doesn't</u>) the *Orient Express* run any more?
9. Here (is, <u>are</u>) your tickets for the carnival.
10. She (<u>doesn't</u>, don't) know how to swim the butterfly stroke.

4. Have the students combine the following pairs of sentences:

1. Daniel Boone is a legendary hero. Johnny Appleseed is a legendary hero.
2. Television doesn't give all the news. Radio doesn't give all the news.
3. Encouragement makes a job easier. Praise makes a job easier.

Have the students exchange papers and check for subject-verb agreement.

5. Have each student write four sentences in the present tense generalizing about the opinions of the other students in the class. (Choose a topic that students might have a strong opinion about.) Each sentence must use one of the following indefinite pronouns as subject: *anybody, most, all, everyone.* Have students read their sentences. Check for subject-verb agreement. Then poll the class to check how accurate the generalization is.

Section 10

Using Verbals

Section Objectives

1. To recognize infinitives and infinitive phrases
2. To recognize participles and participial phrases
3. To recognize gerunds and gerund phrases

Preparing the Students

Read and discuss this page. Remind the students that they have already encountered words that can be used as more than one part of speech.

Write the following sentences on the chalkboard, underlining the italicized words:

1. Gary came onstage *to sing*.
2. Gary *sang*.
3. *Singing* powerfully, Gary pleased the crowd.
4. Gary's *singing* was a hit.

Point out that the underlined words are all forms of the verb *to sing*, but that in three of the sentences the words are used differently from most verbs. Explain that Section 10 will show the students three additional uses for verb forms in sentences.

Additional Resources

Mastery Test—See pages 51-52 in the test booklet. Recommended for use after teaching the chapter.

Reinforcement Exercises—See pages 520-521 in the student text.

Skills Practice Book—pages 160-167.

Duplicating Masters–pages 160-167.

You have learned that there are eight parts of speech. The eight parts of speech are these:

nouns	verbs	adjectives	conjunctions
pronouns	adverbs	prepositions	interjections

In addition to the eight parts of speech, our language contains three other kinds of words. These are **infinitives, participles,** and **gerunds.** These words are called verbals. A **verbal** is a word that is formed from a verb but acts as another part of speech.

In this chapter you will study the three kinds of verbals, and learn how they are used in the sentence.

511

Part 1

Objective

To recognize infinitives and infinitive phrases

Presenting the Lesson

1. Read and discuss this page. Have the students suggest alternative infinitives and infinitive phrases for those in the sample sentences; for example:

We wanted *to win*.
We tried *to call*.
Chris learned *to play a flute*.
We tried *to build the dog a house*.

2. Read and discuss page 513. Have the students suggest alternative infinitives and infinitive phrases for the sample sentences.

3. Do Exercise A on page 514 orally. Then assign and discuss Exercise B on page 514.

Individualizing the Lesson

Less-Advanced Students

1. Before the students begin the Exercises, remind them to look for *to* +*verb* and to include all modifiers in the phrase. Have them underline the infinitive in each phrase.

2. Warn the students that one sentence in Exercise B has two infinitives.

Advanced Students

Have the students explain how each infinitive phrase in the Exercises is used in its sentence. Then have them analyze each infinitive phrase, identifying any objects and modifiers.

Part 1   Infinitives

The **infinitive** is the name of the verbal that usually appears with the word *to* before it. *To* is called the **sign of the infinitive.**

to go   to see   to run   to walk

The word *to* is often used as a preposition. It is a preposition if it is followed by a noun or pronoun that is its object. *It is the sign of the infinitive if it is followed by a verb.* Notice these examples:

We went *to the park.* (prepositional phrase)
We wanted *to swim.* (infinitive)

We stayed *to the end.* (prepositional phrase)
We tried *to dive.* (infinitive)

Because the infinitive is formed from a verb, it is like a verb in several ways. The infinitive may, for example, have an object. It may also be modified by adverbs.

Chris learned *to run a lathe.*
   (*lathe* is the direct object of the infinitive *to run.*)

We tried *to give the dog a bath.*
   (*dog* is the indirect object and *bath* is the direct object of *to give.*)

You will need *to work fast.*
   (*fast* is an adverb modifying *to work.*)

Linda wanted *to drive the car to the station.*
   (*car* is the object of *to drive*; *to the station* is an adverb phrase modifying *to drive.*)

The infinitive with its objects and modifiers is an **infinitive phrase.**

Uses of the Infinitive Phrase

Infinitives and infinitive phrases can be used (1) as nouns, (2) as adjectives, or (3) as adverbs.

You remember that nouns are used as subjects and objects of verbs. Infinitives and infinitive phrases can be used as subjects, as objects, and in other ways that nouns are used.

Subject	*To leave early* is sometimes impolite.
	(*To leave early* is the subject of *is.*)
Object	Sue wanted *to leave.*
	(*to leave* is the object of *wanted.*)

Infinitives and infinitive phrases can be used as modifiers. If the infinitive or infinitive phrase modifies a noun or pronoun, it is used as an adjective. If it modifies a verb, adjective, or adverb, it is used as an adverb.

Adjective	The catcher is the player *to watch.*
	(*to watch* modifies the predicate noun *player.*)
Adverb	Tickets for the big game are hard *to get.*
	(*to get* modifies the predicate adjective *hard.*)
Adverb	Rick went *to see the doctor.*
	(*to see the doctor* modifies the verb *went.*)

The Split Infinitive

Sometimes a modifier is placed between the word *to* and the verb. A modifier in this position is said to split the infinitive. Usually, a split infinitive sounds awkward and should be avoided.

Awkward	Ann expects to *easily* win.
Better	Ann expects to win *easily.*

Reinforcement Exercise

Assign and discuss Exercise A on page 520.

Optional Practice

Have the students complete each of the following sentences with infinitives. Then have them tell how the resulting infinitive phrases are used.

1. Dan tried _____ through the underbrush.
2. We were not allowed _____ up the stairs.
3. _____ is my favorite job.
4. Would you like _____ baseball?

Extending the Lesson

Have each student find a newspaper headline that uses an infinitive. Have the students display these in class. Discuss how each infinitive or infinitive phrase is used. Have the students revise any split infinitives and discuss the relative effectiveness of each version.

Exercises Find the infinitives and infinitive phrases.

A. Find the infinitives and infinitive phrases in these sentences. Write each infinitive or infinitive phrase. Be prepared to tell how it is used in the sentence.

> EXAMPLE: They were ready to drop the whole thing.
>
> Infinitive phrase: *to drop the whole thing*
> (used as an adverb describing *ready*)

object   1. Mary and I plan to watch the Neil Diamond TV special.

object   2. Mr. Anderson wants to explain the new procedures.

subject   3. To finish this project by Monday is my goal.

object   4. We tried to remember the address.

object   5. We plan to visit Washington.

object   6. Judy and I were told to bring our registration cards to orientation.

adverb   7. The vet came to see our horses.

adjective   8. This is the best book to use.

adverb   9. Bill ran to get a flashlight.

adjective   10. Sue still has homework to do.

B. Follow the instructions for Exercise A.

adjective   1. This is the path to follow.

adjective, predicate noun   2. The best thing to do is to wait.

object   3. Would you like to eat breakfast at the pancake house?

subject   4. To read the first two chapters of this book is our assignment.

adjective   5. Amy has someone to help her.

object   6. Do you want to go shopping tomorrow?

object   7. He wanted to sail up the coast to Alaska.

object   8. Did you remember to buy film?

object   9. Remind me to fill out the application form tonight.

object   10. Do you want to play tennis after school?

Part 2 Participles

You remember that one of the principal parts of the verb is the **past participle.** The past participle is formed by adding *-d* or *-ed* to the present tense: *walk-walked.* The past participles of irregular verbs do not follow this rule and have to be learned separately: *bring-brought, ring-rung.*

There is another kind of participle, called the **present participle.** All present participles are formed by adding *-ing* to the present tense of the verb: *bring-bringing, ring-ringing, walk-walking.*

Participles can be used as adjectives. They can modify nouns or pronouns:

> *Smiling,* Jan accepted the award.
> (*Smiling* is a present participle modifying the noun *Jan.*)

> *Lunging,* he hit the fence.
> (*Lunging* is a present participle modifying the pronoun *he.*)

Because participles are formed from verbs, they can have objects and be modified by adverbs. The participle with its objects and modifiers forms a **participial phrase.**

> *Turning the pages,* Barb found an old letter.
> (*Turning the pages* is a participial phrase modifying Barb; *pages* is the object of the participle *turning.*)

> *Turning suddenly,* Jean bumped into Mrs. Wood.
> (*Turning suddenly* is a participial phrase modifying *Jean.* The word *suddenly* is an adverb modifying the participle *turning.*)

> *Completely exhausted,* the swimmer crawled out of the pool.
> (*Completely exhausted* is a participial phrase modifying *swimmer. Completely* is an adverb modifying the participle *exhausted.*)

515

Reinforcement Exercise

Assign and discuss Exercise B on page 520.

Optional Practice

Have the students write sentences that include the following participial phrases. The students should write two sentences for each phrase, one in which the phrase appears at the beginning, and one in which the phrase appears at the end.

1. paddling downstream
2. hidden behind a bush
3. following me
4. rushing to the car

Have the students exchange papers to check for correct usage.

Extending the Lesson

Have each student find five participial phrases in a short story. Discuss the meaning that each participial phrase adds to its sentence.

Exercises Find the participles and participial phrases.

A. Write down the participles and participial phrases in these sentences. Show which word the participle modifies.

EXAMPLE: Flipping the switch suddenly, Ron picked up two possums in the flashlight beam.

Participle *flipping* modifies the noun *Ron*.
Participial phrase flipping the switch suddenly

runners 1. Exhausted, the runners crossed the finish line.
skaters 2. Moving effortlessly, the skaters danced across the ice.
Jim 3. Jumping clear, Jim opened his parachute.
she 4. Crossing the old bridge, she passed the old general store.
pie 5. Frozen, the pie tastes even better.
parts 6. Tested in our laboratories, the parts are strong.
glue 7. Spread thin, the glue dries in an hour.
Jim 8. Looking through binoculars, Jim could see the skyline quite clearly.
center 9. Concentrating deeply, the center sank the free throw.
goalie 10. Moving quickly, the goalie blocked the kick.

B. Follow the directions for Exercise A.

Mr. Mill 1. Seeing the rain, Mr. Mill waited.
she 2. Clutching the receiver tightly, she listened.
ball 3. The ball ricocheted, hitting the taillight.
passengers 4. Waiting patiently, the passengers quietly stood in line at the gate.
back 5. Driving hard, the quarterback dived over the goal line.
Lisa 6. Holding her pigeon, Lisa showed us the leg band.
trucks 7. Watch for gravel trucks leaving the quarry.
we 8. Fascinated by the talk, we listened without a sound.
paperback 9. He forgot that paperback lying on the table.
Nancy 10. Breathing hard, Nancy crossed the finish line.

Part 3 Gerunds

A **gerund** is a verb form that is used as a noun. Gerunds can be used in any way that nouns are used:

Swimming is good exercise.
(*Swimming* is a gerund, the subject of *is*.)

Karen likes *riding*.
(*Riding* is a gerund, the object of *likes*.)

The time for *wrestling* is changed.
(*Wrestling* is a gerund, the object of the preposition *for*.)

Because gerunds are formed from verbs, they can have objects and can be modified by adverbs. Because they are used as nouns, they can also be modified by adjectives.

Riding a horse scares Kitt.
(*Riding* is a gerund; *horse* is the object of *riding*.)

Running uphill is difficult.
(*Running* is a gerund; *uphill* is an adverb modifying *running*.)

Careful reading requires concentration.
(*Reading* is a gerund; *careful* is an adjective modifying *reading*.)

Gerunds can also be modified by prepositional phrases:

Cycling in city traffic is frustrating.
(*Cycling* is a gerund; *in city traffic* is a prepositional phrase modifying *cycling*.)

A **gerund phrase** consists of a gerund with its modifiers and objects.

Part 3

Objective

To recognize gerunds and gerund phrases

Presenting the Lesson

1. Read and discuss this page. Emphasize that gerunds always end with *-ing* and always are used as nouns. Have the students suggest alternative gerunds and gerund phrases for each of the sample sentences; for example:

Jogging is good exercise.
Karen likes *sailing*.
The time for *practicing* is changed.
Climbing a ladder scares Kitt.
Typing quickly is difficult.
Successful baking requires concentration.
Waiting for a bus is frustrating.

2. Do Exercise A on page 518 orally. Assign and discuss Exercise B.

3. Read and discuss **Distinguishing Between Gerunds and Participles** on page 519. Stress that participles act as modifiers and gerunds act as nouns. Tell the students that a simple way to test for a gerund is to try substituting a pronoun for the word or phrase. If the sentence makes sense, the word is a gerund or the phrase is a gerund phrase. Have the students try substituting *this* or *that* for *walking, walking fast*, and *trying* in the example sentences.

4. Assign and discuss the Exercise on page 519.

Individualizing the Lesson

Less-Advanced Students

1. Before the students begin the Exercises on this page, remind them to look for *-ing* words used as nouns and to include all modifiers and objects as part of each phrase.

2. Have the students circle the gerund in each phrase in Exercise B on this page.

3. Work with the students to complete the first two items in the Exercise on page 519. Then have them complete the Exercise independently.

Advanced Students

Have the students identify the objects and modifiers in the gerund phrases in the Exercises on this page.

Reinforcement Exercise

Assign and discuss Exercise C on page 521.

Optional Practice

1. Have the students write sentences that include the following gerund phrases. The students should write two sentences for each phrase, one in which the phrase is used as a subject, and one in which the phrase is used as a direct object or an object of a preposition.

1. studying in the library
2. canoeing alone
3. sleeping late
4. telling jokes

Have the students exchange papers to check for correct usage.

Exercises Find the gerunds and gerund phrases.

A. Find the gerunds and gerund phrases. As your teacher directs, show how the gerund is used.

EXAMPLE: Planning the sports meet was fun.

Planning: gerund, subject of *was*
Planning the sports meet: gerund phrase

1. Skydiving takes nerve. subject
2. Becky read an article on weaving. object of preposition
3. Cleaning the attic was not my idea of a good time. subject
4. Washing that wall took all afternoon. subject
5. Painting the scenery took more time than we thought. subject
6. Part of the journey included canoeing down a river. object
7. Putting on a play takes teamwork. subject
8. Chris enjoys baking. object
9. Skating on the lake in winter is fun. subject
10. That dog specializes in digging. object of preposition

B. Follow the directions for Exercise A.

1. Joe learned fencing last summer. object
2. Writing that essay was a difficult assignment. subject
3. Learning Russian requires homework. subject
4. Visiting Dallas was interesting. subject
5. Jack has always liked reading. object
6. Wearing sunglasses rests her eyes. subject
7. They got sick from overeating. object of preposition
8. Clare likes walking in the rain. object
9. Eating outside was cooler. subject
10. Driving to Alaska was a long, interesting journey. subject

Distinguishing Between Gerunds and Participles

The gerund, like the present participle, is formed by adding *-ing* to the present tense of the verb. How can you tell whether a word is a gerund or a participle? It depends upon how the word is used. If it is used as a modifier, it is a participle. If it is used as a noun, it is a gerund.

Walking is good exercise.
   (*Walking* is a gerund, the subject of *is*.)

Walking fast, we overtook the boys.
   (*Walking* is a participle modifying *we; fast* is an adverb modifying *walking*.)

Trying is half the battle.
   (*Trying* is a gerund, the subject of *is*.)

Trying, Brenda pushed harder.
   (*Trying* is a participle modifying *Brenda*.)

Exercise Distinguishing between gerunds and participles.

For each sentence, write down the gerund or participle and say which it is. Be prepared to explain why it is a gerund or a participle.

1. Watching television bothers his eyes. gerund, subject
2. Watching television, Terry noticed the colors were wrong again. participle, modifies Terry
3. Fixing steps was Mr. Buswell's specialty. gerund, subject
4. Fixing a sandwich, Gerry listened to the sportscast. participle, modifies Gerry
5. Cleaning is done every Saturday. gerund, subject
6. Cleaning the car, Pat found her notebook. participle, modifies Pat
7. Removing the tree was difficult. gerund, subject
8. Panning for gold, the old man waded into the stream. participle, modifies man
9. Moving quickly, the paramedics aided the victims. participle, modifies paramedics
10. Swimming is good for most people's health. gerund, subject

2. Have the students add gerunds or gerund phrases to complete the following sentences:

_____ cheers me up.
My family always enjoys _____.
By _____, I save time.
_____ is harder than _____.

Extending the Lesson

Have each student find a sentence containing a gerund phrase in an advertisement. Use these sentences to create an exercise like those on page 518.

These Reinforcement Exercises may be used for additional practice as needed. Each exercise may be used after the text page indicated in parentheses.

Review

If you have not assigned these Exercises before this time, you can use them as an excellent Section Review.

Mixed Review

The following exercises provide review of the concepts and skills presented in this chapter.

A. Find the verbals. Write the verbals and verbal phrases in these sentences. Tell whether the verbal is an infinitive, a participle, or a gerund. A sentence may contain more than one verbal.

1. Jane and Jeff were exhausted from running in the marathon. P,G
2. Encouraged by the cheering crowd, the football team won the game. P
3. Playing backgammon is a pleasant pastime. G
4. I am going to the bank to deposit my paycheck. I
5. Grace preferred to live in the city. I
6. Showing her I.D. badge, the employee entered the factory. P
7. Painting the house, Gary dripped paint on the patio. P
8. This thriller is a good book to read on a stormy night. I
9. Windsurfing is a combination of surfing and sailing. G,G,G
10. Look at all those people waiting in line. P

Reinforcement Exercises — Review

Using Verbals

A. Find the infinitives and infinitive phrases.
(Use after page 514.)

Find the infinitives and infinitive phrases in these sentences.

1. We hope to visit Washington this summer.
2. To satisfy his curiosity is impossible.
3. Ask them to come with us.
4. We hope to go to the movie on Sunday.
5. I still have a couple of windows to wash.
6. We were just starting to eat the other half of the pizza.
7. Jill proceeded to explain her proposal.
8. Andy is teaching us to float.
9. To go around by the bridge takes too long.
10. Wendy was planning to go to the beach.

B. Find the participles and participial phrases.
(Use after page 516.)

Find the participles and participial phrases in these sentences.

1. Flopping frantically, the trout got off the wharf.
2. Speaking quietly, the librarian explained the reference book to me.
3. Look at the cat carrying its kitten in its mouth.
4. Racing wildly, the horses cross the finish line simultaneously.
5. Elated, Beth told us the news.
6. Cleaning the garage, John found some interesting old newspapers.
7. Bought second-hand, the motor lasted three years.

8. Snorting and kicking, the pinto refused to wear a saddle.
9. Walking slowly, Laura and her dog watched the sunset.
10. Made in Japan, the tape recorder was a money-maker.

C. Find the gerunds and gerund phrases.

(Use after page 518.)

Find the gerunds and gerund phrases in these sentences.

1. Tracy likes making pottery.
2. Skydiving requires skill and an adventurous spirit.
3. Talking on the phone tires Mr. King.
4. Walking is good exercise and a healthful habit.
5. Reading is my favorite pastime.
6. Have you forgotten about mowing the lawn?
7. Paneling the den was Dad's idea.
8. You will never get rich by wishing.
9. In basketball, quick thinking is essential.
10. Driving over Highland Pass takes about an hour.

D. Distinguish between gerunds and participles.

(Use after page 519.)

Write down the gerund or participle for each sentence, and say which it is. Be prepared to explain why it is a gerund or a participle.

1. Swimming fast is all right for short spurts. gerund, subject
2. Swimming fast, he reached the dock first. participle, modifies he
3. Talking a mile a minute, Jan explained her tardiness. participle, modifies Jan
4. Thinking on your feet is not always easy. gerund, subject
5. Talking doesn't take any effort for Pat. gerund, subject
6. Thinking fast, he avoided the collision. participle, modifies he
7. Waiting on tables is very hard work. gerund, subject
8. We saw the plow coming up the hill. participle, modifies plow
9. Finishing the last question on the test, Maria sighed with relief. participle, modifies Maria
10. Playing tennis is Michelle's favorite sport. gerund, subject

B. Identify verbals and their uses.

Copy each sentence. Write the verbals or verbal phrases and tell what kind they are. If the verbal functions as a noun, tell whether it is used as a subject or object. If the verbal is used as a modifier, tell whether it is used as an adjective or adverb.

1. Spinning like a top, the skater finished his routine. P (adj.)
2. Spinning wool into yarn is an ancient art. G (subj.)
3. The fairy tale character tried to spin straw into gold. I (obj.)
4. The trees, bent by fierce winds, touched the ground. P (adj.)
5. Angela went to Phoenix to visit her sister. I (adv.)
6. Evan earns money by building birdhouses. G (obj.)
7. Defeated, the boxer slumped in his corner. P (adj.)
8. Every contestant hoped to qualify for the finals. I (obj.)
9. Playing the piano well requires practice and dedication. G (subj.)
10. The ironed shirts were put in the drawer. P (adj.)

Using Grammar in Writing

1. Have the students use participial phrases to combine the following pairs of sentences:

1. Sue was using Tom's old rod. She caught the only fish.
2. Paddle tennis is played on a platform. Paddle tennis doesn't require as large a court as tennis does.
3. The musicians travel from town to town. They play jazz concerts.

2. Have each student write five sentences about activities that are named by gerunds, such as *hiking, sailing, cooking, painting, writing, running, swimming,* or *traveling*.

Section 11

Capitalization

Capitalization refers to the use of capital letters. To capitalize a word means to begin a word with a capital letter.

Capital letters help a reader to understand what he or she reads. For example, they make the reader notice important words. These might be people's names or the names of specific places. In addition, capitals point out the first word in each sentence. They show the reader where each new thought begins.

This section contains two sets of rules for using capital letters correctly. The first set shows you how to recognize and capitalize proper nouns and adjectives. The second set explains when to capitalize the first word in a group of words.

Just as you treat special people with respect, you use capital letters to show that certain words are special. To write well, you must know which words need to be capitalized. As you write, refer to the rules in this section.

Section Objectives

1. To recognize and capitalize proper nouns and adjectives
2. To capitalize first words in sentences, lines of poetry, quotations, parts of letters, and outlines
3. To capitalize titles correctly

Preparing the Students

Read the introduction on this page.

Write the following on the chalkboard:

sEctiOn 11
caPitAlizAtioN

Explain that the use of capital and lower-case letters in written English follows certain well-established rules. When the rules are not followed, a piece of writing has an odd appearance. Tell the students that Section 11 will help them remember when to capitalize words.

Encourage the students to refer to Section 11 whenever they have questions about capitalization in their writing.

Additional Resources

Diagnostic Test—See page 6 in the test booklet. Recommended for use before teaching the chapter.

Mastery Test—See pages 55-56 in the test booklet. Recommended for use after teaching the chapter.

Reinforcement Exercises—See pages 535-537 in the student text.

Skills Practice Book—pages 168-176.

Duplicating Masters—pages 168–176.

Proper Nouns and Adjectives

Objective

To recognize and capitalize proper nouns and adjectives

Presenting the Lesson

1. Read and discuss pages 524 and 525. Have the students explain why each example is written with a capital or lower case letter. Have the students give additional examples for each rule.

2. Assign and discuss Exercise A on page 525 and Exercise B on page 526.

3. Read and discuss pages 526 and 527. Have the students give more examples for each category.

4. Assign and discuss Exercises A and B on page 528.

5. Read and discuss pages 529 and 530. Have the students give more examples.

6. Assign and discuss Exercises A and B on pages 530 and 531.

Individualizing the Lesson

Less-Advanced Students

1. For Exercises A and B on pages 525 and 526, have the students tell which rule applies whenever they capitalize a word.

2. For the Exercises on page 528, have the students check their capitalization by asking themselves, "Is this a specific place?"

3. For the Exercises on pages 530 and 531, have the students tell

Capitalize proper nouns and proper adjectives.

A **common noun** is the name of a whole group of persons, places, or things. A **proper noun** is the name of an individual person, place, or thing. A **proper adjective** is an adjective formed from a proper noun.

COMMON NOUN	PROPER NOUN	PROPER ADJECTIVE
person	Elizabeth	Elizabethan
country	Spain	Spanish
city	Paris	Parisian

Proper nouns occur in great variety. The following rules with their illustrations will help you solve the capitalization problems that proper nouns and proper adjectives present.

Names of Persons

Capitalize the names of persons and also the initials or abbreviations that stand for those names.

J. R. R. Tolkien   **J**ohn **R**onald **R**euel **T**olkien
Ella **T. G**rasso   **E**lla **T**ambussi **G**rasso

Capitalize titles used with names of persons and also the initials or abbreviations that stand for those titles.

Rev. M. R. Eaton   **S**enator Smith   **D**r. Patricia Ryan

Do not capitalize titles used as common nouns:

Have you seen your doctor?   She is the company president.

Capitalize titles of people whose rank is very important, even when these titles are used without proper names.

The **P**resident of the United States

The titles *Mr., Mrs., Ms.,* and *Miss* are always capitalized.

Family Relationships

Capitalize such words as mother, father, aunt, and uncle when these words are used as names.

Note that when the noun is modified by a personal pronoun, it is not capitalized.

Hello, **M**other. Is **D**ad home yet?
My **a**unt is going to visit us next week.

The Pronoun *I*

Capitalize the pronoun *I*.

Is he taller than **I**?

The Deity

Capitalize all words referring to the Deity, to the Holy Family, the Bible, and to religious scriptures.

God	the **L**ord	the **B**ible
Allah	the **V**irgin **M**ary	the **B**ook of **E**xodus

Capitalize personal pronouns referring to the Deity.

God spoke to **H**is prophets.

Exercises Use capital letters correctly.

A. Number your paper from 1–10. Copy the following sentences. Change small letters to capital letters wherever necessary.

1. I told my mother that ͥi had a doctor's appointment.
2. She said, "Please ask ᴰdr. ᴴhernandez to call me."

which rule applies whenever they capitalize a word.

Advanced Students

Have the students write sentences applying each capitalization rule discussed in this Section.

Reinforcement Exercises

Assign and discuss Exercises A, B, and C on pages 535-537.

Optional Practice

1. Have the students make two columns, labeling one *Proper Nouns* and the other *Common Nouns*. Have the students list pairs of nouns, such as *aunt* and *Aunt Rita* in the two columns.

2. Conduct a capitalization bee, following the procedures for a spelling bee. Present names and titles to each team alternately, drawing from the examples given on pages 524-530. Ask whether the words should be capitalized. Students who give incorrect responses are eliminated from the game.

Extending the Lesson

Assign one or two of the capitalization rules to each student, and have the student find an example of the use of the rule in a magazine. Have the students cut out the examples they find and use them to make a bulletin board display of capitalization rules and examples.

3. The new teacher is from ᴾparis, ꟳfrance.

4. He is a ᴾparisian.

5. Would you tell ᴹmom ᴵi'll be a little late for dinner?

6. The first book of the ᴮbible is the ᴮbook of ᴳgenesis.

7. My mother asked ᴬaunt ᴿrose if ᵀtad and ᴹmaria could stay for lunch.

8. Please take this message to the principal, ᴸlynn.

9. She says that ᴹms. ᴴholchak is not in her office.

10. Some names for ᴳgod are ᴶjehovah, the ᴸlord, and the ᴬalmighty.

B. Follow the directions for Exercise A.

1. There are seven cities in the ᵁunited ˢstates named ˢspringfield.

2. The largest is in ᴹmassachusetts.

3. Our country is sometimes called a ᴶjeffersonian democracy.

4. The new student is ᵀtoshio ᴷkitagawa. His sister is ᴹmieko.

5. Both of them were born in ᴶjapan.

6. Which ᶜcairo do you mean?

7. Is it the one in ᴱegypt or the one in ᴵillinois?

8. Speakers were ᴹmr. ˢs. ꟳf. ᴾpaulson, ᴹms. ᴶj. ᴾp. ᴾperez, and ᴹms. ᴾp. ᴰd. ᶜcardelo.

9. All of my aunts and uncles live in ᶜcalifornia.

10. It was ᶜcaptain ˢsherman who gave ˢsue and ᵀted the booklets on bicycle safety.

Geographical Names

In a geographical name, capitalize the first letter of each word except articles and prepositions.

The article *the* appearing before a geographical name is not part of the geographical name and is therefore not capitalized.

Continents: Europe, Asia, Africa, Australia

Bodies of Water: the Pacific Ocean, Puget Sound, the Columbia River, Hudson Bay, the Straits of Magellan, Lake Superior, the English Channel, the Arabian Gulf

Land Forms: the Mississippi Delta, the Cape of Good Hope, the Mojave Desert, the Atlas Mountains, Pike's Peak, Dismal Swamp

Political Units: Oak Park, Los Angeles, Commonwealth of Puerto Rico, First Congressional District, Utah, Great Britain, the Azores

Public Areas: Badlands National Monument, Grant Park, Shawnee National Forest, the Battery, the Black Hills, Zion National Park

Roads and Highways: Oregon Trail, Lincoln Highway, Broad Street, 34th Avenue, Tri-State Tollway, Riverside Freeway, Drury Lane, Route 23

Directions and Sections

Capitalize names of sections of the country but not of directions of the compass.

Industrial production was high in the **N**orth.
We headed **s**outh for our vacation.
The pioneers moved **w**est over the Oregon Trail.
The first English settlements were along the **E**ast **C**oast.
The frontier moved **w**estward.
The **S**outhwest is our fastest-growing region.

Capitalize proper adjectives derived from names of sections of the country. Do not capitalize adjectives derived from words indicating direction.

an **E**astern school	a **n**orth wind
a **W**estern concept	a **s**outherly course

Exercises Using capital letters correctly.

A. Number your paper from 1–10. Find the words in the following sentences that should be capitalized. Write the words after the proper number, using the necessary capital letters.

1. Many wagon trains left from independence, missouri.
2. The trail took them first to fort kearney, nebraska.
3. Then they followed the north platte river to fort laramie.
4. The pioneers crossed the rocky mountains at south pass, wyoming.
5. After they crossed the rockies, the trail split into three parts.
6. The oregon trail went to the pacific northwest.
7. The mormon trail went to salt lake city, utah.
8. A third trail crossed the great basin of nevada and utah.
9. It crossed the sierra nevada mountains at donner pass.
10. Many frontiersmen followed these trails westward. Correct

B. Follow the directions for Exercise A.

1. The trans-canada highway crosses the entire width of canada.
2. Of the seven continents, asia and africa are the two largest.
3. Next week we elect the representative from the eighth congressional district.
4. The track championships will be held in morton township.
5. In the bay of naples there is an island called capri.
6. The blue grotto is a famous tourist attraction on capri.
7. Lake baikal is the world's deepest freshwater lake.
8. The lake is in siberia, in the soviet union.
9. We had our family picnic at the lincoln park zoo.
10. Last summer, we drove along the gulf of mexico to new orleans and then north to memphis.

Names of Organizations and Institutions

Capitalize the names of organizations and institutions, including political parties, governmental bodies or agencies, schools, colleges, churches, hospitals, clubs, businesses, and abbreviations of these names.

General Motors Corporation   Children's Hospital
Oakwood High School   St. Mark's Church
University of Southern California   **U.S.C.**

Do not capitalize such words as *school, college, church,* and *hospital* when they are not used as names:

the basketball team of our school

Names of Events, Documents, and Periods of Time

Capitalize the names of historical events, documents, and periods of time.

Battle of Hastings   Treaty of Paris   Age of Discovery
World War II   Bill of Rights   Middle Ages

Months, Days, and Holidays

Capitalize names of months, days, and holidays, but not the names of seasons.

March   Labor Day   summer
Friday   Fourth of July   Feast of the Passover

Races, Languages, Nationalities, Religions

Capitalize the names of races, languages, nationalities, and religions and adjectives derived from them.

Native American   African   Lutheranism
French   Buddhism   Episcopalian

School Subjects

Do not capitalize the names of school subjects, except course names followed by a number.

Algebra I   History of Civilization II
social studies   physical education

Remember that the names of languages are always capitalized.

English   Spanish   German   Hebrew

Ships, Trains, Airplanes, Automobiles

Capitalize the names of ships, trains, airplanes, and automobiles.

U.S.S. *Constitution*   *Cutlass*
Santa Fe Chief   *Spirit of St. Louis*

B.C., A.D.

Capitalize the abbreviations *B.C.* and *A.D.*

The first Olympic Games were held in 776 **B.C.**
The Norman Conquest took place in **A.D.** 1066.

Exercises Use capital letters correctly.

A. Number your paper from 1–10. Write the words in each sentence that should be capitalized. Use the necessary capital letters.

1. Our car was made by american motors corporation.

2. We saw a honda accord, a chevy monza, and a ford fairmont before buying the buick skylark.

3. My sister is class president at pulaski high school.

4. I registered for ancient history I, algebra II, social studies, english, and music.

5. In 1898 the treaty of paris ended the spanish-american war.

6. The fourth of july is an important date in american history.

7. The declaration of independence was signed on july 4, 1776.

8. My favorite subjects are home economics, english, and physical education.

9. The first woman to fly across the atlantic ocean was amelia earhart.

10. In 44 b.c. julius caesar was assassinated.

B. Follow the directions for Exercise A.

1. In a.d. 1492 columbus landed on an island in the west indies.

2. The prophet muhammad founded the religion of islam.

3. His followers are called moslems or muslims.

4. The u.s.s. *constitution* is also called "*old ironsides.*"

5. The *broadway limited* runs between new york and chicago.

6. The new head of brookston hospital is dr. margaret allen.

7. The new social studies teacher is from munich, germany.

8. The head nurse in the emergency room at st. luke's hospital is jeffrey adams.

9. The spanish, russian, french, and german clubs at hersey high school sponsored an international bazaar.

10. My sister is studying russian at u.c.l.a., and my brother is a european history major at u.s.c.

First Words

Objectives

1. To capitalize first words in sentences, lines of poetry, quotations, parts of letters, and outlines
2. To capitalize titles correctly

Presenting the Lesson

1. Read and discuss pages 532 and 533. Have the students give additional examples for each rule.
2. Assign and discuss Exercises A and B on pages 533 and 534.

Individualizing the Lesson

Less-Advanced Students

1. Warn the students that the Exercises apply preceding rules as well as the rules on pages 532 and 533.
2. Have the students identify which rule is applied each time they capitalize a word in the Exercises.

Advanced Students

Have the students investigate contemporary poetry that does not use capitalization. Ask the students to explore the reasons for and the effects of this lack of capitalization.

Reinforcement Exercise

Assign and discuss Exercise D on page 537.

Optional Practice

Have the students list, without any capitalization, their favorite books,

First Words

Sentences and Poetry

Capitalize the first word of every sentence and the first word in most lines of poetry.

My sister likes tennis. She is the captain of her team.

Lines of poetry:

Grow old along with me!
The best is yet to be . . .

Sometimes, especially in modern poetry, the lines of a poem do not begin with a capital letter.

Quotations

Capitalize the first word of a direct quotation.

Ralph Waldo Emerson said, "Hitch your wagon to a star."

Do not capitalize the first word of the second part of a divided quotation unless it starts a new sentence.

"Well," he said, "what you say is quite true."
"I agree," he said. "What you say is quite true."

Letters

Capitalize the first word, words like *Sir* and *Madam,* and the name of the person addressed in the greeting of a letter.

Dear Ms. Gomez   Dear Dr. Perkins   Dear Mr. Castillo

In the complimentary close, capitalize the first word only.

Yours very truly   Sincerely yours

Outlines

Capitalize the first word of each line of an outline.

I. Improve your handwriting.
   A. Form letters carefully.
      1. Watch *a, e, r, l,* and *t.*

Titles

Capitalize the first word and all important words in the titles of books, poems, short stories, articles, newspapers, magazines, plays, motion pictures, works of art, and musical compositions.

Articles (the words *a, an,* and *the*), conjunctions, and prepositions are not usually considered important words. However, note that an article, a conjunction, or a preposition used as the first word of a title must be capitalized.

Book	*The Good Earth*
Story	"*A Game of Catch*"
Play	*The Miracle Worker*
Magazine	*Sports Illustrated*

Exercises   Use capital letters correctly.

A. Number your paper from 1–10. Write the words that should be capitalized. Use the correct capital letters.

1. eleanor roosevelt said, "no one can make you feel inferior without your consent."

2. walt whitman wrote a famous poem about lincoln entitled "o captain! my captain!"

3. the famous humorist will rogers, who was of indian descent, said, "my forefathers didn't come over on the *mayflower*, but they met the boat."

movies, television shows, stories, and songs. Then have students exchange lists and add correct capitalization to the titles.

Extending the Lesson

From a short story, read a passage of dialogue as a dictation. In class, check the students' transcriptions for capitalization.

533

4. I. american history
   A. the war for independence
      1. battle of bunker hill

5. "don't go," he said. "i haven't explained yet."
6. for my birthday I got a subscription to *seventeen*.
7. the morning paper is the *herald tribune*.
8. very sincerely yours,
9. "hurry up!" father said. "if we don't leave soon, we'll be late."
10. we went to see the play *fiddler on the roof*.

B.   Follow the directions for Exercise A.

1. dear mrs. weiss:
2. Robert Frost wrote "the death of the hired man."

3. I. business letters
      A. correct business letter form
         1. heading

4. the recent issue of *sports illustrated* has complete coverage of all the hockey teams.

5. he would answer to "Hi!" or to any loud cry
      such as "Fry me!" or "Fritter my wig!"
      to "What-you-may-call-um!" or "What-was-his-name!"
      but especially "Thing-um-a-jig!"

6. the article "images of youth past" appeared last fall in an issue of *life* magazine.
7. Meg finally got to the airport. she asked, "has the plane left?"
8. "i'm afraid so," Janet replied. "we're too late."
9. i have always enjoyed *the wizard of oz*, but I was thoroughly entertained by the stage production of *the wiz*.
10. i think *the call of the wild* is jack london's best book.

534

Reinforcement Exercises—Review

Capitalization

A. Use capital letters correctly. (Use after page 526.)

Number your paper from 1–10. Find the words in the following sentences that should be capitalized. Write the words beside the proper numbers and capitalize them correctly.

1. Warren e.[E] burger[B] was appointed chief[C] justice[J] of the supreme[S] court[C] by president[P] nixon[N] on may[M] 21, 1969.

2. Is aunt[A] theodosia[T] dad's[D] favorite sister?

3. The reverend[R] doctor[D] martin[M] luther[L] king[K], Jr. received the Nobel Peace Prize in 1964.

4. Our drama class went to see carol[C] channing[C] in the musical *Hello, Dolly!*

5. Most people think i[I] look like mom[M], but actually I have my dad's brown eyes and hair.

6. The poet hilda[H] doolittle[D] was known by her initials h.d.[H.D.]

7. Indian civilizations flourished in both peru[P] and mexico[M] before the arrival of the spanish[S].

8. Allyson would like to become a doctor. Correct

9. Should I send the invitation to ms.[M] anita[A] schilling[S] in care of mr.[M] and mrs.[M] albert[A] romani[R]?

10. Tadeusz kosciuszko[K], a famous polish[P] army officer, fought on the side of the american[A] colonists.

B. Use capital letters correctly. (Use after page 528.)

Copy the following sentences, changing small letters to capital letters wherever necessary.

1. The gaspé[G] peninsula[P] is part of the province of quebec[Q].

A. Use capital letters correctly. Rewrite the following passage, correcting the capitalization errors. (There are 37 errors in the passage.)

the latest project of nasa, the national aeronautics and space administration, is the space shuttle. the shuttle is a reusable spaceship that is launched like a rocket, orbits like a satellite, and lands like an airplane.

in april of 1981 the space shuttle *columbia* made its first flight. launched from cape canaveral, florida, the shuttle circled the world 36 times and landed at edwards air force base in the mojave desert. john w. young was the commander, and robert l. griffin was the pilot.

at least 44 flights have been planned for the shuttle. three additional shuttles, *challenger, discovery,* and *atlantis,* will join *columbia.* who knows how far the shuttle will take us? robert freitag, a nasa official, says, "i'm convinced that by 1990 people will be going on the shuttle routinely—as on an airplane."

B. Use capital letters correctly. Copy these sentences. Capitalize words where necessary.

1. the straits of magellan, at the tip of south america, join the atlantic and the pacific oceans.

2. general motors, ford, and chrysler are the largest auto manufacturers in the united states.

3. we are reading *to kill a mockingbird* in my english class.

4. the rev. j. t. nelson is teaching a course that compares the bible, the torah, and the koran.

5. debby and mom went to springfield mall, but my dad and i stayed home.

6. "where," said pat, "is my *seventeen* magazine?"

7. the brown-dappled fawn
   bereft of the doe
   shivers in blue shadow
   of the glaring snow.

8. the roman empire came to an end in the fifth century a.d.

9. during the middle ages, european knights joined the crusades and traveled east to free jerusalem from the moslems.

10. dear sir:
    please send me your latest electronics catalog.
    sincerely,
    allen lasko

Using Mechanics in Writing

Have the students collect specific information about their town or city, including government officials' names, points of interest, historical monuments, parks, unusual buildings, and local industries. Then have the students write letters about their locale, using capitalization correctly. Pairs of students might check each other's work.

2. My parents were delighted to see the chicago skyline as we drove south along lake shore drive.

3. Which are taller, the rocky mountains or the andes mountains?

4. In one presidential election, the republicans won every state except the commonwealth of massachusetts and the district of columbia.

5. The isthmus of panama in central america was a likely place to build a canal.

6. At that spot, the distance between the caribbean sea on the north side and the gulf of panama on the south is only forty miles.

7. Have you noticed that people from the midwest speak differently than people from the east?

8. If you are interested in civil war history, be sure to visit vicksburg national park when you're in the south.

9. By the time we got off of that hot beach, my mouth felt like the gobi desert, the sahara desert, and death valley rolled into one.

10. Lake geneva borders switzerland on the north and france on the south.

C. Use capital letters correctly. (Use after page 531.)

Number your paper from 1–10. After the proper number, copy the words from each sentence that should be capitalized. Use the necessary capital letters.

1. Those three blue fords are still parked in front of rosemont baptist church.

2. So far only six students have signed up for algebra I.

3. The period from a.d. 500 to a.d. 1000 is sometimes called the dark ages.

4. The five countries involved in the six-day war were israel, egypt, syria, jordan, and iraq.

5. Next year ^{R}rosemont ^{H}high ^{S}school will have a winter break during the second week of ^{J}january.

6. We have to memorize the ^{G}gettysburg ^{A}address for our history assignment.

7. A big company like ^{L}legrow, ^{I}inc., probably has two or three doctors who work for it.

8. Most of the people in ^{G}green ^{B}bay, ^{W}wisconsin, are ^{C}catholic.

9. The ^{G}gregory ^{A}art ^{M}museum is closed on ^{M}memorial ^{D}day and ^{C}christmas.

10. The people of ^{S}switzerland speak either ^{F}french, ^{G}german, or ^{I}italian.

D. Use capital letters correctly. (Use after page 534.)

Number your paper from 1–8. Find the words in the following sentences that should be capitalized. Write the words after the proper numbers, using the necessary capital letters.

1. "^{T}there will be a quiz tomorrow," said Mr. Sims, "and it will cover Chapters 1 and 2."

2. ^{H}have you ever read the poem "^{S}song of ^{M}myself" by ^{W}walt ^{W}whitman?

3. ^{M}my teacher says that *^{T}the ^{A}adventures of ^{H}huckleberry ^{F}finn* is a more enjoyable book than either *^{T}tom ^{S}sawyer* or *^{T}the ^{P}prince and the ^{P}pauper*.

4. I. ^{S}shakespeare's plays
    A. ^{C}comedies
        1. *^{A}as ^{Y}you ^{L}like ^{I}it*
        2. *^{M}much ^{A}ado ^{A}about ^{N}nothing*

5. ^{O}our school library subscribes to *^{N}newsweek*, *^{T}time*, and *^{U}u.^{S}s. ^{N}news and ^{W}world ^{R}report*.

6. ^{D}death, be not proud, though some have called thee ^{M}mighty and dreadful, for thou art not so . . .

7. ^{B}because I was raised in the city of ^{C}chicago, I really enjoy reading the poem "^{C}chicago" by ^{C}carl ^{S}sandburg.

8. ^{B}both sculptures, *^{M}moses* and *^{D}david*, are by ^{M}michelangelo.

Section 12

Punctuation

When you read, you probably do not think much about the punctuation used. But if it were not there, you would be bothered by its absence. You would not know where sentences began or ended. You might not be sure which words were meant to go together.

Punctuation marks are signals. For example, by putting quotation marks in the right places, you can show your reader precisely where a person's exact words begin and end. You can use the apostrophe to show where letters have been left out of contractions. You can show pauses between thoughts, and you can emphasize points that you consider important.

This section will help you use punctuation marks correctly. End marks, commas, semicolons, colons, hyphens, apostrophes, and quotation marks all have uses that can be understood both by the reader and the writer. If you want your reader to get the exact meaning from your writing, give the right signals by using these marks in the right places.

Section Objectives

1. To use end marks correctly
2. To use commas correctly
3. To use semicolons and colons correctly
4. To use hyphens correctly
5. To use apostrophes correctly
6. To use quotation marks correctly

Preparing the Students

Copy the following paragraph on the chalkboard:

When you read you probably do not think much about the punctuation used but if it were not there you would be bothered by its absence you would not know where sentences began or ended you might not be sure which words were meant to go together

Discuss with the students how their reading of the paragraph is affected by its lack of punctuation. Read this page. Stress the importance of punctuation as an aid to understanding. Tell them that studying the rules in Section 12 will help them to punctuate correctly.

Additional Resources

Diagnostic Test—See page 7 in the test booklet. Recommended for use before teaching the section.

Mastery Tests—See pages 57-58 in the test booklet. Recommended for use after teaching the section.

Reinforcement Exercises—See pages 568-575 in the student text.

Skills Practice Book—pages 177-192.

Duplicating Masters—pages 177-192.

End Marks

The punctuation marks that show where sentences end are called **end marks.** They include *periods, question marks,* and *exclamation points.*

The Period

Use a period at the end of a declarative sentence.

A **declarative sentence** is a sentence that makes a statement. It is the kind of sentence you use when you want to tell something.

My brother delivers newspapers.

A declarative sentence is often shortened to one or two words, especially when answering a question.

Where are you going to put this macramé planter?
Over there. (*I am going to put it over there.*)

Use a period at the end of an imperative sentence.

An **imperative sentence** is a sentence that requests or tells someone to do something.

Please close the door.

If the imperative sentence also expresses excitement or emotion, an exclamation point is used after it.

Look out!

Use a period at the end of an indirect question.

She asked us whether we liked strawberries.

An *indirect question* is the part of a statement that tells what someone asked, but that does not give the exact words of the person who asked the question.

Use a period after an abbreviation or after an initial.

Dr. Marla E. Corona   P.O. Box
Rev. John L. Haeger, Jr.   2:30 P. M.

Periods are omitted in some abbreviations. If you are not sure whether an abbreviation should be written with or without periods, look up the abbreviation in your dictionary.

FM (*frequency modulation*)
UN (*United Nations*)
FBI (*Federal Bureau of Investigation*)

Use a period after each number or letter that shows a division of an outline or that precedes an item in a list.

(An Outline)   (A List)

I. Poets   1. eggs
  A. American   2. milk
    1. Robert Frost   3. butter

Use a period in numerals between dollars and cents and before a decimal.

$18.98   2.853

The Question Mark

Use a question mark at the end of an interrogative sentence.

An **interrogative sentence** is a sentence that asks a question.

Has anyone seen my dog?

The above sentence gives the exact words of the person who asked the question. It is called a *direct question.* A question mark is used only with a direct question.

Do not use a question mark with an indirect question. Instead, use a period.

An *indirect question* is the part of a statement that tells what someone asked, without giving the exact words.

Kelly asked whether anyone had seen her dog.

The Exclamation Point

Use an exclamation point at the end of an exclamatory sentence.

Tim, look out!

Use an exclamation point after an interjection or after any other exclamatory expression.

An **interjection** is a word or group of words used to express strong feeling. It may be a real word or simply a group of letters used to represent a sound. It is one of the eight parts of speech.

Hurrah!   Wow!

Exercises Use end marks correctly.

A. Copy the following sentences, adding the necessary punctuation. Be prepared to tell what punctuation marks you used and why you used them.

1. Where did I put my new sweater?
2. Wow! that was quite a football game!
3. What is Dr. Harrigan's phone number?
4. Where is Sgt. Leslie's office located?
5. Help! I can't get this door open!
6. I was supposed to meet Tom at 10:30 A.M.
7. Dr. James Coogan, Jr. is going to talk about lifesaving.
8. Mary, look out!
9. Our art supplies will cost more than ten dollars, and I have only $8.25.
10. My appointment with Dr. Wagner is at 11:15 A.M. on Friday.

542

B. Follow the directions in Exercise A.

1. Dr. Elizabeth McMinn is our school principal.
2. Please send your requests to Franklin's, Ltd., P. O. Box 552, New York, New York 10014.
3. While in Washington, D.C., where did you stay?
4. One mile is equal to 16 kilometers.
5. Luis asked if he could help me with my homework.
6. I have two broadcast bands on my radio: AM and FM.
7. UNICEF is the children's organization of the UN.
8. Your appointment is at 9:30 P. M.
9. The Rev. James M. Butler, Jr. will be the guest speaker at the ceremonies.
10. Will you mail these coupons to the Clark Company, Inc., 301 E. Walton Place, Price, Utah 84501?

The Comma

Commas are used to separate words that do not belong together. In speaking, we can keep words apart by pausing. In writing, we must use commas.

Commas in a Series

Use a comma after every item in a series except the last.

The items in a series may be single words, or phrases, or clauses.

Words	The flag is red, white, and blue.
Phrases	The dog ran out the door, down the steps, and across the lawn.
Clauses	How kangaroos run, what jumps they can take, and how they live are explained in this book.

The Comma

Objective

To use commas correctly

Presenting the Lesson

1. Read and discuss pages 543 and 544. Stress that commas used after items in a series help avoid confusion. Discuss the difficulties a reader would have with the sentences on this page if commas were omitted.

2. Assign Exercises A and B on pages 544 and 545. Discuss why each comma is needed.

3. Read and discuss pages 545 and 546. Have the students give additional examples of sentences with introductory words, phrases, clauses, and interrupters that should be set off with commas.

4. Assign and discuss Exercises A and B on pages 546 and 547.

5. Read and discuss page 547. Write the terms *noun of direct address* and *appositive* on the chalkboard, and make sure all students can define them.

6. Read and discuss page 548. Demonstrate the punctuation of quotations. First have a student make a statement. On the chalkboard, write the statement as a quotation, complete with explanatory words. Stress the correct placement of commas. Then write the statement as an indirect quotation, showing how it should be punctuated.

7. Read and discuss page 549. Review the difference between a compound sentence and a compound predicate (pages 473 and 474).

8. Assign and discuss Exercises A and B on pages 549 and 550.

9. Read and discuss pages 550 and 551. Stress the need for the comma after the last part of a date or location.

10. Assign and discuss Exercises A and B on pages 551 and 552.

11. Read and discuss pages 552 and 553. Have the students suggest alternative restrictive and nonrestrictive clauses for each example sentence.

12. Assign and discuss Exercises A and B on pages 553 and 554.

Reinforcement Exercises

Assign and discuss Exercises B–F on pages 568-572.

Use commas after the adverbs *first, second, third,* and so on, when these adverbs introduce a series of parallel items.

> There are three ways to get good marks: first, pay attention; second, take notes; third, study.

When two or more adjectives precede a noun, use a comma after each adjective except the last one.

> They drove away in a bright, shiny, expensive sports car.

Sometimes two adjectives are used together to express a single idea made up of two closely related thoughts. Adjectives so used are not usually separated by a comma.

> Our house is the little green one.
> Look at the big round moon.

When you say the two sentences above, notice that you do not pause between the adjectives.

Exercises   Use commas correctly to separate items.

A.   Number your paper from 1–10. Copy the following sentences and add commas where necessary.

1. A strong, northerly wind swept the snow against the front door.

2. That little green TR7 belongs to my sister. Correct

3. Red, white, and blue bunting decorated the speaker's stand.

4. We went to the store and bought chicken, corn, baked beans, and lemonade mix.

5. The race car skidded, did a complete turn-around, and blew out its right front tire.

6. At the movies, I like fresh, salty, buttery popcorn.

7. Strong, gusty winds blew across the lake.

8. My sister can play the guitar, the banjo, and the mandolin.

544

9. In order to finish the scenery, do the following: first, nail the supports together; second, paint the backdrop; and third, put away all unnecessary tools and paint.

10. Sue finished her homework, made a telephone call, and went to bed.

B.   Follow the directions for Exercise A.

1. The committee discussed, analyzed, and accepted the proposal.

2. A fluffy, tiger-striped cat was sitting on our porch swing.

3. A small rabbit scooted across our doorstep, through the evergreens, and under our back porch.

4. Handball, racquetball, and squash are similar sports.

5. Bowling, tennis, and jogging are my favorite activities.

6. A long, sleek, black limousine pulled up in front of the bank.

7. James, Joan, and Greg helped design the posters.

8. We need crepe paper, balloons, and tape to decorate the gym.

9. The speaker stated the hard, clear facts.

10. The magician pulled a green scarf out of the air, spread it flat on the table, and pulled a pigeon out from under it.

Commas After Introductory Words, Phrases, or Clauses

Use a comma to separate an introductory word, phrase, or clause from the rest of the sentence.

> Yes, I will go.
> After circling twice, the airplane landed.
> Although Dick needed help, he said nothing.

The comma may be omitted if there would be little pause in speaking.

> At first I didn't know what to do.

Individualizing the Lesson

Less-Advanced Students

1. Urge the students to read each sentence in the Exercises aloud before deciding where the commas should be placed. Alternatively, read each sentence aloud in class before the students complete the Exercises independently.

2. When discussing the Exercises, have the students tell why each comma is placed where it is and which rule applies.

3. Before students begin work on Exercise B on page 550, help them determine which groups of words are appositives.

4. Warn the students that two of the sentences in Exercise A on page 549 do not need commas.

5. In the Exercises on pages 553 and 554, have the students test for nonrestrictive clauses by dropping each clause from the sentence and deciding whether the meaning changes.

Advanced Students

Have the students identify the grammatical constructions used in series in Exercises A and B on pages 544 and 545.

Optional Practice

1. Read paragraphs from textbooks that the students use in other subjects as dictation exercises. Have students exchange papers and check the use of commas.

2. Choose paragraphs from textbooks or from a short story in the students' literary anthology. Have the students explain why each comma is used.

Extending the Lesson

1. Have each student find published examples of commas used for five of the reasons given on pages 543-553. Discuss the examples in class.

2. Have two students conduct a brief conversation. Then have the class write out the dialogue, using commas correctly with quotations.

Commas with Interrupters

Use commas to set off words or groups of words that interrupt the flow of thought in a sentence.

Anne, to tell the truth, was quite happy.
The report, moreover, is altogether inaccurate.

Exercises Use commas to set off words correctly.

A. Copy these sentences. Add commas where necessary.

1. No, I don't think the library is open on Sundays.
2. After circling the airport for an hour, we finally landed.
3. Although the game was postponed until Friday, we had practice every morning.
4. Yes, I have finished the dishes.
5. The exam, however, will be given as scheduled.
6. Mrs. Cassini, to tell the truth, was quite pleased with our panel discussion.
7. Since the Cubs lost their last ten games, they will not be in the play-offs.
8. The results of the student survey, however, will not be revealed until next week.
9. No, the mail has not been delivered.
10. Even though we arrived early, we still didn't get good seats for the basketball game.

B. Follow the directions for Exercise A.

1. After we went on the hayride, we had a barbecue and played volleyball.
2. Yes, the garage has been cleaned out.
3. The game, consequently, was postponed.
4. The latest weather report, however, has predicted rain for the weekend.
5. Although the heavy snow tied up the morning traffic, most companies and businesses were open as usual.

546

6. Yes, the intramural track meet is tomorrow.

7. Since Mardi Gras is such a celebrated occasion in New Orleans, most schools there take a holiday.

8. It is doubtful, however, that the weather will change our plans.

9. No, the garage sale isn't until next week.

10. If you look carefully at these old tintypes, you will see how different dress and housing used to be.

Commas with Nouns of Direct Address

Use commas to set off nouns of direct address.

The name of someone directly spoken to is a **noun of direct address.**

> If you look, Peggy, you will see the book I mean.
> Your firefighters did well, Captain.
> Be careful, children, when you cross the street.

Commas with Appositives

Use commas to set off most appositives.

An **appositive** is a word or group of words used directly after another word to explain it.

> The speaker, *a famous explorer,* told about Papua, New Guinea.

An appositive may have a prepositional phrase within it.

> The leader, *the person on horseback,* moved away.

Nouns used as appositives are called **nouns in apposition.** When the noun in apposition is a short name, it is not usually set off by commas.

> This is my friend Rhoda.

Commas with Quotations

Use commas to set off the explanatory words of a direct quotation.

The "explanatory words" used in giving a direct quotation are such brief statements as *Tina said, Christie answered,* or *Bill asked.*

Kate shouted, "Keep your eye on the ball!"

In the sentence above, the explanatory words come *before* the quotation. A comma is then placed after the last explanatory word.

Now look at this quotation:

"I can't find the key," said Patty.

If the explanatory words come *after* the quotation, as in the example above, place a comma within the quotation marks after the last word of the quotation.

Sometimes a quotation is separated into two parts by the explanatory words. This is often done to add variety to the sentence construction. Here is an example:

"The spacecraft," the announcer said, "has just been launched."

The sentence above is an example of a *divided quotation.* A comma is used after the last word of the first part. Another comma is used after the last explanatory word.

Do not confuse direct and indirect quotations. Indirect quotations are *not* set off from the rest of the sentence by commas.

Sylvia said that she had studied for at least an hour.

The Comma in a Compound Sentence

Use a comma before the conjunction that joins the two main clauses in a compound sentence.

Kimberly seemed to agree, and no one else objected.

In a very short compound sentence with the clauses joined by *and*, it is not necessary to use a comma if there is no turn or change in the thought. Always use a comma before *or* or *but*, since these words do change the direction of the thought.

Pete finally arrived *and* we started off.
Pete arrived, *but* it was too late to go anywhere.

Do not use a comma before the *and* that joins a compound subject or a compound predicate.

Sally turned on the radio and sat down to read a magazine.

Exercises Use commas correctly.

A.   Copy these sentences. Add commas where needed.

1. "Cheerleading tryouts will be held tonight," began the announcement, "and all students are invited to participate."
2. The team captain, the player in blue, is a good student.
3. I read *Roots*, but I preferred the television series.
4. I enjoy reading science fiction novels, but I also enjoy reading mysteries.
5. She ran down the stairs and raced down the sidewalk.   Correct
6. Ms. Leoni, our new science teacher, was born in Italy.
7. Sir Georg Solti, the famous conductor, directs the Chicago Symphony Orchestra.
8. When you are finished, Kurt, will you help me?
9. Maria finished her tennis practice and then went directly to play rehearsal.   Correct
10. John Hancock, one of the signers of the Declaration of Independence, was from Massachusetts.

B. Follow the directions for Exercise A.

1. "Wally," said Barbara, "has a good suggestion."
2. Linda showed me her present, a cassette tape recorder.
3. I will wash the car, but I don't have time to wax it.
4. I asked Ms. Wright, our science teacher, about lasers.
5. Andrés Segovia, the classical guitarist, will play at Orchestra Hall in May.
6. Will you come with me, or would you rather stay here?
7. Mrs. Watkins, our P. E. teacher, was a member of the U. S. Olympic swim team.
8. We played soccer for an hour, and then we went inside for lunch.
9. "Please take the dog for a walk," said Dad.
10. Pam, this is my brother Paul.

Commas in Dates

In dates, use a comma between the day of the month and the year.

July 4, 1776   December 7, 1787

In a sentence, a comma follows the year.

The postmark read September 10, 1981, but we didn't receive the letter until yesterday, October 2.

Commas in Locations and Addresses

Use a comma between the name of a city or town and the name of its state or country.

Miami, Florida
Munich, Germany

In writing an address as part of a sentence, use a comma after each item.

Forward our mail to 651 Sentinel Drive, Newark, New Jersey 07124, where we will be moving next month.

Note that you do *not* place a comma between the state and the ZIP code.

Commas in Letter Parts

Use a comma after the salutation of a friendly letter and after the complimentary close of a friendly letter or a business letter.

Dear Tim,   Yours sincerely,

Exercises Use commas correctly.

A. Copy the following sentences. Add commas where necessary.

1. The bombing of Pearl Harbor on December 7, 1941, marked the beginning of World War II for the United States.

2. On August 14, 1945, Japan surrendered to the Allies.

3. The stock market crash on October 29, 1929, marked the beginning of the Great Depression.

4. On August 20, 1974, Nelson A. Rockefeller was nominated for the office of Vice President.

5. Send your requests to Mr. R. Joseph Roller, 180 North Capitol Avenue, Denver, Colorado 80202.

6. The first state, Delaware, entered the Union on December 7, 1787.

7. The first transcontinental railroad was completed on May 10, 1869, in Promontory, Utah.

8. In 1874, Joseph Glidden of DeKalb, Illinois, invented barbed wire.

9. The President of the United States lives at 1600 Pennsylvania Avenue, Washington, D. C. 20500.

10. George Washington was inaugurated in New York City on April 30, 1789, at Federal Hall.

B. Follow the directions for Exercise A.

1. Because my parents work for the government, I have lived in Fairbanks,Alaska,and Madrid,Spain.

2. The Lewis and Clark expedition began on May 14,1804, in St. Louis,Missouri,and returned there on September 23,1806.

3. John H. Glenn, Jr. became the first American to orbit the earth on February 20,1962,aboard the *Friendship* 7.

4. We ordered our uniforms from the J. C. Wood Company, P. O. Box 5835, Richmond,Virginia 23220.

5. The 1982 World's Fair was held in Knoxville,Tennessee.

6. The charter flight will visit Helsinki,Finland,and Stockholm,Sweden.

7. My sister was born in Tokyo,Japan,on January 1,1965, and I was born in Frankfurt,Germany,on January 1,1968.

8. On August 26,1920,the amendment that gave women the right to vote was adopted.

9. The Great Chicago Fire of 1871 supposedly started in the barn at Mrs. O'Leary's,558 DeKoven Street,Chicago,Illinois.

10. Dear Jill,

  Would you please send me the Harrisons' new address? I'd appreciate it.

    Your friend,
    Tom

Commas with Nonrestrictive Clauses

Use commas to set off nonrestrictive clauses.

A **nonrestrictive clause** is one that merely adds an idea to the sentence. The sentence would be complete and the meaning would be definite without it.

A **restrictive clause** is one that is essential to the meaning of a sentence. If a restrictive clause is dropped out of the sentence, the meaning changes.

Nonrestrictive:	Cheryl White, whom I have known for years, will go to Purdue in the fall.
	Cheryl White will go to Purdue in the fall.
Restrictive:	Cheryl White is the only person in our school who is going to Purdue.
	Cheryl White is the only person in our school.

Restrictive clauses are often used to identify or point out the person or thing they modify. Without this identification, the meaning of the sentence would not be clear. Nonrestrictive clauses, on the other hand, add no essential meaning to the sentence.

Restrictive:	Janice is the girl *who found the money.* (which girl?)
Restrictive:	This is the book *that has the map.* (what book?)
Nonrestrictive:	Janice, *who is very alert,* found the money. Janice found the money.
Nonrestrictive:	This book, *which has pictures,* is my choice. This book is my choice.

Commas To Prevent Misreading

When no specific rule applies, but there is danger of misreading, use a comma.

Who she is, is a mystery.

Exercises Use commas correctly.

A. Number your paper from 1–10. Decide where commas should be used in the following sentences. Write the word before the comma, add the comma, then write the word after the comma. If no commas are necessary, write *Correct* after the appropriate number.

1. My grandparents, who are very active people, have just completed a tour of South America.

2. Our dog, who recently had puppies, is very protective of her litter.

3. This is the bicycle that I repaired and painted.

4. The speed limit, which is strictly enforced, has reduced traffic accidents.

5. This is the autobiography that I read for class.

6. Mrs. Kruse is the person who owns that flower shop.

7. Those students who are finished with the test may leave.

8. Kyle, who is my best friend, is moving to Japan next month.

9. The Wades, who live next door, are well known ocean-ographers.

10. The bus that I told you to take stops at that corner.

B. Follow the directions for Exercise A.

1. This camera, which has many features, is the best buy.

2. Ms. Larson is the teacher who coaches the volleyball team.

3. The letter you were waiting for has finally arrived.

4. Our neighbor, who is an excellent gardener, helped us with our rock garden.

5. The coach, who anticipated a tough defense, shifted her team to a zone offense.

6. This Super Suds detergent, which is heavily advertised on television, has had increased sales.

7. Mr. Hansen, who is our club sponsor, will be my English teacher next year.

8. Tomoko Pham is the only student in our school who is from Southeast Asia.

9. That is the book that has all the color photographs in it.

10. Rita Coolidge, who is touring with another singer, will be in Dallas next week.

The Semicolon

Use a semicolon to join the clauses of a compound sentence when no coordinating conjunction is used.

Dan has finished his homework; Darcy has not begun hers.

When there are many commas in the clauses of a compound sentence, separate the clauses themselves with a semicolon.

McCurdy of Illinois made the most spectacular shot of the game, a toss from mid-court; and Indiana, which had been favored to win, went down to defeat.

When there are commas within items in a series, use semicolons to separate the items.

Hartford, New Haven, and Norwich, Connecticut; Springfield and Worcester, Massachusetts; and Pine Bridge, Mt. Kisco, and Chappaqua, New York, have all tried this experiment.

Use a semicolon before a conjunctive adverb that joins the clauses of a compound sentence.

Conjunctive adverbs commonly used are *therefore, however, hence, so, then, moreover, besides, nevertheless, yet,* and *consequently*.

It was a sunny day; however, it was quite cool.

The Colon

Use a colon after the greeting of a business letter.

Dear Sir or Madam: Ladies and Gentlemen:

Use a colon between numerals indicating hours and minutes.

10:00 P.M.

Objective

To use semicolons and colons correctly

Presenting the Lesson

1. Read and discuss pages 555 and 556. Stress that when a colon is used before a list, the statement before the list must indicate clearly that a list of things, and not merely one or two things, will follow.
2. Assign and discuss Exercises A and B on pages 556 and 557.

Individualizing the Lesson

Less-Advanced Students

Make sure that the students can identify the rule for each semicolon and colon required in the Exercises. Have the students first identify the compound sentences in the Exercise before adding punctuation.

Advanced Students

Have the students revise sentences 1 and 10 in Exercise B so that colons are not required.

Reinforcement Exercise

Assign and discuss Exercise G on page 572.

Optional Practice

Have the students decide which compound sentences in Exercises A and B on page 549 – 550 would be acceptable with semicolons rather than commas and conjunctions.

Extending the Lesson

Have each student find a published example of a compound sentence that uses a semicolon in place of a coordinating conjunction and an example of a sentence in which a list is introduced by a colon.

Use a colon to introduce a list of items.

> If you are trying out for the team, bring the following things: a pair of gym shoes, your P.E. uniform, and your consent form.

If there would be no pause in speaking, no colon is used before the list of items.

> If you are trying out for the team, bring a pair of gym shoes, your P.E. uniform, and your consent form.

Exercises Use semicolons and colons correctly.

A. Copy the word before and after each missing punctuation mark and add the correct punctuation mark.

1. Jon prepared dinner; Paula set the table.
2. Grinning broadly, Lee crossed the finish line 10 feet ahead of the others; however, the grin faded when the judges told her she had been disqualified.
3. San Francisco, Los Angeles, and Oakland, California; Dallas and Houston, Texas; and New York and Buffalo, New York, have professional teams.
4. It was a clear day; moreover, it was perfect for swimming.
5. Allen, wash the car; Jenny, clean up the yard; Joan, take the dog for a walk.
6. New animals in the collection include a cheetah, an okapi, and a harpy eagle from Africa; a tiger, two peacocks, and a rhinoceros from India; a snow leopard from Tibet; and two caribou, a Kodiak bear, and an arctic fox from Alaska.
7. Bring three things to class tomorrow: your text, paper, and a blue or black pen.
8. You will need to meet me between 830 and 845 A.M.
9. Dear Madam:
     This letter will confirm your reservation.
10. It was a cold autumn day; however, it was quite sunny.

B. Follow the directions for Exercise A.

1. Please stop at the store and bring these items home: a gallon of milk, a can of tomatoes, and a box of crackers.

2. Tracy was reading a mystery; Sandy was hooking a rug.

3. I know that there is not much time; nevertheless, the work must be finished by 5:30.

4. Mother's plane arrives at 6:55 P.M.; Dad's will land at 7:15 P.M.

5. Jim studied hard for the test; yet, he thought it was one of the hardest ones he'd ever taken.

6. The Pep Club will handle ticket sales; the cheerleaders will help with the ushering.

7. Our bus leaves at 7:15 A.M.; my sister's bus doesn't leave until 8:30 A.M.

8. The snow was blinding; however, the school bus arrived on time at 8:15 A.M.

9. The running back made a spectacular drive to the goal, a 47-yard run; and the defense, which couldn't get organized, was stunned.

10. Bring these items to sewing class on Monday: tracing paper, your pattern, thread, and pins.

The Hyphen

Use a hyphen if a syllable of a word must be carried over from one line to the next.

> In the library you will find several authorita-
> tive books on solar energy.

Only words of two or more syllables can be divided at the end of a line. Never divide words of one syllable, such as *height* or *worse*.

A single letter must not be left at the end of a line. For example, this division would be wrong: *a-waken*. A single letter

The Hyphen

Objective

To use hyphens correctly

Presenting the Lesson

1. Read and discuss pages 557 and 558. Have the students give additional examples of each function of the hyphen. Encourage students to use a dictionary to determine whether a noun or adjective is hyphenated and to check syllabification.

2. Assign and discuss the Exercise on page 558.

Individualizing the Lesson

Less-Advanced Students

Show the students how to locate and interpret syllabification in a dictionary entry.

Advanced Students

Do the Exercise orally.

Reinforcement Exercise

Assign and discuss Exercise H on page 573.

Optional Practice

Have the students use a dictionary to decide how to hyphenate each of the following words at the end of a line:

manufacture	decide
opportunity	writing
announcement	detour
elevator	

Extending the Lesson

Supply each student with a page from a newspaper for a hyphen hunt. Have students find as many uses for hyphens as possible.

must not appear at the beginning of a line, either. It would be wrong to divide *sanitary* like this: *sanitar-y*.

Use a hyphen in compound numbers from twenty-one through ninety-nine.

twenty-three cents   forty-two students

Use a hyphen in fractions.

We won a two-thirds majority.

Use a hyphen or hyphens in such compound nouns as *great-aunt* and *commander-in-chief*.

Use a hyphen or hyphens between words that make up a compound adjective used before a noun.

This is an up-to-date edition.
But: This edition is up to date.

Exercise Use hyphens correctly.

Number your paper from 1–15. After the proper numbers, write the words that should be hyphenated. Add the necessary hyphens. Use your dictionary if you need to.

1. We received the store's new, up-to-date catalog.
2. In ten years I will be twenty-three years old.
3. We saw that the lawn was half cut. Correct
4. One-sixth of the students voted for Pam.
5. Ninety-three students in all voted in the election.
6. Maurita won the election by a three-fourths majority.
7. You must write out the amount of the check: one hundred twenty-three dollars and fifty-six cents.
8. Our great-grandmother celebrated her ninety-fifth birthday.
9. The postage for this package is sixty-two cents.
10. About sixty-eight percent of the residents voted in the special election.

11. When were your great-grandparents born?

12. The man had a well-to-do look about him.

13. Thirty-two students were chosen to go to the speech contest.

14. Chester A. Arthur was the twenty-first President.

15. The President of the United States is the Commander-in-Chief of the Armed Forces.

The Apostrophe

One of the most frequent uses of the apostrophe is its use in forming the possessive of nouns. Before you form the possessive of a noun, be sure to notice whether the noun is singular or plural.

To form the possessive of a singular noun, add an apostrophe and an s.

girl + 's = girl's   man + 's = man's
boy + 's = boy's   Ross + 's = Ross's

To form the possessive of a plural noun that does not end in s, add an apostrophe and an s.

men's   women's

To form the possessive of a plural noun that ends in s, add only an apostrophe.

drivers + ' = drivers'   pilots + ' = pilots'

Use an apostrophe and an s to form the possessive of indefinite pronouns.

someone + 's = someone's   anybody + 's = anybody's

Never use an apostrophe in a possessive pronoun.

ours   yours

The Apostrophe

Objective

To use apostrophes correctly

Presenting the Lesson

1. Read and discuss pages 559 and 560.
2. Assign and discuss Exercises A and B on pages 560 and 561.

Individualizing the Lesson

Less-Advanced Students

Have the students identify the words that make up each contraction in the Exercises.

Advanced Students

Do the Exercises orally.

Reinforcement Exercise

Assign and discuss Exercise I on page 573.

Optional Practice

Have the students take turns writing singular or plural nouns on the chalkboard. Call on other students to make each noun possessive.

Extending the Lesson

Have the students read a page from a local newspaper, checking the use of apostrophes. Compile a list of errors noted by the students and include these in a class letter to the editor.

Use an apostrophe in a contraction.

In a contraction, the apostrophe simply replaces one or more omitted letters.

he's = he is	aren't = are not	I'm = I am
it's = it is	isn't = is not	I've = I have
won't = will not	don't = do not	we've = we have

Use an apostrophe to show the omission of numbers in a date.

the class of '80 (the class of 1980)

Use an apostrophe and *s* to form the plurals of letters, figures, and words used as words.

two *m*'s   four *6*'s   *and*'s and *but*'s

Exercises Use apostrophes correctly.

A. Copy these sentences, inserting apostrophes where they are needed.

1. We've heard that there won't be a show today.
2. Beatrix Potter's most famous work is *The Tale of Peter Rabbit*.
3. Her writings and illustrations are well known in children's literature.
4. Billie Holiday's life and music were portrayed in the movie *Lady Sings the Blues*.
5. Diana Ross's performance as the jazz musician earned her an Oscar nomination.
6. Soichiro Honda's company has been producing motorcycles and cars in Japan since the 1940's.
7. I've always liked the silent movies of Buster Keaton and Charlie Chaplin.
8. All of the teachers' meetings are held in the library.
9. Babe Didrikson Zaharias's autobiography reveals her intense love for athletics and her zest for life.

10. *The Miracle Worker* is a play about Helen Keller's childhood and Annie Sullivan's efforts to help the blind and deaf Helen.

B. Follow the directions for Exercise A.

1. The 1's and the 7's in this ledger are difficult to distinguish.

2. The graduating classes of '82 and '83 bought a new digital scoreboard.

3. Although she was the first woman to go into space, Valentina Tereshkova's name is not well known.

4. We've heard Beverly Sills's performance at the opera.

5. Someone's moped is parked in the Burtons' driveway.

6. Isn't the girls' gymnastics meet on Saturday?

7. Clara Barton's dedication in a volunteer nurse corps led to her founding of the American Red Cross.

8. S. E. Hinton's novel, *That Was Then, This Is Now,* is one of the best books we've read this year.

9. Jenny's sister and Paula's brother are both interns at St. Mary's Hospital.

10. Nurses' training programs are extensive and demanding.

Quotation Marks

Quotation marks tell your reader that you are quoting directly the exact spoken or written words of another person.

Use quotation marks at the beginning and at the end of a direct quotation.

Donna said, "My cat's eyes shine in the dark."

Quotation marks are *not* used with indirect quotations:

Donna says that her cat's eyes shine in the dark.

Quotation Marks

Objective

To use quotation marks correctly

Presenting the Lesson

1. Read and discuss pages 561-564. Point out the placement of commas and quotation marks in the sample sentences.

2. Assign and discuss Exercises A and B on pages 564 and 565.

3. Read and discuss **Using Quo-**

tation **Marks for Titles** on page
566. Have the students suggest
examples of each type of work.
Write these on the chalkboard.

4. Assign and discuss Exercises
A and B on pages 566 and 567.

Individualizing the Lesson

Less-Advanced Students

1. Read the sentences in Exercises A and B on pages 564 and
565 aloud before the students try to
punctuate them. Exaggerate the in-
flections and pauses to help the
students recognize the quoted parts
in each sentence.

2. Have the students identify
each kind of title used in Exercises A
and B on pages 566 and 567.

Advanced Students

1. Have the students revise the
sentences in Exercise B on page
565, moving the explanatory words
to other locations. Discuss the effect
on each sentence, and have the
students decide which versions are
most effective.

2. Have the students write original titles in each category listed on
page 566. Tell them that these may
be humorous.

Reinforcement Exercises

Assign and discuss Exercises J
and K on pages 574 and 575.

Optional Practice

Read a passage of dialogue from
a short story as a dictation exercise.
Have the students exchange papers
to correct the punctuation. Discuss

Sometimes a direct quotation is broken into two or more
parts by explanatory words. In such a case, each part of the
quotation is enclosed in quotation marks.

"Do you think," Bill asked, "that you could help me with
the dishes?"

The second part of a divided quotation starts with a small
letter, as in the example above, unless it begins a new sentence
or unless it is a proper noun.

"We got drenched," said Bob. "We had no umbrella."

The first part of a divided quotation is followed by a comma
that is placed *inside* the quotation marks.

"Before you leave," said Mrs. Lazar, "I want to talk to you."

Explanatory words in a divided quotation are followed by
either a comma or a period *outside* the quotation marks. A
comma is used after the explanatory words if the second part
of the quotation does not begin a new sentence. A period is
used after the explanatory words if the second part of the
quotation is a new sentence.

"When you arrive," said Carol, "ring the doorbell."
"I can't go," said Janet. "I have to study."

Explanatory words at the beginning of a sentence are followed by a comma *outside* the quotation marks. The period at
the end of the sentence is placed *inside* the quotation marks.

Mother said, "There is someone to see you."

Explanatory words at the end of a sentence are followed by
a period. The quoted words at the beginning of the sentence
are followed by a comma *inside* the quotation marks.

"There is someone to see you," Mother said.

Place question marks and exclamation points inside quotation marks if they belong to the quotation itself, but outside if they do not belong to the quotation.

> Dad asked, "Has Mike closed the garage doors?"
> Did Mother say, "Be home by five o'clock"?
> "Look out!" Terry shouted.

You may wonder how to use quotation marks when you are quoting *two or more sentences of a single speaker*. Notice how the following quotation is punctuated.

> "Is the club going to meet tomorrow?" asked Sue. "I wasn't sure whether we had decided to meet tomorrow or the next day. We have important things to discuss."

Only one set of quotation marks would be needed if the example read as follows:

> Sue asked, "Is the club going to meet tomorrow? I wasn't sure whether we had decided to meet tomorrow or the next day. We have important things to discuss."

When a quotation is long, it may consist of two or more paragraphs. In such a case, open each of the paragraphs with a quotation mark, but do not use an end quotation mark until the whole speech is finished.

> "There are many ways in which every individual can conserve energy on a daily basis," began the speaker.
> "For example, turning off lights, radios, stereos, or televisions when we're really not using them saves a lot of electrical power.
> "Being conscientious about our means of travel is beneficial to energy conservation, too. Do we unnecessarily travel by car when we could walk, cycle, or use public transportation? All of these considerations seem minor, but if everyone made an effort to conserve a little energy every day, we'd all benefit enormously."

the reasons for the placement of quotation marks in each quoted passage.

Extending the Lesson

Have each student find a published example of a divided quotation.

563

When you are writing *dialogue* (conversation), begin each speaker's part with a new paragraph, even if the speeches are quite short.

> "It's Saturday again, and here we all are," said Larry.
> "Yes, it's Saturday all day today," Ted joked.
> "It's a wonderful day!" said Anne, happily.

With a quotation *inside another quotation*, single quotation marks are used. Here is an example:

> "It was Patrick Henry," declared Liz, "who said, 'Give me liberty or give me death!'"

Notice that the whole quotation is enclosed in quotation marks. The quotation within the quotation is enclosed in single quotation marks. A comma precedes the single quotation marks at the opening on the inner quotation. Notice how the quotation marks ('") come together at the end of the sentence.

Exercises Use quotation marks correctly.

A. Copy the following sentences. Add the necessary quotation marks and other punctuation marks. Use capital letters where necessary.

1. "Have the committee members come yet?" asked Molly. "They are supposed to set up the tables and chairs."
2. "It was Martin Luther King, Jr.," reported Tanya, "who said, 'Injustice anywhere is a threat to justice everywhere.'"
3. "Would you mind," asked Cindy, "if I borrowed your bicycle?"
4. Didn't the teacher say, "We'll meet in the gym at 10:30"?
5. "Andrea," Sally said, "may I borrow your camera this weekend?"

6. Our history teacher told us John Paul Jones is supposed to have said, "I have not yet begun to fight."

7. Kristen inquired, "Was it Amelia Earhart who said, 'Courage is the price that life exacts for granting peace'?"

8. "Bill kept saying, 'It's just one of those things,'" said Nancy.

9. "In his inaugural address," said Sherry, "John Kennedy stated: 'And so, my fellow Americans, ask not what your country can do for you; ask what you can do for your country.'"

10. "Will you organize the committee," asked Sara, "and order the decorations?"

B. Copy the following sentences. Add the necessary quotation marks and any other punctuation marks. Use capital letters where necessary.

1. "In her autobiography," said Anna, "Eleanor Roosevelt wrote: 'Life was meant to be lived, and curiosity must be kept alive. One must never, for whatever reason, turn his back on life.'"

2. "Isn't it getting too late," Roger asked, "for us to start making plans for an all-school play?"

3. "In what ways have you, as an individual, conserved energy?" began our guest speaker.

4. "There's the doorbell," said Uncle Thomas, "Will you answer it, Ramon?"

5. "That's the game!" yelled the announcer, "The Yanks have won the Series!"

6. "There's someone to see you," my sister said, "and it looks as if he's bringing back the jacket you lost."

7. "Is it Burger King or McDonald's whose motto is 'You deserve a break today'?" asked Debbie.

8. "Bill said, 'I will drive you to school,'" explained Peg.

9. "Joan, have you seen that movie yet?" asked Dan.

10. "I never heard of such a thing," said my mother quietly. "Are you sure that is what he said?"

Using Quotation Marks for Titles

Use quotation marks to enclose chapter titles, titles of magazine articles, titles of short stories, essays, or single poems, titles of television and radio programs, and titles of songs or short pieces of music.

Chapter title	Chapter 3, "Americans in London"
Magazine article	"Images of Youth Past"
Short story	"The Headless Horseman"
Essay	"My First Article"
Poem	"The Raven"
Television program	"Sixty Minutes"
Song	"The Star-Spangled Banner"

When you write the titles of whole books or of plays, magazines, newspapers, works of art, long musical compositions, and motion pictures, do not use quotation marks. Instead, underline the titles, like this: The Light in the Forest. Such titles should be underlined when you are writing in longhand or when you are typing. Use a single underlining, not a double one. Written or typed words that are underlined are set in a special style of type in printing. This style is called *italics*.

Exercises Use quotation marks and underlining correctly.

A. Number your paper from 1–10. Copy the following sentences, adding quotation marks around titles or underscoring titles where necessary.

1. I liked the story "The Monkey's Paw."

2. For my poetry assignment, I read "Macavity: The Mystery Cat."

3. Read the first chapter, "Discovery in the New World," for tomorrow.

4. The television program "The Little House on the Prairie" deals with problems and pleasures of pioneer life.

5. Some of James Thurber's stories are "The Very Proper Gander," "The Shrike and the Chipmunks," and "The Owl Who Was God."

6. Our band played the theme from Rocky and the theme from Star Wars.

7. The Charlie Chaplin movie The Gold Rush and Harold Lloyd's film Safety Last are two well known silent comedies.

8. Did you see the movie One on One?

9. Read Chapter 2, "How We Came to the River."

10. The Love Bug is a movie about a Volkswagen.

B. Follow the directions for Exercise A.

1. "God Save the Queen" and "America" have the same melody.

2. Two of Jack's favorite programs are "The Today Show" and "Hill Street Blues."

3. We read the novel The Call of the Wild and the short story "Brown Wolf" by Jack London.

4. "Adjö Means Goodbye" by Carrie A. Young is the story of a friendship.

5. My essay entitled "Youth Today" won an honorable mention in the poetry and prose contest.

6. One Flew Over the Cuckoo's Nest won the Academy Award for the best picture in 1975.

7. "Old Man River" is a song from the musical Showboat.

8. Last week's editorial was entitled "The Mess in City Government—What Are You Doing About It?"

9. Barry Manilow, who has recorded such songs as "I Write the Songs" and "Mandy," has also written many popular advertising slogans and jingles.

10. My favorite poem is "The Revolt of the Machines" by Stephen Vincent Benét.

Reinforcement Exercises

These Reinforcement Exercises may be used for additional practice as needed. Each exercise may be used after the text page indicated in parentheses.

Review

If you have not assigned these Exercises before this time, you can use them as an excellent Section Review.

Mixed Review

The following exercises provide review of the concepts and skills presented in this chapter.

A. Use commas correctly. Rewrite the following letter. Insert commas where they are needed.

Photo-Art Inc.
7245 Lake Street
Fresno, California 93706
Dear Sir or Madam:
I recently ordered a T-shirt, a mug, and a key chain from your catalog, but I did not receive the correct merchandise. First of all, a child's T-shirt was sent instead of an adult's. Secondly, the mug, a plastic one, arrived with a broken handle. Thirdly, the acrylic key chain, which was to hold a picture of my niece, had a picture of a complete stranger in it!
The president of your company is quoted in your catalog as saying, "Satisfaction is guaranteed." If you can fill my order correctly by April 1, 1983, please do so. If you cannot fill the order by then, however, please refund a check for $12.87.
Sincerely,
Raymond Stone

Reinforcement Exercises — Review

Punctuation

A. Use end marks correctly. (Use after page 542.)

Copy these sentences, adding the necessary punctuation.

1. The order was issued by Capt. Thomas E. Conklin.
2. Jackie! Watch out!
3. Tomorrow night Dr. Linda Marshall and Mr. Mark Leopold will lecture on law enforcement.
4. Our tour of the FBI Building in Washington, D.C., begins at 8:00 A.M. sharp.
5. Did you know that Prof. Stevens is teaching in St. Louis?
6. Wow! That relay race was exciting./!
7. Rev. Martin T. McDaniel will speak at the lecture hall at 9:00 P. M.
8. Marcia's report for U. S. history is on the subject of NATO.
9. Be careful! There's broken glass in that bag./!
10. Mr. and Mrs. Barrett will chaperone the canoe trip.

B. Use commas correctly. (Use after page 545.)

Number your paper from 1–10. Copy the following sentences. Add commas where necessary.

1. If I know David, he would beg, borrow, or even work to go on that camping trip.
2. That long, sleek, silver Jaguar belongs to Dr. Weston.
3. Leaves and branches were strewn all over the front yard, the driveway, and the flower bed.

4. While searching the ground for clues, the detectives discovered a thin, razor-sharp knife.

5. A feisty, mischievous poodle dashed across the newly seeded lawn.

6. Are you sure that only Ginny, Pat, and Terry need rides?

7. I washed the car, waxed it, and polished all of the chrome.

8. To get to the ice rink, go two blocks north, turn right, and park in the junior high school lot.

9. If you want to conserve gasoline, do the following: first, start and stop your car gradually; second, drive at a steady speed; third, don't keep the engine running unnecessarily.

10. While in New Orleans, we visited the French Quarter, rode down the Mississippi on a riverboat, and heard many jazz bands perform.

C. Use commas correctly. (Use after page 546.)

Number your paper from 1–10. Copy the following sentences and add commas where necessary.

1. Yes, I've read several Agatha Christie mysteries.

2. After the photographs have been developed, we can choose one for the newspaper.

3. Gary, to tell the truth, was quite satisfied with the test results.

4. The results of the election, however, will not be posted until tomorrow morning.

5. No, the test will not be given until Monday.

6. Although the game had to be postponed, the dance went on as planned.

7. The office fire was, consequently, a setback for the business.

8. Your decision, moreover, will affect our plans.

9. After running fifteen laps around the gym, the team practiced its defensive plays.

10. Yes, the wrestling meet will be held at the high school.

B. Punctuate correctly. Rewrite the following paragraph. Add the necessary punctuation marks.

"Welcome aboard, ladies and gentlemen," said the pilot's voice over the intercom system. "I am Captain John J. Hayes, and my co-pilot today is Captain Mark Singer. We'll be making intermediate stops in the following cities: Nashville, Tennessee; Mobile, Alabama; and Orlando, Florida. Our estimated arrival time in Miami, Florida, is 6:30 P.M. Our flight stewards will be happy to help you in any way they can; don't hesitate to ask for assistance. Our in-flight movie will be Rocky. Now settle back and have a pleasant flight."

Using Mechanics in Writing

1. Have the students write sentences using colons to introduce each of the following lists:
   1. books, newspapers, magazines
   2. scissors, paste, a ruler
   3. remove the old paint, sand the surface smooth, apply the new paint

2. Have the students combine the following pairs of sentences, punctuating correctly:
   1. The northern swift fox is native to Canada. It is an endangered species.
   2. Limpa is made with fruit and nuts. Limpa is a Swedish bread.
   3. Strawberries are in season in June. Apples ripen in the fall.
   4. A roaring fire warmed the room. Violin music filled the air.
   5. The park is open. No camping is allowed.

3. Have the students write letters to friends. In their letters they should relate an anecdote about something that happened in school recently, using dialogue.

4. Have the students write descriptive paragraphs, using at least three hyphenated adjectives.

5. Have the students write one-paragraph reviews of television programs, books, stories, and movies. Check for the correct use of quotation marks and underlining.

D. Use commas correctly. (Use after page 550.)

Number your paper from 1–10. Copy the following sentences, adding commas where they are needed.

1. Bruce Jenner, the Olympic decathlon champion, was the guest speaker at our school.

2. If you look closely into the microscope, Barb, you will see thousands of living organisms.

3. Margaret Hillis, the famous conductor, directed the symphony at Carnegie Hall.

4. "Weather patterns are changing" explained Mrs. Hammill, "and no one is quite sure why."

5. Maria Tallchief and Martha Graham, women famous in the world of dance, have performed all over the world.

6. Severe drought, the worst in twenty years, hit the Great Plains last summer.

7. Joyce, would you please start a fire in the fireplace?

8. The ballet was in town for a week, and every performance was sold out.

9. Curling, a sport played on ice with brooms, is a rigorous game.

10. Running and swimming are physically demanding activities, but they are the top two sports for staying in shape.

E. Use commas correctly. (Use after page 552.)

Copy the following sentences. Add commas where necessary.

1. Please have the package sent to Ms. Kathy Murphy, 2439 North Granville Avenue, Marion, Ohio 43302.

2. All the letters had to be postmarked by January 1 to be considered. Correct

3. Dear Mrs. Brannstrom,

   Thank you for the birthday gift. It was greatly appreciated.

                        Yours sincerely,
                        Michael Flynn

4. We visited Bellingrath Gardens in Theodore, Alabama, and the capitol buildings in Jackson, Mississippi, while vacationing last summer.

5. The Omni International Hotel in Atlanta, Georgia, has a huge indoor ice rink, six movie theaters, and countless shops.

6. My father was born on February 6, 1939, in Duluth, Minnesota, and I was born on February 6, 1969, in Evanston, Illinois.

7. The Superdome in New Orleans, Louisiana, and the Astrodome in Houston, Texas, are phenomenal structures.

8. When you say "Kansas City," do you mean Kansas City, Missouri, or Kansas City, Kansas?

9. On July 4, 1876, celebrations for our nation's one hundredth birthday were held in Philadelphia, Pennsylvania.

10. Ray Kroc opened his first McDonald's restaurant on April 15, 1955, in Des Plaines, Illinois.

F. Use commas correctly. (Use after page 554.)

Number your paper from 1–10. Decide where commas should be used in the following sentences. Write the word before the comma, add the comma, and then write the word after the comma. If no comma is necessary, write *Correct*.

1. Whatever you do, do well.
2. Janice and Laura are the ones who started the ski club. Correct
3. This magazine, which has beautiful color photos, is one of my favorites.
4. Laura Eaton, who has been my friend for years, has moved to Arizona.

5. Franklin Delano Roosevelt was the only American President who was elected to four straight terms in office. Correct

6. Before eating, my goldfish darts rapidly around its bowl.

7. After we ate, the horses had to be cared for.

8. Paul's camera, which has a telephoto lens, is ideal for sports pictures.

9. While moving, our family stayed at a motel.

10. Mrs. Hogan is the teacher who sponsored the dance. Correct

G. Use semicolons and colons correctly. (Use after page 557.)

Copy the word before and after each missing punctuation mark and add the correct punctuation mark.

1. Jack passed the history test; I failed it.

2. The guidebook suggested buying these items: leather from Barcelona, Spain, or Florence, Italy; wool from London, England, or Edinburgh, Scotland; and crystal from Waterford, Ireland, or Stockholm, Sweden.

3. When he finally decided to buy Mrs. Daniels's old car, my brother was happy; however, he was miserable when the transmission fell apart three months later.

4. The concert tickets went on sale at 9:00 A.M.; by 9:45 A.M. they were all sold.

5. Dear Sir:
Enclosed you will find your refund check for nine dollars.

6. Keith cleaned out the garage; I painted the storm windows.

7. To make the punch, you will need the following ingredients: lime sherbet, lemon juice, and ginger ale.

8. At 8:30 A.M. the following students are to report to the gym: Doug Smith, Beth Schleker, and Lynn Kimball.

9. Please bring these items to the testing room: two pencils, an eraser, and a spiral notebook.

10. At 7:30 A.M. Mary jumped out of bed and started getting dressed; then she remembered that it was Saturday.

H. Use hyphens correctly. (Use after page 559.)

Copy the following sentences. Add hyphens wherever they are needed.

1. Ninety-two is the best golf score Julie has ever shot.
2. Mr. Perez's daughter-in-law is an up-and-coming politician.
3. Jake's still-life paintings are much better than his portraits.
4. The save-the-trees resolution passed the City Council with a three-fifths vote of approval.
5. Last week Louis saw an accident involving twenty-two vehicles.
6. Gina's great-great-grandfather founded the town of Chenoa.
7. Kelly's Lake, once a quiet, out-of-the-way resort, is now a dirty, evil-smelling swamp.
8. Eighty-eight children applied to the camp; no more than forty-one could be accepted.
9. My great-aunt and my great-grandmother are both ninety-one years old.
10. Eighty-five percent of the student population participated in the Toys-for-Tots campaign.

I. Use apostrophes correctly. (Use after page 561.)

Number your paper from 1–10. Copy the following sentences. Add apostrophes where they are needed.

1. The head coach's decision to have two extra practices was helpful.
2. The actress's jeweled costume looked as if it weighed at least fifty pounds.
3. I don't think that the art supplies we ordered will be enough.

4. Scott wondered if a member of Congress's salary was as high as a nurse's.

5. The *m*'s and *n*'s in this note look alike.

6. It's supposed to snow this weekend, so we'll probably be able to go skiing.

7. Don't you think it would have been fun to grow up during the 50's?

8. The girls' swimming meet and the boys' basketball game are on the same day.

9. Since the municipal park's tennis courts were being used, Sandy and Lisa played on the high school courts.

10. The junior high school's choir and orchestra, and the high school's freshmen chorale, will perform at the new shopping mall.

J. Use quotation marks correctly. (Use after page 565.)

Number your paper from 1–10. Copy the following sentences. Add the necessary quotation marks and other punctuation marks. Use capital letters where necessary.

1. "Will the student council sponsor the car wash," asked our principal, "or should another club be responsible?"

2. "If we win tonight," said Coach Strand, "we'll definitely play in the holiday tournament."

3. "I think it was Ben Franklin," replied David, "who said, 'A penny saved is a penny earned.'"

4. "Who said, 'The test is really easy'?" asked Pat.

5. "I wonder," said Wendy, "if anyone wants to go to the art fair."

6. Trisha asked, "was it Tolstoi who wrote, 'If you want to be happy, be'?"

7. Juanita inquired, "What time is play rehearsal tomorrow?"

8. Yolanda said, "It was Mark Twain who wrote, 'Always do right. This will gratify some people, and astonish the rest.'"

9. "Did you see the movie with Katharine Hepburn and John Wayne?" asked Debbie. "It was on television last night."

10. "Mr. Pierce said, 'Do the first eight questions,'" said Nancy. "He didn't say anything about the last two."

K. Use quotation marks and underlining correctly.
(Use after page 567.)

Number your paper from 1–10. Copy the following sentences, adding quotation marks around titles or underlining titles where necessary.

1. The movie Gone with the Wind appeared on television for the first time in 1976.

2. Many adults enjoy watching "Sesame Street" as much as their children do.

3. The prize-winning student essay was entitled "The Future Belongs to Me."

4. Our class read two of Poe's short stories: "The Tell-Tale Heart" and "Murders in the Rue Morgue."

5. Have you ever read the poem "Paul Revere's Ride" by Longfellow?

6. Eve Merriam's two poems "Thumbprint" and "Sometimes" are two of my favorites.

7. The first chapter of David Copperfield is called "I Am Born."

8. The March issue of National Geographic has an interesting article about the Sahara entitled "Caravaning Through the Desert."

9. My Fair Lady is based on a play called Pygmalion.

10. The television program "The Little House on the Prairie" is based on a novel by Laura Ingalls Wilder.

Section 13

Spelling

It is important for you to have good spelling skills. You will use these skills when you write friendly and business letters. You will use them when you write reports on all subjects at school. You will use them when you fill out job applications. If you care about what others think of you and what you have to say, you will want to be able to spell words correctly.

There is no simple way to teach you how to spell. However, there are several methods you can use to attack your spelling problems. These methods are discussed in this section.

Section Objectives

1. To use general techniques for improving spelling skills
2. To use techniques for mastering the spelling of particular words
3. To become familiar with spelling patterns and rules
4. To distinguish and spell correctly homonyms and other words often confused

Preparing the Students

Ask the students if they would submit a job application or an essay or a business letter that they knew had spelling errors. Discuss why and how they try to avoid spelling errors, as well as the kind of impression that correct spelling makes.

Then write the following on the chalkboard.

> Your going to be studing spelling and improveing you're skills.

Have students point out the four spelling errors. Read and discuss this page. Tell the students that using the guidelines in Section 13 would prevent these four errors, as well as many others.

Additional Resources

Diagnostic Test—See page 8 in the test booklet. Recommended for use before teaching the chapter.

Mastery Test—See pages 59-60 in the test booklet Recommended for use after teaching the chapter.

Reinforcement Exercises—See pages 590-591 in the student text.

Skills Practice Book—pages 193-198.

Duplicating Masters—pages 193-198.

How To Become a Better Speller

Objective

To use general techniques for improving spelling skills

Presenting the Lesson

Read and discuss page 578. Encourage the students to begin putting these techniques into practice.

Individualizing the Lesson

Less-Advanced Students

Work with the students to compile a class list of words that are frequently misspelled in the students' writing. Use the steps on page 578 to begin conquering these demons.

Advanced Students

Encourage proofreading of all written work. Advanced students are sometimes careless about spelling in their own work but do a good job of editing someone else's work. Try having the students exchange rough drafts for their next writing assignment.

Optional Practice

Have students suggest memory devices for these spellings: *bargain, realize, eighth, regular,* and *parallel*.

Extending the Lesson

Have the students review previously-written compositions and list all words they have misspelled more than once. Have them look up correct spellings, and quiz each other.

How To Become a Better Speller

1. Find out what your personal spelling demons are and conquer them. Go over your old composition papers and make a list of the words you misspelled on them. Keep this list and master the words on it.

2. Pronounce words carefully. It may be that you misspell words because you don't pronounce them carefully. For example, if you write *probly* for *probably*, you are no doubt mispronouncing the word.

3. Get into the habit of seeing the letters in a word. Many people have never really looked at the word *similar*. Otherwise, why do they write it *similiar?*

Take a good look at new words, or difficult words. You'll remember them better. Copy the correct spelling several times.

4. Think up a memory device for difficult words. Here are some devices that have worked for other people. They may help you, either to spell these words or to make up your own memory devices.

> a**cq**uaint (*cq*) To get a**cq**uainted, I will *seek you*.
> princi**pal** (*pal*) The princi**pal** is my *pal*.
> princi**ple** (*ple*) Follow this princi**ple,** *please*.
> business (*i*) *I* was involved in big business.

5. Proofread everything you write. In order to learn how to spell, you must learn to examine critically everything you write.

To proofread a piece of writing, you must read it slowly, word for word. Otherwise, your eyes may play tricks on you and let you skip over misspelled words.

6. Learn the few important spelling rules given in this section.

How To Master the Spelling of Particular Words

1. Look at the word and say it to yourself. Be sure you pronounce it correctly. If it has more than one syllable, say it again, one syllable at a time. Look at each syllable as you say it.

2. Look at the letters and say each one. If the word has more than one syllable, divide the word into syllables when you say the letters.

3. Write the word without looking at your book or list.

4. Now look at your book or list and see whether you spelled the word correctly. If you did, write it again and compare it with the correct form again. Do this once more.

5. If you made a mistake, note exactly what it was. Then repeat steps 3 and 4 above until you have written the word correctly three times.

Rules for Spelling

The Final Silent e

When a suffix beginning with a vowel is added to a word ending in a silent e, the e is usually dropped.

create + -ion = creation   grieve + -ing = grieving

graze + -ing = grazing   relate + -ive = relative

fame + -ous = famous   continue + -ing = continuing

579

How To Master the Spelling of Particular Words

Objective

To use techniques for mastering the spelling of particular words

Presenting the Lesson

Read and discuss the guidelines on page 579. Practice each step with difficult-to-spell words suggested by the students.

Optional Practice

Have the students practice the guidelines with the following words: *resistance, attendance, committee, condemn,* and *height*.

Extending the Lesson

Have the students read a short story, select two unfamiliar words, and memorize their spellings, using the guidelines on page 579.

Rules for Spelling

Objective

To become familiar with spelling patterns and rules

Presenting the Lesson

1. Read and discuss the rules and examples on pages 579 and 580. Make sure that the students understand the definitions of *suffix,* vowel, and *consonant.*

2. Assign and discuss Exercises A and B on pages 580 and 581.

3. Read and discuss the rules on page 581.

4. Assign and discuss the Exercise on page 582.

5. Read and discuss the rules on pages 582 and 583.

6. Assign and discuss the Exercise on page 583.

7. Read and discuss the rules on pages 583 and 584.

8. Assign and discuss the Exercise on page 584.

Individualizing the Lesson

Less-Advanced Students

Have the students tell which spelling rule applies to each word that they spell or correct in the Exercises.

Advanced Students

Have each student write one additional example word for each spelling rule.

Reinforcement Exercises

Assign and discuss Exercises A, B, C, D, and E on pages 590-591.

Optional Practice

Hold a traditional spelling bee in which individuals or teams compete in spelling words that you read aloud.

Extending the Lesson

Have the students create crossword puzzles using the example words that appear on pages 579-584.

When a suffix beginning with a consonant is added to a word ending in a silent e, the e is usually retained.

spite + -ful = spiteful   taste + -ful = tasteful
state + -ment = statement   move + -ment = movement
voice + -less = voiceless   wide + -ly = widely

The following words are exceptions:

truly   argument   ninth   wholly

Words Ending in *y*

When a suffix is added to a word ending in y preceded by a consonant, the y is usually changed to i.

crazy + -ly = crazily   puppy + -s = puppies
seventy + -eth = seventieth   silly + -ness = silliness
hilly + -est = hilliest   marry + -age = marriage

Note the following exception: When *-ing* is added, the *y* does not change:

scurry + -ing = scurrying   carry + -ing = carrying
ready + -ing = readying   worry + -ing = worrying

When a suffix is added to a word ending in y preceded by a vowel, the y usually does not change.

employ + -ed = employed   stay + -ing = staying
play + -er = player   relay + -ing = relaying

Exercises   Spell words and their suffixes.

A.   Find the misspelled words. Spell them correctly.

1. Who is <u>driveing</u> us home today?   driving
2. After <u>writeing</u> the letter, I <u>hurryed</u> to mail it.   writing, hurried
3. Let's end the <u>arguement</u> before leaving.   argument
4. Ice <u>skateing</u> must be done gracefully.   skating
5. My homework was done <u>sloppyly</u> and hastily.   sloppily

6. That's the sillyest program I've ever seen. silliest
7. You had me almost believeing your story! believing
8. Grandpa remembers horse and carryage days. carriage
9. The shiny new car is as noisey as our old rattletrap. noisy
10. Have you truly considered the statment? statement

B.   Add the suffixes as shown and write the new word.

1. write + -ing writing
2. amaze + -ment amazement
3. care + -ful careful
4. dirty + -er dirtier
5. happy + -ly happily
6. stay + -ing staying
7. spray + -er sprayer
8. relate + -ion relation
9. hurry + -ing hurrying
10. glory + -ous glorious
11. pray + -er prayer
12. employ + -er employer
13. lazy + -est laziest
14. shiny + -ness shininess
15. enjoy + -ment enjoyment
16. skinny + -er skinnier
17. mystery + -ous mysterious
18. thirty + -eth thirtieth
19. bounty + -ful bountiful
20. sleepy + -er sleepier

The Addition of Prefixes

When a prefix is added to a word, the spelling of the word remains the same.

re- + elect = reelect
mis- + spell = misspell
im- + moderate = immoderate
il- + legible = illegible

mis- + direct = misdirect
re- + enter = reenter
dis- + satisfy = dissatisfy
ir- + regular = irregular

The Suffixes -ness and -ly

When the suffix -ly is added to a word ending in l, both l's are retained. When -ness is added to a word ending in n, both n's are retained.

normal + -ly = normally
real + -ly = really

open + -ness = openness
thin + -ness = thinness

Exercise Spell words with prefixes and suffixes.

Find the misspelled words in these sentences and spell them correctly.

1. The cast imobilized my leg. immobilized
2. Our garden is carefuly tended. carefully
3. An ireplaceable vase was broken. irreplaceable
4. The uneveness of the road is annoying. unevenness
5. We are learning about iregular verbs in French class. irregular
6. The teacher remphasized the point. reemphasized
7. I have spent money unecessarily. unnecessarily
8. That was an ilegitimate move. illegitimate
9. The mispelling was totaly unnecessary. misspelling, totally
10. That painting is beautifuly framed. beautifully

Words with the "Seed" Sound

Only one English word ends in *sede: supersede.*
Three words end in *ceed: exceed, proceed, succeed.*
All other words ending in the sound of *seed* are spelled *cede:*

   concede   precede   recede   secede

Words with *ie* and *ei*

When the sound is long *e* (ē), the word is spelled *ie* except after *c*.

I Before *E*

| relieve | grieve | field | pierce |
| belief | piece | pier | reprieve |

Except After *C*

| conceit | conceive | perceive | |
| ceiling | receive | receipt | deceive |

582

The following words are exceptions:

either   weird   species
neither   seize   leisure

Exercise **Spell words with the "seed" sound and words with *ie* and *ei* correctly.**

Find the misspelled words in these sentences and spell them correctly.

1. When was Louisiana <u>ceeded</u> to the United States? ceded
2. Hercules' <u>sheild</u> was made of gold. shield
3. There's one <u>peice</u> of pecan pie left. piece
4. Nixon <u>preseeded</u> Carter as President. preceded
5. Will aspirin <u>releive</u> this headache? relieve
6. The town was <u>siezed</u> after a fierce battle. seized
7. The clerk <u>proceded</u> to write a receipt. proceeded
8. My leisure hours <u>excede</u> my work hours. exceed
9. The paint on the <u>cieling</u> is chipped. ceiling
10. I babysit for my <u>neice</u> every weekend. niece

Doubling the Final Consonant

Words of one syllable, ending in one consonant preceded by one vowel, double the final consonant before adding a suffix beginning with a vowel.

1. These words double the final consonant if the suffix begins with a vowel.

grab + -ing = grabbing   drug + -ist = druggist
dig + -er = digger   slim + -est = slimmest

The rule does not apply to these one-syllable words because two vowels precede the final consonant.

clear + -est = clearest   loot + -ing = looting
treat + -ing = treating   peel + -ing = peeling

2. The final consonant is doubled in a word of more than one syllable:

> When it ends in one consonant preceded by one vowel.
> When it is accented on the last syllable.

re·gret′   per·mit′   de·ter′

The same syllable is accented in the new word formed by adding the suffix:

> re·gret′ + -ed = re·gret′ted
> per·mit′ + -ing = per·mit′ting
> de·ter′ + -ence = de·ter′rence

If the newly formed word is accented on a different syllable, the final consonant is not doubled.

> re·fer′ + -ence = ref′er·ence
> pre·fer′ + -ence = pref′er·ence
> con·fer′ + -ence = con′fer·ence

Exercise Double the final consonant.

Add the suffixes as shown and write the new word. Indicate with an accent mark (′) where each word is accented.

plug′ging	1. plug + -ing	11. sleep + -ing	*sleep*′ing
prefer′ring	2. prefer + -ing	12. swim + -er	*swim*′mer
control′ler	3. control + -er	13. hot + -est	*hot*′test
pref′erence	4. prefer + -ence	14. trim + -ed	*trimmed*
big′gest	5. big + -est	15. fat + -est	*fat*′test
remit′tance	6. remit + -ance	16. heat + -ing	*heat*′ing
slim′mer	7. slim + -er	17. scoot + -er	*scoot*′er
tug′ging	8. tug + -ing	18. motor + -ist	*mo*′torist
permit′ting	9. permit + -ing	19. slug + -er	*slug*′ger
treat′ing	10. treat + -ing	20. drag + -ing	*drag*′ging

Words Often Confused

The following words are often misused. Many of the words are homonyms. **Homonyms** are words that sound alike or are spelled alike but have different meanings. You must be careful not to confuse them.

As you study these homonyms and other words that are often confused, notice how their meanings differ. Try to use the right word at the right time.

accept means to agree to something or to receive something willingly.

except means to exclude or omit. As a preposition, *except* means "but" or "excluding."

> Did the teacher *accept* your explanation?
> Students who behaved well were *excepted* from the penalty.
> Everyone smiled for the photographer *except* Jody.

all ready means completely prepared or ready.

already means previously or before.

> The cast and crew are *all ready* for dress rehearsal.
> Linda has *already* arranged the chess tournament.

capital refers to the large letter used to begin the first word in a sentence, etc. It also refers to the seat of government in a state or country.

capitol refers to the building where a state legislature meets.

the Capitol is the building in Washington, D.C., where the United States Congress meets.

> We use *capital* letters to begin such proper names as New York City and Abraham Lincoln.
> Is Madison the *capital* of Wisconsin?
> Protestors rallied at the state *capitol*.
> A subway connects the Senate and the House in the *Capitol*.

Words Often Confused

Objective

To distinguish and spell correctly homonyms and other words often confused

Presenting the Lesson

1. Read and discuss pages 585-588. Tell the students that these words often cause spelling problems because they sound alike. Stress the differences in meaning, as illustrated in the sample sentences.

2. Assign and discuss Exercises A and B on pages 588 and 589. Have the students use the definitions of the words to tell which word is appropriate in each sentence.

Individualizing the Lesson

Less-Advanced Students

1. Help the students to memorize the definitions of the words often confused. Have them quiz each other on the words and their meanings.

2. For each of the Exercises, have the students write not only the correct word but also its definition.

Advanced Students

Have the students write guidelines for the use of these words that are often confused: *peek-peak, advise-advice, council-counsel,* and *sight-site-cite*.

Assign and discuss Exercise F on page 591.

Optional Practice

Have the students write original sentences illustrating the correct use of the words on pages 585-588.

Extending the Lesson

Have each student find two or more published examples of the correct use of some of the words that appear on pages 585-588.

des′ ert is a dry, sandy region with little vegetation.
de sert′ means to leave or abandon.
dessert (note the change in spelling) is a sweet food, such as cake or pie, served at the end of a meal.

> The Sahara in North Africa is the world's largest *desert*.
> The night guard did not *desert* his post.
> Alison's favorite *dessert* is chocolate cake.

heal means to make well, to cure.
heel refers to the back part of a person's foot or of a shoe.

> If the wound is clean, it should *heal* fast.
> When the *heel* of my shoe came off, I walked lopsidedly.

hear means to listen to or to take notice of.
here means in this place.

> When the TV is on, we can't *hear* the doorbell.
> The softball team practices *here* on the south field.

hoarse describes sound that is harsh and grating; especially a voice.
horse is a large strong animal that can pull loads or carry a rider.

> When I get a cold, I am usually *hoarse* for a week.
> Farm *horses* used to pull plows and do other work that tractors do now.

its is a pronoun that shows possession.
it's is a contraction for *it is* or *it has*.

> Sanibel Island is known for *its* beautiful beaches.
> *It's* great weather for a picnic!

loan refers to something given for temporary use and expected to be returned.
lone refers to the condition of being by oneself, alone.

> I gave that shirt to Max as a gift, not a *loan*.
> The *lone* plant in our backyard is really a weed.

lose means to mislay or to suffer the loss of something.
loose means free or not fastened.

> That tire will *lose* air if you don't patch it.
> My little brother has three *loose* teeth.

peace means calm or quiet, freedom from disagreements or quarrels.
piece refers to a portion or part of something.

> If you want *peace* and quiet, go to the library.
> A *piece* of the scenery crashed onto the stage.

principal describes something of chief or central importance. It also refers to the head of an elementary or high school.
principle is the basic truth, standard, or rule of behavior.

> Declining enrollment is the *principal* reason for closing the school.
> We will get our diplomas from the *principal*.
> One of my *principles* is a belief in total honesty.

quiet refers to freedom from noise or disturbance.
quite means truly or almost completely.

> Observers must be *quiet* during the recording session.
> I was *quite* worried when Kevin didn't return.

stationary means fixed or unmoving.
stationery refers to paper used for writing letters.

> The steering wheel moves, but the seat is *stationary*.
> Rex wrote on special *stationery* with his name on it.

their means belonging to them.
there means in that place.
they're is a contraction for *they are*.

> All the campers returned to *their* cabins.
> I keep my coin collection *there* in those folders.
> Lisa and Tammy practice hard, and *they're* becoming very good at soccer.

to means toward, or in the direction of.

too means also, very, or more than enough.

two is the number 2.

> The President flew *to* France for the conference.
> Megan is healthy, and she is happy, *too*.
> *Two* of my friends will be on TV tonight.

weather refers to atmospheric conditions such as temperature or cloudiness.

whether helps to express choice or alternative.

> Computers will soon be able to predict the *weather*.
> Val had to decide *whether* to tell the truth or to save Bob from feeling hurt.

who's is a contraction for *who is* or *who has*.

whose is the possessive form of *who*.

> *Who's* going to the recycling center?
> *Whose* parents will drive us to the movie?

your is the possessive form of *you*.

you're is a contraction for *you are*.

> What was *your* time in the fifty-yard dash?
> *You're* heading the canned food drive, aren't you?

Exercises   Use words often confused.

A.   Choose the correct word from those given in parentheses.

1. Every country (accept, except) China sent delegates.

2. The nurse's aide had (all ready, already) been trained.

3. The Senator met us on the steps of the (capital, capitol, Capitol) in Washington.

4. Did you and David make apple turnovers for (desert, dessert)?

5. If your (heal, heel) hurts, maybe your shoes aren't the right size.

6. Stand (<u>here</u>, hear) where you can (here, <u>hear</u>) the music better.

7. The bluejay has a (horse, <u>hoarse</u>) call that sounds like a squeaky gate.

8. The magazine prints letters from (<u>its</u>, it's) readers.

9. Toby (<u>accepted</u>, excepted) the gift.

10. Will you (lone, <u>loan</u>) me a pencil?

B. Follow the directions for Exercise A.

1. The pedals on this bike seem (lose, <u>loose</u>).

2. I'd like a (<u>piece</u>, peace) of watermelon, please.

3. When the school (<u>principal</u>, principle) entered the P.T.A. meeting, everyone clapped.

4. Please be (quite, <u>quiet</u>) while we study.

5. The Berkowitzs prefer a houseboat to a (<u>stationary</u>, stationery) house.

6. The networks announced (<u>their</u>, there, they're) fall schedules in the newspaper.

7. Do you think it's (to, <u>too</u>, two) dark to ride our bikes?

8. Even during cold (<u>weather</u>, whether), we walk to school.

9. (Who's, <u>Whose</u>) purse is this on the floor?

10. I admire (<u>your</u>, you're) self-confidence.

Reinforcement Exercises

These Reinforcement Exercises may be used for additional practice as needed. Each exercise may be used after the text page indicated in parentheses.

Review

If you have not assigned these Exercises before this time, you can use them as an excellent Section Review.

Mixed Review

The following exercises provide review of the concepts and skills presented in this chapter.

A. Correct spelling errors. Find the misspelled words. Write them correctly.

1. Your the new student council president, aren't you?
2. Marcy doesn't easily beleive rumors.
3. Making a U-turn on this street is ilegal.
4. His strength is truely amazing.
5. That type of car is usualy quite expensive.
6. The bank recieved the loan payment today.
7. The Secret Service men preceeded the President into the airport.
8. Cal tried scrubing the dirt out.
9. Its a beautiful day for a football game.
10. The number of people who were admited was limited.
11. The toaster made a wierd noise before it broke.
12. Carol excepted the collect phone call.

Reinforcement Exercises — Review

Spelling

A. Add suffixes to words ending in silent e and y.
(Use after page 581.)

Add the suffixes as shown. Write the new word.

enjoyable 1. enjoy + -able	6. believe + -able believable
icy 2. ice + -y	7. hurry + -ed hurried
carrying 3. carry + -ing	8. continue + -ing continuing
earliest 4. early + -est	9. employ + -er employer
wasteful 5. waste + -ful	10. create + -ing creating

B. Add prefixes correctly. (Use after page 582.)

Find the misspelled words. Spell them correctly.

1. It's unecessary to change your plans. unnecessary
2. If you mispell more than two words, you must retake the test. misspell
3. Sharon was dissappointed with the test results. disappointed
4. All traffic was imobile after the heavy snowfall. immobile
5. Several cars were parked ilegally in the loading zone. illegally

C. Add suffixes -ness and -ly. (Use after page 582.)

Find the misspelled words. Spell them correctly.

1. Jill's openess made her an easy person to talk to. openness
2. I realy don't believe Mike actualy said that! really, actually
3. The van was illegaly parked by the fire hydrant. illegally
4. The uneveness of this writing is hardly acceptable. unevenness
5. Eventualy the rain stopped. Eventually

D. Spell words with the "seed" sound and words with *ie* and *ei*. (Use after page 583.)

Find the misspelled words. Write them correctly.

1. Mrs. Barnett <u>succeded</u> Mr. Smyth as corporate treasurer. succeeded

2. Lee believed that the cieling needed to be repainted. ceiling

3. After we receive all of <u>the reciepts</u>, we will <u>procede</u> with payment. receipts, proceed

4. All cars must <u>yeild</u> to the workmen and not <u>excede</u> the limit of 40 M.P.H. yield, exceed

5. Her <u>neice</u> and nephew were here for a <u>breif</u> visit. niece, brief

E. Double the final consonant. (Use after page 584.)

Add the suffixes as shown and write the new word.

1. drop + -ed	4. slug + -er	7. run + -er	1. dropped	6. referring
2. run + -ing	5. begin + -ing	8. plant + -ing	2. running	7. runner
3. put + -ing	6. refer + -ing	9. big + -est	3. putting	8. planting
			4. slugger	9. biggest
			5. beginning	

F. Use easily confused words correctly. (Use after page 589.)

Choose the correct word from those given.

1. The campers are (<u>all ready</u>, already) for their cookout.

2. I began each sentence with a (<u>capital</u>, capitol) letter.

3. After Seth's broken leg is set, it will begin to (heel, <u>heal</u>).

4. Do you know the (<u>horsepower</u>, hoarsepower) of that engine?

5. (Its, <u>It's</u>) time for Marcia's swimming lesson.

6. Did the Bulldogs (<u>lose</u>, loose) their final game?

7. We printed our (stationary, <u>stationery</u>) in the school workshop.

8. Our class reporter took (to, too, <u>two</u>) stories (<u>to</u>, too, two) the editor of the school paper.

9. (<u>Who's</u>, Whose) the announcer on this radio station?

10. (Your, <u>You're</u>) interested in current events, aren't you?

13. Dr. Jolsen <u>refered</u> Kim to an allergy specialist.

14. Mr. Blackman just celebrated his <u>ninetyeth</u> birthday.

15. This argument is <u>totaly</u> ridiculous.

1. You're		9. It's	
2. believe		10. admitted	
3. illegal		11. weird	
4. truly		12. accepted	
5. usually		13. referred	
6. received		14. ninetieth	
7. preceded		15. totally	
8. scrubbing			

Using Mechanics in Writing

1. Have the students practice editing each other's written work to correct spelling errors. Have each student write a paragraph explaining what makes a person a hero. Have them exchange papers and read the paragraphs carefully for spelling.

2. Have each student read an article in a daily newspaper and list all misspellings and typographical errors. Have the student write a letter to the editor of the newspaper, reporting his or her findings.

Section 14

Outlining

Section Objectives

1. To organize ideas for an outline

2. To recognize a topic outline and its function

3. To use correct form in a topic outline

Preparing the Students

Tell the students to imagine that they will be writing a report on astronauts. Write the following outline on the chalkboard:

U.S. Astronauts

I. Qualifications for astronauts
II. Training of astronauts
   A. General training
   B. Mission-oriented training
III. First U.S. astronauts
   A. Alan Shepard, Jr. in 1961
   B. Virgil Grissom in 1961
   C. John Glenn in 1962
   D. M. Scott Carpenter in 1962
   E. Walter Schirra in 1962
IV. Outstanding accomplishments of astronauts
   A. Walk in space
   B. Landing on the moon
   C. Joint flight with U.S.S.R.
   D. Space shuttle

Discuss how the outline would help in organizing the report. Talk, too, about the general purposes of outlines. Read the introduction on pages 593 and 594. Tell the students that Section 14 will help them to write effective outlines.

Additional Resources

Reinforcement Exercise—See pages 598-599 in the student text.

Skills Practice Book—page 199.

Duplicating Masters—page 199.

When you sit down to write a composition, where do you begin? Once you have gathered all the information you need, how do you organize it?

For both of these questions, an **outline** is a good answer. An outline is a condensed plan for a piece of writing. The ideas that crowd your head when you write can become confused unless you have a plan. An outline will help you put your ideas into a logical order.

Outlining also makes writing easier. Many experienced writers use outlines to prepare for writing. They find that outlining gives them a head start in writing a well-organized composition.

In the chapters "Writing the Composition" and "Writing the Report" you learned to group ideas in logical order. An outline is an accepted form for diagraming that order. The same form can be used for any topic and for any kind of composition. Outlines help you to write reports and other explanatory compositions, as well as narrative and descriptive papers. For these reasons, outlining is a valuable skill to learn.

Organizing an Outline

To begin an outline, you should have a clear idea of the purpose of your composition. Then determine the main ideas that you want to develop. These main ideas will be the **main points** in your outline.

Next, consider how you can develop or explain each main point. The supporting ideas for these points will become **subpoints** in the outline. Consequently, related ideas will be grouped together.

Finally, decide which scheme to use for ordering the main points. While time sequence works well for some topics, order of importance is better for others. The best order is the one that makes your topic clearest and easiest to understand.

When you have completed an outline, you will have the skeleton for a composition. By filling in details and building paragraphs around related ideas, you will create a solid composition.

Writing Topic Outlines

A **topic outline** is an informal kind of outline. Topic outlines use words or phrases instead of complete sentences. Topic outlines are effective for organizing compositions.

A topic outline follows. Notice that it does not use complete sentences. Pay attention to the grouping of subpoints under related main ideas.

STREETCARS: YESTERDAY'S BUSES

I. History of the streetcar
    A. Introduction in 1831
    B. Popularity during the 19th century
    C. Decline during the 1930's
        1. Because of cars
        2. Because of buses
II. Description of horse-drawn streetcars
    A. Design
    B. Speed
III. Description of electric streetcars
    A. Power
        1. From overhead wires
        2. From underground wires
    B. Design
    C. Speed
IV. Effect of streetcars on cities

Using Outline Form

Outlines use a precise form that does not vary. Here are some rules to follow:

1. Write the title of your composition at the top of the outline. The introduction and the conclusion are usually not considered parts of the outline.

2. Arrange numbers and letters of headings in the following order: first Roman numerals for main points, then capital letters for subpoints. Next, Arabic numerals are used. Small letters are used for details under these ideas, then numbers in parentheses for details developing the details, and, finally, small letters in parentheses for subdetails. The arrangement on the next page shows clearly which ideas belong together. Note the placement of periods.

595

Topic Outlines.
  2. Have students study the topic outline on page 595.

Using Outline Form

Objective

To use correct form in a topic outline

Presenting the Lesson

1. Read and discuss pages 595 and 596. Show the students how each rule is applied in the sample outline.
2. Assign and discuss the Exercise on pages 596 and 597.

Individualizing the Lesson

Less-Advanced Students

Help the students to see the relationship between ideas in the partial outline in the Exercise before they complete it.

Advanced Students

Have the students write a similar outline for a dish they know how to prepare.

Reinforcement Exercise

Assign and discuss the Exercise on page 598.

Extending the Lesson

Have each student outline directions for doing or making something.

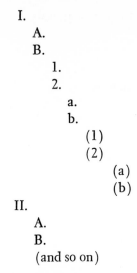

I.
  A.
  B.
    1.
    2.
      a.
      b.
        (1)
        (2)
          (a)
          (b)
II.
  A.
  B.
  (and so on)

3. Indent all headings in the outline. Place letters and numbers of all headings directly underneath the first word of the larger heading above.
4. Do not use a single subheading. There must be at least two. A heading should not be broken down if it cannot be divided into at least two points.
5. Use the same kind of word or phrase for all headings of the same rank. If, for example, A is a verb, then B should be a verb, too.
6. Begin each item with a capital letter. In a topic outline, do not end headings with periods or other punctuation.

Exercise Make an outline.

Look at the partial outline on the next page. Copy it on your paper. Then complete the outline by adding the following headings where they belong.

Necessary toppings	Pepperoni
Baking time	With oregano mixed in
Mushrooms	Prepare the dough
Ingredients	Shape the dough

DIRECTIONS FOR MAKING PIZZA

I. Gather the necessary equipment
   A. Recipe
   B. Pizza pan or pizza stone or baking sheet
   C. Ingredients

II. Light the oven

III. Prepare the dough
   A. Mix ingredients for the dough
   B. Knead the dough
   C. Shape the dough
   D. Place dough in pan

IV. Spread toppings on dough
   A. Necessary toppings
      1. Tomato sauce
         a. Made from canned pizza sauce
         b. Made from canned tomato sauce or paste
            (1) With parmesan cheese mixed in
            (2) With oregano mixed in
            (3) With other spices mixed in
      2. Sliced mozzarella cheese
   B. Optional toppings
      1. Sausage
      2. Pepperoni
      3. Mushrooms
      4. Green peppers
      5. Sliced or chopped onion
      6. Other things you like

V. Bake the pizza
   A. Oven temperature
   B. Baking time

Reinforcement Exercise

Review

This Reinforcement Exercise may be used for additional practice as needed or as an excellent Section Review.

Using Mechanics in Writing

Have the students do some initial research and then make an outline for a report on one of these topics: the Olympic Games, Voice of America, scuba diving, ballet. Have the students exchange outlines to check for correct outline form.

Reinforcement Exercise — Review

Outlining

Complete an outline. (Use after page 597.)

Copy the partial outline. Insert the following headings where they belong in the outline.

National	Entertainment
Lead story	Newspaper name
Letters to the editor	Date
Movies	The Congress
	News section

DISSECTING A NEWSPAPER

I. Front page
  A. Newspaper name
  B. Date
  C. Weather
  D. Pictures
  E. Lead story

II. News section
  A. International
  B. National
    1. Important news from Washington
      a. The Congress
      b. The President
    2. Big stories with national interest
  C. Local

III. Editorial page
  A. Editorials
  B. Letters to the editor
  C. Opinion columns
  D. Cartoon
  E. Masthead

IV. Other
    A. Features
    B. Business
    C. Sports
    D. Entertainment
       1. TV and radio
       2. Movies
       3. Plays and concerts

INDEX

445–447, 451, 469–472, 494–
495, 502–503, 549–550
correlative, 445–447, 451
subordinating, 478–479, 481–
485, 495–496
Conjunctive adverbs, 44–46, 49,
555–557
Connectives, 437–440, 445–447
Connotation, 179–181
Consonance, 283
Context clues to word meaning,
2–9, 12–13
Contractions
apostrophe in, 365–366, 560–
561
negative, 317–318, 430
possessive pronouns or, 365–
366, 374–375
Conversation, writing. *See*
Dialogue.
Coordinating conjunctions, 30–31,
48, 329, 445–447, 451, 469–
472, 494–495, 502–503, 549–
550
Correlative conjunctions, 445–
447, 451
Cross-reference cards, 201

Dash, 5
Dates
apostrophe in, 560–561
comma in, 550–552, 571
in headings of letters, 239, 242
Declarative sentences, 540, 542–
543, 568
Definite article, 415
Definition
to develop compositions, 122,
145–146
to prove facts, 176
to develop paragraphs, 82–85,
101–102, 107

Definitions of words
from context, 2–9, 12–13
in dictionaries, 25, 27
necessary parts in, 84–85, 101,
107, 145
Demonstrative pronouns, 357–
358, 372–373, 413–414
Denotation, 179
Dependent clauses. *See*
Subordinate clauses.
Descriptive compositions, 131,
133–134, 139–141
Descriptive paragraphs, 92–98, 107
Dewey Decimal System, 194–197
Diacritical marks, 23–24
Diagraming
adjective clauses, 486–487
adverb clauses, 484
adverbs, 316
compound sentences, 470, 473
direct objects, 325
imperative sentences, 322
indirect objects, 325
noun clauses, 490–491
predicate words, 328
prepositional phrases, 443
simple sentences, 315–316, 319,
321–322, 330, 473
Dialogue in drama, 301
Dialogue, writing, 564
Dictionaries, 15–27, 203–207
abridged, 203
alphabetical order in, 16, 27
definitions of words in, 25, 27
finding words in, 20–21
guide words in, 17–19, 27
about language, 204
pronunciation of words in, 22–24
syllables in, 21–22, 27
synonymy in, 26–27
thesauruses, 204, 206–207
unabridged, 203

Direct objects of verbs, 323–326,
335–336, 456–457, 461, 463,
466–468
adverb or, 324, 335
compound, 329–331, 336, 362–
363, 467–468
gerunds as, 517–519, 521
infinitives as, 513–514, 520
noun clauses as, 489–492, 497
pronouns as, 359–361
in sentence patterns, 456–457,
461, 463
Direct questions, 541
Direct quotations, 548, 561, 564–565
Directions, following, 214–215
Divided quotations, 548, 562,
564–565
doesn't, don't, 505–506
Double negatives, 430–431, 435
Doubling the final consonant,
583–584, 591
Drama, 301–305
Drawing conclusions, 230–231

Encyclopedias, 160, 205–207
End marks, 540–543, 568
See also Exclamation point,
Period, Question mark.
Envelopes, addressing, 258–259
guidelines for, 258
Essay, 291, 293–295
Example(s)
to develop compositions, 122,
148, 150
to develop paragraphs, 79–80, 107
Exclamation point (or mark),
542–543, 568
after interjections, 448, 542
with quotation marks, 563, 565
at end of sentences, 540, 542, 568
Exclamatory sentences, 542
Explanatory compositions, 131,

133–134, 141–151
Explanatory paragraphs, 99–107

Facts
checking, 173, 183–184, 191
clarifying, 185–187
crediting sources for, 172–173,
186–187
opinions or, 157–158, 176–179, 191
Facts or figures in writing. See
Compositions, Paragraphs, Reports.
Fiction, 297–305
definition, 297
forms of, 297
drama, 301–305
short stories, 297–301
purpose of, 297
Fiction books in library, 194, 197–198
Figures of speech, 288–290
Final copy
of compositions, 129–131, 134
of paragraphs, 58–59
of reports, 173, 218
First draft
of compositions, 120–125, 134
of paragraphs, 55, 59
of reports, 168–173, 218
First-person
compositions written in, 135–137
paragraphs written in, 88–90
personal pronouns, 352–355
Foot, 285
Foreshadowing, 301
Formal language, 128
Fractions, hyphen in, 558
Fragments of sentences, 310–311,
315, 333, 481–482
Free verse, 285
Friendly letters, 238–242
Future perfect tense of verbs,
383–384, 408
Future tense of verbs, 382–384, 408

Object form of pronouns, 358–361
Objective case. *See* Direct object of the verb, Indirect object of the verb, Object form of pronouns Objects of prepositions.
Objective writing, 295
Objects of gerunds, 517
Objects of infinitives, 512–514
Objects of participles, 515
Objects of prepositions, 325, 438–442, 450
  compound, 362–363, 443
  gerunds used as, 517–519, 521
  noun clauses as, 489–492, 497
  nouns as, 325, 438, 441
  pronouns as, 325, 359–361, 438, 441
Objects of verbs. *See* Direct objects of verbs, Indirect objects of verbs.
Onomatopoeia, 283
Opinion
  in compositions, 146–151
  fact or, 157–158, 176–179, 191
  in paragraphs, 104–106
  in reports, 157–158
Oral tradition, 274–280
  definition, 274
  forms of, 274–280
    ballads, 279–280
    legends, 274–277
    tall tales, 277–278
Order, letter of, 252–254
Order of importance
  in compositions, 117–119, 131, 145–150
  in paragraphs, 54
  in reports, 165
Outlines, 593–599
  capitalization in, 533–534, 537, 596
  form for, 595–596

  main points in, 594–595
  period in, 541
  for reports, 165–167, 597–599
  subpoints in, 594–595
  topic, 594–595

Paragraphs, 61–107
  chronological (time sequence) order in, 88–91, 99, 107
  definitions in, 82–85, 101–102, 107
  descriptive, 92–98, 107
  details in, 53–54, 59, 73–77, 92–98, 107
  developing, 73–85, 105
  example(s) in, 79–80, 105, 107
  explanatory, 99–107
  facts or figures in, 77–80, 103, 105, 107
  first draft of, 51, 55, 59
  first person, 88–90
  incident(s) in, 81, 103, 105, 107
  kinds of, 87–107
  logical order in, 54, 95–96, 99, 105–106, 107
  main idea in, 62–70, 73–85, 107
  narrative, 88–91, 107
  narrowing a topic for, 52, 59, 68–70
  opinion in, 104–106
  persuasive, 105–106
  pre-writing steps for, 52–54, 59
  process of writing, 51–59
  proofreading, 56–59
  rewriting, 51, 56–59
  appealing to the senses, 74–77, 92–98, 107
  spatial order in, 95–98, 107
  specific details in, 73–77, 92–98, 107
  third person, 90–91
  topic sentence in, 59, 65–71, 76–85, 101–107

purpose for, 153, 156–157
planning questions for, 159
research for, 160–163
rewriting (revising), 173
spatial order in, 165
subjects for, 154–155
topic sentence in, 170-171
Request, letter of, 250–252
Research for reports, 160–163
Research skills *(See also* Study
skills), 220–223, 225–231
drawing conclusions, 230–231
taking notes, 223
using graphic aids, 227–230
reading, 225–226
SQ3R, 220–222, 225, 232
Respellings of words in dictionary
for pronunciation, 22–23, 27
Restrictive clauses and phrases,
41–44, 49, 552–553, 569
Return address, 258–259
Revising
compositions, 126–131, 134
paragraphs, 56–59
reports, 173, 218
Rhyme, 284
Rhyme scheme, 284
Rhythm, 285
R.S.V.P., 244
Run-on sentences, 59, 107, 332, 337

Salutation (greeting) in letters, 239,
249, 551, 555–556
Satire, 295–296
Scanning, 225
Scenes, 301
Second person pronouns, 352–355
"*See*" and "*See also*" cards, 201
Semicolon, 555–557, 572
in compound sentences, 30,
471–472, 494–495, 555–557
before conjunctive adverbs,

44–46, 49, 555–557
in a series, 555–557
Senses used in writing, 74–77, 92–
98, 107, 139, 288
Sentence combining, 29–49
Sentence fragments, 59, 107, 310–
311, 315, 333, 481–482
Sentence patterns, 453–463
Sentences, 309–337, 453–463,
465–497
agreement of subject and verb
in, 499–509
clauses in, 476–492, 495–497
combining, 29–49
commands (imperative
sentences), 321–322, 334–
335, 540, 542–543, 568
complete, 309–313, 333
complete predicate in, 312–315,
333–334
complete subject in, 312–315,
333–334
complex, 476–492, 495–497
compound, 30, 469–478, 480,
494–495, 549–550, 555
compound parts in, 329–331,
336, 467–468, 473–476
compound predicate in, 467,
473–476
compound subject in, 329–331,
336, 362–363, 467–468,
502–503
compound verb in, 329–331,
336, 467–468, 473–476
declarative, 540, 542–543
exclamatory, 542
fragments of, 310–311, 315,
333, 481–482
imperative (commands), 321–
322, 334–335, 540, 542–543
interrogative (questions), 321–
322, 334–335, 541–543

613

Managing Editor: Kathleen Laya
Senior Editor: Bonnie Dobkin
Assistant Editor: Elizabeth M. Garber
Production Assistant: Julie Schumacher

Director of Design: Allen Carr
Design Assistants: Ken Izzi, Marcia Vecchione,
    Mary E. MacDonald

Acknowledgments

Sources of Quoted Materials

The American Foundation for the Blind: For an excerpt from "Three Days to See" or "The Seeing See Little" by Helen Adams Keller, first appeared in *The Atlantic Monthly*. Brandt & Brandt Literary Agents, Inc.: For an excerpt from *Harvey* by Mary Chase; copyright © 1953 by by Mary Chase; copyright © 1943 by Mary Chase (under the title *The White Rabbit)*; copyright © 1944 by Mary Chase (under the title *Harvey*); copyright © renewed 1971 by Mary Chase, copyright © renewed 1972 by Mary Chase, copyright renewed 1981 by Mary Chase. William Collins + World Publishing Company, for entries from *Webster's New World Dictionary of the American Language*, Students Edition; copyright © 1976 by William Collins + World Publishing Company, Inc. Crown Publishers, Inc.: For "The Ballad of Casey Jones" taken from *A Treasury of American Folklore*, edited by B. A. Botkin; copyright 1944, 1972 by B. A. Botkin. Frank Marshall Davis: For "Rain" by Frank Marshall Davis. Barthold Fles, Literary Agents for Alida Malkus: For "The Hurricane" by Pales Matos, from *Favorite Poems Old and New* by Helen Ferris, translated by Alida Malkus; copyright by Alida Malkus. Harper & Row Publishers, Inc.: For "Cynthia in the Snow" (text only, p. 8) from *Bronzeville Boys and Girls* by Gwendolyn Brooks; copyright © 1956 by Gwendolyn Brooks Blakely. For "Where Would You Be?" (text only), from *The Rose on My Cake* by Karla Kuskin; copyright © 1964 by Karla Kuskin. For specified selections (text only, pp. 78-79—"The Largest Mosquito Ever Seen"), from *Whoppers, Tall Tales and Other Lies* by Alvin Schwartz (J. B. Lippincott); text copyright © 1975 by Alvin Schwartz. Hastings House, Publishers, Inc.: For "Advice to Travelers" by Walker Gibson, from *Come As You Are;* copyright © 1958 by Walker Gibson, originally appeared in *Saturday Review*. Houghton Mifflin Company: For four lines from "Sky Diver," from *A Short History of the Fur Trade* by Adrien Stoutenburg; copyright © 1968 by Adrien Stoutenburg. Henry Lincoln Johnson: For "Your World" by Georgia Douglas Johnson. Alfred A. Knopf, Inc.: For "African Dance," from *Selected Poems of Langston Hughes* by Langston Hughes; copyright 1926 by Alfred A. Knopf, Inc. and renewed 1954 by Langston Hughes. For a four-line excerpt from "Wash" by John Updike, from *Telephone Poles and Other Poems;* copyright © 1962 by John Updike. Little, Brown and Company: For an excerpt from pages 18-20, slightly adapted from *The Dog Who Wouldn't Be* by Farley Mowat; copyright © 1957 by The Curtis Publishing Company; © 1957 by Farley Mowat. Liveright Publishing Company: For "in Just-" by E. E. Cummings, from *Tulips & Chimneys* by E. E. Cummings; copyright 1923, 1925 and renewed 1951, 1953 by E. E. Cummings; copyright © 1973, 1976 by The Trustees for the E. E. Cummings Trust, copyright © 1973, 1976 by George James Firmage. Patricia Ayers for Eve Merriam: For "Inside a Poem," from *It Doesn't Always Have to Rhyme* by Eve Merriam; copyright © 1964 by Atheneum Press. For "Alarm Clock," from *Finding A Poem* by Eve Merriam; copyright © 1970 by Eve Merriam, published by Atheneum. William Morrow & Company, Inc.: For "Surf," from *The Sidewalk Racer and Other Poems of Sports and Motion* by Lillian Morrison; copyright © 1977 by Lillian Morrison, by permission of Lothrop, Lee & Shepard Books (a Division of William Morrow & Co.). The New Yorker Magazine, Inc.: For an excerpt from "Catalogue" by Rosalie Moore; copyright © 1940, 1968 by The New Yorker Magazine, Inc. Oxford University Press: For an excerpt from "The Sword in the Stone," from *Stories of King Arthur and His Knights*, retold by Barbara Leonie Picard; copyright 1955 by Oxford University Press. G. P. Putnam's Sons: For "Is There Life on Earth?" from *Have I Ever Lied to You?* by Art Buchwald; copyright © 1966, 1967, 1968 by Art Buchwald. Viking Penguin, Inc. and The Bodley Head: For "The Open Window," from *The Complete Short Stories of Saki* by H. H. Munro; copyright 1930 by The Viking Press, Inc.; copyright renewed 1958 by The Viking Press, Inc. For four lines from "Lone Dog," from *Songs to Save a Soul* by Irene Rutherford McLeod. Wesleyan University Press: For "The Base Stealer," from *The Orb Weaver* by Robert Francis; copyright © 1948 by Robert Francis. The authors and editors have made every effort to trace the ownership of all copyrighted selections in this book and to make acknowledgment for their use.

Photographs and Illustrations

Cover: Photo Researchers: George Porter

James L. Ballard: 14, 28, 152, 192, 212, 260, 272, 308, 498.

Magnum: Charles Harbutt, ii, 50, 174; David Hurn, xx; Paul Fusco, 60, 86, 338, 376, 452, 522; Eve Arnold, 72, 410; Martin Dain, 108; Wayne Miller, 132; Burk Uzzle, 236, 464; Constantine Manos, 350, 436, 510; Hiroji Kubota, 538; Mark Godfrey, 576; Costa Manos, 592.

Bob Masheris: 274, 276, 279, 281, 283, 284, 286, 289, 294, 298, 299, 300.

Class Record

Name

Diagnostic Test 1. Simple and Compound Sentences																		
Diagnostic Test 2. Using Nouns and Pronouns																		
Diagnostic Test 3. Using Verbs																		
Diagnostic Test 4. Using Modifiers																		
Diagnostic Test 5. Using Prepositions and Conjunctions																		
Diagnostic Test 6. Capitalization																		
Diagnostic Test 7. Punctuation																		
Diagnostic Test 8. Spelling																		
Mastery Tests																		
Chapter 1. Developing Your Vocabulary																		
Chapter 2. Using the Dictionary																		
Chapter 3. Sentence Combining																		
Chapter 5. Writing the Paragraph																		
Chapter 6. Developing the Paragraph																		
Chapter 7. Different Kinds of Paragraphs																		
Chapters 8 and 9. Compositions																		
Chapter 10. Writing the Report																		
Chapter 11. Clear Thinking																		
Chapter 12. The Library and How To Use It																		
Chapter 13. Study and Research Skills																		
• Cumulative Mastery Test—Composition																		
Mastery Tests																		
Section 1. The Simple Sentence Parts 1–4																		
Parts 5–8																		
Section 2. Using Nouns																		
Section 3. Using Pronouns																		
Section 4. Using Verbs: Parts 1–4																		
Parts 5–8																		
Section 5. Using Modifiers																		
Section 6. Using Prepositions and Conjunctions																		
Section 7. Sentence Patterns																		
Section 8. Using Compound and Complex Sentences																		
Section 9. Making Subjects and Verbs Agree																		
Section 10. Using Verbals																		
• Cumulative Mastery Test—Grammar and Usage																		
Section 11. Capitalization																		
Section 12. Punctuation																		
Section 13. Spelling																		
• Cumulative Mastery Test— Capitalization, Punctuation, and Spelling																		

Individual Student's Record

May be duplicated for each student's use

Name _____

	Score	Comment

Diagnostic Tests

Diagnostic Test 1.   Simple and Compound Sentences   _____   _____

Diagnostic Test 2.   Using Nouns and Pronouns   _____   _____

Diagnostic Test 3.   Using Verbs   _____   _____

Diagnostic Test 4.   Using Modifiers   _____   _____

Diagnostic Test 5.   Using Prepositions and Conjunctions   _____   _____

Diagnostic Test 6.   Capitalization   _____   _____

Diagnostic Test 7.   Punctuation   _____   _____

Diagnostic Test 8.   Spelling   _____   _____

Mastery Tests

Chapter 1.   Developing Your Vocabulary   _____   _____

Chapter 2.   Using the Dictionary   _____   _____

Chapter 3.   Sentence Combining   _____   _____

Chapter 5.   Writing the Paragraph   _____   _____

Chapter 6.   Developing the Paragraph   _____   _____

Chapter 7.   Different Kinds of Paragraphs   _____   _____

Chapter 8 and 9.   Compositions   _____   _____

Chapter 10.   Writing Reports   _____   _____

Chapter 11.   Clear Thinking   _____   _____

Chapter 12.   The Library and How To Use It   _____   _____

Chapter 13.   Study and Research Skills   _____   _____

- Cumulative Mastery Test—Composition   _____   _____

Section 1.   The Simple Sentence: Parts 1–4   _____   _____

Parts 5–8   _____   _____

Section 2.   Using Nouns   _____   _____

Section 3.   Using Pronouns   _____   _____

Section 4.   Using Verbs: Parts 1–4   _____   _____

Parts 5–8   _____   _____

Section 5.   Using Modifiers   _____   _____

Section 6.   Using Prepositions and Conjunctions   _____   _____

Section 7.   Sentence Patterns   _____   _____

Section 8.   Using Compound and Complex Sentences   _____   _____

Section 9.   Making Subjects and Verbs Agree   _____   _____

Section 10.   Using Verbals   _____   _____

- Cumulative Mastery Test—Grammar and Usage   _____   _____

Section 11.   Capitalization   _____   _____

Section 12.   Punctuation   _____   _____

Section 13.   Spelling   _____   _____

- Cumulative Mastery Test—Capitalization, Punctuation, and Spelling   _____   _____

620

Scope and Sequence

Vocabulary Development

Word Origins

	Pink 1	Plum 2	Brown 3	Aqua 4	Silver 5	Gold 6	Red 7	Green 8
History of Language, Borrowed Words, Compound Words, Clipped Words, Words from Names or Initials, Echoic Words, Technical Words		25	2–6		2–8	2–8	2–19	
		25–26	3–6, 11–13		3–11	3–11	1–2, 5, 14–15, 16, 18–19	
		214, 244	337–338, 353			500–501	9–10, 28	

Language Acquisition

	Pink 1	Plum 2	Brown 3	Aqua 4	Silver 5	Gold 6	Red 7	Green 8
Using Word Parts To Unlock New Words			7–10	7–11	2–8	461–464	22–27	
Root Words, Prefixes, Suffixes			8, 10, 13	9, 12, 13	3–11	461–464	22, 25–26, 27–28, 38	
			338	402, 423	484–485, 517	565	11–12, 28	
Using Context Clues To Discover Meanings			25–26	2–5	4–16			2–9
Definition, Restatement. Examples. Comparison and Contrast			27, 29	3–6, 13	15–21			3–9, 12–13
			340	401	486–487, 517			9, 28
Using the Dictionary To Learn About Words	23–27, 35	55–63	16–23	143–154	223–234	200–208	28–33	15–26, 203–205
Using Alphabetical Order and Guide Words To Find the Word. Understanding the Pronunciation. Finding the Best Definition	23–28, 30, 35–36	56–66	17–24, 28	144–155	223–235	200–209	28–33, 38–39	16–27, 206–207
	154–158, 172	228–232, 246	339, 353	415–416, 425	515–516, 522	527–528	13–14, 28	11–12, 28

Language Enrichment

	Pink 1	Plum 2	Brown 3	Aqua 4	Silver 5	Gold 6	Red 7	Green 8
Developing Specific Vocabulary	37–43	16–23, 154–162	85, 226–229, 243–244	94–95, 236–247, 288, 375–376	108–110, 185	13–24, 107–108, 412, 466–468	34–37, 61–79, 106–109, 586–590	10–11, 26, 73–76, 92–97, 585–588
Rhymes, Homonyms, Homographs. Synonyms, Antonyms. Words Referring to the Senses	37–44, 47–48	16–24, 30, 154–162, 166	86, 89, 228–229, 246	95–96, 237–247, 288, 377	111, 185–186	14–27, 108, 417, 469	36–39, 62–72, 109, 590–593	11–13, 27, 76–77, 97–98, 588–589, 591
	160–163, 165, 173	210–213, 216, 244, 272–274, 277	363, 376	411, 433–434	497, 529–530, 550	527–528, 513, 565	14, 16–17, 28–29	10, 12, 18, 28–29

☐ **Teaching Pages**
(Explanations and examples in the text and T.E.)

▨ **Exercises**
(All pages containing exercises for the concept)

▦ **Reinforcement**
(Grades 1–6: Practice Pages in T.E.; Grades 7–8: Diagnostic and Mastery Test Booklets)

Composition

Sentences

	Pink 1	Plum 2	Brown 3	Aqua 4	Silver 5	Gold 6	Red 7	Green 8
Using Words for Specific Purposes Clarity and Precision. Persuasion (judgment words. connotations. slanting). Creative Expression (simile. metaphor). Vocabulary To Match the Situation (levels of language)	45	154–164	226–229, 236–241	15–20, 93–100, 244	199–206	13–24, 363–366, 415	34–35, 120–123, 158–161	10–12, 25–26, 175–182, 185–186
	45–46	154–166	228–229, 242	17, 21, 95–101, 245	201–208	14–27, 366, 417	36–37, 39, 120–121, 123, 161	11–13, 25–27, 177–182, 187
	164	272–277, 290	364, 376	412, 433–434	494, 511–512	527–528	14, 16–17	10, 18, 23, 28, 29
Writing Good Sentences	50–60	32–52	47–56	31–45	39–63	29–57	319–344	309–332
Writing Complete Thoughts	50–62	32–54	50–59	33–51	43–67	31–63	321–351	311–337
	166–171	217–227, 245	341, 353	394, 403–404	474, 488–491, 518	490–491, 504–507	1, 33	1, 30–33
Avoiding Run-On Sentences. Combining Thoughts Correctly				53–57	69–71	66–75, 274–276, 298–300	41–56, 344, 491–501	29–47, 332, 465–491
				55–59	71, 74	67–75, 299–301, 306	42–59, 344–345, 351, 494–505	30–49, 337, 467–492, 493–497
				405–406, 424	475, 492–493, 518	508–510, 532, 547–548	33, 50	4–5, 47–48
Combining Sentences				56–57	74–80	66–75, 298	41–56	29–47
				58–59	74–81	67–75, 299–301, 306	43–59	30–31, 33–49
				406	494	508–510, 532, 547–548	15	13
Writing Interesting Sentences					199–206	13–24	56, 61–79, 99–100, 106–108, 120–123, 336–337, 492–493	10–12, 73–76, 87–107
Using Specific Words and Details, Using Strong Verbs, Using Figurative Language					201–208	14–27	56–57, 62–72, 101–103, 109, 120–121, 123, 337, 501, 505	11–13, 76–77, 89–106
					511–512	437–438, 502–503, 531	16–17	14–21

☐ **Teaching Pages**
(Explanations and examples in the text and T.E.)

▨ **Exercises**
(All pages containing exercises for the concept)

▨ **Reinforcement**
(Grades 1–6: Practice Pages in T.E.; Grades 7–8: Diagnostic and Mastery Test Booklets)

Process of Writing

	Pink 1	Plum 2	Brown 3	Aqua 4	Silver 5	Gold 6	Red 7	Green 8
Pre-Writing	117–128	141–146, 169–170	98–99, 175–181, 263–268	115–117, 196–199, 238–242, 298–307	84–85, 90, 110, 119, 123, 293–297, 311–314, 341–352	78–79, 84, 104–112, 116–128, 233–237, 247–248, 310–316	81–84, 89, 99–101, 106–107, 118, 123–124, 136–143, 155, 172–182	52–54, 59, 76, 95, 99, 112–118, 134, 141, 146,148, 154–167
Choosing and Narrowing a Topic. Determining Purpose and Audience. Gathering and Organizing Information	117–128	141–146, 169–170	99, 177–181, 263–268	115–117, 198–199, 239–242, 301–307	111–112, 119, 123, 294–297, 314, 343–352	108–113, 118–129, 233–237, 250, 310–317	101–103, 137–143, 172–183	113–119, 155–167
	196–201	266–267	357, 375, 377	422, 430, 432, 441–442	496, 499–500, 531, 535–536, 551–552	515, 536–537, 540, 549–550, 566, 568		
Writing the First Draft	129	147–150, 172	91–103, 181–185, 233, 267	117, 200, 243–244, 307	86, 90, 110, 298–302, 315–317, 353–356	80, 84, 238–241, 318–320	85, 89, 131, 143–148, 155, 183–188	55, 59, 76, 107, 120–124, 131, 134, 168–173
Single Paragraphs. Compositions, Reports	129	147–150, 172	93, 99–103, 182–185, 233, 267	117, 200, 245, 307	111–112, 299–302, 312–317, 353–356	239–241, 318–320	144–148, 184–189	121–125, 169–173
	202	268, 269–270	348, 358–360, 363, 365–366, 375	442	536	549		
Revising	130	151–152, 173–174	104–105, 186, 197, 233, 268–270	118, 201, 246–247, 308–309	87, 90, 110, 302–305, 356	80, 84, 242–243, 321	86–89, 131, 149–153, 155, 189	56–58, 59, 107, 126–128, 131, 134, 173
Refining Ideas, Organization, and Word choice	130	151–152, 173–174	105–107, 187, 197, 271	120, 203, 247, 309	111–112, 305, 317, 356	126–129, 243, 321	151–152, 189	128, 173
	202	271		443	576–587	549		
Proofreading	130	151–152, 173–174	106–107, 187, 269–270	118–119, 201–202, 310–312	87–90, 91, 110, 302–305, 311, 356	80, 85, 243–245, 248, 321	86–89, 131, 149–151, 189	56–57, 59, 126–128, 134, 173
Correcting Errors in Form, Grammar, Usage, Capitalization, Punctuation, and Spelling	130	151–152, 173–174	106–107, 187, 271	120, 203	111–112, 305, 317, 356	243–245, 321	152, 189	128, 173
	202	271	365–366, 392–397	443, 470–475	576–587, 531	549, 591–603		
Proofreading Symbols			105, 186	120, 202, 311	88, 302	81	86, 149–150	56, 126–127
See also: Narrative Paragraph, Descriptive Paragraph, Explanatory Paragraph, Persuasive Paragraph			105, 187	120, 203	303	81, 242–243		
			392	443, 470	531			

Composition (continued)

Paragraphs	Pink 1	Plum 2	Brown 3	Aqua 4	Silver 5	Gold 6	Red 7	Green 8
The Concept of the Paragraph	127–128	142–144	91–102	103–117	82–83, 98–103	87–101	91–101	61–67
Definition, Identifying the Main Idea, Finding and Writing Topic Sentences	127–128	142–144, 152	93–103	106–117	98–105	90–101	93–95, 97–99, 101–103	64–71
	200–201	266, 271, 291	347, 355, 359–360	413–414, 425	495–496, 519	511–512, 513	18–19	14–15
Developing a Paragraph			101–102	117, 196	107–112	103–112	105–131	73–84, 107
Specific Details, Examples, Facts and Figures, Definitions *See also:* Narrative Paragraph, Descriptive Paragraph, Explanatory Paragraph			103	117	108–113	108–113	81–84, 109–110, 111–112, 113–115	76–85
			348	414	497–498, 519–520	513–515, 533	20–21	16–17, 28–29
The Narrative Paragraph	111–112, 123, 125, 128–129	142–151	175–182	195–200	116–119	116–118	118–120	88–91, 107
First Person or Third Person Narrator, Identifying Main Events, Use of Chronological Order, Writing a Paragraph	123–126, 128–130	142–152	177–182	198–200	119, 127	118, 129	120–121	89–91
	198–199, 201	266–271	357–358, 375	427–428	499–500, 520 ˜	515–516, 534	22, 29	18–19
The Descriptive Paragraph	111–112, 119, 127	154–164, 167–172	231–233	235–244	120–123	119–123	61–79, 121–124	92–95, 107
Choosing Words and Details, Use of Logical Order, Writing a Paragraph	119–120, 127, 129–130	154–166, 168–174	232–233	237–245	123, 127	123, 129	62–72, 124–125	97–98
	197, 200	272–281	363, 375	433–434	499–500, 519–520	515–516, 534	22, 29	18–19
The Explanatory Paragraph			189–197	250–254	124–126	124–128	96–99, 125–129	99–107
Paragraphs That Give Instruction ("How"), Paragraphs That Define ("What"), Paragraphs That Give Reasons ("Why"), Paragraphs That Persuade			190–197	251–254	125–126	126–129	129–130	100–106
See also: Process of Writing			359–360, 375	436	500, 520	515–516, 534	23, 29	19

☐ **Teaching Pages**
(Explanations and examples in the text and T.E.)

▨ **Exercises**
(All pages containing exercises for the concept)

☐ **Reinforcement**
(Grades 1–6: Practice Pages in T.E.; Grades 7–8: Diagnostic and Mastery Test Booklets)

Compositions

Compositions	Pink 1	Plum 2	Brown 3	Aqua 4	Silver 5	Gold 6	Red 7	Green 8
The Concept of a Composition					289–292	229–230, 233	133–135	109–113
Definition, Basis in Personal Experience					292	233–235		113
					531, 551			
The One-Paragraph Composition	127–128	141–151, 167–183			93–103, 115–127	103–113, 115–129	91–131	61–70
	127–129	142–152, 168–184			97–105, 119–127	90–91, 101, 118–129	93–130	64–71
	200–202	266–271, 278–281, 291			495–500, 519–520	511–514	18–21, 22–23	19, 28–29
The Concept of a Composition (continued)					291–305	229–245, 247–259	133–168	110–112
The Composition of Five or More Paragraphs					292–305	233–244, 250–259	137–168	
					531–532	537–540	24–25	20–21
Planning the Composition				260	110, 293–297	104–112, 116–128, 233–237	136–142	112–118
Choosing a Subject, Narrowing the Topic, Gathering Ideas, Finding Sources, Taking Notes, Organizing Ideas, Making a Writing Plan				261	111–112, 294–297	108–113, 118–129, 233–237	137–139, 140, 142	113–119
					531, 551	537–538, 540, 549–550, 566	24, 25, 29	20–21
Writing the Composition					110, 298–302	238–241	81–89, 143–148	120–131
Introductory Paragraph. Body. Conclusion					111–112, 299–302	239–241	144–146, 147–148	67, 70, 121–130
					531–532	537–538	24–25	14, 19, 24
Revising the Composition	130	173–174		261	110, 302–305	242–243	149–153	126–128, 131
Revising for Content				261		126–129, 243	151	128
					111–112, 305	549		
Proofreading	130	173–174			110, 302–305	243–245, 248	149–152	126–128
					111–112, 305	243–245	152	128
See also: Process of Writing					532	549		

Composition (continued)

Compositions (continued)

	Pink 1	Plum 2	Brown 3	Aqua 4	Silver 5	Gold 6	Red 7	Green 8
Kinds of Compositions Narrative (First and Third Person), Descriptive, Explanatory (Paragraphs That Give Instructions, Paragraphs That Define, Paragraphs That Give Reasons, Paragraphs That Persuade)				257–261	115–127	247–259	155–168	133–151
				259–261	119–127	250–255	157–158, 161, 165, 168–169	138–151
See also: Process of Writing					499–500	539–540		21

Reports

	Pink 1	Plum 2	Brown 3	Aqua 4	Silver 5	Gold 6	Red 7	Green 8
The Concept of a Report			260–262	295–297	341	309	171	153
Definition, Basis in Study and Research			262	298				
			365	441				
Planning the Report			263–266	275–279, 299–306	342–352	310–316	172–182, 191–215, 595–598	154–167
			263–266	276–279, 301–307	343–352	310–317	172, 173, 174, 176, 179, 182, 194–214, 598–601	155–167
			366, 377	438, 441–442	535–536, 552	549–550, 568	26, 29	22
Writing the Report			267	307–312	353–356	318–321	81–89, 183–189	168–173
			267	307	355–356	318–321	184–185, 187, 188, 189	169–173
			366		536	549–550	26, 29	22
Revising the Report			268	308–309	356	321	89, 153, 189	173
Revising for Content			271	309	356	321		173
						549		
			269–271	310–312	356	321	89, 189	173
Proofreading			271	313	356	321		173
			391–397	443, 469–475		549		

Stories, Narrative Compositions

	Pink 1	Plum 2	Brown 3	Aqua 4	Silver 5	Gold 6	Red 7	Green 8
Planning a Story		141–147	175–181	257–261	307–314, 377–389	390–404	156–158	87–91, 109–119, 131
Characters. Setting. Plot		142–147	177–181	261	310–314, 379, 385, 389	394, 401, 404	157–158	89–91, 113–119
		267–268	357, 375		533–534, 550			20–21
Writing a Story	129	148–150	181–185	260–261	315–317, 389	390–404	156–158	120–131, 133–151
Introduction, Body, Ending	130	148–152	182–185	261	316–317, 389	394–404	157–158	121–122, 124, 138, 144–147
		268–271	358		534			20–21, 28

Related Writing Skills

	Pink 1	Plum 2	Brown 3	Aqua 4	Silver 5	Gold 6	Red 7	Green 8
Writing a Book Report	64–73	117–129	256–257	273–274	35	222		
Title, Author, Main Characters, Setting, Plot, Evaluation	64–74	118–130	256–257	274	35	222		
		256–260	104–105, 186–187					
Writing Friendly Letters		85–86, 93–95	274–278	317–320	361–364	326–329	237–243	238–241
Form of Friendly Letters		86, 93–96	278	321	364	329–330	243–245	240–242
		242–243	367–368, 377	444	537, 552	551		
Social Notes: Invitations, Replies to Invitations, Thank-You Notes, Bread-and-Butter Notes	113, 115	87–89	283–287	323–325	365–367	330–335	245–250, 257	242–245
	113–116	87–90, 96	287	324–325	368	335–336	248, 251	246
	194–195	239–240	368, 377		537, 552	551		
Writing Business Letters				327–330	367–372	336–339	251–257	246–255
Form of Business Letters, Order Letters, Letters of Request, Letters of Complaint				331	373	340	256	252, 254, 256
				444–445	538, 558	552		
Writing Envelopes		91–92	279–282	322, 331	374–375	340–341	258–261	256–259
		91–92	282	322, 331–332	375	341	260	259
		241	367		537			

Speaking and Listening

Speaking	Pink 1	Plum 2	Brown 3	Aqua 4	Silver 5	Gold 6	Red 7	Green 8
Nonverbal Aspects			118–121	190	335, 411	372–374	264–265	
Using Body Movement To Express Emotion or Ideas				190		373–374		
Social Conversation	1–3, 9	7–10	31–45, 132	16–29, 123–127		371–377, 383–385	263, 268, 271	
Using the Telephone, Taking a Message, Giving Directions, Making Introductions, Casual Discussion	2–3, 9–10	7–10, 14 208	34–45, 133	21–29, 127	323	373–378, 384–385, 387	268–269, 271	
Speaking to Groups	15, 29, 47, 64–73	10, 129	118–121, 256	131–132, 315	357–359	382	263–266, 269–270	
Oral Reports, Demonstration Talk	15, 29, 47, 64–73	10–13, 129 209	121, 256	137, 315	358–359	382	270	
Reading Aloud			122–126	315		367–369, 379, 381		
			126	315		369–370, 379–380		
Telling a Story			215–222	187–193	329–338			
			218–223	188–193	331–339			
Making Announcements				16–17, 128–129			266–267	
				17, 129, 131			267	
Making Introductions to Groups							271	
							271	
Discussions			127–129	135–141	319–324	385–387		262–265, 267–271
			129	138, 141	320–325	386–387		266, 271
Interviewing	13–14	11					277	262–263
	13–14	11–12					277–278	262
Giving a Speech							272–283	
							273–283	

Listening

	Pink 1	Plum 2	Brown 3	Aqua 4	Silver 5	Gold 6	Red 7	Green 8
Listening for Specific Purposes	5–6	9–10	136–138	132–133, 282–292	319–324	359–369	284–285, 294–298	261–271
Following Directions, Listening for Information, Listening for Motive and Bias, Listening to Literature	1, 5, 16, 17, 31, 49, 63, 65, 67, 75, 93, 111	1, 9–10, 15, 31, 55, 67, 85, 97, 117, 131, 141, 153, 167	139	133, 284–293	320–324	361–369	285	262, 271
	146, 172	209		439–440				
Manners in Listening	4	129	138	132–133	323–324	361–362	283–284	
	4	209				361–362		
Evaluation Evaluating Others' Speaking Skills, Evaluating Personal Listening Skills					323–324	361–366	283–285	269–271
					324	361–366	285	271

Study and Research Skills

Clear Thinking

	Pink 1	Plum 2	Brown 3	Aqua 4	Silver 5	Gold 6	Red 7	Green 8
Using Facts			109–111, 127–129	97–99, 250–251	319–324	109–112, 126–128, 257–259	126–129	175–178, 183–187
Differentiating Between Fact and Opinion, Clarifying Facts, Using Facts To Make Judgments			111–112, 129	100, 251	320–325	110–112, 128, 259	129–130	177–178, 184–187, 191
			349, 355	435		540		23–24, 29
Logical Reasoning			113–115	93–100	319–322	20–24	283–285	178–182, 188–190
Recognizing Generalizations, Stereotypes, and Slanted Language; Identifying Cause and Effect			115	95–101	320–322	21–25, 27	285	179–182, 190–191
			349, 355	412		502–503		23–24
Organizing Ideas	11–12, 117–118, 123	143–145, 155–162, 169	266–267	240–242, 252–254, 304–306	85, 90, 110, 117–119, 121–126, 295–297, 313–314, 347–352	105–108, 119–128, 314–316	91–95, 105–129, 140–142, 155–169, 180–182, 278–280	73–84, 87–107, 115–118, 133–151, 163–167, 593–596
Classifying, Outlining, Sequencing	11–12, 16, 117–118, 123–124	143–146, 155–162, 166, 169–172	267	242, 253–255, 305–307	111–112, 119, 123–126, 296–297, 315, 347–352	108, 123, 126, 128–129, 317	93–95, 142, 157–169, 182–183, 280–281	76–85, 89–106, 116, 118–119, 138, 141, 144, 146, 147, 151, 167, 596–599
	148, 196, 198–199, 205	266–267, 272–274, 277–279	365, 375	434, 436, 442	531, 533, 535–536	515–516, 538, 540, 550, 566	18–23, 25	14, 16–21

Study Skills

Study Skills	Pink 1	Plum 2	Brown 3	Aqua 4	Silver 5	Gold 6	Red 7	Green 8
Understanding the Assignment						132–133	218–219	214–216
						133–134	220	216
						517, 533	27	
Setting Up a Study Area					24–26	134	220–221	217
					26–36			
						517	27	
Types of Reading					27–32	137	227	225–226
Skimming, Scanning, In-depth (Study-type) Reading					28–32, 36	138–139	228	226
						517	27	
Making a Study Plan					26	135–136	221–222	217–219
Organizing Time, Setting Long and Short-Term Goals					26, 36	136	223	219
Using a Study Method						137–138	223–224, 234	220
S Q 3 R (Study, Question, Read, Recite, Review)						138	224–225	221–222
						517, 533	27	
Note-Taking			264–266	116, 301–307	344–352, 397, 399	137–138, 313–317	177–178, 226, 231	223–224
Restating in Your Own Words, Separating Fact from Opinion, Evaluating Sources, Using Modified Outline Form			264–266	116, 303–307	346–352, 398, 399	138–139, 314–317	178, 231–232	224
			349, 366	441, 442	535–536	549, 550	26, 27	27
Using Graphic Aids					358	137	228–229	227–230
Pictures, Diagrams, Charts, Maps, Graphs					358		230	230–231
							27	27
Test Taking				205–209			232–234	232–234
How To Prepare for a Test, Taking the Test, Types of Questions				207, 209			235	234–235
							27	

Research Skills

Research Skills	Pink 1	Plum 2	Brown 3	Aqua 4	Silver 5	Gold 6	Red 7	Green 8
Using the Dictionary	23–27, 35–36	56–63	16–23	144–153	223–234	200–208	28–33	179–180
Using Alphabetical Order and Guide Words To Find the Word. Recognizing the Information in an Entry. Finding the Right Meaning. Using the Synonymy	23–28, 30, 35–36	56–66	17–24, 28	145–154	224–235	200–208	28–33	180–181
	154–158, 172	228–232, 246	339–340, 353	415–416	515–516, 522	527–528	13–14	11–12
Using the Library		118–122	252–254	263–271	209–218	211–220	191–203	193–202
Kinds of Books (Fiction/Nonfiction). Book Arrangement and Classification. Dewey Decimal System. Card Catalog		118–122, 130	252–254	265–272	211–219	213–221	193–204	197–198, 202
		257, 260		438	513–514, 522	529–530		25–26, 29
Using Reference Books				275–279	220–221, 341	224–227	175, 204–215, 227, 277	203–211
Table of Contents and Index. Encyclopedia. Almanacs. Atlases. *Readers' Guide to Periodical Literature*. Other Reference Works				276–279	221	227	207–214, 277–278	206–211
				439	514	530		25–26, 29
Using People as Resources	13–14	9–11			330–331		277	261–263
Finding a Good Source. Interviewing	13–14	9–12	128		331		277–278	262

Appreciation of Literature

Nonfiction

	Pink 1	Plum 2	Brown 3	Aqua 4	Silver 5	Gold 6	Red 7	Green 8
Biography					212	405–406	306	
						406–407	306	
						557, 570		
Autobiography					390–393	407–409	304–305	
					391–393	409	305	
					540, 553	557		
Other Types of Nonfiction					394–399	410–411	302–303	291–296
Journals. Diaries. Anecdotes. Feature Articles. Essays. Satires					396–399	411	305	293, 294–295, 296
					540, 553	557, 570		

Fiction

Fiction	Pink 1	Plum 2	Brown 3	Aqua 4	Silver 5	Gold 6	Red 7	Green 8
Oral Tradition			256	192–193		390–396	288–293	274–279
Legend. Myth. Fable. Folk Tale, Tall Tale, Ballad			256	193		394, 396	289, 291–292, 293	277, 278, 280
						557, 570		
Short Story	1, 17, 31, 49, 63, 75, 93, 111, 139–140	1, 15, 31, 55, 67, 85, 97, 117, 131, 141, 153, 167, 195–198				396–404	307–310	297–300
Fantasy. Realistic Fiction						401, 404	311	301
						557, 570		
Elements of Fiction							307	297
Mood, Narrator, Point of View, Theme							311	301
Setting			178, 181–184	258–261	378–379, 389	390	307	297
			178	259, 261	379–380	394, 401, 404	311	301
					539, 553	557, 570		
Characters			176–177, 181–184	258–261	378–379, 389	390	307	297
			177, 185	259, 261	379–380	394, 401, 404	311	301
					539, 553	557, 570		
Plot			179–180, 181–184, 216, 217	188–189	380–389	390	307	297
			180, 182, 185, 218	189	382–383	394, 401, 404,		301
					539, 553	557, 570		

Drama

	Pink 1	Plum 2	Brown 3	Aqua 4	Silver 5	Gold 6	Red 7	Green 8
Definition. Plot. Character. Setting. Stage Directions. Terms of Production. Oral Interpretation					401–415		311–314	301–305
					410–415		315	305
					541–542, 553			

Poetry

	Pink 1	Plum 2	Brown 3	Aqua 4	Silver 5	Gold 6	Red 7	Green 8
Listening to or Reading Poetry	1, 17, 31, 37, 49, 63, 75, 93, 111	1, 15–18, 31, 55, 67, 85, 97, 117, 131, 141, 153, 167	236–247, 296–297, 301	282–293, 341–342, 345	173, 202, 207, 277–286, 426, 427, 460	380–381, 412–416	294–301	
					281–287	381		
				439–440	529–530, 550			
Reading Poetry Aloud			243–245	290–292		379–381		
Analyzing Poetry	37–38	17–18	235–246	281–292	202–205, 277–286	412–416	294–301	280–290
Structure, Images, Rhythm, Rhyme, Alliteration, Assonance. Consonance. Onomatopoeia, Personification. Simile. Metaphor, Mood	37–38	17–18	239–247	284–293	204–207, 281–287	416–417	298–299, 300–301	287, 290
			364, 376	439–440	529–530, 550	558		

Books

	Pink 1	Plum 2	Brown 3	Aqua 4	Silver 5	Gold 6	Red 7	Green 8
Finding a Good Book	64	118	254–255	264, 269–271	210–219	212	192	193–197
		118, 122	254–255	265, 272	211–219	213	192–193	197–198
				437	513–514, 522			
Sharing a Book	63–73	118–129	256–257	273–274	35	222		
	64–74	118–130	256–257	274	35	222		
		256–260						

☐ **Teaching Pages**
(Explanations and examples in the text and T.E.)

▨ **Exercises**
(All pages containing exercises for the concept)

▨ **Reinforcement**
(Grades 1–6: Practice Pages in T.E.; Grades 7–8: Diagnostic and Mastery Test Booklets)

Grammar

Sentences

	Pink 1	Plum 2	Brown 3	Aqua 4	Silver 5	Gold 6	Red 7	Green 8
Identifying Sentences	50–54	32–34	47–49	31–34	39–42	30–31	319–325, 343–344, 354	309–316, 332
Definition, Distinguishing Between Sentences and Fragments, Run-on Sentences	50–54, 62	32–34	50, 58	33, 35, 49–50	43, 64	31, 58	343–344, 344–345, 350–351, 355	313, 332–333
	166–167, 171	217	341, 353	394, 403, 424	474, 488, 518	490, 504	1, 33, 53	1, 30, 48, 53
Kinds of Sentences	55–57	39–42	51–53	36, 38	44–48	32–34	334–335, 542	540
Declarative	55–58, 61–62	39–42, 46, 48, 50, 52, 54	53–54, 58–59	38–39, 50	47–49, 64–65	33–35, 58	335–336, 349, 545–546, 570	542–543, 568
	168–169, 171, 174	220–221, 223–227, 245	332, 341	394, 404, 423	474, 488	490, 504	32	7
Interrogative	55–56, 59	39–40, 43	51–53	37–38	44–48	32–34	334–335, 338, 544	321, 541–542
	55–56, 59–60, 62	39–40, 43–44, 46, 48, 50, 52, 54	53–54, 58–59	38–39, 50	47–49, 64–65	33–35, 58	335–336, 338–339, 349, 545–546, 570	322, 334–335, 542–543, 568
	168, 170–171, 174	220, 222–227, 245	332, 341	394, 404, 423	474, 488	490, 504	32	7
Imperative		45–47	51–53	37–38	44–48	32–34	334–335, 339–340, 542	321–322, 540
		45–48, 50, 52, 54	53–54, 58–59	38–39, 50	47–49, 64–65	33–35, 58	335–336, 340, 349, 545–546, 570	322, 334–335, 542, 568
		223–227, 245	332, 341	394, 404, 423	474, 488	490, 504	32	7
Exclamatory		49–51	51–53	38	44–48	32–34	334–335, 544–545	542
		49–52, 54	53–54, 58–59	38–39, 50	47–49, 64–65	33–35, 58	335–336, 349, 545–546	543, 568
		225–227, 245	341	394, 404, 423	474, 488	490, 504	32	7

Teaching Pages
(Explanations and examples in the text and T.E.)

Exercises
(All pages containing exercises for the concept)

Reinforcement
(Grades 1–6: Practice Pages in T.E.; Grades 7–8: Diagnostic and Mastery Test Booklets)

	Pink 1	Plum 2	Brown 3	Aqua 4	Silver 5	Gold 6	Red 7	Green 8
Sentence Parts: The Subject	51–52	35–36	55–56	32, 40–41	50–52	35–36	320–321	312–313, 315–316, 329–330, 455, 466–467
Complete Subject	51–52, 62	35–36, 38, 54	57, 59	33, 42, 49–51	52–53, 65–66	36–37, 59	321, 346	313, 331, 333–334, 454–463, 467–468
	166	218, 227, 245	342	394, 403	489, 518	491, 505		
				43–44	56–57	45	322–323	314–316, 466
Simple Subject—Definition				44–46, 51	58, 66	45–46, 60–61	323, 346–347	316–317, 329, 336, 493
				394, 404	490	491, 506, 532	1, 30	31, 53
		45		37	61	50	335, 339–340	321–332
Understood Simple Subject		45			61–62, 67	50–51, 62	340	322, 334–335
					491	506	33	32
Finding the Simple Subject: The Subject in Unusual Positions, in Declarative Sentences, The Subject in Interrogative and Exclamatory Sentences					59–60	46–48	336–337, 338–341, 513–514	320–322, 500, 505
					60, 67	47–49, 61–62	336–337, 338–342, 513–515, 516–518	334–335, 493, 501, 506, 507, 509
					490–491	506	1, 32–33, 43, 49, 52, 53	1, 31–32, 37, 50, 53, 54
						51–52, 296–297	332–333, 472–473, 511	329–330, 467
Compound Subject						52–54, 62–63, 297–298, 305–306	333, 348–349, 472–474, 477, 512, 517	331, 336, 467–468
						507	31, 47, 51	1, 3, 33, 36, 49, 54
Sentence Parts: The Predicate	53–54	37	56	32, 40–41	50–52	35–36	320–321, 495	312–313, 315–316, 330, 455, 466–467
Complete Predicate	53–54, 62	37–38, 54	57–59	33, 42, 49–51	52–53, 65–66	36–37, 59	321, 346, 495–496	313, 331, 333–334, 455, 460, 463, 467–468
	167	219, 227, 245	342	394, 403	489, 518	491, 505	49	1

Grammar (continued)

Sentences (continued)

	Pink 1	Plum 2	Brown 3	Aqua 4	Silver 5	Gold 6	Red 7	Green 8
Sentence Parts: The Predicate (continued)	95, 97	99–101	142–148	44–45, 157–160	53–55, 143–145	37–38, 157–158	322–323, 325–326, 354	314–316, 378
Finding the Simple Predicate, or Verb	95–98	99–102	144–149, 159–160	160, 173	55, 66, 144–146, 167	38–39, 59, 159–160, 161	323–327, 346–347, 355, 385–386	314–316, 334–335, 379, 454–463, 493
	184–185, 193	247	350, 356	397, 404, 417, 459–468	477, 489, 503	491, 505, 521, 532	1, 30, 33, 34, 35, 49, 53–54	1, 31, 32, 53
Identifying Main Verbs and Helping Verbs			150–152	163–165	147–149	39–41, 160–161	328, 362	317–318, 380–383, 402–403
			151–153, 160	164, 166, 174	148–150, 167–168	41–42, 59–60, 181–182	329–331, 347–348, 363–364, 387	318, 381–384, 403, 407–409
			351, 356	418, 426	503	490, 522	2, 30–31, 35	3, 31–32, 39
Finding Separated Parts of the Verb				165	150	43, 162	330, 362–363	317–318, 380–384
				166, 175	151, 167–168	43–44, 60, 180–181	330–331, 348, 363–364, 387	318, 381–385
				419	503	490, 522	2, 34, 35	31, 39
Finding Verbs in Unusual Order: Questions, Commands, Sentences Beginning with *There*					59, 60, 156–157	46–48	336–337, 338–341	319–321, 505
					60, 61–62, 67, 158, 169	47–49, 61	337, 338–342, 349–350	320, 322, 334–335, 506, 509
					490, 491, 505	493, 521	32, 33, 34, 52	32
Linking Verbs (Definition)				222	166	166–167, 195, 272	360–361	327–328, 378–379, 412, 413, 421–422, 459, 466–467
				222	166	167–168, 182–183	361–362, 386–387	328–329, 336, 379, 413–414, 422, 459, 462–463
				394, 397, 403, 417, 459		523	35	38
Identifying the Direct Object					152–157, 165–166	163–164, 180	356, 358	323–324, 456–457
					157, 165–166, 168	164–165, 180, 182	357, 359–360, 362, 385	324, 326, 336, 456–457, 461, 463, 493
					504	522, 526	34, 39, 53	32–33

	Pink 1	Plum 2	Brown 3	Aqua 4	Silver 5	Gold 6	Red 7	Green 8
Sentence Parts: The Predicate (continued)							396–397	324–325, 457
Identifying the Indirect Object							397–398, 406	457, 461, 463
							39, 53	32
Identifying a Predicate Noun or Pronoun					166	195	326, 354, 360–361, 386–387, 398–399, 412–413	327–328
					166	195	361–362, 386–387, 399–400, 406, 413	328–329, 336, 458, 462, 463
					478, 507	526	35, 39, 53	33
Identifying a Predicate Adjective				222	252	265, 272	326, 354, 360–361, 430–431	327–328
				222	252	265, 272	361–362, 430–431, 439–440	328–329, 336, 459, 462, 463
				429		542	35–43	4, 33
Compound Predicate						54, 296–297	332–333, 472–473, 495	329–330, 467
						55–56, 63, 297–306	333, 348–349, 473–474, 495–496, 502–503	331, 333–334, 467–468
						507, 546	31, 49	1, 33
Sentence Structure	50–59	31–52	47–56	31–45	39–63	29–54	320–323, 495	309–332, 466–467, 476–477
Study of the Simple Sentence	50–62	32–52, 54	50–59	31–45	43–67	31–63	321, 323–326, 495–496, 502–503	311–337, 467–468, 493
	166–171, 174	217–227, 245	341–342, 353	394, 403–404	448, 474, 488	490–491, 504–507	1, 30–33, 50	1, 30–33, 47, 53
Definition and Study of the Compound Sentence				53–57	74	298–300	41–45, 332–333, 491–499	469–476
				55–59	74	299–301, 306–307	43, 57, 333, 494–505	469–476, 494–495
				405–406	478, 494, 518	546–547	49–50	1, 47, 53

Sentences (continued)

	Pink 1	Plum 2	Brown 3	Aqua 4	Silver 5	Gold 6	Red 7	Green 8
Sentence Structure (continued)							53–54	476–491
Definition and Study of the Complex Sentence							54–55, 59	479–492 495–497
								47, 48, 53
Clauses: Subordinate, Adverb, Adjective, Relative, Noun, Restrictive, Nonrestrictive							53–54	476–491, 552–553
							54–55, 59	479–492 495–497, 553–554, 571–572
								47, 48
Diagraming							325, 332–333, 337, 338, 340, 341, 394–395, 396–397, 403, 429, 431, 446, 466, 493	315–316, 319, 322, 325, 328, 330, 470, 473, 484, 485–486, 490–491
Sentence Patterns		32	49	31, 47	63	57	445, 479–480	453–454
Significance of Word Order		32	50	48	63	57	480, 486, 489	454–460, 463
								46
N V Pattern				89, 173	139	153	481	455
				89, 173	139	153	481, 486, 489	455, 461, 463
							48	46
N V N Pattern						180	482	456
						180	482, 487, 489	456, 459, 463
							48	46
N V N N Pattern							483	457
							483, 487, 489	457, 461, 463
							48	46
N LV N Pattern					166	195	484	458
					166	195	484, 488, 489	458, 462, 463
							48	46

	Pink 1	Plum 2	Brown 3	Aqua 4	Silver 5	Gold 6	Red 7	Green 8
Sentence Patterns (continued)				222	252	272	485	459
N LV Adj. Pattern				222	252	272	485, 488, 489	459, 462–463
							48	46

Parts of Speech

	Pink 1	Plum 2	Brown 3	Aqua 4	Silver 5	Gold 6	Red 7	Green 8
Nouns	76–78	68–69	61–63	61–62	129–130	141–142	389–390	340–342
Definition	76–78, 92	68–70, 84	63, 72	63, 74	130, 140	142–143, 154	390, 404	342, 348, 449
	175, 203	233, 238, 246	333, 343	395, 407	476, 501	492, 519	3, 38, 54	2, 34, 45, 53
Singular and Plural Nouns	79–80	71, 74	67–68	68–70	133–134	146–148	400–401, 507	343–344
	79–82, 92	71–74, 84	68, 73	70, 75	135, 141	148, 155	401, 406–407, 508, 516	345, 348
	176–178, 183, 203	234, 238, 246	333, 343–344	395, 408, 424	476, 502	492, 520	39	8, 35
Common and Proper Nouns	83–86	75–81	64–65	66	131	143–144	391	340–342
	83–86	75–84	66, 72–73	67, 74	132, 140	144–146, 154–155	391–392, 404–405	342–348
	179–181, 203	235–238, 246	333, 343	395, 407	501	519	38, 55	2, 6, 34, 55–56
Possessive Nouns			69–70	71–72	136–138	149–151	402–403, 561	346, 559–560
			71, 73	73, 75	138, 141	151–152, 155	403, 407, 576	346–347, 349, 560–561, 573–574
			344, 373	395, 407	476, 502	492, 520	39	35
Use of Nouns as Subjects		69	63	64, 89	139, 165, 166, 252	153, 180, 195, 272	393, 507	312–316, 319–321
		69	63	65, 89	139, 165, 166, 252	153, 180, 195, 272	393–394, 405, 508	313, 316–317, 333–336
							39, 53	44, 45
Use of Nouns as Direct or Indirect Objects of Verbs, or as Objects of Prepositions					152–153, 165	163–164, 180	356–358, 394–397	323–325, 330
					153, 165, 168	164–166, 180, 182	357, 359–360, 385–386, 395–398, 405–406	325–326, 331, 335–336
					504	522	34, 35, 39, 46, 53	1, 38, 53, 54

Parts of Speech (continued)

	Pink 1	Plum 2	Brown 3	Aqua 4	Silver 5	Gold 6	Red 7	Green 8
Nouns (continued)		70	63		166	166–167, 195	398–399	327–328, 330
Use of Nouns as Predicate Words		70	63		166	167–168, 195	400, 406	328–329, 331, 336
						523	35, 39, 53	38
Verbs	93–97	97–101	141–148	157–160	143–145	157–158, 166–167	326, 353–361, 412, 430–431	378, 421–422, 466–467
Definition; Action and State-of-Being (or Linking) Verbs	94–98, 110	98–102	144–149	158, 160, 174	144–146, 167	159–160, 167–168, 181, 182–183	327, 355, 357, 359–362, 386–387, 432, 434–435	379, 422, 433, 449
	184–185, 193, 204	247, 289	350, 356	394, 397, 403, 417, 429, 468	477, 503	493, 521, 523	35	31, 38, 45, 53–54
Main Verbs and Helping Verbs			150–152	161–165	147–150	160–162	362–363	317–318, 380
			151–153	162–166, 173–176	148–151, 167–168	162–163, 181–182	363–364, 387	318, 381, 407
			351, 356	418–419, 426	503, 510	505, 522	2, 31, 35	3, 31, 39
Forming the Present Tense of Regular Verbs	99–100	103	163–165	180–181	191–192	169–170, 353–354	364–365, 507–508	382–383, 385–386, 499–500
	99–100, 109–110	103–104	166, 173	181	195	170–171, 183, 355	366, 387, 508	383–384, 386, 408, 501, 507–508
	186–187, 193, 204	248	334, 352, 356	397, 421, 459–468	509	523, 555–556	36	3, 39
Forming Past Tenses of Regular Verbs	101–102	107	167–170	182–183	193	169–170, 353–354	364–365, 367–368	382–383, 385–386
	101–102, 108, 110	107–108	171–173	182–184	193	170–171, 183, 355	366, 387	383–384, 386, 408
	188–189, 193, 204	250, 289	334, 352, 356	421	509–510	523, 555–556	36	3, 39, 40
Using Principal Parts of Verbs To Form Other Tenses					194	169–170, 353–354	364–365, 367–368	382–386
						170–171, 183, 355	366, 387	382–386, 407–408
						523, 555–556	36	39
Forming Tenses of Irregular Verbs	97, 103–106	105–106, 109–114	169–173	167–168, 184–185	154–155, 196–197	169–170, 355–357	369–384, 508–509	387–406, 500
	97–98, 103–110	105–106, 109–116	171–173	168, 185	155, 168	170–171, 183	370–384, 387	389–408, 501, 507–508
	185, 190–193, 204	249, 251–255, 289	334, 356, 379–390	419, 426, 459–468	504, 510, 521, 555–574	523, 555–556	2, 36–37	3, 39, 40–41

	Pink 1	Plum 2	Brown 3	Aqua 4	Silver 5	Gold 6	Red 7	Green 8
Verbs (continued)						163–164	358	323–325, 466–467
Transitive and Intransitive Verbs						164–166, 182	359–360, 386	325–326, 335–336, 468
							34, 35	32, 52, 53
Active and Passive Verbs								402–403
								403, 408–409
								41
Verbals: Gerunds, Infinitives, Participles							367	511–519
								514, 516, 518–521
See also Usage: Verbs								51–52, 54
Adjectives		154–162	199–205	211–216	237–244	261–264	427–428	411–412, 415
Definition, Kinds (*what kind, how many, which ones*), Articles		154–162, 166	203–206, 212	213–217, 223–224	239–245, 253–255	263–265, 273	429, 439	413–414, 416, 432, 449
		272–274, 277, 291	361, 376	398, 429–430	523–524, 577	495, 541–542	4, 42, 54	4, 42–43
Proper Adjectives					418	266–267	428, 522	413
					418–419, 429	267–268, 274	429, 439, 523–524, 536–538	414, 432
					543	541	55	6, 54, 55
Predicate Adjectives				222	252	265, 272	430–431, 449–450, 485	327–328, 412
				222	252	266, 272, 274	430–432, 439–440, 450–452, 454–455, 485, 488	328–329, 336, 413–414
						542	35, 43	53
Comparative and Superlative Forms		163–164	207–208	218–221	248–249	270–271	432–433	423–425
		163–164	209, 213	221–222, 225	250–251, 255	271, 275	433–434, 440–441	425–426, 431, 434–435
		275–276, 290	362	430	480, 524, 549	495, 542	43	
Pronouns Classed as Adjectives							435–436	413
See also Usage: Adjectives and Avoiding Confusion of Adjectives and Adverbs							436–437	414

Grammar (continued)

Parts of Speech (continued)

	Pink 1	Plum 2	Brown 3	Aqua 4	Silver 5	Gold 6	Red 7	Green 8
Adverbs			210–211	227–229	257–259	277–278	443–444	324, 416–417
Definition. Kinds (*how. when. where. to what extent*)			211–213	229–230, 233	259–260, 266	278–279, 284	444–445, 453	324, 417–443
			362, 376	431	481, 525, 528	496, 543	4, 44, 47, 54	4, 42–43, 44, 54
Comparative and Superlative Forms				231	260–261	278–279	448	426–428
See also Usage: Adverbs *and* Avoiding Confusion of Adjectives and Adverbs				232–233	261, 266–267	280–281, 284–285	448–449, 454	428, 434–435
				432	481, 526, 549	496, 544	45	43
Pronouns	87–88	132–138	75–76	77–78	173–175	185–186	409–417	352, 354, 367
Definition, Personal Pronouns, Compound, Forms of Pronouns	87–90, 92	132–140	77, 87	79, 80	175–176, 187	187, 196	411, 413–417, 423–425	353–355, 371–372, 375, 449
	182–183,	261–265, 290	345, 354	396, 409, 425	478, 507	494, 525, 536	3, 40, 54	2, 36–37
Possessive Pronouns			83–84	87	184–185	194	415–416, 421, 435–436, 562–563	360, 365–366, 413, 559
			84, 88–89	88, 91	185–186, 189	194	415–416, 421–422, 440–441, 563–564	360–361, 366, 414
			346	410	478, 508	494, 525	40, 43	2, 37
Demonstrative Pronouns							436	357, 367–368, 413, 429
							436	357, 368, 372–373, 375, 414, 431
								37, 45, 54
Indefinite Pronouns							421	355–356
							421–422, 425	356–357, 372–373
							41	36–37, 50
Interrogative Pronouns								358, 364
								358, 364–365, 372–373
								36, 37
Relative Pronouns								488–491
								492, 497
								48, 54

	Pink 1	Plum 2	Brown 3	Aqua 4	Silver 5	Gold 6	Red 7	Green 8
Pronouns (continued)	87	133–135, 137	78–79	80–82, 85–86, 89	177–178, 183	188	410–413, 417, 509–510	358–360, 367
Use of Pronouns as Subjects of Sentences	87–88, 92	133–140	80, 87–88	82, 86, 89, 90	179, 183–184, 187, 188	189, 196–197	411, 413, 417, 423–425, 510–511, 519	360–361, 368, 375
	182–183, 203	261–263, 265, 290	345, 354	396, 409–410	478, 507–508	494, 526, 536	3, 40–41, 54	2, 3, 36–37, 50, 54
Use of Pronouns as Predicate Pronouns					180	190	412–413	327–329, 358–360, 458
					180, 188	190–191, 197	413	328–329, 336, 360–361, 458, 462–463
					507	494, 526, 536	3, 40–41	2, 36–37
Use of Pronouns as Direct or Indirect Objects of Verbs	88	133, 135, 138	81	83–86	181–183	191–192	414	359–360, 362
	88, 92	133–136, 138–140	82, 88	84, 86, 91	182–184, 188–189	193, 197	414–415, 424	361, 363
	182–183, 203	261–262, 264–265, 290	345, 354	396, 409–410, 425	478, 507–508	494, 526	3, 40–41	2, 36–37
Use of Pronouns as Objects of Prepositions			81	83–86	181–183	191–192	461–463	359, 360, 362
			82, 88	84, 86, 91	182–184, 188–189	193, 197	462–463, 475	361, 363
See also Usage: Pronouns			345, 354	396, 409–410, 425	478, 507–508	494, 526, 536	3, 40, 46, 54	2, 36–37
Conjunctions					74–75	296–297	472–473	437, 445–446, 469–487
Definition, Coordinating, Correlative, Subordinating					74–75	297–298, 305–306	473–474, 477	446–447, 451, 469–487
					494	546–547, 568	5, 47, 54	5, 45, 46, 54
Combining Parts of Sentences, Sentences, or Clauses				56–57	72–75	296–297	491–499, 511	467–491
				58–59	73–75, 79–81	297–299, 306	494–505, 512, 517	467–491, 494–497
				406	493–494	508, 532, 546–547	47, 50	47, 48
Prepositions					269–274	288–289	457–472	324–325, 437–443
Definition, Object of Preposition, Prepositional Phrase					270–275	289–290, 304	459–467, 468–472, 475–477	325–326, 439–444, 449–451
					527–528, 549	526, 545, 568	5, 46–47, 54	5, 44–45, 54
Interjections						437	545	448–449, 542
Definition						437–438, 454	545, 570	449, 542
						561	57	45

Usage

Verbs

	Pink 1	Plum 2	Brown 3	Aqua 4	Silver 5	Gold 6	Red 7	Green 8
Problems with Making the Subject and Verb Agree	99–100	103–104	164–165	180–181	191–192	169–170, 344–345, 353–354	507–514	499–505
General Rules for Agreement of Subject and Verb	99–100, 107, 110	103–104	166–173	181	195	170–171, 183, 345–347, 351, 355	508, 510–515, 516–519	501–509
	186–187, 193	248	352, 356	397, 421		553	2, 51	3, 36, 49, 50, 54
Difficulties in Identifying the Simple Subject					59, 156–157	46–50, 347–350	513–514	319–322, 500–504
					60, 67, 158, 169	47–51, 61–62, 348–351	514, 515, 518	320–322, 501, 509
					490–491, 505	506, 553–554	1, 30, 32–33, 51, 52, 54	3, 36, 49–50
Verb Choice with a Compound Subject or an Indefinite Pronoun as Subject						347, 349	511	355, 502–504
						348–350, 351	512, 517, 519	356–357, 502–505, 507–508
						554	2, 51	3, 36, 49–50, 54
Irregular Verbs	97, 103–106	105–106, 109–114	169–170	167–168, 184–185	154–155, 195–197	355–357	368–384	387–406, 505
"To Be," Other Commonly Used Irregular Verbs	97–98, 103–110	105–106, 109–116	171–172	168, 176, 185	155, 168		369–384	389–408, 506, 509
	185, 190–193, 204	249, 251–255, 289	350–352, 379–390	419, 422, 426, 459–468	504, 509–510, 527–555	555–556, 573–590	2, 51	3, 39, 40–41, 49, 50, 54

Pronouns

	Pink 1	Plum 2	Brown 3	Aqua 4	Silver 5	Gold 6	Red 7	Green 8
Using the Correct Form of Personal Pronouns	87	133, 135, 137	78–79	80–82, 85–86	177–178, 183	188	409–413, 417	351–375, 358–360, 362, 367
Using Pronouns as Subjects of Sentences	87–88, 92	133–140	80, 87–88	82, 86, 90	179, 183–184, 187, 189	189, 196–197	411, 413, 417, 423–425	360–361, 363, 368, 375
	182–183, 203	261–265	345, 354	396, 409–410, 425	478, 507–508	494, 526	3, 40–41, 54	2, 36–37
Using Pronouns as Predicate Pronouns					180	190	412–413	359–360, 362
					180, 188	190–191, 197	413, 423	361, 363
					507	494, 526	3, 40–41	2, 36–37
Using Pronouns as Direct or Indirect Objects of Verbs, or as Objects of Prepositions	88	133, 135, 138	81	83–86	181–183	190–193	414, 461–462	359–362, 367–368
	88, 92	133–136, 138–140	82, 88	84, 86, 91	182–184, 188–189	193, 197	414–415, 462–463, 475	363, 368, 375
	182–183, 203	261–262, 264–265	345, 354	396, 409–410, 425	478, 507–508	494, 526	3, 40–41, 46	2, 36–37

Pronouns (continued)

	Pink 1	Plum 2	Brown 3	Aqua 4	Silver 5	Gold 6	Red 7	Green 8
Distinguishing Between Demonstrative Pronouns and Demonstrative Adjectives			202		246	268–269	436–437	367–368, 429
			203–204		247, 255	269, 275	437, 441	368, 375, 431
					524	495, 542		54
Other Problems		134	85	85	178	347	418–421	352, 355, 369
Including Using *I* or *Me* Last, Coordinating Pronouns and Antecedents, and Agreement of Verb with Indefinite Pronoun as Subject		134	86, 89	86	179, 187	348	418–422, 425	353, 356–357, 370, 375
See also Grammar: Parts of Speech. Pronouns			346, 354	409, 425	507	554	41, 43	2, 35, 37, 50

Adjectives

	Pink 1	Plum 2	Brown 3	Aqua 4	Silver 5	Gold 6	Red 7	Green 8
Forming Comparisons and Using Them Correctly		163–164		218–221	248–250	270–271	432–433	423–425
Correct Use of Comparative and Superlative Forms. Special Cases (including *good better best*)		163–164		220–221, 225	250–251, 255	271, 275	433–434, 440–441, 454	425–426, 431, 434–435
	275–276, 290		362, 376	426	524, 549	495, 542	43	43, 54

Adverbs

	Pink 1	Plum 2	Brown 3	Aqua 4	Silver 5	Gold 6	Red 7	Green 8
Forming Comparisons and Using Them Correctly				231	260–261	279–280	448	426–428
Correct Use of Comparative and Superlative Forms. Special Cases (including *well better best*).				232–233	261, 266–267	280–281, 284–285	448–449, 454	428, 431, 434–435
				432	526, 549	496, 544	45	43
Avoiding Double Negatives			157	171	163–164	178–179	452	421
			158, 161	172, 177	164, 170	179	452, 455	431, 435
			351	420	506	524		43

Avoiding Confusion of Adjectives and Adverbs

	Pink 1	Plum 2	Brown 3	Aqua 4	Silver 5	Gold 6	Red 7	Green 8
					262–264	281–283	449–450	419, 421–422
Choosing Between Adjective and Adverb Forms of a Modifier, Using *Good* and *Well* Correctly					263–265, 267	282–283, 285	450–452, 454–455	420, 422–423, 433–434
					526, 549	544	4, 45, 54	4, 42–43, 45

☐ **Teaching Pages**
(Explanations and examples in the text and T.E.)

▨ **Exercises**
(All pages containing exercises for the concept)

▨ **Reinforcement**
(Grades 1–6: Practice Pages in T.E.; Grades 7–8: Diagnostic and Mastery Test Booklets)

Words Often Confused

	Pink 1	Plum 2	Brown 3	Aqua 4	Silver 5	Gold 6	Red 7	Green 8
Using Troublesome Pairs of Verbs Correctly, Recognizing and Using Correctly Homonyms and Other Words Often Confused, Possessive Pronouns and Contractions		19–20	85	375–376	159–161, 185	172–177, 466–468	382–384, 415–416, 562–563, 586–590	365–366, 404–406, 585–588
		19–20	86, 89	376–377	160, 162, 169, 185–186	172–178, 183, 469	382–384, 416, 424, 563–564, 576, 590–593	366, 374–375, 406, 409, 588–589, 591
		211, 244	346	452, 475	505, 508	524, 565	8, 37, 54, 60	3, 8, 37, 41

Clauses

	Pink 1	Plum 2	Brown 3	Aqua 4	Silver 5	Gold 6	Red 7	Green 8
Subordinate, Adverb, Adjective, Relative, Noun, Restrictive, Nonrestrictive							53–54	476–491, 552–553
							54–55, 59	479–497, 553–554, 571–572
								47, 48

Mechanics

Capitalization

	Pink 1	Plum 2	Brown 3	Aqua 4	Silver 5	Gold 6	Red 7	Green 8
The Word *I*	87	134, 176	291	337	418	420	523	525
	87–88, 92	134, 176	292, 300	338, 344	418–419	421, 430	524, 536–539	525–526
	182–183	282	335, 369, 392, 397	399, 446	544	497, 559	6, 55, 61	6, 55–56, 61
Proper Nouns	83–84	75–77, 176	64–65, 290–294	66, 336–339	131, 417–423	143–144, 419–422	391, 522–523, 529	342, 523–527
Personal Names and Titles, and Their Abbreviations; Names of Buildings, Streets, Cities, States, Countries	89–92	75–78, 84, 176	65, 72–73, 292–295, 300	67, 74, 337–340, 344	132, 140–141, 418–423, 429–430	144–146, 154–155, 421–423, 430–431	391–392, 404–405, 523–524, 529, 536–539	342, 348, 525–526, 528, 535–537
	179	235–236, 238, 246, 282	335, 343, 354, 369–370, 378, 397	399, 446, 471	482, 501, 543	497, 559	6, 38, 55, 61	2, 6, 34, 55–56, 61
Months, Days, and Holidays	85–86	79–82, 176	293	339	422	422	527	529
	85–86	79–82, 84, 176	294–295, 300	339–340, 344	423, 430	423–425, 430	527–528, 536–539	530–531, 535–537
	180–181, 203	237–238, 282	343, 369, 397	399, 446	482, 543	497, 559	6, 55, 61	6, 34, 55–56, 61
Nationalities, Races, Religions; Names for the Deity and Scriptures; Geographical Names and Directions; Organizations; Events and Documents; Other Nouns				339	423	420, 423–424	391, 526–528	529–530
				339–340, 344	424, 430	421, 424–425, 430–431	391–392, 404–405, 527–529, 536–539	530–531, 535–537
				446, 474	482, 543	497, 559	6, 55, 61	2, 6, 34, 61

Mechanics (continued)

Capitalization (continued)

	Pink 1	Plum 2	Brown 3	Aqua 4	Silver 5	Gold 6	Red 7	Green 8
Proper Adjectives					418	419–424	428, 522–523, 525	413, 524, 527
					418–419, 429	421–425, 430–431	429, 523–524, 526, 536–539	413–414, 525, 528
					482, 543	497, 559	6, 55, 61	6, 55
First Words	57, 59	41, 43, 47, 51, 177	51–53, 295	36, 340	425	425	530	532
Sentences	57–62	41–44, 47–48, 51–54, 177	54, 58–59, 297, 301	38–39, 50, 340–341, 345	426, 430–431	426–427, 430–431	531–532, 538–539	533–534, 537
	169–171, 174, 205	221, 222, 224–227, 283–291	332, 335, 370, 377, 392–397	399, 446, 470–475	482, 544	497, 560	6, 56, 61	6, 56
Lines of Poetry, Quotations, Letters, Outlines		89, 177	295–296	306, 319–320, 340–341	349–350, 363–364, 425–427	329, 425–428	530–533	532–538, 562, 595–596
		89–90, 95–96, 177	297, 301	321, 331, 341–342, 345	364, 426–427, 430–431	329–330, 426–431	531–532, 534–535, 538–539	533–534, 537, 564–565, 596
		240, 242–243, 283	332, 335, 366, 370, 377–378, 395	399, 444, 447, 472	482, 537, 544	497, 551, 560	56, 61	6, 56
Titles		118, 182	298	342–343	428	428–429	533	533
		118–120, 130, 182	299, 301	343–345	428, 431	429–431	534–539	533–534, 537
		256, 288–289	335, 370	399, 447, 473	482, 544	497, 560	6, 55–56, 61	6, 56, 61

Punctuation

	Pink 1	Plum 2	Brown 3	Aqua 4	Silver 5	Gold 6	Red 7	Green 8
The Period	57	41, 47, 178	51–53	36–37, 347	44–48, 433	32–34, 433–434	335, 542–543	539–542, 563–564
Sentences	57–58, 61–62	41–42, 47–48, 52, 54, 178	305–306, 315	38–39, 50, 349–350, 363	47–49, 64–65, 436, 452	33–35, 58, 435–436, 454	335–336, 545–546, 570	542–543, 564–565, 568
	169, 171, 174, 205	221, 224, 226–227, 245, 284, 291	332, 336, 341, 371, 378, 392–397	400, 404, 448, 470–475	483, 488, 545	498, 504, 561	7, 57, 62	7, 57, 62
Initials, Abbreviations, Outlines		76, 178	304–305	306, 348–349	349–350, 434–436	434–435	543–544	541, 595–596
		76, 84, 178	305–306, 315	349–350, 363	436, 452	435–436, 454	545–546, 570	542–543, 568
		284	371, 397	400, 448	483, 545	498, 561	7, 32, 57, 62	7, 57, 62

Mechanics (continued)

Punctuation (continued)

	Pink 1	Plum 2	Brown 3	Aqua 4	Silver 5	Gold 6	Red 7	Green 8
The Question Mark	59	43, 179	51–53, 306	37, 350	44–48, 437	32–34, 437	335, 544	541–542, 563
Sentences	59–60, 62	43–44, 48, 52, 54, 179	54, 58–59, 306, 315	38–39, 50, 350–351, 363	47–49, 64–65, 437, 452	33–35, 58, 437–438, 454	335–336, 545–546, 570	542–543, 564–565, 568
	170–171, 174, 205	222, 224–227, 245, 285	332, 341, 371, 378, 392–397	400, 404, 448, 470–475	483, 488, 545	498, 504, 561	7, 32, 57, 62	7, 57, 62
The Exclamation Point		51, 179	51–53, 307	37, 351	44–48, 438	32–34, 437	335, 544–545	542, 563
Sentences		51–52, 54, 179	54, 58–59, 307, 316	38–39, 50, 351, 364	47–49, 64–65, 438, 452–453	33–35, 58, 438–440, 454	335–336, 545–546, 570	542–543, 564–565, 568
		226–227, 245, 285	341, 371, 392–397	400, 404, 448, 470–475	483, 488, 545	498, 504, 561	7, 32, 57, 62	7, 57, 62
Interjections					438	437	545	448, 542
					438, 452–453	438–439, 454	545–546, 570	542–543, 564–565, 568
					545	511, 561	7, 57	7, 57, 62
The Comma		82, 89, 91, 180–181	308–309	319–320, 352–355	363–364, 439–440	329, 441, 443	240–242, 258, 556–557	238–239, 249, 258, 550–551
Uses in Letters and Other Writing: Dates, Addresses and Locations, Letter Parts		82, 89–92, 95–96, 180–181	309–311, 316	321, 331, 353–356	364, 440–441, 453	329–330, 440–444, 454–455	244, 256, 260, 557–558, 574	252, 254, 259, 551–552, 570–571
		240–243, 286	372, 378, 392–397	400, 444, 449, 472	483, 537, 546	498, 551–552, 561, 569	7, 57, 61	7, 57
Uses in Sentences: Series, Introductory Words, Nouns of Direct Address, Quotations, Compound Sentences, Appositives, Interruptors, Nonrestrictive Clauses, For Clarity			308–310	352–355	439–440	438–443	42–45, 50, 53–56, 496–497, 546–555	29–47, 471–476, 543–549, 552–553, 561–564
			309–311, 316	353–356	440–441, 453–454	439–444, 454–455, 457	43–46, 50–51, 53–59, 497–501, 503–505, 547–556, 570–574	544–547, 549–550, 553–554, 564–565, 568–572
			372, 378, 392–397	400, 449, 472	546–547, 554	498, 561, 571	7, 50, 57, 62	7, 47, 57, 62
The Semicolon						448	492, 558	44–47, 471–472, 555
						448, 456	559, 575	45–49, 472, 556–557, 572
						563	58, 62	58, 62

	Pink 1	Plum 2	Brown 3	Aqua 4	Silver 5	Gold 6	Red 7	Green 8
The Colon				329, 359	369, 445	337, 447	254, 558	249, 555–556
				331, 359	373, 445, 454	340, 448, 456	256, 559, 570	252, 254, 556–557, 572
				450	538, 547, 552	552, 563	7, 58, 62	7, 58, 62
The Apostrophe			69–70, 311	71–72, 356–357	136–138, 441	149–151, 444–445	402–403, 561	346, 559
Possessives			71–73, 312, 317	73, 75, 357–359	138, 141, 442, 453–454	151–152, 155, 445, 455	403–407, 561, 563–564, 576	346–347, 349, 560–561, 573–574
			344, 378	400, 408, 409	483, 502, 548	498, 520, 562	7, 39, 58, 62	7, 35, 58, 62
Contractions and Other Omissions		27–28, 181	154–155, 312	169, 357–358	163, 442–443	445	415–416, 562–563	365–366, 560
		27–28, 30, 181	156, 160, 312, 317	169, 170, 177, 357–359	163–164, 171, 443, 453–454	446, 455	415–416, 423–424, 563–564, 576	366, 374–375, 560–561, 573–574
		215–216, 244, 287	351, 373, 378	364–365, 400, 420, 449	438, 506, 548	498, 562, 571	7, 58, 62	3, 7, 58, 62
Plurals of Letters, Figures, Words Used as Words							563	560
							563–564, 576	560–561
							58, 62	58, 62
The Hyphen					444	446	559–560	557–558
					445–446	446–449, 455–456	560, 575	558–559
					547	498, 562	58, 62	7, 58, 62
Quotation Marks			313	360–361	446–450	429, 449–452	564–568	561–566
			313–314, 317	361, 365	447–450, 454	429, 451, 452, 457	565–569, 576–577	564–567, 574–575
			374, 378	400, 450, 475	483, 548, 554	562–563, 571	7, 58, 62	7, 58, 62
Underlining		118, 182	314	362	450–451	428–429, 453	568	566
		118–119, 130, 182	314, 317	362, 365	451, 455	453, 457	189, 569, 577	566–567, 575
		256, 288–289	374, 378	400, 450, 473, 475	548	563, 571	7, 55, 56, 57	56, 61

☐ **Teaching Pages**
(Explanations and examples in the text and T.E.)

▨ **Exercises**
(All pages containing exercises for the concept)

▨ **Reinforcement**
(Grades 1–6: Practice Pages in T.E.; Grades 7–8:
Diagnostic and Mastery Test Booklets)

Mechanics (continued)

Spelling

Spelling	Pink 1	Plum 2	Brown 3	Aqua 4	Silver 5	Gold 6	Red 7	Green 8
Study Plan for Spelling				368–370		460–461	579–581	577–579
				370				
Rules for Common Problems			165, 168, 207–208	181–182, 371–374	192–193	461–462, 465	26–27, 400–401, 581–582, 585, 586	343–344, 579–580, 583–584
Problems with Adding Suffixes: Final *e*, Final *y*, Doubling the Final Consonant			171, 173, 209	181–182, 371–374	193	462–463, 465, 470–471	27–28, 401, 406–407, 582–583, 586, 593	345–348, 580–581, 584, 590–591
			352	421, 450–451	502	499, 565	8, 59–60, 62	8, 59–60, 62
Adding Prefixes; Adding the Suffixes *-ly* and *-ness;* Spelling Words with the *seed* Sound; Spelling Words with *ie* and *ei*				370–371, 374	185	463–464	583–585	581–583
				371, 374, 377	185	463–464	584, 585, 593	583, 590–591
				450–451		470–471, 499, 564–565	8, 59–60, 62	8, 59–60, 62
Homonyms and Other Words Often Confused			85	368–369, 375–376		466–468	415–416, 562–563, 586–590	585–588
			85, 89	377		469	416, 424, 563–564, 576, 590–593	588–589, 591
			346	425, 475		499, 565	8, 60, 62	8, 37

Proofreading

	Pink 1	Plum 2	Brown 3	Aqua 4	Silver 5	Gold 6	Red 7	Green 8
Checking Sentences for Grammatical Correctness; Checking Paragraphs for Form; Checking Punctuation, Capitalization, and Spelling; Rewriting for Appearance	130	151, 173	106–107, 187, 269–270	118–119, 201–202, 310–312	87–90, 91, 110, 302–305, 311, 356	81–82, 85, 242–243, 321, 460	81–89, 153	51–59, 578
	130	151, 173–174	106–107, 187, 271	120, 203	111–112, 305, 317, 356	243, 321	152	131
See also: Process of Writing: Revising; Compositions, Reports	202	280–281, 291	365–366, 392–397	443, 469–475	555–574	591–603	1, 6–8, 18–21, 29, 33, 38, 47, 50, 53–54, 55–62	1, 2, 4, 6, 7, 8, 43, 50, 54, 62

Outlining

	Pink 1	Plum 2	Brown 3	Aqua 4	Silver 5	Gold 6	Red 7	Green 8
Form. Use in Note-Taking. Use in Planning a Report			263–266	116, 301–307	349–352	315–316, 428, 435	180–182, 595–598	223–224, 593–596
See also: Composition: Reports; Study and Research Skills: Clear Thinking			263–266	116, 303–307	352	317, 429, 436	182, 599–601	596–598
			366, 377	442	536	550, 560		